Nixon's Civil Rights

Dean J. Kotlowski

Nixon's Civil Rights

Politics,

Principle,

and

Policy

Harvard University Press

Cambridge, Massachusetts and London, England

2001

Library of Congress Cataloging-in-Publication Data
Kotlowski, Dean J.
Nixon's civil rights: politics, principle, and policy / Dean J. Kotlowski.
p. cm.
Includes bibliographical references and index.
ISBN 0-674-00623-2 (cloth : alk. paper)
1. Civil rights–United States–History–20th century.
2. Affirmative action programs–Government policy–United States–History–20th century.
3. United States–Politics and government–1969–1974.
I. Title.

JC599.U5 K65 2001
323′.0973′09047–dc21   2001039278

In memory of my grandparents,
George K. Kari and Grace R. Kari,
my first teachers

Acknowledgments

Many people provided assistance in researching and writing this book. I think Bryon (Scott) Parham and William Joyner for helping me navigate the Nixon presidential materials at the National Archives in College Park, Maryland. Susan Naulty at the Richard Nixon Library and Birthplace in Yorba Linda, California, opened new material on Richard Nixon, as did Herbert Pankratz of the Dwight D. Eisenhower Library in Abilene, Kansas. Also helpful were Michael C. Sutherland at the Occidental College Archives (Robert H. Finch Papers); William H. McNitt at the Gerald R. Ford Library; William Cooper at the University of Kentucky (Creed C. Black Papers); Dallas R. Lindgren at the Minnesota Historical Society; Thomas Rosenbaum and John LeGloachec at the Rockefeller Archive Center; Dwight Miller and Wade Slinde at the Herbert Hoover Presidential Library. I am grateful to the staff at the Indiana University Library, especially the departments of government publications and microforms, for their many courtesies.

Financial assistance made my research possible. I thank the University Graduate School, women's studies program, and history department at Indiana University for grants-in-aid of research. The Gerald R. Ford Foundation, Bentley Historical Library at the University of Michigan, Everett McKinley Dirksen Congressional Leadership Research Center, Caterpillar Foundation, and Rockefeller Archive Center provided travel grants that allowed me to expand my research base. In the project's latter stages I received research grants from the history department at Ohio University, John F. Kennedy Library, Lyndon B. Johnson Library, and Charles R. and Martha N. Fulton School of Liberal Arts at Salisbury University in Maryland.

This book originated as a dissertation in the department of history at Indiana University. During my eleven years in Bloomington, a city I came to love, many people influenced both me and this project. The members of my dissertation committee gave freely of their time and worked hard to improve this study. Michael E. McGerr encouraged me to place Nixon's policies within the ideology of the Republican Party. James M. Diehl's high academic standards and his skepticism about revising "Tricky Dick" inspired me to strengthen my argument. George I. Juergens taught me the importance of smooth writing and good storytelling whether on paper, in the classroom, or among friends. Irving Katz's command of both U.S. political history and the English language improved my prose; his fellowship, keen editorial eye, and wit were sources of strength as I completed this book.

My greatest intellectual debt is to my adviser, fellow Nixon scholar, and friend, Joan Hoff. She was the model dissertation adviser, providing incisive criticism, intellectual stimulation, and absolute freedom to pursue my research as I saw fit. Her wry humor and steadfast faith in my abilities eased the writing process, and her sound advice and professionalism will forever inspire my scholarship and teaching.

A number of other scholars read portions of this study. I thank Mary Frances Berry, Bruce J. Dierenfield, Robert H. Ferrell, Katherine Jellison, Heiko Muehr, David M. Pletcher, Lana Ruegamer, and John David Skrentny for commenting on individual chapters. Dean Jacobs and David McNab offered helpful comments on Chapter 7. My greatest regret is that my first mentor at Indiana University, John Edward Wilz, did not live to see the dissertation's completion and the book's publication. Nevertheless, his devotion to students and his demand for excellence remained with me every step of the way.

Two close friends read and commented on this book. Dean J. Fafoutis, known for his critical eye and editor's pen, marked up each chapter, improving prose immeasurably. He also provided comradeship during my "freshman" year as a faculty member at Salisbury University. From start to finish, Ricky Earl Newport read each chapter countless times, striking out superfluous phrases here, expressing skepticism (or support) there. No other person put so much into this book, and I am deeply grateful.

Over the years, other friends offered encouragement and much-welcomed diversions from the chores of study and writing. Thanks to Andy Evans and Lydia Murdoch, Greg Ference, Victoria Gonzalez, Katherine Jellison, Kay McAdams, Mikal Mast, Lino Nicasio, Tim Pursell, Gerry and Carolyn Sherayko, and Tracy Uebelhor. A special thanks goes to the Mast family—Chuck, Muggs, Mikal, and Anja—for their fine hospitality during one of my last research trips to Washington, D.C.

As this project moved toward publication, several people kept up my spirits. Gillian Berchowitz, Mary Anne Reeves, Holly Panich, Rick Dodgson, and Kara Dunfee helped to make my year at Ohio University both productive and enjoyable. I thank all of my colleagues at Salisbury University for providing a supportive environment in which to teach, study, and write. I am especially grateful to G. Ray Thompson, my department chair, and fellow history professors Mike Lewis and Melanie Perreault, who began teaching at S.U. the same year I did.

At Harvard University Press, Jeffrey Kehoe believed in this project from the start and offered wise advice for turning the dissertation into a book. It was a great pleasure to work with Kathleen McDermott and Elizabeth Suttell. Amanda Heller, a superb copyeditor, greatly improved my prose. Once again, my friend Carolyn Sherayko did an excellent job compiling the index. The *Journal of Policy History, The Historian,* and *Business History Review* granted permission to reprint material from my previously published articles. A. James Reichley allowed me to quote from transcripts of his interviews with Nixon and Ford administration officials.

Last but not least, I thank my family for all they have given. My aunt and uncle, Donna and Salvatore Manuele, taught the importance of education, persistence, and patience in the pursuit of goals. My father,

ACKNOWLEDGMENTS

Roger J. Kotlowski, offered wise counsel, understanding, and financial support to see this project to its conclusion. My brother, Darin, and his wife, Amy, have been sources of strength. My sister (and best friend), Donna Slater, never let me lose faith in myself, nor did her husband, Mike. My three nephews—Michael, Nathan, and Ryan—have been constant sources of joy. My stepfather, Ronald C. Belcher, never ceases to amaze me with his concern and common sense. Mostly I thank my mother, Gail Belcher, for unrivaled love and the example of optimism, generosity, and "true grit." Finally, with my dedication, I begin to repay my greatest debt.

Contents

Prologue: Deeds versus Words   1

1   Flexible Response: Southern Politics and School Desegregation   15

2   Open Communities versus Forced Integration: Romney,
     Nixon, and Fair Housing   44

3   The Art of Compromise: Extending the Voting Rights Act   71

4   Jobs Are Nixon's Rights Program: The Philadelphia Plan
     and Affirmative Action   97

5   Black Power, Nixon Style: Minority Businesses
     and Black Colleges   125

6   A Cold War: Nixon and Civil Rights Leaders   157

7   Challenges and Opportunities: Native American Policy   188

8   Stops and Starts: Women's Rights   222

Epilogue: In the Shadow of Nixon   259

Notes   273

Select Bibliography   381

Index   389

Prologue: Deeds versus Words

"When the historical record of the first four years is written," President Richard Nixon wrote in 1973, "I am confident it will show that this Administration did far more in the fields of civil rights and equal opportunity than its critics were willing to admit."[1] There is much evidence to support that claim. The Nixon administration implemented affirmative action and set-aside programs for minority-owned companies. It desegregated southern schools and reformed Native American policy. Attorney General John N. Mitchell was not jesting when he advised African American leaders in 1969 to "watch what we do, rather that what we say" in the area of civil rights.[2] Yet the president's courtship of conservative southern whites and forceful denunciation of busing, labeled the "southern strategy" by contemporary critics, continues to eclipse his policies in general histories of the Nixon era.[3] Leonard Garment, a liberal Nixon aide, correctly asserted that the president's enforcement of civil rights "was for the most part operationally progressive but obscured by clouds of retrogressive rhetoric."[4]

Nixon's public policies appear even more confusing when placed alongside his private remarks. Nixon's views on race are plain: while doubting black equality, he still opposed bias. In the presence of aides, the president could sound as bigoted as any southern segregationist, asserting that "there has never been an adequate black nation and they are the only race of which this is true."[5] But this self-made man parted with segregationists in believing that African Americans deserved the opportunity to compete with whites. "Praise or blame, acceptance or rejection," Nixon wrote one citizen, "should be personal matters based upon individual achievement and not the accident of color or birth."[6] "It's clear that not everybody is equal," the president lectured one aide, "but we must ensure that anyone might go to the top."[7]

Early revisionist scholars, wrestling with such conflicting behavior, shifted credit for the administration's policies away from Nixon. Hugh Davis Graham saw the energy for civil rights initiatives originating in the Democratic-controlled Congress, federal courts, and bureaucracy, not the Oval Office. Graham, a historian, stressed the importance of process over personality, following in the footsteps of political scientists such as James Q. Sundquist and Hugh Heclo, who studied the participation of Congress, interest groups, and bureaucrats in policy making. The presidential historian Joan Hoff analyzed Nixon's advisory system and viewed his policies as contingent on whether he received and accepted advice from conservative or liberal aides.[8] These writers' works have enhanced our knowledge of Nixon's decision making and the larger policy-making environment. Perhaps unintentionally, however, they have depicted this intelligent, powerful president as either hopelessly enigmatic or the mere extension of others.[9]

Biographers and later revisionists have striven to integrate Nixon into this story. Tom Wicker, a journalist and biographer of Nixon, discussed U.S. Supreme Court decisions against segregated schools before affirming that Nixon "conceived, orchestrated and led the administration's desegregation effort."[10] The historian Melvin Small used the Contested Document File, a cache of White House materials opened in 1997, to link the president to domestic policy decisions. "Despite his rhetoric and unsavory role in exacerbating racial polarization over busing," Small maintained, "Nixon could have boasted, had he wanted to, about his progressive civil rights policy."[11] Unfortunately, civil rights occupied at most a chapter in each of these balanced studies.

Building on the works of Graham, Hoff, Wicker, and Small, this book explores more deeply the attitudes and assumptions of the president and his aides, "Nixonians," and how their actions modified the civil rights debate. Although Nixon did not make policy in a vacuum, without reference to the courts, Congress, or public, the internal story of how the GOP reacted to and reshaped civil rights during the 1970s remains heretofore untold. What appeared at first glance to be a severe case of presidential split personality—moderate deeds matched against reactionary words—becomes understandable when placed alongside the civil rights dilemmas of the late 1960s as well as Nixon's persona, agenda, and decision-making style.

This study emphasizes four themes. First, Nixon's policies tried to accommodate a number of social forces emerging from the 1960s. Responding to pro–civil rights sentiment, the president espoused economic gains for minorities, then played to white backlash by denouncing "forced integration." Second, as practical politicians, Nixonians channeled grassroots demands for change into established institutions, providing increased funds to federal offices handling civil rights. Third, Nixon's policies drew on "moderate Republicanism," later known as "modern Republicanism," a tradition which dated to the party's birth and influenced presidents such as Herbert Hoover and Dwight D. Eisenhower. Envisioning the small, independent producer as the bedrock of society, Republican moderates used state power selectively, to ensure equal opportunity and social mobility.[12] Fourth, this type of moderation became a device to unify the GOP, for Nixon knew that his party would never gain majority status if either its liberal or conservative wing was "sliced off."[13]

Sallyanne Payton, an African American adviser to Nixon, has argued that the Nixon administration was "trying to achieve some progress, subject to political constraints and in light of its determination to make the GOP the majority party."[14] His divisive rhetoric notwithstanding, Nixon compiled a creditable record on civil rights. The gap separating the president's deeds and words is not hard to fathom, given the national mood of the late 1960s.

❖❖

Nixon became president at a critical point in the history of the civil rights movement, a time when some Americans feared that the movement had run its course while others saw it accelerate. Support for integration remained high among black and white liberals, and federal courts, impatient over delaying tactics, demanded desegregation of schools. But the movement began turning in new directions. Many African Americans rejected interracial alliances in favor of separatism and "Black Power." Other groups, such as Native Americans and women, copied the goals and tactics of the African American rights revolution. Such changes challenged the idea, with which Nixon had grown up, that white males were the natural leaders of American society. The president's team, assuming office in 1969, governed within a less ordered, more contentious, and more democratic social milieu.

By 1969 Americans had grown accustomed to presidential initiatives on race. President Harry S. Truman had responded to pressure for civil rights by forming a committee to study race relations. He signed an executive order abolishing segregation in the armed forces and proposed laws, which Congress rejected, to end poll taxes and ensure fair employment. Under Truman, argued the historians Donald R. McCoy and Richard T. Ruetten, the president "became the prime educator for the need to secure the rights and dignity of all citizens."[15] It was a legacy to which Eisenhower, Truman's Republican successor, added. He completed the task of desegregating the armed forces, quietly pressed for desegregation of public facilities in Washington, D.C., and won passage of minor legislation to enhance voting rights. Yet, save for the dispatch of federal troops to Little Rock, Arkansas, he failed to implement the Supreme Court's ruling in *Brown v. Board of Education* (1954), which outlawed racially segregated schools. Although Eisenhower did not press the cause of equal opportunity beyond symbolic gestures, his actions encouraged "a public expectation of civil rights advance within a framework of political moderation and consensus."[16]

Organized protest shattered that fragile consensus. During the 1960s, nonviolent direct action forced Democratic presidents John F. Kennedy and Lyndon B. Johnson to address racial equality with moral fervor, moving beyond the narrow, legalese rhetoric of the Eisenhower White House. They proposed and won passage of laws to abolish segregation in public facilities and guarantee African Americans access to employment, the ballot, and housing, measures that would have been unthinkable a decade earlier.[17] Yet the formula of mass protest plus new acts yielded more progress in the South, where segregation had been etched into law, than in the North, where racial injustice and economic inequality were bound together. Frustration led to rioting in urban areas, calls for black separatism, not racial integration, and white backlash, in which voters in the South and in suburbs throughout the country stressed maintaining law and order over progress on civil rights. The GOP scored gains in the congressional elections of 1966, and even Johnson, heralded as "the last president to offer committed leadership that challenged racial injustice," began playing down civil rights.[18] "Flawed Giant," a catchphrase that the historian Robert Dallek has applied to LBJ as president, could sum up his reputation as a leader on race.[19]

Although civil rights was an issue which no president could ignore, Nixon has been charged with doing just that. As will be discussed in Chapter 6, Daniel P. Moynihan, Nixon's adviser for urban affairs, wrote a memorandum in 1970 arguing that race could benefit from a period of "benign neglect" in public discourse. A Harvard sociologist and adviser to both JFK and LBJ, Moynihan had captured Nixon's attention with ideas for welfare reform, but interestingly never emerged as White House ombudsman on civil rights. When Moynihan's missive appeared in the *New York Times,* critics pounced on Nixon for sanctioning a retreat on civil rights enforcement, which he did not. Nixon, in fact, would build on the legacy of LBJ, whose legislative triumphs of 1964, 1965, and 1968 required both fine-tuning and implementation. Key sections of the Voting Rights Act of 1965 were set to expire in 1970, and the weak Fair Housing Act of 1968 required application. The Equal Employment Opportunity Commission, established under the Civil Rights Act of 1964, lacked enforcement powers, and the type of authority appropriate for the commission was a question left to Nixon. In his 1969 inaugural the president addressed race with these modest words: "The laws have caught up with our conscience. What remains is to give life to the law."[20]

Regarding civil rights, Nixon weighed many of the same considerations as his predecessors. The political scientist Mark Stern viewed both JFK and LBJ as "political schemers" who "maneuvered, made promises, and maneuvered again as political necessity dictated." "Political idealists," or movement activists, Stern asserted, transformed both presidents into champions of racial justice.[21] Nixon's outlook on the civil rights movement also proved reactive and politically driven, though his calculus and policy responses were unique.

To account for the president's policy intentions, the obvious must be stressed: Nixon was an extremely complex man. He possessed a multifaceted personality, pursued contradictory aims, and structured his staff accordingly. The president's aides have alternately depicted him as cynical, manipulative, and realistic or idealistic, courageous, and pugnacious. Presidential assistant H. R. Haldeman warned against making "easy conclusions" about Nixon since in his case "the obvious is probably wrong."[22] Using the president's complexity to explain his behavior, rather than dismiss him as inscrutable, affords him some credit for his government's achievements and blame for its failings.[23]

Three considerations–political expediency, practicality, and principle–molded Nixon's civil rights policies. Politics was Nixon's prime concern, and he pursued a flexible agenda, seeking the most votes with the fewest promises. The president's aim was to get himself, not other Republicans, elected to office. A resourceful skipper, he read the compass of public opinion, then trimmed his sails. As vice president, when such issues were fresh, Nixon expressed interest in school desegregation and fair employment. Becoming president after a decade of civil unrest, he stressed "deeds over words" in assisting blacks and cultivated white voters in the South and in the suburbs. In urging welfare reform, he chose to appeal not "to people on welfare, or to the unemployed, or to the Blacks" but to "the working poor" and the "taxpayer."[24]

Nixon used symbolic gestures to woo white southerners. The president told aides to publicize the administration's tentative approach to school desegregation. Nixon chose as his spokesman in the South Vice President Spiro T. Agnew, a saucy critic of the so-called liberal eastern establishment and defender of the former Confederacy as it continued to wrestle with the issue of school desegregation.[25] "Of course," Agnew wrote a friend, "we hope to provide an alternative to George Wallace–

so do the Democrats. But [ours] will be a responsible, authentic and sound alternative to his negative appeal."[26] To Nixon, "PR" was a vital part of leadership because, as he explained, "those who write about politics really care more about style than substance."[27]

Nixon courted minorities gingerly. The president argued "that politically we have very little to gain from some groups and possibly a considerable amount to gain from others." Although African Americans voted Democratic, he sanctioned some symbolic gestures to "knock down the idea that the President and his Administration are 'anti-Negro' or that we 'don't care.'" Nixon saw greater chances for breakthroughs among Hispanics and other Catholics, especially Poles and Italians, who seemed conservative. The president ordered aides to keep this analysis top secret because "it indicates my thinking with regard to what we *ought* to do from a political standpoint and also what we *must* do from the standpoint of Presidential leadership."[28]

Practical concerns shaped Nixon's civil rights policies. By "practical" I refer to the president's pragmatic response to the day-to-day challenges of governance. Nixon and his aides were realists and improvisers who analyzed the national mood, problems at hand, and alignment of political forces. They knew that the Vietnam War had undermined public confidence in government. They understood that LBJ's Great Society legislation had failed to end the twin nightmares of racism and poverty, and white backlash was erupting. Nixonians were sensitive to any sign of rioting.[29] In an off-the-record interview in 1970 with one journalist, the president "mentioned the possibility of further racial troubles" since "anything can happen in the hot weather of summer."[30]

Nixonians also knew that liberalism was "down but not out." They noticed civil rights proponents present within interest groups, the bureaucracy, and the judiciary. Facing a Democratic-controlled Congress and a GOP torn between moderates and conservatives, the president declined to follow either a purely liberal or conservative course. In each chapter of this book we will see how Nixon responded to grassroots pressure and civil rights advocacy, whether Democratic or Republican. Senator Ted Kennedy, Democrat of Massachusetts, influenced Native American policy, and Senators Phil Hart, Democrat of Michigan, and Hugh Scott, Republican of Pennsylvania, shaped the Voting Rights Act of 1970. Nevertheless, Nixon remained ahead of the Democrats on issues of tribal self-determination, black colleges, and minority business enterprise.

Philosophy was the third influence on Nixon's policies. Philosophy is a set of assumptions, not a static ideology, from which Nixonians referenced and reacted to events. Sensing the "American system" to be under fire from various dissenters, the president and his aides offered to extend the opportunities they had known to disadvantaged groups. Largely self-made men who had risen to leadership positions in business, law, and politics, they extolled opportunity, hard work, and success. As moderate Republicans, they used state power to open a range of choices to their fellow citizens. Recalling the 1930s, Nixon rejected a "stand-pat attitude in the view of massive unemployment which I saw on all sides around me," but remained committed to local autonomy and individualism: "I would probably rate myself at that period as being progressive in my political thinking, in the TR sense but definitely not new deal in the FDR sense."[31] In other words, the president approved of federal programs likely to advance opportunity and mobility.

Nixon proposed to lift disadvantaged groups into higher-paying jobs. He believed that integration should be enforced in the workplace, not in schools or neighborhoods. That is why he espoused some affirmative measures, such as hiring goals to achieve fair employment, while rejecting others, such as busing for school desegregation. This jobs strategy dated to Nixon's years as vice president, when he chaired a committee to stop bias in companies with government contracts.[32] Nixon opposed discrimination which prevented blacks from attending the nearest school or owning a home in a neighborhood of their choice. But he would not "force" races together. "I am convinced that while legal segregation is totally wrong, forced integration of housing or education is just as wrong," the president wrote in 1970.[33]

Nixon's multiple motives accounted for his sporadic boldness and frequent vacillation on civil rights. On issues of minority business enterprise and Native American self-determination, where political, practical, and philosophical concerns entwined, the president acted forcefully. Regarding affirmative action, a more controversial program, he first advanced swiftly, then retreated, then allowed federal agencies to pursue their own fair employment remedies. In the areas of school and residential integration, anathema to many white voters, Nixon flinched.

Nixon's populist instincts cemented his varied motives on civil rights. The president did not call himself a "populist," nor did he identify with such self-styled populists as the agrarian radicals of the 1890s or George Wallace. Rather, Nixon's populism stemmed from his self-image as an outsider lacking privilege, wealth, and an elite education. This scrapper championed the "little guy" against people born with social advantages. In 1972 he ordered a 50 percent reduction in executive positions at the CIA partly because "its personnel, just like the personnel in State, is primarily Ivy League and Georgetown set rather than the type of people that we get into the services and the FBI."[34] On racial issues, such resentment saddled Nixon with the same prejudices of the middle-class whites whom he claimed to represent. Yet it also instilled an aversion to artificial barriers that prevented people from rising as far as their talents permitted.

Perhaps the one thing more complicated than Nixon's policies was his attitude toward race. Born in 1913, the year that Woodrow Wilson introduced segregation into the federal service, he was a product of a racially segregated society. He grew up in Whittier, California, where no African Americans lived and only two blacks, including a "shoeshine boy," worked.[35] Nixon had no black friends and read little African or African-American history. Addressing the Alfalfa Club in Washington, D.C. in 1965, he joked that the people of the Congo were dissatisfied with American Peace Corp volunteers: "They complain that they are too *thin*." The audience laughed, suggesting that American views of Africa still had not progressed beyond Tarzan films and their depiction of black cannibals.[36] As president, Nixon made patronizing remarks that some African Americans were "good negroes" or "our negroes."[37]

Nixon's prejudice against some groups seemed to grow as he came into greater contact with them. "In talking with him at various times," one of Nixon's law school classmates wrote, "he seemed to have a distinct prejudice against the Japanese and Chinese . . . with whom he had had contact most of his life."[38] The same held true for Mexicans, also present in California; the president once ordered aides to recruit "some honest Mexicans" for federal jobs and privately referred to one Latino as a "wetback."[39] Nixon's most forceful denunciations of bias against African Americans occurred early on, during his years at Duke University Law School, while his bigoted remarks surfaced in the White House, after years of meeting with black leaders and observing the rise and splintering of the civil rights movement.

Nixon's class bias, bigotry, and belief in opportunity all surfaced in his attitude toward Jews. The president hated wealthy liberal Jews, who, he believed, wielded great power. According to Nixon, chain stores were "dominated by Jewish interests" with "a notorious reputation in the trade for conspiracy," and "the Arts" were synonymous with "left-wing" Jews.[40] Politics fed his prejudice. "We are *not* going to get the rich Jews who like rich Christians tend to be soft-headed and liberal," Nixon told one aide. "Go after the middle-income [Jews]."[41] He ordered tax audits of Jewish Democrats, whom he labeled "cocksuckers."[42] Yet he followed a nondiscriminatory course by naming to federal posts Jewish Americans such as Arthur Burns, Herbert Stein, William Safire, Henry Kissinger, and Leonard Garment. The president also backed Israel.[43] He did not fear Jewish presence in the art scene and accepted the advice of Garment to increase federal funding of the arts: "A small cost—lets do it—(But no modern art at the White House!)."[44] On an anti-Semitic continuum of one to one hundred, Garment argued, giving his friend the benefit of every possible doubt, "my personal experience would put Nixon somewhere between 15 and 20," which he rated "much like the rest of the world."[45]

Garment's defense aside, Nixon was no run-of-the-mill bigot. He was brought up as a Quaker, a tolerant religious sect that had opposed slavery. Tom Bewley, an attorney in Whittier, California, recalled how Nixon "was very much on the side of the Jehovah's Witnesses, who were under legal attack."[46] Wallace Newman, his Whittier College football coach and a Cherokee, aroused Nixon's concern for Native American issues. Moving from Whittier, a Quaker school, to Duke University Law School, the Californian became upset at the sight of segregation Dixie-style. One classmate recalled Nixon's being "shocked and disturbed at the prevalent North Carolina treatment of the negro population as an inferior group," and another claimed that he "looked upon the issue of the treatment of the negro in the South as a moral issue and condemned it very strongly."[47]

As vice president, Nixon feared that American racism might push the nations of Africa and Asia into the Soviet camp. During the 1950s, he established rapport with Martin Luther King, Jr., and met with President Kwame Nkrumah in Ghana.[48] His early belief in equal opportunity did not vanish. "President Nixon invited me when he spoke at a military base near Meridian, Mississippi," the civil rights leader Charles Evers recalled. "And when he saw the state police bar me from the podium, he touched my heart by seating me way up front, as his special guest."[49] Nixon clearly could question the abilities of blacks and other minorities yet also think that they deserved the chance to compete with whites. Overall, his belief in civil rights proved shallow, intellectual, and abstract rather than intense, emotional, and engaged.

Nixon's prejudice seems less shocking if we eavesdrop on other presidents.[50] After discussing his views on civil rights, Truman added, "But personally I don't care to associate with niggers."[51] At times Johnson also referred to blacks as "niggers" and once promised a fellow Texan, "I'm gonna try to teach these nigras that don't know anything [about] how to work for themselves instead of just breedin'."[52] Such comments were not confined to southerners, nor to members of Truman's or Johnson's generations. Moynihan once told the civil rights leader James Farmer that "what your people need are some of our genes." Farmer "searched his face looking for some sign that the man was jesting" and "found none."[53] The frequency of Nixon's slurs might be exceptional, but their existence was not.

Institutional and social momentum roused Nixon into moving on rights-related matters. The "emergence" of civil rights as a "national issue" coincided with the rise of presidential power under Franklin D. Roosevelt.[54] And it was a stroke of fate that Nixon entered the White House as the struggle for racial equality entered a crucial phase. But it was a matter of choice that this Republican decided to be active in domestic affairs, approving procedures and initiatives that would have lasting impact.

Nixon was no laissez-faire conservative. Early in 1969, Haldeman jotted in his diary that the president was "determined to show action, be different." According to a later entry, White House liberals had to restrain Nixon: "Moynihan points out that he *can't* have a Domestic Program. Not any money available, and politically impossible anyway. Better just to try to get rid of the things that don't work, and try to build up the few that do."[55] On the matter of decor, Nixon ordered aides to replace a White House portrait of Warren G. Harding, a GOP stand-patter, with one of Herbert Hoover, a moderate of sorts.[56] With Moynihan, Garment, and John D. Ehrlichman, his domestic policy chief, at his side, Nixon addressed national problems. "You have handled the development of programs with superb organizational ability," he wrote Ehrlichman in 1972, "and substantively have seen to it that they have come out along the lines of my own thinking."[57] Conservative Nixon speechwriter Patrick J. Buchanan lamented that the president would never "satisfy" the "hard right ideologues" because he "is an activist in domestic policy."[58]

Nixon chose to guide foreign policy himself and entrust the details of domestic policy to subordinates since he did not consider the latter as critically important as the former. "Mistakes in domestic policy can be rectified," the president explained. "Very seldom is that the case where a major foreign policy mistake is made."[59] Yet if foreign policy was his "bag," Nixon was not as indifferent to domestic affairs as some of his critics have alleged.[60] The president, Garment argued, knew that "an effective domestic policy" provided the political strength "to conduct an effective foreign policy."[61] "Passion issues," Ehrlichman told Tom Wicker, "such as busing or school integration engaged him because they called on his political skills and knowledge. Less emotional questions, such as revenue sharing, were too technical or administrative to catch his interest."[62] In fact, during March 1970 the president was "pushing for more free time to work out his civil rights/school position."[63] Labor Secretary George P. Shultz recalled that Nixon liked to deal with domestic policy when his aides advanced a course of action. The president was a veteran campaigner, well versed in politics, well informed on policy; his more liberal initiatives did not materialize, as if by magic, because "he believed in nothing."[64]

Sound decision making was one thing Nixon strongly believed in.[65] The president preferred a "formalist" approach, using "an orderly policy-making structure" with "well-defined procedures, hierarchical lines of communication and a structured staff system."[66] Several names, procedures, and tactics reappeared in his handling of civil rights. The president delegated authority to a coterie of lieutenants and outlined his views in memoranda, meetings, and remarks jotted in the margins of his daily news summaries. His aides served as liaison to cabinet secretaries, informing them of the presidential will. Nixon directed his team to settle civil rights matters, when possible, through court enforcement or administrative action rather than legislation. This chain of command allowed Nixon to focus on foreign policy, except when court rulings, in areas such as school desegregation, spurred him to take a more direct role in policy discussions. Significantly, Nixon's moderate staffers tended to policy matters while his conservative advisers dealt with political strategy (Harry Dent and Charles Colson) or public relations (Haldeman), encouraging the gap between the president's deeds and words.

I refer to the president and his aides as "Nixonians" to stress their collective outlook rather than play down tactical differences. A Nixonian was any member of the administration who viewed civil rights in terms of "political practicality." Whether liberal or conservative, Nixonians usually placed the president's political interests before practical concerns, such as solving a given problem, or morality. They were self-made men who preferred to settle disputes through established channels; Agnew, for example, privately defended his criticism of anti-war demonstrators by claiming that "perpetual protest is disruptive of the democratic process."[67] By seeing civil rights as a matter of "right versus wrong," Housing Secretary George W. Romney and the Reverend Theodore M. Hesburgh, C.S.C., chair of the U.S. Commission on Civil Rights, were un-Nixonian. In contrast, Garment and Raymond Price, a speechwriter, shared Romney's and Hesburgh's belief in racially integrated schools and neighborhoods, but they deferred to Nixon's will on such matters.

The "lead" Nixonian was Ehrlichman, a political moderate who emerged as the president's "idea broker" for domestic policy. A lawyer from Seattle, Ehrlichman joined Nixon's campaign staff in 1960, espousing no particular philosophy, save to elect his chief president. Ehrlichman reflected the tactician in Nixon, mediating between liberal staffers such as Garment and conservatives such as Buchanan.[68] He emerged as the president's alter ego in home affairs; Nixon, using words that might have applied to himself, listed Ehrlichman's virtues: "an orderly mind," "convincing," "tough," and "effective on television."[69] Ehrlichman, like Nixon, was pragmatic on civil rights, where he once compared progress to the "ground game" in football: advances are "ground out" without "long bombs" or sudden "touchdowns."[70] If "Coach" Nixon set the game plan, Ehrlichman, his quarterback, called the plays.

At times it worked the other way. Nixon's aides were adept at coaxing him to adopt policies which seemed liberal. Moynihan, a gifted writer of memoranda, stoked the president's interest in welfare reform, persuading Nixon to endorse a scheme to guarantee poor families a minimum income. Garment, also eloquent, helped draft the president's positions on school desegregation and fair housing, and even persuaded him to sign the Voting Rights Act of 1970. Nevertheless, undo stress should not be placed on the influence of presidential aides, for Moynihan, Garment, and Ehrlichman did not bewitch Nixon into accepting liberal policies against his will.

The legacies of Nixon's civil rights decisions are manifold, though four stand out. First, the president and his aides shifted the aims of civil rights policy from integration of neighborhoods and schools toward economic opportunity and black separatism. Second, Nixon influenced the manner in which presidents addressed civil rights with a "deeds over words" formula that his successors have copied. Third, Nixon helped set the Republican Party's race-based political agenda through his "southern strategy." Last, by responding to demands from the Native American and women's rights movements, his administration acknowledged that the issue of civil rights no longer applied to African Americans alone.

Grassroots activism combined with congressional, judicial, and bureaucratic pressure set the stage for Nixon's policies. But the president's own decisions loomed large. In the end, he helped move the nation away from integration and gestures on behalf of racial equality and toward civil rights methods that were low-key, bureaucratized, and job-oriented. How a small collection of white males worked to contain, advance, and reshape sentiment for civil rights is the subject of this book.

1

Flexible Response: Southern Politics and School Desegregation

"Legally segregated education, legally segregated housing, legal obstructions to equal employment," Richard Nixon wrote in 1972, "must be totally removed."[1] That statement might shock some of the president's critics, who argued that he had retreated from civil rights to win the votes of conservative white southerners.[2] Modifying this thesis, more recent scholars have concluded that the president was neither a segregationist nor a conservative on the race question.[3] The challenge remains to reconcile Nixon, the politician who appealed for white southern votes, with Nixon, the desegregator of Dixie's schools.

In dealing with the South, especially regarding education, Nixon worked to reconcile his many roles: politician, practical reformer, and opponent of de jure segregation. Possessing no political "strategy" or master plan, the president improvised to keep options open. He appealed for votes in all regions of the country, offering symbolism more than substance. As for school desegregation, he sought a moderate policy that allowed him to carry out court mandates in accordance with his beliefs and without alienating voters in Middle America. The result of these competing political and personal considerations was a twofold compromise. While making token gestures of political support to conservative whites, Nixon quietly ended de jure segregation in the South. But he declined to tackle de facto segregation in the North and decried busing.

The Politics of Ad-Lib

Nixon pursued a flexible, opportunistic political agenda, seeking the maximum number of votes with minimal commitments. During the elections of 1960 and 1968, the Republican nominee campaigned as a moderate and cultivated southern conservatives only when expedient. As president, Nixon used symbolic appeals to win over likely supporters in the South and other regions. By basing his appeals on token gestures and public relations, the president was free to pursue conservative and moderate voters.

During the election of 1960, Nixon took a middle-of-the-road position on civil rights. In seeking the Republican presidential nomination, the vice president faced pressure from Governor Nelson A. Rockefeller of New York, a liberal and rising GOP star, who urged federal solutions to several problems, including civil rights.[4] The governor favored Justice Department lawsuits against segregated schools, laws to end bias in labor unions, an executive order prohibiting discrimination in federally assisted housing, and "equal access to public facilities."[5] After meeting with the governor, Nixon, an earlier supporter of civil rights legislation, vowed "aggressive action" to remove the "vestiges" of segregation and discrimination.[6] Rockefeller reviewed the GOP plank on civil rights, then declared himself "gratified with [the] result."[7]

During the fall campaign, Nixon made small appeals to white southerners. He told aides to contact any southern Democratic leader likely to defect from the Kennedy-Johnson ticket, made overtures to chronically disgruntled Democrats such as Senator Harry F. Byrd of Virginia, and sent southern newspapers information on his entire public record.[8] Nixon's courtship of white southerners did not preclude appeals to voters across the country, since he pledged to campaign in all fifty states. And he remained wary of this early southern strategy but deemed it "worth trying."[9] On election day, the vice president took four southern states: Kentucky, Virginia, Tennessee, and Florida.

While Nixon courted white southerners, he made only halfhearted appeals to African Americans. Following the midterm elections of 1954, the vice president wrote one supporter, "I sometimes almost give up hope that we will ever be able to make much progress among the so-called minority groups, but we of course must continue to try."[10] During the 1960 campaign, Nixon appealed to African Americans through advertisements in black newspapers and endorsements from celebrities such as the former Brooklyn Dodger Jackie Robinson. On the surface, Kennedy went further by condemning the jailing of Martin Luther King, Jr., which the Republican nominee had declined to do. Mostly, Nixon chose to stress Kennedy's shortcomings on civil rights instead of his own positive record.[11] Accordingly, he earned just one third of the African American vote and lost the election by a slim margin.[12] Such returns suggested that Nixon could not compete for black votes, and he needed to focus on more likely supporters.

Nixon's move toward wooing southern whites was not original. By the 1960s, Raymond A. Moley, a onetime New Dealer turned laissez-faire advocate, was admonishing Republicans, particularly Nixon, to court southern conservatives by soft-pedaling civil rights and expounding states' rights and limited government.[13] Bryce N. Harlow, congressional liaison chief under Eisenhower, urged the GOP "to go after votes where they can be gotten," in the farm belt, southern states, and Catholic suburbs, rather than waste effort "on these passion groupings," meaning blacks, whom he deemed "blindly addicted to Democratism."[14] In 1964, after President Lyndon B. Johnson pushed a civil rights act to outlaw racial segregation in public accommodations, GOP presidential nominee Barry M. Goldwater campaigned for white southern votes and carried five Deep South states.[15] Clearly, Democratic policies had opened Dixie to Republican appeals.

The Democrats countered Republican overtures with ones of their own. JFK sought to appease conservative southern Democrats by naming segregationists to the federal judiciary. At the party's national convention in 1964, LBJ opposed the seating of the pro–civil rights Mississippi Freedom Democratic Party in favor of a lily-white delegation from that state.[16] As the federal government sandblasted the foundations of racial inequity, both parties built bridges to southern conservatives.

During the congressional election campaign of 1966, Nixon taunted Democrats about this paradox while courting moderate whites. He advised southern Republicans to forsake "the fool's gold" of racist votes in favor of human rights, states' rights, individual initiative, and "peace without appeasement." According to Nixon, states' rights was not an "instrument of reaction" but a way to reform health care and social welfare programs, an idea he later revived under the "New Federalism."[17] By 1968 Nixon knew the difficulty of carrying the Deep South, with its segregationist tradition.[18] He instead focused on capturing such "outer South" states as Florida, Kentucky, and Virginia, which were "symbolic of Middle America."[19]

During the 1968 election, Nixon steered toward the center. In seeking the GOP presidential nomination, he again jousted with Rockefeller, who recommended funds to "rebuild the Nation's slums" and laws ensuring "open housing." "Government must seize the initiative and actively pursue that which is right," he declared, proclaiming the liberal Republican creed.[20] Rockefeller's staff disparaged their rival's vacillation, with Graham T. Molitor, a pollster, noting that "Nixon's words often suggest secondary meanings or include qualifying addendums."[21] Yet the GOP front-runner had been closer to Rockefeller than Goldwater on domestic issues, and, as Molitor conceded, he "consistently supported civil rights legislation in Congress, as Vice President, and during the last seven years."[22] Nixon knew when to press ahead and when to hedge on civil rights.

Nixon's campaign for the presidential nomination in 1968 involved cautious courtship of southern conservatives. In approaching Dixie politicians such as Senator Strom Thurmond, Republican of South Carolina, he tried to avoid civil rights and emphasize issues, such as maintaining a strong national defense, on which they agreed.[23] Prior to the party's convention, when pressed on school desegregation, Nixon wavered. He told Thurmond and other southerners that he opposed the busing of children to achieve integration and backed "freedom-of-choice" plans (usually a delaying tactic) when such plans desegregated schools. Then Nixon reaffirmed his approval of the Supreme Court's decision in *Brown v. Board of Education* (1954).[24] Such waffling helped him win over southern Republicans and secure the nomination. He even predicted that Thurmond's support would prove "decisive" in blunting the appeal of the segregationist American Independent Party candidate, former governor George C. Wallace of Alabama.[25] Although Nixon did not owe his nomination to Thurmond, he had incurred a political debt.

Throughout the fall campaign, Nixon presented himself as a centrist by avoiding stands on specific issues and endorsing conservative values associated with suburban, middle-income Americans: hard work, traditional morality, patriotism, and law and order. Regarding desegregation, he stuck to a middle course, opposing coercive enforcement while making no promise to repeal the achievements of the civil rights revolution. Nixon thus positioned himself between the liberal Democratic nominee, Vice President Hubert H. Humphrey, and the segregationist Wallace.[26]

Nixon's strategy worked, but barely. He captured 43 percent of the popular vote and carried most of the Middle and Far West as well as Thurmond's South Carolina and the Upper South states of North Carolina, Virginia, Tennessee, Kentucky, and Oklahoma.[27] The closeness of the election left the president-elect with two questions. Without neglecting civil rights, could he maintain the support of moderate white southerners who, along with liberals, had read into his campaign double-talk a pledge to ease pressure for desegregation?[28] Could he gain the allegiance of Wallace voters and enhance his reelection prospects without appearing overtly racist and offending his centrist base?

As president, Nixon noted that the Old South, emerging from its Democratic shell, would be "terribly important" to his reelection. The president concluded that GOP gains in Dixie over the past decade meant one thing: "*That's* where the ducks are."[29] Upon learning that a Justice Department official had urged the adoption of a "hardline Northern political strategy" which would "write off the South" for the next presidential election, Nixon exploded: "(1) get me a report (2) this is utterly stupid."[30] Accordingly, he proposed a dinner to honor former governor James F. Byrnes of South Carolina and named to government office two of Thurmond's former aides, J. Fred Buzhardt and Harry S. Dent, Jr. Nixon urged his department chiefs to make the appointment of white southerners a priority, and he himself attempted to place on the Supreme Court two conservative southerners, Clement F. Haynsworth, Jr., and G. Harrold Carswell.[31] Mostly, Nixon's southern strategy employed "PR." He ordered his staff to stress the administration's seemingly tentative approach to school desegregation and chose as his southern spokesman Vice President Spiro T. Agnew, a brazen and increasingly popular critic of both eastern liberals and African American radicals.[32]

Nixon's interest in the South should not be exaggerated since his appeals extended to all regions. In 1969 the president agreed with the argument of Harry Dent, his southern political adviser, that "this Administration has no Southern strategy but rather a national strategy which, for the first time in modern times, *includes* the South, rather than *excludes* the South."[33] The president met with southern politicians not as a separate group but with representatives of other regions, and he approved "a good propaganda campaign" to dispel "the idea that there is any lessening of interest in the Northeast."[34] During 1970 and 1971, Nixon urged White House special counsel Charles W. Colson, a New Englander, to win the favor of ethnic groups and labor unions in the North. As the election of 1972 approached, he admonished aides against "writing off" any one state or region.[35]

This national strategy practiced the politics of exclusion or inclusion as circumstances dictated. By 1969 the president viewed African Americans as strong Democrats and expended little effort to gain their votes. The National Association for the Advancement of Colored People (NAACP), he complained, "would say [my] rhetoric was poor [even] if I gave the Sermon on the Mount."[36] Husbanding his appeals for likely disciples, Nixon in 1970 ordered H. R. Haldeman, his chief of staff, to "get some symbolic things for Poles, Italians, Mexicans—no more Blacks."[37] On civil rights, he warned aides not to "expect any credit for what you do, or any real PR gains, just do what is right and forget it."[38] The president did not write off the black vote entirely. After the Republican Party scored modest gains in the elections of 1970, he proclaimed an "open door" policy, telling advisers to "pay attention" to African American concerns and "do what is right . . . If we don't alienate [blacks] like Goldwater did, we should get about twenty percent of their vote."[39] But wooing African Americans never became a priority with Nixon.

Nixon was if nothing else a guileful politician. On the volatile issue of civil rights, he avoided making commitments to both blacks and whites, liberals and conservatives. This stance hardly constituted strong moral leadership, but it allowed him to respond flexibly to the imperatives of governing. The bones he tossed to southern conservatives belied a moderate policy agenda.

Politics versus Policy: Nixon's Dual Agenda

Contrary to conventional wisdom, expediency did not always govern Nixon's domestic policies. Pursuing a dual agenda, the president often separated political and policy decisions. He followed the recommendations of conservative advisers on which voting blocs to court but then entrusted policy formulation to his more moderate lieutenants. While cultivating conservative white southerners and blue-collar ethnic voters, Nixonians paradoxically tackled welfare reform, desegregated schools, and developed affirmative action programs for the building trades.

In 1969 Nixon agreed with political advisers on electoral objectives while slighting their counsel on domestic policy. Dent wrote the president a memorandum depicting the southern states as ripe for Republican picking if he took a number of steps, including easing pressure for school desegregation. Nixon found Dent's ideas appealing and forwarded the memorandum to cabinet officers handling civil rights.[40]

The president's interest in this memorandum proved to be an exception. The White House largely shelved Dent's advice on policy, since his assignment involved politics—acting as a liaison with the South.[41] Nixon and his domestic policy advisers, Daniel P. Moynihan and John D. Ehrlichman, excluded Dent from the process of drafting the administration's welfare reform proposal, the Family Assistance Plan (FAP).[42] The president included Dent only when he sought to mobilize southern support for FAP.[43] When Nixon suddenly urged Ehrlichman to involve Dent in "anything that you possibly can" relating to domestic affairs, a staff member replied, "Mr. Ehrlichman has taken note of this request and will include Mr. Dent where he deems it appropriate."[44] The president pressed no further. On school desegregation, Dixie's "voice" often went unheeded; by 1971, staff members simply filed away Dent's memoranda rather than forwarding them to Nixon.[45]

The president also concurred with the suggestions of Kevin Phillips, an aide to Attorney General John N. Mitchell. In his book *The Emerging Republican Majority* (1969), Phillips forecast that liberalism's excesses would soon propel white southerners and blue-collar ethnics into the Republican Party.[46] Nixon read the book, then instructed aides to "use Phillips as an analyst—study his strategy—don't think in terms of old-time ethnics, go for Poles, Italians, Irish, must learn to understand silent majority . . . don't go for Jews and Blacks."[47] Phillips urged the president to hasten this realignment by moving to reduce the role of the federal government in American life. Nixon agreed.[48]

Yet the role of conservative leader ill suited Nixon. His pre-presidential career, covering the years 1946 to 1968, spanned an age when Democrats expanded the welfare state and successful Republican politicians, such as Eisenhower, trimmed laissez-faire tenets to fit popular programs.[49] As Eisenhower's vice president, he mastered the precepts of "modern Republicanism"—limited use of state power to enhance opportunity—by taking "a very moderate, forward-looking position" on federal funding of health care, education, and welfare.[50] Nixon privately lauded programs such as Social Security for making "important contributions to our society" and scored rightists for dismissing them as "Socialism," which only ruins "the moral fibre of the people."[51] "[I] don't think," he said during a cabinet exchange on education in 1957, "any of our fellows should be under [the] impression that it's a popular thing to oppose fed. action."[52] As early as 1966, he backed cost of living increases for Social Security recipients.[53] President Nixon dismissed a proposed campaign by big business to revise labor legislation as *"Nuts!"* and he rejected cuts in agricultural and veterans' programs as "dangerous politically."[54] Nixon wished to prune the costs, excesses, and failures of the New Deal and Great Society without scrapping them outright.

Doubting that voters wanted a purely conservative agenda, Nixon charted a centrist course. He directed aides to "go gung-ho for blue collar Catholics but *not* [with a] hard right reactionary philosophy."[55] He agreed with Ehrlichman, his domestic policy chief, that the wisest political course lay in an agenda of conservative and liberal programs. "Very few initiatives will be truly in the center," Ehrlichman asserted. "They will fall on one side or the other. Our domestic policy job, as I have understood it up to now, was to insure some *balance*."[56]

Nixon's moderation tarnished his relations with the right. Presidential speechwriter Patrick J. Buchanan, an unflinching conservative, once compared the task of defending Nixon before rightists to that of "Christians marching into the Lion's Den."[57] Republicans in Congress grumbled that the president's programs were "aping the Great Society."[58] Groups such as the American Conservative Union blasted Nixon's welfare reform proposal, and conservative columnists griped that the president tilted leftward in patronage and policy.[59] Goldwater warned of "real trouble à la Eisenhower" if Nixon did not "start rooting out holdover Democrats."[60] In 1969 Haldeman noticed the president's concern "about reports (especially Buchanan's) that conservatives and the South are unhappy. Also he's annoyed by constant right-wing bitching, with never a positive alternative."[61] Nixon also considered the leaders of the Young Americans for Freedom "nuts and second-raters."[62] Knowing that "the far right" would never support his Family Assistance Plan, the president insisted that rightists defend him "on foreign policy instead of nitpicking here, there and everywhere."[63]

Nixon sometimes advocated programs such as welfare reform and affirmative action that hardly benefited his white, middle-class base. Structural, personal, and political factors accounted for such an intricate agenda. The president compartmentalized the White House staff: Ehrlichman coordinated domestic policy; Dent and Colson handled blocs of voters; Haldeman looked after public relations.[64] Such division allowed Nixon to separate political and policy objectives. He also set domestic goals, such as moving poor people from public assistance to jobs, which stemmed from personal philosophy as well as political calculation.[65] Assuming the incongruous roles of moderate reformer and conservative populist, appealing to white southerners, enabled Nixon to adjust to shifting political tides. If the president's initiatives at times stemmed from expediency, at other times he adopted policy independent of politics or simply tailored it to public opinion.

Nixon and School Desegregation: A Middle Course

Nixon's complex policy making emerged most clearly in his handling of school desegregation. Seeking a "middle course," the president in 1969 chose to desegregate schools through Justice Department litigation. Since this approach offended many white southerners, it is questionable whether Nixon had swapped civil rights enforcement for southern votes as his critics complained.

Throughout his career, Nixon had tried to sound reasonable on desegregation. In 1964 he denounced racial segregation but backed "an orderly transition" to desegregated schools without hauling children "from one school to another in order to force integration in an artificial and unworkable manner."[66] As president, Nixon, noticing "two extreme groups," those "who want instant integration" and others who favor "segregation forever," affirmed his preference for "a middle course."[67] He privately expressed a willingness to apply federal power to "break down all barriers . . . between an individual and his rights and between one race and another" without forcing "the races together."[68]

To Nixon, quality education was the key to success. "Because of my own experience," he told the journalist Stewart Alsop in 1958, "I feel very strongly about educational opportunities for people in the lower brackets."[69] As president, Nixon invested in elementary and vocational education, which, he predicted, "will provide for the needs of those who otherwise will never become useful members of our society."[70] Such class bias aside, Nixon considered education especially important for minorities. "Too many of the blacks aren't prepared, they can't make it," he told the journalist Richard L. Wilson, off-the-record, in 1970. "Education is the answer and it is a long process."[71]

To ensure equal opportunity, Nixon compiled a solid, if unspectacular, record. From 1957 to 1968 he supported every major civil rights law passed by Congress, outshining future presidents Ronald Reagan and George Bush, who both opposed the Civil Rights Act of 1964.[72] As vice president, Nixon chaired a committee to stop discrimination in companies receiving government contracts and drew praise from Martin Luther King, Jr., for his "intense interest in solving the civil rights problem."[73] Unlike Eisenhower, Nixon endorsed the *Brown* decision. The vice president also sent his two daughters to desegregated schools and in 1957 denounced as "disgraceful" the obstruction of desegregation by Arkansas governor Orval Faubus.[74] Nixon's actions can be traced to numerous motives, including expediency; his denunciations of inequality certainly lacked fervor. Still, his record could not have been amassed without some commitment to equal rights.[75]

Nixon's belief in equal opportunity partly derived from his Quaker faith and "family tradition" against bias.[76] Patriotism was another source, since he privately defined the "reason for America's greatness" as its belief "in freedom and opportunity for all." World War II encouraged that sentiment. "I could not accept Hitler's idea of a master race," he wrote. "I cannot accept the equally false principle of an inferior race." With an eye toward the Third World, Nixon worried that racism hindered America's capacity to prevail in the cold war.[77] As vice president, he declared that segregation impeded education and wasted talent.[78] "In the national interest, as well as for the moral issues involved," Nixon privately informed Eisenhower, "we must support the necessary steps which will assure orderly progress toward the elimination of discrimination."[79]

For Nixon, dismantling this racial caste system required patience and attention to local opinions. Before assuming the presidency, Nixon backed desegregation at a gradual pace and with minimal application of federal power. In 1960 he wrote, "To me it is morally wrong to segregate human beings on the basis of race," but admitted that "it is difficult to change patterns that have prevailed for many years."[80] He assured one citizen that "in the long run education and persuasion, rather than compulsion, are the most effective weapons in dealing with this problem at the national level."[81] In 1960 he noted that desegregation suits against districts in the "hard core" states "would result in much havoc and close schools." *"Not now,"* he scribbled.[82] Nixon was a desegregationist, albeit a hesitant one.

As president, Nixon gauged the political fallout of his desegregation policies before acting. After consenting to deny tax-exempt status to lily-white private schools, he jotted: "I believe we have to do what is right on this issue. But again let us be under no illusion that we are badly hurt politically."[83] On desegregating public schools, Nixon conceded that "we have to do what's right, but we must separate that from politics and not be under the illusion that this is helping us politically."[84] This refrain appears over and over in his discussions of civil rights.

In fashioning his stance on desegregation, Nixon struggled to harmonize ideological, pragmatic, and political instincts. While he exhorted aides to "do what is right," caution prevented him from strongly pressing ahead. It is hard to know for certain whether Nixon's remarks about "doing right" were posturing. Suffice it to say, his moderate course resulted from neither high-minded idealism nor pure opportunism but a politician's attempt to reconcile philosophical assumptions with self-interest.

Like his predecessors, Nixon grasped the perils of crafting desegregation policy, which was apt to offend either civil rights liberals or racial conservatives. In 1952, before he had achieved national office, prior to the *Brown* decision, and when federal expenditures on education were slight, Nixon endorsed withholding funds from segregated schools.[85] It was the tactic that Johnson, armed with greater amounts of federal aid, employed in the 1960s, with meager results. LBJ's administration drafted guidelines requiring schools to desegregate by a set date or lose their assistance. But it enforced such guidelines inconsistently and "had no intention of pressing the issue beyond the bounds of political reality in the North."[86] Pressed by Mayor Richard J. Daley, Johnson restored funds to Chicago schools accused of noncompliance. Only in March 1968 did the Department of Health, Education, and Welfare (HEW) set a deadline, September 1969, for desegregation of all southern schools. There was much work to do; in districts where funds had been terminated, only 2 percent of black students attended desegregated schools in 1968.[87] Since HEW had packaged this new mandate as "guidelines," not requiring a presidential signature, rather than "regulations," possessing the force of law, LBJ had not signed off on the deadline.[88]

Johnson was uneasy with HEW's punitive policy. To appease southern Democrats, he proceeded with caution. Upon reading that HEW planned to investigate a segregated school system in Georgia, Johnson ordered aides to "go over very carefully with [Attorney General Nicholas de B.] Katzenbach—Have K. talk to the two Senators."[89] When, in 1967, HEW began drafting its school desegregation statement, LBJ inquired, "Has anyone with political sensitivity looked at these guidelines?"[90] A year earlier, Douglass Cater, a White House staffer handling education policy, had attacked HEW for transforming the commissioner of education into "policeman, judge and jury" and for hurting, by withholding federal dollars, "those whom the programs were designed to help, *i.e.* the poor disadvantaged Negro children."[91] Cater urged the president to adopt instead financial incentives to encourage desegregation, then unveil the strategy in a Rose Garden address. Johnson rejected the latter advice. "Talk to [Joe] Califano," he scrawled, referring to another aide. "I'm speaking too much."[92] LBJ doubtless preferred that the cabinet, federal courts, and his successor absorb the fallout from this ticking time bomb.

Pressure for change came from the federal courts. After neglecting school desegregation for over a decade, the Supreme Court began insisting on solid evidence that districts were complying with *Brown*. In *Brown II*, issued in 1955, the court charged federal district courts with implementing desegregation, but set no timetable, urging instead a "prompt and reasonable start" and compliance with "all deliberate speed."[93] During the 1960s, federal courts and HEW permitted schools to use voluntary freedom of choice plans as a means to desegregate. But such plans seldom yielded anything beyond token integration, since black parents wanted to send their children to better-financed white schools while white parents refused to enroll their offspring in underfunded black schools.[94] The high court, impatient with such heel-dragging, ruled freedom of choice plans unacceptable in *Green v. New Kent County* (1968), ordering a rural Virginia district to "come forward with a plan that promises realistically to work, and promises to realistically work *now*."[95] Although the Court had not ruled all freedom of choice plans unconstitutional, it had shifted the onus of desegregation from blacks to school boards, meaning that no future administration could copy LBJ and invoke the "freedom of choice" shibboleth.

With pressure for school desegregation growing, Nixon wanted to appear more reasonable than Johnson and still carry out the law. In so doing, the new president contributed to the misleading impression that LBJ favored quick desegregation while he resisted progress. At the outset, the Nixon administration spoke with two voices. HEW Secretary Robert H. Finch began enforcing guidelines drafted by the Johnson administration, while Attorney General John Mitchell recommended Justice Department lawsuits against districts refusing to comply with *Brown*.[96] The distance between these methods was not very great since neither man ruled out using the other's policy if his own failed to yield results.

Despite surface differences, Finch and Mitchell had personal similarities. Both were friends of Nixon who had managed his campaigns for the White House, Finch in 1960, Mitchell in 1968.[97] Both thought like politicians. Mitchell wanted the GOP to appeal to southerners, while Finch opposed writing off African Americans.[98] Both looked for practical means to end segregation. Seeking to "get the heat out of" school desegregation, Finch began his HEW tenure by denying money to five southern districts, then offered to restore aid if those schools desegregated.[99] Mitchell's public image as a conservative was not quite accurate. Aides closest to the attorney general detected no "clear-cut ideological viewpoint," and he sought a "workable" desegregation policy that would avoid termination of funds.[100] During an early meeting with civil rights leaders, Mitchell criticized previous administrations for "haphazard" desegregation suits and promised to "establish a pattern" that would "make a big impact."[101] Bradley H. Patterson, Jr., a liberal White House staffer, was "impressed" by Mitchell's "good judgment" on desegregation.[102]

Mitchell and Finch differed most sharply in management and "PR"; unlike Finch, Mitchell distanced himself from more liberal subordinates and cultivated a conservative image. The attorney general named Jerris Leonard, a Wisconsin Republican, to head the department's civil rights division and then embraced Leonard's novel plan to file a desegregation suit against an entire state, Georgia.[103] At the same time, Mitchell opposed rigid adherence to the 1969 deadline for desegregation.[104] Segregationists such as Thurmond thus breathed fire upon Leonard while professing "the greatest respect" for Mitchell.[105] Finch received no such praise. To head HEW's Office of Civil Rights he named Leon E. Panetta, a liberal Republican from California who was outspoken, headstrong, and possessed a flair for offending southern whites. Panetta endorsed the 1969 deadline, then pragmatically urged extending it another year for majority black schools.[106] Some southern whites complained that HEW practiced a double standard, while others denounced the department as a liberal bastion, with Finch its hapless captive.[107] Finch, reported one South Carolinian, "is undoubtedly the most detested national figure in the state."[108]

To clarify his policy, Nixon opted to desegregate schools through Justice Department litigation. Mitchell's more cautious strategy coincided with Nixon's desire to avoid the upheaval that often accompanied government-imposed deadlines.[109] The president disliked HEW's cutoff strategy because it fanned confrontation and denied schools much-needed aid. "When funds [are] cut off," he explained, sounding like Cater, LBJ's aide, the "law has failed. [You have] neither integration [n]or education."[110] Nixon sympathized with districts facing the loss of federal funds. When Governor Richard Ogilvie, Republican of Illinois, requested time to meet desegregation deadlines for Chicago, a problem left from the Johnson years, Nixon asked, "Why can't we let up in such a case[?]"[111] Accordingly, he chose to play down cutoff procedures in favor of what he deemed a "more realistic approach."[112]

Mitchell's strategy was attractive politically, for it seemed to decelerate desegregation and shift responsibility for enforcement from the executive branch to federal courts. In February 1969 Nixon conferred with his top domestic advisers "about problems with Southerners, *i.e.,* busing, guidelines, appointments, etc."[113] One month later the president relayed word to Finch and Mitchell that few Americans favored a "speedup of desegregation."[114] Nixon hoped to enforce desegregation without alienating white southerners.

At first the president was reluctant to tell his friend Finch that he had opted for Mitchell's desegregation policy. In February 1969 Nixon instructed Mitchell to "work on what Finch can do."[115] One month later, Haldeman's meeting notes recorded a weakening of patience: "P[resident] wants guidelines changed . . . P. feels change in guidelines sh[ou]ld be drastic. [N]o arbitrary guidelines."[116] Yet it was not until May that Nixon met with Finch to chart the administration's course. After discussing the fate of recalcitrant districts in South Carolina, the president informed the secretary that hereafter HEW desegregation plans were to "(a) be developed in method and content in such a manner as to be inoffensive to the people of South Carolina and (b) . . . be satisfactorily applicable in any subsequent case or cases." He then directed Finch to devise with Mitchell a "long-range plan" for desegregating schools through "the use of U.S. Federal District Court actions rather than administrative compliance procedures."[117] Nixon then ordered Finch and Mitchell to draft a statement explaining the revised policy.[118]

The Finch-Mitchell statement of July 1969 satisfied neither supporters nor opponents of desegregation. Mitchell wanted a "PR statement" casting President Johnson's desegregation policy as anti-southern and

Nixon's as "evenhanded" and "equitable."[119] The final draft affirmed Mitchell's litigation strategy but dropped the September deadline. Civil rights leaders promptly lambasted the change. "It's almost enough to make you vomit," remarked Roy Wilkins, executive secretary of the NAACP.[120] In a dispassionate analysis, the syndicated columnists Roscoe and Geoffrey Drummond noted that JFK and LBJ "had eight years to bring about school desegregation. Mr. Nixon has had six months. The crunch will come with future enforcement."[121] The response of southern whites was mixed. Dent described "southern reaction" to the statement as "very good."[122] Others believed that Nixon merely had exchanged one club for another. Dent's old boss, Senator Thurmond, withheld judgment "until I see how this new policy is administered."[123]

Thurmond had reason for caution. At most, Nixon sought to modify, not halt, the drive for desegregation. Just days after the joint statement became public, the Justice Department filed lawsuits against racially segregated schools, and by autumn 1969 a record number of children had entered desegregated schools.[124] Many southerners concluded that the new administration was not easing pressure for desegregation. "We hear talk of delay," complained Governor Robert E. McNair, Democrat of South Carolina, "and then we see the Nixon Administration go into court."[125] Many voters were livid. A lawyer warned his fellow Tennesseans not to count on Nixon to preserve segregation: "There does not appear to be any relief at all from this source."[126] "The Republican Party," fumed another man, "has done more to wreck our Southern schools since they have been in power than the Democrats did."[127]

Nixon intervened to delay desegregation only once. In that instance, the president's motive had little to do with enhancing his reelection prospects. In 1969 Senator John Stennis, Democrat of Mississippi, denounced desegregation plans for his state as "so sweeping" that they "cannot possibly work." In discussions with HEW, he protested, "the talk was always for moderation of the guidelines, but when the action comes it is always severe, even more severe than in prior administrations."[128] Needing Stennis's vote to pass the antiballistic missile program (ABM), Nixon put off desegregation deadlines for school districts in Mississippi.[129] In August 1969, with Stennis voting with the majority, ABM cleared the Senate, 51 to 50.[130] Two weeks later Finch asked the

Fifth District Court of Appeals to give thirty-three Mississippi school districts more time to desegregate.[131]

The decision to drop the deadlines backfired. Civil rights groups sued the holdout schools, and the Justice Department, siding with the districts, pleaded for more time. Although two lower courts upheld the department's motion, the Supreme Court did not. On October 29, 1969, the high court, in *Alexander v. Holmes County*, unanimously ordered southern schools "to terminate dual school systems at once and to operate now and hereafter only unitary schools."[132] The decision marked the culmination of the court's impatience with delays by southern whites. Nixon's one attempt at postponement for political reasons had lent an unintended push to the cause of desegregation.[133]

During 1969, the president's school desegregation policy–an assortment of starts and stops, forward thrusts and backward slides–seemed so haphazard that it is hard to believe the White House consistently pursued a southern strategy.[134] Given Nixon's balancing of personal concerns with public duties and conflicting advice, such hedging was not surprising. By going into court, the president allowed the judiciary to set the pace of desegregation.

Delivering on Desegregation

The *Alexander* decision compelled the president to dismantle the South's dual system of education much faster than he had expected; the question became how to do it. At first Nixon responded cynically to the Supreme Court's mandate, telling aides, in language reminiscent of Andrew Jackson, "Let's see how they enforce it."[135] But in formulating desegregation policy, Nixon had refused to meddle in pending court cases and never contemplated defying judicial edicts.[136] Throughout 1970 he continued to search for a moderate solution with the help of his advisers: low-key persuasion of southerners.

The *Alexander* decision bewildered the White House. One day after the ruling, the president pledged to enforce the law.[137] Yet Nixon and his advisers had no inkling *how* to enforce it. In January 1970 the president's domestic advisers considered appointing a "blue ribbon southern group" to study the school desegregation question.[138] Meanwhile, Buchanan urged Nixon to abandon the issue: "The era of Re-Construction is over; the ship of Integration is going down; it is not our ship . . . we ought not to be aboard."[139] During a meeting with Senator Richard B. Russell, Democrat of Georgia, the president, in the words of one aide, "evidenced extreme perplexity over what to do."[140] Later, Nixon told Haldeman: "[We should] develop a careful plan for schools. [We] can't go on fuzzing the issue. Need to give P[resident] options . . . [The] prob[lem] is no one has sat down and done this. We have just reacted—never got ahead of it."[141]

Philosophical, political, and practical considerations guided Nixon's response to *Alexander*. While conceding there were "no votes" in desegregating southern schools, the president lectured aides that the "law requires deseg[regation]—and it is right. Carry out the law."[142] He told Ehrlichman that there was "no good pol[itics] in P[at] B[uchanan]'s extreme view: seg[regation] forever" because it was "bad law."[143] In handling the politics of desegregation, the president enlisted moderate southerners, representatives of what he called "decent opinion."[144] Yet Nixon's overriding goal was to enforce the law without disrupting the education of children. After reading that rash desegregation could "destroy" the South's public school system, he wrote Ehrlichman: "I would like to know what I *can* do about this. I don't give a damn about the Southern Strategy—I care a great deal about decent education."[145]

Struggling to "get ahead" of the school desegregation question, Nixon limited the scope of *Alexander*. The president distinguished between two types of racial segregation, de jure and de facto. Under de jure segregation, southerners passed laws to force blacks and whites to attend separate schools. De facto segregation, common in the North, emerged when blacks and whites attended separate schools because they lived in separate communities. Nixon exhorted aides to "do only what the law requires": attack de jure segregation and ignore de facto segregation.[146] The White House, in March 1970, issued a lengthy statement reiterating the president's support for the *Brown* decision as well as his opposition to busing children to end de facto segregation. By ducking the matter of de facto segregation, Nixon declined to move beyond "desegregation" toward "integration."[147] He told Ehrlichman: "Believe [we] sh[ou]ld carry out deseg[regation] . . . Integ[ration] not wave of future. No massive program."[148] If officials were uncertain whether segregation was one type or the other, the president directed them to "call it de facto and drop it."[149] By distinguishing between de jure and de facto segregation and combating only the former, Nixon hoped to steer the courts away from compelling integration across the country.[150]

Put another way, Nixon favored neighborhood schools on a nonsegregated basis: children, regardless of race, would attend the school nearest their home. "Whatever degree of bussing is necessary to follow that concept," wrote Stanley Blair, an Agnew aide, "is the am[oun]t of bussing [the president] supports."[151] Nixonians used this neighborhood school idea to counter southern segregationists. "The President has been saying all this time," Ehrlichman assured Governor Claude Kirk of Florida, "that he is against forced bussing for purposes of achieving racial balance, that the policy of this Administration is for neighborhood schools." "You're pretty g . . d . . . good," Kirk replied. "How do you do these things without me?" "Mirrors," said Ehrlichman.[152]

In separating desegregation from integration, Nixon had concocted a moderate position that was attractive politically, if not always legally. An article by Alexander M. Bickel, a law professor at Yale University, distinguishing desegregation from integration influenced the president's thinking. Under the Nixon-Bickel formula, the administration assumed responsibility only for removing barriers to equal educational opportunity, that is, formal segregation as it had been practiced in the South. They would not take the next step and attack informal patterns of segregation by, as Nixon had put it, forcing the races together. Although the Supreme Court in 1971 rejected this distinction and permitted integration via busing, in 1970 the president believed that he had found a middle course.[153]

Nixon's dealings with subordinates underscored his desire for moderation. With Ehrlichman acting as broker, the president allowed liberal White House counsel Leonard Garment to draft the desegregation message. Ehrlichman then sent Garment's draft to Buchanan "for comment."[154] Dissatisfied with this balancing act, Nixon confided to Haldeman and Ehrlichman that he had to assume responsibility for school desegregation. While hoping "we can find one man to whom I can turn," the president resolved that "this man should not be Garment because of his bias in one direction, or Buchanan because of his bias in another."[155] Others remained outside the loop. Conservative advisers Dent and Bryce N. Harlow had to plot ways of voicing their concerns about desegregation. Nixon had even less patience with liberals. In early 1970 he removed Panetta as chief of HEW's Office of Civil Rights.[156] In so doing, the president served notice that he would not desegregate schools in a high-handed fashion.

Nixon used persuasion to promote desegregation. Rather than assign blame for the problem, he involved southerners of both races in its solution. With the support of advisers of differing philosophies–Ehrlichman, Garment, and Dent–Nixon established a cabinet-level committee on school desegregation. Agnew chaired the panel and Labor Secretary George P. Shultz, a moderate Republican, coordinated its efforts.[157] Shultz's committee formed advisory committees of prominent blacks and whites in seven states to bring districts into compliance with *Alexander*.[158] Shultz's group stressed negotiation and interracial cooperation over federal coercion. It assigned funds to districts slated for desegregation and financed television advertisements to encourage respect for the law.[159] The cabinet committee thus shifted the debate from *whether* to *how* the South would desegregate schools.

The committee faced hurdles in establishing state committees. Segregationists, such as Governor John J. McKeithen, Democrat of Louisiana, and Senator Edward J. Gurney, Republican of Florida, resisted their formation. Mississippians opposed the use of local committees, as did a group of Atlantans who considered themselves "urbane, sophisticated, cultured, and liberal," reported L. Patrick Gray, the cabinet committee's staff assistant. "The majority demonstrates skepticism, suspicion, and a strong dislike for the policies of the Nixon administration."[160] The staff of the cabinet committee–Gray, James Clawson, and Robert C. Mardian–did yeoman's work, compiling names, interviewing candidates, and stroking egos, to assemble citizens' committees in each state.[161]

While the cabinet committee brought the federal government into the desegregation process as a partner, the president wanted it to remain a silent one. Nixon predicted that "high profile, overly aggressive Fed[eral] actions will make the problem worse."[162] He thought that bragging will "get us no votes in the North while gravely abrading the entire South."[163] As the new school year neared, the president reminded subordinates "*not* [to] make a big deal of all we're doing . . . *Quietly* do our job . . . [Don't] be sucked into praising our 'great record'

... *Low profile* is the key."[164] To ease desegregation policy making, Garment proposed organizing a "Tranquility Base" instead of a "war room," while Jerris Leonard suggested a benign name for a telephone assistance center: "Dial-a-Desegregationist."[165]

Civil rights liberals were pressing hard for desegregation, and a few Nixonians appeared flustered. The U.S. Commission on Civil Rights prepared a report that accused the government of lax enforcement. Leonard denounced the document as "replete with inaccuracies," and, during one meeting, bullied Howard A. Glickstein, the commission's staff director: "I am going to shove this report up your ass." He wailed, "Thurmond goes for my throat, [liberal senator Walter] Mondale for my midsection, but you, Mr. Glickstein, are the worst, you go for my nuts." He threatened that "if this report comes out, there is going to be blood in the streets, and it is going to be yours, Mr. Glickstein."[166] This tantrum did not prevent publication of the study, which scored the civil rights efforts of the entire government, not just the administration.[167] Leonard's reference to "blood in the streets" underscored White House anxiety over the impact of desegregation.

Despite attempts to sell the president's policy as moderate, many whites still found it aggressive. A Georgian told one official, "You will have as much chance of succeeding in this endeavor as you would have in explaining to your wife that adultery is merely a joyous frolic."[168] White northerners also complained. "For God's sake go along with Mr. Thurmond," a constituent wrote House Minority Leader Gerald R. Ford, "& fight this damned forced integration. Last time I voted for Nixon but unless things change—I & *many* others will vote for Wallace" in 1972.[169]

Conservative Republicans protested the administration's enforcement of school desegregation as too strict. A "furious" Representative George Bush, Republican of Texas, claimed that "it is literally killing me in my Senate campaign" against Democrat Lloyd Bentsen.[170] Two southern Republicans, Thurmond and Senator John Tower of Texas, seethed over Nixon's policy. Dent reported that Thurmond "is convinced the Administration wants to alienate him . . . *Senator Tower* is never satisfied. Now he is upset over law suits against 45 Texas school districts."[171] Hoping Nixon would ease pressure for desegregation, Thurmond and Tower learned that he would go only so far in meeting their demands.

Nixon grew anxious. After reading criticism by Thurmond and Tower, he issued a series of orders demanding "no more catering to liberals and integrationists to our political disadvantage."[172] Nixon affirmed that he was "a conservative, does not believe in integration, will carry out the law, nothing more."[173] On August 10, a jittery president informed Haldeman that he had changed his mind about the school desegregation message of March 24, now thinking "it went too far."[174] Such vacillation was to be expected. In an election year, Nixon worried about the impact of desegregation on white southern voters. Furthermore, he was about to implement what no president had even attempted: full-scale desegregation of southern schools. To remain resolute with memories of Little Rock, multiplied by one thousand, lurking in his mind would have been a feat. But rather than subvert the high court's mandate by accepting token desegregation, as Dent had advised, Nixon soothed white sensibilities *and* carried out the *Alexander* decision.[175]

To encourage compliance with the law, the president conferred with prominent southerners during the summer of 1970. Sounding familiar themes, he told members of the South Carolina state advisory committee that the South must no longer be treated as a separate region and that the power of the federal government "has in a way failed when it can only be used to coerce."[176] In meeting southerners, Nixon sometimes placed principle ahead of politics. After agreeing to journey to New Orleans to nudge the Louisiana state advisory committee into supporting desegregation, the president acknowledged, "It'll be harmful politically but it will help the schools so we'll do it."[177] At other times Nixon used personal diplomacy to mend political fences. On August 6 he brought to the White House Senators Thurmond and Tower, other conservative members of Congress, and Republican Party officials to listen to their grievances and assure them that desegregation would be carried out as fairly as possible.[178] Participants in such meetings usually found the president persuasive.[179] Nixon's penchant for keeping a low public profile belied his behind-the-scenes leadership in resolving the desegregation problem.

As autumn 1970 neared, the president monitored school desegregation through Edward L. Morgan, an aide to Ehrlichman. Morgan concurred with Nixon's low-key approach and even advised that all desegregation meetings remain *"absolutely quiet."*[180] The president, of course, was in command of policy. To "balance the South," he agreed to let Justice support an NAACP suit against Michigan's freedom of choice statute. He also gave HEW funds to schools in Jackson, Mississippi, before securing authorization from Congress. Nixon refused to dispatch more federal attorneys to the South, enlisted local lawyers and "friendly" members of Congress, and opposed sending in federal marshals "unless I order it."[181] The judiciary, the president reasoned, "has given us such a severe requirement that we ought not go one step beyond what the Court absolutely requires."[182]

It worked. A confluence of presidential leadership, federal persuasion, Supreme Court rulings, Justice Department lawsuits, and the threat of HEW denying holdout districts federal aid broke white southern resistance. Out of a total school population of 3 million, only 186,000 African American children attended desegregated schools in the South prior to 1969. During autumn 1969, after the Nixon administration began to desegregate schools via litigation, 600,000 southern blacks entered desegregated schools.[183] Justice Department lawsuits compelled recalcitrant districts to implement desegregation plans that they had previously drawn up but refused to carry out.[184] In 1970, after the *Alexander* decision, 2 million more African Americans were attending desegregated schools.[185] In this sense, Nixon was the greatest school desegregator in American history.

Although the Supreme Court had forced the president's hand, *Alexander* alone did not ensure school desegregation. "There will not be anything like total desegregation in the South in September 1970," predicted an HEW regional director, "unless the administration, this time, has the will to enforce the law promptly and consistently."[186] In 1970, at least, Nixon had the will. He shrewdly gave the South the opportunity to comply with the Court's mandates peacefully, with little coercion.[187] While he did not threaten to deny federal funds to schools, that option remained available. After years of defying *Brown,* southern whites chose to retreat with dignity rather than continue fighting.

Nixon and the South: Toward Reelection

Despite Nixon's interest in capturing the white southern vote, politics alone never determined his civil rights policy. Consequently, the president's relations with southern conservatives remained tenuous. As the next election approached, he used a variety of measures to solidify his southern base.

Examples of southern displeasure with the president's civil rights policy abound. Thurmond voiced disappointment over Nixon's failure to back freedom of choice plans.[188] A few southerners opposed the president's policy of aiding minority businesses. Uncertain of the initiative's merits, Senator John L. McClellan, Democrat of Arkansas, stalled passage of the president's budget for the Office of Minority Business Enterprise.[189] Thurmond asked Stans to justify a program "whereby a businessman who is a member of the minority race is to be given preferential treatment when he bids on government contracts."[190]

To secure his southern flank, Nixon employed gestures of goodwill. In May 1971 he toured Alabama and lauded the South for its progress in school desegregation.[191] One month later the president privately praised southern contributions to American life and directed aides to have his remarks reprinted across the region.[192] After learning of southern concerns over the minority business project, government officials worked to assure Senators McClellan and Thurmond that the program was viable and proper.[193] To build additional bridges, the president, in 1971, offered to meet with "Southern Democrats who have been consistently with us" to "thank them for their support" on foreign policy votes.[194]

Because Nixon's "southern strategy" proved more symbolic than substantive, support for the president's reelection was not assured. During the midterm elections of 1970, Republicans gained just one Senate seat in the South.[195] With 1972 approaching, two scenarios concerned the White House. The first was "the likelihood that the Democratic Party will move strongly toward the center" and compete for the moderate vote.[196] Second, Nixon and his aides fretted that Wallace might launch another independent campaign and take conservative votes away from the president.[197]

To prevent both scenarios, Nixon rallied his supporters and went after his opponents. The president reached out to moderates, reminding Dent that "our appeal must not be restricted to the old guard southerners."[198] To undermine the candidacy of Senator Edmund S. Muskie of Maine, a centrist Democrat, Nixon proposed setting up a front group, "Liberals for Muskie," to mail broadsides citing the senator's liberal voting record to southern Democrats.[199] To damage Wallace's prospects, the White House funneled money to Wallace's opponent in Alabama's gubernatorial primary. After Wallace won, Nixon adopted a "carrot and stick" policy. Mitchell's Justice Department probed charges of graft in Alabama. The president then made friendly overtures to the governor as he awaited announcement of Wallace's plans.[200]

As the next campaign approached, Nixon's domestic policies seemed to lurch to the right more than ever before. In 1971 the president ordered his aides to stress the work requirement of the Family Assistance Plan to shore up conservative support.[201] When Associate Justices John M. Harlan and Hugo Black resigned from the Supreme Court in September 1971, Nixon saw a "good chance" to score points with rightists by naming strict constructionists.[202] The president mostly emphasized his opposition to busing. After the high court, in *Swann v. Mecklenberg County* (1971), sanctioned busing to achieve integration, Nixon commanded Elliot L. Richardson, the liberal Republican who had replaced Finch as HEW secretary in 1970, to "do what the law requires and not *one bit* more."[203] With court rulings threatening his anti-busing position, the president told Ehrlichman to "get legislation or a const. amendment [prohibiting busing] ready as an option as soon as possible. I reject the advice of Richardson, Garment et al. to relax & *enjoy it*."[204] In March 1972 Nixon went on television to criticize busing and ask Congress for a moratorium against it. Although the moratorium never passed, he had carried the day politically by identifying himself with anti-busing sentiment.[205]

Nixon's eleventh-hour conversion to conservatism was more apparent than real. In accenting FAP's work provisions, the president conceded, "What I am looking for is symbolism to be perfectly candid."[206] He privately noted that "Moynihan–income strategy is right. We have to cast ourselves as reformers."[207] After appointing conservatives to the high bench in 1971, he considered naming to the next vacancy "a middle-of-the-road guy," Elliot Richardson.[208] Although Nixon disagreed with busing for philosophical as well as political reasons, his priority remained quality education. Upon learning that schools had curtailed art and music programs to finance court-ordered integration, Nixon searched for some means, within "political reality," to fund busing.[209]

According to one Senate aide, the president was "playing a very cute and deceptive game," opposing busing in word while carrying out integration in fact.[210]

That comment requires explanation, since it calls into question the president's well-known opposition to busing. Nixon stressed his aversion to busing in battleground states, such as Michigan, where the policy was especially unpopular among whites. In private he sounded more responsible, conceding that he could not "talk like Wallace does."[211] At a meeting with the cabinet committee on school desegregation in 1972, Nixon, restating his support for "quality education," argued "that legally segregated education is inferior education" and opposed "any solution that would, in effect, 'turn back the clock.'"[212] Such remarks explain why he wavered between a constitutional amendment against busing and the more modest legislative ban. Morgan wanted to keep liberals "convinced we are doing what the Court requires, and our conservative Southern friends convinced that we are not doing any more than the Court requires." *"Good! Keep it up,"* Nixon replied.[213] Yet the public heard his racially divisive anti-busing rhetoric.

Combining conservative words with moderate policies, Nixon forged a right-center coalition. Yet the price was confusion. "In my view," admitted Richardson in 1971, "Nixon's political course is subject to too much of this zigzag, and it has hurt him more than helped him."[214] One White House staffer accurately forecast that liberals would overlook progress in school desegregation and accuse the administration of timidity "in its enforcement of civil rights laws in pursuit of a so-called southern strategy," while conservatives "will charge it has been too vigorous."[215] For Ehrlichman, Nixon's agenda lacked focus: "Our policy is we have no domestic policy. We have a body of folklore."[216]

During the election of 1972, Nixon's success in the South turned on fate more than anything else. The prospect of a centrist Democratic candidate evaporated when the party nominated an unreconstructed antiwar liberal, Senator George S. McGovern of South Dakota.[217] The threat to the president's right flank vanished when Wallace, paralyzed after an assassination attempt, declined to launch a third-party bid.[218] Thus, the president gained the votes of moderates and conservatives and carried Dixie.[219] Even if Nixon's goodwill gestures and low-key approach to desegregation aided his triumph, the outcome might have been otherwise had Democrats chosen a centrist or had a third-party candidate appealed for conservative support.

The Southern Strategy in Retrospect

The legacy of Nixon's "southern strategy" is as varied as the man who practiced it. On the positive side, the president did not surrender completely to demands for a Thermidorian (or "Thurmondorian") reaction on civil rights. In fact, he and his aides desegregated southern schools on an unprecedented scale. Yet their posture involved little moral leadership, all but excluded African Americans from Nixon's electoral coalition, ignored de facto segregation in the North, and failed to bridge racial division. The president's course had greater impact on the civil rights policy debate, by moving it away from integration, than on strengthening the Republican Party in the South.

If the president's intricate policies, contradictory goals, and ambiguous legacy have invited diverse interpretations, one has become particularly fashionable: Nixon was the political midwife of the new conservatism. By crafting a message tinged with populism, social conservatism, and even racism, he delivered Wallace voters into the waiting arms of the Republican Party. According to this interpretation, Nixon's activities helped to elect Ronald Reagan and George H. W. Bush to the presidency and elevate Representative Newt Gingrich, Republican of Georgia, to the Speakership of the House of Representatives in 1994. Moreover, Nixon occasionally exploited "hot button" socioeconomic issues, such as affirmative action, crime, and race, that politicians have since used to divide the electorate.[220]

While there is much truth in this interpretation, especially regarding the racial alignment in presidential elections, it remains flawed. Placing Nixon squarely within a conservative tradition would have shocked the intellectual fathers of the New Right as well as diehard segregationists.[221] In light of the rightward turn of the GOP beginning with the nomination of Barry Goldwater in 1964, moderation, Nixon-style, represented a detour.

Nixon, if anything, helped to delay his party's resurgence in the South and in Congress. In pursuing the presidency, he chose the easy path of cultivating conservative southern Democrats, neglecting Dixie's

Republicans, and playing down his own party affiliation. In 1960 Nixon told GOP speakers below the Mason-Dixon line "to make their appeal—not for the purpose of making the South Republican—but for carrying the South for the Nixon-Lodge ticket."[222] As president, he continued to court southern Democrats, considered replacing the GOP with an "Independent Conservative Party," and declined to campaign for Republican congressional candidates in 1972, telling advisers "to quit talking about the New Republican Majority."[223] To the extent that Reagan, Bush, and Gingrich benefited from Nixon's appeals, it was only in a general sense. Their successes were their own.

Rather than being a Republican partisan or a conservative visionary, Nixon juggled his own complex views, popular ideals and prejudices, and competing pressures. Understanding that segregation was wrong, that whites did not consider themselves racists, that public opinion was turning against the civil rights movement's perceived excesses, the president trod cautiously.[224] On segregated schools, he employed court enforcement, then persuasion, tackling de jure segregation in the South, not de facto segregation in the North. In one sense, Nixon followed a "southern" strategy by holding the South to a higher standard than the North. That he was able to pursue such a course without offending southern whites underscores the power of his symbolic appeals, his acumen, and his luck.

The president's actions marked a turn away from compulsory racial integration. Nixon continued to argue that integration via busing was unconstitutional, even after the Supreme Court had ruled otherwise. Realizing the unpopularity of busing, liberals of both parties shunned it. In 1964 New York senatorial candidate Robert F. Kennedy opposed the "compulsory transportation of children over long distances" on the grounds that it "doesn't make much sense." Hubert Humphrey also began distancing himself from this tactic, and Nelson Rockefeller signed a bill forbidding busing without the consent of school boards.[225] "The Democrats weren't all that excited about busing, either," recalled George McGovern. "It is not the happiest way to deal with civil rights issues, so I never felt that that was one of [the Nixon administration's] chief failings."[226] The high court got the message. In *Milliken v. Bradley* (1974), it rejected a comprehensive plan for racial integration across district lines in Detroit's school system.[227] While some busing proceeded, most notably in Boston, the issue faded as Presidents Gerald R. Ford, Jimmy Carter, and Ronald Reagan opposed forced integration.[228]

Moreover, the tradition of presidents assuming a low profile on school desegregation continued after Nixon. In 1977 Arthur S. Flemming, chair of the U.S. Commission on Civil Rights, informed President Carter that desegregation was proceeding in communities where leaders had endorsed "the Constitutional requirement of equal opportunity in education." He urged Carter to take the next step and invite prominent Americans to the White House in order to organize a "National Citizens Committee for the Desegregation of the Nation's Schools."[229] The president declined, arguing that his administration would use its "existing authority" to desegregate schools. "It is too early to call a conference, which would probably duplicate your own extant recommendations," he wrote.[230] Instead, Carter proposed giving additional funds to "advisory groups" working to foster desegregation.[231] By substituting local committees and increased dollars for visible presidential leadership, Carter was following in Nixon's footsteps.

If Nixon's school desegregation strategy failed to remedy all inequities in education, it provided what he wanted most: a flexible response to a nettlesome issue. His policy on housing bias paralleled that of school desegregation. In both cases the president espoused the narrower principle of nondiscrimination, rejecting "forced integration" of schools and neighborhoods.

2

Open Communities versus Forced Integration:
Romney, Nixon, and Fair Housing

President Nixon's school desegregation and fair housing policies had some similarities and some differences. As with school desegregation, Nixon defined open housing as nondiscrimination, meaning that housing should not be denied on the basis of race. Rather than impose federally subsidized housing on suburbs, under what Nixon called "forced integration," Attorney General John N. Mitchell would sue, on a case-by-case basis, individuals suspected of bias in the sale or rental of housing. Litigation again became the preferred means to fight bias, an approach that seemed reasonable since, unlike in the case of school desegregation, the president had evinced barely a glint of interest in fair housing during his early public career. The Fair Housing Act of 1968 had passed during a period of white backlash against civil rights agitation, at a time when Nixon was courting white suburbanites.[1] But since he had opposed bias in other areas such as education and employment, Nixon tepidly backed fair housing during the 1968 campaign and his years in the White House.[2]

Secretary of Housing and Urban Development (HUD) George W. Romney challenged Nixon's reticence. The former Michigan governor attacked, with moralistic fervor, the widening economic gulf between the races, which left many whites residing in comfortable suburbs while poor blacks endured a harsh life in urban slums. Like Jack F. Kemp, President George H. W. Bush's HUD secretary, Romney emerged as sympathetic to African American concerns. But the two men's goals differed. Kemp sought to rebuild inner cities through "enterprise zones," that is, the use of tax breaks to spur business investment in blighted neighborhoods, while Romney strove to move blacks from cities into suburbs.

In their bout over fair housing, Nixon and Romney sparred for three rounds. During round one, covering 1968 and 1969, Nixon backed fair housing in a tentative, low-key manner. In round two, running from 1969 to 1970, Romney promoted "open communities" by denying federal aid to lily-white suburbs. Then, between 1970 and 1972, or round three, Nixon asserted that integration must not be "forced" on white neighborhoods, compelling Romney to work with the White House in tailoring more modest fair housing guidelines.

Limited Commitment: Nixon and Fair Housing

Like most politicians of his era, Nixon never marched in the vanguard of the struggle for open housing. He supported the Fair Housing Act of 1968, but only quietly. Wary of offending white suburbanites, President Nixon initially displayed no interest in pressing the matter and allowed the federal departments, particularly Justice, to enforce it.

For most of the twentieth century, a web of formal and informal discriminatory practices had prevailed in the housing industry. Restrictive covenants barred minorities from owning a given dwelling, and many real estate brokers, assuming that racial integration would lower property values, steered African Americans away from homes in white neighborhoods. If a black person managed to purchase a house in a white area, realtors sometimes engaged in "blockbusting," raising the bugbear of integration to sway other whites to sell their homes. Real estate boards, in turn, defended zoning laws that forbade the construction of low-income housing.[3] Some whites even resorted to mob violence to dissuade blacks from infringing on their turf.[4]

In the years after 1945, presidents offered only token support of fair housing. Harry S. Truman, who opposed restrictive covenants, achieved just a "modicum of desegregation" in housing.[5] President Dwight D. Eisenhower, devoted to limited government, proved "incapable of moving beyond symbolism to an open confrontation with racial inequities in basic human services, employment, and housing."[6] President John F. Kennedy belatedly fulfilled a campaign promise to sign an executive order prohibiting discrimination in federally assisted housing. But the national government did not formally outlaw bias in housing until 1968, when Lyndon B. Johnson occupied the White House.[7]

Early in his career Nixon maintained a low profile on housing discrimination. When a group of southern segregationists, upset with the vice president's support of desegregation and fair employment, planned to embarrass him by selling a black family a home in his Washington neighborhood, Nixon let his subordinates respond. "I would say he couldn't care less," remarked Rose Mary Woods, his secretary, when she learned of the plot.[8] Yet Nixon's silence hardly constituted strong leadership. During the 1960s he continued to address housing bias cautiously; a position paper, probably from 1967, had him supporting nondiscrimination clauses only for federally assisted housing. The paper rejected federal legislation, "which the vast majority of [this] country virulently opposes," to outlaw bias in housing on the grounds that such a step would "inflame" racial tensions. Nixon, like most Republicans, upheld the right of local authorities to implement their own fair housing remedies and "advance at [their] own pace."[9] In its deliberate tone the paper resembled Nixon's various statements on school desegregation.

Nixon opposed a federal fair housing law for three reasons. He argued that 95 percent of blacks would be unable to take advantage of "open housing" during their lifetimes, since they lacked the means to buy homes.[10] He saw minority economic development, not racial integration of schools and neighborhoods, as the key to progress in civil rights, and he derided fair housing as a "will-o'-the-wisp," an empty gesture advanced by liberals.[11] Finally, Nixon feared a growing white backlash, warning, "It is important to bring down the barriers, but these (open housing) demonstrations have reached a point of diminishing returns."[12]

As a presidential candidate, Nixon modified his stance by supporting the Fair Housing Act of 1968. Prospects for passing the bill brightened when "Old Switcheroo," Senate Minority Leader Everett M. Dirksen, Republican of Illinois, abandoned his opposition and voted with moderate Republicans and liberal Democrats to end a southern filibuster. The Senate, by a margin of 70 to 21, then approved a fair housing measure for 80 percent of the nation's housing. At the request of Senator Charles Percy, Republican of Illinois, Nixon "made some calls" to Republicans on behalf of the measure, although Mike Manatos, LBJ's liaison to the Senate, asserted that "the only votes we got were those we got ourselves."[13] The bill faced stiff resistance in the House of Representatives, where Minority Leader Gerald R. Ford, Republican of Michigan, favored a scaled-back version covering 60 percent of housing.[14]

Nixon and Governor Nelson A. Rockefeller of New York both urged Ford to accept the Senate's bill without changes.[15] Nixon sent Ford a letter from the civil rights leader Clarence Mitchell requesting help in passing it. He also discussed the matter with the minority leader over the telephone.[16] In the end, pressures for approval in the aftermath of Martin Luther King, Jr.'s, murder proved too great. In April the Senate bill cleared the House, 250 to 172, and Johnson signed it into law.[17]

Nixon's own "switcheroo" on fair housing reflected several concerns. Fair housing coincided with his belief in equal opportunity and his endorsement of the civil rights acts of 1964 and 1965. Remembering how cities had simmered with racial strife over the previous three summers, Nixon, like Dirksen, saw fair housing as a means to cool unrest. Besides, if Republican leaders thwarted this law and the cities erupted in violence, Democrats might blame them in the upcoming presidential campaign. Needing to fend off the liberal Rockefeller, his closest rival for the GOP nomination, Nixon backed fair housing to please moderate Republicans, including Percy.[18]

Even with such mixed motives, he deserves some praise for supporting the Fair Housing Act. In so doing, Nixon went against public opinion, especially in suburban areas and in the South. Residents of suburban Houston became enraged when their congressman, George Bush, voted for the Fair Housing Act. The youthful Republican perhaps supported the act to make up for his opposition to earlier civil rights legislation. In any event, Houstonians flooded Bush's office with more than one thousand letters denouncing fair housing. "I am surprised," one woman sarcastically wrote, "you are not with Mr. Nixon in the black people's march [at King's funeral] on Tuesday in Atlanta. We Shall Overcome."[19]

In truth, the Fair Housing Act (officially Title VIII of the Civil Rights Act of 1968) was a rather tame measure. Although the law prohibited a number of discriminatory practices, including blockbusting, it failed to specify its aim, whether to attack bias or to integrate white suburbs. The 1968 act provided for little in the way of enforcement, aside from litigation by the Justice Department. Had voters read the law's fine print, they might have perceived it as a symbolic stroke against bias.[20]

With fair housing so volatile, candidate Nixon did not raise the issue to woo minorities. In Philadelphia he remarked, "I am not going to campaign for the black vote at the risk of the suburban vote." The GOP candidate only vowed not to "say anything or do anything which will cause the Negroes to lose confidence in me."[21] Such hedging was pure Nixon, and it worked. In 1968 the Republican nominee polled 48 percent of the suburban vote, against 42 percent for the Democrat, Hubert H. Humphrey, and 10 percent for George C. Wallace, the independent candidate. Given Nixon's razor-thin margin of victory, a half-million votes, suburbanites certainly had helped elect him president.[22]

During 1969, Nixon, with an eye toward his suburban constituency, kept the issue of open housing away from the White House. After the Fair Housing Act went into effect, in 1969 Assistant Attorney General for Civil Rights Jerris Leonard, a moderate Republican, filed twelve lawsuits against people suspected of bias in housing. He initiated forty such suits the following year.[23] Meanwhile, urban affairs chief Daniel P. Moynihan, a liberal Democrat, publicly criticized residential segregation.[24] But Moynihan, perhaps seeing little chance to sway Nixon on this issue, focused on winning presidential support for welfare reform instead.

Within the White House, concern about open housing surfaced in a pair of obscure reports. During his first year in office, Nixon, concentrating on foreign policy, named sundry task forces to propose solutions to domestic problems. Arthur F. Burns, his chief domestic adviser, established eighteen such panels at the end of 1968, and John D. Ehrlichman, Burns's successor, formed sixteen additional task forces a year later.[25] One panel, on urban renewal, urged "a strong national policy" of "carrots and sticks" to shift low- and medium-income housing from ghettos to suburbs.[26] Another, on low-income housing, pressed the government to use its community assistance programs to "overcome racial and economic discrimination" in housing.[27] Both reports called for something beyond court enforcement of fair housing: the use of federal power to integrate suburbs.

The president vehemently rejected such counsel. After reading that the Task Force on Low-Income Housing wanted to link federal aid to a suburb's progress on racial integration, Nixon scrawled: "E[hrlichman]. I am *absolutely* opposed to this. Knock it in the head now."[28] Such a response was not surprising. Since these panels tapped private citizens, not government officials, they were free to propose sweeping reforms, which others would have to implement.[29] After the president rebuffed later proposals from his Task Force on Women's Rights and Responsibilities, Commission on Population Growth, and National Advisory Council on Minority Business Enterprise, this approach to policy making soon faded away.

Political expediency was the main reason Nixonians dodged the question of fair housing. Their breed of Republicans—middle-of-the-road, pragmatic, and politically astute—knew that suburbanites opposed a muscular open housing program. Throughout the struggle for civil rights, politicians rarely mustered the courage to defy white opinion. That remained the task of moral crusaders.

George Romney: The Crusader as Dissenter

If Nixon's administration generally lacked crusaders, George Romney proved a notable exception. The housing secretary, unlike the president's other advisers, viewed civil rights issues in terms of morality and justice rather than political pragmatism. Instead of gauging the political fallout of a given policy, the onetime American Motors president and Michigan governor ascertained the "right" course and forged ahead.

Romney, to be sure, seldom emerged as the administration's knight-errant, slaying dragons by the score. In a manner reminiscent of Woodrow Wilson, whom he liked to quote, Romney sometimes carried his missionary fervor too far, offended powerful people and key constituencies, and stumbled into political thickets.[30]

Three key aspects of Romney's character molded his public stance on civil rights. First, in an odd way, Romney's Mormon faith left him sensitive to racial intolerance. Born in Mexico, where his parents had fled to escape American laws against polygamy, Romney experienced prejudice at an early age. After his family returned to the United States, Romney's playmates questioned his nationality by tagging him "Mex." Yet he remained loyal to Mormonism, a religion hostile to African Americans. Until the 1970s, the church held that blacks bore the mark of Cain and were ineligible for the clergy. Caught between his own brushes with bigotry and his church's racism, Romney accepted Mormon practice, then campaigned for civil rights outside his church. He fought for open housing during World War II, and as Michigan's governor during the 1960s marched in demonstrations organized by the National Association for the Advancement of Colored People.[31] Mormon theological racism, one Michigan Democrat noted, had led Romney to overcompensate and stand up for racial equality. This Democrat accurately predicted that the governor's ardor would repel white suburbanites and GOP conservatives.[32]

Second, a religious zeal fired Romney's approach to public service. As a young man he had served as a Mormon missionary, and friends later detected an evangelical strain in his undertakings.[33] Looking toward the election of 1964, President Kennedy feared a race against the squeaky-clean Romney, whom he considered "an evangelist" cloaked in "God" and "Mother."[34] Dismayed by the presidential bid of the conservative senator Barry M. Goldwater in 1964, Romney told GOP leaders that he was ready to run against the Arizonan in a "crusade" for moderate Republican principles.[35] Frustrated with Romney's insistence on locating low-income housing in a Chicago suburb, Ehrlichman once sighed that the housing secretary "wanted to be a crusader."[36] Romney, joked a black official at HUD, "is an evangelical kind of cat."[37]

Finally, Romney's leadership style of bold advances and awkward retreats lacked guile. In 1964 the headstrong Romney offended Goldwater by refusing to endorse him and by tarring the GOP's right wing as extremist.[38] When their paths later crossed, the Michigan governor avoided the Arizonan. "I intended to catch up with you after the dinner," Romney explained, "but left a little early to watch the Michigan-UCLA [championship] basketball game."[39] In 1967, after presidential candidate Romney uttered an impolitic remark about having been "brainwashed" by military commanders in Vietnam, he lost ground and withdrew from the race before the first primary.[40] During his tenure at HUD, Romney embraced open housing but recruited few black employees for his department. When a group of African Americans chased after the secretary to press this matter, Romney purportedly raced down ten flights of stairs to avoid them.[41] Accustomed to getting his own way in business and in Michigan politics, Romney was more adept at taking a public stand than at accepting criticism, compromising his beliefs, or forming coalitions.

Romney's leadership style differed from Nixon's. Although both men were moderates, Nixon trimmed his beliefs to suit public opinion. Using carefully scripted statements to placate conservative as well as centrist Republicans, Nixon performed like a virtuoso in the fine art of waffling, while Romney never progressed to being more than a rank amateur. And Nixon was quick to flash his party loyalty when it was in his interest. The man whom Lyndon Johnson once labeled a "chronic campaigner" stumped for Goldwater in 1964 and for Republican congressional candidates two years later. So it was the opportunistic Nixon, not the moralistic Romney, who captured the GOP's nomination in 1968.[42] "I can't change myself to fit what people want," Romney conceded. "I'm not a political animal in that sense. I'm no Lyndon Johnson or Richard Nixon."[43]

During most of the 1960s, Nixon and Romney remained cordial. They first corresponded in 1960, when Romney urged presidential candidates Nixon and Kennedy to begin addressing the burning issues of the day.[44] Nixon considered the American Motors president a "comer"; in 1962 he told Eisenhower that "if [Romney] can avoid alienating too many of the party leaders," he would capture the governorship and become "a real power on the national scene."[45] After he lost California's governorship while Romney prevailed in Michigan, Nixon appeared to pass the baton, urging Romney to fight "for our cause."[46] LBJ's White House worried that he might do just that. In 1966 one Johnson aide expressed concern that "Governor Romney will win reelection by such a wide margin" that "Republicans will nominate him for President in 1968."[47]

Presidential ambition turned Nixon and Romney into rivals. The former vice president angled for the Republican nomination in 1964 while trying to dissuade the Michigan governor from launching his own presidential bid.[48] As the election of 1968 neared, Nixon described Romney as a formidable foe: "With his messianic streak, he might go on to the bitter end."[49] In fact, the governor dropped out early, but he opposed Nixon almost to the "bitter end." Romney endorsed Rockefeller over Nixon and then, at the GOP convention, fought against the nomination of Nixon's running mate, Governor Spiro T. Agnew of Maryland.[50]

Why, then, did Nixon name Romney to his cabinet? The president-elect wanted to appease Republican moderates, and Leonard Garment, a liberal aide, had touted Romney for the housing post: "He certainly has the stature, is a superb administrator in both business and government, and is highly acceptable to blacks and others concerned with the neglected 'people problems' of housing."[51] Romney's experience with voluntary action, a core Republican principle, perhaps also proved appealing.[52] Finally, although Nixon recognized Romney's independence, he had not yet grasped its full extent.[53]

Romney emerged as a leading dissenter from administration procedures and policies. The housing secretary, in accordance with the president's wishes, launched "Operation Breakthrough" to increase the supply of low- and medium-income housing, and he chaired a cabinet committee to encourage voluntary action.[54] Yet Romney objected to Nixon's use of White House staffers as policy gatekeepers and to his downgrading of the cabinet as a decision-making organ. "Romney really stirred up," jotted White House chief of staff H. R. Haldeman in 1969; "wants appointment but P[resident] won't see him until his volunteer program is fully worked out. Poor E[hrlichman] has to handle and George ain't easy. Is reaching the crisis stage with threats of quitting."[55] Upset that no one had briefed him on "revenue sharing," Nixon's program to aid cities, Romney asked whether Ehrlichman's Domestic Council was a "policy instrument" or just "window dressing."[56]

The president had cause for avoiding his housing secretary; on domestic matters, Romney proved to be headstrong and much more eager than Nixon to use federal power. When the president, under revenue sharing, sought to dispense grants to locales "without strings," the housing secretary clamored for federal oversight.[57] Romney helped persuade Nixon to continue LBJ's costly Model Cities program. To arrest inflation, he advocated wage and price controls even before the president adopted this policy. Romney believed that a measure of disagreement would sharpen Nixon's decision making.[58] But in the president's view, he went too far.

An irritated Nixon tried to force Romney to resign. Early in 1970 the president ordered Bryce N. Harlow, a political adviser, to "do some moseying around" regarding the Michigan Senate race. He wanted Harlow to contact two Michigan Republicans, Minority Leader Ford and Republican National Committeewoman Elly Peterson, and "get them to create a hassle." Then, he said, they should send out feelers to "have Geo[rge] come [and] save the party."[59] This plot went nowhere. In 1970 Democratic senator Philip A. Hart won reelection by swamping Lenore Lafount Romney, the housing secretary's wife. George Romney remained entrenched at HUD.[60]

Such underhandedness was quite unnecessary. As Garment proved, it was possible to advocate a left-of-center agenda and remain a team player within Nixon's White House. Garment, a onetime clarinet player in Woody Herman's jazz band, had practiced law in Nixon's New York firm during the 1960s. The hippest member of the president's inner circle turned out to be one of the most liberal, with Haldeman tagging the former Democrat "Lenny Government."[61] Garment coordinated civil rights matters and favored racial integration, which, he conceded, "won't solve all our problems" but had to be carried out or "we will lose the cities and much more."[62] Garment lost this argument, and the policy battles he did win derived partly from his unique personal relationship with Nixon.[63] Yet Garment, unlike Romney, never tried to force the president to take a particular position.

Under Nixon, Romney's approach to governance was out of place. The president and his top aides were pragmatic managers, coldly mixing principle with opportunism. According to White House staffer Stephen Hess, Nixon had not run his election campaign as a "crusade" and had refused to push a domestic agenda "with zealotry." Inevitably, the "zealous" Romney became an object of scorn, in Hess's opinion, a "blowhard."[64] "Romney's enthusiastic piety," quipped Nixon speechwriter William Safire, "caused critics of his Presidential effort in 1968 to say he only wanted the Presidency as a steppingstone."[65]

Romney and Open Communities

Romney's "crusading dissension" emerged most clearly in the arena of housing discrimination. To achieve "open communities," Romney and his aides drafted an ambitious but flawed plan to link federal aid to a locale's record on integration. When one of the first communities slated for such pressure resisted, Romney found his campaign in shambles. With Nixon again fuming, White House officials began to assert control over fair housing policy.

Romney and his aides opposed residential segregation. The housing secretary, early in 1969, hinted that he might propose a federal law to strike down zoning ordinances which prohibited low-income housing.[66] Four years later he flailed away at the evils—"crime, drug abuse, inadequate education"—associated with the "concentration of the poor" in cities.[67] At HUD, Assistant Secretary for Equal Opportunity Samuel J. Simmons and Assistant Secretary for Metropolitan Development Samuel C. Jackson, both African Americans, favored a mixture of pressures and incentives to prod suburbs to accept low-income housing. Undersecretary Richard C. Van Dusen, a Detroit attorney and Romney protégé, directed HUD's open housing effort.[68] Van Dusen, who shunned the label "integrationist," was a liberal Republican committed to bringing the races together. He once refused to fund a federal housing project unless it included whites as well as blacks.[69]

Disregarding the political danger signs, Romney and his aides thrashed out their ideas for "open communities" during a meeting at Camp David in 1969. Van Dusen argued that pork barrel projects provided them with leverage to use for "objectives." "So what are our objectives?" he asked. Simmons's goal was a "truly integrated society," while Jackson conceded that economic and social integration was "far more controversial" than racial integration. Romney denied that economic strides for minorities alone would lead to integration. Believing that restrictive zoning had to end as well, the secretary favored a policy of "carrots and sticks" whereby local governments seeking federal subsidies had to remove housing barriers to blacks. HUD counsel Sherman Unger agreed, urging Romney to "keep [an] overall box score of prog[ress] in a given community, & be sure there's balance. [It] can be done quietly."[70] Unger's emphasis on "quiet" enforcement underscored white middle-class antipathy toward integration.

Did open communities conflict with the president's housing program? Since Nixon had provided little direction on the issue, Romney was simply filling a policy vacuum. The secretary no doubt believed that his program meshed with the law, court rulings, and Nixon's own statement on school desegregation, which sought a "free and open" society. Yet HUD officials had construed the Fair Housing Act very broadly, as a mandate for integration.[71]

Romney surely knew that he was moving beyond the president's open housing stance. The Justice Department under Mitchell and Leonard used litigation to seek remedies for individual victims of housing bias.[72] Romney, in contrast, favored a more active remedy in which communities had to show nondiscrimination by accepting low-income housing. Nixon never endorsed this policy, and HUD officials never cleared it with him.[73] Instead, they merely rummaged through speeches by the president and his aides, collecting quotations to justify their course. Jackson suggested that integration coincided with Nixon's post-election pledge to "bring us together," an interpretation at odds with the president's pronounced opposition to busing.[74]

In 1969 Romney named a task force to draft a strategy for open communities. Moved by Moynihan's speech "Toward a National Urban Policy," the panel defined an open community as "one in which choices are available, doors are unlocked, opportunities exist for those who have felt walled within the ghetto."[75] It proposed building public housing in suburbs and compelling these projects to rent to minorities. The task force endorsed giving loans to aspiring home owners and rebuilding low-income housing, demolished under urban renewal, in suburbs.[76] To strengthen their case, task force members cited the Fair Housing Act, which vaguely prohibited HUD from subsidizing bias, and the Housing and Urban Development Act of 1968, which expanded funding of low-income housing and water and sewer projects.[77]

Yet open communities faced obstacles. A HUD report conceded the pervasiveness of segregation, with suburbanites equating low-income people with "delinquency," "family disorganization," and "poor maintenance of housing and grounds." Some African American leaders, seeking to preserve their power bases, favored keeping blacks in urban ghettos. Romney's aides realized that suburban integration was "extremely sensitive" and "would arouse major political opposition."[78] So, rather than argue over "*whether* we should work toward open communities," HUD's task force debated "*how explicit* we should be in announcing our goals."[79]

To overcome these obstacles, Romney, guided by his task force on open communities, charted a high-risk course. In 1970 Romney tucked into HUD's legislative package an amendment prohibiting restrictive zoning laws.[80] Then, after weighing a range of proposals, he elected to use HUD grants as leverage to spur communities into accepting low-income housing. His task force, to test this policy, targeted areas with high employment and few dwellings for poor minorities: Long Island, Cook County (Illinois), and the suburbs of Dallas, Boston, Newark, Buffalo, and Los Angeles.[81] HUD's Chicago office pressed for integration of Warren, Michigan, a white, working-class, largely Catholic suburb of Detroit. Romney and Van Dusen informed Warren officials that their community would not receive a $3 million urban renewal grant until they accepted low-income housing.[82] Since Nixon had refused to withhold federal funds from segregated schools, it is hard to imagine him approving HUD's threats.

No civil rights initiative developed on Nixon's watch was as sincerely devised or poorly executed as open communities. The housing secretary amateurishly assumed that a political consensus was not a prerequisite for this policy. Romney never sought presidential approval of his bill to outlaw discriminatory zoning laws. When the Budget Bureau adjudged the measure "consistent with the objectives of the Administration," Romney simply submitted it to the House Committee on Banking and Currency.[83] Outflanked by the committee's chair, Wright Patman, a Texas Democrat with forty-two years of congressional service, the bill never reached the House floor. Four of the six Republican committee members, who represented suburban districts, voted against it.[84] Nixon could not have rescued this controversial measure, and the White House Office of Congressional Liaison, headed by William E. Timmons, a conservative, would have provided little aid and comfort.

Nonetheless, Romney, new to Washington politics, should have tried to enlist greater support from the White House.

Romney kept Nixon in the dark on the ultimatum to Warren. During a meeting with the president, in May 1970, the housing secretary mentioned open communities but with little elaboration.[85] After learning of HUD's interest in open communities, Ehrlichman told Romney that the White House needed to review his plans. The secretary, perhaps with crossed fingers, replied that the bill against zoning requirements was the "only specific element of such a policy" and HUD was still reviewing its options.[86] By this time, of course, Romney's threat to Warren had progressed beyond the drawing board.

It remains unclear why Romney declined to brief Nixon on open communities. The housing secretary, remembering previous scuffles, probably feared that the president or his underlings would squelch this program. Perhaps he tried to broach the issue and Nixon rebuffed him. Romney's bruised pride over earlier White House slights no doubt influenced his stance. Forcing a confrontation, he might have reasoned, was the only way to draw presidential attention to this matter.[87]

If Romney wanted to bypass the White House and take on the white suburbs, he needed to enlist fellow integrationists. This he failed to do. In 1969 the NAACP had begun to challenge the constitutionality of restrictive zoning laws.[88] The organization later declared fair housing to be the "area of civil rights" most requiring "national action."[89] Yet the secretary never consulted with this natural ally nor with any like-minded white liberals. Romney's "lone-wolf" style of leadership began with daring advances, not patient coalition building.

Romney's biggest error was to underestimate the extent of white suburban racism. Warren, with 30 percent of its workers black but 99 percent of its residents white, offered a classic example of residential segregation.[90] But the community was a racial tinderbox. When an African American family moved into Warren in 1967, whites picketed their home and hurled rocks through their windows. Local police stood aside, forcing then-Governor Romney to send state troopers to restore order.[91] The HUD secretary clearly wanted to test open communities in an area with which he was familiar. Yet he ignored Warren's violent past.

HUD's ultimatum ignited a firestorm throughout Detroit's overwhelmingly white suburbs. "U.S. Picks Warren as Prime Target in

Move to Integrate All Suburbs," blared the *Detroit News*.[92] "I don't want HUD shoving stuff down our throats," responded the mayor of nearby Royal Oak. "It's not right."[93] Racial and class enmity shaped many reactions. "I resent those [rich] do-gooders who stand on a [soap] box but live behind a wall," fumed one town supervisor.[94] When Romney arrived in Warren to meet with city officials, picketers waved placards of defiance: "Warren Does Not Need HUD or Romney," "Romney Take Your Urban Renewal to Bloomfield Hills," "Open Housing in Bloomfield Hills? Never." Bloomfield Hills, the town where Romney lived, was an upscale, exclusively white suburb situated fifteen miles northwest of Warren.[95]

All this *Sturm und Drang* forced Romney into another awkward retreat. During his meeting with Warren officials, the housing secretary denied that he had singled out their city for a policy of "forced integration."[96] He explained that HUD's rules applied to the nation; they sought "voluntary" integration and set no quotas.[97] After a councilwoman asserted that "we do not need your money," Romney shot back, "My dear lady that is wonderful. . . I am not trying to force any money on Warren."[98] His point about opposing quotas, while true, was a side matter.[99] Romney had used Warren as a testing ground, and tying HUD grants to progress on racial integration was the basis of his policy.

Romney shifted back and forth on the matter of urban renewal for Warren. In July 1970 he promised to give the city HUD money with no strings attached. A month later he told a Senate panel that Warren would receive no funds until it formed an open housing board.[100] When reporters tried to quiz him on occurrences in the Detroit suburb, an "angry and flustered" Romney dashed away from them.[101] Warren residents, late in 1970, laid the issue to rest, voting down a motion to establish an open housing board.[102] A cartoon in the *Detroit Free Press* bitingly captured the secretary's predicament. Clad in a zigzag-striped sweater, in the fashion of *Peanuts'* Charlie Brown, a distraught Romney gazes at his kite ("HUD") which has become tangled in a tree ("housing problems"). He exclaims, "Good Grief!"[103]

Had the president backed Romney, HUD's efforts in Warren might have fared better. But there was no chance of gaining Nixon's support. Events in the Detroit suburb confirmed what the president had long suspected: that middle-class whites fiercely opposed anything that smacked of compulsory integration. "George Romney found out in Warren," Nixon explained to aides, "that there's as much racism in the North as in the South."[104] After reading that the HUD secretary still backed suburban integration, the president ordered Ehrlichman to "stop this one."[105] Ehrlichman informed Romney that a fair housing policy "has yet to be developed and adopted by this Administration."[106] With Romney acting from an obtuse zeal and Nixon ducking for cover, the Warren imbroglio showed both men at their worst.

If implemented in less racially polarized towns or in a less coercive manner, open communities had the potential to become an effective policy of integration. Since many communities depended on federal assistance for public works, Romney and Van Dusen understood their influence, as did officials in Warren. Open communities offered a quicker route to integration than Nixon's glacial litigation strategy, which responded only to individual complaints of discrimination. But Romney and Van Dusen were better at conceiving the open communities policy than at implementing it.

The policy, with its strange blend of noble intentions, moral fervor, secrecy, threats, and brashness, posted few gains. "The more HUD seeks to expand the supply of low and moderate income housing in the suburbs in a highly publicized, breast-beating manner," argued Lawrence M. Cox, assistant HUD secretary for urban renewal and housing management, "and the more coercive the techniques it uses, the more doomed to failure the effort will be."[107] This Cassandra-like memorandum did not reach Romney until after HUD had attacked segregation in Warren. "When there is too much pressure for what ought to be," the housing secretary later admitted, "it prevents what can be."[108] Still, Romney had achieved one important thing: he had forced the open housing issue onto Nixon's agenda.

Nixon: "No Forced Integration"

During round three of the contest between Nixon and Romney, covering the years 1970–1972, the administration at last adopted a middle-of-the-road housing policy. Additional dialogue, more give-and-take, and greater presidential attention helped end the sparring. Romney abandoned policies to force integration on suburbs while Nixon and Mitchell stepped up Justice's prosecution of housing bias. Combining the president's political savvy with the housing secretary's sense of justice, White House officials revised slightly the administration's fair housing policy.

The open communities policy spurred Nixon to clarify his stance on fair housing. The president preferred to prosecute individual cases of discrimination because "forced integration" was, in his opinion, impractical. Nixon told aides that open housing meant ensuring that "anyone can buy a house" anywhere. Yet he did not think that racial integration should begin with the construction of low-income housing in affluent suburbs. The president, stressing local autonomy, argued that communities had a right to be "uniform," consisting of valuable single-family homes without the blight of low-income high-rises. Catering to his political base, Nixon predicted that residents of upscale Bel Air, California, would resist the imposition of "cheap houses." He saw no harm in existing housing patterns and zoning laws so long as they upheld the economic, not racial, integrity of suburbs.[109] To enable minorities to purchase homes in suburbs, Nixon wanted to "upgrade blacks economically" and assure them "freedom of movement."[110] In so doing, the president sought gradual, voluntary integration.

He also wanted to preserve ethnic enclaves in major cities. The president told Ehrlichman that "forced integrated housing" went "far beyond the color problem," since ethnic groups such as "Italians, Mexicans, Irish" favored keeping their "exclusive neighborhoods."[111] How strongly Nixon believed this argument is difficult to say. It certainly coincided with his support for separate minority institutions (discussed in Chapters 5 and 7). But the president was bowing to political reality, since he wanted to court Catholics more than African Americans. In citing the need to maintain ethnic communities, Nixon blurred the distinction between race and ethnicity, an error his Republican and Democratic successors would repeat.

To solidify his position, Nixon decided to rid himself of the troublesome Romney. Following the GOP's lackluster showing in the midterm elections of 1970, the president informed his staff that he wanted to shore up his suburban base and make changes in his cabinet. Ehrlichman predicted that Romney would resign over the suburban integration issue because he and Van Dusen "really believe in forced in-tegr[ation] of housing." Nixon repeated that he himself "deeply *dis*be-lieves in it," arguing that the government "can't force blacks into housing–or we'll have a war. It just won't work–we'll get reseg[rega-tion]" through white flight. Nixon urged his staff to nail every Demo-cratic senator and congressmen to the cause of "compulsory integrated housing." He planned to paint Romney as a proponent of forced inte-gration and then compel him to quit. Nixon ordered Mitchell and Ehrlichman to secure the secretary's resignation.[112]

Romney, at that point, reversed course and cast himself as a team player. At a session with Mitchell late in 1970, the HUD secretary de-fended his fair housing efforts as "cautious" and "lawyer-like."[113] During a discussion with Ehrlichman, he argued that both the law and the courts had rejected discrimination in housing. Yet Romney now repu-diated "forced integration" and "federally directed uniform zoning."[114] When Mitchell informed the housing secretary that his stance re-mained out of step with Nixon's, Romney shrewdly replied, "How is it possible to know with certainty that we are on a collision course when [HUD's] policies have not yet been determined?" The former crusading dissenter now invited the president, Mitchell, and Ehrlichman to "es-tablish a procedure to determine what you think HUD policies should be."[115] After another meeting with Mitchell, Romney agreed to duck the fair housing issue in public.[116] Slipping into the open communities quagmire seemed to awaken the secretary's survival instinct and readi-ness to compromise.

While a determined president continued to press for Romney's resig-nation, an equally tenacious housing secretary clung to his office. In November 1970 Nixon ordered Ehrlichman to make any fair housing guidelines so stringent that Romney would find them impossible to support and thus quit.[117] The president rejected withholding federal aid from communities that resisted low-income housing, telling reporters that "forced integration of suburbs is not in the national interest."[118] To ease Romney's departure, Nixon dangled before him the ambassador-ship to Mexico, the country of his birth. The secretary, however, wanted to remain at HUD to help draft the fair housing policy, and the president ultimately agreed to let him stay.[119] Unwilling to fire Romney, Nixon began the new year with his old HUD secretary.

Nixon declined to sack Romney for several reasons. The secretary, by adopting an accommodating posture, preempted any charge of insubordination. Nixon, weary of trying to nudge Romney out, reasoned that his forceful housing secretary might prove useful as a salesman for administration programs.[120] He doubtless worried that replacing Romney would offend GOP moderates. Having already fired Leon E. Panetta, HEW's civil rights chief, and Interior Secretary Walter J. Hickel, the president feared that another dismissal would signal disarray within the government.[121]

Nixon also understood that dismissing Romney would not end the controversy over open housing. The U.S. Commission on Civil Rights and the General Services Administration were urging federal agencies to select construction sites where housing was available to the poor and minorities.[122] During 1970, officials at the Housing and Justice departments drafted guidelines to disperse federal buildings and housing into suburbs.[123] Moreover, the Third Circuit Court of Appeals, in *Shannon v. Romney* (1970), ordered HUD to "give more attention to social and racial factors in reviewing project and site proposals." The department's ardent liberals seized on this decision to clamor for open housing rules. "We *urgently* need a site selection policy for all HUD-assisted housing," argued Simmons.[124]

Nixon saw such court rulings as opening "a can of worms" from which liberal judges might demand integration. He wanted a policy that "waffles" open housing and "gets [the White House] out of it."[125] As with the dilemma he faced in school desegregation, Nixon needed to fence in integrationist judges and bureaucrats, then pull his team together behind a middle-of-the-road policy.

To deal with fair housing, Nixon employed the same methods he had used to craft school desegregation policy. The president formed a working group, like the cabinet committee on school desegregation, that included officials from the departments of Justice, HUD, and HEW and the White House. Nixon continued to coordinate policy making through Ehrlichman, who again blocked liberal and conservative staff members from pressing their own agendas.[126] When an option paper by Garment seemed slanted in favor of integration, Ehrlichman sent it back for revision.[127] Also as with school desegregation, Nixon tapped Raymond K. Price, his liberal speechwriter, to draft a message explaining his fair housing policy.[128] In both cases, recalled Bradley H. Patterson, Jr., Garment's assistant, Nixon avoided "personal dialogue and participation with the responsible Cabinet officers."[129]

In truth, Nixon's decision making for fair housing was more hierarchical than that for school desegregation. The reason is simple. The cabinet officials handling school desegregation, HEW secretaries Robert H. Finch and Elliot L. Richardson, Labor Secretary George P. Shultz, and Attorney General Mitchell, subordinated their views with the president's, and Nixon freely discussed policy with them. In dealing with fair housing, and his resident loose cannon, the president exercised greater caution. White House staffers scanned Romney's speeches and alerted their superiors whenever the secretary strayed from Nixon's aims.[130] Although Ehrlichman allowed Romney and his lieutenants to sketch a presidential message on fair housing, HUD's paper only slightly resembled Price's final draft.[131] Nominally inclusive and White House–centered, Nixon's policy making strove to pacify Romney and to limit his influence.

Yet Romney would not stay corralled on the issue of racial segregation in suburban St. Louis. To preempt the construction of a federally assisted apartment complex, residents of Black Jack, Missouri, incorporated their community and passed an ordinance barring multifamily rental housing. Romney, suspecting racial bias, asked the Justice Department to prosecute the city in 1970.[132] Mitchell, hardly eager for a fight, demurred until the federal courts had ruled on local zoning laws. Trying to hang onto his job, Romney went along with Mitchell.[133] Then, after the Supreme Court, i n *Kennedy Park Homes Association v. City of Lackawanna, N.Y.* (1971), deemed a zoning code to be racially biased, he resumed the drumbeat for action against Black Jack.[134] Ehrlichman, scrambling to respond, urged Romney to "avoid any further requests by employees of your department to the Justice Department for action in the Black Jack case."[135] The White House discovered that Romney could not be ignored entirely.

Romney's pressure, Ehrlichman's mediation, and Price's writing skills provided Nixon with a middle-of-the-road response. Price's statement, released in 1971, pledged "firm enforcement of laws relating to equal housing opportunity."[136] It separated economic from racial segregation and attacked only the latter: "We will not seek to impose economic integration upon existing local jurisdictions; at the same time, we will not countenance any use of economic measures as a subterfuge for racial discrimination."[137] The government would determine, case by case, whether discrimination amounted to one type or the other. Nixon's message urged the attorney general to sue localities that changed their land use laws in order to exclude minorities. It also allowed federal agencies to consider the matter of racial concentration when selecting sites for their projects.[138]

Given that a high percentage of the poor were minorities, the message's distinction between economic and racial integration was absurd. Yet Nixon liked its waffling, its rejection of forced integration, and its stress on court enforcement. "Excellent statement," he scribbled. "We shall lose on it politically—but the law and justice of the issue require it."[139]

The administration backed up its words with deeds. Just days after the White House released its statement, Mitchell, with Nixon's blessing, filed suit against six perpetrators of housing bias, including the city of Black Jack. The Black Jack case marked the first time that the government had charged a city with using its zoning powers to discriminate on the basis of race. Between 1971 and 1974, the Justice Department annually filed an average of thirty-five lawsuits against persons or communities practicing racial bias in housing.[140] Also, Romney and his aides drafted regulations to shift subsidized housing into the suburbs. These guidelines, published late in 1971, did not make HUD grants conditional on a community's acceptance of low-income housing, but gave preference to projects that promised to disperse minority groups from central cities.[141] By pressing for action on Black Jack and for these guidelines, Romney proved to be a fairly effective champion of fair housing when he worked (or was allowed to work) within administration structures.

In the short run, Justice Department lawsuits and HUD guidelines gave the administration a credible one-two punch on open housing. The Supreme Court, in *James v. Valtierra* (1971), upheld Nixon's distinction between economic and racial segregation, finding only the latter to be unconstitutional.[142] Although integrationist civil rights leaders rejected such hairsplitting—NAACP chief Roy Wilkins called it "hogwash"—they softly applauded the president's housing message. Wilkins, impressed by Mitchell's flurry of lawsuits, dubbed Nixon's statement a "ray of hope" in the fight for fair housing.[143] NAACP board member Stephen G. Spottswood, who had labeled the administration "anti-Negro" in 1970, called Nixon worthy of "cautious and limited approval" in 1971.[144] Unlike his school desegregation statement, the president's fair housing paper scored points with the high court and civil rights leaders; both groups apparently had adapted to Nixon's hedging on integration.

By the 1970s, moreover, NAACP officials were acknowledging the political complexity of fair housing, and, like Nixon, saw merit in expanding economic opportunity to ensure social mobility. In 1971 Gloster Current, an NAACP staff member, reported on growing segregation in urban areas, noting that black income, at 61 percent of white income, "further reduces the freedom of movement." The integrationist wing of the civil rights movement, Current argued, faced a political dilemma because "white suburbanites are expected to continue resisting racial and economic integration while blacks will continue to seek ways of preserving their new-found political base in the racially segregated inner city."[145] If Current did not conclude, as Nixon had, that the nation was not ready for forced integration of housing and education, his tone nevertheless waxed pessimistic.[146] William R. Morris, director of housing programs for the NAACP, forwarded Current's memorandum to Wilkins, calling housing "a far cry from the simplistic fair housing theme we tackled (unsuccessfully) in the 1950s and 1960s."[147]

In the long run, Nixon continued to oppose "scattered-site" housing to force integration. After learning of HUD's site-selection rules, the president commanded Ehrlichman to make sure that Romney and his aides "carry out *my views.*"[148] When Mayor Richard J. Daley of Chicago objected to construction of a low-income apartment complex in a white neighborhood, the president ordered his team to "get back into the case on Chicago's behalf to try and help Daley."[149] But since the construction had been ordered by a federal court, not HUD, Nixon could not assist the mayor. The Supreme Court, in *Hills v. Gautreaux* (1976), found opponents of the project to be racially biased and upheld the suburban site.[150] Although Nixon worried that liberal judges might demand integration, he still clung to court enforcement as the most moderate remedy for both school desegregation and open housing.

Nixon continued to play politics with fair housing. He even tried to trap his rivals into supporting an integrationist bill, the Ribicoff Amendment. To stress that "suburbs are not the white sanctuary," Senator Abraham A. Ribicoff, Democrat of Connecticut, pressed for racial balance in suburban schools.[151] Nixon political aide Charles W. Colson labeled Ribicoff's bill "the greatest piece of political gold to drop in our laps in a long while," since "any Senator who sponsors or endorses this measure is unequivocally on record as favoring forced suburban integration."[152] Colson, with approval from Nixon and Haldeman, followed the Senate's debate and marked which Democrats backed the bill. Although White House officials shed no tears when the upper chamber, in 1971, rejected Ribicoff's amendment, 51 to 35, Colson bubbled with glee when prominent Democrats such as Hubert Humphrey of Minnesota, George S. McGovern of South Dakota, Edward M. Kennedy of Massachusetts, and Edmund S. Muskie of Maine voted "aye."[153] Ribicoff's amendment and Romney's open communities gave Nixon opportunities to gird suburbanites for a stronger program of integration. Yet he refused to follow up.

As the election of 1972 approached, HUD officials pressed for integration discreetly and unsuccessfully. The department overrode the objections of Jewish residents and those of Senator James L. Buckley, Conservative of New York, by approving a $30 million low-income housing project for the Forest Hills section of New York City.[154] After hearing of such efforts, Ehrlichman said that "Romney and Van Dusen have jobbed us on the integration of the suburbs business."[155] HUD counsel Sherman Unger no doubt encouraged the White House to think even less of Romney when he relayed word that Assistant Secretary Simmons "reports to Larry O'Brien," chair of the Democratic National Committee, and that Assistant Secretary Jackson "speaks against Agnew and Mitchell." Unger, a onetime proponent of open communities, now denied that HUD had any right to cut off federal money. He described Frank Fisher, head of the Chicago office, where the Warren plan had hatched, as a holdover from "either JFK or LBJ" and disloyal to the current administration.[156] With underlings like Unger, no wonder Romney was in hot water once again.

Between 1972 and 1974, debate on open housing narrowed as the Nixon administration continued to shun "forced integration." Romney, influenced by either the upcoming election or pressure from Ehrlichman, began to sound a more conservative tone.[157] In 1972 he extolled voluntary integration, promising not to ram low-income housing "down the throats of people in every suburb in this country."[158] Frustrated by ongoing battles with Ehrlichman and by his lack of access to the president, Romney resigned late in 1972. With his departure, integration waned. Romney's successors, James T. Lynn and Carla A. Hills, were unwilling to disperse subsidized housing to suburbs or to interfere with local zoning.[159] Without a cabinet member pushing open housing, the president let the Justice Department handle the issue.

Nixon further derailed integration by downsizing the public housing program. Since the government planned to build fewer dwellings, any scattering of public housing was unlikely to yield much integration. Nixon's plan stemmed from a reform impulse as well as political expediency. "I have driven through these areas," he told Lynn in 1973. "Some of the worst housing in this country has been federally built, supported and operated." "Our goal," the president explained, "is to get the Federal Government out of the public housing business, not because we don't care, but because we truly care." To enable the poor to move from these complexes, Nixon considered reintroducing his Family Assistance Plan to boost their income.[160] He halted construction of new subsidized housing and proposed direct housing allowances for the poor. Opposed by big-city mayors and liberal Democrats, who accused the government of abandoning its commitment to provide shelter, Nixon's proposal went nowhere.[161] But it did set an important precedent. During his first term, President Ronald Reagan slashed funding for public housing, without granting the kind of cash payments that Nixon had proposed.[162]

Nixon's unwillingness to press for suburban integration was predictable. It is difficult to believe the president would have backed federally inspired integration, given his aversion to it. "An open society does not have to be homogeneous or even fully integrated," Nixon declared, in language that had become commonplace by the 1990s. "There is room for many communities."[163] Still, he might have made his case without resorting to racial code words such as "forced integration," which, Simmons noted, raised "doubts in the minds of Black Americans as to our intention to enforce the law."[164] Nixon enforced fair housing in accordance with his political interests, his beliefs, and whatever he deemed practical. He cared little for what blacks thought of his rhetoric.

Aftermath: The Withering of Integration

As with school desegregation, Nixon's open housing policy defined the outlines of the debate for two decades. His rhetoric of supporting open housing while opposing forced integration became standard jargon for national politicians, who used litigation to attack specific cases of housing bias. Administrative efforts to compel integration, such as open communities, tapered off.

During the presidential election of 1976, candidates of both parties parroted Nixon on fair housing. Three contenders for the Democratic nomination, Representative Morris K. Udall of Arizona, Senator Henry M. Jackson of Washington, and Governor Jimmy Carter of Georgia, all pledged to enforce open housing without forcing the integration of white environs.[165] "I see nothing wrong," Carter declared, "with ethnic purity [of neighborhoods] being maintained. I would not force racial integration of a neighborhood by government action."[166] Civil rights leaders and other candidates quickly pounced on Carter for his "ethnic purity" remark.[167] "That's not a phrase I would have used to describe any of my policies," wrote President Gerald R. Ford, with perhaps a snicker at his chief rival's faux pas. The president privately affirmed his belief in "diversity" and the government's "obligation to make certain [that] all constitutional rights are fully protected."[168] But Ford, the man who had resisted the Fair Housing Act, refused to impose integration on a white neighborhood, which he deemed an "ethnic treasure."[169] Ford, like Nixon and Carter, saw America as a mosaic of different cultures, not a melting pot.[170]

Nixon, Ford, and Carter all confused ethnicity with race. Preserving the ethnic purity of neighborhoods signaled more than a nostalgic effort to retain the social composition of Chicago's Greek-populated Halstead Street, San Francisco's Chinatown, or the largely Polish-American community of Cheektowaga, New York, a suburb of Buffalo. It meant that blacks would remain concentrated in inner cities while suburbs, with their mixture of European stock, stayed overwhelmingly white. Nevertheless, this rhetoric of celebrating diversity reappeared in later presidential campaigns. And Nixon's other civil rights policies, such as supporting minority businesses, black colleges, and Native American self-determination, acknowledged the vitality of distinct cultures.

With integration fading as a political issue and a national goal, Nixon's successors continued his policy of fighting housing bias through litigation. At first none of them matched Nixon's average, between 1971 and 1974, of thirty-five fair housing lawsuits per year.[171] Prosecution of housing bias expanded only after Congress passed the Fair Housing Act of 1988. This law prohibited discrimination against handicapped people and families with small children, permitted HUD to enter cases involving bias, and widened the definition of real estate discrimination.[172] The Justice Department, with these weapons in hand, filed eighty-one fair housing suits in 1992 and 120 the following year.[173]

While litigation remained the preferred method to enforce open housing, scattered-site policies languished. Many federal agencies shifted their installations into suburban areas only when affordable space was not available in cities. Others refused to require suburbs to provide housing on a nondiscriminatory basis. The Housing and Community Development Act of 1974, which paid lip service to dispersing low-income housing, contained many loopholes.[174] Most HUD secretaries lacked either the will or the resources to push for integration. Carter's housing secretary, Patricia Roberts Harris, an African American, issued murky site-selection regulations which conflated suburban integration with the goal of "rehabilitating" blighted dwellings in central city areas.[175] Kemp's enterprise zones sought to expand opportunities for minorities within cities. Henry G. Cisneros, President Bill Clinton's housing secretary, tried to revive dispersal policies only to find little support from his president or among white suburbanites.[176] Given the federal government's belt-tightening to shrink its budget deficits, HUD lacked the means to achieve significant integration through scattered-site methods.[177]

The waning of scattered-site policies helped keep America racially segregated. Between 1970 and 1990, the proportion of African American families living in central cities declined only slightly, from 62 to 59 percent.[178] Attitudes toward open housing, moreover, seemed frozen in a time warp. Whites believed that interracial neighborhoods rarely last and that influxes of minorities cause property values to plummet and crime rates to soar.[179] Meanwhile, many poor minorities endure harsh lives in inner cities. In 1993 Cisneros spent a night in a public housing project in Chicago and "painted an eerie portrait of waking to morning fog and young corpses, victims of gang warfare."[180]

It would be foolhardy to blame racial segregation on Nixon alone. Suburban whites opposed any steps beyond token integration, and national politicians have catered to such sentiments. In 1972 John E. Barriere, director of the Democratic Steering Committee of the U.S. House of Representatives, described "forced integration" as "political poison ivy."[181] Even Romney, one of the few leaders brash enough to tackle the issue, faltered when he encountered white racism in Warren. Poverty, of course, remains entwined with issues of race, gender, lack of employment opportunities, and disintegration of family units. Location is only one factor. Still, a policy of integration might have brought these other topics home, compelling middle-class whites to address them.

The retreat from integration need not have been inevitable. Since Nixon was the first president to enforce the Fair Housing Act, his policies set important precedents. He might have lessened residential segregation through tactics of court enforcement and low-key persuasion, which he had employed to desegregate schools. Instead, he placed political expediency and conservative principles ahead of civil rights and construed open housing narrowly, favoring voluntary integration at a slow pace. To judge from more recent census figures, the country has followed Nixon's track. The most troubling aspect of the president's policy was his strident rhetoric, which no doubt discouraged integrationists from making their case. Since the early 1970s, topics of open housing and suburban integration have almost vanished from public discourse.

Nixon's championing of white suburban values did not mean that he shut African Americans out of the political process. The president backed voting rights for minorities, and he supported affirmative action and aid to minority-owned businesses as ways to enhance economic opportunity. But when it came to electoral politics, Nixon pandered to his white base.

3

The Art of Compromise:
Extending the Voting Rights Act

"During my vice presidency," Richard Nixon recalled in 1993, "I was lonely in arguing for voting rights."[1] That statement, however embellished, contained an element of truth.[2] Nixon was one of the Eisenhower administration's strongest advocates of voting rights legislation. And his early commitment did not exactly vanish.

Practicing the fine art of political compromise, President Nixon enhanced protection of voting rights for blacks. At first he sought to woo southern conservatives who despised the Voting Rights Act of 1965 for placing the South under federal oversight. Rather than renew that law, which was set to expire in 1970, Nixon and Attorney General John N. Mitchell proposed a substitute that would have abolished literacy tests nationwide and repealed "pre-clearance," the section that required southern states to clear voting laws in advance with the Justice Department. In the end, the president signed a bill to extend the Voting Rights Act for five years, until 1975, as liberals wanted, and to end literacy tests, as he and Mitchell had urged. Civil rights forces obtained the best of both bills.[3]

Nixon's pragmatism proved to be the chief reason for his endorsement of minority voting rights. This professional politician believed in "ballots, not bullets"; dissenters must express themselves within "the system," in voting booths rather than in the streets. Nixon knew that vetoing the Voting Rights Act of 1970 would alienate minority groups and further divide the country at a time when citizens were protesting his military incursion into Cambodia and the shootings of antiwar demonstrators at Kent State University. He signed the revised Voting Rights Act for a most unheroic reason, to prevent the "goddamn country" from "blow[ing] up."[4] Nevertheless, Nixon deserves mild praise for helping to nationalize voting rights and for approving the new act.

Nixon and Voting Rights: The Pre-Presidential Years

Before becoming president, Nixon had supported voting rights rather consistently. During the 1950s, Republicans such as Dwight D. Eisenhower saw voting as a way to empower blacks and avoid undertaking "politically risky and philosophically objectionable" actions on behalf of civil rights.[5] Eisenhower and Nixon replaced tough enforcement of school desegregation, a searing issue among white southerners, with protecting voting rights, an idea that appealed to most Americans, as the focus of civil rights policy.

Eisenhower approved legislation to protect the voting rights of African Americans. In 1955 Attorney General Herbert A. Brownell drafted a four-part civil rights bill that granted new injunctive and litigative powers to the Justice Department to help minorities gain access to the ballot. Partly to please liberal northern Republicans, partly to empower African Americans, the president approved Brownell's proposal.[6] "We believed," recalled Brownell, "that once black citizens had the right to vote . . . they would have a 'level playing field' and the same opportunity to achieve their political goals as all other citizens."[7] For his part, Eisenhower viewed Brownell's bill as the "mildest" civil rights remedy possible.[8] Despite the president's occasional gestures to white southerners, noted Ann Whitman, Ike's secretary, the president was "adamant on the fact that the right to vote must be protected."[9]

Vice President Nixon weighed the same considerations and came to the same conclusions as Eisenhower. He expressed "deep personal abhorrence" of "intimidation and economic reprisals against Negroes who attempt to exercise their right to vote."[10] While serving in the House of Representatives, he voted in 1947 and 1949 to abolish poll taxes and to continue debate on this subject. As vice president, he urged cabinet officials not to raise the issue of the poll tax, arguing that there was no chance of getting the Democratic-controlled Congress to eliminate it.[11] But Nixon saw Brownell's civil rights bill as a way to crack the Democratic Party's North-South axis and woo blacks at the same time. When courting African Americans, he often cited his opposition to the poll tax and his support of voting rights legislation.[12]

Nixon strongly endorsed Brownell's bill. After months of heel-dragging by southerners in the House, the vice president pushed for speedy consideration of the measure in the Senate. He backed Senator Paul Douglas, Democrat of Illinois, and Senate Minority Leader William Knowland, Republican of California, when they attempted to skirt the Judiciary Committee and bring the bill directly to the Senate floor. Nixon also lobbied against an amendment advanced by Senate Majority Leader Lyndon B. Johnson, Democrat of Texas, to guarantee a jury trial to anyone cited for contempt in a civil rights case.[13] Although LBJ had invoked a cherished American right, the vice president, like many observers, knew that lily-white southern juries would not convict violators of African American rights.[14] At a meeting with Republican congressional leaders, Nixon "stressed that there must be no compromise regarding the jury trial issue," because "this is where the whole program could be vitiated."[15] The vice president tried to strike a pose that civil rights advocates would find appealing. Johnson strove to do likewise, while enticing fellow southerners to support a moderate bill.[16]

After the Senate passed the jury trial amendment, Eisenhower and Nixon became incensed. "It saddens me," the president told congressional leaders, "that 18 southern senators can bamboozle everyone about jury trial[s]."[17] At another session Nixon criticized the "so-called liberal forces," including Senator Douglas, labor leaders, and "NAACP lobbyists," who, in clamoring for compromise, had placed loyalty to the Democratic Party before civil rights. Democratic senators Mike Mansfield of Montana and John F. Kennedy of Massachusetts, the vice president fumed, "all sing [that] this is not a bad bill."[18] Of course, the NAACP's priority was civil rights enforcement, not helping Democrats thump the Grand Old Party. And Republican presidential aspirants Nixon and Knowland had played to the galleries as much as their opposition. But the vice president was correct about one thing: his party had favored a stronger bill, and the Democrats had weakened it.

In responding to the jury trial amendment, Eisenhower talked tough, then acceded to the Senate's watered-down bill. "I'm just an amateur in politics," he remarked, less than truthfully. "But . . . when a fellow tries to hit me over the head with a brickbat I look for something to hit him back with."[19] Nixon opposed sending the bill to a House-Senate conference committee, where Democrats could kill it and then blame Republicans.[20] Partly for that reason, partly to appease GOP liberals who wanted some sort of bill, Eisenhower and Nixon accepted the Senate's version.[21] They knew that a veto would ax the bill's other provisions, to organize a civil rights division within the Justice Department and to form a commission to probe civil rights violations. Nixon considered the current measure "much better than no bill at all."[22] Eisenhower agreed, and signed the Civil Rights Act of 1957.[23]

Nixon's stance earned praise from African American leaders. Martin Luther King, Jr., thanked him for his "assiduous labor and dauntless courage" in making the Civil Rights Act "a reality."[24] After LBJ accused the vice president of opportunism in opposing the jury trial amendment, Percy L. Prattis, an African American newspaper editor, defended Nixon, complaining that no politician "can express himself [on] a controversial public issue without becoming the object of narrow-minded charges of political motivation."[25] "As far as I'm concerned," Jackie Robinson, the former Brooklyn Dodger, wrote Nixon, "a man's motives don't mean a thing as long as he is attempting to do good."[26]

Such accolades failed to conceal the fact that the Civil Rights Act of 1957 proved to be as toothless as its critics had predicted.[27] In 1959 the United States Commission on Civil Rights advanced a new plan permitting the president to dispatch registrars into communities where blacks had complained of unfair voting practices. Eisenhower allowed his Justice Department, now headed by William Rogers, to fashion a more modest bill allowing federal courts to assign referees to locales where violations of voting rights had occurred.[28] The attorney general no doubt reasoned that this proposal was the most he could pry from the Democratic-controlled Congress, with its strong southern accent.

After some hesitation, Nixon endorsed Rogers's bill. To Roy Wilkins, executive secretary of the NAACP, he pledged "vigorous support" for "substantive legislation" and agreed that the Civil Rights Commission's plan "should be seriously considered."[29] Yet when one commission member, the Reverend Theodore M. Hesburgh, C.S.C., president of the University of Notre Dame, asked for his support, Nixon paused. "I have given [Hesburgh] a non-committal answer," he told Rogers, "but I would like to get your views on his position since I imagine he speaks for a fairly sizeable body of opinion in the country."[30] With another election on the horizon, the vice president considered Rogers's court-enforcement plan sensible and moderate.[31] He assured Jackie Robinson that the administration's referee approach would yield results, stressing that "*there will be* a continuing civil rights bill this year."[32]

The vice president's predictions proved partly correct. In May 1960 President Eisenhower signed a bill embodying the voting referee concept.[33] But the Civil Rights Act of 1960 turned out to be as weak as the one passed in 1957. Both laws provided African Americans with legal tools to overcome discriminatory voting practices such as poll taxes and literacy tests. But neither act outlawed those practices. The 1960 law established labyrinthine procedures, involving litigants, Justice Department officials, and federal courts, before the federal government sent referees into the South. And Eisenhower's Justice Department proved a less-than-vigorous enforcer, filing just ten voting rights suits between 1957 and 1960.[34]

Nixon, too, considered the 1960 act ineffective. During the presidential election of 1960, he conceded that states had the authority to set voting qualifications, but he supported new federal efforts to prevent "excessive" use of literacy tests to exclude voters. Balancing federal enforcement against respect for states' rights, he favored national legislation "to accept the completion of primary grades" as "prima facie evidence of literacy for voting purposes."[35] Later on, as president, he followed up with a bill to abolish literacy tests altogether.

While many observers cheered the vice president as the administration's resident civil rights advocate, Nixon had not earned a standing ovation. Without doubt, his support for voting rights laws and his opposition to poll taxes and the jury trial amendment stemmed from principle. At the same time, Nixon had acceded to a watered-down act in

1957. In 1960 he probably should have backed Hesburgh's voting registrars scheme, which presaged the effective Voting Rights Act of 1965. The political motive behind Nixon's advocacy cut two ways. So long as the vice president sought African American votes, civil rights leaders could count him among their friends. As Nixon looked to southern whites for support, his commitment to voting rights slackened, at least on the surface.

Once Nixon left office, he placed principle ahead of politics. In 1965 he endorsed President Johnson's voting rights bill, which abolished literacy tests in the South and empowered the federal government to send examiners into the southern states to register African Americans. Responding to demonstrations for voting rights in Selma, Alabama, LBJ personally asked Congress to pass this legislation.[36] Two days earlier Nixon had made a less publicized appeal, urging Republicans to remain true to the party's "Lincoln tradition" by supporting laws "that will serve the cause of equal rights." The party, he said, "must not compromise its strong position on civil rights for the purpose of gaining votes in Southern states."[37] This point suggests that the thought of courting white southerners had already crossed his mind. Nevertheless, in retirement, he grudgingly praised Johnson for securing civil rights legislation, his "big achievement."[38]

Nixon also backed voting rights legislation to temper the civil rights movement's tactics. In 1964 he assailed nonviolent direct action for breeding "disrespect for [the] law" and creating "an atmosphere of hate and distrust." In an early nod to white backlash, Nixon denied that civil disobedience was needed to pass civil rights legislation, and he argued that mass protests had "divided our people at home and discredited us abroad."[39] The former vice president hoped that a strong voting rights law would channel political participation into established institutions, where grievances could be aired and resolved quietly. Unlike to civil rights leaders, who emphasized the goal of racial justice, means and ends were equally important to politicians like Nixon.

Throughout the 1950s and 1960s Nixon was able to champion voting rights because white southerners were not a central part of the Republican coalition. During and after the presidential campaign of 1968, however, he strove to lure southern whites into his camp. Before accepting his party's nomination for president in 1968, Nixon hinted to southern

Republican leaders that he was opposed to regional legislation, a not-so-veiled reference to the Voting Rights Act. As president he tried to navigate between the demands of civil rights advocates and those of white southerners. Like Senate Majority Leader Lyndon Johnson in the 1950s, Nixon learned the hazards of governing from a broad-based coalition.

The Nixon Administration and Voting Rights, 1969

In 1969 President Nixon found himself appeasing myriad groups on renewal of the Voting Rights Act. On the surface, he made token appeals to white southerners by offering to soften the act and apply it nationwide. In fact, the administration's voting rights bill grew out of advice from various political and judicial sources. The president, moreover, privately reaffirmed his support of voting rights and his willingness to bargain with liberals to renew the current act. As with the school desegregation issue, Nixon's symbolic "southern strategy" confused his supporters and drew fire from liberals and civil rights advocates.

When President Johnson departed the White House, he left behind some unfinished business: Sections IV and V of the Voting Rights Act were due to expire in 1970. Section IV, the heart of the act, voided literacy tests in seven southern states where fewer than 50 percent of eligible voters had cast ballots in 1964. The 50 percent turnout stipulation was known as the "trigger" because it activated Section V, the act's insurance policy. Section V required states falling under Section IV to "pre-clear" any changes in their voting rights laws with the Justice Department or the District of Columbia Court of Appeals. Although the Voting Rights Act helped to register nearly 1 million African Americans between 1965 and 1970, LBJ offered little guidance on how or whether to renew it. His Justice Department did not begin to study the merits of renewal until late in 1968.[40] As with school desegregation and fair housing, Johnson passed this knotty issue on to Nixon.

In 1969 civil rights leaders and politicians of almost all stripes advocated the status quo. House Minority Leader Gerald R. Ford, Republican of Michigan, Representative William McCulloch, Republican of Ohio, the ranking minority member of the Judiciary Committee, and Representative Emanuel Celler, Democrat of New York and chair of the Judiciary

Committee, proposed extending the Voting Rights Act for another five years. Liberal senators such as Jacob Javits, Republican of New York, Minority Whip Hugh D. Scott, Republican of Pennsylvania, Vance Hartke, Democrat of Indiana, and Edward Kennedy, Democrat of Massachusetts, drafted a similar bill.[41] Civil rights leaders Roy Wilkins and Clarence Mitchell, Washington lobbyist for the NAACP, supported these efforts and exhorted Nixon to renew the Voting Right Act.[42]

But members of the Commission on Civil Rights clamored for something more: the prohibition of literacy tests nationwide. In March 1969 Howard A. Glickstein, the commission's staff director, urged his compatriots to "endorse extension of the Act on a broader basis." Agreeing, Hesburgh, the commission's chair, noted that television provided "complete political coverage" to all citizens "even if they can't read." Another commissioner shrewdly noted that literacy tests prevented Mexican Americans from voting in Texas, which did not fall under the current law.[43] Hesburgh advised Nixon to extend the Voting Rights Act and then seek legislation to "ban the use of literacy tests nationwide."[44]

The United States Supreme Court weighed in on the side of Hesburgh and Glickstein. In *Gaston County v. United States* (1969), the high tribunal struck down a North Carolina literacy test, reasoning that unequal educational opportunities in the state had the "effect" of denying voting rights to African Americans. By focusing on this test's results rather than its intentions, the court questioned the legitimacy of all literacy tests.[45] Both the Commission on Civil Rights and the Supreme Court were moving toward a national ban on literacy tests.

To complicate matters, white southerners sought to alter the Voting Rights Act. Segregationists such as Representative William Colmer, Democrat of Mississippi, and Senator Sam J. Ervin, Democrat of North Carolina, wanted the act to wither away.[46] Conservative southern Republicans preferred to remove the Voting Rights Act's regional stigma. Republican national committeeman Howard H. "Bo" Callaway, a Georgian who privately denounced the law as a slap "in the face" of the South, was willing to accept "a tough voting rights bill, so long as it [is] applied equally to all sections of the country."[47] "John, this is extremely important to us," he wrote Mitchell. "I believe most Southerners would feel that the Nixon administration broke a strong commitment to the South if it allowed an extension of the present bill."[48] Early in

1969 southern Republican state chairs exhorted the attorney general to draft a voting rights bill for "the nation as a whole without regional discrimination."[49]

To southern Republicans, nationalizing the Voting Rights Act represented a badge of regional honor as well as smart politics. Party leaders deemed the law arbitrary and unfair. Since fewer than 50 percent of eligible Georgians had voted in 1964, the state fell under the law, while Texas, where more than half the eligible population had voted, did not. Richard H. Poff, Republican of Virginia and a member of the House Judiciary Committee, objected to the act's 50 percent net because it snared his state, which the Commission on Civil Rights had cleared of any racially motivated barriers to voting. Poff also opposed extending the current law because it was regional.[50]

Interestingly, such sentiments had animated politicians as early as 1965. Senator Joseph D. Tydings, a liberal Democrat from Maryland, had proposed amendments to apply LBJ's voting rights bill across the nation since "not all instances of discrimination are limited to Alabama, Mississippi, Georgia, and Louisiana."[51] Before endorsing Johnson's bill, Ford and McCulloch had endorsed safeguarding the voting rights of all adults with at least a sixth-grade education. Four years later, Callaway, conceding that "the right to vote should not be restricted because of race," favored reviving the Ford-McCulloch measure.[52]

In responding to these pressures, the Nixon administration swayed back and forth. In February 1969 Mitchell and Jerris Leonard, assistant attorney general for civil rights, met with civil rights leaders and hinted that they favored extending the Voting Rights Act, with perhaps a few changes.[53] That same day the president ordered the attorney general to study whether the act should be extended or revised.[54] So began a lively debate. Leonard, a liberal Republican, implored Mitchell to use the *Gaston County* ruling to press for a national ban on literacy tests. At the same time, White House counselor Arthur F. Burns, a conservative Republican, urged Nixon to read *Gaston County* narrowly and retain literacy tests for voters who had failed to complete the sixth grade. Burns also proposed supplanting pre-clearance with court enforcement and forming a commission to study voter fraud.[55]

As the debate unfolded, the president stood "above the fray," except to reiterate his desire for a national voting rights law. "What is [the] status on this?" Nixon asked John D. Ehrlichman, his top domestic policy adviser, emphasizing that he was "against current law since it ignores some states (like Texas)."[56] By broadening the Voting Rights Act, the president no doubt hoped to satisfy southern Republicans, continue his support for voting rights, and firm up his "national strategy" of appealing for votes in all regions of the country.

In refashioning the Voting Rights Act, Mitchell weighed the government's obligations to enforce the law against political and practical concerns. As a lawyer, the attorney general knew that he had to carry out the high court's *Gaston County* ruling, which he rightly viewed as a strike against all literacy tests. He rejected as legally unsound Burns's plea to maintain such tests and accepted Leonard's appeal to prohibit literacy tests altogether.[57] When Harry S. Dent, Jr., Nixon's southern political adviser, allowed that outlawing literacy tests nationwide "may be grudgingly acceptable to many southern leaders," the attorney general was given pause.[58] In the end, Mitchell arrived at a pragmatic reason for eliminating literacy tests, telling a House panel, "I want to encourage our Negro citizens to take out their alienations at the ballot box, and not elsewhere."[59]

GOP congressional leaders provided little guidance on voting rights. When Mitchell proposed sending voting examiners to all regions, McCulloch seconded the idea as a way to "substantially improve" the current law.[60] But when he advocated prohibiting literacy tests nationwide, McCulloch protested and urged a simple extension of the Voting Rights Act. Other leaders then joined the debate, sparking "confusion about who stood where."[61] By the next leadership meeting, no consensus had emerged. Liberal Republicans such as Hugh Scott favored extending the Voting Rights Act, while such staunch partisans as Senator Roman L. Hruska of Nebraska advised Nixon to keep his campaign pledge to end regional legislation. Conservatives such as Minority Leader Everett M. Dirksen of Illinois and Richard Poff supported a bill to forbid all literacy tests, provided such a ban was temporary.[62] Northerners who defended literacy tests for their region while rejecting them for the South clearly exhibited a regional bias.

In truth, GOP leaders acted from a variety of motives. Since Scott and McCulloch had helped to draft the Voting Rights Act, they resisted efforts to tamper with their prized handiwork. By insisting on a *temporary* ban on literacy tests, Dirksen and Poff defended states' rights: in the absence of overt bias, states would retain the power to set voting requirements.[63] But most Republicans understood the influence of civil rights leaders. Scott, for example, warned Nixon that civil rights groups viewed the Voting Rights Act as their "Magna Carta," "militantly" favored its extension, and would reject the attorney general's alternative. If the president wanted to end all literacy tests, Scott advised, he should send Congress a separate bill.[64]

Nixon and Mitchell would have done well to heed Scott's advice. By extending the Voting Rights Act and then submitting legislation to end all literacy tests, the president could have claimed that he had remained true to voting rights and to the spirit of the *Gaston County* decision while nationalizing the act, as he had promised. But Nixon could not resist making a strong, symbolic appeal to southern Republicans. Mitchell drafted a substitute bill, even though he predicted that the House Judiciary Committee and "the House itself likely will pass a simple 5-year extension of the [Voting Rights] Act."[65]

Stitching together moral, legal, and political advice, Mitchell's voting rights bill was a classic example of artless compromise. Section I, by banning literacy tests nationwide until January 1, 1974, bowed to the Commission on Civil Rights and to conservative northern Republicans, who opposed ending these tests permanently. Section II restricted state residency requirements for voting in presidential elections.[66] Although White House aide Daniel P. Moynihan, a liberal Democrat, claimed credit for this idea, its author is unknown. Moynihan only argued that the idea was "good Republican politics," probably because Republicans generally enjoyed higher incomes and greater mobility than Democrats.[67] Section III granted the attorney general authority to send voting examiners and observers to any part of the country. Section IV replaced pre-clearance with court enforcement, whereby the attorney general would sue locales practicing racial bias in voting. Finally, Section V formed a commission to study both discrimination and fraud in voting.[68]

Mitchell's bill was quite odd. One wonders why the attorney general agreed to the last two ideas, since they came from Burns, the man who had misread the *Gaston County* decision. The attorney general's proposal straddled many contradictory ideals: respect for states' rights (by ending pre-clearance), national standards for voting, and litigation to safeguard civil rights.

This hydra-headed bill gave each interest group a reason to slay it. Civil rights leaders and liberals howled over the abolition of pre-clearance and called the effort to nationalize the law needless. To Clarence Mitchell, the bill represented a "sophisticated, calculated, incredible" attempt to undermine voting rights.[69] According to the *New York Times,* its "genuinely good features," such as uniform residence requirements, disguised its "impossibly bad ones," such as the abandonment of pre-clearance.[70] Many moderate Republicans objected to banning all literacy tests. "The Administration creates a remedy for which there is no wrong," McCulloch complained, "and leaves grievous wrongs [in the South] without adequate remedy."[71] The Commission on Civil Rights protested the ending of pre-clearance and then opened fire on the proposed commission to study voting rights, which it deemed a rival.[72] A few right-wing Republicans rejected national residence requirements for voting as an assault on states' rights.[73] Segregationists had little to cheer. Sam Ervin called Mitchell's bill and the Voting Rights Act extension "two peas from the same pod."[74] Only GOP officials from the South accepted the attorney general's bill, because it partly met their demands.[75]

The White House overcame these objections with a lobbying blitz. During hearings before the House Judiciary Committee, the usually gruff Mitchell made a strong pitch for national application of voting rights. Casting himself as a reformer and his liberal critics as stodgy conservatives, the attorney general argued that literacy tests denied voting rights to all persons lacking education, including residents of northern ghettos and non-English speakers. Meanwhile, Bryce N. Harlow, congressional liaison chief at the White House, mapped out an alliance between conservative Republicans, who backed the president out of party loyalty, and southern Democrats, who, when forced to choose, preferred Mitchell's bill to the current law. To shepherd his bill through the House, Nixon enlisted Minority Leader Ford, who, after first supporting extension of the act, had kept silent throughout the GOP's wrangling over voting rights.[76] Ford labeled Mitchell's bill "more fair and equitable" than the simple extension, and he urged his colleagues to back it.[77] A bipartisan coalition in the House did just that, passing the administration bill, 208 to 203, in December 1969.[78] Clarence Mitchell branded the vote "a scurrilous attack on constitutional rights."[79]

Did the administration's bill threaten voting rights? Yes and no. The attorney general's effort to repeal pre-clearance represented a setback. According to one Mississippian, new black voters continued to face gerrymandering and economic pressure when trying to cast their ballots.[80] Requiring states to continue to pre-clear new voting laws with the federal government seemed a worthy insurance policy. The Commission on Civil Rights correctly labeled Mitchell's substitute remedy, litigation, "tedious and time-consuming," for such enforcement harked back to the limp civil rights acts of 1957 and 1960.[81] To make matters worse, the administration's bill placed the burden of proof in voting rights cases on the federal government, not the states.

To be sure, pre-clearance was not a panacea. The drafters of the Voting Rights Act had not envisioned this device as the key to enforcement. States practicing bias seldom submitted voting laws to the Justice Department for approval, and, until 1969, the department had filed just one lawsuit to force compliance.[82] But nationalizing pre-clearance *and* initiating new suits would have been a more constructive way to reform voting rights.

Critics stood on shakier ground when they labeled Mitchell's substitute a "southern bill" to woo racists.[83] The proposed repeal of pre-clearance failed to satisfy old guard southerners who preferred no bill to the administration's. In truth, the attorney general's patchwork measure stitched together input from myriad quarters, including the Commission on Civil Rights and the Supreme Court. His political aim seemed narrow, merely to settle a campaign debt with southern Republicans who wanted a national voting rights bill. Even within this group one heard dissent. Senator John Tower of Texas opposed the national ban on literacy tests as "suicide for the Republican Party."[84] William E. Timmons, a Nixon aide, agreed, noting that the "illiterate seldom vote Republican."[85]

Critics were wrong to play down the bill's national ban on literacy tests. In 1970 the Commission on Civil Rights confirmed what it, the Supreme Court, and the attorney general had claimed: that literacy tests in the North had "a racially discriminatory effect." The commissioners, using census data, found that greater numbers of blacks had failed to register to vote in states with literacy tests than in states without them.[86] Clarence Mitchell was right to worry that banning all literacy tests would ignite a congressional "squabble," causing the Voting Rights Act to expire by default.[87] But to question John Mitchell's motives is not to deny the justice of ending literacy tests nationwide.

Nixon, for his part, emphasized the expansive elements of Mitchell's bill over its repeal of pre-clearance. Prior to the House vote, the president jotted down his thoughts on the Voting Rights Act: "(1) it had worked for South, (2) I want *no retreat,* (3) it should be national–*Uniform Residence Requirements.* Any Bill which accomplishes that will have my approval."[88] He then ordered aides to hang tough on sections of the administration's bill that encompassed the "whole country": literacy tests and residence requirements. As for the rest, including pre-clearance, Nixon expressed "no obj[ection] to compromise."[89]

A number of forces pushed the president toward compromise. Nixon, the earlier champion of voting rights, had reemerged. The president, in another sense, simply resolved to horse-trade on a difficult issue. A memorandum from liberal adviser Leonard Garment urged renewal of the Voting Rights Act and reinforced Nixon's stance.[90] Yet the president did not deserve much praise for sounding a conciliatory note. If anything, he earned a stiff reprimand for not reassuring African Americans about his purposes.

African Americans probably would not have listened to a presidential appeal. By the end of 1969, civil rights leaders had wearied of Nixon, especially his "go-slow" approach to school desegregation.[91] Lacking experience on civil rights, Mitchell proved uninspiring. "How does a Wall Street lawyer approach this [voting rights] problem?" asked Roy Wilkins, even before the attorney general had taken his official oath.[92] Except for white southerners and a few GOP politicians, observers found Mitchell drab and dour. Dean Acheson, hardly the picture of youth, vigor, and charisma, dismissed him as an "old fart."[93] In 1970 Nixon himself admitted that his attorney general had made "a lousy spokesman."[94] Nevertheless, the president could have tried to offer more reassurance on voting rights.

Nixon's opposition to renewing the Voting Rights Act in its original form spotlighted a major pitfall of his civil rights policy. In public he seemed overly sensitive to the concerns of white southerners and insensitive to those of African Americans. Such a stance offended liberal and moderate northern Republicans who backed civil rights and resented the president's fond gazes toward Dixie. These GOP senators deserted Nixon on his nomination of southerners to the Supreme Court, as well as on his revised voting rights bill.

The Voting Rights Truce of 1970

Congressional pressure, combined with advice from White House liberals, reinforced Nixon's willingness to compromise on voting rights. Without consulting the president or any White House staff member, Senate Minority Leader Scott reached out to liberal Democrats and revised the administration's bill. This center-left alliance restored the preclearance clause and added an amendment to lower the voting age to eighteen. Although Nixon preferred a compromise bill without the eighteen-year-old vote rider, the Senate's version met most of his stipulations.

Minority Leader Scott, in pressing for compromise, acted from three considerations. The first was his strong personal belief in equal rights. Scott, throughout his Senate career, had voted for every civil rights bill and nearly every amendment or appropriation to promote racial equality. He pushed for the Civil Rights Act of 1960 and co-sponsored the landmark act of 1964.[95] "I believe," Scott asserted, "that any citizen who is good enough to fight for the security of all the States of the Union is good enough to vote in any of them."[96] Clarence Mitchell remarked that Scott never wanted for "logical answers when debating the civil rights issue."[97] The senator did not always play advocate, of course. Although Scott backed Nixon's Philadelphia Plan to set minority hiring goals for construction trades, he did so quietly "so as not to stir up" unrest among white blue-collar workers.[98]

Scott's political compass also led him to support voting rights. He courted the large minority population in his state, Pennsylvania, and formed close ties with civil rights leaders. After Scott endorsed renewal of the Voting Rights Act in 1969, the senator's staff asked Clarence Mitchell to spread the word among black voters.[99] As the debate on voting rights moved into 1970, when the senator faced reelection,

Scott's aides urged him to hog the limelight. In April they dissuaded the minority leader from announcing that the president supported Scott's compromise bill since "it might be considered to dilute your role in the passage of the extension."[100] No less a politician than Nixon, Scott espoused civil rights more vigorously and, at times, in a more calculated way.

Scott's independent streak occasionally set him against the administration. As a matter of conscience, he voted against Nixon's nomination of Judge Clement F. Haynsworth, Jr., of South Carolina to the Supreme Court, believing that Haynsworth had engaged in "conflict of interest."[101] Upset over Nixon's public indifference toward civil rights, the Pennsylvanian urged him to issue a statement on race "to allay the widespread fear that this Administration does not list this concern among its highest priorities. I know otherwise."[102] The president demurred. In 1972 Scott helped scuttle Nixon's busing moratorium.[103] Yet the senator's periodic sparring with the White House should not be exaggerated. Scott voted with the administration 78 percent of the time in 1969, endorsing 72 percent of Nixon's domestic programs and 95 percent of his foreign policy initiatives.[104]

These considerations—adherence to principle, political opportunism, and independence—informed Scott's leadership style. The Pennsylvanian, who became minority leader in 1969, ranked voting his conscience first. Serving his state came second, leading Republican senators third, and pushing administration programs last. "As a Senator," he remarked, "I cannot subordinate my own conscience nor the welfare of Pennsylvania for what some feel is the tradition of complete, unbending support for the Executive department's viewpoints."[105] Although his record exhibited less high-minded independence than he laid claim to, Scott, unlike Ford, his House counterpart, did sometimes refuse to play "fetch and carry" with the White House.[106]

Without seeking Nixon's approval, Scott reached out to Democrats, listened to fellow Republicans, and modified the administration's bill. Even before the House passed Mitchell's measure, Scott huddled with two liberal Democrats, Philip A. Hart of Michigan and Birch E. Bayh of Indiana, to plot ways of propelling a voting rights bill through the Senate.[107] Hart urged Sam Ervin's Subcommittee on Constitutional Rights to report a voting rights measure by March 1, 1970.[108] When Ervin offered to produce a bill after presenting one on electoral college reform, Hart and Scott rejected this attempt at delay.[109] The minority leader knew that Senator Barry M. Goldwater, Republican of Arizona, wanted to end all residency requirements for voting.[110] And Scott realized that any bill had to retain enough "national" provisions, such as ending all literacy tests, to pass muster with Nixon.[111] Democratic and Republican liberals were pressing Nixon to move on voting rights.

Scott and Hart welded the toughest enforcement provisions of the administration's bill, a national ban on literacy tests and uniform residency requirements, onto the Voting Rights Act of 1965. To appease Goldwater, Scott reduced the administration's proposed residency requirement from sixty to thirty days.[112] The final bill retained preclearance, as northern liberals wanted, and applied it to non-southern states where fewer than 50 percent of eligible minority citizens had voted in 1968, another "national" proviso for the president.[113] Hart's staff outlined the compromise, and Scott introduced it in the Senate.[114] Again the contribution of Senate Democrats was crucial. "Senator Hart's staff man, Burt Wides, has done a mammoth job on this bill," a Scott aide noted.[115] The two senators then recruited moderates and liberals of both parties, including a majority of members of the Judiciary Committee, as co-sponsors.[116]

On one issue Scott and Hart followed their younger liberal colleagues. Democratic senators Kennedy and Bayh had prepared the rider to lower the voting age to eighteen. Bayh argued that young people were "far better prepared to exercise the responsibilities of citizenship than at any previous time" because of increased access to education.[117] Proponents of lowering the voting age also contended that if eighteen-year-olds were old enough to fight in Vietnam, they were old enough to vote.[118] Senate Majority Leader Mike Mansfield fastened the Kennedy-Bayh measure onto the voting rights bill, and Senator Marlow W. Cook, a GOP moderate from Kentucky, seconded Mansfield's motion.[119] Inserting an amendment to the Scott-Hart bill was an astute way to sidestep Ervin's subcommittee, which had held hearings on lowering the voting age in 1968 but had failed to report a bill.[120]

Although the eighteen-year-old vote amendment raised the eyebrows of conservatives, who deemed it an unconstitutional invasion of states' rights, it did not undermine the compromise bill. On March 13, 1970, Scott-Hart breezed through the upper chamber, 64 to 12, with eleven of the nays coming from southerners.[121] The broad coalition that had favored renewing the Voting Rights Act early in 1969 had resurfaced to endorse a stronger measure. And, thanks to Bayh and Kennedy, Nixon could not evade the issue of lowering the voting age.

The president viewed these events with scant enthusiasm but put up only token opposition. When forced to choose between the House bill and extending the current voting rights law, Nixon told aides that he "firmly" backed the former, which was a national bill.[122] Yet he proved apathetic to Scott's maneuvers, a reflection of the president's earlier willingness to compromise, as well as poor staff work. Nixon assigned the chore of driving his voting rights bill through the Senate to Mitchell, who had almost no experience in dealing with Congress, and to Harlow, who had left the Office of Congressional Liaison three months earlier to become White House counselor. Neither man developed a plan to win passage of this bill, and Nixon did not seem to care.[123] This laissez-faire approach was not unusual. In 1969 Ford had set strategy for the House vote on voting rights while Harlow and Mitchell handled the Haynsworth nomination. On the latter vote, GOP moderates deserted the ship and sank the nomination.[124]

There was another reason for presidential inattention to voting rights. During 1970 Nixon had more urgent business before the Senate: the Supreme Court nomination of Judge G. Harrold Carswell. In keeping with his symbolic "southern strategy," Nixon selected Carswell, a Floridian of limited intellect and with a segregationist past, after the Senate rejected Haynsworth.[125] The president then attempted a trade-off: he focused on winning votes for the judge, a nod to southern racists, while tacitly accepting most of Scott-Hart, as liberal Republicans desired. During a meeting with congressional leaders on March 3, Nixon listened to Scott discuss voting rights without objecting. He then talked up the Carswell nomination.[126]

Nixon found it awkward to back away from his bill in public. On March 5 he told his press secretary to "be sure we stand w/House version on voting rights."[127] But a month later, on April 8, the day the Senate rejected Carswell, Nixon informed aides that he was "OK" with most provisions of the Senate's bill.[128] The president was not the only one walking a tightrope. Scott made up for his independence on voting rights by backing Carswell.[129]

Nixon opposed only one part of Scott-Hart, the eighteen-year-old-vote amendment.[130] He told Ehrlichman to "give someone direct orders [and] responsibility to stop this highest *priority*."[131] That Nixon turned to his "can-do" domestic policy chief and not to Mitchell and Harlow, who often failed to lead Congress, underscored his seriousness. The president warned of "constitutional chaos" if Congress trampled on states' rights and passed this amendment.[132] A number of legal experts also questioned whether Congress possessed the authority to lower the voting age.[133] In a sense, Nixon brought this problem on himself. By revising the Voting Rights Act, the president unwittingly invited liberals and moderates to offer revisions of their own.

The president's rhetoric shrouded his chief motive for resisting the eighteen-year-old vote: political vulnerability. From polls he knew that most young people leaned Democratic and represented an obstacle to his reelection bid.[134] During the campaign of 1968, Nixon had endorsed the eighteen-year-old vote, if passed by the states, and promised college students an "open administration that will welcome dissent."[135] Yet President Nixon did not push for a lower voting age, and he remained wary of youthful dissenters, notwithstanding his spontaneous nocturnal tête-à-tête with antiwar protestors at the Lincoln Memorial during the invasion of Cambodia in May 1970.[136]

Nixon employed a number of means to defeat or delay the eighteen-year-old vote. The president moved discreetly, for he did not want to offend young voters if his plans went awry. "How to defeat the 18 year old vote & still make P appear to favor it" was, an unidentified White House aide jotted, the *"gut issue."*[137] Rather than lower the voting age by statute, Nixon pushed for a constitutional amendment, hoping that it would not pass until after his reelection. When Scott-Hart traveled to the House, he vowed to support it if lawmakers would excise the eighteen-year-old vote proviso.[138] Nixon asked House Judiciary Committee chair Emanuel Celler, who doubted the constitutionality of a statute to lower the voting age, to run some interference. Meanwhile, the White House kept up the drumbeat for a constitutional amendment. Charles W. Colson, soon to emerge as one of Nixon's top political advisers, asked constitutional scholars to write letters opposing a congressional act to lower the voting age.[139] Legal testimony and organized pressure were the same futile tactics Nixon had used in pressing for Senate approval of the Haynsworth and Carswell nominations.[140]

These machinations yielded nothing. Celler decided to back the Scott-Hart bill with the eighteen-year-old-vote rider.[141] Liberal Republicans in the House, including John B. Anderson of Illinois and Donald Riegle of Michigan, backed the Senate bill. In their view, Scott-Hart combined the best elements of the current law and the administration's bill with an amendment that "gives our young people an opportunity to really participate in our system and undercuts those who would advocate overthrow of the existing system."[142] William E. Timmons, who had succeeded Harlow as congressional liaison chief, counted 180 votes against Scott-Hart, not enough to derail the eighteen-year-old vote. In June the House approved the Senate's bill, 272 to 132.[143] Nixon now had to decide whether or not to sign it.

Determined either to thwart or get credit for enfranchising eighteen-to-twenty-year-olds, Nixon decided that if a veto could be upheld, he would reject Scott-Hart. If not, he would approve it. "Otherwise," the president calculated, "we will be in a position of having . . . the bill become law and those affected by it remembering that we opposed it." Political opportunism had overwhelmed Nixon's constitutional scruples, for he still thought the eighteen-year-old vote proviso was "unconstitutional."[144]

Nixon's liberal advisers put forth the strongest case for signing the revised voting rights bill. Raymond K. Price, a speechwriter, conceded that a veto might prevent young people from voting in 1972 and please conservative southerners. But he contended that "the right to vote is one thing that practically all Americans agree on," adding that to align "ourselves with the Thurmonds and Eastlands on this one" would "invite the label of blatant racism." A veto, Price went on, "would trigger shock, revulsion, and despair" among blacks and have a "damaging impact on our capacity to govern."[145] Garment, Price's friend, assured Nixon that the political fallout of enfranchising eighteen-year-olds was slight, for young people voted sporadically, and not all of them were liberal. Calling voting rights an "explosive issue," Garment concluded that a "veto could have a devastating impact on our chances (already questionable) of getting through the summer without major violence."[146] With fresh memories of ghetto rioting, of students demonstrating against the Vietnam War, and of national outrage following the shootings of antiwar protesters at Kent State and Jackson State universities, the president could not afford to overlook Garment's last point.

There were other reasons why the Garment-Price argument packed a powerful punch. Garment and Price, skilled wordsmiths, often outflanked their conservative rivals and wound up drafting the president's statements on issues such as school desegregation and fair housing. On voting rights, their foes seemed especially inept. Assistant Attorney General William H. Rehnquist urged a presidential veto on the grounds that the eighteen-year-old vote rider was both "unconstitutional" and an exercise in "masochism" for the GOP.[147] Justice Department officials thrashed out a veto message while Nixon's conservative congressional advisers, Harlow and Timmons, argued that a presidential rejection could be sustained in Congress.[148] Yet they seemed reluctant to press the issue, perhaps knowing that opposing the right to vote was politically risky. Since the congressional liaison staff had failed to deliver on Haynsworth and Carswell, Nixon probably did not trust their forecasts anyway. Finally, Garment and Price appeared to gain an ally in Ehrlichman, who, during the early months of 1970, had grown weary of Nixon's rightward drift, symbolized by the Carswell nomination.[149] While it is unclear whether Ehrlichman used his power as gatekeeper to suppress memoranda by Timmons and Rehnquist, he may have ensured that Garment and Price received more than a fair hearing.

Nixon, not wanting to thwart voting rights, accepted the compromise bill. He twice informed his staff that if the measure dealt only with blacks, he would approve it.[150] The president privately expressed no qualms about the bill's "merits."[151] Of course, the idea of scuttling the eighteen-year-old vote proved tantalizing. Nixon argued that the "politically best course" was a veto, for he saw "no mileage" in enfranchising eighteen-year-olds, complaining, "[We] will lose votes if we sign it." Yet Nixon worried that rejecting the entire voting rights bill would drive minorities and young people into the streets, as Garment and Price predicted: "[I] am concerned re volatile situation . . . & real danger of [the] country blowing up."[152] "Intuition" convinced this real-life Hamlet that the "black problem"–that is, not alienating African Americans from the political system–was "overriding."[153] So on June 22 the president signed the Voting Rights Act of 1970.[154]

Nixon's remarks upon signing the bill hinted at his deliberations. The statement, drafted by Price and revised by Nixon, admitted that the president had nearly vetoed the act on the grounds that the eighteen-year-old vote rider was unconstitutional, a phony argument. To ensure minority voting rights, Nixon set aside his reservations. He praised the Voting Rights Act of 1965 as "a symbol of open participation in the political process" and called its registration of voters "evidence that the American system works" and "an answer to those who claim that there is no recourse except to the streets." The president lauded the act's new sections, which he had advocated: a temporary ban on all literacy tests and uniform residency requirements for voting.[155]

This self-serving pronouncement ignored Nixon's political motives. In reviewing Price's draft, the president crossed out all references to the act's effectiveness "in the South," another symbolic gesture to white conservatives.[156] Yet Nixon's statement captured his belief that the right to vote must not be abridged. His reference to voting as legitimizing "the American system" and discouraging street demonstrations highlighted the president's chief reason for signing this law.[157]

Nixon's decision drew mostly favorable responses. Roy Wilkins lauded the president for citing "the safeguarding of the Negro's right to vote" as his "prime consideration," and Clarence Mitchell called Nixon's action "an act of statesmanship."[158] But southern segregationists declined to sing the president's praises. Senator Strom Thurmond, Republican of South Carolina, penned a tart letter to the chief executive, accusing Nixon of breaking his campaign pledge by signing "regional" legislation. That the new Voting Rights Act voided literacy tests nationwide and applied pre-clearance to some northern districts failed to move the South Carolinian. He had wanted the president to reject the bill as "unconstitutional" and "unjust."[159] As with school desegregation, Nixon sought Thurmond's political support but refused to bind himself to the policy whims of this unreconstructed southerner.

The president's signing of the Voting Rights Act did not signal a permanent shift to the left, any more than his sporadic wooing of southern conservatives denoted an unbending right-wing agenda. Having zigged toward the liberals, Nixon again zagged toward conservatives. "Perhaps Cambodia & Kent State," he wrote aides in September 1970, "led to an overreaction by our own people to prove we were pro-student, [pro]-blacks, [pro]-left. We must get turned around on this before it's too late." The president wanted to stress "anti-crime, anti-demonstrations, anti-drug, anti-obscenity" to "get with the mood of the country which is fed up with the liberals."[160]

Such sentiments came and went. After making little headway with a "law and order" message during the elections of 1970, Nixon declared an "open door" policy to court young people and minorities. In 1971, as his own reelection neared, the president ordered his troops to "get some 18 year olds to move our way."[161] Nixon welcomed to the Oval Office Elvis Presley, an icon to many young people, in the first-ever encounter between the president and "the King."[162] He even proposed a new organization to mold young people into Republicans. "Make it 'out' to wear long hair, smoke pot and go on the needle," Nixon told conservative speechwriter Patrick J. Buchanan. "Make it 'in' to indulge the lesser vices, smoking (cigars preferably–non-Castro!) and alcohol in reasonable qualities on the right occasions."[163] With such far-fetched schemes, the president struggled to reach the under-thirty crowd.

On voting rights Nixon emerged as a man of multiple motives and some indecision, neither a crusader nor an outright villain. From the standpoint of expanding voting rights, he was correct to nationalize the Voting Rights Act but incorrect in trying to expunge pre-clearance. Civil rights leaders, in contrast, were incorrect to dismiss the nationwide ban on literacy tests but correct in defending pre-clearance. By compromising, both sides sculpted the Voting Rights Act of 1970, which influenced the debate on voting rights over the succeeding two decades.

Voting Rights after Nixon

By accepting the eighteen-year-old vote, retaining pre-clearance, and nationalizing voting rights, the president altered national policy. After Nixon left office, the Voting Rights Act became something more than a device to enfranchise African Americans in the South. It became a means to ensure the political power of minority groups across the United States.

Ironically, the Nixon administration reinforced the one provision of the Voting Rights Act of 1970 that the president disliked: the eighteen-year-old vote. Upon signing the act, Nixon pushed for review of this rider in court. He also vowed to back a constitutional amendment to enfranchise eighteen-year-olds if the Supreme Court struck down this proviso. Behind the scenes, Nixon searched for litigants to challenge the rider and asked Mitchell to oppose it.[164] But since the president had signed the act, the attorney general had to defend Congress's right to lower the voting age.[165] In 1970 the Court upheld the eighteen-year-old vote rider only for presidential elections.[166] To avoid alienating these new voters, eighty-five senators sponsored a constitutional amendment granting them the vote in all elections. Within three months, thirty-eight states ratified what became the Twenty-sixth Amendment.[167] By urging a constitutional amendment, Nixon helped enfranchise eighteen-year-olds in time for the election of 1972.

Nixon's decision, after considerable pressure, to retain pre-clearance proved to be another important, albeit unintended, change. During the 1970s, the Supreme Court read pre-clearance broadly, as a means to promote minority officeholding instead of a means to preempt unfair voting practices.[168] Such an interpretation had merit. In 1975 African Americans accounted for 26 percent of the South's population but held only 3 percent of its elected offices.[169] The high tribunal thus upheld reapportionment to establish majority black districts.[170] Such reasoning flowed from the court's *Gaston County* decision, which had focused on the effect, not the intent, of voting laws. So the Supreme Court used affirmative action to enhance minority voting strength and officeholding.

Nixonians would not have agreed with such an expansive definition of pre-clearance. Even after the president signed the Voting Rights Act, which retained this procedure, the attorney general continued to fight it. In 1971 Justice Department officials drafted new pre-clearance guidelines which required the federal government, not the states, to prove that electoral laws were racially biased.[171] Civil rights groups denounced the regulations, forcing Senate liberals and White House aides such as Garment and Ehrlichman to fashion yet another compromise.[172] In the end, Mitchell gave in and kept the burden of proof upon the states.[173]

Notwithstanding its reservations about pre-clearance, Nixon's Justice Department far exceeded LBJ's in filing objections to voting laws.[174]

The Johnson administration reviewed only a handful of voting laws and rarely disputed them. Between 1971 and 1974, Justice Department officials examined 4,211 statutes and rejected 183.[175] Three factors prompted this flurry of enforcement. First, since pre-clearance now applied to northern as well as southern states, more voting laws were referred to the government to scrutinize. Second, Mitchell unwittingly strengthened enforcement by reorganizing the Justice Department's civil rights division into separate sections for voting, housing, and employment. He thus installed a cadre of voting rights advocates within the federal bureaucracy.[176] Finally, even though Nixon and Mitchell seemed cool to pre-clearance, they "went with the flow" by enforcing and legitimizing this proviso. Originally crafted to reinforce voting rights, pre-clearance "turned out to be the most important section of the Act" by the 1970s.[177]

Not all of the administration's good work was inadvertent. By nationalizing the Voting Rights Act, Nixon and Mitchell proved farsighted. The Voting Rights Act of 1970 applied pre-clearance to four counties with significant Hispanic populations: Apache County, Arizona; Imperial County, California; and Kings (Brooklyn) and New York (Manhattan) counties in New York.[178] When the act next came up for renewal in 1975, debate focused on how to expand it further. Young urban black leaders called for more attention to the North. "There are more blacks denied the right to vote in Chicago than live in the entire State of Mississippi," declared the Reverend Jesse Jackson, sounding a lot like John Mitchell five years earlier.[179] Upset with voting rights violations in Texas, Hispanic American leaders favored extending pre-clearance to the Southwest.[180] The longtime civil rights lobbyist Clarence Mitchell, in contrast, again emphasized protecting black voting rights in the South. He urged flat renewal of the act and accused Mexican American leaders of thwarting this goal. One observer recalled Mitchell pointing his finger at representatives of the Mexican-American Legal Defense and Education Fund "and saying, you want to take us back to the dark days of 1963, with lynchings in Mississippi."[181]

President Gerald R. Ford, like Nixon, agreed to expand the reach of the Voting Rights Act. Joseph L. Rauh, Jr., a white lawyer and civil rights advocate who had worked with Clarence Mitchell, struck a bargain between African American and Hispanic leaders. Rauh proposed added provisions to protect the rights of Spanish-speaking Americans, and Majority Leader Mike Mansfield then pushed such a measure through the Senate.[182] In 1975 Ford signed the amended bill, which renewed the Voting Rights Act for seven years, applied pre-clearance to areas with unregistered "language" minorities, and permanently abolished literacy tests.[183] In so doing, he completed the process of "nationalizing" voting rights begun under Nixon.

With advances came setbacks. By nationalizing the Voting Rights Act, policy makers moved away from the act's original mission, to enfranchise southern blacks, and scrambled the voting rights picture. As the act lost its coherence, judges filled the vacuum, with mixed results. By the 1990s, federal courts, turning against affirmative action, had invalidated as gerrymandering many of the black districts fashioned over the previous two decades.[184] Moreover, politicians and civil rights leaders who viewed voting rights as a panacea for the problems of African Americans grew disillusioned. While acknowledging that the 1965 act had broadened the political base, the historian Steven Lawson called it "a marginal instrument for black economic advancement."[185]

Nixon understood these limits. The president and his team knew that an agenda based on school desegregation, fair housing, and voting rights would crash against the rocks of white backlash. They sought to move the civil rights debate away from integration and toward minority economic development. In so doing, Nixon could play down integration in education and housing, anathema to his white base, and still claim that he had not neglected civil rights.

4

Jobs Are Nixon's Rights Program:
The Philadelphia Plan and Affirmative Action

"Incredible but true," declared *Fortune* magazine at the time of President Richard M. Nixon's death in 1994. "It was the Nixonites who gave us employment quotas."[1] "Affirmative action," a term used by Presidents John F. Kennedy and Lyndon B. Johnson, evolved naturally and logically from earlier federal efforts to fight job bias.[2] But it was a Republican president who backed "goals and timetables" to raze barriers to minority employment. Nixon, recalled the civil rights leader James Farmer, was "the strongest president on affirmative action—up to that point."[3]

It was Nixon's pragmatism that led him to back affirmative action. In the aftermath of urban rioting, with the civil rights movement still active and whites turning against integration in education and housing, the president sought to address economic grievances. In 1969 White House urban affairs chief Daniel P. Moynihan urged Nixon to dissolve the "great black urban lower class" and co-opt "militant" African Americans by making them "judges, professors, congressmen, cops." "How better to give persons an interest in the continued viability of the system," Moynihan ventured, "I do not know."[4]

Nixon saw economic opportunity as the key to social mobility, racial peace, and national stability. "This country," he wrote in 1972, "is not ready at this time for either forcibly integrated housing or forcibly integrated education."[5] But America was ready for integration in employment because, the president told aides, "jobs are more important to Negroes than anything else."[6] The journalist David Hawkins summed up the president's vision when he noted, "Jobs are Nixon's 'rights' program."[7] Yet in practice, Nixon's fair employment policy involved ample give-and-take, and his support of affirmative action proved fragile. The president's earliest orders on fair employment called for increased efforts; hiring targets came later. When affirmative action angered blue-collar ethnics, he flinched. Sporadic presidential leadership freed federal officials to apply their own affirmative action standards, with varying results.

While the public debate on affirmative action turned on whether such programs established "goals" or "quotas," the president's decentralized policy making spawned three models of enforcement: statist, corporatist, and minimalist. By pressing for hiring goals and strongly threatening sanctions, some of Nixon's ranking civil rights appointees–Arthur A. Fletcher, J. Stanley Pottinger, and William H. Brown III–imposed statist remedies on federal contractors in Philadelphia, universities receiving federal aid, and private industry. Hometown plans, to desegregate construction work outside Philadelphia, embodied corporatist principles of voluntarism, local planning, and government suasion. To end bias in federal employment, the Civil Service Commission preached minimalism, that is, hazy guidelines and persuasion in lieu of coercion.

To Nixon, each model had a virtue. Statist remedies brought immediate results, while corporatist and minimalist methods coincided with Republican principles of local autonomy and limited government. With Nixon sometimes endorsing, sometimes containing, and sometimes ignoring bureaucratic initiatives, affirmative action developed in fits and starts.

The Origins of the Philadelphia Plan

The idea of affirmative action developed gradually, as the federal government moved to open the lily-white building trades to racial minorities. Throughout the 1950s, minimalist policies of investigation and persuasion secured few construction jobs for African Americans. During the 1960s, Labor Department officials slowly moved to implement the Philadelphia Plan, a statist program of race-based hiring goals for the construction industry.

Racial discrimination in the construction trades was pervasive. To maintain a scarce labor supply, construction unions restricted admission to their apprenticeship programs. Although leaders of the American Federation of Labor–Congress of Industrial Organizations (AFL-CIO) supported the Civil Rights Act of 1964 and paid lip service to equality of opportunity, union locals declined to recruit African Americans.[8] "When I was a plumber," AFL-CIO president George Meany once remarked, "It never [occurred] to me to have niggers in the union!"[9] In 1967 African Americans made up just 8 percent of construction trade unionists, and out of a brotherhood of 330,000, the plumbing, sheet metal, electrical, asbestos, and elevator trades had only 1,400 black members.[10]

To attack discrimination in employment, President Dwight D. Eisenhower applied minimalist solutions. He established the President's Committee on Government Contracts, chaired by Vice President Nixon, to end bias in firms doing business with the government. Sensitive to the prerogatives of Congress and the wishes of southern politicians, Eisenhower directed committee members to promote "equality" through "persuasion" rather than coercion. He warned Nixon that the committee must not evolve into a fair employment practices commission with the power to issue sanctions.[11] Consistent with the GOP's laissez-faire creed, Nixon's committee would end job bias gradually, by resolving individual complaints through cooperation. The committee reserved the right to cancel contracts only when "absolutely necessary."[12]

By chairing the government contracts committee, Nixon gained a firsthand understanding of job discrimination. He called bias "a waste of urgently needed manpower" and deemed a program of equal opportunity "the right thing to do."[13] According to Labor Secretary James P.

Mitchell, vice chair of the committee, the vice president became a strong voice for fair employment.[14] At a cabinet meeting in 1959, Nixon acknowledged that "whenever a group of Negroes gets into a desegregated school" it became "big news," but improved education was useless if minorities failed to break into "professional white collar areas."[15] Nixon brought these assumptions to his own presidency, where he placed jobs ("results") ahead of "token" integration.[16]

Populist instincts, and political expediency, shaped Nixon's approach to fair employment. He admired self-made men more than persons born to wealth and privilege, an attitude consistent with his own experience. Rising from lower-middle-class origins to national leadership on the strength of drive and ability, the vice president embodied the American Dream. The notion of equal opportunity, giving all individuals the chance to rise as far as their talents permitted, proved a key thread in the tangled skein of Nixon's life.[17] Moreover, he saw a mild fair employment policy as appealing to blacks without offending whites.[18] As head of the contracts committee, Nixon earned scattered praise from African Americans, although white liberals charged him with trepidation, and southern conservatives accused him of going to "extremes" to "cultivate the Negro vote."[19] After visiting the South in 1956, White House press secretary James C. Hagerty reported that whites associated Nixon "with the Negro difficulty" and that "not one person" supported the vice president's reelection.[20]

Such responses reinforced Nixon's desire to enforce equal opportunity according to Eisenhower's minimalist guidelines. The government contracts committee urged federal agencies to practice fair employment. It reviewed charges of bias case by case, then coaxed employers into reforming their employment practices.[21] The committee ruled out quotas to compel minority hiring and never canceled a contract of an employer suspected of discrimination.[22] Pleased with the AFL-CIO's work in promoting noncommunist labor unions overseas, Nixon did not press for integration of unions.[23]

As a result, Nixon's committee secured few skilled jobs for blacks. While AFL-CIO officials cited statistics showing progress in admitting blacks, Meany (a member of the committee) refused to compel union locals to admit them. In one breakthrough, the committee found employment for three African American rodmen on construction projects in Washington, D.C. In 1960 the NAACP justly complained that at this pace blacks would require 138 years to secure equal employment in the skilled crafts.[24]

A balanced assessment of the contracts committee came from its last director, Jacob Seidenberg. In 1960 Seidenberg wrote a summary report that lauded the committee for securing jobs for minorities and for giving fair employment policy "considerable status." He singled out Nixon and Mitchell as two men whose "interest and concern never lagged." On the negative side, Seidenberg lamented the committee's organizational defects and inadequate funding. He recommended legislation to recognize the committee's work, the blacklisting of employers practicing discrimination, and the extension of fair employment rules to labor unions.[25] His counsel was far from complete; Seidenberg failed to address whether numerical hiring goals were proper remedies for bias.

Lingering discrimination in the building trades provoked unrest. In 1963 the NAACP braved police violence in picketing Philadelphia's white-dominated building trade unions. Similar protests in 1969 delayed construction projects at the University of Washington, Tufts University, and the State University of New York at Buffalo.[26] African American demands for admittance to unions aroused resentment.[27] In Chicago a probe of union bias propelled rank-and-file workers into the streets. "I had to wait my turn . . . getting my apprenticeship," complained one white protester. "Why should these guys be given special consideration, just because they happen to be black?"[28]

In fighting bias, Democratic presidents John F. Kennedy and Lyndon B. Johnson proved slightly more assertive than Eisenhower. Following the outburst of strife in Philadelphia in 1963, Kennedy directed his Committee on Equal Employment Opportunity to monitor hiring practices on federal construction projects. Johnson signed Executive Order 11246, which affirmed the government's commitment to promote "equal employment opportunity" in companies holding federal contracts. While both presidents put "affirmative action" in their executive orders, neither JFK nor LBJ endorsed specific goals or timetables for desegregating the construction unions.[29]

Moves toward affirmative action came from the Labor Department. Between 1965 and 1967 the department's Office of Federal Contract Compliance (OFCC) inched toward the forbidden terrain of hiring quotas. The agency at first required bidders on government contracts to submit written affirmative action plans for minority employment. It later adopted a "more result-oriented approach" in which the government awarded contracts to companies that set targets for hiring minorities. To avoid the "quotas" prohibited under Title VI of the Civil Rights Act of 1964, LBJ's Labor Department developed numerical "goals" for construction contractors in St. Louis, Cleveland, and Philadelphia.[30]

To proponents of affirmative action, the difference between goals and quotas was more than semantic. While both methods used numerical hiring ratios, they differed in flexibility and degree of enforcement. Under a quota system, employers who failed to hire a specific number of minorities faced immediate sanctions. A policy of goals, in contrast, punished only a contractor who failed to demonstrate a "good faith effort."[31] Opponents of affirmative action, however, rejected such distinctions, arguing that numbers were numbers. U.S. Comptroller General Elmer B. Staats, for example, deemed the Johnson administration's "Philadelphia Plan" a scheme to promote racial "quotas," not "goals." In November 1968 he ruled the plan in violation of the Civil Rights Act of 1964. Preparing to turn over the reins of governance to Nixon, LBJ declined to press the issue, and his administration dropped the Philadelphia Plan.[32]

By drafting hiring goals, Johnson administration officials pioneered a statist remedy that went beyond the vague regulations and conciliation methods of Nixon's contracts committee. Yet early in 1969 the United States Commission on Civil Rights criticized OFCC for failing to set minimum standards for the agency's programs and to blacklist contractors suspected of bias.[33] Later that year, the A. Philip Randolph Institute, a civil rights think tank, reproached the government for not prodding contractors "into undertaking positive moves to end discrimination."[34] Johnson's administration had tested but not institutionalized government-inspired affirmative action.

A "Little Extra Start": The Revised Philadelphia Plan

By embracing and defending numerical goals, President Nixon and his advisers made permanent the practice of affirmative action. In 1969 the new president reaffirmed the government's commitment to opening construction unions to minorities. Then, moved by assorted considerations, he endorsed a revised version of the Philadelphia Plan.

The Philadelphia Plan's rebirth was tied to basic economics: the scarcity of skilled construction workers had inflated the cost of new housing. Nixon did not request hiring goals, merely greater enforcement of fair employment. Responding to a task force report, the president, early in 1969, asked Labor Secretary George P. Shultz and Housing and Urban Development Secretary George W. Romney to study the impact of "restrictive practices of construction unions" on the housing industry.[35] A week later he specifically urged them "to work on problems of discrimination in the building trade unions" as well.[36]

These routine directives spurred officials in the Housing and Labor departments to study discrimination in the building trades.[37] Drafted by Undersecretary Richard C. Van Dusen, the HUD paper confirmed that racial discrimination was one culprit in the shortage of skilled workers and spiraling housing costs. It urged "forceful, effective enforcement" of the statutes and executive orders "requiring affirmative action."[38] The Labor Department's report, a rambling overview of problems facing the construction industry, danced around the issue of discrimination.[39] Although HUD seemed to be taking the lead against employment bias, the Labor Department soon became the prime force behind the rejuvenation of the Philadelphia Plan.

Shultz and his team advocated numerical goals to secure better jobs for African Americans. The secretary's commitment to racial equality was plain; he informed one labor leader that "I am deeply interested in civil rights matters and feel the Department of Labor can—and should—play a significant role in assuring equal opportunities to all Americans."[40] Early in 1969 Shultz threatened to withhold government contracts from southern textile mills that rejected a "reasonable program of affirmative action."[41] Four months later he decreed that contractors must make written commitments to correct any deficiencies in their equal employment posture.[42] "I believe," the secretary added, "the affirmative action concept is indispensable to the President's domestic program."[43]

With Shultz's support, Assistant Labor Secretary Arthur A. Fletcher, one of the ranking blacks in the government, redrafted the Philadelphia Plan in June 1969. The revised plan required federally assisted contractors on projects exceeding $500,000 to show good faith in hiring minorities, "Negro, Oriental, American Indian, and Spanish-surnamed." After consulting contractors in the Philadelphia area, OFCC was to establish numerical ranges for employment of these groups, with the focus on blacks.[44] Iron trade unions working on federal projects would have to employ between 5 and 9 percent blacks in 1970, with ranges increasing each year thereafter. Apparently sweeping in its mandate, the revised Philadelphia Plan covered just five counties in eastern Pennsylvania. Moreover, only employers who declined to show good faith in meeting OFCC targets faced losing their contracts.[45] Nevertheless, by permitting hiring ratios and punishment of negligent contractors, Fletcher's Philadelphia Plan revived the statist model of affirmative action.

External pressure influenced Nixon's fair employment policy. During a meeting with the president in 1969, Roy Wilkins, executive secretary of the NAACP, expressed a "sense of urgency" about racial problems, especially in areas of employment and "the enforcement of FEP clauses in Federal Contracts."[46] Nixon then ordered a study of bias in the construction trades. After the Commission on Civil Rights, the Leadership Conference on Civil Rights, an umbrella organization based in Washington, and Senator Harrison A. Williams, Jr., Democrat of New Jersey and chair of the Subcommittee on Labor, all reproached the government for lax enforcement of contract compliance, Shultz issued his ultimatum to the southern textile mills.[47] Before announcing the revised Philadelphia Plan, Fletcher offered to meet with Wilkins to discuss problems of "mutual concern."[48] Afterward, Herbert Hill, labor director of the NAACP, praised Shultz for supporting the plan.[49] If civil rights groups failed to form alliances with sympathetic bureaucrats and politicians, they nonetheless roused the administration to adopt a more active fair employment stance.

The revised Philadelphia Plan encountered formidable opposition, some of it expected, some not. Ignoring the plan's emphasis on goals and "good faith efforts," George Meany termed it a program of quotas and deadlines, which he rejected as "completely unacceptable."[50] For the second time, Comptroller General Staats ruled that the Philadelphia Plan mandated quotas and violated the Civil Rights Act of 1964.[51] Senate Minority Leader Everett M. Dirksen, Republican of Illinois, agreed and threatened to rally the appropriations committees in Congress to deny funding for the plan.[52] The minority leader told the president that to Senate Republicans, "this thing is about as popular as a crab in a whorehouse."[53] After Dirksen's death in September 1969, Senator Sam Ervin of North Carolina, chair of the Judiciary Committee, picked up the gauntlet. To prove that the Philadelphia Plan breached the Civil Rights Act of 1964 (a law he had voted against), Ervin convened hearings. Senators who usually backed Nixon administration programs, right-wing Republicans and southern Democrats, had united to oppose the plan.[54]

Did the Philadelphia Plan establish quotas? Absolutely not, said officials in the Labor Department. In public, Shultz and Fletcher distinguished between quotas, which compelled employers to hire a set ratio of African Americans, and goals, which simply established numerical ranges for minority employment.[55] Labor Department solicitor Laurence H. Silberman and Attorney General John N. Mitchell agreed with such reasoning and found no conflict between the Philadelphia Plan and the Civil Rights Act of 1964.[56]

It remains unclear whether these practical men believed strongly in the distinction between goals and quotas. Fletcher's overriding objective was to secure decent jobs for blacks. Reminded years later of the charge that the plan had established quotas, Shultz justified it on the basis of past discrimination: "We found a quota system [in the construction industry]. It was there. It was zero." Silberman privately wrestled with the distinction between goals and quotas. He came to favor less coercive, corporatist remedies and later lamented that the administration had opened a Pandora's box in pressing for goals.[57]

Why did Nixon endorse a scheme to set racial goals? The desire to check housing costs led him to open the construction trades to more workers. The Philadelphia Plan had garnered wide support within the administration, from the conservative Mitchell to liberal White House staffers Moynihan, Leonard Garment, and Bradley H. Patterson, Jr. The appeals of Shultz, a reasonable, soft-spoken former dean of the University of Chicago's School of Business, no doubt moved Nixon as well.[58] Assistant Secretary Fletcher also proved persuasive, reminding reporters that the "way we put a man on the moon in less than ten years was with goals, targets and timetables."[59] Fletcher "transfixed a Cabinet meeting" when he pleaded for economic development for blacks.[60]

Furthermore, Nixon's thinking on fair employment policy had shifted from favoring minimalism and persuasion to endorsing some form of state-sanctioned justice. During the 1950s Nixon remained wedded to the limited government and pro-business tenets of the GOP, and he flatly opposed establishing a national fair employment practices commission with authority to police discrimination in the private sector.[61] During the presidential campaign of 1960, Nixon backed legislation to recognize the work of his government contracts committee and "end the discriminatory membership practices of some local labor unions."[62] In its final report, Nixon's committee advised employers to adopt "a positive policy of nondiscrimination."[63] Yet its chair failed to specify any "positive" steps to resolve this problem. "Under no circumstances," Nixon wrote an aide, "should the recommendations be more detailed than they are."[64]

Over the next decade, Nixon's views evolved. The riots that racked American cities during the sixties forced national leaders to acknowledge that economic status, not just race, continued to separate blacks from whites.[65] While privately supporting equal opportunity, Nixon questioned whether giving African Americans an "equal chance" would be sufficient.[66] Before launching his second presidential bid, Nixon, in words worthy of LBJ, told reporters that "people in the ghetto have to have more than an equal chance. They should be given a dividend."[67] He followed up in the new year, promising to give "everybody an equal chance at the line and then giving those who haven't had their chance, who've had it denied for a hundred years, that little extra start that they need so that it is in truth an equal chance."[68] To Nixon, the Philadelphia Plan became one "extra start" for blacks struggling to obtain decent jobs and enter mainstream society. After the president embraced the plan, Fletcher declared that the "Nixon Administration now has a civil rights vehicle."[69]

The historian Hugh Davis Graham has contended that Nixon pushed the Philadelphia Plan to pit the twin pillars of the Democratic Party, labor unions and civil rights groups, against each other.[70] To be sure, Nixon was cunning and capable of such Machiavellian thinking. So too was Fletcher, who predicted that "marriages between civil rights and labor people are going to come apart," freeing "civil rights people to go . . . after their own issues on their terms."[71] But among the factors leading the president to sign on to the plan, political revenge was of lesser importance. There is no evidence of presidential interest in dividing the Democrats during July 1969, when Nixon first defended the plan before congressional leaders. Nixon did not resolve to use the Philadelphia Plan to split the opposition until later that year, after labor unions and civil rights groups had coalesced to block the confirmation of Clement F. Haynsworth, Jr., to the Supreme Court.[72]

Nixon's partisan reason for endorsing the Philadelphia Plan was rather obvious; as a Republican, he saw organized labor's shortcomings more clearly and moved against them more forcefully than the Democrats had. Leaders of both wings of the Republican Party had called for an end to bias in unions. In 1960 Governor Nelson Rockefeller of New York, a liberal Republican, proposed granting the National Labor Relations Board authority "to refuse to certify unions that discriminate in membership."[73] Eight years later Governor Ronald Reagan of California, a conservative, attacked discrimination by labor unions: "When less than 3% of the union membership in California comes from our minority communities, there is something wrong."[74] By supporting the Philadelphia Plan, Nixon could do something positive for minorities and pull his party together against a common adversary: organized labor.

From the standpoint of broadening Nixon's political base, however, the Philadelphia Plan carried few benefits. Beginning in 1969, the president strove to cultivate conservative white southerners and blue-collar ethnics, not African Americans and civil rights organizations. He held meetings with AFL-CIO chief Meany and other labor leaders to win their support.[75] Since the Philadelphia Plan favored blacks and antagonized union leaders, conservative southerners, and blue-collar ethnics, it hardly advanced Nixon's long-term electoral objectives. Understanding this fact, the president's conservative political aides opposed the program. "While there may be much justification for the Philadelphia Plan in the Labor Department," presidential adviser Harry S. Dent argued, "the recent hearings on more integration of the building trades unions in Chicago put this Administration in an adverse position with regard to union members."[76] As with school desegregation policy, Nixon read Dent's memorandum but did not follow its recommendations.

In approving the Philadelphia Plan, Nixon placed economics and civil rights ahead of political expediency. During a meeting with Republican congressional leaders in July 1969, the president conceded that there were votes to be gained in courting construction unions. But he argued that "the Republican Party has 'temporized' too long" over the problem of building trades discrimination and it was "essential" to "break the bottleneck." The failure to employ minorities, he said, had driven the cost of housing to alarming heights.[77] A few months later, after reading Meany's "scathing" critique of the Philadelphia Plan, Nixon second-guessed his own decision: "While our 'liberals' won't agree, this [program] hurts us. With our constituency, we gained little on the play."[78]

To the extent that politics influenced Nixon's endorsement of the Philadelphia Plan, it was politics defined broadly as the pursuit of power and prestige at others' expense. Disturbed over "tight union control of labor supply," the president noted that this plan "challenges" the unions' control.[79] Defending his prerogative to set fair employment policy, Nixon resolved to overturn the comptroller general's "very sweeping" veto of the Philadelphia Plan.[80] Furthermore, this program enabled him to claim credit for progress in an area where the opposition had faltered; Nixon privately crowed that Democrats "are token-oriented" while "we are job-oriented."[81] The Republican president relished exercising power and confounding critics with bold initiatives.

Together these motivations made Nixon and his subordinates effective sponsors of the Philadelphia Plan. During 1969 he met on three occasions with Republican congressional leaders to defend the plan and plead for support.[82] Meanwhile, officials in the departments of Labor and Justice and within the White House lobbied members of Congress to back the program.[83] When the Senate late in 1969 considered an amendment to kill the Philadelphia Plan, the president rallied his lieutenants. House Minority Leader Gerald R. Ford, Republican of Michigan, and Senate Minority Leader Hugh D. Scott, Republican of Pennsylvania and Dirksen's successor, exhorted their troops to reject the amendment.[84] A White House message, hastily typed out by Bradley Patterson, reiterated that the Philadelphia Plan "does not set quotas; it points to goals."[85] Three days before Christmas, Nixon threatened to hold Congress in session to reconsider the plan if it went down to defeat. His full-court press paid off. On December 23 a coalition of liberal Democrats and moderate Republicans salvaged the Philadelphia Plan, allowing Congress to adjourn and the president to toast a pre-holiday victory.[86]

In truth, Nixon's support for the Philadelphia Plan proved tenuous. Because he accepted the plan for no single reason, the president lacked an overarching motive for extending affirmative action. Nixon's choice of civil rights remedies shifted with the prevailing winds. The economic factors that led him to endorse the Philadelphia Plan would change. Since the program cut against his reelection strategy, he never felt comfortable with it. While a few African Americans applauded Nixon's defense of the plan, and the president saw it as a device to quiet black criticism of his administration, integrationist civil rights leaders such as Clarence Mitchell of the Leadership Conference on Civil Rights denounced it as a tool to divide the Democratic coalition.[87] Accordingly, Nixon ordered his chief of staff, H. R. Haldeman, to "be sure our P.R. types make it clear we aren't adopting policy for the purpose of being 100% Negro & winning their votes. We know this is not possible."[88]

The Philadelphia Plan Neglected and Enforced

Needing labor unions' support for his Vietnam policy and anti-inflation program of wage and price controls, Nixon showed little inclination to extend the Philadelphia Plan after 1969. By approving the program, however, the president had signaled his support for affirmative action. Accordingly, Nixon appointees in the federal departments, walking a tightrope between too little and too much enforcement, expanded the Philadelphia Plan.

Presidential support of the plan waned as Nixon questioned the wisdom of adopting a policy to appease liberal constituencies such as young people and blacks. "Will continue to do what is right—as P[resident]," Nixon said in 1970, "q[uestion] is—what is right politically . . . re sign[ing] [the] 18 yr vote [and] Phil. Plan."[89] To prevent the president's policies from careening to the right, domestic policy chief John D. Ehrlichman defended the Philadelphia Plan for driving "a wedge between the Democrats and labor which has stretched the membrane." But he also appealed to the president's moderation: "If we administer it without undue zeal it can become a 'slow and reasonable' approach to civil rights." Nixon agreed.[90]

Inspired by Nixon's earlier endorsement, cabinet members and their immediate subordinates modified and extended the Philadelphia Plan.

In 1970 and 1971 the Labor Department pressed hiring goals on businesses with federal contracts exceeding $50,000 and widened those goals to include women as well as racial minorities.[91] Over the next three years, Labor Secretary Shultz and his successor, James D. Hodgson, encouraged business, labor, and civil rights organizations in American communities to confer and design their own plans to bring disadvantaged groups into the building trades.[92] Hodgson predicted that these voluntary "hometown plans" would prove superior to government-imposed solutions such as the Philadelphia Plan. Hometown plans, he argued, covered private construction, while imposed plans dealt only with federally funded projects.[93] Coinciding with the president's stress on local authority–the "New Federalism"–governors and mayors helped negotiate hometown plans. By 1973, fifty-six such plans existed in cities across the country.[94]

The Labor Department lacked the means and will to make hometown plans successful. Embodying the notion of "corporatism," in which bureaucrats invite segments of society to resolve problems voluntarily, hometown plans employed negotiation and mediation rather than coercion and punishment. Corporatism had roots in the moderate wing of the GOP, dating back to Herbert Hoover.[95] But in the case of building trades discrimination, where unions resisted change, the corporatist remedy proved inadequate. Although department officials threatened to impose their own plans upon recalcitrant communities, they seldom did.[96] Lacking funds and personnel, the Labor Department failed to police the mushrooming number of hometown plans.[97]

Officials charged with enforcing hometown and imposed plans shunned tight enforcement. Undersecretary of Labor Silberman, who favored the corporatist model, proposed using a "plain government hack" to review the Philadelphia Plan because, he argued, "we don't want someone who will expose all of its crevices."[98] When contractors complained of "unrealistic" hiring goals under Washington's government-imposed plan, Silberman reconsidered those goals.[99] Labor Department bureaucrats sometimes tried to duck responsibility for contract compliance. Criticized for barring a contractor who failed to meet targets under El Paso's hometown plan, William J. Kilberg, a Labor Department lawyer, blamed the Department of Transportation.[100] Within other agencies, officials proved equally timid. HUD undersecretary

Richard C. Van Dusen rejected fixed goals for Detroit's hometown plan, reminding one subordinate, "We should have in mind the potential criticism of Federal coercion and arbitrary quotas."[101]

The persons overseeing hometown plans proved to be good Nixonians; moderate and pragmatic, they understood that bias had to end without saddling business, a key constituency, with excessive federal regulations.[102] Fletcher, a liberal Republican, endorsed a blend of threats and rewards to encourage contractors to reform their employment practices. Ronald Reagan favored hometown plans because they respected states' rights and were "voluntarily initiated."[103] With Republicans united behind an ostensibly well-intentioned policy, Nixonians had little incentive to beef up contract compliance.

Had the administration imposed its own plans on communities, integration of building trades would have quickened. Under the Philadelphia Plan, the most famous imposed plan, with its blend of threats and incentives, contractors exceeded federal hiring goals.[104] "I think it's working," a Filipino electrician said. "There are three of us here as a result of the Plan."[105]

Advertised as the "Atlanta Plan," "Buffalo Plan" or "Tacoma Plan," hometown solutions resembled the Philadelphia Plan in name only.[106] Unmitigated flops, they drew wide criticism. In New York, a state official called hometown plans an abdication of federal responsibility.[107] The NAACP also berated the government for lax enforcement.[108] Fletcher himself called Chicago's voluntary plan "a failure"; civil rights groups labeled it a "sham."[109] Finding the results of New York's plan "inadequate and disappointing," Mayor John V. Lindsay, a Republican turned Democrat, exhorted Labor Department officials "to impose a Philadelphia-type plan on all Federally-aided construction in our City."[110] They took no action. Underscoring this hit-or-miss enforcement, contract compliance officials failed to develop any plan for Baltimore.[111] As a result, minorities made little progress in gaining admission to the construction trades.[112]

Apathy, interstaff squabbles, and political pressures blocked reconsideration of hometown plans. In 1971 Fletcher prodded the White House to rethink its fair employment policy for the construction industry. He found few allies. Protecting his turf, Undersecretary of Labor Silberman defended the hometown plans.[113] Moderate-to-liberal White House staffers Ehrlichman, Garment, and John R. Price favored modifying the program but advanced few alternatives.[114] Since Shultz had departed the Labor Department to become Nixon's budget director in 1970, he did not partake in the debate. And Charles W. Colson, White House liaison to unions and organized groups, opposed any policy changes that might alienate blue-collar voters in the upcoming presidential contest. "I don't want to argue the merits," he declared. "I am sure the Department and Mr. Fletcher are absolutely right. I am equally convinced that this is political dynamite."[115]

Colson's opposition to strengthening contract compliance proved significant. By 1971 the New England native had become, along with Ehrlichman and Haldeman, one of the president's three most trusted advisers on domestic affairs. Unlike Ehrlichman, who handled policy, and Haldeman, who looked after scheduling and public relations, Colson specialized in political strategy—and skulduggery. This self-proclaimed "anti-liberal Nixon fanatic" reinforced Nixon's hatred of the press, bureaucrats, and antiwar protesters.[116] Ehrlichman also complained of Colson's influence as a broker "bringing pressure to bear on the President (and his staff) in behalf of special groups."[117] Yet Nixon remained "greatly impressed" with Colson's work.[118] Colson strove to expand his domain and sway domestic policy. Late in 1970 he warned White House aides that Meany opposed the administration's proposal for welfare reform, arguing that "the Family Assistance Plan is counterproductive politically to our efforts with the average middle-class working man and the labor movement."[119]

But Colson, a bigot and a crass opportunist, was unqualified to offer advice on delicate race-related issues. After describing a series of projects to court Polish Americans, he quipped, "We really should get some fat Japs as well," a tasteless reminder of a remark by Vice President Spiro Agnew.[120] Such insensitivity alienated White House liberals. "Garment," Colson wrote, "is convinced I am anti-semitic and anti-arts (both true)."[121] He even offended conservatives by treating them as just another voting bloc. Patrick J. Buchanan rebuked him for making comments such as, "See what Sops are available to conservatives."[122] Colson's right-wing position on civil rights stemmed from electoral considerations, the need to woo blue-collar voters, not laissez-faire principles.

If Colson failed to persuade the president to abandon "FAP," he succeeded in weakening the Philadelphia Plan. In 1971 Colson outflanked his moderate colleagues and forged a consensus to rid the Labor Department of Fletcher. He began by circulating Fletcher's most inflammatory statements, including one in which Fletcher had termed the construction trades "racist."[123] Colson warned Haldeman that such words had alienated blue-collar workers: "We must deal with this."[124] He next approached Kenneth Cole, Ehrlichman's deputy, and personnel chief Frederic V. Malek about finding a new position for Fletcher. "I would be overjoyed to enlist you as a supporter in this cause," Colson wrote Cole. "Believe me there is much good we can do."[125] He reminded Malek to keep his memoranda on Fletcher "in the utmost confidence. I consider them of enormous sensitivity obviously."[126] Colson then warned Ehrlichman that "the situation involving Arthur Fletcher and minority hiring plans in major cities is deteriorating very, very rapidly."[127] His effort climaxed with a meeting between the president and New York Building Trades president Peter J. Brennan, a steadfast critic of affirmative action, when Nixon agreed to transfer Fletcher.[128] By late 1971 Fletcher had left the Labor Department for the United Nations, taking with him any remaining chance for revitalizing contract compliance.[129]

Colson's influence reflected Nixon's shifting domestic agenda. Whereas in 1969 the White House had focused on expanding employment opportunity for minorities and holding down housing costs, by 1971 the president was seeking union support for his Vietnam and anti-inflation policies and for his own reelection.[130] Assuming the role of conservative populist, Nixon ordered Colson to court labor leaders "in the construction trade, the Teamsters, etc., who are our friends." The president saw no reward in coddling "congenial left wingers" in the United Auto Workers and Garment Workers unions, whom he deemed "not only hopeless Democrats, but also hopeless pacifists." Instead, Nixon wooed George Meany–"an all out Democrat, but a great patriot"–and other "leaders in the labor movement who are basically conservative."[131] In July 1971 the president told Haldeman that there were many ways to appeal to workers: "Jobs is the main one, but the racial issue and a lot of others can also be used."[132] Shortly thereafter Nixon remarked that he "was not int[erested] in pushing Phil. Plan."[133]

During 1972 and 1973 Nixon and the Labor Department displayed less and less interest in affirmative action. Bidding for union votes during his reelection campaign, the president lambasted "quotas" as "anti-ability."[134] Comfortably reelected, he appointed conservatives to ranking government positions, called for cutbacks in expenditures, and preached the gospel of Franklin Delano Roosevelt: "Reward the friends, punish the enemies, and build something that is strong."[135] In a sop to hard hats, Nixon named Peter Brennan labor secretary.[136] Unsympathetic to affirmative action, Brennan forbade state and local officials from imposing additional fair employment requirements on federally assisted construction.[137] He proposed replacing Philadelphia's imposed plan with a hometown solution. When John Buggs of the Commission on Civil Rights replied that hometown plans have "led to few, if any, noticeable results," Brennan defended them as exercises in "voluntarism."[138]

If the president's commitment to affirmative action wavered, it did not vanish. Nixon never disavowed the Philadelphia Plan, and he declined to make affirmative action a major issue in the 1972 campaign. When pressed, he simply restated his support for numerical goals and distinguished them from the dreaded quotas.[139] To make his position "perfectly clear," Nixon had Garment draft a statement separating goals from quotas.[140]

In fact, Nixon sanctioned hiring goals for positions in his second administration. The president informed Haldeman that "two out of five" political appointments should go to minority ethnic groups, especially Mexicans, Poles, and eastern Europeans, whom he thought important to his electoral base. Nixon deemed African Americans a lower priority, although, he warned, "certainly we don't want to be in a position where we are not putting qualified Negroes into jobs."[141] By approving additional hiring goals, Nixon showed a willingness to retain affirmative action remedies and extend them to include new groups. In succeeding decades, Hispanics, American Indians, and Asian Americans would also benefit from this policy.

In the long run, the Philadelphia and hometown plans set important precedents. They sanctioned numerical goals to measure employment of disadvantaged groups. And, by defending the Philadelphia Plan in 1969, Nixon declared his support for such methods. The federal courts followed suit. In *Griggs v. Duke Power Co.* (1971), the Supreme Court skirted the legislative ban on quotas and upheld the constitutionality of results-oriented targets.[142] Armed with intermittent support from the White House, the high court's blessing, and the Labor Department's examples, officials in other branches of the federal government extended race- and gender-based hiring targets to white-collar work.

Affirmative Action and the Professional Class

In extending affirmative action to the federal civil service, colleges, and businesses, Nixon administration officials used different strategies and achieved varying results. Regarding the civil service, where minimalist methods prevailed, minority hiring proved limited. But statist remedies forced open the doors of universities and giant corporations. The president's moderate compass led him to approve both enforcement models.

Although the federal government did not fall under the equal employment requirements of the Civil Rights Act of 1964, by 1969 there was hope for progress in federal minority hiring. In January LBJ's Justice Department issued a scathing critique of the government's fair employment practices.[143] Robert J. Brown, Nixon's liaison to minority groups, pressed Robert E. Hampton, chair of the United States Civil Service Commission, and Ehrlichman's staff to enhance fair employment policy.[144] Nixon at that point ordered the Civil Service Commission to review the government's hiring practices.[145]

The Civil Service Commission resisted substantive change. In a throwback to the 1950s, Hampton favored persuasion to encourage minority hiring and defended the existing merit system.[146] Guarding the commission's authority, Hampton drafted Executive Order 11478 urging federal offices to take "positive action" to eliminate bias.[147] Since the order failed to spell out numerical goals for departments to follow in hiring disadvantaged groups, Brown dismissed it as "more of the same."[148] Perhaps viewing Hampton's minimalist approach as a "slow and reasonable" solution, however, Nixon signed the executive order.[149]

Government officials implemented Nixon's executive order haphazardly. Hampton promised agencies a "credible program" of affirmative action that "will not dwell on numbers."[150] To preempt charges of "reverse discrimination," he announced in 1970 that the commission would ease pressure for minority hiring.[151] Nixon reluctantly endorsed this decision, noting that "it puts us in a bad light."[152] A year later, the chameleonlike Hampton permitted agencies to adopt realistic employment "goals" that did not conflict with merit-based recruitment.[153]

With these blurry guidelines, federal offices developed their own fair employment policies. Some agencies simply upgraded job training programs or placed minorities and women in token positions.[154] Others experimented with numerical targets or bypassed the merit system in favor of results-driven proportional representation.[155] A government committee reported in 1975 that the Civil Service Commission "is not consistent internally with respect to what it expects agencies to do–and what it permits them to do–to meet equal employment opportunity objectives."[156]

Under such a muddled policy, minority groups and women gained few high-paying federal jobs. The Civil Service Commission routinely released figures suggesting that these groups were entering the federal service at a record pace in grades nine through twelve.[157] Yet they had little success securing positions in grades thirteen to eighteen; in 1975 minorities constituted only 5 percent, and women just 4.5 percent, of federal employees at the highest levels. Moreover, during Nixon's presidency, the proportion of all federal employees who were minorities grew negligibly from 19.3 to 20.4 percent.[158].

Officials in the Department of Health, Education, and Welfare, in contrast, applied specific admissions and hiring ratios to higher education. President Johnson's Executive Order 11246 required colleges and universities receiving federal aid to draft affirmative action plans.[159] During Nixon's term, J. Stanley Pottinger, Leon E. Panetta's successor as director of HEW's Office of Civil Rights, threatened to withhold funds unless university officials developed programs to recruit minorities and women.[160] Unlike Hampton, Pottinger approved of numerical goals to measure the admission and hiring of these groups. He solicited advice from civil rights leaders and from other bureaucrats and, like the president, packaged his policy as one of flexible goals to "evaluate good faith efforts" instead of "rigid" quotas.[161]

In implementing his statist policy, Pottinger proved either unable or unwilling to separate numerical goals from quotas. One member of the

Commission on Civil Rights wondered if HEW had not adopted stiffer rules for universities than for contractors.[162] In 1971 Sidney Hook, a well-known philosophy professor at New York University, scolded Pottinger for introducing an illegal "quota system."[163] White House staffer Bradley Patterson quickly defended Pottinger, pointing out that "his task is to deal with hundreds, perhaps thousands, of institutions of higher learning–and he can't *do* that job (with finite numbers of people) unless he uses gross measurements."[164] Yet Pottinger once remarked that he had found *no* evidence of quotas in faculty hiring.[165] Fairly or not, it seemed that Pottinger never saw a goal he didn't like.

Pottinger's actions ignited a firestorm. Recalling how private universities had used ratios to exclude Jews, American Jewish groups rejected goals as "quotas."[166] African American leaders, in turn, considered such criticism an assault on civil rights. Representative Louis Stokes, Democrat of Ohio, called Hyman Bookbinder, Washington representative of the American Jewish Committee, a "racist."[167] To promote understanding, the American Jewish Committee in 1972 asked presidential candidates Nixon and George S. McGovern to explain their positions. Both men endorsed hiring goals in one breath and condemned quotas in another.[168] A Harvard University official justly lamented that neither candidate had risen "to a statesmanlike stature" by urging "an end to the domestic quibble" over affirmative action.[169]

Opposed to rigid quotas, Nixon tried to undo Pottinger's handiwork. The president in 1973 demanded an end to education "quotas,"[170] and Caspar W. Weinberger, the new secretary of HEW, ordered a review of his department's regulations.[171] But the Watergate scandal swept this issue from the president's agenda. The Equal Employment Opportunity Act of 1972, signed by Nixon with little fanfare, permitted individuals to sue universities suspected of bias.[172] Accordingly, Labor Department officials and Nixon's hand-picked successor, Gerald R. Ford, did not ease enforcement. Ford's labor secretary, John T. Dunlop, actually nudged HEW bureaucrats to accelerate their policing of university affirmative action programs.[173] Aided by an odd mixture of bureaucratic zeal and inertia, numerical goals flourished as minorities and women entered college in record numbers.[174]

With the aid of the Equal Employment Opportunity Commission (EEOC), disadvantaged groups had begun to secure jobs in corporations as well. Nixon, for his part, sought an activist but restrained EEOC. To stop overzealous enforcement, the president in 1969 changed personnel at the commission. When EEOC chair Clifford L. Alexander, a Democrat, convened hearings on employment bias, Nixon exercised his presidential prerogative and chose to designate a Republican chair for the commission.[175] After he learned that Senate Minority Leader Dirksen had charged Alexander with harassing business and vowed to get him fired, the president's resolve stiffened, and he asked, "Why not get rid of this guy?"[176] A White House spokesman then announced Alexander's dismissal.[177] While critics protested that Nixon had caved in to Dirksen, the president had reached his decision much earlier.[178]

Alexander's ouster did not undermine the government's prosecution of bias; Nixon's choice to head the EEOC, William H. Brown III, an African American lawyer from Philadelphia, became a champion of affirmative action. Soft-spoken and clever, Brown alternately appealed to Nixon's best intentions, forged alliances to strengthen the commission, trimmed his sails to suit the presidential will, and pressed his own agenda. While endorsing Nixon's job-oriented policies, the EEOC chair flatly rejected Attorney General Mitchell's adage "Watch what we do, not what we say." He also adjudged Nixon's job training and technical education policies to be "of little value if the private sector is allowed to continued to treat equal opportunity as a matter of corporate largesse."[179]

Brown first secured more funds for EEOC. Backed by Garment, the commission chief persuaded the president to endorse a budget of nearly $16 million for 1970.[180] Nixon then wrote Senate Majority Leader Mike Mansfield, Democrat of Montana, and Dirksen's successor, Minority Leader Scott, to gain their support. The president ordered the Bureau of the Budget to request $19 million for EEOC in 1971.[181] Nixon's promotion of Labor Secretary Shultz, co-author of the revised Philadelphia Plan, to budget director in 1970 reinforced the White House's commitment.[182] By 1972, EEOC's budget had ballooned to $29.5 million, up from $13.2 million in 1968. Higher outlays financed a quadrupling of the commission's staff, to over 1,600 people.[183] These increases did not come easily. In 1970 Senator Milton T. Young, Jr., Republican of North Dakota, reported "considerable opposition" within the Appropriations Committee to enlarging EEOC's budget.[184] Nixon's motives were not entirely high-minded, since he saw hiking the budget as a way to improve his "image" with minorities and liberals.[185] Still, the president had to know that more resources for EEOC meant greater enforcement.

In seeking enforcement powers for EEOC, Brown followed Nixon's wishes. Under Title VII of the Civil Rights Act of 1964, EEOC resolved complaints of discrimination through investigation and mediation.[186] But, backed by civil rights groups, liberal members of Congress moved to add teeth to the commission. In 1969 senators Harrison Williams, Democrat of New Jersey, and Jacob R. Javits, Republican of New York, sponsored a bill granting EEOC power to issue cease and desist orders.[187] Worried about a meddlesome bureaucracy tormenting businesses, Minority Leader Dirksen opposed the bill.[188] In keeping with his court enforcement remedies for school and housing segregation, Nixon favored a scaled-down plan, endorsed by Dirksen, authorizing EEOC to sue employers suspected of bias.[189] Seeking the strongest machinery, Brown at first favored cease and desist. After the president's views became apparent, he proclaimed court enforcement the most effective weapon against discrimination.[190]

The administration's proposal sparked a three-year debate. Liberals, African American leaders, women's groups, and labor unions contended that cease and desist powers would expedite resolution while court enforcement, involving countless lawsuits, would prove agonizingly slow.[191] Businessmen as well as moderate and conservative Republicans responded that cease and desist would transform EEOC into a quasi-judicial body with powers of prosecutor, judge, and jury. Reluctant to bestow such sweeping authority on one agency, these groups favored the traditional (and, they thought, tamer) remedy of court adjudication.[192]

Unfortunately, this debate obscured the effectiveness of court enforcement. Behind the alarmist rhetoric of civil rights advocates and the heel-dragging of conservatives, few people grasped that cease and desist would transform EEOC into a court and require it to reach decisions through "impartial analysis."[193] The capacity to sue, as White House aide Stephen Hess noted, enabled EEOC to perform as a prosecutor and "advocate" the cases of disadvantaged groups.[194] Many observers forgot that some of the civil rights movement's greatest gains had come via litigation.[195] Unable to persuade Nixon to back cease and desist, Brown began to see the virtues of litigation.[196] After the president signed the Equal Employment Act of 1972, embodying the court-enforcement approach, the EEOC chair used his new authority to open private industry to minorities and women.[197]

Brown compelled corporations to adopt state-inspired hiring goals. His purpose was to tackle patterns of discrimination in large companies, not individual complaints.[198] In his most notable achievement, Brown forced the American Telephone and Telegraph Company to pay $15 million to past victims of bias and to develop numerical goals for hiring women and minorities.[199] He predicted "wider fallout" from the AT&T settlement "as companies start to move on their own initiative to bring themselves into compliance with the law."[200] During 1972 and 1973, EEOC filed 141 lawsuits against some of the nation's biggest companies.[201] Private industry got the message; by mid-decade terms such as "goals" and "timetables" had entered the corporate lexicon. A regimen of increased funds, court enforcement, and Brown's leadership had transformed EEOC from emaciated onlooker to muscular enforcer of civil rights.

Civil rights leaders embraced Brown's work. In 1973 Clarence Mitchell urged Brown's reappointment as chair.[202] Impressed with EEOC's successes, Americans for Democratic Action chair Joseph L. Rauh, Jr., recanted his earlier support of cease and desist.[203] And Brown enhanced his credibility with civil rights groups by naming liberal Democrats to his staff.[204] Black leaders often credited affirmative action gains to Brown rather than Nixon.[205]

In fact, Nixon tacitly endorsed Brown's statist enforcement. The president considered Brown "a good man."[206] The EEOC chief, after all, promised to follow a presidential order to avoid the appearance of harassing businesses.[207] Brown appreciated Nixon's "personal support" and "stated conviction that I have the kind of sensitivity and dedication he wants leading equal employment opportunity."[208] Timing aided the commission's efforts; several EEOC lawsuits occurred after the election of 1972, when dodging impeachment, not pacifying business, dominated the president's attention.[209] Stringent enforcement conformed with Nixon's focus on jobs. "The impression I got," declared Clarence

Mitchell after a meeting with White House officials, "was that they wanted the Equal Employment Opportunity Commission to succeed."[210] If Nixon did not sign off on Brown's settlements, he surely knew of the well-publicized ones, such as AT&T, and did not impede them.

Brown's strong leadership stirred controversy. Other commissioners scolded him for secrecy and arbitrary decisions, and for allowing EEOC's backlog to swell to over sixty thousand complaints.[211] Hampton, the administration's chief foe of hiring goals, accused the EEOC chair of poor management.[212] A spirited defense by Garment could not salvage another term for Brown.[213] With the president preoccupied with Watergate, White House chief of staff Alexander M. Haig, Jr., and personnel chief Jerry Jones probed Brown's managerial failings and urged his replacement. Yet neither the AT&T settlement nor EEOC's enforcement strategy figured in their deliberations. Jones was more upset with Brown's appointment of Democratic staffers and "an organizer for Cesar Chavez."[214] Brown's removal did not mean less enforcement. Nixon named John H. Powell, Jr., who commanded the trust of civil rights advocates, as EEOC's new chair.[215]

Statist affirmative action provided increased employment opportunities. The percentage of female college graduates in the general population rose from 11 in 1970, to 17 in 1980, to 24 in 1990.[216] Over the same period, the proportion of the African American population that had graduated from college climbed from 8 to 11 to 15 percent. From 1972 to 1979, the proportion of office managers who were female jumped from 42 to 63 percent, while the proportion of African Americans so employed rose from 1 to 2 percent. But blacks and women gained few high-ranking positions, and under the corporatist hometown plans, neither group entered the building trades in great numbers.[217] In 1972 women constituted 0.6 percent and blacks 9 percent of skilled construction workers. Seven years later, they constituted, respectively, 1.6 and 9.7 percent of such workers.[218]

Why did Nixon condone tough affirmative action for Republican constituencies such as corporations but not for labor unions? No doubt he believed that white professionals and business executives would support him come what might; labor needed some bait. After agreeing to business's plan for court empowerment, the president may have deemed it time for strong gestures on behalf of civil rights. Nixon's populist instincts played some role as well. He extolled the "ordinary working guy" who "never went to college" for his patriotism, character, and "guts." He showed less respect for the university-trained "new managerial business class," who lacked "character or guts."[219] The president once dismissed the chief executive officers of major corporations as "softheaded" and "putty in the hands of dese and dose labor guys."[220] As a self-made man, Nixon understood the importance of enhancing opportunity. As a politician, he often catered to the prejudices of potential constituents. The concerns of silver spoon–fed, diehard Republican corporate officials were not priorities, so the corporations received statist affirmative action.

Goals, Quotas, and the Administrative State

Since Nixon was often disengaged from the making of fair employment policy, it is difficult to discern his views on each affirmative action program. This much is certain: the president believed in economic opportunity in the abstract and desired a balanced, politically safe policy. His timely support helped to institutionalize affirmative action over the next two decades.

Sometimes actively, sometimes passively, the multifarious Nixon exploited statist, corporatist, and minimalist methods. When the bold, principled president wanted to confound critics or to advance civil rights, he embraced statist policies such as the Philadelphia Plan. When Nixon the coalition builder sought to woo labor leaders without alienating moderate Republicans, the corporatist hometown plans suited him. When he saw the need for restraint, as in the case of the civil service, the president endorsed minimalism. When preoccupied with other matters, he left decisions to subordinates such as William Brown, who pushed their own agenda. A policy existed for each side of Nixon's persona. Rather than search for an imaginary middle ground, he achieved balance by endorsing both liberal and conservative programs.

If we are to understand the origins of affirmative action, the abstruse, self-serving distinction between goals and quotas is less than useful. Since quotas were illegal, policy makers espousing numerical goals had to expend considerable energy differentiating them from quotas. The more officials tried to separate the two concepts, the more their distinctions seemed arbitrary, even artificial. In applying affirmative action to universities, Stanley Pottinger believed that his policy employed flexible goals. Both Jewish groups and Nixon, of course, disagreed.

Discriminating between goals and quotas only served the interest of politicians who wished to expand opportunities for minorities and women without angering white males. The affirmative action measures Nixon adopted were goals; those he rejected were quotas. Concern with what constituted legitimate or illegitimate affirmative action missed an essential point. As the economy weakened in the mid- and late 1970s, white males needed assurance that affirmative action gains for disadvantaged groups would not come at their expense. In failing to make this case, political leaders such as Nixon, George McGovern, and especially Jimmy Carter, who served during a time of recession, left all affirmative action open to criticism.

Nixon's on-again, off-again support of affirmative action nonetheless wrought important policy changes. The administration sanctioned new methods to fight bias. Disadvantaged groups could now seek redress from the federal bureaucracy as well as through demonstrations, legislation, voting, and litigation. "The civil rights movement has not . . . slowed down," observed liberal senator John Sherman Cooper, Republican of Kentucky, in 1971. "It is moving in a different manner in the same direction. Many reforms can be accomplished in a quiet way through the mechanisms provided by our Constitution."[221] By enhancing the bureaucracy, Nixon cemented the gains of the civil rights revolution.[222]

The president's policies helped move the civil rights debate away from legal equality and toward economic opportunity. Nixon's reiteration that "we are job-oriented" cannot be dismissed as a publicity ploy, for it coincided with several administration programs and with the agenda of civil rights advocates. In 1967 Senators Javits and Philip Hart, Democrat of Michigan, urged Congress to "direct its efforts to a new phase of the civil rights struggle—economic opportunity and the problems of our urban areas."[223] Six years later the Reverend Jesse Jackson considered holding demonstrations "at the Department of the Treasury to emphasize the black economic struggle."[224] Unlike Nixon, liberals and civil rights groups viewed affirmative action as a supplement to other civil rights policies, such as busing and housing integration.

Finally, the president's distinction between goals and quotas *temporarily* assuaged the sting of race- and gender-based targets. During the administration of Jimmy Carter, federal officials extended numerical hiring targets, with the Democrat Carter, like Nixon, backing "flexible affirmative action programs using goals" over "inflexible quotas."[225] In 1981, 68 percent of Americans favored "affirmative action programs" so long as such programs did not impose "rigid quotas."[226] Although President Ronald Reagan tried to chip away at affirmative action, he still favored "voluntary" hiring goals for firms and unions.[227]

Indicative of his tenuous support for affirmative action, Nixon never ranked this policy among his greatest achievements. During an interview in 1977, the former president defended his civil rights record while claiming that "nobody is interested in this anymore."[228] His memoir, running over one thousand pages, devotes two pages to affirmative action.[229] Yet when the GOP's right wing attacked this policy as "preferential treatment," he defended it. In 1990 Nixon warned President George Bush against attacking racial quotas, noting that since the 1950s the civil rights label on the Republican Party "was indelible." Then he counseled, "There is no reward for going after the anti-quota vote."[230]

In the 1990s, the right-wing assault on affirmative action prompted a few liberals to praise Nixon's record. Such nostalgia is justified. By defending numerical goals in 1969, the president allowed the practice of affirmative action to develop. His motives were not always impeccable. At times he wavered. But even if Nixon often shunned his offspring, he still must be acknowledged as the sire of affirmative action.

5

Black Power, Nixon Style: Minority Businesses and Black Colleges

While President Richard M. Nixon tentatively embraced affirmative action, he championed "black capitalism" with gusto. "What we have to do," declared candidate Nixon in 1968, "is to provide an opportunity for every American, for black Americans, for Mexican-Americans, and others who haven't had an equal chance, not just to be a worker . . . but to be a manager and an owner."[1] President Nixon established the Office of Minority Business Enterprise (OMBE), expanded federal procurement from firms owned by African Americans and Hispanic Americans, and laid the basis for contract set-asides from minority-owned firms. He also funneled aid to the nation's predominantly black colleges, the largest minority-run enterprises in the United States.

In taking these actions, Nixon co-opted a fashionable concept: Black Power. During the 1960s, many African Americans rejected the civil rights movement's traditional stress on nonviolence, interracial coalitions, and government measures to alleviate poverty and achieve integration. Leaders such as Malcolm X, Stokely Carmichael, and Floyd

McKissick trumpeted separatism and endorsed the need for all-black institutions and economic independence.[2] "The American black man," wrote Malcolm X, "should be focusing his every effort toward building his *own* businesses, and decent homes for himself."[3]

Nixon and Malcolm X, however similar their ends, were not kindred spirits. Nevertheless, with many whites wary of racial integration and anti-poverty programs, penny-wise politicians came to support some black separatist ideas. In 1968 Nixon advocated "black ownership, . . . black pride, black jobs, black opportunity and yes, black power in the best, the constructive sense of that often misapplied term."[4] Black Power was an oppositional but elastic concept which the Republican candidate stretched into a mainstream proposal for black capitalism.

The president and his aides sought to replace the melting pot concept, whereby distinct ethnic and racial cultures disappear, with one blending economic opportunity and separatism. Nixon's statements on school desegregation and fair housing defined an "open, pluralistic society" as one in which the individual enjoys "open choices" and "the mobility to take advantage of those choices," but he played down the importance of integration: "We cannot be free, and at the same time be required to fit our lives into prescribed places on a racial grid—whether segregated or integrated."[5] Nixon proclaimed this rhetoric "excellent" and urged his aides to quote it.[6] Respect for minority institutions also underpinned Nixon's policy of supporting Native American tribal self-government. So the administration infused badly needed cash into viable minority institutions, black colleges and businesses, that would, in the president's view, contribute to the movement of minorities into the middle class—and maybe the Republican Party as well.

Nixon, like President Lyndon B. Johnson, proposed a program to raise minority incomes, hoping to ease the unrest that had overwhelmed cities during the 1960s. His plan advanced Republican ideals of self-reliance and private enterprise, and it appeared to put Nixon ahead of liberals in responding to trends within the black community. By inviting blacks to acquire a stake in the free market economy, it seemed inclusive without foisting integration upon white schools and neighborhoods. In fact, the president publicized his minority business policies to quell criticism that he was indifferent to civil rights.

The minority enterprise policy unfolded in three major stages. Nixon first espoused black capitalism during the election of 1968. Throughout 1969, or phase two, minority enterprise faltered as the policy, run by the Commerce Department, became mired in organizational difficulties. Phase three, spanning the years 1970–71, saw the program's maturation as government officials, guided by White House staffers, expanded procurement from minority-owned firms, deposited federal funds in minority banks, and secured OMBE's first budget. At the same time, another set of advisers worked on a related policy, boosting aid to black colleges. Although not complete, by late 1972 the contours of a useful but limited new civil rights effort had emerged.

The Birth of Black Capitalism

Nixon's support for minority entrepreneurship emerged during the presidential campaign of 1968. In response to the urban race riots, he voiced a message that combined repression with reform. Appealing to whites uneasy over crime, Nixon rejected violence as a protest tactic and pledged to uphold law and order. To heal racial tensions and extend opportunity to ghetto residents, he espoused aid to minority enterprises.

Viewing urban violence through the lens of financially comfortable suburbanites, Nixon and his all-white staff insisted on maintaining law and order above all else. According to one Nixon aide, "the Black Power militants" were wrong since "there are no extenuating circumstances for violence."[7] Campaign workers sometimes attributed crime to minorities. On a news dispatch detailing the murder of a policeman by one youth, a Nixon adviser jotted, "RN–note–This was probably a Negro youngster."[8] Nixon himself publicly criticized the report of the National Advisory Commission on Civil Disorders for its "undue stress" on white racism as a cause of urban unrest.[9]

To deal with civil disorders, Nixon's more conservative advisers endorsed increased use of police squadrons, derided Great Society programs to improve conditions in slums, and offered individual initiative as the solution to poverty. Nixon's conservative speechwriter Patrick J. Buchanan favored confronting rioters with "maximum essential force at the earliest possible moment."[10] In a memorandum to Nixon, the economist Alan Greenspan rejected the liberal notion that federal anti-poverty projects would raise minority incomes and lower the crime rate. He further attacked left-wing politicians for stressing that "capitalism *is* exploitation and therefore Negroes, being non-owners of property, are being exploited." To resolve the problem, Greenspan proposed shifting federal policy from "reparations for past exploitation" to measures that "help Negroes help themselves."[11] But he failed to propose any specific policies to achieve that aim.

Although they responded more sympathetically to African American concerns, Nixon's more moderate aides reached similar conclusions. "There's a real danger," wrote the speechwriter Raymond K. Price in 1967, "in letting the rash of riots harden attitudes into a simple formula of 'it's us against them.'" The Long Island native attacked liberal Democrats "who, faced with a riot, beat their breasts in a chorus of collective mea culpas" and white conservatives "who don't recognize the cultural gulf between the ghetto and suburbia." Yet Price did not fully grasp that "gulf" himself. He proposed solving the urban problem by replacing "the Negro habit of dependence" with "one of independence" and "personal responsibility."[12] In so arguing, Price, like Greenspan, neglected white racism and blamed its black victims.

As the presidential primaries approached, Nixon's liberal and conservative aides recommended appeals to disadvantaged groups. Price wanted Nixon to advocate greater investment of "our resources in an enterprise that raises the level of the whole society."[13] Perhaps remembering Nixon's earlier support of civil rights, Buchanan wrote: "We ought to be thinking of material that will make points with the Negro. These people are not locked into LBJ; they are not particularly hostile to RN . . . and maybe some of them can be sold on RN."[14] If Price and Buchanan represented opposite ends of the political spectrum, both men, like their boss, balanced principle with expediency.

Nixon wove together the strands of his advisers' thinking. Realizing that mounting crime had made voters "angry," the Republican candidate called for expanded police forces and lambasted Supreme Court rulings that limited the ability of law enforcement officers to grill suspects and secure confessions.[15] "The most fundamental civil right," Nixon told Bostonians in February 1968, "is the right to be safe from violence." While acknowledging that "force is needed," he proclaimed that "force alone is not enough." To forestall "violent revolution," the Republican candidate endorsed peaceful means to achieve "the progress revolutionaries talk about but seldom deliver upon."[16] By assuming the role of reformer, Nixon sought to blunt the appeal of fist-clenched black separatists.

A few months later Nixon set out specific remedies for the urban crisis. In a pair of radio broadcasts titled "Bridges to Human Dignity," the candidate offered poor blacks not "dependency" but "a piece of the action."[17] He proposed tax incentives to corporations investing in depressed neighborhoods, expansion of tutorial assistance and job training, and government loans to fledgling minority entrepreneurs and homeowners. "Black extremists are guaranteed headlines when they shout 'burn' or 'get a gun,'" he noted. "But much of the black militant talk these days is actually in terms far closer to the doctrines of free enterprise than to those of the welfarist 30's."[18] On that last point, Nixon conveniently failed to mention his own previous support of New Deal–like programs.

The idea of fostering minority enterprise had merit. In 1969 blacks and Hispanics, accounting for 17 percent of the population, owned 4 percent of the nation's businesses and held just 1 percent of its total business assets.[19] Minority enterprises tended to be small-scale and service-oriented. No minority-owned company made *Fortune* magazine's list of the one thousand largest American businesses, and 58 percent of black businesses were in the retail and service sectors.[20] The low level of minority entrepreneurship stemmed from many factors, including shortage of capital, lack of technical and managerial skill, and competition from larger, better-financed white firms. Failure rates for minority-owned companies remained high, and African Americans held business in low esteem. "More often than not," Abraham S. Venable, a Commerce Department official and an African American, declared in 1967, "many Negro businessmen are a symbol of frustration and hopelessness rather than an example of achievement, success, and leadership."[21] Minority entrepreneurs needed encouragement and dollars.

Since LBJ had already begun to help minority entrepreneurs, Nixon's proposal for black capitalism was less original than he let on. Congress in 1967 passed anti-poverty amendments that boosted the Small Business Administration (SBA) budget to $2.65 billion and required the agency to funnel half its loans to blacks and whites in ghetto areas.[22] During the latter half of 1968, SBA chief Howard J. Samuels packaged the government's minority enterprise programs as "Project OWN."[23] He recommended increasing SBA loans to fledgling minority entrepreneurs and expanding federal procurement from firms owned by blacks, Puerto Ricans, Mexican Americans, and American Indians. Samuels also wanted bankers to lend money to minority entrepreneurs and industrialists to offer technical guidance.[24] During the final months of 1968, 5.7 percent of SBA money went to minorities, a small but respectable percentage considering that many blacks were poorly educated and Hispanics had drawn little attention from the federal government.[25] Both Johnson and Nixon used affirmative action and minority enterprise as crisis management tools, that is, as policies to promote minority economic development and thus allay urban unrest.[26]

Yet minority entrepreneurship had not been a Democratic priority, and Project OWN, begun in 1968, smacked of election year politics. In February 1968, after Vice President Hubert H. Humphrey had expressed interest in the issue, Undersecretary of Labor James J. Reynolds depicted the administration's efforts as flagging and urged "large, coordinated steps on all fronts."[27] LBJ thereupon formed an interagency task force to study ways of aiding minority entrepreneurs. Samuels was the head cheerleader, telling Johnson that "the clearest message coming from the poor" was their desire for "a piece of the action."[28] While Humphrey's staff also used that sanguine phrase, officials at the Bureau of the Budget stressed the risks of start-up businesses and called programs to support minority entrepreneurs "more easily defended on grounds of 'political economy' than of 'economics.'"[29] Even LBJ's task force warned against both "overstating" the benefits of such a policy and allowing the president to publicize it.[30] Such advice might have appealed to a person not seeking office.

Nixon moved to outdo Johnson. Aiding small entrepreneurs advanced opportunity, social mobility, and economic independence, ideas associated with moderate Republicans. President Eisenhower had established the Small Business Administration in 1953, and Nixon himself defined the role of government as "to do for people what they cannot do for themselves: to open up new opportunities, to mobilize private energies to meet public needs . . . to create a climate that enables every person to fulfill himself."[31] A new program to assist minority entrepreneurs would further this aim.

A relentless scrapper, Nixon respected aspiring entrepreneurs who took chances more than stereotypical self-satisfied corporate executives who preferred management to risk. Such attitudes began in his youth, when Nixon's father, a nickel-and-dime grocer, purchased gasoline from the upstart Richfield Oil Company instead of the Standard Oil Corporation.[32] "We have to make these [small] businesses work," Nixon told his Council for Urban Affairs in 1969.[33] "I know we can't go back to mom-and-pop grocery stores," the president later admitted to his cabinet, "but does everything have to be sold in a super-market?"[34] When discussing big business, Nixon could sound nasty. After reading that insurance companies might avoid compensating victims of an airplane crash, he ordered an aide to "get on this–Don't let these bastards get out of paying this claim."[35] But Nixon was no trustbuster. Like Herbert Hoover, he endorsed "sensible forms of industrial togetherness," and directed Attorney General John N. Mitchell to "keep a close watch" on the antitrust division with its "professional *anti-business* jerks."[36]

In many ways the archetypal representative of bourgeois values such as sobriety, thrift, and self-reliance, Nixon felt compelled to impart these values to minority groups. In the words of Sallyanne Payton, an African American member of Nixon's White House staff, the president would close the economic gap between the races by "getting more Black people to behave like whites," that is, "get into business, go to school, become homeowners."[37] What was at stake for Nixon was social stability: "People who own their own homes don't burn down their neighborhoods."[38] Expanding the black middle class, he wrote in 1967, would address "the causes of the Negro problem rather than its symptoms."[39]

Nixon's emphasis on black capitalism pleased conservatives and left liberals scratching their heads. Such right-leaning periodicals as *Time* and the *Wall Street Journal* termed the Republican candidate's proposals "thoughtful" and "promising."[40] In New York, James L. Buckley, the Conservative Party's candidate for the United States Senate, parroted Nixon by praising the "spirit" of "militant black leaders who have been preaching black initiative, black capitalism, and yes, black power." Buckley, who later won a Senate seat with President Nixon's support, embraced Black Power advocates as comrades in arms in the conservatives' crusade against "that huge monster on the banks of the Potomac."[41] Of course, neither Buckley nor Nixon approved of the angry, even violent, rhetoric of some Black Power leaders.

African American reaction to Nixon's initiative proved mixed. Floyd McKissick, the black separatist president of the Congress of Racial Equality, echoed the Republican candidate: "Handouts are demeaning. They do violence to a man, strip him of dignity, and breed in him a hatred of the system."[42] Black capitalism, however, drew little praise from integrationist civil rights leaders or from the African American press. They found Nixon's "law and order" rhetoric racially divisive and the candidate himself untrustworthy. The Reverend Ralph David Abernathy, who succeeded Martin Luther King, Jr., as head of the Southern Christian Leadership Conference, registered his disapproval. Abernathy backed liberal governor Nelson A. Rockefeller of New York for the Republican nomination, then endorsed the Democratic nominee, Hubert Humphrey, in the general election. The Leadership Conference on Civil Rights hardly took notice of Nixon's black capitalism proposal.[43] The *Pittsburgh Courier* later accused Nixon of seeking to divide African Americans and undermine "black power as a political force."[44] More likely, the Republican's black capitalism proposal merely highlighted existing differences among African Americans.

Liberal politicians gradually endorsed Nixon's goals. At first, Rockefeller puzzled over how to respond to his rival's black capitalism proposal. After the governor had backed public and private spending to rebuild slum areas, Jeffrey Geilich, a liberal aide, advised him to attack black capitalism as "segregationist."[45] But Graham T. Molitor, Rockefeller's pollster, dubbed black capitalism a "stroke of political genius," a clever attempt to steal a militant slogan. "The only criticism we can suggest," Molitor argued, "is a carping one of challenging Nixon's noncommitment to a government-assisted solution."[46] Rather than carp, Rockefeller decided to mimic Nixon by favoring federal aid to minority-owned small businesses.[47]

Liberal Democrats followed Nixon's lead as well. To relieve urban blight, Humphrey advanced an $8 billion "Marshall Plan" modeled after

Great Society programs. He belatedly backed increased aid to minority businesses, almost in response to Nixon, even though he had supported both civil rights and aid to small businesses during his years in the Senate. The *New York Times* also endorsed black capitalism, while cautioning that "most Negroes, like most whites, are not going to be entrepreneurs," and pointing out the shortcoming of Nixon's black capitalism.[48]

If minority enterprise emerged as a "sexy issue," Nixon's failure to address other civil rights matters at similar length suggested that, unlike LBJ, he saw this scheme as a cure-all. Since the candidate certainly did not intend to convey such a message, why did he? Relying exclusively on their own values and intuitions, Nixon and his aides underestimated the complexity of African American social and economic concerns. They ignored the fact that discrimination in home sales and wage scales helped keep African Americans in urban ghettos. Like many white liberal sociologists, Price partly attributed black dependency to the legacy of "slave culture."[49] During the election of 1968, at least, Nixon made no effort to broaden his understanding. When one correspondent inquired what blacks other than the basketball star Wilt Chamberlain were advising Nixon on racial problems, Nixon's brain trust–Buchanan, Greenspan, and H. R. Haldeman–told their subordinates to say nothing.[50] So Nixon presented black capitalism as both a panacea and a fait accompli.

Between election day and his inauguration, Nixon heightened African American expectations. Either buoyed or shaken by his narrow victory, the president-elect vowed to "bring the American people together" and "bridge the gap between the races."[51] To do that, he reached out to African Americans, who had voted overwhelmingly for Humphrey. Before taking the presidential oath, Nixon promised black leaders that he would "do more for the Negro than any president has ever done."[52] He would start by assisting separate minority institutions, such as businesses and colleges.

Growing Pains: The Office of Minority Business Enterprise

During 1969, or phase two, Nixon's black capitalism program scored few gains. Like his other civil rights policies, Nixon first left minority enterprise to a cabinet official, Commerce Secretary Maurice H.

Stans, and withdrew to handle other matters. Hampered by excessive promises, a narrow focus, and structural woes, not to mention meager funding, bureaucratic infighting, and popular skepticism, the infant program struggled to take its first steps.

Before announcing his policy for black capitalism, Nixon remained true to form by calculating its pluses and minuses. In private, the president termed aiding minority businesses "long overdue" and a "high priority." "Politically," he allegedly told Stans, "I don't think there are any votes in it for us, but we'll do it because it's right."[53] At the same time, Nixon understood the program's "enormous problems." "*Any* small business," he wrote Stans, "has a 75% chance of failing," and a "*minority* small business has a 90% chance of failing—good luck."[54] The president knew that high crime rates made ghetto businesses risky ventures. At a meeting with GOP congressional leaders early in 1969, Nixon lamented that "'black capitalism' [funding] will have to go to Mexicans and Indians" and then described "how the first black supermarket complex in Delaware shut down because of dozens of robberies."[55]

Such reservations did not cool the president's enthusiasm. After taking office, Nixon formed a cabinet committee on minority enterprise. In accordance with the committee's advice, particularly that of Stans, the president pressed for immediate results. On March 5, 1969, he signed Executive Order 11458 founding the Office of Minority Business Enterprise within the Commerce Department.[56] As was the case with his affirmative action policies, Nixon bypassed Congress and allowed federal departments, in this case Commerce, to develop policy.

Although the president did not get involved with OMBE's operations, he supported its efforts, at least verbally. Nixon discussed black capitalism with advisers, conferred with African American business leaders, and appointed a national advisory council to study minority enterprise.[57] In handwritten notes he stressed the rewards of business ownership—"dignity, pride, self-respect"—for disadvantaged groups.[58] Contrary to what he told Stans, Nixon saw this program as his "best polit[ical] theme" regarding middle-class blacks, who made up, he estimated, 20 percent of the African American vote.[59] "Everything we can do," argued Nixon political aide Harry S. Dent, Jr., "to increase minority business holdings, minority home ownership, and more jobs for minorities, will in the long run mean more to the minorities and help increase our political favor."[60]

Minority business enterprise fit within the president's ad lib political strategy. "Like most politicians," Dent recalled, "Richard Nixon did not hesitate to work for votes on both sides of even such an emotional issue as the race question."[61] Nixon, as discussed in Chapter 1, made overtures to white southerners, then backed a policy which achieved record school desegregation and sporadically courted blacks. OMBE became a key political initiative. To win over conservative whites, the president often welcomed criticism from civil rights leaders. But when African American denunciation grew strident, Nixon would tell aides to publicize OMBE's work to show his concern for minority rights.[62]

Outside advice reinforced Nixon's commitment to minority business enterprise. Early in 1970 the president met with a group of professors from Harvard, Columbia, and the University of California at Berkeley. These academics advised him to "shift [domestic] policy to helping and backing the strong, instead of putting all effort into raising up the weak." They also contended that whites "have to give the black middle class a cultural legitimacy," an idea that sounded like Nixon's "Bridges to Human Dignity."[63] During a meeting with senior advisers and members of Congress in 1971, the president promised to "appeal to Negroes" through "jobs, schools, opportunity" and the idea of "freedom of movement."[64] Nixon had already expressed such ideas in his statements on school desegregation and fair housing.

Commerce Secretary Stans appeared suited to the task of running the minority enterprise effort. Although known for his button-down conservatism during his years as Eisenhower's budget director, the Minnesotan embraced black capitalism. A self-described "Horatio Alger–type" who had risen from working-class origins to build a major accounting firm, the commerce secretary believed in expanding opportunity and rewarding success.[65] As a fund-raiser for Nixon's presidential bids, Stans sensed "vote-getting potential" in minority business enterprise. "With a relatively small budget impact," he wrote domestic policy chief John D. Ehrlichman, "this is one program which can put the Administration in a good light with the Blacks without carrying a severe negative impact on the majority community, as is often the case with civil rights issues."[66] Self-made, pragmatic, and politically astute, Stans typified the men around Nixon.

Stans worked hard to foster black capitalism. Along with colleagues in the cabinet, the commerce secretary persuaded Nixon to drop the narrow "black capitalism" slogan and rally Hispanics and Native Americans under the banner "minority business enterprise."[67] Stans also drafted the president's executive order establishing the Office of Minority Business Enterprise. To build up the program, the commerce secretary, in keeping with his conservative Republican background, favored voluntary cooperation between the public and private sectors. Stans urged the presidents of Ford Motor Company and McDonald's to increase the number of minority-owned dealerships and franchises.[68] He also promoted Minority Enterprise Small Business Investment Corporations (MESBICs). Funded by SBA and private sponsors, MESBICs loaned money to minority entrepreneurs.[69] In 1970 Stans traveled about the country to build public support for minority entrepreneurship.[70]

Despite these actions, the minority business program floundered in 1969. No less than the president, Stans raised expectations about the policy's prospects. The commerce secretary publicly promised to gain commitments for one hundred MESBICs by June 30, 1970, and he succeeded.[71] Yet landing commitments was one thing; breathing life into these hideously named creatures was quite another. Worried that Congress might not approve, the Bureau of the Budget proved hesitant to fund MESBICs. The private sector, sensing little profit, often balked.[72] By July 1970 the Commerce Department had licensed thirteen MESBICs. A year later it had approved a total of only thirty-four.[73] Publicizing this program was important, but policy makers historically have oversold new initiatives, and Stans, like Nixon, should have been more sober in gauging OMBE's initial impact.

The administration widened the gap between promise and performance by limiting OMBE's mission. After the cabinet committee on minority entrepreneurship weighed proposals to build the program, Stans stressed that OMBE "will not become involved with individual cases or with programs at the operational level." In forgoing a legislative mandate, he restricted the agency to "stimulation and coordination" of existing public and private programs.[74] Stans respected the domain of the General Services Administration (GSA), which oversaw procurement, and that of SBA, which made loans, leaving OMBE without the "necessary clout" to fulfill its mission.[75] Furthermore, the secretary and OMBE's first director, Thomas F. Roeser, formerly a public relations specialist at Quaker Oats Company, developed few yardsticks to measure the program's progress. By mid-1969, OMBE had secured only two assistance grants for minority businesses.[76]

To be fair, most of OMBE's problems lay beyond Stans's reach. There is no evidence that Nixon wanted a broader mandate for the agency, and the decision to exclude Congress from policy making was understandable. Conservative members of the House Select Committee on Small Business had scorned LBJ's funneling of SBA loans to minorities as "discrimination in reverse." Yet if Nixon planned to shun Congress, he might have directed the policy more closely. Noting that federal departments of equal rank rarely bend to one another, an SBA official proposed using a White House adviser, not a cabinet officer or new agency, to oversee minority enterprise. This advice never received consideration, and White House coordination of minority enterprise did not begin until 1970, after the policy had already faltered.[77]

Why did White House officials forgo brokering the minority business effort? New to governance, the president and his staff had not grasped the challenges of launching a brand-new agency. On top of defining OMBE's functions, crafting an agenda, and publicizing the policy, the commerce secretary and OMBE's director spent considerable time gathering data, hiring staff, establishing regional offices, persuading business leaders to serve on the National Advisory Council on Minority Business Enterprise, and trudging through endless reports, paperwork, and strategy sessions. To develop ideas, Stans also established three task forces, on capital development, construction, and government contracting. The commerce secretary surely qualified for overtime pay. Yet OMBE's structural problems remained unsolved.[78]

OMBE's difficulties included staff inexperience and frequent changes in leadership. Trained in public relations, Roeser, OMBE's director, was a poor administrator; he left the agency after just six months.[79] To enhance OMBE's standing with minority groups, the commerce secretary replaced Roeser with an African American, Abraham S. Venable.[80] Described by Stans as "amiable" and "husky," Venable possessed managerial experience and brought stability to OMBE. After Venable departed, in 1971, John L. Jenkins, a black lawyer and a former business executive, assumed command of the agency. While there is no evidence that Jenkins proved less able than Venable, all these comings and goings took their toll as the OMBE struggled to gain its footing.[81]

OMBE also endured paltry funding. For two and a half years, Stans and his aides worked without a budget for the wobbly agency. To reduce inflation fueled by the Vietnam War, Nixon in 1969 set out to pare back such Great Society programs as the Office of Economic Opportunity and the Job Corps. The commerce secretary panhandled other departments for funds. With its amorphous duties, revolving-door leadership, and dependence on other departments for its livelihood, OMBE hardly earned the respect of fellow agencies during its first year in business.[82]

Turf fights between OMBE and SBA hindered the minority enterprise policy. Both agencies possessed different prerogatives and goals. Section 8(a) of the Small Business Act of 1953 gave SBA the power to award government contracts to small or "non-competitive" firms and to lend money for business ventures. While OMBE chief Roeser urged more aid to blacks, SBA chief Hilary Sandoval, the ranking Hispanic in the Nixon administration, doubled the volume of SBA loans and 8(a) contracts to all minorities during 1969. The rivalry between the two agencies grew "furious" as Roeser and Sandoval jousted over who would announce the government's first grants.[83]

Personality conflicts did not help matters. Arguing that Sandoval lacked sufficient business experience for the SBA post, Stans had urged Nixon not to nominate him. After the appointment went through, Stans and Sandoval reached "a suitable degree of surface harmony."[84] But it remains doubtful whether the SBA chief ever won Stans's confidence. One Republican Party official noted that Sandoval did not get along with the secretary of commerce.[85]

In this context, coordinating the minority business effort became taxing. To secure private funding for MESBICs, the Office of Minority Business Enterprise and Small Business Administration operated on different planes. OMBE officials appealed to corporate leaders' sense of "social involvement" and won some commitments. SBA, by contrast, made its pitch "on a strictly profit and loss basis" and sometimes frightened sponsors away from these high-risk ventures. Accordingly, Stans told Venable to have MESBIC applications sent to OMBE, not SBA.[86] There was further evidence of a lack of teamwork. SBA officials in 1971 had to request a briefing on OMBE's programs.[87] Three years later a White House staffer lamented that the two agencies "have often failed to cooperate" on minority business efforts.[88]

Divided between separatists and integrationists, African American leaders expressed dismay over OMBE's first-year blues. Separatists who favored the program bit their tongues as the agency endured growing pains.[89] Yet integrationist groups such as the Leadership Conference on Civil Rights opposed the policy for reviving the "discredited doctrine of 'separate but equal.'"[90] Many integrationists questioned the value of small, minority-owned businesses in corporate America and advised blacks to seek positions in giant corporations. Federal Reserve governor Andrew F. Brimmer, an African American, rejected black capitalism as "one of the worst digressions that has attracted attention and pulled substantial numbers of people off course."[91] The debate among separatists and integrationists, which continued more or less throughout the 1990s, prevented African Americans from uniting to lend a hand with the minority business policy.

African American leaders emphasizing the benefits of economic progress disagreed with the integrationists. The problem with minority enterprise, prominent black executives and leaders of the National Urban League contended, lay in its execution, not its conception. Whitney M. Young, Jr., executive director of the National Urban League, chided Nixon for leaving the program "in shambles" and Stans for failing to name a representative from his organization to the National Advisory Council on Minority Business Enterprise.[92] Stans and his aides responded by vowing to include an Urban League official, and in fact did keep in contact with the organization's leadership.[93]

Appeasing Jackie Robinson proved more difficult. The former baseball player and Nixon supporter, who had become a corporate executive, endorsed the president's minority business initiative in 1969. Yet within a few months Robinson grew angry with the program's meager returns.[94] After Stans met with Robinson and other African American business leaders to urge patience, the onetime Brooklyn Dodger shot back, "I don't think anyone can ask us for patience. Black people have shown a tremendous amount of patience." Considering the newness of the program, the commerce secretary was justified in seeking a measure of forbearance. In fact, Robinson later praised Stans's dedication. But Robinson's critique boded ill for winning over black business leaders.[95]

Not all black businessmen took such a jaundiced view of the administration's program. In 1970 Milton O. McGinty, an African American civil servant turned entrepreneur, defended OMBE's aims by citing his own success: "I know that there is a place in the business world for the minority entrepreneur—despite the contentions by some people that minority businessmen will tend to operate 'Mom and Pop' stores." Finding criticism of the program to be more political than constructive, he dismissed efforts to win over civil rights leaders as "not essential," since black capitalism targeted only "a very small minority within the minorities."[96] His last point hit the mark. If Nixon, Stans, and civil rights leaders had accepted minority enterprise for what it was, a small program with useful but limited impact, and then worked to build it without indulging in rhetorical flourishes, they might have achieved quicker results and allayed skepticism.

OMBE failed to impress minorities and members of Congress. Venable reported "widespread suspicion and distrust" within the "minority community" over the "sincerity" of the government's commitment. He recounted complaints over the agency's lack of money, influence, and achievements as well as concerns that black capitalism would prove either "a myth" or a formula for subsidizing "a few black fat cats."[97] During Senate hearings late in 1969, Charles H. Percy, Republican of Illinois, termed OMBE's record "inadequate" and the government's planning lax.[98]

Such criticism prodded the White House to act. Nixon's domestic policy chief, John D. Ehrlichman, summoned officials from the White House, Commerce Department, and SBA to review the policy and quiet discontent. "The whole minority business area needs a push," Moynihan noted.[99] As with his policy making on school and housing desegregation, Nixon began to centralize decision making within the White House.

The Maturing of Minority Business Enterprise

Throughout 1970 and 1971, or phase three, minority enterprise began to yield results. Credit for its gains belongs to White House aides Robert J. Brown and Leonard Garment, who helped coordinate the policy, to the ever zealous Stans, to Republican appointees within the departments, and to Nixon, who generally backed his troops. These concentric policy-making circles expanded procurement from minority-owned firms, deposited unparalleled funds in minority banks, refined OMBE's functions, and secured a budget for the agency.

Robert J. Brown, White House liaison to minority groups, really forced the issue of minority procurement. Late in 1969 Brown drafted a presidential memorandum inviting federal agencies to help "set goals" to expand purchases from minority firms.[100] Unlike the Philadelphia Plan for bringing minorities into the construction trades, Brown's plan called for decentralized, voluntary decision making, with agencies drafting their own targets. Since the minority business policy needed a boost, Brown's ideas drew support from liberal White House aides Moynihan and Garment, moderates such as Ehrlichman, and even conservatives such as Bryce Harlow.[101] Arguing that banks preferred to loan money to businesses with government contracts, Moynihan called procurement "the most powerful engine the Federal establishment has to promote minority enterprise."[102] General Services Administration head Robert L. Kunzig agreed. A longtime civil servant and former Nixon campaign aide who had chaired OMBE's interagency task force on procurement, Kunzig contended that "virtually nothing will be accomplished without [a presidential statement]."[103] On December 5, Nixon signed Brown's memorandum.[104]

The new memorandum reinforced Stans's policies and spawned the first minority contract set-asides. Before Nixon signed Brown's memorandum, Stans read it to members of OMBE's task force on procurement and signaled his support. Agents from the Small Business Administration then presented procurement goals for minority businesses under Section 8(a), the act which suspended competitive bidding on federal contracts for small firms. During fiscal years 1970 and 1971, SBA proposed to award $38 million and $100 million, respectively, in contracts to small minority-owned businesses under 8(a). The task force also drafted procedures for agencies to follow in meeting these goals. General Services chief Kunzig alone pledged to purchase $10 million worth of goods from minority businesses during fiscal year 1970.[105] In 1971 Nixon endorsed procurement goals for minority firms under 8(a).[106] Although SBA did not achieve the target of $100 million until 1972, policy makers, under the aegis of Brown, Garment, and Stans, had begun contract set-asides for minorities.[107]

Why did SBA fail to meet its aims sooner? For one thing, the 8(a) program encountered resistance from the Defense Department, the government's largest procurer, and from Congress. Defense Secretary Melvin R. Laird objected to an SBA-proposed contract with tiny Garland Foods of Dallas that ran 36 percent above the lowest bid. Laird relayed word to Sandoval that members of the House Appropriations Committee were up in arms over purchases "used for economic development or for payment of subsidies."[108] In 1970 the Senate Appropriations Committee considered an amendment by Senator Allen J. Ellender, Democrat of Louisiana, to limit price differences between small and large firms to no more than 10 percent under the 8(a) program.[109] While fiscal conservatism influenced Ellender and his colleagues, they perhaps disliked a program that seemed to favor minorities.

White House staffers broke the bottleneck. Ehrlichman's intervention helped secure the contract for Garland Foods.[110] Although he did not technically handle minority enterprise, budget director George P. Shultz proved an important ally. The former labor secretary, who had helped to fashion affirmative action and school desegregation policies, backed Garment, Brown, and Ehrlichman by providing SBA with funds to cover the gap between competitive and noncompetitive bids under 8(a).[111] Garment got tough with the departments by requesting reports on their purchases from minority-owned businesses.[112] By coordinating minority enterprise from the White House, where there were officials both committed to the program and close to the levers of presidential power, Nixon fortified this policy.

Yet Nixon refused to apply procurement goals to minority construction firms. The idea of using very precise goals, similar to those in the Philadelphia Plan, sprang from two officials at the Housing Department, Undersecretary Richard C. Van Dusen and Assistant Secretary for Equal Opportunity Samuel J. Simmons.[113] Van Dusen met with his fellow undersecretaries and endorsed the "Los Angeles Plan."[114] This grassroots proposal called for setting aside a certain volume of federal contracts for minority-owned construction firms in Los Angeles.[115] Simmons, chair of OMBE's task force on construction, overcame the indifference of other departments and unveiled the plan in 1970.[116] To extend the Los Angeles Plan, Simmons and Stans drafted orders for each agency to prepare "a comprehensive plan with specific goals for fostering minority enterprise in the construction industry."[117] Their emphasis on a "comprehensive" plan with "specific" goals differed from Brown's earlier, more vague memorandum, which only encouraged agencies to fashion their own targets. Garment advised Nixon to approve Simmons's memorandum and expected him to sign it. He was shocked when the president refused.[118]

Although it remains unclear why Nixon rejected goals for construction contracts, philosophical and political factors must have influenced his decision. By urging a "comprehensive" plan with "specific" goals, Simmons scared the president. As discussed in Chapter 4, Nixon distinguished between flexible goals, which he supported, and rigid quotas, which he opposed. The Simmons memorandum reached the president's desk at the worst possible time, in July 1971, when Nixon had begun to court blue-collar workers and play down other affirmative action policies such as the Philadelphia Plan. Nixon the politician sensed that whites backed minority enterprise conditionally and would reject programs which overtly favored blacks. White contractors and members of Congress such as Senator Strom Thurmond, Republican of South Carolina, already had voiced disapproval of "preferential treatment" for minorities.[119] Former Nixon aide John McClaughry, who had helped draft the "Bridges to Human Dignity" address in 1968, even questioned the propriety of promoting a separate "minority" business program.[120]

If political expediency was Nixon's prime motivation in rejecting the Simmons memorandum, he miscalculated; Thurmond's concerns aside, Republicans backed minority enterprise and might have accepted specific goals for construction contracts. In 1970 the Senate Republican Policy Committee declared minority enterprise to be consistent with the GOP's pro-business tenets.[121] Governor Ronald Reagan of California praised SBA "boot straps" programs to assist minority entrepreneurs.[122] And, with an eye toward his Mexican American constituents, Senator John Tower, Republican of Texas, denied that "more business opportunities for minorities" meant diminished opportunities for other groups, since America boasted "substantial amounts" of untapped capital and resources.[123] Stans crafted a sensible response to the critics of procurement goals: "Small business generally has had similar preferences in the past and this step merely notes the need for minorities to participate."[124] But Nixon failed to make this case.

The president's opposition to contracting goals for minority construction firms did not undermine the procurement effort. Van Dusen and Simmons continued to enforce the Los Angeles Plan for minority contractors in California. SBA and GSA proceeded to secure contracts for small minority-owned firms under the 8(a) program. Garment and Brown kept after agencies and departments to purchase goods from minority-owned firms.[125] Between 1969 and 1975, 8(a) procurement from minority firms sprang from $9 million to $250 million. During the years 1970–1975, purchases from minority businesses increased 265 percent, to $475 million.[126] Although the United States Commission on Civil Rights later faulted the government for not doing more to procure goods from minority firms, the Nixon administration, beginning almost at ground zero, compiled an impressive record.[127]

Another network of policy makers increased federal deposits in minority-owned banks. The movers behind this program included Undersecretary of the Treasury Charls Walker, Alan Steelman, director of the National Advisory Council on Minority Business Enterprise, and, of course, Stans, Venable, Brown, and the omnipresent Garment. To raise desperately needed capital, Brown, with Stans's support, recommended placing government revenues in banks that made loans to minority businesses.[128] The proposal ran into opposition from Treasury Secretary David M. Kennedy and his staff, who predicted it would "generate political pressures to re-locate deposits for the benefit of other interest groups."[129] Garment and Walker reassessed their plans. Backed by Stans, Brown, and Steelman, the two men decided to aid minority-owned banks directly.[130] In so doing, they would provide capital for minority business ventures, bolster financial institutions, and pay homage to another form of black separatism. By late 1971, Stans and Walker were promising to pump $100 million into minority-owned banks, with one third of the money coming from the federal government.[131]

The bank deposit program encountered stiff resistance from familiar quarters. Andrew Brimmer, an African American governor of the Federal Reserve Board, held tightly to his belief in integration; he doubted the viability of separate black banks and rejected measures to strengthen them. Federal Reserve chair Arthur F. Burns, a conservative economist and a former White House staffer, also wondered whether such a policy would yield significant returns. Members of Congress unfriendly to civil rights questioned the program's propriety. Independent senator Harry F. Byrd, Jr., of Virginia accused the government of forcing federal contractors to deposit money in minority banks.[132]

Learning from past mistakes, Stans and his allies set credible targets, recruited powerful patrons, and worked together to overcome these critics. They persuaded Nixon to endorse the $100 million target.[133] To reach the goal of $65 million in private deposits, Garment and Stans wrote the presidents of major corporations such as General Motors, Heinz, and Swift Meats.[134] Garment and Walker developed goals for federal agencies to follow in placing their funds in minority banks. When officials at the departments of Labor and Health, Education, and Welfare dragged their heels, Garment ordered them to get moving.[135] By October 1971, the government had exceeded its targets, securing nearly $200 million in new minority bank deposits.[136]

Hardly a panacea for minority enterprise, the bank policy still posted commendable gains. Federal deposits in minority banks swelled from $35 million to more than $80 million during the period 1971–1973. Between 1970 and 1973, total public and private deposits in such banks surged from nearly $400 million to over $1 billion. From 1970 to 1974 the number of minority-owned banks in the country almost doubled, from twenty-eight to fifty.[137]

Policy makers rounded out the minority enterprise program by expanding OMBE's powers and funding the agency. The National Advisory Council on Minority Business Enterprise, in its final report, proposed merging OMBE, SBA, and the Economic Development Administration (EDA), which provided general economic assistance, into an "agency for expanded ownership" at an additional cost of $350 million.[138] Stans objected to this grandiose scheme, partly because EDA had not played a key role in minority enterprise.[139] Finding little "meat" in the expanded ownership idea, Garment and his deputy, Bradley Patterson, agreed.[140] With Garment's support, Stans and his aides drafted their own plan, which called for an assistant secretary of commerce for minority enterprise, added oversight powers and money for OMBE, local OMBE affiliates, and legislation to ease the development of MESBICs.[141]

Nixon endorsed Stans's proposals. In 1970 the management-conscious president informed Ehrlichman that he wanted to merge SBA with OMBE, as the advisory council had urged.[142] But Stans argued that such tinkering would "impose a reorganization within a reorganization." The result would "only confuse everyone" and again sow doubt among minorities about "the Administration's commitment." The secretary advocated "greater thrust to the existing program" through new legislation.[143] Nixon agreed. He submitted Stans's proposals to Congress and signed an executive order to enhance OMBE's coordinating duties.[144]

Stans secured OMBE's first budget. Between 1969 and 1971, the agency obtained its operating funds from other departments. To finance technical assistance grants and new OMBE affiliates, Stans and his lieutenants requested a budget of $188 million in fiscal year 1972.[145] With the administration seeking to restrain inflation through wage and price controls and spending cuts, budget director Shultz and Ehrlichman offered $130 million over two years. Disappointed, the commerce secretary took his case to the president. Nixon grumbled that "it is *ridiculous* to have Stans appeal this item." Wielding the budget ax, he approved $40 million and $60 million, respectively, for OMBE during fiscal years 1972 and 1973.[146] Stans's appeal probably saved OMBE from deeper cuts, given Nixon's budget-slashing mind-set. In fact, Stans's funding request for technical assistance was high enough to please the Congressional Black Caucus and modest enough to deflect criticism from fiscal conservatives on Capitol Hill.[147]

Minority Business Enterprise: A Balance Sheet

Stans's legislative proposals helped define OMBE's mission for the next two decades. At Nixon's behest, Congress passed legislation to foster

MESBICs, though it did not establish an assistant secretary for minority enterprise. OMBE, later known as the Minority Business Development Agency, continued to referee minority enterprise policy. The agency also dispensed grants to trade associations and nonprofit groups that provided managerial and technical assistance to minority entrepreneurs.[148]

By late 1971 the outlines of minority business policy were set, although OMBE was not scandal-proof. The agency's reputation suffered when White House staffers such as Robert Brown, Frederic Malek, and Kenneth Cole used it to advance Nixon's reelection. After hearing that "one of our most stalwart black supporters in Texas" had applied for an OMBE grant, Brown wrote, "I would like to see him funded (by letter contract if necessary)."[149] Some applicants for OMBE grants or federal contracts were required to declare their support for the president. The chair of the Watts Labor Community Action Committee complained of "almost unbearable" pressure to get "in line" behind Nixon's reelection bid or lose a $1.5 million contract. Derek Hansen, an OMBE employee, resigned, charging that the agency's "main purpose was political."[150]

After Nixon's reelection, White House officials continued to use OMBE for ill-gotten political gains. In January 1973 Jim Brown, the former football player, who had backed the president's reelection, applied for a $327,000 OMBE grant to finance his Black Economic Union (BEU). Brown's organization had received a $100,000 grant the previous year, though, according to Tod Hullin, an Ehrlichman aide, it had "accomplished absolutely nothing." Nevertheless, Hullin prepared an option paper on whether or not to raise BEU's stipend to $250,000 for 1973. "Any increase would be *blatantly* political," Hullin admitted, with embarrassing candor, because an "increase in funding is not justified on the merits." Ehrlichman approved the $250,000 grant, then scrawled in response to Hullin, "Consider full funding on assessment of performance."[151]

Corruption also tainted SBA's 8(a) program. Members of the SBA's procurement staff handed out contracts to some "minority" firms that were in fact mostly owned by whites. When SBA chief Thomas Kleppe moved against such deception, the white partners allegedly "got the 'blacks' to 'cry' that SBA was trying to kill the 8(a) Program."[152] In 1973

Kleppe issued new 8(a) rules requiring that *"actual ownership* and *control* must be in the hands of the eligible minority" and that participating small businesses must demonstrate "viability."[153] Kleppe proved less sensitive to the appearance of favoritism; he defended an $863,000 contract under 8(a) to Cade Services, a firm owned by former White House staffer Robert Brown.[154]

The policy implications of such goings-on should not be exaggerated. Politics had influenced earlier small business programs; during the 1950s many Republicans envisioned SBA as a patronage plum, an agency "committed to political ends."[155] OMBE scandals paled in comparison to the White House's "shakedown" of major corporations to finance Nixon's reelection.[156] As early as 1969, Stans had urged the president to oppose a "Clean Elections Bill" to limit campaign contributions.[157] That bill never passed.

Yet OMBE continued to be plagued by oversights dating to the period 1969–1971. During most of the 1970s, OMBE did nothing to help other disadvantaged groups, such as women. A few minority business leaders found OMBE unresponsive and its programs fragmented.[158] In 1974 members of President Gerald R. Ford's staff studied the problems, and Ford responded by signing another memorandum urging more interdepartmental cooperation.[159] OMBE's chief difficulty encompassed money, not procedure. "The academic argument of one agency or the other is not the one we should get involved in," stated Berkeley G. Burrell, president of the National Business League, an African American organization. "What is needed is a much greater commitment by the government."[160]

Nixon's successors declined to increase funds for OMBE. The agency's $60 million budget for fiscal year 1973 remained steady under Presidents Ford and Jimmy Carter, then dropped under Ronald Reagan and George Bush.[161] During Bush's presidency, Stans served on a commission to revive OMBE, with little success.[162] President Bill Clinton's allotment for the Minority Business Development Agency, OMBE's successor, amounted to $38 million in 1994.[163] It remains uncertain whether a larger office, the proposed "agency for expanded ownership," could have fended off budget cuts during the frugal nineties.

By the 1990s, more groups were fighting for a slice of the pie. By espousing minority enterprise, Nixon encouraged non-black minorities, especially Hispanics, to form businesses. By 1989, 234 state and local set-aside programs, covering African Americans, Hispanics, American Indians, Asian Americans, Eskimos, Aleuts, and women, had emerged.[164] The expansion of set-asides yielded mixed returns. On the positive side, other disadvantaged groups gained access to public contracts. In 1979 President Carter signed Executive Order 12138, which prohibited bias against female entrepreneurs, and the Women's Business Ownership Act of 1988 authorized the federal government to promote women's business enterprises.[165] But some locales have tried too hard to satisfy all groups. Richmond, Virginia, included Aleut- and Eskimo-owned businesses in its set-aside program even though there was no evidence of Aleut or Eskimo entrepreneurs in that city.[166] Critics who dismiss set-asides as favoritism have stressed such excesses, and the Supreme Court in 1989 insisted on tighter rules for fighting discrimination in public contracting. "Proper findings," Justice Sandra Day O'Connor wrote in *City of Richmond v. Cronson,* "are necessary to define both the scope of the injury and the extent of the remedy necessary to cure its effects."[167] The *Cronson* decision called into question the legality of set-asides.

During the 1980s and 1990s, the minority business effort faced other challenges. SBA corruption neither began nor ended with Nixon. According to a federally funded study in 1986, whites owned 20 percent of the "minority" businesses receiving set-aside contracts. During the mid-eighties, an independent counsel investigated Attorney General Edwin Meese III for improperly lobbying on behalf of Wedtech, a minority-owned defense supplier. By the 1990s, critics were assailing the minority business effort from all angles. Some lamented the scant funding for MESBICs.[168] A few claimed that SBA set-asides made minority firms dependent on the government.[169] Up to that point, minority business enterprise had enjoyed bipartisan support as "compassionate capitalism," with set-asides becoming legal under Carter and lasting through Reagan and Bush.[170] Then, right-wing critics of affirmative action gathered strength and took deadly aim at set-asides. In 1996 Clinton declared a three-year ban on new set-aside programs.[171]

Despite occasional losses, the minority enterprise balance sheet showed a net profit. Between 1969 and 1991, federal grants and loans to minority-owned firms jumped from $200 million to $7 billion while government purchases from such firms grew from $83 million to $17 billion. A good deal of this progress occurred during the Nixon and Ford years. By 1976, eighty-two MESBICs had been formed. Fifty-six of the top one hundred black-owned firms in 1981 had emerged between 1969 and 1976. From 1969 to 1987, the total number of minority-owned businesses quadrupled from 320,000 to 1.2 million.[172] During the 1970s, of course, spending on most federal programs rose along with economic and population growth. Yet Nixon intended to expand opportunities for minority firms and did so within a short time.

Undeniably, the advance in minority enterprise also can be traced to nongovernmental factors. The talent and initiative of individual entrepreneurs helped spur minority business growth.[173] As African Americans and other minorities gained access to higher education, partly as a result of affirmative action, they obtained technical and managerial expertise and were able to form "capital intensive" firms specializing in computer and business services, manufacturing, and large-scale retailing.[174] As blacks and Hispanics entered college in larger numbers and secured higher-paying jobs, their earning power grew, and they were able to patronize minority-owned firms in their communities. The development of a "black consumer market" and the growth of black banks expanded the volume of capital available to minority enterprises.[175] Even so, given the risks of small business ventures, one wonders where minority entrepreneurs would have been without the policies, especially set-asides, that Nixon and Stans set in motion.[176]

The minority enterprise program's greatest contribution was intangible. In 1970 Stans told Nixon that they had "crossed the 'Continental Divide' of the minority enterprise program" as criticism had fallen off.[177] In 1972 Californians organized a dinner to honor Van Dusen, Simmons, and the Los Angeles Plan. Over two thousand minority business leaders saluted Stans at a similar banquet in Washington that same year. In 1984 one thousand black and Hispanic entrepreneurs sponsored yet another testimonial dinner to thank Nixon and Stans for the minority enterprise program.[178] Although Stans was not the policy's lone architect, minority business leaders rightly sensed his zeal and remembered him as "really committed" to it.[179]

By the 1970s, the concept of minorities owning businesses had gained currency. In September 1970, eighteen months after Nixon formed OMBE, *Black Enterprise* appeared on newsstands. *Ebony* and *Jet,* two other African American periodicals, published business news and ran articles on the emerging black middle class.[180] Federal aid to minority businesses, moreover, won grudging support from integrationists. In 1975 Roy Wilkins, executive secretary of the NAACP, said that such policies had been effective "to a limited extent," although their "failures are often highlighted" and they suffered from "too much red tape & politics."[181] "We would rather own A&P than burn it," declared the Reverend Jesse Jackson, the young African American leader sounding a lot like Nixon.[182] Such themes found their way into mass culture. *The Jeffersons,* one of the most-watched television sitcoms of the 1970s and 1980s, featured the travails of George Jefferson, a swaggering, self-made dry cleaning tycoon from Harlem. Jefferson was a Republican, and the show's theme song was "We're Movin' On Up."[183]

Not all minorities aspired to own businesses, nor did the Nixon administration deserve sole credit for these developments. But as Stans asserted in 1996, "Our publicized national efforts created a climate in which business ownership became a new hope for the minorities."[184] He might have added that the president also sought to aid long-established minority-owned enterprises.

Beyond Integration: Black Colleges

The Nixon administration's respect for separate minority institutions surfaced in its aid to black colleges. Since the end of the Civil War, these schools had been the largest minority-run enterprises in the United States. In addition to facing competition for talent and funds, the nearly one hundred predominantly black colleges came under pressure to integrate or merge with other institutions.[185] Did an end to segregated schools mean the end of black colleges? Nixon believed not. "Black schools are not necessarily inferior," he told Ehrlichman in 1972.[186]

Nixon strove to narrow court rulings that mandated desegregation of southern universities. In 1970 Leon Panetta, HEW's ardent integrationist, requested plans to end the "racial identifiability" of black colleges in favor of a "unitary system of education."[187] After the president sacked Panetta for antagonizing much of the white South over desegregation of secondary schools, federal courts pressed for collegiate integration.[188] In 1973 Nixon rejected the argument that black colleges had to end for the sake of integration; such a course would disrupt the education of African Americans, jeopardizing "a whole generation of graduates from the black colleges."[189] In desegregating Louisiana's state universities, officials at the Justice Department and within the White House worked with that state's congressional delegation and black colleges to limit court decisions and preserve African American institutions.[190] Nixon also supported separate minority institutions through his pro-tribal, anti-assimilationist Native American policy.

The president's support for black colleges went beyond his reluctance to press integration. Not unlike liberal private organizations such as the Ford and Rockefeller foundations, the administration bolstered these schools with additional money.[191] In 1969, after African American college students requested increased funding for predominantly black universities, the president ordered HEW Secretary Robert H. Finch to follow up "if there is anything we can do."[192] In 1970 Nixon personally promised the heads of black colleges more funds, advising them to "watch what we do."[193] He commanded Haldeman and Ehrlichman to get $100 million in grants for black colleges to send the message "I care."[194] Nixon reminded his aides to dispense these grants and claim credit for the administration. He also encouraged black college presidents to draft further recommendations.[195]

White House interest in blacks was clear. Presidential aides Garment and Brown embraced the cause of the black colleges and corresponded with their presidents.[196] Nixon, moreover, met with black college presidents after the killing of antiwar protesters at Kent State and Jackson State universities, at a time when he needed to display concern for students and higher education in general.[197] After the GOP scored few gains in the elections of 1970, the president expressed a desire to appeal to minorities by assisting the black colleges.[198] Nixon privately affirmed that "any higher education is better than no higher education," adding that if most African Americans attended black colleges, "we should find ways to find more support for them."[199]

Presidential interest in black colleges was nothing new. In 1963 President John F. Kennedy asked the presidents of the Ford and Rockefeller foundations to increase their financial contributions to these institutions.[200] He invited corporate, educational, and civic leaders to the White

House in an effort to raise $50 million for the United Negro College Fund and scribbled a personal note to Laurance S. Rockefeller, president of the Rockefeller Brothers Fund: "This I know is a matter with which you are very familiar–and on which you have done much–I hope you can come."[201] President Johnson endorsed the goal of $50 million, calling improved facilities for black colleges "an imperative need."[202] Title III of the Higher Education Act of 1965 enabled Johnson to fund financially strapped "developing institutions," including black colleges.[203]

President Nixon used Title III to assist separate black colleges. During the summer of 1970, President James E. Cheek of Howard University wrote Nixon a memorandum which tied the fate of black colleges to changing aims within the civil rights movement. Put simply, Cheek suggested that blacks desired institutions of their own and requested more federal dollars to preserve black colleges. After reading this memorandum, Nixon ordered Finch, who had moved into the White House as a counselor, and HEW Secretary Elliot L. Richardson to "follow up and report."[204]

By assisting black colleges, Nixon could boost economic development, black separatism, and African American moderates. "It is vitally important," the president explained to Haldeman, "to have Black colleges going strong and to maintain them so that Blacks develop the capacity to run something themselves." Since many African Americans lacked education and expertise, Nixon predicted that whenever large-scale institutions "are integrated the whites are inevitably going to dominate." Besides, he added, building up black colleges was "one way we can encourage the good Blacks," such as President Cheek, who "seems willing to work with us." But "this can only be done with money," Nixon affirmed.[205]

Nixon's administration significantly enlarged federal aid to black colleges. Finch, Garment, Brown, Richardson, and Ehrlichman proved instrumental in sculpting this policy. One day after the president had signed off on Cheek's memorandum, Brown and Finch assured reporters that more federal aid to black colleges was on the way.[206] Richardson then dispensed $29 million in HEW funds to black colleges during fiscal year 1970. Other agencies, probably coaxed by Brown and Garment, followed suit.[207] Yet the policy ran into opposition from officials at the Office of Management and Budget. Arguing (accurately) that black colleges already received a greater share of federal aid than other institutions in proportion to their enrollment, assistant budget director Richard P. Nathan opposed pumping more money into them.[208] Ehrlichman ended the deadlock by approving an additional $15 million in grants to black colleges under Title III of the Higher Education Act.[209] From 1969 to 1973, Title III subsidies to black colleges tripled from $30 million to $100 million.[210] Federal outlays to these schools grew from $108 million to $167 million between 1969 and 1971.[211]

While it is tempting to attribute Nixon's policy to staff or interest group pressure, to the president's thirst for "PR," or to his political machinations, Nixon's commitment to black colleges remained strong. He presented a personal check to the United Negro College Fund in 1971.[212] A year later, Frank A. Rose, the former president of the University of Alabama, credited Nixon's funding with abetting "the development of 112 Black Colleges" which had been "ignored by past administrations."[213] The president thereupon let his staff know that aiding black colleges remained "one of *his* priorities."[214] In 1973, while preoccupied with Watergate, Nixon made time to meet again with black college presidents and restate his support for their schools.[215]

The impact of Nixon's policies was threefold. By reining in integration, the president preserved the racial distinctiveness of black colleges. During the 1970s, African Americans entered predominantly white schools in record numbers, thanks to the government's affirmative action measures. At the same time, black colleges had little success in recruiting white students.[216] With white colleges becoming more inclusive and historically black schools eager to attract students, African Americans planning to attend college enjoyed greater educational choices than ever before. To extend access to higher education, Nixon and his aides also expanded grants and loans to low-income students.[217]

Nixon's policies, to some extent, helped strengthen black colleges academically. In 1970 independent and state-assisted black colleges received 12.5 percent and 9.7 percent of their income, respectively, from federal grants. Five years later the national government was providing 21 percent and 13 percent of operating costs, respectively, for these schools. Between 1970 and 1975, black colleges used these additional funds to increase the percentage of faculty members holding doctorates and the number of volumes in their libraries. Partly as a result, the proportion of their alumni accepted by graduate schools grew as well.

Most of these gains occurred at state-affiliated schools, which depended less on federal support.[218] Enrollment in all black colleges grew 50 percent from 1969 to 1977, and government funds helped these schools weather a decade of transition.[219]

Mostly, Nixon's efforts helped to shape an emerging national consensus in favor of black colleges. In its study *Between Two Worlds* (1970), the Carnegie Commission on Higher Education envisioned black colleges as instilling a sense of community and building a new black professional class. Such colleges, the commission argued, were in a position, "above all, to speak for the Negro in American education."[220] In 1970 Vernon E. Jordan, executive director of the United Negro College Fund, called the black college "as American as apple pie and as crucial to the welfare of the country as Harvard or Yale."[221] President Ford appeared in a television spot to urge contributions to the United Negro College Fund, and President Carter, following Nixon's lead, met with the heads of black colleges to pledge his support.[222] In 1980 participants at an HEW conference restated the principle that "black colleges should exist in this society."[223] By the 1980s, Title III aid to black colleges had grown to $130 million dollars per year, making it the largest non–research-based institutional subsidy to colleges.[224]

If Nixon's opposition to integration constituted the chief weakness of his civil rights policy, as liberals charged, it was in one respect a strength. Aversion to busing and scattered-site housing enabled Nixonians to see the virtue in nurturing some predominantly black institutions. From the vantage point of the 1990s, when many African Americans favored a degree of separatism, as well as expanded opportunities, one senses an irony. Regarding minority businesses and black colleges, Nixon and Stans, even with their mixed motives, now appear more "politically correct" than such diehard integrationists as Leon Panetta and Andrew Brimmer.

Coherence within Nixon's Agenda

The Nixon administration's affirmative action and minority enterprise policies were a matched set. Reflecting their self-made, moderate Republican backgrounds, Nixonians crafted measures to enhance training and economic opportunity for minority groups. Affirmative action opened doors to previously all-white schools, while federal aid invigorated black colleges. For individuals willing to start their own businesses, the administration proved supportive. Nixon and his aides geared their efforts to people who were, like themselves, upwardly mobile and middle class.

The president's vision, usually unstated, crept into White House correspondence. Nixon lauded one man for exemplifying "what the minority business program is all about," that is, "opening the full range of business opportunity to all by removing the inherited and institutional barriers to entry."[225] Taken out of context, this letter reads like hyperbole. Within the framework of Nixon's deeds, its words do not ring hollow.

The most radical aspect of Nixon's program was the president's willingness to move beyond the melting pot. As Republican moderates committed to individual choice, local authority, and voluntary solutions, Nixonians hated federal programs to force the races together outside the workplace. When a fair number of blacks expressed a desire for separatism and greater economic power, the administration acted. In this respect, Nixonians and Black Power advocates made strange bedfellows indeed.

This is not to suggest that the Nixonians' outlook and programs were foolproof. Showing their gender bias, the men who crafted Nixon's policies never considered that women wished to own businesses. Partly reflecting their class backgrounds, the president and his team tailored policy to members of minority groups who either were middle class or aspired to join the middle class. They largely overlooked the plight of the poor who lacked such aspirations. To be fair, Nixon offered poor Americans direct payments under his Family Assistance Plan if they accepted job training. FAP, hampered by presidential inattention and rejected by a Democratic-controlled Congress, never became law.[226]

Nixon and his aides learned an important lesson from their efforts to expand economic opportunity. Policies which encouraged a measure of racial separatism and/or offered economic assistance to disadvantaged groups could be sold as moderate alternatives to liberal programs. Nixonians decided to court black leaders who seemed sympathetic to their policies. Responding to "Red Power," they backed Native American self-determination. And they slowly moved to extend economic opportunities to women.

6

A Cold War: Nixon and Civil Rights Leaders

Why has it taken so long to credit Richard Nixon with some advances in civil rights? For one thing, Nixon alienated civil rights leaders and African Americans. The president who dragged his heels on integration of suburbs and northern schools made few addresses to the nation on civil rights, and he inflamed racial tensions through his "southern strategy." Incensed black leaders criticized Nixon harshly. Their critique has remained the standard interpretation of Nixon's policies.

Nixon's relations with civil rights leaders resembled a cold war. Each side became suspicious of the other, saw their rivalry in ideological terms, and engaged in hyperbole. Yet realizing they had to deal with each other, the antagonists on rare occasions cooperated in areas of mutual benefit. In a scaled-down version of the half-century-long antagonism between the United States and the Soviet Union, Nixon and civil rights advocates endured frosty relations punctured by infrequent, fleeting thaws. The parallel should not be pushed too far. Unlike the cold war, this rivalry was not between well-matched adversaries. As the nation's leader, Nixon should have been more sensitive to the concerns of a minority group that had only recently secured its rights.

Yet the cold war analogy conveys a sense of the racial polarization of the early 1970s. It highlights how many African Americans expressed their alienation indirectly, through angry rhetoric rather than riots or civil disobedience. To Nixon, relations with civil rights leaders involved power politics with both sides jousting to influence policy. With the civil rights community divided between separatists and integrationists, the president practiced *Realpolitik* by cultivating black leaders who might benefit from and support his policies.

Nixon used four strategies to deal with civil rights leaders. First, he generally evaded civil rights issues in public. Second, when expedient, he tried to pacify his critics through conferences or official statements explaining his policies. Third, Nixon confronted his detractors, such as when he removed the Reverend Theodore M. Hesburgh, C.S.C, an integrationist, as chair of the United States Commission on Civil Rights. Last, Nixon occasionally sought partnerships with civil rights groups, such as the National Urban League, which shared his aims. Together, these practices suggest formal, distant, even cold relations between the White House and civil rights leaders.

Nixon's cold war with civil rights leaders sprang from several sources. The legislative triumphs of the 1960s inspired civil rights advocates to expect increased support from the federal government, making the task of governing more difficult for Nixonians, who sought a middle course between the liberal state and the conservative doctrine of laissez-faire. Moreover, many black leaders were liberal and saw integration as central to solving racial problems. The president did not. Politically, he focused on winning white votes and interpreted black criticism as partisan whining. A series of public relations missteps by Nixon alienated civil rights leaders, hindering efforts at dialogue. Mostly, tension sprang from the different weight that each side gave to civil rights. For blacks, racial equality was a moral issue requiring the highest priority. To Nixon it was a lesser concern, one that he usually viewed in terms of political practicality or duty rather than right versus wrong.

Uneasy Entente: Vice President Nixon and Black Leaders

Before descending into cold war, Nixon and civil rights leaders started out as allies of convenience. As vice president, Nixon had wooed two well-known African Americans: Martin Luther King, Jr., and Jackie Robinson. But when the vice president refused to risk white disfavor and back civil rights more strongly, King and Robinson criticized him. Nixon in turn grew disillusioned and curbed his contacts with black leaders.

During the 1950s, Nixon and King established a formal working relationship. The vice president first met the strategist of the Montgomery Bus Boycott in 1957, when he and King traveled to Ghana to commemorate that nation's independence. After exchanging pleasantries, Nixon invited King to visit him in Washington, and the civil rights leader accepted. King's advisers urged him to prepare diligently for the coming encounter, which members of the African American press compared to a "summit conference." On June 13 King and an associate, the Reverend Ralph David Abernathy, conferred with the vice president for two hours.[1]

During their meeting, the Alabama minister lectured, and the vice president, like a dutiful pupil, took copious notes. King pressed for federal enforcement of school desegregation, which, he assured Nixon, most southern whites did not favor but seemed "willing to accept." King stressed that his Southern Christian Leadership Conference (SCLC) was working to register 3 million black voters. If the effort succeeded, he affirmed, "we can solve [the civil rights] problem [and] won't need [the] Fed[eral] gov[ernmen]t." Accordingly, he urged Nixon to support the voting rights bill before Congress. While King stressed his movement's commitment to nonviolence, Abernathy wondered how long their followers could avoid violence.[2]

King's words reinforced and influenced Nixon's approach to civil rights. To implement the *Brown* decision, Nixon aimed for moderation, partly to appease white southerners who were willing to accept school desegregation. He backed voting rights to shift responsibility for civil rights matters to African Americans. The vision of new black voters, gratefully loyal to the GOP, surely appealed to Nixon. Abernathy's point, that the movement might abandon nonviolence if its aims went unfulfilled, perhaps sounded an alarm bell in Nixon's mind. During his meeting with King, the vice president stressed his own efforts to end bias in companies holding federal contracts.[3] As president, Nixon continued to stress the importance of jobs over integration.

Nixon and King left this meeting as partners—of a sort. Both men endorsed the Civil Rights Act of 1957 to protect voting rights and opposed efforts by southern Democrats to weaken it. The civil rights leader applauded the vice president for lobbying against a southern-sponsored amendment requiring jury trials in civil rights cases. After this amendment passed, King still urged Nixon to accept "the present bill," which he considered "far better than no bill at all."[4] Nixon agreed, and predicted that the law would yield results if blacks "register and vote."[5] A grateful King sent the vice president a copy of his book *Stride toward Freedom* (1958), with the inscription: "To my friend, Honorable Richard Nixon. Through our conversation and correspondence, I know of your intense interest in solving the civil rights problem facing our nation . . . With warm personal regards."[6] Such flattery aside, King correctly grasped that Nixon possessed at least some commitment to racial equality.

The Nixon-King partnership proved tenuous. Both men were cagey, had different goals and constituencies, and never really trusted each other. As the leader of a reform movement, King concentrated on specific aims and demands, in particular registering black voters and desegregating southern schools. Nursing presidential ambitions, Nixon guarded against becoming attached to one racial group or to such a volatile issue as civil rights. After meeting with Nixon, King remarked that the vice president mixed enthusiasm for racial equality with pragmatism and projected sincerity on a wide range of issues. "If Richard Nixon is not sincere," King wrote in 1958, "he is the most dangerous man in America."[7]

Nixon paid a political price for consorting with King. In 1958 Virginia segregationists circulated handbills painting the vice president as an integrationist and the lapdog of African Americans. Above the caption "Vice President Richard M. Nixon Has Been an NAACP Member for Over 10 Years!" snapshots showed Nixon greeting King in Washington, holding hands with black women in Harlem, and hugging a tribal leader in Ghana.[8] One of the vice president's aides ordered copies of these "smear sheets" for distribution in black districts.[9] Such cynicism aside, the flyers suggested that at least a few white southerners had grown angry over Nixon's associations and had organized to undermine him.

As the presidential election of 1960 neared, Nixon began to court southern whites and distance himself from black leaders.[10] His correspondence with King descended to trite expressions of goodwill.[11] When a group of civil rights leaders, including King, asked to meet with the vice president early in 1960, Nixon balked: "Contact that civil rights group that has been wanting to come in to see me and tell them that I would like to see them but that I am completely booked this week—or whenever they asked for . . . Tell them I have to go to Florida and have commitments that I just can't break."[12] Later, in August, Nixon made and broke an appointment with Roy Wilkins, executive secretary of the National Association for the Advancement of Colored People.[13] The vice president had neither written off the black vote nor become an outright opponent of civil rights. Yet he increasingly cultivated white southerners.

The fall campaign put greater distance between Nixon and King. After police in Atlanta arrested the civil rights leader during a lunch counter sit-in, John F. Kennedy, the Democratic nominee, telephoned the minister's wife, Coretta Scott King, to console her. Robert F. Kennedy, JFK's campaign manager, then called a local judge to secure King's release.[14] Although civil rights leaders and concerned citizens urged the vice president to condemn the jailing of King, he refused.[15] Nixon's advisers did not want their candidate to offend white southerners by taking a public stand. "This is too hot for us to handle," scribbled one campaign aide.[16] E. Frederic Morrow, a black aide to President Eisenhower, unsuccessfully implored Nixon to contact either the governor of Georgia, the mayor of Atlanta, or King's family.[17]

The Kennedys were not exactly valiant warriors in the fight to release King, nor was Nixon AWOL. Louis Martin, a black aide to JFK, remembered that Robert Kennedy became concerned over King's jailing only after hearing that Nixon planned to blame the Democrats, who governed Georgia.[18] The younger Kennedy later conceded that JFK needed to campaign for black votes: "He [had] voted in favor of the jury trial amendment, so there were some reservations about him on that. Nixon didn't have a bad record as far as Negroes were concerned, so they were reasonably interested in him."[19] In fact, the vice president had telephoned Attorney General William P. Rogers to ask whether the government had authority to intervene in King's case.[20] It would have been "completely improper for me or any other lawyer to call the judge," explained Nixon. "And Robert Kennedy should have known better than to do so."[21] Yet Nixon voiced no personal concern for King in public.

The Republican nominee's low-key response could not match JFK's display of sympathy for King and his movement. Kennedy's telephone call, Morrow recalled, "just electrified the Negro community so that just to talk about Nixon in a Negro group was considered treason."[22] R. Sargent Shriver, JFK's brother-in-law, described the gesture as "a shot of lightning in the middle of the night."[23] As if by magic, the Democratic nominee managed to erase his own lackluster civil rights record and solidify the backing of African Americans. "When the call to Mrs. King was made," remembered Franklin Williams, a Kennedy aide, "and when Daddy King [the Reverend Martin Luther King, Sr.], as a leading black Baptist minister, announced that this was sufficient for him to change his support from Nixon to Kennedy, that was like an electric shock through the black community."[24] Even Robert H. Finch, Nixon's campaign manager, conceded that the "King incident undoubtedly shifted a great many votes away that we might otherwise have gotten."[25] The vice president took only a third of the black vote and lost the election by just 113,000 votes. This so-called master politician had learned an important lesson about the power of symbolism.

Nixon's seeming indifference to King's arrest ended their relationship. While the vice president did not blame African Americans for his loss, he knew that Kennedy's telephone call had cost him black votes.[26] Nixon and King never again corresponded, and when an aide urged the defeated candidate to write to people who had expressed concern over King's arrest, Nixon refused.[27] King might have expected such pettiness. "I had known Nixon longer [than JFK]," King recalled in 1964. "And yet, when this moment came, it was like he had never heard of me." He deemed the vice president "a moral coward" for being "unwilling to take a courageous step and take a risk" for racial equality.[28] Given Kennedy's own tepid support of civil rights as senator and as president, perhaps he too was a moral coward. Yet King assessed correctly Nixon's reluctance to apply government power to attack racial injustice. Neither friend nor foe, he allowed political expediency to influence his public stance on civil rights.

As his relationship with King soured, Nixon wooed another African American icon, Jackie Robinson. As the first African American to play major league baseball, Robinson "graphically symbolized and personified the challenge to the vicious legacy and ideology of white supremacy."[29] "The colored fans applauded Jackie every time he wiggled his ears," quipped one black sportswriter.[30] Robinson did more than that. His base-stealing stirred fans of all races, who had not experienced such electricity since Ty Cobb had run the base paths for the Detroit Tigers in the 1920s.[31] After retiring from baseball in 1956, Robinson joined the Chock Full O' Nuts Coffee Company as an executive. He also wrote a column for the *New York Post*. So Nixon knew that the onetime Dodger was in a position to influence black opinion. Nixon perhaps reasoned that Robinson's Republican business background would make him more pragmatic and less exacting on civil rights than King. That assumption proved wrong.

Love of sports drew the vice president and Robinson together. A self-described "sports nut," Nixon conversed freely with athletes, starting with Robinson.[32] He first met the Brooklyn Dodger by chance, during the Republican National Convention of 1952. After congratulating him for hitting a home run that day, Nixon reminisced about the first time he had watched Robinson compete, in football. The man who had ridden the bench at Whittier College described how Robinson, playing halfback for UCLA, had sprinted for a long touchdown against Oregon. "While Robinson had undoubtedly met a lot of notables in his career," recalled an observer, "nevertheless I was sure there was one person he would never forget."[33] According to Brooklyn slugger Duke Snider, the vice president attended games at Ebbets Field and discussed baseball with Robinson.[34] Nixon and King never established such rapport. Civil rights was King's life, while this was not true of Nixon.

Robinson's triumph over racial prejudice probably reinforced the vice president's belief that discrimination was wrong. Nixon's private racist comments, in which he questioned the ability of blacks to compete with whites, did not prevent him from arguing that bias wasted talent. He knew that had baseball remained segregated, Robinson would have missed competing against some great players and white fans would have missed his home runs and stolen bases. Sallyanne Payton, one of the president's black aides, argued that white males of Nixon's generation often backed the aspirations of "exceptional individuals." They "carried a sense of injustice" about the memory of someone "they admired deeply" who was denied opportunities because of race. Robinson may have triggered such thoughts in Nixon because, despite his "conventional racist prejudice," Nixon "profoundly" respected the former Dodger.[35] President Nixon cited Robinson's example–that the first person to challenge a barrier must be "the best"–when he considered naming an African American woman to the federal bench.[36] His affinity for exceptional individuals reinforced Nixon's own racist belief that only a few blacks could succeed. Yet this theory helps to explain his support for fair employment and for minority businesses as well as his overtures to Robinson.

Robinson and Nixon became political partners. The baseball hero applauded the vice president for supporting the Civil Rights Act of 1957 and for opposing Governor Orval Faubus's obstruction of school desegregation in Little Rock. "Tell the Vice President," he informed Nixon's secretary, "it made us feel good to have [him] act like the kind of a man we need and we knew he was."[37] In Robinson's opinion, the vice president's travels to Asia and Africa had educated him about the concerns of "colored people."[38] As the 1960 presidential campaign approached, Robinson preferred Senator Hubert H. Humphrey, Democrat of Minnesota, but also spoke highly of Nixon. In one of his newspaper columns Robinson wrote "that many people whom I've talked with, whose first concern is civil rights, would not hesitate to support Vice President Nixon."[39] Through such statements he shrewdly encouraged leaders of both political parties to solicit black votes and back civil rights.

Robinson's praise rekindled Nixon's courtship. "While you disclaimed any pretensions toward being a political expert," he wrote Robinson, "it seems to me that you handled this subject with the same agility which you always show on the baseball diamond."[40] Fred Lowery, a staff member, urged Nixon to make a pitch for the ex-Dodger's support because he "is more or less considered sort of a God" among blacks.[41] The vice president agreed to a meeting, and Robinson left the encounter "more convinced [than] ever of the rightness of his support of Nixon."[42]

In wrapping up Robinson's endorsement, Nixon scored a coup over Kennedy. Robinson resented JFK's courtship of southern segregationists, especially Governor John Patterson of Alabama. Foreshadowing Nixon's own "national strategy," Kennedy pleaded that he had an obligation to listen to public officials from every region of the country. "You can't satisfy everybody," Robinson responded. "You're either for or against the practices that Patterson stands for."[43] After JFK named Senator Lyndon B. Johnson of Texas, the author of the jury trial amendment, as his running mate, Robinson threw up his arms in disgust. In September 1960 he left the *New York Post* to campaign for Nixon.[44]

Like Kennedy, Nixon learned that Robinson tolerated no detours on the path to racial equality. The former ballplayer resented Nixon's reluctance to campaign in Harlem. When the Republican nominee refused to second the pledge of his running mate, Henry Cabot Lodge, to name an African American to the cabinet, Robinson grew angrier. After Nixon declined to speak out for the jailed King, Robinson considered quitting the campaign.[45] Like King, he discovered that the vice president would not campaign for civil rights at the expense of white votes.

Because Nixon and Robinson had invested so much in their relationship, they parted gradually and somewhat reluctantly. In 1962 the former vice president congratulated Robinson on his election to baseball's Hall of Fame and sought Robinson's support in his bid for the California governorship.[46] The baseball hero consoled Nixon after he lost that election and announced his retirement from politics: "I hope that you will reconsider, Dick, because it is the great men people attack. You are good for politics; good for America."[47] Robinson turned away from the GOP, endorsing the Democratic nominees for president in 1964 and 1968.[48] Although he resented Nixon's catering to white conservatives, Robinson never recanted his earlier support of Nixon and offered to help the new president bridge the racial gap.[49] "I believe [Nixon] does have sincerity in many areas," Robinson wrote a friend in 1969, "but I believe his commitments are such [that] he has to be cautious."[50] Sadly, the president replied to Robinson through insipid form letters.[51]

Nixon's dealings with King and Robinson convinced him that civil rights advocates were self-centered, ungrateful, and fickle. That King and Robinson came to view the vice president in the same way failed to register with him. Nixon simply dismissed blacks as chronic Democrats. "As far as this particular vote is concerned," he told Eisenhower late in 1960, "it is a bought vote, and it is not bought by civil rights."[52] Expecting no political "payoff," President Nixon enforced civil rights with little fanfare. He courted black voters sporadically and wooed more likely supporters: whites in the South and in the suburbs.

Antagonism: Nixon versus the Integrationists

President Nixon's relations with other integrationist civil rights leaders proved chillier than his previous dealings with King and Robinson. African American leaders such as Roy Wilkins, Ralph Abernathy, and Clarence Mitchell resented, among other things, Nixon's "go-slow" policy on school desegregation and his southern strategy. They refused to credit the president with any advances in civil rights. Although neither side took into account the other's position, Nixon allowed minor scuffles to escalate into mutual suspicion, hyperbole, confrontation—and cold war.

It did not begin that way. There was a part of Nixon, admittedly small, that wanted to bridge racial divisions. On the advice of Leonard Garment, his in-house liberal, Nixon hosted a White House gala to honor jazz great Duke Ellington on his seventieth birthday, April 29, 1969. The evening sparkled with dancing and unforgettable music, making it the most carefree cultural event of Nixon's presidency. The soul singer Lou Rawls began with a blues number, "Goin' to Chicago"; Dizzy Gillespie played the trumpet; the president, seated at the piano, led the chorus of "Happy Birthday," then awarded the Medal of Freedom to "Edward Kennedy . . . Ellington."[53] After the Nixons bade their guests good night, around midnight, the East Room, like the old Cotton Club, began to swing. Rose Mary Woods, Nixon's secretary, danced with Ellington while Labor Secretary George P. Schultz paired up with the dancer Carmen de Lavallade. The old mansion rocked with the sound of jazz, leading one person to joke that the president might emerge pajama-clad to evict the partygoers.[54]

African Americans applauded Nixon's gesture. "He really made history tonight," the singer Mahalia Jackson said. "Nixon," one musician raved, "did something no one else has ever done—this is the first time an American black man was honored at the White House."[55] "America generally," opined *The Afro-American Voter*, would never "forget this precedent breaking honor to a good man."[56] As Nixon's relations with civil rights leaders deteriorated, he would renew his contacts with African American celebrities.

Nixon also tried to establish dialogue with civil rights leaders. He understood that many blacks had read his campaign rhetoric of "law and order" as an appeal to white backlash. Assuming the presidency after a era of mass protests and racial riots, Nixon had to enlist civil rights advocates in order to govern and "bring us together." After taking office, he asked Father Theodore Hesburgh, who favored racial integration, to chair the U.S. Commission on Civil Rights. "P[resident] met with Civil Rights Commission and came out all jazzed up," jotted chief of staff H. R. Haldeman. "Wants to make something of the Commission, and utilize its staff productively."[57] He also decided to meet with Wilkins and Abernathy.

Nixon had to make some hard sells. Weary after eleven years on the Civil Rights Commission, Hesburgh agreed to serve as chair for only one year, then urged the president to increase the commission's budget: "I know that I can count on your personal support in this effort."[58] Wilkins and Abernathy proved more skeptical. During the presidential campaign of 1968, Abernathy had endorsed Humphrey, while Wilkins had criticized Nixon's refusal to withhold federal funds from segregated schools. When the president-elect invited Wilkins to his inauguration, the NAACP chief declined. He later attended a White House dinner and sensed a "change in mood" from the days of LBJ: "Everything was stiff, formal, artificial." To break the ice, Nixon asked Wilkins to speak up "if I do anything wrong."[59] The NAACP chief took the president up on his offer.

Wilkins, in public, tried to sound hopeful. In a speech on January 28, 1969, the civil rights leader vowed to "work with any Administration, any Congress, any section of a political party or any president" to advance the cause of civil rights. Referring to the civil rights acts of 1964, 1965, and 1968, he argued that the movement's "greatest and most telling victories have come through bipartisan activity." Wilkins, moreover, found "more than mere hints" in Nixon's inaugural address that issues of civil rights, full employment, and improved housing would be high on the new president's agenda. "Where we are forced into the position of adversaries," he added, "we will press our views, in President

Nixon's own words, 'in peaceful competition . . . in enriching the life of man.'"[60] "Peaceful competition" was one of Nixon's euphemisms for the ongoing Soviet-American rivalry.

Nixon's second meeting with Wilkins, in the Oval Office, proved cordial. Familiar with the corridors of power, the NAACP chief mixed criticism with advice for the new administration. Wilkins expressed mild dismay with Health, Education, and Welfare Secretary Robert H. Finch for postponing desegregation deadlines in five southern school districts. He also conceded "that the President should be given a chance to work out his [own] programs and policies." Wilkins urged Nixon to place more blacks in federal jobs, enforce fair employment guidelines in firms with government contracts, and extend the Voting Rights Act. Since many of his aims coincided with Nixon's, the NAACP leader left the meeting "impressed with the President's knowledge and grasp of the[se] problems."[61] Yet unlike Wilkins's relationship with Johnson, his relations with Nixon did not develop into an alliance to advance specific civil rights measures.

Nixon's engagement with Abernathy, in May 1969, proved confrontational. The two men had different backgrounds, personalities, and philosophies. As a protest leader, Abernathy, unlike Wilkins, could not hide his contempt for practical politicians. At the beginning of the meeting, he rebuked Nixon and his cabinet for ignoring an SCLC drive to organize striking hospital workers in South Carolina. Abernathy then recited a wish list of new federal programs to enhance social welfare, achieve fair employment, and create jobs. His rhetoric waxed lofty and patronizing: "Let history record that this Administration, of which little was expected, was the one which made America truly keep its long-deterred promise to all of its citizens." "You are right," the president responded. "Any Administration owes justice to every American." Nixon argued that most of his cabinet had started out poor, all believed in opportunity, and they "really [were] *trying* to find answers." "Most of us haven't known the kind of poverty you have seen," Nixon concluded. "We don't want other Americans to know it."[62] Unlike Wilkins, Abernathy publicly denounced his meeting as "fruitless" and "disappointing."[63]

Each side interpreted this skirmish differently. Abernathy maintained that his constituency, poor and nonwhite, faced great challenges and required vigorous government support beyond Nixon's program of affirmative action, aid to black businesses, and modest increases in social spending.[64] Nixonians, pragmatic policy makers to the bone, dismissed Abernathy. "The poor deserve better," concluded Nixon's liberal speechwriter Raymond K. Price. "The Urban Affairs Council placed itself at [Abernathy's] disposal, prepared to discuss specifics, and he wasted its time with posturing, attitudinizing, sermonizing, and with pleading and wheedling directed not at the problems of poverty, but at the requirements of his own brand of confrontation politics."[65]

The president had expected Abernathy to blow off some steam for the benefit of other African Americans. During a White House meeting, Senate Minority Leader Everett M. Dirksen of Illinois recounted his own two-hour session with Abernathy and declared that he had "had enough." Nixon cynically described Abernathy as a "limited fellow" who "doesn't have much" and was only "after dough."[66] The civil rights movement, he expounded, "is badly split in a leadership fight between CORE [Congress of Racial Equality], Whitney Young [of the National Urban League], Mrs. King, Rev. Abernathy and others."[67] But Nixon later projected Abernathy's contentiousness onto African Americans in general, becoming "pretty fed up with blacks and their hopeless attitude."[68]

The showdown with Abernathy reinforced Nixon's opinion that civil rights leaders preferred confrontation to compromise, and it undermined Nixon's liberal aides who wanted the president to confer with blacks. Urban affairs chief Daniel P. Moynihan, the meeting's architect, apologized for Abernathy's "unconscionable" behavior.[69] Nixon reassured his beet-faced assistant, "Moynihan—I thought *you were the rude one!*"[70] The tussle with Abernathy strengthened White House advisers who opposed engagements with African American leaders. "Abernathy went out and stabbed us on TV," Haldeman wrote. "Proved again there's no use dealing honestly with these people. They obviously want confrontation, not solutions."[71] "For the next four years," remembered domestic policy chief John D. Ehrlichman, "anyone who suggested that the President meet with a group of blacks could expect to hear about Moynihan's meeting with Ralph Abernathy."[72]

The Abernathy meeting influenced the president's flawed public posture on civil rights. "The problem as I see it," Nixon told Moynihan, "is that [blacks] don't think that I care. We must demonstrate to them we *do* care by our actions and not just by our words."[73] This position evolved into a low-key "deeds not words" approach which inhibited the president from selling his programs for affirmative action and minority business enterprise. It also prevented him from reassuring blacks that his "national" voting rights bill and his school desegregation policy, stressing lawsuits over withdrawal of funds, did not involve retreats. Although the "deeds over words" formula provided Nixon with cover to court white southerners, it carried a price.[74] Without words of support, many blacks assumed that Nixon had either moved backwards or was standing still on civil rights enforcement.

Few African Americans praised Nixon. In July 1969 Carl Rowan, an LBJ associate turned columnist, puzzled over the "atmosphere of estrangement" between the White House and African Americans. Rowan lauded Nixon for enforcing school desegregation and fair housing in Chicago: "It all suggests that Nixon isn't trying to move the country backwards in the field of race relations. It suggests that he isn't even the pussyfooter that some people suspected." The columnist blamed the president's unpopularity on black antipathy toward the GOP and on Nixon's overtures to white southerners. Rowan concluded that "where Mr. Nixon is entitled to the applause of the black community, he ought to get it."[75] Civil rights leaders ignored such advice.

Throughout 1969 the downward spiral continued; black leaders criticized Nixon's policies, the president's public relations missteps mounted, and African American disillusionment grew. Wilkins scorched the administration for "scrapping" school desegregation guidelines and turning the "clock back" by failing to renew the Voting Rights Act.[76] Clarence Mitchell, legislative tactician for the Leadership Conference on Civil Rights, an NAACP-affiliated group, lobbied against Nixon's voting rights bill and his nomination of conservative southern judges to the Supreme Court.[77] After Nixon salvaged the Philadelphia Plan, Dr. John A. Morsell, assistant executive director of the NAACP, still considered the president's civil rights record "a mixed bag" with "more negative aspects than positive aspects."[78]

The president claimed, unconvincingly, that his persona prevented his making a stronger appeal to civil rights leaders. Nixon believed that "Presidents who are not strong do not win and, more important, cannot lead the country." This would-be "tough guy" once forbade public relations aides from "making me appear [to be] something I am not, making me soft, benign."[79] His right-wing advisers played to such sentiments. "We can get RN to give an impassioned pro–Civil Rights speech, tearing into Southern and Northern reaction, and with tears running down his cheeks, sing 'We Shall Overcome,'" argued the speechwriter Patrick J. Buchanan. "But that is not RN's style."[80] These arguments were self-serving. During conversations with King and Robinson, Nixon had expressed commitment to racial equality. If the president had given a pro–civil rights speech, it might have undermined his appeals to conservative white southerners, which Buchanan encouraged.

Nixon's cold war with the integrationists stemmed from philosophical differences as well as poor "PR." Like Abernathy, Wilkins and Clarence Mitchell believed that civil rights policy entailed something beyond creating jobs. "Efforts to foster small ghetto business or tax incentives that encourage industry to help employ the poor," declared the Leadership Conference, "must be reluctantly accepted for what they are–sincere but inadequate attempts to cope with severe problems."[81] The group also warned of a crisis as "grave" as the Civil War if the government refused to integrate schools and neighborhoods promptly.[82] Nixon favored economic opportunity over integration and showed no sensitivity for the other argument. In fact, he expressed interest in a constitutional amendment to ban busing: "We should bite the bullet now and hard, if it's called racism, so be it!"[83]

In truth, Nixon and the integrationists often differed over the means and degree of change. Beneath his racially divisive rhetoric, the president sought to slow, not halt, desegregation of southern schools. "Man, that Nixon's really cracked down," remarked Charles Evers, an NAACP leader in Mississippi, in 1970. "There's not a school in this state that some blacks aren't in."[84] Yet Evers was almost the only African American leader to applaud Nixon. Perhaps other black leaders believed that they needed to criticize the president to appease their followers. More likely, civil rights leaders, accustomed to reproaching Nixon, found it difficult to reverse course. During an off-the-record interview, the journalist Richard L. Wilson asked the president "when it would dawn on Negro leaders that his policies really are promoting desegregation." Nixon sighed, "Maybe they simply didn't want to admit that."[85]

Both civil rights leaders and Nixon contributed to this cold war. Having seen the federal government enact civil rights legislation and declare war on poverty, many African American leaders unrealistically wanted Nixon to govern as they imagined a liberal would, attacking segregation and poverty with the full force of the national government. They should have known that moderate Republicans were more reluctant to wield federal power than liberal Democrats. Even Lyndon Johnson proved less than vigorous in enforcing school desegregation and affirmative action. Within this context, Nixon's policies were not entirely negative, as both Rowan and Evers noted.

Yet the president was more responsible for this cold war. As the nation's leader, Nixon had a duty to listen to all groups and rise above his critics. This seasoned politician should have known that protest leaders often demand rapid change and ignored their rhetoric. Instead the president who had promised an "open" administration in his inaugural address acted like a spurned suitor and gave up courting civil rights leaders. Nixon thus missed a chance to cooperate with them in areas, such as fair employment, where they agreed with him. And it is hard to believe that a presidential appeal for racial justice would not have eased tensions to at least some degree.

In 1970 Nixon became even more discouraged with African American criticism and withdrew further from addressing civil rights. He thought about publicizing the Philadelphia Plan to quiet his critics, but then took a "very low key" stance on civil rights in his State of the Union address.[86] After reading of black leaders "publicly charging us with genocide," the president scrawled, "It is an almost hopeless holding action at best. Let's limit our public actions and $ to the least we can get by with."[87] In fact, Nixon would increase funding of civil rights enforcement and then rail against African American leaders in private. He rejected a proposal to designate King's birthday a national holiday with the words *"No Never."*[88] "Black leaders in the U.S. do not have great confidence in the Nixon Administration," declared the diplomat Ralph J. Bunche. "I share this view."[89]

Haldeman, who oversaw scheduling and "PR," no doubt influenced Nixon's low profile on civil rights. After Charles Evers called liberal

Democrats "the black man's main hope" to fight racism, Haldeman noted that such statements prove "we have *nothing* to gain by cooperating" with such leaders.[90] The former advertising executive wondered how "we can possibly be expected to accomplish anything when we are constantly under black attack & are thus forced *away* from positive steps."[91] Rather than force the president away from "positive steps," African American criticism perhaps pushed him to enforce civil rights when he saw little political reward in doing so.

Members of the Commission on Civil Rights also expressed dissatisfaction with Nixon's leadership. On Christmas Eve 1969, Howard A. Glickstein, the commission's staff director, alerted Hesburgh to America's "deep and serious moral crisis." He told the Notre Dame president, "You have the potential to become the moral leader of this country. It does not appear that the President is going to provide that leadership."[92] Believing that the administration was not integrating schools fast enough, Hesburgh decided to remain as chair of the commission.[93]

During 1970, Nixon's civil rights posture acquired a name: "benign neglect." In a memorandum to the president, Moynihan argued that the Johnson administration's policies had struck down discrimination and raised black incomes. Yet African Americans remained alienated from "the system." "The time may have come when the issue of race could benefit from a period of 'benign neglect,'" Moynihan contended. "We may need a period in which Negro progress continues and racial rhetoric fades." "I agree," Nixon jotted.[94] One wonders how any policy of "neglect" could be "benign" if blacks felt as alienated as Moynihan claimed.

Moynihan's memorandum provoked more controversy. James Farmer, the former leader of CORE who worked for Finch at HEW, leaked this "outrageous" document to the press.[95] "The Moynihan memorandum," opined the *New York Times,* "is cold comfort for Negroes and whites alike who have watched the low–not to say disappearing–profile of the Administration in several areas of civil rights."[96] Moynihan protested that the phrase "benign neglect" was neutral, coming from a 130-year-old report on British policy toward Canada. In Nixon's opinion, reporters had given Moynihan a "bad rap."[97] Neither Moynihan nor the president realized that they implicitly had compared civil rights policy to British colonialism.

Moynihan gave a name to what had become since 1965 the standard presidential posture on civil rights. White discontent over the Watts riot in August 1965 had forced President Johnson "to mute his public commitment to black rights."[98] In 1966, LBJ considered releasing a message on civil rights when Congress was out of session. "Who wants more coverage?" he asked an aide.[99] But Johnson's "benign neglect" differed from Nixon's. LBJ did not give his retreat a name that sounded like a conscious effort to ignore civil rights. Besides, Johnson enjoyed greater confidence among African Americans, since he had secured passage of the Civil Rights Act of 1964 and the Voting Rights Act of 1965.

The flap over "benign neglect" forced Nixon to take steps to appease the integrationists. In March 1970 he released a statement reiterating his support for school desegregation without mandatory busing. The president ordered Ehrlichman to prepare a "fact sheet" listing the administration's achievements in civil rights. "I believe," Nixon scribbled, "the record is impressive on things done (Phil. Plan etc.) & things advocated (Family Assistance [Plan])."[100] He later told aides it was "OK" to invite Wilkins to the Oval Office, "if he wants to come in."[101] Although Nixon possessed a knack for offending civil rights leaders, he feared that breaking off relations would provoke even more criticism.

Civil rights leaders dismissed the president's gestures. The Leadership Conference rejected Nixon's policy of fighting de jure segregation in the South but not de facto segregation in the North.[102] While Nixon's meeting with Wilkins seemed cordial, the NAACP chief blasted the president one month later: "The [less] said about [Nixon] the better–if it were not for many other dedicated people working in government, the Nixon policies would make us very, very depressed."[103] "The general feeling in the black community," noted Arthur Fletcher, a Labor Department official, "was that the Administration doesn't give a damn." James Farmer declared the racial climate "worse than it had been at any time since the early 1960s."[104]

On civil rights, black leaders preferred personal appeals to legalistic statements. In mid-1970, Stephen G. Spottswood of the NAACP labeled the Nixon administration "anti-Negro."[105] In a public letter, Garment defended the president for adopting the Philadelphia Plan, proposing funds to desegregate schools, and signing a Voting Rights

Act covering the entire nation.[106] Spottswood replied that the administration had dragged its feet on desegregation and voting rights and that
the Philadelphia Plan had been "a flat failure."[107] Although the critique
came before the administration desegregated a record number of
schools, in autumn 1970, and before the Philadelphia Plan yielded results, Spottswood rightly identified Nixon's vacillation. His "anti-
Negro" remark underscored the movement's sense of alienation; since
the Nixonians controlled the government, denouncing their policies
was one of the few weapons remaining to civil rights leaders.

Such rebukes put Nixon's liberal advisers on the defensive, hindering
any rapprochement. Garment labeled Spottswood's "anti-Negro" remark "self-destructive slander," and Moynihan privately called it an "act
of idiocy."[108] "You have every right," Moynihan told the president, "to
be bitter at [this] destructive denunciation of you." Nixon replied, *Pat I
understand.*[109] So did the NAACP, belatedly. "If we knock [the admin-
istration] regardless of what they do," declared an NAACP staffer in
1971, "what incentive will they have for doing anything."[110]

As the elections of 1970 approached, Nixon made fewer overtures to
civil rights leaders. "We can't win over our enemies—youth, black, Jew,"
he explained.[111] The president ruled out conferences with Jewish leaders
and sanctioned meetings with blacks only "to show we care."[112] He told
Haldeman to invite just one African American to each White House dinner.[113] And Nixon displayed a growing immunity to black criticism. After
Clarence Mitchell called Nixon the weakest post–World War II president
on civil rights and the first to generate "general uneasiness" among blacks,
the president sighed, "Here he goes again."[114]

Nixon tolerated less dissent from integrationists within the government. Beginning in 1970, the Commission on Civil Rights cooperated
with the Leadership Conference on Civil Rights to fight anti-busing
legislation. "Although the Commission has always maintained active liaison with private civil rights organizations," Glickstein noted, "in the
past year this activity has taken on more significance."[115] When the
agency prepared a study criticizing the government's enforcement of
civil rights, Garment pressed Hesburgh to withhold it. He refused, arguing that any delay would undermine the panel's independence.[116]
After the 1970 elections, Nixon considered replacing Hesburgh and finally did so after his own reelection in 1972.[117] Although the new chair,

Arthur S. Flemming, never became a White House "errand boy," the removal of Hesburgh had compromised the commission.[118]

Nixon's showdown with Hesburgh was only one battle in his cold war with integrationists. While some clashes were inevitable, and civil rights leaders also heightened tensions, the nation's leader lacked magnanimity, to say the least. After reading that few urban blacks looked to leadership from Senator Edward W. Brooke, an African American Republican from Massachusetts, Nixon scribbled that Brooke was "too responsible for them–This shows why they talk ok in private and lash out in public."[119] The president increasingly shunned integrationist leaders and sought a "responsible" African American leadership.

Détente: The Black Silent Majority and the Open Door

Nixon cultivated a moderate alternative to the established, liberal civil rights leadership. The president wooed upwardly mobile blacks under his "open door policy," a cliché straight out of American diplomatic history. But such gestures and slogans did little to enhance Nixon's standing among African Americans.

Nixon's advisers urged him to court blacks who favored his policies. Robert J. Brown, an African American, pressed him to offer "positive reinforcement" to "the many black people who share the aspirations of white people for education and success." Brown advised the president to build on his minority business program by aiding historically African American universities as well as black wage earners, working mothers, and students.[120] In his "benign neglect" memorandum, Moynihan identified a "silent black majority." "It is mostly working class," he argued. "It is politically moderate (on issues other than racial equality) and shares most of the concerns of its white counterpart . . . The more recognition we can give to it, the better off we all shall be."[121] Charles V. Hamilton, an African American political scientist, saw members of this "silent Black majority" as neither "Uncle Toms nor militants." Rather, they aspired to financial security, wanted their children to attend college, and exhibited a "patriotic, law-abiding, tax-paying 'this is my country too' sense."[122] The term "silent Black majority" was really a misnomer. By 1969 the black middle class constituted a tiny fraction of one minority group.

Nixon thought that appealing to African American ministers and "Brown's negro businessmen–bankers–Elks" might win him some votes. He circled Moynihan's reference to "silent black majority" and wrote, "Let's poll this & then go after the probably 30% who *are potentially on our side*–Garment *et al.* are directing our appeal to the wrong groups (both in case of negroes & whites)."[123] With Nixon's blessing, black conservatives launched the "Black Silent Majority Committee."[124] This middle-/working-class group espoused "constitutional government, law, order, and justice." It opposed "revolutionaries" and vowed to "break the 'welfare-liberalism' stranglehold that has bound too many blacks for too long."[125] Although the Washington-based committee established chapters in all fifty states, its vague, rather negative agenda drew little support outside the GOP.[126]

During 1970, Nixon saw the "silent Black majority" as the only African American constituency worthy of his attention. As pragmatic, self-made men, Nixonians shared the values of upwardly mobile blacks. The president's populist instincts also led him to embrace middle-class blacks: "Gov't & press impose on Negroes a l[eader]ship they don't want. We must *not* play to that."[127] To Nixon, the middle class was "the traditional power structure of the Black community," and courting it enabled him to ease his conscience.[128] "[The president] broods frequently over problem of how we communicate with young and blacks," Haldeman wrote in his diary. "It's really not possible, except with Uncle Toms, and we should work on them and forget [the] militants."[129] Practicing *Realpolitik,* Nixon would exploit divisions within the black community. "[He is] going again on his determination not to play to blacks and professional civil righters," Haldeman noted. "Is convinced we gain nothing . . . Key is to limit all our support and communication to the good blacks and totally ignore the militants."[130] From Haldeman's diary, it remains unclear whether Nixon or Haldeman described the moderates as "Uncle Toms." Still, the use of such terms showed a strain of racist paternalism within this White House.

Cultivating the black silent majority was more than a sinister attempt to divide African Americans. In 1970 a group of Nixon's liberal advisers, including Garment, Fletcher, and Farmer, concluded that "the traditional black leadership had been created by Democratic Administrations and would never embrace a Republican Administration." They urged the administration to "look to its own ranks for potential new leaders for the black community."[131] Although they overestimated the partisanship of civil rights leaders such as Wilkins, the criticism leveled at the White House by integrationists encouraged Nixon to seek an alternative black leadership.

Timing influenced Nixon's courtship of "moderate" African Americans. Before releasing his school desegregation statement in 1970, the president solicited input from black administration officials.[132] Partly to calm the uproar over Moynihan's "benign neglect" memorandum, Nixon visited with a delegation of African American ministers.[133] To offset Spottswood's charge that the administration was "anti-Negro," Nixon conferred with members of the National Insurance Association, an African American group. Yet he also talked with this organization because White House officials deemed it "constructive" and appreciative of the president's minority business policy.[134] Similarly, Nixon also agreed to meet with a group of African American doctors.[135]

Since Nixon and middle-class blacks possessed similar aims, their meetings ran smoothly. The president stretched his session with black administration officials to an hour and a half and found it "pretty productive."[136] Nixon appointed Robert Brown as liaison to the National Insurance Association and vowed to help this organization of black businessmen enhance African American identity and self-respect and strengthen black colleges and businesses.[137] During his meeting with black ministers, the president pledged funds for charitable and job-training projects. "I don't want any excuses on this," he told Ehrlichman, "even if you have to find the money in the White House emergency fund." Nixon wanted to give the ministers money that the Office of Economic Opportunity normally "wasted." "I realize that they will take some cream off the top too," he added with characteristic cynicism, "but probably not quite as much." The president ordered Ehrlichman to "send a $100 contribution from me; ask them that it be kept anonymous, in accordance with our usual policy."[138] Since Nixon had contributed to the United Negro College Fund, he was clearly capable of helping out black groups whose goals he deemed worthy.

Meetings with African American moderates helped soothe the president's bitterness. After conferring with black ministers, Nixon informed Haldeman that "[we] have to have Negroes" at White House events.

"Always have blacks–at least two," he commanded. To build up a middle-class black leadership, the president wanted to cultivate EEOC chair William H. Brown III, who shared his goal of expanding economic opportunities for minorities.[139]

Nixon's alternative African American leadership did not include Black Power advocates. The president, with cause, viewed young urban black leaders as prone to incite violence. In 1970 Eldridge Cleaver of the Black Panther Party (BPP) vowed to "cause destruction, to drag this decadent system of capitalism over the cliff."[140] Influenced by such statements, Nixon saw the Panthers as enemies of the republic and repressed them with vengeance. He continued Johnson's policy of using the FBI to monitor and harass the Black Panthers.[141] "The FBI," reported Tom Charles Huston, a White House aide, in 1969, "correctly views the BPP as the most serious internal security threat in the country today."[142] After reading that Leonard Bernstein's wife had thrown a party to raise money for the Panthers, Nixon privately condemned "the complete decadence of the American 'upper' class intellectual elite."[143]

Nixon's aversion to the Black Panthers probably prejudiced him against less militant Black Power leaders, such as Floyd McKissick of CORE. McKissick's agenda meshed with Nixon's; the former once said, "If a man is broke and hungry, he needs bread and money, not [to] sit down beside a white man."[144] But since McKissick opposed the president's policy in Vietnam, he received only a telephone call from Moynihan and a presidential handshake during the election of 1972.[145]

During 1970, Nixon's African American support barely held steady. Gallup Polls between March and June showed that only 29 percent of blacks approved of the president's job performance. By year's end, that figure had not changed.[146] To make matters worse, the GOP, espousing a racially divisive "law and order" message, had scored few gains in the elections of 1970. Looking to the next presidential contest, a Harris Poll of likely voters put Senator Edmund S. Muskie, Democrat of Maine, ahead of Nixon by 6 percentage points. Another poll had the two men in a dead heat.[147] In an earlier poll, blacks favored Muskie to Nixon by 73 percent to 17 percent.[148]

As a result, Nixon proclaimed an "open door policy." He explained to GOP leaders, "I would like the Republican party to be the party of the open door, a party with its doors open to all people of all races and all parties."[149] Nixon approved meetings with groups, such as young people and blacks, whom he earlier had dismissed as "enemies."[150] The open door policy sought to win back moderate Republicans more than minorities; the president told aides, "[We] won't [win] black or youth votes but must convince others that we are willing to communicate."[151] Nixon's latest slogan, which acknowledged that the GOP had not always practiced openness, yielded no significant returns.

Nixon opened his door to blacks outside the civil rights leadership. He considered naming Edward Brooke, the only African American U.S. senator, to the Supreme Court,[152] and he sought Brooke's support "to knock down the argument of many of our Negro friends who might consider some facets of the revenue sharing plan to be anti-Black."[153] The president revisited an earlier strategy and courted black celebrities. In mid-1970 he named Pearl Bailey, star of Broadway's *Hello, Dolly!* and champion of poor children, his "Ambassador of Love." In 1970 the vivacious singer, who sometimes performed at the White House, chatted with Nixon about the challenges facing young people. The president gave Bailey the Heart-of-the-Year Award, and reappointed her Ambassador of Love with diplomatic license plates.[154] The vocalist accepted, but requested a new title, "Roving Ambassador of Love," because, as she put it, "Honey, I get around a lot."[155]

Nixon's "open door" policy fostered détente with liberal African American leaders, such as the Congressional Black Caucus. Nine black representatives, all Democrats, had formed the caucus in response to the president's evasiveness on civil rights. When these representatives had asked to meet with Nixon in 1970, he refused, saying that he would see them as members of Congress but not as a racial caucus.[156] The caucus retaliated by boycotting the president's State of the Union address in 1971.[157] Nixon's hair-splitting made no sense, for he had met with other African American groups, and his minority business program recognized the need for separate black institutions. The president no doubt feared that a meeting with the Black Caucus would turn quarrelsome, like his encounter with Abernathy. Such pettiness again blinded Nixon to a politically more astute course.

Under the open door policy, Nixon finally met with the Congressional Black Caucus in March 1971. Stiff and formal, the encounter resembled a peace conference between two adversaries. The caucus presented Nixon with sixty recommendations running from welfare reform to increased enforcement of civil rights laws to expediting American withdrawal from Indochina.[158] Nixon formed a White House panel to answer them. Garment, who worked on the response, found agreement in aims, some differences in funding, and disagreement on just eight issues, including busing. "To borrow a phrase from diplomacy: This has been a useful exchange," he concluded.[159] Members of the Black Caucus agreed. The White House response, a 115-page laundry list of Nixon's achievements in civil rights, failed to move them.[160] Yet, as Representative William L. Clay, Democrat of Missouri, noted, "At least we are at the point where we can discuss the areas of disagreement between us."[161]

Nixon also made overtures to Whitney Young of the National Urban League. During the president's first two years in office, relations with Young remained icy. Nixon met with Young late in 1968 and considered him for a cabinet post. Their relationship quickly cooled when the Urban League chief began to attack the president's evasiveness on civil rights.[162] "I think Young may have drawn the sword to go all the way to get King's mantle and . . . to satisfy the militants," Nixon reckoned.[163] When a citizen suggested inviting the Urban League leader to the White House, the president instructed Ehrlichman to "*ask* [*Young*] *warmly* . . . but don't do it."[164] Young claimed that he scolded the government to prod it to act, but that reasoning failed to sway Nixon. The president considered asking the Urban League's contributors to "cut off" funding if Young did not soften his tone.[165]

Such skulduggery overlooked Young's own moderation and pragmatism. As early as 1960, Young had stressed the importance of self-help and entrepreneurship in building African American communities. In 1968 he launched the "New Thrust," a program to funnel Urban League resources into ghetto areas.[166] Sterling Tucker, the program's director, wanted to transcend the debate between integrationists and separatists. He predicted that there would be "segregated black ghettos in the major cities of the United States for many years to come, and the real question was how one should go about developing better education and other opportunities in the ghettos."[167] Young's New Thrust promoted "ghetto power" by "concentrating our resources" within central cities while "at the same time holding fast to our commitment to integration."[168]

An agenda of self-help, economic opportunity, and ghetto power sounded quite Nixonian. But the Urban League needed cash to carry out it out. In 1970 Young sent out peace feelers, urging blacks to work with the administration when possible.[169] Under the open door policy, Nixon decided to meet with Young.

Arranged by Garment, the conference with Young, in December 1970, brought out the president's best side. Nixon praised both the Urban League and its leader. He asked if any of his cabinet officers had visited the League's national headquarters, then added, "I have and I encourage you all to do the same."[170] After describing the Urban League's financial woes, Young noted, "Maybe we will have to get a new President." "You mean," Nixon quipped, "a new president of the Urban League."[171] As in his relations with black ministers, the president hoped to use the Urban League to bypass the government's social service and job-training bureaucracy, which he deemed wasteful. Nixon promised to disburse government contracts, research grants, and manpower training subsidies to the Urban League, and named Garment as liaison to the organization.[172] He closed the meeting with a tribute: "What's good for the Urban League is good for America."[173] "It sure helps to go to the top," replied one Urban League staff member.[174] "The President was really great," remembered Bradley H. Patterson, Jr., Garment's assistant.[175]

Nixon and Young planted the seeds of a partnership. "I was greatly encouraged," Young wrote the president, "by your obvious concern and interest, and by the positive leadership which you demonstrated in the meeting."[176] Such flattery cannot be taken at face value, of course. Yet Nixon backed up his promises with dollars. After the conference, he telephoned Young to update him on the funds' status.[177] The president then urged aides to publicize these grants because "we have been doing good things in this field for 2 years—with no credit."[178]

The Young episode, like the meeting with black ministers and unlike the Abernathy imbroglio, acted as a tonic on Nixon. The president took seriously Young's advice to name black judges to federal courts in the South, telling Ehrlichman that "we do need some appointments of this type."[179] He even softened his stance toward a fallen civil rights hero. In January 1971 Nixon decided to spread the word that he would sign a bill designating King's birthday a national holiday.[180] The president incorrectly guessed that Congress was about to pass such a measure by wide margins. Whatever his motivation, Nixon's position on a King holiday had changed after the meeting with Young.

After Young died, in 1971, Nixon took an unprecedented step and spoke at his graveside. The president wrote the eulogy and clearly saw himself in Young: "He was a complex man, and he understood the complexities of the society in which he lived . . . Whitney Young will be remembered as a doer, not a talker."[181] Considerations of political expediency were never far from Nixon's good deeds; he ordered aides to send copies of his eulogy to black leaders.[182] African Americans applauded the president. "He could not have spoken so movingly of Whitney Young's career as a civil rights leader," opined the *Chicago Defender,* "unless he too had a vital, personal stake in the struggle for equality."[183] Such words recalled the president's gestures toward Ellington and Bailey and echoed earlier praise by King, Robinson, and Young.

The partnership with the Urban League flowered, thanks to Garment, Ehrlichman, and budget director George P. Shultz. Garment and Shultz had scraped together $21 million worth of federal subsidies for the Urban League. According to Arnold R. Weber, Shultz's deputy, these efforts had impressed the League's leadership, making a "follow-up" meeting unnecessary.[184] As Garment, Ehrlichman, and Shultz continued to pump money into the Urban League, Vernon Jordan, Young's successor, thanked them privately. "He explained," Ehrlichman recalled, "that he'd lose his credibility with his constituency if he openly praised the Nixon Administration."[185] Jordan often warned Garment and Ehrlichman when he planned to attack the president.[186] Nixon accepted this underhanded arrangement partly because he was a political realist who understood Jordan's dilemma. Besides, the president wanted "to work w/UL" because he now deemed its leaders "responsible."[187] Two years into his presidency, Nixon decided to overlook the civil rights movement's internal politics and its rhetorical sallies. By 1972 Ehrlichman could remark, "We have a good record with the Urban League in terms of our co-partnership."[188]

Nixon's rapprochement with the Urban League did not mean that he had deserted his southern and suburban strategies. As the election of 1972 approached, the president reckoned that African Americans would vote Democratic and began to slam shut his open door. In 1971 Nixon, goaded by Haldeman and Buchanan, considered financing an independent African American presidential candidate to divide the opposition.[189] In contrast, Ehrlichman's aides, especially Sallyanne Payton, recommended greater attention to blacks. "I see," Payton wrote, "the key to the black vote as a vigorous and visible economic development strategy coupled with the use of credible allies in the black community."[190]

Nixon eventually pursued a watered-down, politically safe version of Payton's strategy. He again secured endorsements from African American celebrities, including the singers James Brown and Sammy Davis, Jr., and the football players Jim Brown and Gale Sayers.[191] Nixon's campaign also released a booklet emphasizing the president's "deeds not words" approach to civil rights.[192] Mostly, Nixon directed his appeals to white voters in the South and in the suburbs by blasting court-ordered busing.

Such tactics earned Nixon few African American votes. With the possible exception of James Brown, who sang "Say it loud–I'm black and I'm proud," none of the black celebrities endorsing the president possessed the influence of a Jackie Robinson. Georgia state representative Julian Bond, an African American, denounced them as "political prostitutes."[193] One wonders if anyone read the president's campaign brochure on blacks, which was only a tad splashier than earlier White House "fact sheets." On election day, Nixon took just 13 percent of the African American vote, one percentage point higher than his showing in 1968.[194] The problem of how to communicate with blacks dogged the president into his second term. "He feels," Haldeman wrote in 1973, "that there is a need for us to show them that we love them in some way."[195] Biting and sarcastic in his remarks about blacks, Haldeman was not a good influence on Nixon.

In pursuing détente with moderate African Americans, Nixon failed to erase his symbolic appeals to white backlash. Had the president stressed the open door policy at the outset, he might have softened black criticism. Since Nixon seldom manned the front lines of civil rights battles, and his public relations on civil rights proved flawed, he paid the price with black voters.

A Legacy of Racial Polarization

The frequent sniping between Nixon's White House and civil rights leaders was both ironic and sterile. The president who deplored the "inflated rhetoric" of the 1960s adopted tactics that seemed calculated to provoke civil rights advocates.[196] Yet Nixon's much-discussed civil rights "retreat" involved words more than deeds. By the same token, Nixon's predecessors usually promised more than they could deliver on civil rights.

Nixon's cold war with civil rights leaders cast a pall over race relations in three respects. First, the president's distance encouraged a "government-in-exile" mentality among some black groups. The Congressional Black Caucus, formed in response to Nixon's evasions, pressed "a continuous black agenda" which was quite liberal.[197] Unlike established civil rights organizations such as the NAACP, the caucus has ventured beyond "rights issues" into social policy, gun control, and raising the minimum wage. It advanced alternatives to Republican and Democratic fiscal policy, and, beginning in 1986, annually proposed its own federal budget of higher taxes and greater funding of social programs.[198]

The Black Caucus's agenda has bedeviled Nixon's successors. Gerald R. Ford met with members of the caucus and impressed them with his easygoing manner. Yet they remained wary of Ford's cuts in domestic programs.[199] Expecting more from Jimmy Carter, the caucus came to dislike the Democrat's fiscal conservatism and his tepid support for the Humphrey-Hawkins full employment bill. A member of the caucus once stalked out of a meeting with Carter. During the same conference, Representative Parren J. Mitchell, Democrat of Maryland, and Vice President Walter F. Mondale, a liberal on civil rights, engaged in a shouting match.[200] In a way, both Carter and Nixon fell victim to the adversarial relationship between liberal activists who in the name of morality asked for much government support, and moderate, pragmatic politicians who never offered enough.

Second, Nixon's "southern strategy," however symbolic and fleeting, helped lay the foundation for the Republican Party's race-based political agenda. President Ronald Reagan and his successor, George Bush, built on Nixon's strong showing among southern whites, suburbanites, and blue-collar workers.[201] They ignored African American voters, except for a small band of black conservatives. Not all Republicans pursued this strategy with equal vigor. Ford conferred with civil rights leaders and proclaimed his own "open door policy."[202] But since Ford opposed busing and accomplished little in civil rights, he took just 15 percent of the black vote in 1976, only 2 percentage points better than Nixon in 1972.[203] Since weaning African Americans away from the Democratic Party required considerable effort in terms of deeds and words, GOP standard-bearers, until George W. Bush in 2000, remained content to march under the banner of an overwhelmingly white party. Interestingly, despite his efforts, the younger Bush fared no better with African American voters.

Third, Nixon's successors more or less followed his example and declined to address civil rights in a major speech. Ford's open door policy encompassed gestures and meetings with African Americans, not high-profile speeches. Carter exceeded Ford (and all previous presidents) in appointing blacks to federal offices but voiced no "highly visible public message" on civil rights.[204] Reagan limited himself to stories of black heroism that came from Hollywood scripts rather than history books. Bush inflamed racial tensions during the presidential election of 1988 when his television spots tied Democratic nominee Michael Dukakis to Willie Horton, an African American convicted of rape. In 1992 Democratic presidential nominee Bill Clinton's most memorable speech on race attacked a black rap singer, Sister Souljah, for urging violence against white people.[205] Yet Clinton became more vocal on civil rights, invoking King's memory in his second inaugural address.

These developments cannot be attributed to Nixon alone. Each president selected his own role models. In exercising leadership, any of Nixon's successors could have looked to JFK's stirring (albeit belated) address on civil rights in 1963 or to LBJ's eloquent appeal for voting rights in 1965. Cowardice and racism, whether conscious or unconscious, partly explained why presidents sidestepped civil rights. The dilemma of racial problems was another factor. After Congress passed the civil rights acts of 1964 and 1965 to end discrimination, racial equality became entwined with questions of how to implement the law, how to close the economic gap between the races, and how to eliminate prejudice. With hundreds of possible solutions, presidents have found it daunting to rally citizens behind one course of action.

During the 1980s and 1990s, events took a turn for the worse. Presidents Reagan and Bush undermined reforms, such as affirmative action, that the Nixonians had put in place.[206] In so doing, they offered minorities less in the way of both deeds and words. The Nixon administration, whatever its shortcomings (and they were manifold), never pursued such a wholesale retreat.

Nixon understood the challenges of his time and opted for what he thought was an easy, politically safe posture, "deeds not words." He discovered that civil rights leaders wanted not just deeds *and* words, but *their* deeds and *their* words. Frustrated, the president largely accepted America's racial polarization and became more selective in choosing which African Americans he would court. Yet there remained a part of Nixon that wanted to solve problems and transcend the old civil rights debates. He would do that by addressing the concerns of other minorities, such as Native Americans.

7

Challenges and Opportunities:
Native American Policy

During the 1970s, Richard M. Nixon's Native American policy evoked fulsome praise and sporadic criticism. Elected tribal leaders, who represented reservation Indians and enjoyed support from the Bureau of Indian Affairs (BIA), applauded his efforts to replace a policy of assimilation with one of tribal self-determination. The Navajo leader Peter MacDonald, a Republican, hailed Nixon as "the Abraham Lincoln of the Indian people."[1] Yet non-elected urban militants not tied to the BIA denounced the whole federal setup. "The so-called self-determination policy of the federal government," complained Russell Means, a leader of the American Indian Movement (AIM), "was designed and intended to bolster rather than dismantle the whole structure of BIA colonialism."[2]

To Nixon, Native Americans were a "safe" minority to help. Because the president was dealing with the Indian movement during its inception, Native Americans, unlike African Americans, proved responsive to gestures from him. Since Indians numbered fewer than 1 million, their problems seemed more manageable than those of blacks. There was popular sympathy for Indian rights, at least at first, and unlike many African American leaders, who preferred integration, Native Americans generally embraced Nixon's anti-assimilationist message. The president's practical, political, and philosophical motives entwined, and he emerged as a forceful public advocate for Indian rights. By addressing the concerns of a small group, Nixon could show empathy for minority rights.

In developing his Native American policy, Nixon drew on his other civil rights programs. He again entrusted policy making to a coterie of moderate aides. Nixon did not think it necessary for Indians to meld into Anglo society, and he recognized the need for separate Native American institutions, a position in tune with his support for minority businesses. Nixon's respect for tribal autonomy was analogous to his use of local committees to desegregate southern schools. As with their support of the Equal Employment Opportunity Commission, Nixonians pumped money into Native American programs and the BIA.

At the same time, Nixon's Native American programs departed from his other policies in important respects. The president more openly supported the aspirations of Indians than those of blacks. Such support did not satisfy all Native Americans, especially young radicals, and Nixon's unfulfilled promises helped spark protests at the Bureau of Indian Affairs and at Wounded Knee, South Dakota. The result was a heated situation quite different from his "cold war" with black leaders. This crisis atmosphere may explain why the president drafted Indian policy in the White House instead of first entrusting it to the federal departments, as he had done with his other civil rights policies.

Within the context of grassroots protest and congressional pressures and constraints, Nixon managed to advance Indian self-determination. Nixonians were especially sympathetic to tribal concerns, settling land claims with the Taos Pueblo, the Yakima, and Alaska's native peoples. They reacted with tact and composure to the militants' often violent protests. But the president did not reorganize the BIA, nor did he end the poverty of urban Indians. Overall, Nixonians were practical reformers, not ambivalent onlookers, on Indian rights.

Native American Policy before Nixon

Compared to those of his predecessors, Nixon's Indian reforms were almost revolutionary. He moved to reverse a century of federal efforts to acculturate Indians into white society. In 1968 the Republican nominee disavowed a twenty-year-old policy of "terminating" tribes to enforce assimilation. He also promised to allow tribes to administer many federal programs themselves.

A policy of "Americanizing" Indians dated from the late nineteenth century. After subjugating Native Americans through military conquest, the federal government sought to abolish tribal life by encouraging Indians to become independent farmers. The General Allotment Act of 1887, or Dawes Act, allowed individual Indians to acquire "allotments" of tribal land and bestowed U.S. citizenship on any Indian who left the reservation for "civilized life." Unlike federal policy toward blacks, which by the 1880s overlooked racial segregation and discrimination in the South, the Dawes Act envisioned a place for Indians in white society. But the law was ethnocentric in that it required Native Americans to act like or "become" Anglos; and it crippled tribes by gradually shrinking the amount of land under their control.[3]

During the middle third of the twentieth century, Native American policy swung from reform to reaction to reform again. In the 1930s the national government approved limited tribal self-government under the "Indian New Deal." John Collier, Franklin D. Roosevelt's commissioner of Indian affairs, granted autonomy to "Indian societies" and respected their "cultural liberty."[4] The Indian Reorganization Act of 1934 suspended allotment laws, restored surplus land to tribes, and set up procedures for tribal constitution writing, incorporation, and self-government. The law was sweeping but imperfect. By stressing written constitutions and elections, it reshaped Indian institutions along Anglo lines, promoting a more subtle form of assimilation. During World War II, even Collier retreated and accented assimilation as a goal of federal Indian policy.[5] Nevertheless, according to one historian, "Collier's Indian New Deal . . . set in motion forces that could never be stamped out."[6]

During the 1940s and 1950s, assimilationists struck back. In 1948 the Hoover Commission on government organization asserted that "assimilation must be the dominant goal of public policy."[7] Right-wing western senators, who were wary of federal authority, devoted to private property, and sensitive to white constituents, opposed Indian self-government. Led by Senator Arthur V. Watkins, Republican of Utah, they urged Eisenhower's Interior Department to "terminate" federal responsibility for tribes and assimilate Indians into white society.[8] Native Americans would then lose all privileges under treaties with the government and become subject to the same laws as whites. In 1953 the Republican-controlled Congress endorsed termination in House Concurrent Resolution 108. Assistant Interior Secretary Orme Lewis asserted that "the Indians never will learn to manage their own affairs and to exercise the full prerogatives of American citizenship unless they are given the opportunity."[9]

During the 1960s, Indian policy began to change. In the face of Native American criticism, the Interior Department curtailed its termination campaign near the close of Eisenhower's term. In 1960 Democratic presidential nominee John F. Kennedy promised not to terminate "treaty or contractual relationships without the consent of the tribes concerned."[10] In his 1968 message on the "Forgotten American," President Lyndon B. Johnson backed "self-help, self-development, and self-determination" for reservation Indians, without disavowing termination.[11] More important, as the Great Society expanded public spending, poor Native Americans qualified for an increasing portion of federal largess.

By 1968 LBJ could see political advantages in addressing Native American concerns. His Indian message won a "generally favorable" response in Congress and drew praise from the *New York Times* as a "welcome sign."[12] Before its release, in March 1968, Johnson ordered aides "to say that no president has ever done more" for Native Americans.[13] The White House moved swiftly on the message, partly to beat Senator Robert F. Kennedy to the punch.[14] Beginning in 1967, the New York Democrat, Johnson's bête noire, chaired a special subcommittee on Indian education; prior to his ill-starred bid for the White House in 1968, Kennedy blasted the inadequacy of reservation schools as "an American tragedy."[15]

Despite such gestures, Indians longed for something more: self-determination. This concept suggested many things. Rural, tribal-based groups such as the National Congress of American Indians (NCAI) urged the government to disavow termination and give tribes greater control over BIA programs, from which they benefited. Meanwhile, young urban Indians, inspired by the "rights-conscious" spirit that had imbued African Americans, attacked "the system" by espousing "Red Power" and founded the American Indian Movement (AIM) in 1968. The urban radicals' program proved murky. Some favored such extreme remedies as abolishing the BIA, a hated symbol of wardship. (Since the bureau served only federally recognized tribes, not off-reservation Indians, urban militants felt free to attack it.) Others built urban centers to showcase what they believed to be Native American culture. Unlike NCAI, which negotiated with the government, urban radicals employed civil disobedience, even violence. They would visit a reservation, where their support was slight, stage a sit-in or armed takeover, and then bargain with government officials before moving on to other targets.[16]

Whatever their differences—age, location, or tactics—Indians rejected the integrationist goals of the black civil rights movement. "In the past," argued the historian Vine Deloria, Jr., "they had experienced so many betrayals through policies which purported to give them legal and social 'equality'" that they distrusted "anyone who spoke of either equality or helping them to get into 'the mainstream.'"[17]

During his early career, Nixon kept an open mind on Indian self-determination. As a California congressman and senator, he represented Native Americans from his district. In 1949 he criticized the Bureau of Indian Affairs for neglecting "the legitimate rights of the American Indian" and for "shameful extravagance."[18] As vice president, he backed education and economic opportunities for Indians, that is, "relocation assistance for those who desire and are able to move away from the reservation and greater industrial development near the reservations for . . . those who prefer to remain in their native surroundings."[19] The vice president did not defend termination. "Our overriding aim, as I see it," he declared in 1960, "should not be to separate the Indians from the richness of their past or force them into some preconceived mold of human behavior."[20] Such words meshed with President Nixon's later argument against "forced integration" of blacks and whites.

In 1968, with another presidential election nearing and Native Americans mobilizing, Nixon vowed to do "all I can" to improve "Indian life and education."[21] In a message to the National Congress on American Indians, he condemned current Indian policy as "unfair," "unwise," "confused," "demeaning," "vacillating," and "tragic." Unlike LBJ, Nixon clearly rejected forced assimilation and termination while endorsing Indians' "right of self-determination." He promised to give tribes "responsibility" over federal programs and to enhance Indian health care, education, and economic opportunity.[22] After becoming president, Nixon set out to realize his "strong commitment to improve the plight of the American Indian."[23]

Skeptical of integration between blacks and whites, the president saw no point in extending such a policy to Native Americans. He also equated the government's treatment of Indians with the liberals' tendency to use federal power at the expense of local or private initiative. Nixon called Native American policy "a bitter example of what's wrong with the bankrupt, old approach to the problems of minorities. They have been treated as a colony within a nation–to be taken care of."[24] Fond memories of his Whittier College football coach, Wallace Newman, a Cherokee, reinforced the president's view. Newman, he told aides, had blamed the government for turning "a once proud people" into "wards."[25] Nixon did not romanticize traditional Native American lifestyles, which he deemed "dirty, filthy, horrible."[26] Still, he believed that Native Americans deserved the opportunity to make their own choices and "should no longer be treated like a colony within a nation."[27]

Although political expediency molded Nixon's stance, he was not really seeking votes. The tiny Indian vote leaned Democratic, and by pursuing a policy of self-determination, he risked offending westerners in Congress.[28] Nixon backed Native American rights for broader political reasons: to enhance his own prestige and to preempt the opposition. Early in 1969 the president ordered aides to "make a study of the Indian Bureau, and particularly Bobby Kennedy's approach to the Indian problem." "He feels very strongly," added chief of staff H. R. Haldeman, "that we need to show more heart, and that we care about people, and thinks the Indian problem is a good area."[29] Here was a way to appease the young people in RFK's constituency, who expressed concern for Indians. Then in 1969, when Senator Edward M. Kennedy, Democrat of Massachusetts, became chair of his late brother's committee on Indian education, he branded Native American policy "a continuing national failure."[30] Seeing Kennedy as a likely opponent in the 1972 presidential contest, Nixon wanted to steal some of the Democrat's "clothes," including such liberal issues as forming an all-volunteer army, to leave "Teddy" as "bare" as possible.[31]

In helping Native Americans, Nixon placed what he called "Presidential responsibility" above politics. "There are very few votes involved," the president wrote John D. Ehrlichman, his domestic policy chief, "and I doubt if many [Indians] will move in our direction." But, he resolved, "a grave injustice has been worked against them for a century and a half and the nation at large will appreciate our having a more active policy of concern for their plight."[32] Here was an area ripe for some statesmanship.

The president moved on Indian rights partly to counter his negative image on African American rights. Nixon seconded the motion of Daniel P. Moynihan, his urban affairs adviser, to pay "greater attention to Indians, Mexican Americans and Puerto Ricans."[33] The president urged Vice President Agnew to sound the theme of "Forgotten Minorities."[34] By entrusting such a touchy subject to his troubadour of invective, best known for saucy, alliterative attacks on liberals and antiwar protesters, Nixon probably looked to avenge his black critics. Among non-black minorities, Native Americans became a high priority. The president even asked both the vice president and the first lady to visit Indian reservations.[35]

To Nixon, reservation Indians were "deserving" of greater responsibilities, apparently because they had shown initiative and eschewed violent protest. He privately characterized Native Americans as "strong, proud, independent and creative and more so if they break away. But we treat them like cattle and they booze it up."[36] The president thought Indians were a minority group of "good size" for whom the right policy "could affect results."[37] "There is a feeling," the journalists Rennard Strickland and Jack Gregory wrote, "that the Indian offers a chance to demonstrate that private enterprise and minority capitalism may yet prove to be the best solution to the problems of poverty, whether Indian, Negro, Puerto Rican or Appalachian."[38]

Nixon could not ignore Native American demands for autonomy. In February 1969 he received a report on Indian problems by Alvin M.

Josephy, Jr., an editor of *American Heritage* magazine and author of a well-known study, *The Indian Heritage of America* (1968). Josephy compared Indian fear of termination to a "psychosis," and he criticized the BIA's unwieldy decision making and its preoccupation with Indians' lands rather than Indians' lives.[39] Josephy's message was clear: reform of the BIA had to come from the White House, as soon as possible.

Average citizens, meanwhile, began to see increasingly sympathetic images of Native Americans. Books by scholars such as Josephy and Deloria depicted Anglo exploitation. Films such as *Little Big Man,* in which a 121-year-old Indian, played by Dustin Hoffman, recalls his life, challenged the stereotype of the murderous savage. In 1972 Marlon Brando refused his Academy Award for *The Godfather* and sent an Indian woman, Sasheen Littlefeather, in his place to condemn Hollywood's earlier portrayal of Indians. A "Keep America Beautiful" television commercial further appealed to white guilt by showing an Indian, Iron Eyes Cody, weeping as Anglos polluted the environment.[40] Public policy had to change to keep up with more sensitive depictions of Native Americans.

Self-determination was an idea whose time had arrived. "This administration," White House aide Leonard Garment wrote in 1969, "can begin a whole new civil rights initiative–for American Indians and Alaskan Natives" with "practically none of the backlash which encumbers efforts to help blacks."[41] When Garment wrote his memorandum, most whites opposed forced integration of the races. So did Native Americans, and so did Nixon.

Self-Determination without Termination

Change in Indian policy came slowly. During 1969 and 1970, Nixonians tinkered with ways to address Indian concerns. But the emergence of Ehrlichman as the president's domestic policy chief, coupled with the seizure of Alcatraz Island by militant Indians, strengthened the hand of Nixon's reform-minded advisers.

The stalemate on Indian policy stemmed from the usual structural and personnel problems that plagued presidents early in their terms. Nixon at first entrusted domestic policy to White House counselor Arthur F. Burns, a friend and a former economist at Columbia University. Conservative and systematic, Burns moved cautiously. After receiving the Josephy report, he advised Nixon to convene the National Council on Indian Opportunity, an advisory panel of tribal leaders and cabinet officers chaired by Agnew, and to appoint "qualified Indians to the Indian Claims Commission and the Bureau of Indian Affairs."[42] The owlish Burns may have been biding his time until he could name his own task force to study the matter. But Stephen Bull, an aide to Haldeman, rightly wondered why Burns did not use the Josephy report, written by an expert, to overhaul the BIA.[43]

Interior Secretary Walter J. Hickel remained enigmatic on Indian rights. Although Hickel increased the number of federal contracts to Indians and appointed Native Americans to the BIA, he neither pressed for nor expounded a new Indian policy.[44] After perusing a draft of Hickel's address to the National Congress of American Indians, White House aide John C. Whitaker, an expert on the environment, lamented that "it doesn't contain a program."[45] NCAI delegates booed the speech. White House aides had to guide the secretary on how to aid urban Indians and draft legislation for Native Americans.[46] As a former governor of Alaska, Hickel perhaps feared that a policy of self-determination would invite Alaska's natives to demand an exorbitant settlement of their pressing land claims. Best remembered for criticizing the invasion of Cambodia and eventually losing his job for it, Hickel provided little leadership on Native American policy.

During the latter part of 1969, Nixon assembled the team that would sculpt his Native American policy. In July the president appointed Louis R. Bruce, a Mohawk and a Republican, as commissioner of Indian affairs. Bruce vaguely promised to change the BIA from "a management to a service organization" by allowing tribes to administer some of its programs.[47] More important, Nixon in October named Ehrlichman to coordinate his domestic policies. The president, as mentioned in Chapter 2, had tapped the onetime Seattle lawyer to settle the feud between Burns and Moynihan over welfare reform. Ehrlichman, who oversaw Native American policy, squelched Burns's plans for a task force on Indian affairs. He wanted to couch the administration's efforts "in terms of action and not more studies." "Good," scribbled Nixon in response.[48]

Ehrlichman allowed White House officials in sympathy with Indian self-determination to review the government's policies. As chair of the National Council on Indian Opportunity, Agnew took a "personal interest" in Indian problems.[49] Barbara Greene Kilberg, a White House fellow familiar with Native American affairs, served as ombudsman. Kilberg and Agnew found allies in Garment and his deputy, Bradley H. Patterson, Jr. With Garment absorbed in other minority issues, Patterson handled the nuts and bolts of Native American policy, such as drafting legislation.[50] Despite sporadic sparring, these moderate-to-liberal aides worked to realize the president's promise of Indian self-determination.

Agnew's concern was not as strange as it may seem. The vice president was the self-made son of Greek immigrants; like other Nixonians, he favored measures to help minorities "who are working diligently within our free system to elevate themselves."[51] In 1966, after Agnew defeated a segregationist to win the Maryland governorship, blacks took a "wait and see" approach toward his administration.[52] Many liked what they saw. Agnew named African Americans to state offices, approved a fair employment code for the executive branch, and won passage of a mild open housing law to prohibit bias in the sale of new homes.[53] "Agnew is amassing record rights gain," proclaimed the *Baltimore Afro-American.*[54] But following a riot in Baltimore, he scolded mainstream black leaders and later denounced the Reverend Ralph David Abernathy's Poor People's March as "lobbyists for opportunism."[55] The stump and the microphone became Agnew's worst enemies on many race-related issues.

For the vice president, Native American affairs represented an opportunity to show constructive leadership. Agnew's staffers, especially C. D. Ward, advised him to use the National Council on Indian Opportunity to help Indians, and he did. From the Department of Housing and Urban Development, the vice president pried additional housing units for Native Americans. He secured a $750,000 grant to send manpower coordinators to reservations and proposed including Native Americans under Nixon's revenue-sharing plan.[56] Such efforts, however small, boosted Agnew. The *New York Times* ran a feature article on the vice president's interest in Indians, and tribal leaders praised Agnew's "spirited leadership" and "unwavering support."[57] The vice president surely relished such praise, for he considered himself to be moderate and "infinitely more complex" than his "public image" as a right-wing firebrand.[58] "I don't feel," Agnew wrote one acquaintance, "that being for Black equal opportunity, open housing and fair play requires me to rationalize or condone prison rioting, family desertion or blatant Black racism."[59] With Indians, the vice president could try to make a fresh start on minority rights.

Late in 1969 Nixon's team faced their first challenge when Indians seized Alcatraz Island in San Francisco Bay. The dispute actually began in 1964, when five Sioux Indians briefly occupied Alcatraz and claimed the former federal prison under the Fort Laramie Treaty of 1868. The controversy resurfaced in 1969, after fire destroyed an Indian center in San Francisco. When Hickel offered to turn Alcatraz into a national park, Native Americans took action. On November 20, fifty Indians navigated the dark, foggy bay. They landed on Alcatraz, claiming it for all tribes "by right of discovery." These latter-day explorers vowed to stay put until Hickel ceded the island to them.[60]

This invasion was something more than an isolated stunt. Indian activists, mostly urban, had organized similar protests on federal lands to highlight treaty violations and to assert Red Power. "We are attacking the whole system by attacking Alcatraz," proclaimed Adam Nordwall, leader of the United Bay Area Council of Indians.[61] By the end of 1969, more than one hundred Indians had made the "Rock" their home. Some of them commuted between Alcatraz and the mainland in the boat *Clearwater,* purchased with money donated by the rock band Creedence Clearwater Revival.[62]

How did Nixonians view these bizarre occurrences? After some venting, Nixon's moderate advisers sought compromise. Garment, with cause, scored the seizure as "confrontation politics" by "an irresponsible, but PR-conscious group."[63] Patterson called it "nihilistic but *superb* showmanship."[64] To calm the waters, they sent Robert Robertson, director of the National Council on Indian Opportunity, to Alcatraz to bargain with the occupants. When Robertson promised to build a park for the Indians on the island, the occupiers, calling themselves the "Indians of all Tribes," said no. They insisted on possession of Alcatraz, where they hoped to build a cultural center, and broadcast their demand over their own network, "Radio Free Alcatraz."[65] The White House declined to cave in to protesters, and the standoff continued.

As the seizure's first anniversary approached, Garment, Patterson, and Robertson had to defend their "watchful waiting" from attacks by less temperate colleagues. Egil M. Krogh, who handled law enforcement issues for Ehrlichman, sided with Coast Guard officials eager to regain Alcatraz's lighthouse.[66] He wanted the Justice Department to "clear the Island."[67] To remove the Indians forcibly, Geoffrey C. Shepard, another White House aide, proposed a set of options worthy of a Hollywood action film, including a "*Commando Operation* conducted at night by Navy Seals" and a *"Dawn Invasion"* complete with "tranquilizer guns."[68] Garment poured cold water on these hotheads by warning that Alcatraz could become "the biggest political sideshow of 1971" if one person died.[69] Remembering the shootings at Kent State University in 1970, Ehrlichman and Nixon agreed to "play it safe."[70]

For two years the government and the Indians played cat and mouse. The occupiers charged five dollars to each Anglo visiting Alcatraz.[71] Before Robertson tried to negotiate with the Indians, they allegedly served him coffee spiked with mescaline, a hallucinogenic drug. "He was to hold a press conference right after the negotiations," reported an amused Patterson, "and if he had drunk that coffee, can you see the result?"[72] The Indians once shot a toy arrow at a tourist boat, then lobbed a "fiery projectile" at a Coast Guard ship. To keep watch, federal officials enlisted a recluse with a telescope in a house overlooking the bay.[73] They later shut off the island's supply of water and electricity.

The Alcatraz occupiers did not lack prominent supporters. The publisher of the *San Francisco Chronicle* gave the Indians a generator, and Ethel Kennedy, Robert Kennedy's widow, telephoned Garment to accuse him of "genocide." Ethel Kennedy also visited Alcatraz, as did the actress Jane Fonda and the comedians Dick Gregory and Jonathan Winters. The public eventually lost interest in the whole escapade, the Indians squabbled among themselves, and most gradually abandoned the island. Federal marshals peacefully removed the last band of fifteen on June 11, 1971.[74]

Nixon's moderate advisers used the occupation to plead for change in Indian policy. "The Alcatraz episode is symbolic," read one unsigned memorandum; "to the Indians and to us it is a *symbol* of the lack of attention to [their] unmet needs."[75] Agnew assumed command by convening the National Council on Indian Opportunity (NCIO) early in 1970. He listened to the concerns of tribal leaders and asked cabinet officials to respond. Dissatisfied with the work of "middle-level" bureaucrats, Agnew told two aides, Robertson and Ward, to draft legislation.[76]

The vice president next urged Nixon to disavow termination "in the most forceful way possible" and allow tribes, "by majority vote," to assume complete control over any federal programs. He advised replacing BIA area offices with centers to ease the "transition from Federal to tribal control."[77] Agnew argued that his proposals would advance the "New Federalism," the president's policy of transferring power from federal to local authorities, and Patterson and Garment agreed.[78] White House aides then began work on a statement explaining Nixon's policy.

Patterson and Garment had more say in drafting the Indian message than Agnew. Patterson broached the idea of a statement and then sketched it. When the vice president's office stepped in, Ehrlichman asked Kilberg to referee.[79] They found allies in Donald Rumsfeld, director of the Office of Economic Opportunity, who rejected termination, and Labor Secretary George P. Shultz, who favored contracting with tribes to permit them to run some federal services. White House aides conferred with few Indians, though they kept in mind NCIO's last meeting.[80] Deeming the work of Agnew's staff to be lackluster, Ehrlichman asked Garment and Patterson to "wrap" up the statement. By July 1970 the embryonic statement had "hatched."[81]

Nixon's Indian message grafted proposals for self-determination onto the existing BIA bureaucracy. The statement renounced termination as "morally and legally unacceptable." "Self-determination among the Indian people," Nixon said, "can and must be encouraged without the threat of eventual termination."[82] He asked Congress to pass a resolution repealing termination and eight bills to advance tribal autonomy, including one appointing an assistant secretary of the interior for Indian affairs to oversee the BIA and an Indian trust counsel authority to protect Native American lands. Under Nixon's legislation, federal agencies would "contract out" educational and health care services to tribes. Indians would be able to assume control over any federal programs as well as lease land and regulate trade on reservations.[83] In drafting these proposals, Garment bypassed Agnew, who had wanted to restructure the BIA, and tapped Kilberg and Harrison Loesch, assistant secretary of the interior for land management.[84] By working with Loesch, Garment eschewed a frontal assault on his department, giving the message a "rather pro-BIA tone."[85]

Nixon's statement won wide acclaim. Indian leaders telephoned NCIO to express thanks.[86] "This represents a complete reversal in the Federal attitude toward Indian affairs," proclaimed Alvin Josephy.[87] The *New York Times* praised the "new Nixon program" for offering "great hope" to Native Americans.[88] The columnist Max Lerner called it a "historic state paper."[89] In 1974 a correspondent for the American Indian Press Association lauded "the famed Nixon Indian Message" as one of the "presidential messages most-quoted by Indians in recent history."[90] Yet Native American radicals were unmoved. "Anything Nixon says is shit," one AIM activist asserted.[91]

Nixon's agenda included blind spots. White House officials tailored policy to the moderate tribal leaders attending NCIO, not the troublemakers camped on Alcatraz. They only offered urban Indians more social service centers, and they did not propose changing the BIA. On the last point, Agnew's office lost out to Garment, who may have reasoned that either Bruce or the new assistant secretary of the interior for Indian affairs would restructure the bureau. But Congress dallied over whether or not to establish this new post.[92]

The White House, in truth, dumped a mammoth agenda before Congress without consulting its leaders or setting priorities. Assistant Secretary of the Interior for Planning Lewis H. Butler compared Nixon's Native American menu to a "smorgasbord."[93] And Ehrlichman's helter-skelter approach to Indian policy making—with first Agnew taking charge, then Kilberg, then Garment—left no one aide responsible for shepherding these bills through Congress. In 1972 Ward rightly identified "this diffusion of authority" as one of the "major problems" with Indian policy.[94] His solution, of course, was to restore the vice president's influence.

In the short run, Nixon was shrewd to wed a bold statement to an ambitious agenda. The Indian message, Patterson recalled, "gave us a target," "guidelines," and "our charter."[95] The size of the legislative package suggested flexible goals. Nixonians surveyed the political landscape and selected specific "targets," starting with Indian land claims.

Legislative Triumphs and Setbacks

In 1970 and 1971 two issues moved to the top of Nixon's agenda: the Taos Pueblo's claim to Blue Lake and the land claims of Alaskan natives. Although White House officials settled these matters, Nixon's other reforms languished on Capitol Hill. By 1972 the president had decided to let Congress set the legislative agenda, while he addressed Indian rights through administrative actions.

The White House first tackled the Taos Pueblo's claim to 48,000 acres around Blue Lake, New Mexico. In 1906 President Theodore Roosevelt had annexed this ground, sacred to the Taos Pueblo, into a national forest. For sixty years the tribe fought to regain its land. In 1940 the Forest Service granted them a fifty-year permit to use the environs of Blue Lake for livestock and timber and for religious ceremonies. The Indian Claims Commission in 1965 ordered the government to settle the dispute with cash, then the usual method of compensation.[96] The Taos Pueblo still demanded possession of the area. Then, with the rise of the Indian movement, Blue Lake came to represent "one of the most egregious acts of federal imperialism."[97] The U.S. House of Representatives in 1968 and 1969 passed bills restoring it to the Taos Pueblo. But the Senate failed to act.[98]

Sensing the popularity of Blue Lake, White House officials snatched the issue. The vice president first learned about this issue while chairing NCIO.[99] Garment advised Nixon to back the House bill, warning that liberal Democratic senators such as Fred R. Harris of Oklahoma and George S. McGovern of South Dakota "are moving to seize this issue." "Since 1906," Garment went on, "this particular issue has snowballed and is now *the* single specific Indian issue."[100] Agnew concurred: "I do want to push for the Indians—full speed ahead."[101] Kilberg oversaw the matter for Ehrlichman, who also backed the tribe's claim. With his advisers in accord, Nixon endorsed the House bill in his Indian statement, and even sat beside Taos Pueblo leaders when he issued the message.[102] In so doing, the president answered the symbolic seizure of Alcatraz with his own brand of symbolism.

Conservatives on the Senate Interior Committee grumbled about Blue Lake. Clinton P. Anderson, Democrat of New Mexico, seeking to protect grazing rights for white ranchers, opposed encouraging "every

Indian tribe that has a claim against the Government to ask for land in lieu of cash."[103] Senator Gordon Allott of Colorado, the committee's ranking Republican, called the Blue Lake bill "a very bad precedent."[104] The committee's chair, Democratic senator Henry M. ("Scoop") Jackson of Washington, feared losing Anderson's vote on the antiballistic missile and kept Blue Lake under wraps.[105] Congressional liaison staffs at the White House and at Interior offered scant direction since no one wanted to get their "neck stuck out on this issue."[106]

With bipartisan support, Nixon's team overwhelmed these pockets of resistance. Although the president knew that Blue Lake might jeopardize Anderson's vote on ABM, he fought for the House bill.[107] Patterson lobbied lawmakers, while Kilberg reminded her colleagues of Blue Lake's symbolic importance.[108] Senators such as Republicans Robert P. Griffin of Michigan, Mark O. Hatfield of Oregon, and Barry M. Goldwater of Arizona and Democrats McGovern, Kennedy, and Harris favored returning Blue Lake. Anderson and his Interior Committee allies then erred by reporting both the House bill and their substitute, which only granted the tribe use of the disputed tract.[109] It was no contest. On December 2, 1970, the Senate voted, 70 to 12, to restore Blue Lake to the Taos. In a way, Nixon simply rode a popular issue to the winner's circle. By exercising timely leadership and by bucking Anderson, who later voted against ABM, he ensured the return of Blue Lake.[110]

Blue Lake remained important symbolically. White House congressional liaison chief William E. Timmons, with an eye on ABM, advised against a public signing because "we rolled Gordon Allott, Scoop Jackson . . . et al on the Floor. A ceremony would rub salt in their wounds."[111] But Garment, eager to spotlight Nixon's refurbished Indian policy, disagreed.[112] "The President did something that has a great deal of meaning to the Indian population," Kilberg added. "He should get credit for it."[113] Nixon agreed, calling Blue Lake "pure symbol[ism]."[114] On December 15, in a theatrical flourish worthy of LBJ, he signed the Blue Lake bill in the State Dining Room, with shawl-clad Taos leaders looking on. Haldeman tried to keep Fred Harris, who also had fought for the law, away from the cameras.[115] Nixon had never tried to hog the limelight so blatantly on an African American issue.

Blue Lake was prologue to a far greater land settlement: the Alaska Native Claims Settlement Act of 1971. Like Blue Lake, this dispute had deep roots, since the federal government had never established title to Alaska's vast, scenic, mineral-rich domain. The Organic Act of 1884, which made Alaska a territory, gave Aleuts, Eskimos, and Alaskan Indians "any lands in their use or occupation or now claimed by them."[116] Even after extending the Dawes Act to Alaska in 1906, the government continued to leave these natives alone. Such "benign neglect" ended with the Alaska Statehood Act of 1958, which allowed the new state to reserve 103 million acres—an area larger than California.[117] Eight native groups formed the Alaska Federation of Natives (AFN) in 1966 and laid claim to 370 million of Alaska's 375 million acres. Interior Secretary Stewart Udall then forbade the state from taking any more land, "freezing" Alaska's economic development and leaving the natives "in a position of real political strength."[118]

At the outset, Nixon's administration lacked the leadership and will to solve the Alaskan riddle. In 1968 candidate Nixon vaguely promised Alaska's aboriginal peoples "just compensation, either in money, lands, royalties or some combination," to end the dispute.[119] Accordingly, Hickel in 1969 proposed giving Alaska's natives $500 million and just 46,000 acres. It is not clear why Hickel offered such a measly land settlement, since as governor he had endorsed 40 million acres for the natives.[120] The secretary may have listened too closely to conservative aides and to Burns and Krogh, who deemed this offer "sound."[121] Without consulting their liberal counterparts or the tribes, Burns and Krogh rubber-stamped Hickel's bill, which contained a termination clause for Alaska's natives.[122] To make matters worse, Kilberg, who favored a princely settlement, conceded that "an anti-native backlash is developing and a segment of the white population is not in favor of supporting the natives' land claims."[123] Nixon's Indian message ducked this controversy and left it to Congress.

Congress failed to untangle the Alaskan knot. In 1970 the Senate passed a bill granting the natives $500 million in cash, $500 million in royalties from minerals, and 10 million acres. Yet native goals shifted with the Arctic winds. The Alaska Federation of Natives first demanded 40 million acres.[124] While AFN weighed the Senate's offer, the Eskimos, who claimed 56 million acres along the oil-rich Arctic slope, turned it aside. To appease them, AFN president Donald R. Wright insisted on 60 million acres and shrewdly reminded Nixon of his generosity on Blue Lake.[125] By that point, policy makers at both ends of Pennsylvania Avenue probably cursed the memory of William H. Seward, the secretary of state who had purchased Alaska from Russia in 1867.

Nixon's moderate-to-liberal advisers revisited the Alaskan impasse. Kilberg and Patterson did the spadework, digging up cryptic facts here, conferring with AFN leaders there. "I got to know Don Wright," Patterson recalled. "We began to hear his side of the story."[126] He also consulted Senator Ted Stevens, Republican of Alaska, and outlined a new bill. But snags developed over the land tally: Kilberg favored giving Alaska's natives 40 million acres, Garment recommended 15 million acres, the Interior Department 5.2 million, the Office of Management and Budget (OMB) 2.9 million. With career bureaucrats at Interior and OMB objecting to a large land giveaway, Garment and Patterson appealed to Ehrlichman for help.[127]

Ehrlichman broke the logjam. He discussed Alaskan claims with Nixon in March 1971, and then huddled with Patterson, Garment, Kilberg, Donald B. Rice of OMB, Frank A. Bracken, Interior's legislative counsel, and Rogers C. B. Morton, Hickel's successor as interior secretary. Ehrlichman laid out Nixon's multiple aims: (1) the Alaskan oil "pipeline issue should be moved toward conclusion"; (2) "The President knows that he has taken a very forthcoming position on Indian affairs and he does not want to renege on this"; (3) "He would like to succeed politically in the State of Alaska."[128] At that point Morton blurted: "Well, hell, why don't we give them 40,000,000 acres and $1,000,000,000?" The participants all agreed, and Patterson typed up the deal.[129]

To build the Alaskan pipeline and a good record on Indian affairs, Nixon accepted the compromise. In 1970 Morton, as chair of the Republican National Committee, had warned the president of the pipeline's economic and political importance, urging him not to delay it "on environmental or any other grounds."[130] Yet in talking with Ehrlichman, Nixon also cited his Indian policy and seemed eager to play statesman. In April 1971 he approved the revised Alaskan proposal at a session with Morton, Stevens, and Wright. Wright lauded the $40 million settlement as "the best and fairest one to emerge from any national Administration or Congressional Committee."[131] The president rarely sought or received such interest group support on African

American issues. In a giving mood, Nixon closed the meeting à la LBJ, by handing out paperweights stamped with the presidential seal.

The revised Alaska claims bill faced more resistance within the executive branch than on Capitol Hill. When Bracken attempted to redraft it "in terms slightly different from our agreement," Ehrlichman roared, "You're not welching on a decision made in my office."[132] Bracken backed down. Patterson and Garment then lobbied lawmakers to support the president's proposal.[133] Although House liberals, opposed to the pipeline, mounted "a furious environmental-based attack on the bill," it passed, 334 to 63.[134] Scoop Jackson, Stevens, and Wright steered the measure through the Senate, 76 to 5, and Nixon approved it in December 1971. By refusing to sign the act until AFN had ratified it, the president remained true to his policy of self-determination.[135]

The Alaskan Native Claims Settlement Act was both landmark and problematic, mixing self-determination with capitalism. It ended aboriginal land titles and granted 40 million acres to twelve native-owned regional corporations. Any Alaskan who was at least one-quarter Eskimo, Aleut, or Indian gained one hundred shares in one corporation. The government paid the corporations $462.5 million in cash and $500 million in royalties from minerals extracted from state-owned land. The settlement nearly equaled the area, 50 million acres, held by Indians in the lower forty-eight states. It allowed Alaskan natives to own choice land and to start mining and timber businesses. Yet some observers disliked the law's accent on corporations, fearing that natives would sell stock to white investors or desert their subsistence-based tribal cultures. And many Native American companies had spoiled the environment.[136]

The Alaskan Native Claims Act advanced two of Nixon's aims: to expand choices for Indians and to aid minority entrepreneurs. Hardly naive, aboriginal leaders fought for the law and AFN ratified it, 511 to 56. To protect its gains, AFN cultivated new leaders and "cultural awareness."[137] In 1987 aboriginals secured legislation limiting the sale of their stock.[138] While some native corporations continue to struggle, others thrive, and most natives deem them "beneficial." "The corporations," concluded *The Economist* in 1996, "have given them political clout, assured them a fair share of Alaska's oil revenues, and provided a measure of economic self-determination."[139]

Despite triumphs on Blue Lake and Alaskan claims, Nixon failed to win approval of his other Indian legislation. During 1970 and 1971 the Senate Interior Committee held hearings on just two administration bills—to form an Indian trust counsel authority and to establish an assistant secretary of the interior for Indian and territorial affairs. By 1971 the Senate had passed only the latter proposal, while the House had not acted at all. During 1971 neither chamber scheduled hearings on the president's other reforms.[140]

Blame for these setbacks begins with conservatives on the Senate Interior Committee. One White House report fingered "Senator Allott and his displeasure with our proposals." Allott, the committee's ranking Republican, influenced the "introduction and sponsorship" of bills, raising a "very serious stumbling block" to winning "any other Republican support."[141] Moreover, other matters preoccupied Congress. "The Interior Committees," argued John Whitaker, "have spent themselves on the Alaskan Claims issue."[142] Immersed in Alaskan claims, Patterson offered vague guidelines for pushing the other bills: "The greatest need is (a) some TLC by Morton and (b) to get those Interior Hearings *going*."[143]

Since the administration had proposed few laws to assist blacks, it seemed lost on how to persuade a Democratic-controlled Congress to approve its Indian bills. Morton, showing little interest in Indian legislation, testified poorly on behalf of the trust counsel measure. Meanwhile, Nixon's congressional liaison office, headed by William Timmons, a conservative, ignored the Native American agenda. With no one adviser choreographing Indian policy, confusion reigned at the White House. In 1971 Agnew promised to resubmit the legislative package and repeal termination through a new congressional resolution. His statement left Kenneth Cole, Ehrlichman's deputy, scratching his head. White House aides never had drafted such a resolution.[144]

Agnew's lapse was not surprising since he did not direct Native American policy. With Patterson and Garment apparently in charge, the vice president's staff freely critiqued their rivals' failings. In 1972 C. D. Ward criticized Indian policy for "much talk and little action," correctly charging the White House, Justice Department, and Interior Department with giving the legislative package "a very low priority." Ward was less accurate in calling Blue Lake "the sole 'success' story" and for dismissing the Alaskan act as "the result of overwhelming economic motivations and not our desire to set things right for the Indian." Yet his frustration was genuine and justified. "We just can't seem to overcome the inertia," Ward told Agnew.[145]

The Indian legislation needed a heavy dose of bipartisan leadership, along the lines of Blue Lake and Alaskan claims. Yet issues such as China, strategic arms limitation, Vietnam, and reelection politics, including dirty tricks, consumed Nixon's attention. And some liberal Democrats proved negligent. "I feel guilty," confessed McGovern, chair of the Senate subcommittee on Indian affairs, "about not having done more for Indians."[146] The president neither solicited nor obtained help from Democrats in Congress.

In 1972 liberals passed legislation on Indian education which Nixon detested. The president in 1970 had weighed whether to form a National Board of Regents for Indian Education or to contract out education services to tribal schools. In keeping with his support for local control, Nixon endorsed the latter option. But Kennedy, chair of the special subcommittee on Indian education, recommended an associate commissioner for Indian education and a National Indian Educational Advisory Council. Patterson opposed funding these new offices, arguing that their functions duplicated those of BIA and NCIO.[147]

Since Kennedy's proposals passed as a part of the Higher Education Amendments of 1972, which also expanded the student loan program, Nixon swallowed hard and signed the act. The White House extracted revenge by delaying nominations to the advisory council and by impounding its funds.[148] With Indian education in dire straits, one wishes that both sides had granted Indian school boards greater funds *and* autonomy.

Sandbagged by liberals and conservatives on Capitol Hill, Nixonians enhanced Indian rights via budgetary and administrative actions. Between 1969 and 1974, the White House doubled outlays for Indian programs, to $1.6 billion. The BIA's budget alone grew from $249 million to $635 million.[149] In 1971 Native Americans "widely credited" Nixon for "submitting the largest Indian budget of any Administration."[150] Under revenue sharing, Nixon's program of grants to strengthen local governments, tribes received $25 million in 1974. To advance business opportunities, the Office of Minority Business Enterprise established an Indian desk.[151]

By propping up the Bureau of Indian Affairs, Nixonians resorted to one of their favorite tactics: bureaucratizing civil rights. To advance African American rights, the president and his charges had pumped dollars into the Equal Employment Opportunity Commission. Yet "bureaucratization" did not work equally well for all minority groups. BIA, much older than EEOC, seemed "establishment-oriented," partly because it represented elected tribal leaders and was submerged within a department, Interior, that had long favored the land claims of white ranchers over those of Indians. Accordingly, urban Indians, unlike radical blacks, assailed the existing federal bureaucracy, especially the BIA.

Nixon, to make matters worse, spent less than $10 million on urban Indians between 1969 and 1974.[152] The White House funded only thirteen centers for urban Indians, and their returns proved "very inadequate."[153] The difficulty lay in Nixon's reliance on the Office of Economic Opportunity, which he tried to abolish in 1973, to help off-reservation Indians. White House staff members preferred to settle high-profile land claims with moderate tribal leaders rather than address the ongoing economic woes of urban radicals. Agnew and Commerce Secretary Maurice H. Stans had wanted to use the Economic Development Administration as the lead agency to aid off-reservation Indians. But Garment, listening to officials at Interior, did not recommend these ideas for the president's Indian message.[154]

Nixon's disregard for urban Indians was the chief failing of his policy. By 1970, the Indian population, nearly 800,000, was almost evenly split between urban and rural.[155] By ignoring city dwellers, the president's Native American policy remained only half complete. Nixon, concluded one Indian journalist in 1974, "left the urban Indians' unresolved issues and unmet needs" to President Gerald R. Ford.[156]

Nixonians did better in organizing new offices to protect Indian land and water rights. While congressional conservatives delayed Nixon's trust counsel bill, liberals clamored for change. Senators Kennedy and John Tunney, Democrat of California, vowed to study conflicts of interest between the Department of Justice, which represented the government in disputes, and the Department of Interior, which represented Native Americans. Late in 1971 William Youpee, president of the National Tribal Chairmen's Association, proposed an alternative: establishing an office of Indian water rights at Interior.[157] Nixon's Indian policy team and the Navajo leader Peter MacDonald approved this idea as an interim measure until Congress passed the trust counsel bill. In 1972 Morton and Attorney General John N. Mitchell agreed to co-ordinate enforcement of Indian rights, and a year later the Justice Department formed its own Office of Indian Civil Rights.[158]

Nixon sidestepped Congress in resolving another land dispute, this one involving the Yakima, a tribe cursed with incredibly bad luck. Under a treaty with the national government, in 1855 the Yakima gained a tract of 21,000 acres around Mount Adams in Washington state. Federal officials then misplaced the treaty's map, and Theodore Roosevelt (again) incorporated Mount Adams into what became Gifford Pinchot National Forest. In 1970 Garment, Loesch, Agnew, and Hickel studied the dispute and proposed returning the Yakima's land. Yet they encountered resistance from career bureaucrats at the Forest Service, backed by Agriculture Secretary Clifford M. Hardin.[159]

Mitchell and Agnew broke this deadlock. Depicting the seizure of Mount Adams as a presidential error, the attorney general drafted Executive Order 11670 restoring it to the Yakima.[160] Agnew urged the president to sign this order as a "further step in the efforts to implement your Indian policy."[161] The congressional liaison staff surveyed opinion on Capitol Hill and found only Allott (again) opposed to the settlement. Nixon approved the executive order on May 20, 1972.[162] If such an expansive view of presidential power proved dangerous during Watergate, it seemed helpful in redressing tribal grievances.

Nixon's administrative actions underscored the strengths and weaknesses of his Indian policy. The return of Mount Adams recalled the White House's successes on Blue Lake and Alaskan claims and its courtship of moderate tribal leaders. But urban Indians received scant attention, and BIA, despised by militants, remained unchanged. Such unfinished business helped to spark new protests.

Nixon Besieged: The BIA and Wounded Knee

Nixonians anticipated more unrest. "Urban Indians," predicted one unsigned memorandum in 1971, "will most likely be creating more confrontations with federal, state and city authorities over the next two years."[163] Protests at the BIA in 1972, and at Wounded Knee, South

Dakota, in 1973, pushed the government to revisit Native American concerns.

Rising unrest derived in part from Nixon's failure to reform the BIA. From the outset, the president wanted to change the agency's operations. At a meeting of the Council on Urban Affairs in 1969, Nixon condemned BIA's "routine bureaucratic mentality," which, he claimed, "hasn't changed since the Bureau started." The president commanded Interior Secretary Hickel to recruit fresh personnel instead of "keeping the same small crowd in and doing things the same way." Hickel assured Nixon that Louis Bruce, the new Indian commissioner, was "not part of the establishment."[164]

But intramural feuding impeded change. In 1970 Bruce, backed by Hickel, vowed to transfer BIA functions to tribes.[165] He began streamlining his bureaucracy and reassigning personnel who represented "the out-of-date-philosophy" of paternalism.[166] Interior Secretary Morton, who replaced Hickel in 1971, regarded Bruce's staff of activists as long on zeal and short on managerial competence. He named career bureaucrats to oversee policy: John Crow became deputy BIA commissioner, and Wilma Victor served as special assistant to the secretary for Indian affairs. Morton tried to shift authority from Bruce to Crow, only to retreat when tribal leaders opposed the change.[167]

Bruce, his critics claimed, had "deluded himself to think that he could do business with the militants." Yet in promoting the "establishment-oriented" Crow, Morton sided with Interior Department officials who favored the land and water rights of white ranchers over Indians.[168] The secretary, by accenting administrative experience over reform, stalled Bruce's efforts.[169]

Instead of backing Bruce, White House staffers haggled over the BIA's place within the president's program for executive branch reorganization. During 1971 Garment and Patterson advised shifting BIA into the proposed Department of Human Resources, while Kilberg suggested moving it into either the tentative Department of Human Resources or that of Economic Development.[170] This tiresome debate ended in the timid proposal to place BIA within a Department of Natural Resources, Interior's proposed successor, pending "an acceptable alternative arrangement" with "Indian leaders."[171] Congress rejected the reorganization scheme, leaving BIA at Interior. By focusing on the bureau's location, not its operations, the White House overlooked Bruce's reforms. That was not surprising, since Garment and Patterson had never made reforming BIA a priority.

Nixon preferred to blame BIA's troubles on Interior, then delay reform. Regarding Indians, he complained during a conference in 1971, "I'm [the] victim of a revol[ution]" and "E[hrlichman] says join them." To prove he had, Nixon cited his generous budgets. Morton, Ehrlichman, and Whitaker, also present at this meeting, conceded the hardships of reservation life: only 15 percent of Indians had electricity and just 5 percent owned telephones. They lamented that "no one has a plan" to address such problems and criticized Bruce and Loesch for exhibiting the backbone of "2 jellyfish." The president wanted Interior to carry out his Indian message and draft a "plan for reservations." But, sensing Bruce's shortcomings, he told Morton to "do the symbols now" and agreed not to go for substantive change until "after the [1972] election."[172]

Native American leaders refused to wait. Moderate tribal groups such as the National Congress of American Indians defended the beleaguered Indian commissioner. Peter MacDonald, speaking for the National Tribal Chairmen's Association, condemned Morton's personnel moves and urged the transfer of BIA to the White House.[173] Such reproaches, coming from friendly sources, stung Nixon. He ordered Morton to "shake up" the bureau, but the order went unheeded, leaving Victor and Crow free to square off against Bruce throughout 1972.[174] A group of radical Indians later attempted to arrest Crow "on charges he was reversing an enlightened Nixon policy."[175]

The wrangling at BIA coincided with rising Indian militancy. During 1971 the American Indian Movement, led by Russell C. Means, an Oglala Sioux, and Dennis J. Banks, a Chippewa, staged protests; in the Black Hills of South Dakota, a site sacred to the Sioux, Means openly urinated while standing atop Mount Rushmore. To stress how whites misused stolen Indian lands, AIM organized a sit-in at an abandoned Nike missile site. It also sought to protect Native American culture while attacking tribal leaders as "too establishment," locked into the BIA. In 1972 AIM followers incited violence in Topeka, Kansas, where white Boy Scouts had tried to perform Indian dances. What AIM lacked in size, having just 4,500 members, it made up for in daring.[176]

The faction-ridden, inert BIA emerged as AIM's next target. Late in 1972, AIM members seized the BIA building. Means and Banks led the "Trail of Broken Treaties," a caravan of militant Indians, to Washington to present their grievances. On November 2, agents of the government and the caravan gathered at the BIA to discuss the protesters' living accommodations. The Indians, nearly four hundred strong and poised to fight, refused to leave until the government guaranteed them shelter. They overturned desks and file cabinets and barricaded doors. They smuggled in firearms and cans of gasoline, creating an atmosphere even "more hairy" than at Alcatraz. The occupiers then held religious ceremonies and applied war paint.[177]

Nixon's advisers used the lessons of Alcatraz. "The way we played it was [with] restraint," Patterson remembered.[178] Officials at the White House and Interior sketched out three aims: (1) "get best press possible"; (2) "Look strong. [Will] not tolerate illegality any longer"; (3) "Defer *violence* until Wed. A.M.," the day after the presidential election.[179] On the evening of the occupation, Ehrlichman sounded impatient: "We better get those people out of there."[180] But after Nixon indicated that he did not want bloodshed to mar his reelection, Justice Department officials sought a court injunction to evict the trespassers. Garment and Frank C. Carlucci, deputy director of OMB, then opened talks to entice them to leave.[181]

The White House's handling of the Trail of Broken Treaties differed from that of Alcatraz. Unlike at Alcatraz, administration officials needlessly raised tensions by seeking an injunction with a deadline.[182] Moreover, since this seizure was taking place in Washington just days before a presidential election, the White House did not want to wait out the occupiers. Garment and Carlucci formed a task force to study their demands, including review of treaties, religious freedom, restoration of Native American lands, and increased funds for Indian health care and education. They then paid $66,000 to transport the Indians home.[183] Such appeasement ended the seizure of the BIA after one week, not nineteen months as at Alcatraz.

In the short run, the occupation of the BIA weakened Nixon's support for Indian rights. The president "took it very hard," recalled Ehrlichman, because he thought he had been responsive to Indian concerns. Seeing Native Americans, like African Americans, as ungrateful,

Nixon vowed that "he was through doing things to help Indians."[184] When Agnew, a week after the occupation, asked permission to continue his work on Indian matters, Nixon labeled the issue a "loser," adding that the vice president "should not be tied to a loser."[185] He later dismissed the BIA as a "classic mess."[186] Such outbursts, so typical of this quick-tempered president, cannot be taken too literally. Nixon did not reverse his Indian policy. Though his aides studied new ways to reform the BIA, the president showed little interest in their plans.[187]

In the long run, the trashing of the BIA further divided moderate tribal officials from urban radicals. Knowing that they could not compete with elected tribal leaders for support on reservations, AIM leaders tried to replace elections with stunts and programs with slogans. They derided "established" tribal leaders as "Uncle Tomahawks," or "apples" who were "red on the outside, white on the inside."[188] Elected tribal leaders replied with harsh criticism. The Inuit leader Joseph Upicksoun branded the Trail of Broken Treaties a "fiasco," while Clarence Hamilton of the Hopi condemned AIM's "trail of destruction." President Richard Wilson of the Oglala Sioux denied AIM's right to speak for his tribe. Wilson soon observed the widening gap between Indians when AIM occupied Wounded Knee on the Oglala reservation.[189]

Native American protest crested during the "Second Battle of Wounded Knee." In February 1973, two hundred members of AIM motored to the Pine Ridge Indian Reservation, converging at the hamlet of Wounded Knee. Means and Banks, backed by tradition-bound Sioux leaders, sought to replace the elected tribal government, headed by Wilson, with a hereditary, hierarchical one. (Means and Banks disliked the existing government because it had been established under the Indian Reorganization Act of 1934.)[190] They also demanded revision of the Oglala Sioux's 105-year-old treaty with the federal government.

To achieve their goals, AIM followers took over Wounded Knee at gunpoint. They stormed a trading post and stole arms. They proclaimed an independent Sioux nation and appealed to the United Nations for recognition. They also seized eleven hostages as "prisoners of war." Wilson, the Oglala Sioux chief, prepared to invade Wounded Knee to eject the outsiders. To preempt violence, U.S. marshals, FBI agents, and BIA police cordoned off the town with armored personnel carriers. AIM members, armed mainly with hunting rifles, dug foxholes and fashioned explosives out of Coca-Cola and Fresca bottles. Over the next three months, the two sides traded gunfire on the grassy South Dakota plain.[191]

Both sides came close to provoking a massacre. On the morning of April 16, sixty AIM members marched to within three hundred yards of a government roadblock. They knelt, assumed firing positions, and pointed their weapons at the roadblock. Mercifully, they withdrew.[192] During one night, April 26, Wilson's forces and AIM fired between six and eight thousand rounds at each other. "A miracle that no one has been killed other than the casualties we have so far," Patterson reported. "Some morning we will wake up to see 8–10 people dead . . . AIM occupiers seem to be lavish with ammunition.[193]

Why the standoff at Wounded Knee? Indian militants wished to settle the score with moderates, such as Wilson, who seemed closely tied to the BIA. AIM sought to grab national attention. Although the White House formed a task force to answer the Trail of Broken Treaties, it had refused to confer with AIM followers charged with plundering the BIA.[194] Wounded Knee mirrored rising militancy within South Dakota. To protest the murder of an Indian by a white man, AIM members earlier had raided, of all places, Custer, South Dakota. They set fire to three buildings, and then rambled northward to Rapid City, where they sacked four bars.[195]

Most important, Wounded Knee, like Alcatraz and Blue Lake, exemplified white mistreatment of Native Americans. In 1890 U.S. troops had slaughtered over one hundred Sioux at Wounded Knee, including forty-four women and eighteen children. Eighty years later, Dee Brown's best-seller, *Bury My Heart at Wounded Knee,* reminded Anglos of this calamity, and Means in 1970 called Wounded Knee "an ideal location for a future demonstration."[196] Patterson labeled "the whole damn thing symbolism, marvelous symbolism. When those guys picked Wounded Knee–what a place!"[197]

In responding to "Wounded Knee II," some administration officials ignored history. In March 1973 Nixon cryptically told aides that he was "for action, even in long run."[198] The law-and-order crowd dusted off its sidearms. Geoffrey Shepard, an aide to Ehrlichman, wondered whether "we can long tolerate such armed takeovers."[199] Health, Education, and Welfare Secretary Caspar W. Weinberger wanted to "isolate . . . Wounded Knee completely, cut off all supplies and bring that operation to an end, followed by arrests and trials."[200] Such bravado had limits. While some Justice Department officials cried for action, no one at Defense drafted an order approving the use of force.[201] Staring at so many armed Indians, the White House, as with Alcatraz and the BIA, recoiled from launching an assault.

Nixon's moderate aides again forged a policy of restraint. "Satisfying law enforcement requirements simply doesn't justify the potential loss of life," warned Colonel Volney F. Warner, military liaison for Wounded Knee.[202] "After a meeting at Justice this noon," a regretful Garment noted, "the options involving real force appear to me to be just about unthinkable."[203] "We could end the siege in a day if the Marshalls attacked," conceded Cole in April. "I believe this would be a mistake . . . We don't need an Indian massacre on our hands." "I agree," scrawled Nixon in reply.[204]

The administration opened talks to resolve the crisis. Means, ever conscious of television cameras, at first scorned plans for a private session. AIM leaders demanded a meeting at the White House, followed by a commission to review the Sioux treaty of 1868.[205] Garment fumed at such fist-pounding: "We aren't just ventriloquists over here." Officials outside both the White House and AIM eventually signed a settlement. Assistant Attorney General D. Kent Frizzell and his deputy bargained with Sioux leaders. (Marlon Brando even offered his good offices.)[206] On May 6, 1973, the occupiers surrendered their arms in exchange for a probe of Wilson's management of the Pine Ridge Reservation. Garment then sent Patterson to Wounded Knee to discuss the Sioux treaty.[207] Nixonians, using some well-worn patience, had avoided a second massacre at that site.

AIM leaders, stung by mounting press skepticism toward their sensational occupations, offered truces with Indian moderates and the White House after Wounded Knee.[208] They appealed to the National Tribal Chairmen's Association (NTCA) and the National Congress of American Indians to form a national coalition for Indian rights. Dennis Banks, extending the olive branch to the White House, bade Patterson a happy new year and thanked him for "all of your assistance and quick response to our calls . . . a job well done." "Brad," Garment joshed, "this is one for the memory book. Point to it with pride and astonish-ment."[209] AIM's sugary rhetoric did not last long. In 1974 Means and Banks denounced NTCA as a "hoax."[210] AIM members also organized a sit-in at a BIA office in Aberdeen, South Dakota, and requested a meeting with federal officials. The government refused.[211]

Nixonians became, if anything, harsher toward AIM. OMB audited federal agencies suspected of channeling money to AIM.[212] The admin-istration, bruised by successive occupations, stepped up its surveillance of troublemakers. Deputy Attorney General Joseph T. Sneed asked his Community Relations Service to report "any indications of future mili-tant action."[213] The FBI also got involved, drafting a report titled "The American Indian Movement: A Record of Violence."[214] Such tactics re-sembled Nixon's repression of the Black Panthers, and were reminis-cent of his disregard for the civil liberties of demonstrators. Yet the Community Relations Service and FBI uncovered only minor Indian unrest. One FBI report relayed such trivia as the travel itinerary of Rus-sell Means's brother, alleged demonstrations to mark Wounded Knee's first anniversary, and AIM's links to the Workers World Party.[215]

Yet White House officials reaffirmed their commitment to Indian self-determination. "I think our policy is right," said Whitaker. "If we have erred, it has been in over-expectation (much like LBJ with the War on Poverty)."[216] He might have cited Nixon's own overselling of minority business enterprise. In fact, the president wanted more public-ity for his policy during Wounded Knee: "Shouldn't we get out a White Paper on our remarkably progressive record on Indians?"[217] White House moderates used the seizure to move Nixon's Indian bills. Wounded Knee, Patterson contended, was "wrapped up in the larger question of how well we've followed up on the effectiveness of our In-dian program."[218] In March 1973 Whitaker resubmitted Nixon's legisla-tive package and then rebuked Congress for failing to act sooner.[219] Nixonians clearly sought to blame Wounded Knee on congressional inaction.

Between 1973 and 1975, Congress approved a spate of Indian re-forms. It restored the Menominee, a Wisconsin tribe terminated in 1961, to federal trust responsibility. Ada Deer, a Menominee leader, lobbied for the Menominee Restoration Act, and White House coun-selor Melvin R. Laird, a former Wisconsin congressman, typed the president's statement of support. In passing this law, Congress all but repealed termination, as Nixon had asked.[220] Both houses also passed the Indian Financing Act of 1974, the president's proposal to lend tribes money through a revolving fund. After Nixon's resignation, they approved the Indian Self-Determination Act of 1975, which allowed federal agencies to contract out services to tribes and expanded Indians' control over their schools.[221] Credit for these advances belongs to tribal leaders and the White House for conceiving them and to Congress for following up. While Means and Banks enjoyed reputations as publicity hounds, prone to employ irresponsible, even dangerous, methods to achieve their ends, AIM's antics had served to remind government officials of their unfulfilled promises to Indians.

Watergate did not cause Nixon's Native American initiatives to drift. The scandal, to be sure, cost the president some of his ablest advisers, including Ehrlichman, who resigned over his role in the cover-up, and Garment, who took over as Nixon's lawyer. Yet the sure-footed Patterson stayed on to handle Native American matters.[222] With Congress cranking out bills, the president only needed to keep his signing pen at hand. And Nixon's personal commitment to Indian rights held firm. In 1974 he endorsed the return of 251,000 acres in Arizona to the Havasupai. Congress a year later granted the tribe 185,000 acres near the Grand Canyon.[223] As it turned out, some of Nixon's most significant reforms came to pass just as his presidency came to an end.

That was one of the many ironies of Nixon's policy. The president who extolled Indian self-determination became upset when radicals took matters into their own hands. The seizures of the BIA and Wounded Knee, in fact, cut two ways. They enraged Nixon's reform-minded aides, diverting their attention from policy questions. Yet such protests to some extent accelerated change. The president, after Alcatraz, issued his Indian message, and Congress, after Wounded Knee, began implementing it. Such were the bookends of Nixon's Native American reforms.

Beyond Termination, Beyond Nixon

Overall, Nixon used firm leadership to expand choices for Native Americans. According to a reporter for the American Indian Press Association, "The Nixon administration . . . has been in the eyes of even the most critical observers one of the most active in Indian affairs since that of . . . President Franklin D. Roosevelt."[224] In truth, Nixon's record eclipsed Roosevelt's, and Nixon's successors continued his reforms. "Existing tribal governments," argued the historian Roger L. Nichols in 1988, "exercise more direct and a wider variety of authority than at any other time in this century."[225]

Many Native Americans fondly recalled Nixon's Indian policy. The majority of tribal leaders, John Whitaker argued in 1996, "will tell you that Nixon did more for Indians than any president since the Second World War."[226] In fact, in 1978 LaDonna Harris, president of Americans for Indian Opportunity, a member of the Comanche tribe, and the wife of Democratic senator Fred R. Harris of Oklahoma, complained of slights from the Carter White House. "This has led those of us in the Indian Community, including AIO, to say that the Nixon Administration was much more accessible," she wrote a Carter aide. "This is very disconcerting for a dyed-in-the-wool Democrat."[227]

Curiously, Nixon enjoyed greater praise and faced more civil unrest from Indians than from blacks. This paradox stemmed from the fact that Native Americans, unlike African Americans, agreed on aims but argued over tactics. Indian leaders, favoring self-determination, included elected tribal officials who had a stake in "the system" and wanted to work within it, and nonelected urban militants who used direct action to show their alienation. Liberal and radical blacks debated the merits of integration versus separation while criticizing the Republican administration, in part to cement their own community. This does not explain why under Nixon urban Indians were more prone to use civil disobedience than blacks. Dissenters, it seems fair to say, are more likely to protest when they think the public will identify with their cause. Urban blacks, after a decade of protests and rioting, enjoyed little support among whites.

Nixon does not merit all the credit for promoting Native American rights. Grassroots advocacy forced issues of self-determination and land claims onto the national agenda, just as African American demonstrations had pressed JFK and LBJ into pushing the civil rights acts of 1964 and 1965. Nevertheless, Nixon assembled an able staff, heeded their advice, and backed them when Native American unrest surfaced. And the president's policy of self-determination meshed with his opposition to forced integration and his support of separate minority institutions.

Nixon's successors built on his policies. Gerald R. Ford reaffirmed the "self-determination without termination" policy, and Jimmy Carter approved legislation to settle land claims with tribes in Rhode Island and Maine, a solution first proposed by Bradley Patterson in 1976.[228] Carter signed bills to safeguard Indian religious practices and to expand Indians' control over their schools.[229] He also established, via executive order, an assistant secretary of the interior for Indian affairs, using Nixonian means to achieve a Nixonian end in a manner that Nixon himself should have thought of.[230] Carter's BIA started the Federal Acknowledgement Project to bring unrecognized tribes under federal jurisdiction.[231] And federal courts, beginning in the 1970s, affirmed Indian sovereignty, the power of "tribes to assert their economic, political, and cultural authority in appropriate spheres."[232] Over a century, the historian Lawrence C. Kelly concluded, national policy had evolved from "virtual denial of tribal sovereignty to almost full recognition."[233]

There was a partial reaction against these practices during the 1980s. By the late 1970s, western ranchers and business leaders had organized to challenge tribal control of Native American property.[234] Ronald Reagan signed the Indian Claims Limitation Act of 1982, which placed limits on Indian land claims not already registered with the Department of the Interior. Reagan slashed funding for Indian health care and education.[235] Yet even Reagan favored self-determination, a "government-to-government relationship" among states, tribes, and federal officials.[236]

Nixon was correct to espouse Indian self-determination, even though this policy was no panacea for a complex set of problems. Since natural resources are finite, whites and Indians continued to clash over access to rivers, lakes, and parcels of land. Native American activists increasingly used litigation, not civil disobedience, to seek redress.[237] A less centralized BIA would have further expanded the range of choices available to Indians. But Carter and Reagan, like Nixon, named panels to restructure the bureau, which then failed to follow up.[238] Nixon should have paid closer attention to Agnew's plan to reorganize the BIA.

Most important, no president has balanced Indian self-government with economic development. Nixon and Carter attacked Indian poverty with more dollars than Reagan, and the percentage of Native American families living below the poverty line shrank from 33.3 to 23.7 between 1970 and 1979.[239] By 1989, following Reagan's budget cuts, that figure had swelled to 27.2 percent, and the poverty rate for Indian families remained three times that of whites.[240] The government, by curtailing assimilation, however justified, risked isolating Native Americans–and their difficulties–from Anglo society.

If Nixonians failed to resolve all Indian problems, they made a strong start. By asserting Indian self-determination, they acknowledged that "civil rights" now reflected the aspirations of other disadvantaged groups, not just blacks. This change became further apparent in Nixon's response to the women's movement.

8

Stops and Starts: Women's Rights

On August 6, 1971, President Nixon had to be "dragged kicking and screaming into the State Dining Room" to address delegates to the American Legion Auxiliary's Girls' Nation. Presidential aide John Andrews called this task "a hardship assignment unmatched since Br'er Fox tossed Br'er Rabbit in that old briar patch." The president soon warmed to his audience: "His soft, light tone of voice, relaxed manner, and whimsical opening comments were perfectly suited to flatter these young ladies *as* young ladies." Nixon called women a "great human resource" and proclaimed: "There should be no bars to women's achievement and contribution. Perhaps one of you will even occupy this office. That can and should happen." He lauded homemakers, telling his audience that "you can do as much, perhaps more, as a good woman."[1]

The meeting with Girls' Nation underscored Nixon's attitude toward women's rights. The president was almost as hesitant to address women's issues as he was to address Girls' Nation. When pushed, Nixon's message to the Second Women's Movement resembled his remarks to Girls' Nation: that women deserved the opportunity to compete with men in the workplace, while those choosing to remain at home deserved equal respect. The president and his aides balanced feminist demands for equal opportunity against traditional gender roles, without abandoning their own sexism. Andrews's patronizing remarks, noting how Nixon's "soft, light tone" was appropriate for "young ladies," were common within the overwhelmingly male White House staff and the wider male world of the late 1960s.

In handling both women's and African American rights, Nixon practiced substitution. In place of integration, the president offered blacks increased economic opportunities and a degree of separatism. Regarding women, he supplanted vigorous support of the Equal Rights Amendment (ERA) with specific programs to help females attain professional careers. Although Nixon questioned the ability of most women–and blacks–to succeed, he agreed to end the barriers to female opportunity. Underlining these policies was the president's class bias, whereby he supported the middle-class aspirations of minorities and women.

In key respects, the president's approach to women's rights departed from his handling of minority rights. Even more than his African American and Native American programs, Nixon's policies for women unfolded in stops and starts. The president tried to dodge the feminist agenda, especially ERA. Then, pressed by Republican women and their own Task Force on Women's Rights and Responsibilities, Nixonians recruited women for federal jobs and developed affirmative action programs. The president granted the United States Commission on Civil Rights authority to investigate discrimination based on sex and signed legislation assuring women access to higher education. But his support for women's rights remained limited. Nixon vetoed a comprehensive child care bill and opposed abortion. While women's rights was not the only new social movement to emerge during the late sixties, Nixonians considered its demands to be more complex and politically more explosive than those of Native Americans, a tiny minority group.

Absent from Nixon's programs for women was a commitment to empowerment, a concept embedded in his minority business and Native American policies. While Nixonians co-opted the separatist rhetoric of Black Power and Red Power, they were too entrenched in male privilege to espouse "womanpower," a term associated with radical feminists seeking to end all types of male domination. Instead, the president and his men haltingly espoused equal opportunity, a narrower idea identified with liberal feminists, to allow women to compete with men in the workforce.

All the President's Men

The president's men first responded to women's rights with "patronizing neglect."[2] Within their masculine culture, Nixonians bantered about women as "better halves" or sexual objects while disparaging their abilities. Pressure from Republican feminists and a presidential task force on women's rights eventually forced gender equality onto Nixon's agenda.

Disregard for women's issues began with the president. After reading criticism that he had placed few women in federal jobs, Nixon jotted, "Much ado about *nothing!*"[3] When the bipartisan National Women's Political Caucus convened, Secretary of State William P. Rogers compared its members to "a burlesque." "What's wrong with that?" the president wisecracked.[4] The sexual remarks continued. While showing the journalist Richard L. Wilson around the White House, Nixon spied a young woman in a miniskirt and quipped "that he liked to keep up with things like that."[5] The president did not like assertive women; he privately referred to a female reporter for *Women's Wear Daily* as a "bitch."[6] Nixon thought feminists were ice-cold fanatics, reincarnations of France's infamous Madame Lafarge. "Liberal women," he joked. "They knitted at the guillotine."[7] In 1993 he described Hillary Rodham Clinton as "steely," adding, "She even *claps* in a controlled way. She's a true-believing liberal."[8] Nixon wanted his wife, Pat, to avoid controversial issues because, as he once wrote, "we don't want her to become like Eleanor Roosevelt."[9]

The president's family life reinforced his patriarchical views. To be sure, Pat Nixon had worked during the early years of her marriage, and as first lady she privately favored women's rights. Yet she mostly played a "supportive, encouraging role" as her husband climbed the political ladder. Nixon, for his part, called his wife his "Dearest Heart" and "Dear One."[10] "I wouldn't have made it without them," the former president said of his wife and two daughters. "The credit belongs to Mrs. Nixon. She's a great, great mother."[11] Whether or not his family actually conformed to this blissful ideal is not really important. Nixon thought it did, and he believed in traditional gender roles.

Nixon had strange ideas about what constituted expanded opportunities for women. During a campaign flight in 1967, he marveled at the ability of airlines to "take raw country girls" and "convert them into efficient hostesses and stewardesses" with "well-modulated voices."[12] Regarding unemployment, Nixon told aides to focus on "the breadwinner in the family as distinguished from youth, women, part-time applicants in the Labor force, etc."[13] The idea of women as breadwinners escaped the president.

But Nixon conceded that exceptionally talented women might rise to leadership positions in the United States. During the race for the 1964 Republican presidential nomination, he did not dismiss the campaign of Senator Margaret Chase Smith of Maine. When asked whether a woman could serve as president, Nixon acknowledged, "Women can . . . hurt us, so as far as I'm concerned . . . [O]f course a qualified woman could be president."[14] He believed that there were a few women, such as Smith, who might contribute to governance if given the chance. Such thoughts were quite common at the time. In 1969, 58 percent of men and 49 percent of women affirmed that they would vote for a qualified woman for president.[15]

Nixon's liberal advisers went a bit further, endorsing equal opportunity while scorning radical feminism and "empowerment." Urban affairs chief Daniel P. Moynihan saw "female equality" as "a major cultural/political force of the 1970s" and recommended "creative political leadership." As for radical feminism, however, Moynihan playfully warned of violence, since "by all accounts, the women radicals are the most fearsome of all."[16] White House counselor Robert H. Finch, who later recruited women for federal jobs, joked of a "Women's Lib" doll, "You wind it up and it runs you down."[17] After reading that the Labor Department planned a "Womanpower Week," White House counsel Leonard Garment, a strong advocate of minority rights and sometime supporter of ERA, advised against presidential support. "I'm not a good judge on this one," he admitted. "I am not sympathetic to the 'movement,' and think this particular suggestion is just plain silly."[18] Domestic policy chief John D. Ehrlichman, who favored Indian rights, said little about women's issues during 1969.

Nixon's conservative advisers, for their part, expressed contempt for women's abilities and equal rights. Vice President Spiro T. Agnew quipped, "Three things have been difficult to tame—fools, women and the ocean. We may soon be able to tame the ocean; but fools and women will take a little longer."[19] The economist Arthur Burns professed ignorance "of any discrimination against the better half of mankind."[20] But sexism was all around Burns. White House chief of staff H. R. Haldeman refused to hire women for advance positions in Nixon's reelection campaign, calling it a "stupid idea which will cause more trouble than it's worth."[21] Appointments secretary Dwight Chapin referred to female staffers as "girls."[22] Alexander M. Haig, Jr., who succeeded Haldeman as chief of staff in 1973, barred women from the White House gym because the "place just isn't suited for ladies." Haig eventually allowed women to use the facility, provided they followed the "buddy system" to ensure their safety.[23] "Let's try it for a while," he conceded. "Then sure[ly] interest will fade."

A few subordinates publicly joked about female sexuality. Press secretary Ronald Ziegler remarked that thirty-two-year-old Constance Stuart, the first lady's press secretary, was suffering from a "menopause problem."[24] National security adviser Henry A. Kissinger, a self-styled "swinger," complained that women seated near him at White House dinners were not pretty enough. (At the next dinner, Kissinger found himself beside the film star Zsa Zsa Gabor.)[25] Labor Secretary Peter J. Brennan was grossly sexist. During his confirmation hearings in 1973, Brennan offered to invite "go-go girls" to entertain bored assembly-line workers.[26] Upon taking office, he compared himself to a sheik inheriting a harem of three hundred women: "I know what's expected of me but I don't know where to start."[27] When a female aide went to testify before a House panel, Brennan cracked, "If you play the right music, she can strip and change."[28] Sexist comments were far more common than racist slurs in Nixon's administration.

Such comments conveyed contemporary male attitudes. "Male dominance," Moynihan wrote, "is so deeply a part of American life that males don't even notice it."[29] Liberal politicians could be just as sexist as Nixonians. Republican governor Nelson A. Rockefeller of New York praised women's intuitive sense of candidates, not their grasp of issues.[30] In 1964 Interior Secretary Stewart L. Udall, a champion of environmental protection, asserted that woman's "intuitive feel for the mystical, her inclination to reverence, her instinct to defend and save those things which will serve her young" made her a strong conservationist.[31] Meanwhile, President John F. Kennedy showed more interest in pursuing sexual liaisons with women than in extending equal rights to them, and President Lyndon B. Johnson privately told risqué jokes that "a later generation of women would label 'sexual harassment.'"[32]

This masculine culture influenced policy making. In 1967 the National Organization for Women (NOW) urged John Macy, chair of the U.S. Civil Service Commission, to lambaste LBJ for failing "to obtain true equality for women" and for "the lack of recent appointments of women."[33] Nixonians at the outset proposed no programs for women, although they had for blacks and Native Americans. Unlike Eisenhower, but like Kennedy and Johnson, Nixon failed to name a woman to his cabinet, thus breaking a campaign pledge to outdo his predecessors in female appointments.[34] Facing a growing women's movement, Nixon listened to liberal advisers, whose support of equality proved erratic. His political aides, meanwhile, endorsed women's rights for a narrow reason—to placate female voters. Accordingly, Nixon's policies usually followed "liberal feminism" and the path of equal rights.

Professional women within Nixon's government attacked sexism. In 1970 Helen Delich Bentley, chair of the U.S. Maritime Commission and one of Nixon's few female appointees, criticized the president for failing to place women in "responsible" posts and for relying on such "empty" gestures as inviting the wives of cabinet members to attend a cabinet meeting. Bentley found many administration officials "positively anti-women."[35] Within this administration, wrote Carol Reavis, an aide to Finch, one of the few Nixonians who pushed the appointment of women, "there is little comprehension of the impenetrable psychological difficulties" facing professional women. Reavis called the White House a "hotbed of petty discriminatory acts" resulting in a "shameful" waste of talent.[36]

Nixonian apathy galvanized other professional women; while Democratic feminists gradually lowered their expectations of the president, Republican women raised their demands. In 1968 Betty Friedan, a Democrat and president of NOW, the leading, but still very small, feminist group, asked candidate Nixon to comment on NOW's "Bill of

Rights." NOW favored passage of the Equal Rights Amendment, equal access to employment and education, day care centers, maternity leave, and reproductive rights for women. Nixon did not reply.[37] Early in 1969 its leaders invited the president to detail his "program to benefit women." Again, no response. By the end of 1969, NOW had retreated to asking Nixon for symbolic gestures, such as naming a woman to the Supreme Court and launching a female astronaut into orbit, to demonstrate his support for women's rights.[38]

Republican women first complained of Nixon's laxness on female appointments, then advanced a feminist agenda similar to NOW's. When Vera Glaser, a correspondent for the North American Newspaper Alliance and former Republican national committeewoman, asked why Nixon had not appointed more women, the president kidded that Glaser should enter government service herself. Elly M. Peterson, assistant chair of the Republican National Committee, reported that the Johnson administration had placed twenty-seven women in policy-making jobs, while Nixon had appointed nine.[39] Out of 1,170 appointments, fewer than twenty went to women, a record one Republican national committeewoman labeled "appalling."[40] Why had Nixonians failed to recruit women? "THE MEN SAID THEY SIMPLY HADN'T THOUGHT OF IT," Peterson complained to Republican National Committee chair Rogers C. B. Morton. She urged Nixon to "push" his cabinet to hire more females.[41]

Pressure grew. Glaser grilled Arthur Burns, then Nixon's chief domestic adviser, on the lack of women in top federal positions. Burns invited Glaser "to make more noise," and she did, giving him data on gender bias and proposals to enhance women's rights.[42] Representative Florence P. Dwyer, Republican of New Jersey, ran with Glaser's ideas, urging Nixon to appoint more women, name an assistant for women's rights, and back "cease and desist" powers for the Equal Employment Opportunity Commission (EEOC) and authority for the Civil Rights Commission to probe bias against women. Like NOW, with its Bill of Rights, she favored passage of ERA, funding for child care, and measures to bar discrimination in education and in federally contracted work. Republican representatives Margaret M. Heckler of Massachusetts, Charlotte T. Reid of Illinois, and Catherine D. May of Washington co-signed Dwyer's memorandum. "None of us are feminists,"

Dwyer affirmed. "We do not ask for special privileges. We seek only equal opportunity."[43] She no doubt shunned the label "feminist" to separate herself from radicals and the Democratic-led NOW.

In truth, Dwyer's agenda, along with NOW's, signaled a nascent movement, class-based and bipartisan, known as "liberal feminism." Liberal feminists were professional women seeking equal opportunity. These middle-class feminists, present in both parties, saw protective laws as restricting their ability to compete in the workplace. Some state laws prohibited female employment in places ranging from mines to shoeshine parlors to poolrooms, while others forbade women workers from cleaning moving machinery, serving alcohol, or lifting heavy objects. By the mid- 1960s, federal courts began using Title VII of the Civil Rights Act of 1964, which prohibited bias against women in employment, to strike down these laws. Republicans Dwyer and Glaser surely backed NOW's goal "to bring women into full participation in the mainstream of American society" in a "truly equal partnership with men."[44] In drafting her proposals, Glaser sought advice from Democrat Catherine East, executive secretary of the Citizens' Advisory Council on the Status of Women, a panel established by President Kennedy.[45]

By the end of 1969, the women's movement had become a featured story on television and radio and in newspapers and large-circulation magazines such as *Look, Life, Time,* and *McCall's.*[46] The president might overlook the demands of Democratic women but not those of feminists within his own party. Moreover, the movement's commitment to opportunity and competition meshed with the bourgeois outlook of Nixonians. Even so, their sexism ensured that the road to equal opportunity would be slow and tortuous.

Nixon responded cautiously to the rising feminist tide. Like JFK, he named a task force, in October 1969, to study women's rights. Dwyer had broached the idea for a presidential commission in February, and Tom Cole, a Burns aide, seconded her motion.[47] Such a study group both coincided with and departed from the president's usual policy making. At the outset, Nixon and Burns established several task forces to consider domestic issues. Yet, except for the National Advisory Council on Minority Business Enterprise, none addressed civil rights per se. The president ruled out a study of Native Americans and moved swiftly to implement tribal self-determination. Given their earlier neglect of women's rights, Nixon and Burns surely considered this latest task force a delaying tactic. Dwyer thought otherwise.

The Presidential Task Force on Women's Rights and Responsibilities, as it was called, ratified most of the liberal feminist agenda. To shape the panel, Glaser and East each sent Burns a list of possible members. Although he rejected most of their proposals, Burns named Virginia R. Allan, a Republican and former president of the National League of Business and Professional Women's Clubs, as chair. Glaser became a member, and East served as staff director.[48] Overall, the panel of eleven women and two men bore a Republican feminist stamp.

Burns and Nixon offered few guidelines for the task force, and Republican feminists filled the vacuum. Burns defined the panel's mission as "to review the present status of women in our society and to recommend what might be done in the future to further advance their rights and responsibilities."[49] This broad mandate mirrored his own ignorance of women's rights; at the task force's first meeting, Burns endorsed equal opportunity by citing insipidly the lesson of World War II. In limiting women to traditional roles ("Kinder, Kuche und Kirke"), Nazi Germany, he asserted, found itself at a military disadvantage against the United States, where women worked in munitions factories. Dwyer's remarks proved more relevant and influential. She circulated her earlier memorandum to Nixon and praised the task force as "a giant step and an indication that President Nixon has seen the light." While Dwyer again rejected the label "feminist," she advised against timidity: "We should join the men and let them know that we are not going to move over any longer."[50]

A Matter of Simple Justice, the report of the Presidential Task Force on Women's Rights and Responsibilities, trumpeted the earlier proposals of Glaser and Dwyer. The panel urged Nixon to name an assistant for women's rights and send Congress a message on discrimination against women. It endorsed ERA as well as legislation to empower EEOC, provide child care and access to education, expand the Civil Rights Commission's charge, and end gender distinctions in Social Security benefits. The panel also favored guidelines to end gender bias among federal contractors, the use of lawsuits against firms suspected of discrimination, and the naming of more women to government offices.

"Women do not seek special privileges," declared Allan, sounding like Dwyer. "They do seek equal rights."[51]

Unprepared for the task force's agenda, top Nixon aides buried it. The president received the report in December 1969 and did not publish it until June 1970. Aversion to women's rights was the most likely explanation for the holdup. The chore of responding to the report fell to Garment, the in-house liberal.[52] But he focused on one issue, clamoring, unsuccessfully, for a presidential assistant for women's rights. "I doubt that it would be an effective addition," wrote Peter M. Flanigan, a personnel adviser. "I agree," scrawled Haldeman, as he shelved the idea.[53] Ehrlichman said nothing on the proposed office.

Within this context, releasing the task force report became a public relations nightmare. Alice L. Beeman, director of the American Association of University Women (AAUW), expressed a "very strong desire that the report be made available to the public."[54] Dwyer called the document "excellent" and urged Nixon to issue it. He demurred.[55] After reading that Republican women planned a meeting on women's rights in April, Garment sent the report to executive branch offices and urged its publication.[56] He was too late. A task force member, probably Glaser, had leaked it to the press.[57] When the White House finally printed the report, Elly Peterson noted that "it landed with a rather dull thud as it was overdue and the President said not one word."[58]

Nixon's political advisers groaned at the delay. Although conservative, they hoped to court women voters by paying lip service to equal rights. Charles W. Colson, White House liaison to organized groups, favored early release of the task force report, noting that women's rights "is beginning to build up a real head of steam."[59] Party leaders agreed. In a memorandum titled "Women–God Bless Them!" Rogers Morton complained, "It is now after June 1st–the report still has NOT been printed." To Morton, such heel-dragging gave Democrats in Congress the opportunity to champion women's rights.[60] Yet the president remained aloof.

Unlike minority rights, gender issues were not on Nixon's agenda. The task force on women's rights was his bastard child, unplanned and unwanted. When its proposals signaled a new social movement, the president ducked for cover. Nixon the politician could not overlook women's rights forever. But he knew how to evade sticky issues such as ERA.

The Artful Dodger: Nixon on ERA

Political pressure, not principle, made Nixon a sporadic supporter of the Equal Rights Amendment. During his years in the U.S. House and Senate, Nixon backed ERA. Later on, he simply referred to his earlier pro forma endorsements. Meanwhile, his staff, lacking a feminist voice, remained divided on ERA. Nixon did not consider the amendment important, even though it emerged as "the symbol of the Second Women's Movement just as the suffrage amendment [had] been for the First Women's Movement."[61]

Before Congress passed it in 1972, ERA had endured a long, tortuous history. Beginning in 1923, Alice Paul and the National Woman's Party campaigned for a constitutional amendment granting women equal rights with men. Other former suffragists, including Carrie Chapman Catt, Florence Kelley, and Jane Addams, opposed such an amendment, believing it would end protective legislation for women workers. Paul's single-minded pursuit of ERA further divided the movement, and the amendment, opposed by such prominent women as Eleanor Roosevelt, faltered in Congress. In 1950 and 1953, the Senate passed ERA with the "Hayden amendment." Senator Carl Hayden, Democrat of Arizona, advanced this rider to retain protective legislation and other "benefits" women enjoyed under current law. The proviso, leaders of the National Woman's Party argued, would defeat the purpose of an equal rights amendment. The ongoing debate between proponents of equal opportunity and defenders of protective measures delayed ERA.[62]

Between 1945 and 1968, every president routinely endorsed the amendment. Aligned with labor unions, which defended protective laws for women, Democrats proved to be lame supporters of ERA. As a senator, Harry S. Truman expressed sympathy for the amendment, then dropped the matter. In 1960 Emma Guffey Miller, a Democratic national committeewoman and chair of the National Woman's Party, drafted JFK's letter backing ERA, though without his approval. Lyndon Johnson originally favored the amendment while in the Senate, but later retreated under pressure from labor-oriented Democratic women.

Eisenhower, a Republican, was more supportive, calling for passage of ERA in his message to Congress in 1957.[63] But he later admitted, "[I] haven't been active enough in doing something about it."[64] With no prospect of passage, ERA represented a cosmetic reform.

Early in his career, Nixon seemed bolder on ERA. Following his election to the House in 1946, he felt pressure from the National Woman's Party to back the amendment.[65] The newly elected representative affirmed his support for ERA, and in 1949 promised Representative Katherine St. George, Republican of New York, to provide "any assistance you may want me to for advancing the [ERA] resolution."[66] Senator Nixon co-sponsored the amendment in 1951. Such actions stemmed from party loyalty as well as concern for women voters. The GOP, with little support among labor union members, proved more forthcoming on ERA.[67] And Republican women dominated the National Woman's Party.

But Nixon did not believe strongly in ERA. "We never had any *push* [from him] that we could see," recalled Alice Paul.[68] As vice president, Nixon replied to leaders of the National Woman's Party via form letters.[69] Nixon's belief in domesticity weakened his pro-ERA stance. In 1959 Amelia Haines Walker, chair of the National Woman's Party, again urged Nixon to back the amendment. His reply avoided mentioning ERA, rejected laws which "unjustly restrict women," and proclaimed that "in the interests of family life, and woman's primary role as a wife and mother, the laws granting women protection . . . should be retained."[70] Nixon asked an aide to "check whether this [reply] is too dangerous. I would like to tone it down a bit."[71] In the final draft he vaguely opposed "legal obstacles" to women's rights and blandly praised the "status and achievements of the American woman."[72] *"Good,"* Nixon scribbled, regarding the watered-down version, "but she'll probably not think it's enough."[73] He was right. Walker quickly protested his retreat on ERA.[74]

Political vulnerability forced Nixon to reaffirm his support. In 1959 Rockefeller, a contender for the Republican presidential nomination, endorsed ERA, and the National Woman's Party pressed Nixon to respond.[75] Meanwhile, aides worried about Nixon's appeal among women. "You have spoken to many a woman's group in the past," John Reagan McCrary wrote, "but never in a manner to gain a national impact."[76] When the National Woman's Party elected Emma Guffey Miller, a Democrat, as chair, Leila Holt, a Republican, read it as "a move to organize women against Nixon."[77] Although polls showed him running strongly among women, the vice president told advisers to "make a special effort to get out the women's vote in the close states."[78] After JFK's nomination, Nixon placed greater weight on the women's vote because "we all know that [Kennedy] has a great deal of appeal to women."[79] With that in mind, Nixon endorsed ERA in September 1960, expressing hope "that there will be widespread support" for it.[80] In 1968 he used the same language to reiterate his approval.[81]

Nixon's stance partly reflected staff advice: campaign aides either ignored ERA or encouraged him to back it for political rather than philosophical reasons. His secretary, Rose Mary Woods, condemned the leaders of the National Woman's Party as "bleeding hearts."[82] In 1960 Leila Holt sent Nixon data on women's growing preference for the GOP, something he could not overlook in a tight race.[83] In 1968 conservative aides Patrick J. Buchanan and Annelise G. Anderson drafted Nixon's statement on ERA, but without conviction. Anderson, an economist, considered the amendment "pointless" but "harmless," adding that not coming out for it when other candidates did would be "unfortunate."[84] Buchanan, a speechwriter in Nixon's White House, opposed ERA. "One prays the silly amendment will perish," he wrote in 1973.[85]

To Buchanan's chagrin, the women's movement soon resurfaced. Radical feminists, like Native American militants, assailed emblems of oppression. They draped the Statue of Liberty with a banner reading "Women of the World Unite!" "It is ironic," said one protester, "that a woman symbolizes the abstract idea of liberty, but in reality we are not free."[86] Radicals from WITCH (Women's International Terrorist Conspiracy from Hell) picketed *Playboy* magazine.[87] In August 1970 liberal feminists staged the "Women's Strike for Equality" to celebrate fifty years of suffrage. In New York they waved signs such as "Don't Cook Dinner! Starve a Rat Today!" and listened to NOW leaders demand abortion rights, child care, and equal pay for equal work. Even more than liberals, radicals attacked prevailing gender roles. One young woman, with hair cropped, hurdled a fence, planted a kiss on a young man, then shrieked, "Hello, you male-chauvinist racist pig!"[88] Meanwhile, a hairdressing appointment at Vidal Sassoon's salon delayed

Betty Friedan's appearance at the strike.[89] It seemed that even well-off liberals were extolling "Women's Liberation." "Emeralds! Aren't they divine?" exclaimed a female character in a *New Yorker* cartoon. "Jack gave them to me to shut up about Women's Lib."[90]

Within this setting, Nixon's "hope" for "widespread support" of ERA came true. Middle-class liberal feminists, committed to equal opportunity, took the lead. Nixon's task force on women's rights and his Citizens' Advisory Council on the Status of Women endorsed the amendment. In 1969 the Women's Bureau at the Labor Department ended fifty years of hostility and backed ERA. In 1970 Representative Martha W. Griffiths, Democrat of Michigan, brought the amendment to the House floor via discharge petition, and it passed, 350 to 15. Gladys O'Donnell, president of the National Federation of Republican Women, urged Nixon to restate his support for ERA, and NOW, with growing membership, pledged to campaign against any politician thwarting the amendment.[91] Even first lady Pat Nixon approved of ERA.[92] The president did not expect such "widespread support" to appear so swiftly—or so close to home.

Among the president's advisers, sentiment for ERA ran wide and shallow. Only Attorney General John N. Mitchell opposed the amendment, arguing that women enjoyed equal rights under the Fifth and Fourteenth Amendments.[93] Other Nixonians saw endorsing ERA as "good politics." "The President has publicly supported this amendment, as has every other politician down through the years," Colson noted. "Fortunately, the good sense and ultimate wisdom of Congress has always kept this ridiculous proposal from being enacted."[94] Congressional liaison chief Bryce N. Harlow called ERA "insane," but favored "routine" acknowledgment of Nixon's earlier support since the president "must be for it . . . *Reason*—it's *political.*"[95] Garment argued weakly that "we have passed the point where reservations about the Equal Rights Amendment make any political or substantive sense."[96] In 1970 Garment prepared an option paper urging Nixon to restate his approval of the amendment. But Ehrlichman said nothing for or against ERA, and the president ignored the issue.[97]

Nixon saw no compelling reason to re-endorse ERA, which had stalled in the Senate. In the fall of 1970, Senator Sam J. Ervin, Jr., Democrat of North Carolina and ERA's fiercest foe, advanced an amendment to retain protective laws for women. A flurry of riders followed. James B. Allen, Democrat of Alabama, proposed a rider to end the Supreme Court's authority over education. The Senate adopted amendments to ERA allowing prayer in public schools and sparing women from the draft. To achieve consensus, Birch E. Bayh, Democrat of Indiana, rewrote ERA, but Congress recessed before considering his compromise.[98] Nixon, meanwhile, left this controversy to the Senate.

Such evasion sowed doubts about Nixon's stance. In 1971 Anne Armstrong, a Republican national committeewoman, inquired if "the President supports the Equal Rights Amendment."[99] Without a staff member overseeing the issue, Nixon's position had become "ambiguous at best."[100] In April 1971 Assistant Attorney General William H. Rehnquist informed the House Judiciary Committee that the president favored ERA. But, like the amendment's opponents, Rehnquist suggested that ERA might void state alimony laws and compel women to serve in the armed forces.[101] Two months later the House Judiciary Committee approved the "Wiggins rider" to exempt women from the draft and retain laws protecting their "health and safety."[102] In protest, Republican women, including Helen Bentley, Dwyer, Heckler, and Reid, petitioned Nixon to endorse an unfettered ERA, warning that the "women's vote in 1972 will be more critical" than ever before.[103] Unlikely to persuade Nixon on ERA's merits, they cited his political vulnerability instead.

ERA's opponents clung to moot arguments. By the mid-1960s, federal courts began to strike down, as sexually discriminatory, protective laws for women. The prospect of drafting women became remote as Nixon moved to form an all-volunteer army.[104] And the Supreme Court could leave political issues such as the draft or alimony to Congress. Most ERA opponents adhered to patriarchy. "I believe in equality," said Representative Charles P. Wiggins, Republican of California and author of the rider, "but not total equality." His GOP colleague Richard H. Poff of Virginia worried that ERA would end state laws allowing men to determine where their families would live. "Well, someone has to decide, and I think it must be the man," insisted Poff. Suppose the man was ill or incapable? "Well," he ventured, "in that case, I think it's alright for the woman to make the decision."[105]

Such arguments sparked an odd debate: White House personnel chief Frederic V. Malek, a conservative, supported ERA, while Garment, a liberal, flinched. "By maintaining our ambiguous-to-negative posture," reasoned Malek, "we risk incurring . . . the hostility of a sizeable segment of women voters in 1972."[106] But Garment recommended a "statement that reaches for the reasonable middle, that quite deliberately assumes a leadership role in discussing the attitudinal complexities of women's rights."[107] The idea sounded patronizing, and it overlooked the fact that few people had read earlier civil rights messages. Garment, in truth, was hedging on ERA. "How will Middle American mothers react to the news that their teenage daughters might be subject to the draft, that their preferred position under alimony, custody and other domestic relation laws could be ended?" he misleadingly asked Ehrlichman.[108] Without consistent advocacy from Garment, who had persuaded Nixon to sign the Voting Rights Act of 1970, ERA stood little chance of winning strong presidential support.

Garment was more committed to minority rights than to women's rights. Like ERA's opponents, he fretted over the amendment's impact and urged Nixon to show "concern not only for those women who want a career but for those who don't and who are concerned with the stability and dignity of the family unit."[109] In 1971 Garment prepared a list of options on ERA, and Nixon agreed to re-endorse it in a letter to House Minority Leader Gerald R. Ford. Then Garment balked; this fervent integrationist moved to block a constitutional amendment prohibiting busing.[110] In a second memorandum, he told Nixon that twenty-two constitutional amendments lay before Congress and most wrapped "complex dilemmas into easy phrases ('Fair Housing,' 'Busing')." Such proposals suggested that "the Constitution isn't working adequately." Garment next advised Nixon to avoid comment on any constitutional amendment, including ERA and anti-busing.[111] In so advising, he sacrificed gender equality for racial integration.

Nixon did not sign the letter to Ford. In 1971 he hoped to make a double play for women's rights by appointing the first woman to the Supreme Court and then endorsing ERA. The two issues became entwined when Nixon told Garment to "hold [the letter of endorsement] until after the Court *appointment*."[112] In the meantime, Pat Nixon pressed her husband to name a woman to one of the court's two vacancies. Unable to locate a qualified conservative woman, Nixon selected Lewis F. Powell, a moderate Virginia lawyer, and Rehnquist, who was no friend of ERA.[113] The first lady, feeling betrayed, "really hit him on his failure to appoint a woman." "Boy is she mad," the president sighed.[114] Amid the fuss, no one brought up the letter on ERA, and Nixon never sent it.

The president's commitment to the amendment, never strong, had weakened during his years in the White House. Nixon came to view the Equal Pay Act of 1963, requiring the same salary for men and women performing the same work, and Title VII of the Civil Rights Act of 1964, which prohibited discrimination based on sex, as sufficient to ensure equal opportunity.[115] His thoughts on equal pay may have come from Garment, who once argued, "Equal pay for equal work–clearly no problem. These other [women's rights] issues–frankly I don't know."[116] Schooled in the law, as were Garment, Rehnquist, and Poff, the president shared their fear that ERA might void all gender distinctions. Wiggins predicted that Nixon would never "go along with this amendment" because he was "a very good Constitutional lawyer."[117]

The president was also a politician, husband, and father; for political and personal reasons, he re-endorsed ERA. The House passed it without amendments, 354 to 23, late in 1971, and Pat Nixon and Julie Nixon Eisenhower urged Nixon to reiterate his approval. "Dear Daddy," Julie wrote, "the Administration should support the Equal Rights Amendment. We have nothing to lose by supporting it more vigorously–and we lose [the] support of many women by sitting back."[118] After discussing ERA with his wife and daughter, Nixon realized that "we absolutely must push this Women's Rights Amendment."[119] "We are stuck with the Equal Rights Amendment regardless of its constitutional deficiencies," he told Rose Mary Woods. "Let's do something dramatic to set the record straight–we are for it."[120] The president wanted to appeal to female voters. Besides, he thought that "Congress could never act [on ERA] this session."[121]

But Congress did act. With one third of the Senate up for reelection, opposition to ERA evaporated. White House counsel John W. Dean III considered the amendment "very popular politically." Nixon, prodded by Dean and Ehrlichman, restated his support in a letter to Senate Minority Leader Hugh D. Scott, Republican of Pennsylvania. Four days later, ERA, with nominal White House support, cleared the Senate, 84 to 8.[122]

After re-endorsing ERA, Nixon declined to campaign for its ratification. Anne Armstrong, who joined Nixon's staff during his second term, wanted to speed the amendment's ratification by having Nixon reiterate his support. The president refused. Influenced by Haldeman, Buchanan, and Kenneth Cole, Ehrlichman's deputy, Nixon noted that his stance was well known and the matter now lay with the states. He understood that a backlash against domestic reform, especially ERA, was surging.[123] "Why we want to get the President back out front, when we don't have to," Buchanan wrote, "on an issue whose hard charges are the Women's Lib crowd is beyond me."[124] Safely reelected, Nixon let Armstrong, a little-known staffer, lobby state legislators.

But ERA needed presidential support. Between 1972 and 1973, thirty of the requisite thirty-eight states ratified the amendment. Only three states endorsed ERA in 1974, just one in 1975, and one more, the last, in 1977. Anti-feminists, women who defended traditional gender roles, led by the conservative activist Phyllis Schlafly, stymied the amendment in crucial states, such as Illinois. Accordingly, a firm statement from the president or first lady would have boosted ERA. Of course, Nixon supported the amendment without passion. Unlike the civil rights movement, the women's movement began in the 1960s, an era of reform, then peaked in the 1970s, a time of rising reaction. Its best-known reform, ERA, did not succeed.[125]

A confluence of popular ferment, organizational strength, consensus, and elite political support was needed to pass any constitutional amendment. Bad timing derailed ERA. It enjoyed popular appeal from 1970 to 1972, but found inconsistent support in the Senate and White House. The amendment passed Congress in 1972, just as the national mood was growing more conservative. By that point NOW lacked the grassroots energy and charismatic national leaders to blunt the emotional appeals of anti-feminists.[126] Schlafly's "lieutenants" descended upon the Illinois legislature carrying baby girls wearing signs which read "Please don't draft me."[127] Moreover, radical feminists refused to campaign for ERA, which they considered a piecemeal reform, until it was too late.

Had Nixon dodged ERA as a congressman, senator, or presidential candidate, its prospects would have improved. Without a record of support, he might have felt compelled to push the amendment through the Senate in 1970, an election year. Also, "had the ERA gone to the states a couple of years before 1972, when the national mood was still ebullient," the historian Elizabeth Pleck argued, "its chances of passage would have increased sharply."[128] Granted, Nixon could not have evaded ERA in 1968, when all presidential aspirants backed it.[129] But the Equal Rights Amendment never received timely presidential support.

Women's rights included more than a proposed constitutional amendment. The goal of liberal feminism, equal opportunity, was narrow enough to be advanced through executive orders and congressional acts. Almost as a substitute for ERA, Nixonians designed affirmative action programs to foster female employment.

"We Are Job-Oriented"–Again

Affirmative action became Nixon's most effective policy for women's rights. Hiring targets for women grew logically and naturally out of efforts to fight employment bias under Johnson and Nixon. Under Revised Order number 4, Nixon's Labor Department used goals and timetables to open high-paying jobs to women. This order coincided with the president's Philadelphia Plan for minorities and his staff's efforts to place more women in federal positions as the election of 1972 approached.

Federal officials and liberal feminists had shaped fair employment policy under Johnson. In 1966 NOW and other liberal feminist groups successfully lobbied EEOC to end want ad distinctions by gender. Two years later Johnson, pressed by NOW, signed Executive Order 11375 mandating affirmative action for women among federal contractors.[130] Yet Harry McPherson, an LBJ adviser, dismissed the order as "not really a major action" which "should not be overplayed."[131] The Johnson administration, which had inconsistently supported the Philadelphia Plan for minorities, did not even consider hiring goals for women.

Under Nixon, inadequate guidelines and liberal feminist criticism produced stricter fair employment rules: Revised Order 4. Lacking interest in women's issues, White House officials at first let federal agencies handle job bias. In 1969 EEOC issued rules that barred contractors from invoking protective laws to deny women jobs.[132] Solicitor of

Labor Laurence H. Silberman, Labor Secretary George P. Shultz, and Undersecretary James D. Hodgson then approved similar rules drafted by their department's Office of Federal Contract Compliance (OFCC). With the report of the task force on women in hand, Garment urged OFCC chief John L. Wilks to complete the guidelines.[133]

OFCC's guidelines defined "affirmative action" narrowly. Employers were to visit women's colleges on recruitment trips, encourage females to apply for jobs, and "use flexible working hours so that women can be hired on a part-time basis."[134] By failing to mandate hiring goals and timetables for women, OFCC's edict fell short of the numerical targets established under "Order #4." This order, signed by Shultz in February 1970, required specific hiring goals for minorities, but not females, on all federally contracted work exceeding $50,000.

Labor Department officials did not extend hiring goals to women for three reasons. First, they failed to solicit feminist views on fair employment and affirmative action. Second, OFCC bore the stamp of male bias; deputy associate manpower administrator Edward Aguirre favored restoring sex-segregated want ads because "some occupations are considered more attractive to persons of one sex."[135] (Mary N. Hilton, deputy director of the Women's Bureau, vetoed the motion, saving OFCC from certain embarrassment.)[136] Third, Hodgson, who succeeded Shultz as labor secretary in 1970, cringed at mandating goals and timetables for every disadvantaged group. He saw Order 4 as a device to "eliminate race and color barriers to equal opportunity," not to resolve "the often different, more difficult and more elusive problems of sex discrimination."[137] Perhaps Hodgson wondered whether hiring targets for women would have to approach in proportion the female share of the population.

Liberal feminists demanded hiring goals along the lines of Order 4, not OFCC's limited guidelines. Representative Florence Dwyer, a Republican, was "deeply disappointed" over the failure to extend the order to sex discrimination.[138] Representative Patsy T. Mink, Democrat of Hawaii, "strongly urged" Hodgson to announce "that Order Number 4 shall apply to sex discrimination."[139] Oregon Democrat Edith Green, Mink's colleague, agreed and rebuked Hodgson for failing to demonstrate "any justifiable differences in terms of women and other minorities."[140] Although not a minority group, women had experienced bias and saw hiring goals as one path to equal opportunity. Favoring the expansion of Order 4, Ann F. Scott, contract compliance coordinator for NOW, told Hodgson, "It is vital that the guidelines be as strong as possible."[141] Such statements highlighted the appeal of affirmative action remedies among liberal feminists.

During the summer of 1970, OFCC faced growing pressure to strengthen its gender discrimination rules. In June, NOW charged 1,300 federal contractors with failing to file affirmative action plans under Executive Order 11375. Bernice Sandler, contract compliance officer for the Women's Equity Action League (WEAL), another liberal feminist group, scolded OFCC for ignoring women's organizations when designing sex discrimination rules.[142] Until OFCC backed hiring goals, Sandler and Scott vowed to communicate with the agency only through Representatives Mink and Green and Senator Margaret Chase Smith.[143] In July, NOW staged protests demanding enforcement of goals and timetables for women.

Hodgson reversed himself on hiring targets. Despite lamenting that some "women's Lib groups are obviously trumpeting some absurdities," the labor secretary detected "genuine interest" among women in "employment opportunities." "We would be ill-advised not to treat this aspect of the subject seriously," he wrote.[144] A former Democrat and labor negotiator with Lockheed Aircraft Corporation, Hodgson responded pragmatically to grassroots pressure, as did other Nixonians. In July 1970 the Justice Department filed its first suit under Title VII of the Civil Rights Act of 1964, charging Libbey-Owens-Ford, a glass manufacturer, with gender bias. Ten days later Hodgson promised to use goals and timetables to assure women employment in federally contracted work.[145] If Shultz quietly championed the Philadelphia Plan for minorities, Hodgson belatedly sponsored hiring targets for women.

Learning from mistakes, Hodgson now consulted with liberal feminists. Elizabeth Duncan Koontz, an African American Democrat who led the Women's Bureau, urged him to enlist groups such as NOW, WEAL, AAUW, and the National Federation of Business and Professional Women's Clubs. Silberman, now undersecretary, and Wilks invited these groups to send agents to design employment goals for women. Ann Scott and other NOW leaders did not merely demand specific goals; they wanted them enforced at once.[146]

Hodgson stressed practical results. He favored a "non-doctrinaire" approach to goals to "make sure what we come up with is relevant to and workable under the actual conditions of the labor market."[147] Accordingly, Silberman and Wilks conferred with business groups such as the Chamber of Commerce, labor unions such as the United Automobile Workers, and liberal feminists, including Sandler of WEAL and Scott of NOW.[148] Silberman again resorted to a corporatist solution, a federally mediated consensus among management, labor, and other interest groups.

By calling for consultation with many different organizations, the corporatist approach delayed hiring goals for women. Hodgson promised to apply specific targets to women in July 1970 but did not order them until December 1971.[149] Impatience mounted. NOW threatened the Labor Department with legal action, while Koontz "tried valiantly to get OFCC to move faster on affirmative action."[150] Silberman, who oversaw OFCC's efforts, spurred Wilks to act: "I am terribly disappointed that I have heard nothing in recent weeks on our sex discrimination consultations."[151]

Under pressure from feminists, Labor Department officials proved diligent, even farseeing, in designing hiring goals. Wilks recommended that the new order on sex discrimination supersede state and local law.[152] Solicitor of Labor Peter G. Nash wanted to require employers to set up child care centers; he also warned that firms might claim a black woman as both a minority and a female hire.[153] Accordingly, Wilks favored separate categories–"minority men," "minority women," and "non-minority women"–for affirmative action plans, and Hodgson agreed.[154] Such proposals went into Hodgson's edict on female hiring: Revised Order 4.

Revised Order 4 was the Magna Carta of female employment. The decree, signed by Hodgson on December 1, 1971, defined women as an "affected class" and directed firms with federal contracts exceeding $50,000 to submit written plans, with goals and timetables, for recruiting them. Unlike the Philadelphia Plan for minorities, Revised Order 4 set no specific ranges. It required contractors to consider various factors, such as the proportion of females in the workforce, availability of skilled women, and number of females seeking employment in devising hiring targets. Like the Philadelphia Plan, Revised Order 4 defined goals as "targets reasonably attainable" through "good faith effort," separating them from "rigid and inflexible quotas."[155] Employers who failed to develop such programs faced cancellation of their contracts. Labor Department officials advertised the order as a means to employ women as managers, professionals, technicians, sales executives, and "craftsmen."[156] Although it did not cover construction work, the order proved far-reaching, touching one third of the American workforce.[157]

Revised Order 4 was not an "embarrassed gesture," nor did it require that goals for women reflect their proportion of the population, as one historian has claimed. The decree stemmed from feminist advocacy and an apparent consensus among business, labor, and interest groups. Since these parties had not settled upon hiring goals for each industry, Revised Order 4 pioneered a trial-and-error method in which employers studied a pool of potential female workers and then established goals and timetables. Feminists did not consider such affirmative action to be preferential treatment, but saw it as one weapon to fight bias.[158]

Nixon did not impede OFCC's use of goals. This self-made man had preached the virtues of opportunity, proclaiming, after approving the Philadelphia Plan for minorities, "We are job-oriented." Tightening gender bias rules had been one proposal of the presidential task force on women's rights, and at some point Nixonians had to support their commission. Moreover, in 1971 Senator Edmund S. Muskie of Maine, a contender for the Democratic presidential nomination, championed sexual equality and scolded the administration "for its failure to implement task force recommendations."[159] Revised Order 4 was partly an answer to Muskie.

White House officials began to recruit women for federal jobs. At the outset Nixon seemed ambivalent on female appointments. When American Women in Television and Radio urged the president to appoint a woman to the Federal Communications Commission, he asked, *"Why Not?"*[160] In 1969 he placed a few women in ranking posts, naming Virginia H. Knauer his special assistant for consumer affairs and Helen Bentley chair of the Maritime Commission. In 1970 he appointed the first female generals in American history, Elizabeth P. Hoisinger of the Women's Army Corps and Anna Mae Hays of the Army Nurse Corps, and hired the first female Secret Service agents. But Nixon's political aides considered these gestures insufficient. Harry S. Dent, Jr., the president's southern strategist, recommended more publicity for individual female appointments, without mentioning their meager numbers.[161] Malise C. Bloch, another aide, noted that females made up 1 percent of the 613 civil service appointments at Grades 16 and above, despite the fact that more women than men voted in presidential elections.[162]

Beginning in 1970, Nixon the politician emphasized female appointments. Reading that Senator Bayh had charged the administration with "dragging its heels" on women's rights, the president referred the matter to Ehrlichman.[163] As the elections of 1970 neared, Nixon conceded "that we have failed to grab the ball on the whole women's business," reminding aides "that we need to do some things to see that women are properly recognized."[164] The president thought that business and professional women, including females in government, were most likely to support him. After the GOP scored few gains in the elections, he stressed the importance of female voters, telling Ehrlichman to "get more women" on his staff and "exploit staff wives" through publicity.[165] Late in 1970 a politically vulnerable Nixon also proclaimed his "open door policy" to woo African Americans and young people.

Nixon's political aides urged the department chiefs to place women in ranking positions. Finch oversaw the effort, while Malek and his assistant Barbara Franklin pushed hiring goals.[166] When associate budget director Arnold R. Weber wondered whether "our knowledge regarding available female talent is yet sufficient to permit the development of reasonable goals," Malek jotted, *"Bull."*[167] Finch denied "that women are a minority–like blacks," but believed that "giving women a fair chance" would "help all groups regardless of race."[168] In 1971 the president ordered his cabinet to design plans to hire females, but told Finch, "I seriously doubt if jobs in gov[ernmen]t for women will make many votes from women."[169]

Although Nixon's order did not mandate hiring goals, Malek and Franklin insisted on them. Affirmative action plans varied according to department. When Secretary of Health, Education, and Welfare Elliot L. Richardson vowed to place three women in supergrade (GS-16 and above) and 175 in mid-level (GS-13 to 15) civil service positions, Franklin lauded HEW's plan as "one of the greatest that I have seen."[170] But most departments required a push. When, for example, Interior Secretary Rogers C. B. Morton proposed adding twenty women in mid-level positions, Malek urged fifty. Except for Housing Secretary George W. Romney, who was immersed in racial integration, department heads replied promptly to the president's order and Malek's pressure.[171] The use of numerical hiring goals for women went beyond Revised Order 4.

Under such plans, women began entering the top grades of the civil service. "Women Flourish in Nixon Regime," the *Maine Telegram* headlined. During 1971 and 1972, the number of women in supergrade posts tripled, from 36 to 105.[172] Nixon named the first six women to the rank of general in the armed forces, the first female rear admiral, and the first female air force general. Women became sky marshals, air traffic controllers, and narcotics agents, and in 1973, for the first time, three females chaired executive branch agencies.[173] White House fact sheets trumpeted such breakthroughs as well as Revised Order 4, proving that the edict had not been "whispered into the wind" by Nixonians.[174]

But obstacles remained. Democratic presidential nominee George S. McGovern noted that, although 105 women held policy-making jobs, they made up just 0.8 percent of all supergrades. The Labor Department compiled the best record, with females occupying 6 percent of supergrade jobs in 1973. At the Departments of Justice and Housing and Urban Development, females held fewer than 1 percent of supergrade positions, and Interior employed no women at this level.[175] Women held no ranking positions in Nixon's reelection campaign. "We don't have to have a woman on top as long as their opinions and suggestions are admitted equally with men," Rose Mary Woods argued.[176] Female employment certainly required greater pressure.

Safely reelected, Nixon responded by naming Anne Armstrong White House counselor with cabinet rank. But she lacked a clear self-identity, signing her communiqués "Mrs. Tobin Armstrong" and answering to "Mrs. A."[177] The newest Nixonian had no assignment; when one staffer proposed that Armstrong tackle cost-of-living issues, Larry Higby, Haldeman's deputy, called her "a natural to handle food prices."[178] Armstrong eventually oversaw projects relating to Hispanics, commemoration of the bicentennial of the American Revolution, and women's rights, which she espoused lightly.[179] To encourage the hiring of female supergrades, she staged "drop-by" meetings with department chiefs.[180] Armstrong did not expand upon Malek's hiring goals, and by 1974 women still occupied fewer than 1 percent of supergrade jobs.[181]

Rita E. Hauser might have brought a stronger feminist voice to Nixon's staff. One of the president's first female appointees, to the United Nations, Hauser had impressed Nixon, who wanted to "use her as extensively as possible" on television.[182] Hauser urged the president to listen to women's groups and recognize "emergent responsible feminism."[183] Her idea for a White House assistant for women's affairs drew praise from such a conservative political aide as Colson. But her influence soon slackened.[184] The president was shocked when Hauser suggested that same-sex marriages might be legal: "There goes a Supreme Court Justice. I can't go that far–That's the year 2000. Negroes [and whites]–OK; but that's too far."[185] When Hauser advocated "new faces" for Nixon's second term, the president noted, "Probably a good idea–But she would end up with too many liberals."[186] Had she been listened to, Hauser could have forced Nixon to reconsider liberal feminism, since she did not champion ERA as the chief remedy for gender bias.[187]

Overall, Malek's hiring goals, however limited and fleeting, and Revised Order 4 established important precedents. In 1972 Congress, at Nixon's behest, granted EEOC the power to sue employers suspected of bias. EEOC chair William H. Brown III, a Nixon appointee, used this authority to prod firms to develop goals and timetables to hire minorities and women. As discussed in Chapter 4, such targets abetted female employment, at least at entry-level positions. They also completed a reversal in public policy. Between 1920 and 1963, the national government had stressed segregated protection for female workers. In 1963, when JFK's Commission on the Status of Women issued its report and the Equal Pay Act passed Congress, federal policy slowly began to recognize women as aspiring professionals, not simply potential mothers. Prodded by liberal feminists, national elites gradually approved laws and executive orders to expand female opportunity, and hiring goals proved the most far-reaching.[188]

Nixon does not deserve great praise for these changes. He and his advisers clung to traditional gender roles, and then agreed to expand opportunity for narrow reasons–to appease a new social force, tap exceptionally talented females, and win the women's vote. But their efforts mirrored the job-oriented thrust of Nixon's programs for minorities. There was less consistency on other women's issues, as Nixonians, instinctively patriarchical and political, pondered the demands of a disgruntled majority.

Legislation–and Limits

While Nixon agreed to enhance female employment, he proved reluctant to expand opportunity in all respects. The president became conservative on day care and abortion, erratic on access to higher education, and reformist on widening the charge of the Commission on Civil Rights and ensuring women equal access to credit. This jagged course reflected his sexism and unfamiliarity with these matters. Even more than with his programs for African Americans and Native Americans, political expediency and staff advice drove the president's policies for women.

Although provision of child care emerged as a concern of working women, only a few Nixonians seemed friendly to the issue. In 1969 Robert J. Brown, liaison to minority groups, backed day care centers for working women under Nixon's welfare reform proposal, the Family Assistance Plan (FAP).[189] Burns, who seldom understood women's issues, seconded Brown's idea as "a move in the right direction."[190] If enacted, FAP would raise spending on preschool and day care programs for poor families by 65 percent, to $400 million. Finch, then HEW secretary, favored a sliding fee scale to allow non-disadvantaged children to enter developmental programs. Within the Labor Department, Assistant Secretary Arthur Fletcher studied child care and Undersecretary Silberman helped to establish Labor's first day care facility. In 1971 Hodgson asked firms to build their own child care centers. Overall, his efforts produced few results, since Revised Order 4 merely mentioned, but did not mandate, child care.[191]

Class bias shaped Nixon's position; he considered child development programs custodial, appropriate for poor youngsters prone to delinquency but not for middle-class children. At first he seemed uncertain. After reading that Finch sought expanded social services for children, the president fumed, "Why can't they keep [this] quiet until I approve."[192] Swayed by Finch and Ehrlichman, Nixon began to see federally funded day care as crucial to the success of FAP, which wedded a guaranteed minimum income to work requirements for welfare recipients. Such a reform, the president argued, would "get children well-treated" and "grow them out of" the psychology and cycle of welfare.[193] He privately called day care "a constructive program that's a long run effort to solve the problem," adding, "Kids shouldn't sit around–they become non-workers."[194] But by late 1969 Nixon was expressing a "dim view" of "costly" child care centers.[195] After FAP failed in Congress, his interest in day care waned.

Without welfare reform, Nixon saw no point to subsidized child care; he believed that women should rear their children at home. The president decided that FAP must make job training optional for mothers with children under age six.[196] By 1972 Nixon regarded federally financed child care centers as an assault on the nuclear family. After scanning a critique of such institutions by the columnist William V. Shannon, he wrote, "He shows that even the libs are having 2nd thoughts about the welfare kick. I totally subscribe to this view." Nixon blasted Israel's communal rearing of children as "cockeyed" and agreed with Shannon that "it is a rare and exceptionally gifted woman who does something more important in the outside world than she does in the first six years" of her child's growth.[197] Support for a few talented females and traditional roles for the rest had formed the crux of Nixon's thinking on women's issues.

Political expediency reinforced Nixon's aversion to child care. In 1971 Congress passed a bill to fund day care centers for the poor and cover child care costs for middle-class families under a sliding fee schedule. HEW Secretary Richardson favored the measure, but he never gained Nixon's approval.[198] The child care bill was attached to an appropriations bill for the Office of Economic Opportunity that the president intended to veto. To Nixon, day care centers were "ok for social workers," whom he despised, but they represented "bad politics."[199] The president opposed "legislation which might take children away from their mothers."[200] He first advised Ehrlichman not to make his veto message "too hard."[201] Then, influenced by Colson and Buchanan, he courted the GOP's right wing with a statement bashing the Child Development Act's "fiscal irresponsibility, administrative unworkability, and family-weakening implications."[202] Nixon called for a policy "to cement the family in its rightful position as the keystone of our civilization."[203] He would not support day care simply to expand opportunities for women.

Nixon's veto message spoke of a bygone age when women did not need day care to pursue careers. Richardson called the statement "a disaster."[204] He grasped its inconsistency, since the president had backed day care for poor children. "I think his argument to that is I don't know where the line is, I know this [bill] is [going] too far," replied Ehrlichman.[205] After veering to the right, Nixon steered toward the center. In 1972 the first lady endorsed "quality day care" for women who "needed to work," while the Republican National Convention approved a compromise plank on child care.[206] The Revenue Act of 1971, signed by Nixon, provided tax deductions for child care expenses. In 1973 HEW Secretary Caspar W. Weinberger completed the cycle, issuing day care rules with a sliding fee scale for low- and medium-income families. Still, by 1976 child care services remained in short supply.[207]

Nixon's veto helped delay child care legislation for two decades. Traditional views on domesticity and motherhood remained commonplace among his successors. President Gerald R. Ford vetoed a child care bill which he claimed infringed on states' rights, while President Jimmy Carter opposed federally funded day care as too expensive. A child care act consisting of block grants, tax credits, and new before- and after-school programs passed Congress in 1990. Yet it provided only "the most minimal help for parents trying to balance jobs and children."[208]

Nixon also proved conservative on reproductive rights, an early crusade of radical feminists. Abortion, recalled feminist leader Ellen Willis, "symbolized our fundamental demand–not merely formal equality for women but genuine self-determination."[209] By the late 1960s, doctors and family planning advocates had begun lobbying to revise or repeal laws against abortion. NOW joined the fight, and by 1972, sixteen states and the District of Columbia had liberalized their abortion laws.[210] Radicals saw control over reproduction as crucial to women's opportunity, sexual freedom, and "self-determination."[211] Nixon, however, supported self-determination for minority groups such as Native Americans, but not women.

Nixon's stance on abortion paralleled his thinking on child care: he backed family planning for poor women but opposed abortion as a basic right of females. The president, swayed by Moynihan, became concerned with the social effects of population growth. In 1969 he vowed to expand family planning services for 5 million poor mothers, ordered studies of new birth control methods, and named a Commission on Population Growth and the American Future.[212] "The president really *cares* about family planning," noted Moynihan in 1970.[213] Even when population control provoked grumbling in Congress, Nixon held firm, telling Moynihan, "Let's continue to press it."[214]

There was little in the president's background that inclined him toward liberalized abortion. During the 1968 campaign, Nixon sidestepped abortion by declaring it a state issue.[215] As president he vowed that his program for population control would never "infringe upon the religious convictions or personal wishes" of any person, a stance that drew praise from the Roman Catholic Church.[216] But as his reelection neared, the president, guided by Colson and Buchanan, used the abortion issue to woo conservative Catholics. Pressed by New York's Terence Cardinal Cooke, Nixon ordered military hospitals to respect local laws prohibiting abortions.[217] As with day care, he grounded his edict on conservative ideals, citing America's "Judeo-Christian heritage" and his own "personal and religious" aversion to "such a drastic and intolerable solution."[218] "We scored a big plus on this one with the Catholic Community," reported Brigadier General James D. Hughes, his military aide.[219] In 1972 Nixon planned to "tilt to the right" and bring a "sharp cutting edge" to his reelection bid by denouncing legalized abortion and marijuana.[220]

Just as his stance on child care changed, Nixon's abortion rhetoric reversed direction. In 1972, after his commission on population growth endorsed abortion on request, Nixon courted political embarrassment when, on the advice of Buchanan and Haldeman, he endorsed Cardinal Cooke's campaign to repeal New York's liberal abortion law. In so doing, he entered a state dispute against a fellow Republican, Rockefeller, who favored New York's revised act.[221] After appeasing the right, Nixon returned to the center. Hauser sent Ehrlichman data showing "a sizeable majority of Americans, including Roman Catholics, now favoring liberal abortion laws."[222] The president decided to leave this matter to the states and privately affirmed that "abortion reform" was "not proper gr[oun]d for Fed[eral] action. W[ou]ld never take action as P[resident]."[223] Nixon the moderate spoke through his wife, who labeled abortion "a personal thing" best left to the states, not the national government.[224] When the Supreme Court ruled in *Roe v. Wade* that women possessed a constitutional right to privacy, and thus abortion, Nixon directed aides to "keep out" of the case.[225]

In a general sense, Nixon's stand began a trend whereby Republican presidents (and Jimmy Carter) condemned abortion and the *Roe* decision. But Nixon's denunciations would lack the fervor of his successors', Reagan and Bush, and he warned against banning abortion and population control in developing nations.[226] By the 1990s, Nixon had come to regret the Republicans' excessive bashing of abortion rights, complaining, "I don't want to hear about abortion. That's people's own business."[227] Quietly, and after much political analysis, Nixon was voicing a libertarian position not unlike that of his Republican contemporary Barry Goldwater.[228] But it came after he had relinquished power. Neither Nixon nor Goldwater discussed abortion primarily in terms of expanding women's reproductive rights.

Nixon, pressed by liberal Democrats, proved more cooperative on ending gender bias in higher education. The Women's Equity Action League and Edith Green, Democrat of Oregon and chair of the House Committee on Education, began the fight against discrimination in education, and Senator Birch Bayh joined their cause.[229] In 1970 Indiana University, Bayh's alma mater, considered imposing an admission "ratio slightly in favor of men," on the grounds that "girls" matured faster than young men, and "if we . . . let in only the best qualified students, we may well have more women than men."[230] Bayh assured one angry constituent that ERA "for which I am fighting would prohibit such discriminatory acts on account of sex in state universities."[231] Even before Congress approved ERA, Bayh and Green cosponsored an amendment, Title IX, which prohibited gender bias in 2,500 post-secondary schools receiving federal aid. Title IX became part of the Higher Education Amendments of 1972, which expanded the student loan program. Nixon signed it, albeit with little fanfare.[232]

But the legislative intent of this terse amendment remained elusive since Green, to speed its passage, had cut off debate. In 1973 HEW officials, led by Gwendolyn H. Gregory of the Office of Civil Rights, drafted rules to implement Title IX and then sent them to Secretary Weinberger. The sticking point involved interscholastic athletics, namely, whether competitive teams must admit both sexes and whether Title IX required equal spending on male and female sports, something which Gregory supported.[233] "I don't think I need to dwell too long on estimating what the President would think of this issue," declared Tod Hullin, an Ehrlichman aide. "Does anybody know what the hell is going on [at HEW]?"[234] So began a lively debate. Liberal feminists backed equal funding for male and female athletics and sexually integrated teams while the male-led National Collegiate Athletic Association (NCAA) denied that Title IX covered sports.[235] Since schools not complying with Title IX faced loss of federal funds, this dispute became quite important.

Nixon, an avid sports fan, took the NCAA's side. When White House aide Geoffrey Shepard misleadingly argued that HEW's Title IX rules would "virtually end athletic scholarships," the president was furious: "The answer is *No!* Tell Weinberger to reassess all this & prepare a bill to go to Congress which I can submit & provide thereby an excuse for not going forward with this monstrosity."[236] With Watergate occupying Nixon's attention, liberal staffers Garment and Bradley H. Patterson, Jr., defended Title IX from attacks by conservative colleagues such as White House counselor William Timmons, who endorsed the weakest enforcement of Title IX, advising, "[Let's] ban the babes!"[237]

Such jockeying produced stalemate. In 1974 HEW's proposed Title IX rules, shaped by Gregory, did not mandate equality of expenditures on collegiate athletics. Rather, they permitted single-sex teams so long as schools funded separate sports teams for men and women. The compromise, however, failed to satisfy the U.S. Commission on Civil Rights, liberal feminists, or college athletic directors, and the debate continued into Ford's presidency.[238]

The excitement over collegiate athletics, fanned by the sort of people who don garish school colors, sing fight songs, and pack football stadiums each autumn, clouded Title IX's importance. The amendment prohibited discriminatory practices, including the "stacked" admission standards considered by Indiana University, and encouraged public colleges and vocational and professional schools to use affirmative action to recruit women. Most females did not want to destroy male athletics, and the loudest cries of impending doom came from colleges offering expensive, income-producing spectator sports such as men's football and basketball.[239] A former center for the University of Michigan football team, President Ford signed Title IX rules in 1975, convinced that men would continue to receive most athletic scholarships.[240] "Our members are terribly disappointed and surprised," wailed Tom Hansen, the NCAA's deputy director. "They can't believe that a football-playing President would do that to us."[241]

Title IX has remained controversial. Feminists derided it as tame, citing NCAA's heel-dragging and the reluctance of HEW's Office of Civil Rights and federal courts to set clear rules for athletic programs. Large universities proved most resistant. During the 1995–96 academic year, colleges without football (Division I-AAA) spent 38 percent of their athletic budgets on women, while schools offering football (Division I-A) reserved just 19 percent of athletic funds for women's sports.[242] Athletic directors complained when schools curtailed men's sports to comply with Title IX. After Syracuse University dropped men's wrestling and gymnastics in order to finance women's sports, U.S. Olympic Committee officials warned that such cuts "will hurt this country's chance to succeed in the Games."[243] "It wasn't the intention of Title IX to take from men," lamented Boston University football coach Tom Masella after the school's board of trustees voted in 1997 to cancel the football program.[244]

But Title IX has opened athletics to women. Between 1971 and 1996 the number of girls playing high school sports grew from 300,000 to 2.4 million, making females 40 percent of all varsity athletes. According to the columnist E. J. Dionne, this trend has encouraged "less teenage pregnancy, higher high school graduation rates, the avoidance of abusive relationships, and success later in life." Federal officials and courts have moved toward more specific Title IX rules, requiring colleges to fund male and female sports in proportion to their male and female enrollments or demonstrate a "continuing history" of expanding athletic offerings for women. As a result, NCAA women's volleyball gained a national following, while women's basketball added to "March Madness" with its own sixty-four-team tournament. U.S. women earned a record number of medals at the 1996 Summer Olympics and captured the gold medal in hockey at the 1998 Winter Olympics, refuting the claim that Title IX would "hurt" the United States in the games.[245] On the twenty-fifth anniversary of Title IX's passage, President Bill Clinton expanded the law to cover schools on military bases and Indian reservations, and Bayh ranked it with the civil rights acts of 1964 and 1965 as "landmarks in securing basic rights for our citizens."[246]

Although Nixon had endorsed each of the laws to which Bayh referred, he proved least enthusiastic about Title IX. Nixon supported more strongly another women's rights issue, expanding the jurisdiction of the Commission on Civil Rights to include gender. Although the president's task force had endorsed a broader mandate, Howard A. Glickstein, the commission's staff director, opposed this reform unless it came with an increase in funding. By early 1972 Nixon surely saw wider authority for the commission as one possible substitute for ERA. At the Office of Management and Budget, officials debated whether to allow the Commission on Civil Rights to probe gender discrimination.[247] Associate OMB director Frank A. Carlucci approved it for "political" reasons, saying, "I think it is probably inevitable and not worth the flack to oppose it."[248] Nixon agreed and in 1972 signed legislation adding gender bias to the commission charge.[249]

Nixon also endorsed legislation to ban discrimination in credit transactions, although he took no personal interest in the subject. In 1973 Senator William Brock, Republican of Tennessee, and Emily Card, his liaison to women's groups, promoted equal access to credit, regardless of gender or marital status. Meanwhile, Justice Department officials were working on a bill to prohibit discrimination in credit on the basis of race, religion, color, national origin, and sex. Sentiment within the House lay with the Brock bill, which was narrower and easier to pass.[250] Armstrong presented the issue to the president's inner circle, and Garment and Weinberger both endorsed equal credit. Nixon backed equal credit in his 1973 message to Congress on housing and in his 1974 State of the Union address. The House and Senate then passed Brock's bill by wide margins, and President Ford signed it in October 1974.[251] Once again, a Republican president substituted nondiscriminatory legislation for vigorous support of ERA.

The Equal Credit Opportunity Act of 1974 marked a watershed, since Congress for the first time passed a bill to advance gender equality that had no racial antecedents. This trend continued when the House and Senate passed the Women's Educational Equity Act (WEEA) of 1974 to fund books and programs to counter "sex-role socialization and stereotyping." As with Title IX and equal credit, WEEA stemmed from feminist advocacy, timely congressional support, and passive White House approval.[252]

There was little in Nixon's background and outlook inclining him to advance women's rights beyond employment. The president, his family's patriarch, disapproved of abortion and day care. An admirer of masculine competition in politics and in sports, he took a narrow view of Title IX's reach. But Nixon responded to bipartisan support for giving broader powers to the Commission on Civil Rights. Such zigging and zagging would bedevil the policy debate on gender equality for two decades.

Unfinished Revolution

The Nixon administration's skittish response to the women's movement is mirrored in the ambiguous status of American women today. Females enjoy greater opportunities in the workplace, but continue to face constraints both at the office and at home. Federal policy recognizes women as breadwinners, but it does not provide them the means to advance as quickly or as far as men.

Since 1960 attitudes about gender roles have changed slowly. In the year Americans elected John F. Kennedy president, "airline stewardess" was perhaps the loftiest position a girl could aspire to, and even that dream "was reserved for white women only—young, slim, and single."[253] Although affirmative action and legislation banning gender discrimination helped expand women's access to education and professional careers, the American workforce remained sex-segregated. In 1995 the bipartisan Glass Ceiling Commission reported that women occupied just 5 percent of senior managerial posts in *Fortune* magazine's one thousand wealthiest companies.[254] The glass ceiling, *Los Angeles Times* columnist Katheryn M. Fong wrote, is made not of "breakable glass" but of "shatter-proof, shock-resistant Plexiglass."[255]

In addition to the glass ceiling, child care remained a crucial concern for female workers. In 1994, 60 percent of mothers with children under age six worked outside the home, and nearly 20 million children received day care from adults who were not members of their immediate family. Child care expenses in the mid-1990s often consumed up to one third of a poor family's income, placing new demands on women and men juggling home and workplace duties. In 1993 Congress offered modest relief, passing the Family and Parental Leave Act to guarantee workers up to twelve weeks of unpaid leave. In contrast, other industrialized nations provide parents paid leave over longer periods of time.[256]

Nixonians made a weak start in addressing these problems. True, they yielded to political pressure and approved affirmative action for females, an epilogue to their job-centered policies for minorities. But regarding concerns exclusive to women, they remained myopic. The president and Garment believed naively that the toothless Equal Pay Act could alter the sex-segregated nature of the U.S. workforce. Explaining why White House communiqués did not address women as "Ms.," Nixon told the reporter Dan Rather, "I guess I am a little old-fashioned, but I prefer 'Miss' or 'Mrs.'"[257] The result of Nixon's outlook and feminist pressure was increased female access to education and employment without the requisite means to advance as far as males.

Nixon's policies for women missed many opportunities. His record on female appointments barely improved on Johnson's, and he did not take a firm stand on behalf of ERA, almost ensuring its defeat. ERA's importance for women's rights may have been overestimated, as radical feminist scholars have argued.[258] But in the hands of liberal federal judges, the amendment might have been used to protect gay rights and women's access to abortion, as its right-wing detractors feared.

Nixonians did not translate their instinct to protect women into a message of empowerment. They could have advocated stiffer penalties against rape and pornography on the grounds that such crimes degraded women and denied them equal rights. F. Lynn May, a Nixon aide, urged a study of rape, calling it "a valid vehicle to show the Administration's concern for women's rights and law enforcement."[259] But May's proposal, advanced in 1974, failed to gain presidential attention. Nixon displayed more interest in fighting pornography, praising celebrities such as Jackie Gleason and Katharine Hepburn for denouncing "smut."[260] He asked the Justice Department to study ways of making foreign films comply with Hollywood's code of decency and named a commission to study pornography. When the panel backed the right of adults to obtain pornography, the president disavowed its report.[261] In his private comments Nixon expressed concern for the impact of "obscene material" on children, not its exploitation of women.[262]

Nixonians were capable of refining conservative principles to address the new social forces of the 1960s. They represented the middle strata of both American society and American politics. In tailoring long-cherished notions of opportunity and social mobility to the demands of new groups, they proved practical and resourceful. They refashioned the angry rhetoric of Black Power into a mainstream proposal to support separate minority businesses and responded sympathetically to calls for Native American self-determination. But on women's rights, the president and his aides were too steeped in traditional roles to offer anything beyond halfhearted leadership. The result was more action on women's rights than in previous administrations, but also a series of stops and starts on the path to gender equality.

Epilogue: In the Shadow of Nixon

"The pattern of civil rights enforcement in Nixon's first term," Leonard Garment shrewdly argued, "was for the most part operationally progressive but obscured by clouds of retrogressive rhetoric."[1] There are many reasons for this dichotomy. Nixon's policies were shaped by pressure from federal courts and a Democratic-controlled Congress as well as his own assumptions. The administration's programs built on moderate Republicanism, a tradition of using the state to enhance social mobility. As early as 1950 Nixon had declared "that a free-opportunity system, to mean anything at all, must mean opportunity for those at the bottom as well as those at the top."[2] Such ideas, embedded in his policies for racial minorities and women, helped to shape the ongoing debate on civil rights.

Nixon's appeals to white resentment and his willingness to foster opportunity fit together politically and practically. He sought to build a "Silent Majority" of working- and middle-class Americans to reelect him president and co-opt or neutralize the dissenters. Nixon wanted African Americans to become white-collar workers, join unions, or form business enterprises; students to forsake the streets for the ballot box; tribal self-government to be strengthened; and women who so chose to enjoy fulfillment outside the home. Remaining controversies would be resolved by federal agencies, generously funded by Nixonians but far away from the White House, or through court adjudication. To citizens who had aired their grievances in the streets, the Nixonian retort was: Go to school, get a job, join the bourgeoisie, vote.

Together, Nixon's policies aimed for selective integration. They used federal power to bring whites and racial minorities together in the workplace, but not in neighborhoods or public schools. Nixon agreed to remove barriers that prevented black people from moving into a given neighborhood and sending their children to the nearest school. But he played down remedies, such as busing and scatter-site housing, to integrate schools and neighborhoods directly in favor of affirmative action in employment. According to Nixon, once blacks became educated and entered skilled trades or professions or opened businesses, they would be able to purchase homes in suburbs. The formula proved expedient, placing Nixon at the center of American politics, on the side of honest toil and gradual, voluntary integration. It resonated among middle-class voters, who reelected him in 1972.

Nixon's programs unfolded within a larger context in which activist federal courts and a Democratic-controlled Congress often forced the president's hand. In *Holmes v. Alexander* (1969), the Supreme Court decreed an immediate end to racially segregated schools in the South, setting up the administration's low-key desegregation drive during 1970. On the Voting Rights Act of 1970, Senator Philip A. Hart, Democrat of Michigan, shared center stage alongside his Republican colleague, Senate Minority Leader Hugh D. Scott of Pennsylvania. Democratic senators Edward M. Kennedy of Massachusetts and Henry Jackson of Washington helped to shape Native American policy, while Indiana's Birch E. Bayh emerged as an important player on lowering the voting age to eighteen, enacting Title IX, and passing the Equal Rights Amendment. Nevertheless, Nixon and his team were something more than disinterested observers, leapfrogging ahead of the Democrats on issues such as tribal self-determination and aid to black colleges and minority-owned businesses.

Regarding the impact of his policies, Nixon remained a fatalist. During an off-the-record interview with the journalist Richard L. Wilson, the president called race the "problem for which there seemed no solution" and predicted that "it would be two or three hundred years before the kind of equality now being demanded could be realized." Repeatedly, Wilson observed, he "kept referring to the insolubility of the problem."[3] It was the sort of response one might expect from a white male politician of Nixon's generation, someone who had not marched on behalf of equal rights. No doubt the president's own prejudices, ongoing black criticism, and the complexity of race-related issues had conspired to provoke this particular outpouring of pessimism.

On one level the president was wrong. His civil rights policies influenced public policy, society, and politics even after he left office. Since both the conservative and liberal positions on many civil rights issues date to Nixon, it is almost impossible to understand American politics today without referring to this complicated presidency.

Nixon's policies influenced U.S. society in three respects. First, they helped minorities enter the middle class. "Affirmative action," argued the civil rights leader Roger Wilkins, "has done wonderful things . . . by enlarging opportunity, and developing and utilizing a far broader array of skills available in the American population."[4] Between 1950 and 1982, the proportion of non-white men in professional or managerial positions grew from 6 to 20 percent, much of the increase coming during and after Nixon occupied the White House. But affirmative action was not an anti-poverty program, for it did not touch all blacks and still left them overrepresented in low-wage, unskilled jobs.[5] "In the economic sphere," the African American historian John Hope Franklin argued, "obviously the black middle class is increasing. But the black under-class is increasing, too."[6]

Affirmative action proved to be both controversial and durable. Conservatives attacked it as preferential treatment and lauded the early goal of the civil rights movement, equality of opportunity, even though America lacked any tradition of color-blind egalitarianism.[7] Affirmative action has become the federal government's chief method to advance civil rights and, as the journalist Salim Muwakkil put it, "a symbol of America's long-denied promise of racial equality."[8] According to Representative Maxine Waters, Democrat of California, many white males acquired a stake in affirmative action since they "have wives, daughters, mothers, and others who are in the work-force, making money to pay the mortgage."[9] In recruiting an ethnically diverse workforce of Asians, Latinos, and African Americans, U.S. firms have gained a cultural advantage over European and Japanese competitors in the race for global alliances and international business deals.[10] Affirmative action, solidified under Nixon, has produced a web of interlocking interests that make its repeal unlikely, perhaps even impossible, for the foreseeable future.

Second, Nixon's policies have meant less racial integration in education and housing. Without pressure from the federal government, suburban integration faded to the point where, by the 1990s, it was "no where to be found on the national agenda."[11] Without busing across entire metropolitan school systems, blacks and whites remained isolated from each other, something Nixon had predicted. "I realize," he wrote Ehrlichman in 1972, "that this position will lead us to a situation in which blacks will continue to live for the most part in black neighborhoods and where there will be predominantly black schools and predominantly white schools in metropolitan areas."[12] But the president had not grasped the long-term consequences of residential segregation.

Since 1968, residential patterns have validated the conclusions of the Kerner Commission, the panel established by President Lyndon B. Johnson to study race relations: "We are rapidly becoming two societies, one black and the other white, separate and unequal."[13] Local zoning laws and school district boundaries kept blacks and whites apart as much as the price of suburban housing. Economic advances, abetted by affirmative action, have allowed some blacks to move to suburbs; but, as Nixon forecast, they usually lived in non-white areas. In only a few instances have white suburbanites overcome their "fear and loathing" and accepted African Americans as neighbors. Service- and information-based industries, whose emergence Nixon did not foresee, located their plants in suburbs, adding new layers onto the walls of segregation. As a result, many cities faced a declining tax base and fewer public resources. Between 1970 and 1990, for example, the number of inhabitants in Camden, New Jersey, the "city of broken wings," fell from 120,000 to 80,000, nearly 70 percent of whom were either children or elderly.[14]

Solutions to these dilemmas have remained cloudy. In 1992 suburbanites for the first time cast the majority of votes in a presidential contest, electing Bill Clinton, a "New Democrat" opposed to excessive federal intervention. Yet racial division, exposed during the Los Angeles riots that same year, haunted many citizens.[15] "Race is an explosive on the tongues of men," said Senator Bill Bradley, Democrat of New Jersey.[16] "Our separation is frightening," Chief Justice Robert Wilentz of the New Jersey Supreme Court declared.[17] Some state courts, such as New Jersey's, have ordered dispersal of low-income housing into suburbs. Yet it was unclear whether blacks would take advantage of these new opportunities, whether suburbanites would accept judicial activism, and whether such policies would be used elsewhere.[18] The remedy, combining court enforcement with state action, was quite Nixonian, even if the fervent rhetoric was not.

Third, the Nixon administration, by its actions, acknowledged that civil rights no longer applied simply to African Americans. Native Americans and women organized to force the national government to address their concerns, and Nixonians replied with varying degrees of sympathy. They weighed the merits of each group's demands against their own philosophical assumptions and political agenda. They agreed that Native American problems cried out for justice and statesmanship and that women deserved opportunities to work outside the home while retaining their special, subordinate roles as wives and mothers.

Then there were the "forgotten minorities"–Irish, Poles and other eastern Europeans, Italians, the Spanish-speaking–who, Nixon thought, should benefit from the era's "rights-conscious" spirit because they were tradition-bound, hardworking, and favorable to him politically. The president courted such groups via messages, appointments, and meetings with such lavishly named organizations as the Sons of Italy Supreme Council and the American Hellenic Educational Progressive Association.[19] Bowing to Italian American sensibilities, Attorney General John N. Mitchell prohibited Justice Department aides from using the terms "mafia" and "cosa nostra" when reporting on organized crime.[20] But, knowing that white ethnics faced little discrimination, the president reserved affirmative action for non-whites.

Spanish-speaking citizens posted a few concrete gains. Although a nationally organized movement was still a few years away, Hispanics were the fastest-growing minority group in the United States, and Nixon offered them jobs and gestures of support. In 1969 he corresponded with the Cuban American celebrity Desi Arnaz, and Senator Barry M. Goldwater, Republican of Arizona, who sympathized with Hispanics, on ways to assist Spanish-speaking Americans. The president established the Cabinet Committee on Opportunities for Spanish-Speaking People (CCOSSP) to study the matter and included Hispanics in his affirmative action programs. Between 1970 and 1972 the number of Spanish-surnamed presidential appointees doubled, and in 1973 the Small Business Administration awarded Hispanics $109 million in loans. In 1970 Nixon backed bilingual education for Hispanic children, a program sanctioned by the Southwest Development Act of 1967.[21] The Department of Health, Education, and Welfare provided additional funds, leading one presidential aide to boast that bilingual education was "flourishing under the Nixon Administration."[22]

Nixon also endorsed efforts to enhance the rights of the elderly. "This is one area where we must play the political game out as skillfully as possible," he wrote in 1971. "Expenditures in this area . . . could prove far more effective politically than in environmental, health and other areas where we will also have great pressures."[23] Unlike LBJ, who failed to include age in his executive orders prohibiting job bias, Nixon seized a "golden" opportunity.[24] In 1972 the president sent Congress a lengthy message on aging, named Arthur S. Flemming the first White House assistant on aging, and directed cabinet officers to end discrimination against older employees. In 1975 Congress outlawed bias on the basis of age in federally funded projects.[25]

Nixon proved less concerned with the rights of disabled people, where the initiative lay with the federal courts and Democratic-controlled Congress. In 1972 Nixon vetoed, as too costly, a $1.7 billion bill to upgrade vocational rehabilitation services for the handicapped. But the next year the president signed a scaled-down version of the same bill which forbade bias against handicapped people in projects receiving federal funds. The civil rights provision, Section V, had little to do with vocational rehabilitation itself and was the handiwork of liberal Democrats such as Representative Charles Vanik of Ohio and Senator Hubert H. Humphrey of Minnesota. Although Nixon's Justice Department later filed amicus curiae briefs in support of the rights of retarded people, civil rights for the disabled received its biggest boost in 1990, when President George Bush signed the Americans with Disabilities Act.[26]

Not all groups shared equally under this expansion of civil rights. Well-organized and enjoying presidential sympathy, Native Americans won the most in terms of symbolic support (Blue Lake) and legislation (Alaskan claims settlement). Hispanic Americans, with an infant movement, made small breakthroughs in government employment, education, and business ventures, even though CCOSSP failed to exercise firm leadership and went out of business in December 1974.[27] White ethnic groups, represented by fraternal and educational, not civil rights, organizations, received token political gestures. Women, a majority group, were both a unique case and a lesser concern. Programs to advance women's rights, resembling the job-oriented ones for minorities, unfolded after a series of false starts. Nixon's motto might have been "Race beats gender" in importance and "Race influences gender" on policy.

The extension of civil rights, however politically inspired and slap-dash, proved both landmark and factious. When, in 1970, the U.S. Civil Service Commission noted the movement of "Negroes, Spanish-surnamed Americans, American Indians, and Oriental Americans" into federal jobs, it identified the minority groups that technically fell under Nixon's Philadelphia Plan and would fall under contract set-asides in coming years.[28] When, during the 1990s, some Republicans discussed making English the official language of the United States, they repudiated a bit of their party's past. In 1971 Nixon aide Charles Colson called bilingual education "a concept close to the hearts of most Spanish-speaking people," one that "towers as a major example of government sensitivity and concern for equal educational opportunities."[29] As the 1990s came to a close, bilingual education remained in place. Nixon's civil rights policies continued to influence American politics, as liberals, centrist Democrats, and conservative Republicans either defended, refined, or exploited aspects of this complex man's varied legacy. While seldom invoking the disgraced president's name, politicians of different stripes campaigned and governed in the shadow of Nixon.

Left-leaning Democrats defended Nixon's most controversial civil rights policy, affirmative action. In 1995 Senate Majority leader Robert

J. Dole, Republican of Kansas, sponsored a bill to end race- and gender-based "goals and timetables" in employment. Meanwhile, Republican governor Pete Wilson of California pressed the University of California to eliminate racial and gender classifications in admitting students. The Reverend Jesse L. Jackson, who emerged as the field marshal for affirmative action, organized protests to disrupt Wilson's meeting with the university's Board of Regents and blasted President Clinton for his stony silence on affirmative action. Jackson also led nationwide boycotts against Mitsubishi Motors and Texaco Oil Company to force them to hire more women and minorities.[30]

This was quite a reversal. Dole and Wilson, Nixon "protégés" and past supporters of affirmative action, courted the GOP's right wing by denouncing "goals and timetables," while Jackson, representing the Democratic left, publicly defended part of Nixon's legacy and threatened to enter the Democratic presidential race unless Clinton spoke on behalf of affirmative action. The president did, vowing to "mend, not end" the policy. Mitsubishi and Texaco, stung by the boycotts, drafted plans to recruit female and minority employees, whereupon Jackson opened a New York office to monitor Wall Street's employment practices. The civil rights movement had come full circle, with Jackson using direct action to protect and extend an administrative measure, affirmative action, which had been prompted by earlier grassroots protest. His move to Wall Street recalled pressure, exerted by Nixon's EEOC, to apply hiring goals to corporations.[31]

Centrist Democrats adopted policies which mirrored those of Nixon. The historian Burton I. Kaufman wrote of Jimmy Carter's civil rights record: "His administration . . . channeled more government contracts to minority firms, boosted substantially the amount of federal deposits in minority-owned banks, strengthened the Justice Department's enforcement of the voting rights statutes, and increased the effectiveness of the Equal Employment Opportunity Commission in settling job discrimination cases. But most of the president's efforts to assist blacks and other minority groups were undertaken through executive and agency actions and their greatest impact was on mid- and upper-income minorities, not the poor."[32] That passage could have summarized the Nixon administration's efforts. It is interesting to count how many Nixonian programs, procedures, and aims–the bank deposit policy, reliance on administrative measures, aid to middle-class minorities–Carter carried forth. This was not surprising. The Georgian emerged as a national leader during the 1970s, and his staff probably looked to Nixon more than LBJ for direction on domestic affairs. Nixon's policies, forged at a crucial phase of the civil rights struggle and implanted in the bureaucracy, cast a long shadow indeed.

There were parallels between Clinton's "New Democrat" rhetoric and moderate Republicanism, since both saw the state as the servant of opportunity. In 1953 Nixon extolled "the general-welfare state," which "seeks to help, not control. It promotes rather than absorbs the free energies of labor, business and the farmer."[33] Clinton echoed that refrain in 1992, when he called for "a government that expands opportunity, not bureaucracy."[34] In his 1997 inaugural address, he put it differently, favoring "a government humble enough not to try to solve all our problems for us but strong enough to give us the tools to solve our own problems for ourselves."[35] The conservative legacy of the 1980s no doubt forced Clinton to accept a more constricted role for the state. "Where are all the Democrats?" the president asked his advisers after reviewing his first budget message. "We are all Eisenhower Republicans. We are Eisenhower Republicans and we are fighting Reagan Republicans."[36] With that in mind, perhaps, Clinton saw reason to praise Nixon's creative but selective use of federal power to protect the environment, fight cancer, and champion health care reform.[37] Rather than taking a "right turn," presidential politics since 1968 has swung, pendulum-like, from moderation to conservatism and back again.

Clinton and Nixon parted ways on civil rights in that the former offered blacks more conversation but less enforcement. Although Clinton's "mend, don't end" posture on affirmative action provided the embattled program with some cover against right-wing attacks, his record, at least through his first four years, was lackluster. He ordered a moratorium on new set-aside programs, failed to name an assistant attorney general for civil rights, and provided scant funds for the EEOC, Office of Contract Compliance, and Minority Development Agency. Clinton's strengths were eloquence and passion, quite evident when he proclaimed his commitment to racial justice. In 1997 he appointed a

White House commission, chaired by the African American historian John Hope Franklin, to engage in an extended "honest dialogue" on race.[38] Nixon had made no comparable appeal for racial harmony.

Neither Nixon nor Clinton was able to enhance civil rights *and* overcome racial division. By whispering "We Shall Overcome," Nixonians gambled that southern conservatives would appreciate their soft words and African Americans their strong deeds.[39] Spiro T. Agnew predicted that "our actions . . . will create an atmosphere that will eventually turn some members of these [minority] groups in our direction without losses elsewhere."[40] In fact, the GOP got what it wanted most, white southern votes, leaving blacks to the Democrats. Clinton's "words over deeds" method placated some Democrats, but his commission endured criticism from biracial citizens, who felt left out; from liberals, who decried its lack of focus; and from African Americans, who expressed skepticism.[41] "The situation [for black America]," said Gerald Reynolds, president of the conservative Center for New Black Leadership, "has deteriorated to the point that we have to do more than just talk. We need to equip people to solve their own problems."[42] Jackson lamented the lack of "significant policy initiatives."[43] Someday, perhaps, a party or administration will deploy both rhetoric and action in the service of civil rights.

Republicans benefited from Nixon's overtures to the white South, which bridged the Goldwater and Wallace movements of the 1960s and the Reagan and Bush presidencies of the 1980s and 1990s. But here Nixon's motives emerged as more selfish, his strategy more improvised, and his ultimate goals less clear than his contemporary critics charged. Using a subtle brand of racial politics, he eased the entry of southern whites, a historically conservative group, into the Republican column in presidential elections. "Nixon," Ehrlichman recalled, "always couched his views in such a way that a citizen could avoid admitting to himself that he was attracted by a racist appeal."[44] The president wanted his stand against busing to be "simple" and "direct," knowing that his "position of responsibility" kept him from talking "like Wallace does."[45] With an insinuated message and moderate programs, Nixon avoided being tagged as the most racist, or most conservative, leader in recent memory.[46]

By century's end, Nixon's shadow faded as the GOP, entrenched in Congress but not the White House, pushed a very conservative agenda.

The Republican leadership—Representatives Newt Gingrich of Georgia and Dick Armey of Texas and Senators Trent Lott of Mississippi and Donald Nickles of Oklahoma—confirmed the party's power base in Dixie. But southern gains came with losses elsewhere, in New England and the Midwest, belying Nixon's carefully crafted "national strategy." Many Americans resented the Republican congressional leaders as too southern, too right wing, and too extreme. They bashed gun control, affirmative action, immigrants, and federal funding of the arts, something President Nixon had backed. They embraced the crusades of the Protestant-led Christian Coalition: unyielding opposition to abortion and gay rights and support for public school prayer.[47] True, Republican rightists imitated Nixon by exploiting racial and cultural cleavages. Yet their most negative remarks made his anti-busing rhetoric seem almost tame by comparison.

Nixon shook his head over the Republican right's ascent. He thought Gingrich's remarks to the 1992 Republican National Convention "a disappointment—but he's a bomb thrower and we need him." Nixon predicted that Texas Senator Phil Gramm's thirst for the White House would go unquenched: "In the TV age, he just doesn't have it." His choice for the 1996 Republican presidential nomination was Bob Dole, the oldest and most moderate candidate. The former president urged Dole to be "conservative" on economics, sound "compassionate" on welfare and health care, and select a "progressive and serious Republican" as his running mate. Nixon advised him to establish "a good relationship" with the religious right without "allowing them to dictate his policies or his campaign."[48] Dole followed most of that advice, won his party's nomination, but lost the election to Clinton. The year 1994 proved to be a political benchmark. That year the GOP lost Nixon but gained Gingrich. The Clinton Democrats, not unlike the Eisenhower-Nixon Republicans of old, then reclaimed the center.

Will Nixon's civil rights legacy enhance his place in history? Probably not. Granted, the question begs information beyond the scope of this book. Nixon's programs appear strong when compared to those of his successors. "I would have to say," Roger Wilkins ventured, "that looked at through the prism of the Reagan Administration, the Nixon civil rights record does not look as bad today as it did in 1971, '72, and '73."[49] But Nixon's motives were too mixed to earn him cheers as the "unanticipated hero" of civil rights.[50] Then there was Watergate. During his second term, many of the president's domestic programs either drifted or faded as the scandal consumed his attention and his staff's time. "History," the historian Stanley I. Kutler wrote, "will record a fair share of the significant achievements of Nixon's presidency, but Watergate will be the spot that will not out."[51] In 1997 Kutler edited and published portions of the White House tapes, revealing some of Nixon's most shabby comments and criminal plots. Together, affirmative action, minority business enterprise, Indian rights, and school desegregation seem unlikely to boost him in the presidential greatness polls.[52]

Rather than a means for rehabilitation, the president's civil rights policy offers a vista on his multifarious persona. Nixon the politician was often harsh, bitter, nasty, shrill, and vindictive. During an off-the-record interview in 1955, he rejected the "myth" that "a man has to be non-controversial" as "'togetherness' bullshit."[53] The historian Stephen E. Ambrose rightly sensed a "meanness of spirit" in his order to do only what the law required on school desegregation.[54] Nixon the coalition builder was an opportunist. After rejecting Jewish voters as unreachable, the president in 1972 decided to host a black-tie dinner for Jewish leaders, including "financial contributors."[55] Nixon the racist dismissed African Americans. At one meeting he noted that there were "good blacks" working in his government. Secretary of State William P. Rogers, a staffer replied, was taking three of them on a trip to Africa. "I'd take one," the president snapped.[56]

Other traits completed this president's character. Nixon the self-made man and moderate Republican expanded opportunity under minority business enterprise, affirmative action, and aid to black colleges. Nixon the statesman reformed Native American policy and responded calmly to Red Power unrest. Nixon the realist listened to liberal members of his own party, enforced Supreme Court edicts effectively, and even compromised with a Democratic-controlled Congress. Nixon the president understood his unique "responsibility" in governing a nation just beginning to express its racial, ethnic, and gender diversity via a rights-conscious spirit. He once expressed a desire "to meet some responsible, young Negroes," adding, "It is very possible that it is difficult to find a group of this type, but I would be open to suggestions."[57] But the impulse to "bring us together" surfaced intermittently, for it marked only one part of Nixon's persona.

Whatever the impact of the president's policies, one thing was clear: these were his programs. Nixon the administrator was well informed, tapping bright advisers, reading their memorandums, and using their ideas to advance his own agenda. It was Nixon who reminded Ehrlichman that "we expect to continue to do a lot for the Negro Colleges."[58] Domestic policy making, at times chaotic and diffuse, reflected Nixon's assumptions, intentions, and periodic vacillation. Credit or blame for his programs cannot be assigned exclusively, or even mostly, to staffers, as if the White House were headless and the nation governed by unseen "iron triangles." The journalist Tom Wicker wrote that "it was Richard Nixon personally who conceived, orchestrated and led his administration's desegregation effort," a fact confirmed by the president's blue ink comments on Edward Morgan's memorandums concerning school desegregation.[59]

We are left to ponder a complex president, a tumultuous era, a mixed record, and an ambiguous legacy. Nixon seemed to foresee as much when he dedicated the Lyndon B. Johnson Library in 1971. After describing the Oval Office, he compared its shape to the presidency itself: "For the President of the United States cannot approach a question from one side or the other; on each issue that comes to the Oval Office there normally are an infinite number of sides and of competing considerations to be resolved or chosen among."[60] It was surely a trite analogy, but one that only a complicated person would have invoked.

Notes

Abbreviations

AIPA American Indian Press Association
ANS annotated news summary
AWDS Ann C. Whitman Diary Series
BHL Bentley Historical Library, University of Michigan, Ann Arbor
CDF Contested Documents File
CF Confidential Files
CMPE *Minutes and Documents of the Cabinet Meetings of President Eisenhower (1953–1961),* ed. Paul Kesaris and Joan Gibson (Washington, D.C.: University Publications of America, 1980)
DDEL Dwight D. Eisenhower Library, Abilene, Kansas
EDS Eisenhower Diary Series
EMLL *President Eisenhower's Meetings with Legislative Leaders, 1953–1961,* ed. William E. Leuchtenburg (Bethesda, Md.: University Publications of America, 1986)
FG Federal Government, White House Central Files
GRFL Gerald R. Ford Library, Ann Arbor, Michigan
HEW Department of Health, Education, and Welfare Series, Creed C. Black Papers, Margaret I. King Library, University of Kentucky, Lexington
HHL Herbert Hoover Library, West Branch, Iowa

HI	Hoover Institution, Stanford University, Stanford, California
HU	Human Rights, White House Central Files
IN	Indian Affairs, White House Central Files
JCL	Jimmy Carter Library, Atlanta, Georgia
JFKL	John F. Kennedy Library, Boston, Massachusetts
JHC	Johnson handwritten comment
LBJL	Lyndon B. Johnson Library, Austin, Texas
LC	Library of Congress, Washington, D.C.
LCCR	Leadership Conference on Civil Rights
MHC	Michigan Historical Collections, Bentley Historical Library, University of Michigan, Ann Arbor
NA	National Archives, College Park, Maryland
NA-LN	National Archives, Pacific Southwest Region, Laguna Niguel, California
NHC	Nixon handwritten comment
NPM	Richard M. Nixon Presidential Materials, National Archives, College Park, Maryland
NPPP	Nixon Pre-Presidential Papers
OF	Official File
PNWH	*Papers of the Nixon White House,* ed. Joan Hoff-Wilson (Lanham, Md.: University Publications of America, 1989)
PO	Press Office
POF	President's Office Files
POS	Press Office Series (Nelson A. Rockefeller Papers)
PPF	President's Personal File
PPP	*Public Papers of the Presidents* (Washington, D.C.: Government Printing Office)
PQ	Procurement, White House Central Files
RAC	Rockefeller Archive Center
RFA	Rockefeller Family Archives
RG	Record Group
RNLB	Richard Nixon Library and Birthplace, Yorba Linda, California
SMOF	Staff Member and Office Files
SOHP	Southern Oral History Program, University of North Carolina, Chapel Hill
SP	Speech File
WHSF	White House Central Files
WHSF	White House Special Files

Prologue

1 Richard M. Nixon to Edward L. Morgan, Mar. 22, 1973, Box 4, Federal Government (FG) 6–15, Domestic Council, White House Central Files

(WHCF), Nixon Presidential Materials (NPM), National Archives (NA), College Park, Maryland.

2 Quoted in Melvin Small, *The Presidency of Richard Nixon* (Lawrence: University Press of Kansas, 1999), 162.

3 Rowland Evans, Jr., and Robert D. Novak, *Nixon in the White House: The Frustration of Power* (New York: Random House, 1971), 133-164; Jonathan Schell, *The Time of Illusion* (New York: Knopf, 1976), 40-49, 77-84; Leon E. Panetta and Peter Gall, *"Bring Us Together": The Nixon Team and the Civil Rights Retreat* (Philadelphia: Lippincott, 1971); Robert Weisbrot, *Freedom Bound: A History of America's Civil Rights Movement* (New York: Plume, 1990), 282-285; John Morton Blum, *Years of Discord: American Politics and Society, 1961-1974* (New York: Norton, 1991), 332-341, 409; Harvard Sitkoff, *The Struggle for Black Equality, 1954-1992* (New York: Hill and Wang, 1993), 212-223; Dan T. Carter, *The Politics of Rage: George Wallace, the Origins of the New Conservatism, and the Transformation of American Politics* (New York: Simon and Schuster, 1995).

4 Leonard Garment, *Crazy Rhythm: My Journey from Brooklyn, Jazz, and Wall Street to Nixon's White House, Watergate, and Beyond* (New York: Times Books, 1997), 220.

5 H. R. Haldeman Diary, Apr. 28, 1969, in *The Haldeman Diaries: Inside the Nixon White House*, ed. H. R. Haldeman (Santa Monica, Calif.: SONY Corporation, 1994), CD-ROM.

6 Nixon to Leonard H. Clark, July 22, 1960, Box 153, General Correspondence, Richard M. Nixon Pre-Presidential Papers (NPPP), National Archives, Pacific Southwest Region, Laguna Niguel, California (NA-LN).

7 Haldeman Diary, Oct. 7, 1971.

8 Hugh Davis Graham, *The Civil Rights Era: Origins and Development of National Policy, 1960-1972* (New York: Oxford University Press, 1990), 301-365; Joan Hoff, *Nixon Reconsidered* (New York: Basic Books, 1994), 80.

9 See "The Nixon Watch Continues," a review of Hoff's book by the historian Richard Norton Smith, *New York Times Book Review*, Oct. 30, 1994, 1.

10 Tom Wicker, *One of Us: Richard Nixon and the American Dream* (New York: Random House, 1991), 487.

11 Small, *Presidency of Richard Nixon*, 176.

12 See Arthur Larson, *A Republican Looks at His Party* (New York: Harper and Brothers, 1956), 202-203; Herbert Hoover, *American Individualism* (Garden City, N.Y.: Doubleday, 1922), 53; Eric Foner, *Free Soil, Free Labor, Free Men: The Ideology of the Republican Party before the Civil War* (New York: Oxford University Press, 1970), 16-18, 191.

13 Nixon off-the-record remarks to Republican congressional staffers, attached to George Pavlik to Bourke B. Hickenlooper, Mar. 3, 1966, Box

49, Political File, Bourke B. Hickenlooper Papers, Herbert Hoover Library (HHL), West Branch, Iowa.

14 Sallyanne Payton, "Remarks at Hofstra," in *Richard M. Nixon: Politician, President, Administrator,* ed. Leon Friedman and William F. Levantrosser (Westport, Conn.: Greenwood, 1991), 183.

15 Donald R. McCoy and Richard T. Ruetten, *Quest and Response: Minority Rights and the Truman Administration* (Lawrence: University Press of Kansas, 1973), 347.

16 Robert Frederick Burk, *The Eisenhower Administration and Black Civil Rights* (Knoxville: University of Tennessee Press, 1984), vi.

17 Carl Brauer, *John F. Kennedy and the Second Reconstruction* (New York: Columbia University Press, 1977), 315–320; Steven F. Lawson, "Civil Rights," in *Exploring the Johnson Years,* ed. Robert A. Divine (Austin: University of Texas Press, 1981), 93–125.

18 Steven F. Lawson, "Mixing Moderation with Militancy: Lyndon Johnson and African-American Leadership," in *The Johnson Years,* vol. 3, *LBJ at Home and Abroad,* ed. Robert A. Divine (Lawrence: University Press of Kansas, 1994), 82.

19 Robert Dallek, *Flawed Giant: Lyndon Johnson and His Times, 1961–1973* (New York: Oxford University Press, 1998), 322–329.

20 Quoted in Schell, *Time of Illusion,* 26.

21 Mark Stern, *Calculating Visions: Kennedy, Johnson, and Civil Rights* (New Brunswick, N.J.: Rutgers University Press, 1992), 233.

22 H. R. Haldeman, "Remarks at the Sixth Annual Presidential Conference: Richard M. Nixon," in *Watergate and Afterward,* ed. Leon Friedman and William F. Levantrosser (Westport, Conn.: Greenwood, 1992), 320–321. On Nixon's complexity, see William Safire, *Before the Fall: An Inside View of the Pre-Watergate White House* (New York: DaCapo, 1975), 97–106; Raymond Price, *With Nixon* (New York: Viking, 1977), 29.

23 Nixon biographer Stephen E. Ambrose explained his role as chronicling Nixon's complexities rather than explaining them. Stephen E. Ambrose, *Nixon,* vol. 2, *The Triumph of a Politician, 1962–1972* (New York: Simon and Schuster, 1989), 9–10.

24 H. R. Haldeman to John D. Ehrlichman, July 19, 1969, Box 3, H. R. Haldeman Files, Contested Documents File (CDF), NPM.

25 Nixon to Haldeman, Sept. 22, 1969, Box 229, Haldeman Files, White House Special Files (WHSF), NPM; *New York Times,* Dec. 7, 1969, 1, 60.

26 Spiro T. Agnew to Thomas L. Karsten, Nov. 25, 1969, Box 87, Series 3, Subseries 5, Spiro T. Agnew Papers, Theodore R. McKeldin Library, University of Maryland, College Park.

27 Nixon handwritten comment (NHC) on Raymond K. Price to Nixon, Jan. 16, 1970, Box 229, Haldeman Files, NPM.

28 Nixon to Ehrlichman, Nov. 30, 1970, Box 12, Haldeman Files, CDF, NPM.

29 Daniel P. Moynihan to Nixon, May 15, 1970, Box 2, John D. Ehrlichman Files, CDF, NPM.

30 Richard L. Wilson, "Visit with President Nixon, June 5, 1970," Box 5, Richard L. Wilson Papers, HHL.

31 Nixon to Patrick J. Buchanan, Feb. 10, 1971, *Papers of the Nixon White House,* ed. Joan Hoff-Wilson, pt. 2, *The President's Meeting File* (Lanham, Md.: University Publications of America, 1989), Fiche 71-2-7 *(PNWH).*

32 Herbert S. Parmet, *Richard Nixon and His America* (Boston: Little, Brown, 1990), 594-619; Hugh Davis Graham, "Richard Nixon and Civil Rights: Explaining an Enigma," *Presidential Studies Quarterly,* 26 (Winter 1996), 103.

33 Nixon to Ehrlichman, Jan. 28, 1972, Box 2, Ehrlichman Files, CDF, NPM.

34 Nixon to Haldeman, May 18, 1972, Box 5, Frederic V. Malek Papers, Hoover Institution Archives (HI), Stanford University, Stanford, California.

35 Wicker, *One of Us,* 416.

36 "Address of Richard M. Nixon," Jan. 23, 1965, and Rose Mary Woods typescript note, Jan. 27, 1965, Box 10, Post-Eisenhower Administration Series, Fred A. Seaton Papers, Dwight D. Eisenhower Library (DDEL), Abilene, Kansas.

37 John D. Ehrlichman meeting notes, Oct. 12 and July 2, 1970, Box 1, Ehrlichman Files, CDF, NPM.

38 Davis Williams to Stewart Alsop, Jan. 22, 1958, Box 47, Joseph and Stewart Alsop Papers, Manuscript Division, Library of Congress (LC), Washington, D.C.

39 H. R. Haldeman meeting notes, June 26, 1970, Box 1, Haldeman Files, CDF, NPM; Ken Hughes, "Absolutely No Sense of Humor," *American Journalism Review* (April 1997), 14.

40 Nixon to Peter M. Flanigan, Mar. 16, 1970, Box 4, President's Office File (POF), CDF, NPM (first quotation); Hoff, *Nixon Reconsidered,* 320 (second quotation).

41 Annotated news summary (ANS), June 28, 1972, Box 3, POF, CDF, NPM.

42 Stanley I. Kutler, *Abuse of Power: The New Nixon Tapes* (New York: Free Press, 1997), 31.

43 Nixon to Ehrlichman, Nov. 30, 1970, Box 12, Haldeman Files, CDF, NPM.

44 NHC on Leonard Garment to James Keogh, Feb. 17, 1969, Box 1, POF, CDF, NPM.
45 Garment, *Crazy Rhythm,* 199.
46 Stewart Alsop, "Nixon Notes," n.d., Box 47, Alsop Papers.
47 Arthur A. Brooks, Jr., to Stewart Alsop and Williams to Alsop, Feb. 5, 1958, Box 47, Alsop Papers.
48 Memorandum of conversation, Mar. 4, 1957, Box 100, Confidential Files (CF), WHCF, Dwight D. Eisenhower Papers, DDEL.
49 Charles Evers and Andrew Szanton, *Have No Fear: The Charles Evers Story* (New York: John Wiley, 1997), 276.
50 See Kenneth O'Reilly, *Nixon's Piano: Presidents and Racial Politics from Washington to Clinton* (New York: Free Press, 1995).
51 Alonzo L. Hamby, *Man of the People: A Life of Harry S. Truman* (New York: Oxford University Press, 1995), 624, 631.
52 Dallek, *Flawed Giant,* 111.
53 James Farmer, *Lay Bare the Heart: An Autobiography of the Civil Rights Movement* (New York: New American Library, 1985), 325.
54 Harvard Sitkoff, *A New Deal for Blacks* (New York: Oxford University Press, 1978), vii.
55 Haldeman Diary, Feb. 12, 1969 (first quotation), and Mar. 11, 1969 (second quotation).
56 Larry Higby to Stephen Bull, Mar. 15, 1969, Box 211, Haldeman Files, NPM.
57 Nixon to Ehrlichman, Apr. 8, 1972, Box 3, Ehrlichman Files, CDF, NPM.
58 Buchanan to Haldeman, Mar. 10, 1970, Box 4, Haldeman Files, CDF, NPM.
59 Nixon to Ehrlichman, Apr. 9, 1972, Box 3, Ehrlichman Files, CDF, NPM.
60 George P. Shultz telephone interview with author, Oct. 25, 1995, Stanford, California.
61 Leonard Garment interview with A. James Reichley, Oct. 19, 1977, Gerald R. Ford Library (GRFL), Ann Arbor, Michigan.
62 Wicker, *One of Us,* 397.
63 Haldeman Diary, Mar. 11, 1970.
64 Shultz telephone interview with author, Oct. 25, 1995. James Farmer quoted in *Nixon: An Oral History of His Presidency,* ed. Gerald S. Strober and Deborah Hart Strober (New York: HarperCollins, 1994), 114.
65 Quoted in Hoff, *Nixon Reconsidered,* 50.
66 See Joan Hoff-Wilson, "The Corporate Presidency: Richard M. Nixon," in *Leadership in the Modern Presidency,* ed. Fred I. Greenstein (Cambridge, Mass.: Harvard University Press, 1988), 179.

67 Agnew to Karsten, Nov. 25, 1969, Box 87, Series 3, Subseries 5, Agnew
   Papers.
68 "John D. Ehrlichman," in *Political Profiles: The Nixon-Ford Years,* ed.
   Eleanora W. Schoenebaum (New York: Facts on File, 1979), 182–188;
   Hoff, *Nixon Reconsidered,* 115–129.
69 Nixon to Ehrlichman, Apr. 8, 1972, Box 3, Ehrlichman Files, CDF, NPM.
70 John D. Ehrlichman telephone interview with the author, Feb. 6, 1995,
   Atlanta, Georgia.

1. Flexible Response

1 Richard M. Nixon to John D. Ehrlichman, Jan. 28, 1972, Box 2, John D.
   Ehrlichman Files, Contested Documents File (CDF), Nixon Presidential
   Materials (NPM), National Archives (NA), College Park, Maryland.
2 See Rowland Evans, Jr., and Robert D. Novak, *Nixon in the White House:
   The Frustration of Power* (New York: Random House, 1971), 133–164;
   Jonathan Schell, *The Time of Illusion* (New York: Knopf, 1975), 40–49,
   77–84; Leon E. Panetta and Peter Gall, *"Bring Us Together": The Nixon
   Team and the Civil Rights Retreat* (Philadelphia: Lippincott, 1971); Kevin
   P. Phillips, *The Emerging Republican Majority* (New Rochelle, N.Y.: Ar-
   lington House, 1969). Historians accepting this argument include Peter
   N. Carroll, *It Seemed Like Nothing Happened: America in the 1970s* (New
   Brunswick, N.J.: Rutgers University Press, 1982), 38–43; Dewey W.
   Grantham, *The Life and Death of the Solid South: A Political History* (Lex-
   ington: University Press of Kentucky, 1988), 177–179; Robert Weisbrot,
   Freedom Bound: A History of America's Civil Rights Movement (New York:
   Plume, 1990), 282–285; John Morton Blum, *Years of Discord: American
   Politics and Society, 1961–1974* (New York: Norton, 1991), 332–341, 409;
   Harvard Sitkoff, *The Struggle for Black Equality, 1954–1992* (New York:
   Hill and Wang, 1993), 212–223; Dan T. Carter, *The Politics of Rage:
   George Wallace, the Origins of the New Conservatism, and the Transformation
   of American Politics* (New York: Simon and Schuster, 1995).
3 Herbert S. Parmet, *Richard Nixon and His America* (Boston: Little,
   Brown, 1990), 602–605; Hugh Davis Graham, *The Civil Rights Era: Ori-
   gins and Development of National Policy, 1960–1972* (New York: Oxford
   University Press, 1990), 301–365; Tom Wicker, *One of Us: Richard Nixon
   and the American Dream* (New York: Random House, 1991), 505; John
   Robert Greene, *The Limits of Power: The Nixon and Ford Administrations*
   (Bloomington: Indiana University Press, 1992), 41–47; Joan Hoff, *Nixon
   Reconsidered* (New York: Basic Books, 1994), 80.
4 Nelson A. Rockefeller press conference, Apr. 14, 1960, Box 5, Press Office Series (POS), Nelson A. Rockefeller Gubernatorial Papers, Record

Group (RG) 15, Rockefeller Family Archives (RFA), Rockefeller Archive Center (RAC), Sleepy Hollow, New York.

5 "Excerpt of Remarks by Governor Rockefeller," June 17, 1960, Box 5, POS, Rockefeller Gubernatorial Papers, RG 15, RFA.

6 "Statement by Governor Nelson A. Rockefeller," July 23, 1960, Box 5, POS, Rockefeller Gubernatorial Papers, RG 15, RFA.

7 "Statement by Governor Nelson A. Rockefeller," July 27, 1960, Folder 110, Box 5, POS, Rockefeller Gubernatorial Papers, RG 15, RFA.

8 Nixon to Leonard W. Hall and Robert H. Finch, July 18, 1960; Nixon to Finch, Aug. 1 and 29, 1960; Nixon to Hall, Finch, and James Bassett, Sept. 7, 1960, Folder 79, Box 12, private papers of Robert H. Finch, Pasadena, California.

9 Nixon to Hall and Finch, July 18, 1960, Folder 79, Box 12, Finch papers.

10 Nixon to Mildred Younger, Dec. 7, 1954, LBM 115, Richard M. Nixon Pre-Presidential Papers (NPPP), Richard Nixon Library and Birthplace (RNLB), Yorba Linda, California.

11 Nixon to Finch, July 18 and Aug. 8, 1960, Folder 79, Box 12, Finch papers; Robert H. Finch Oral History, June 19, 1967, 51–52; Butler Library, Columbia University, New York; "Excerpts from Responses by Vice President Richard Nixon," Jan. 15, 1960, Civil Rights Position Papers, NPPP, RNLB.

12 Hoff, *Nixon Reconsidered,* 78.

13 Raymond A. Moley, "GOP Civil Rights Change Is Urged," *New Orleans Times-Picayune,* Apr. 27, 1951, Box 11, E. Frederic Morrow Records, Dwight D. Eisenhower Library (DDEL), Abilene, Kansas; Moley to Nixon, Nov. 2, 1960, Box 293, Raymond Moley Papers, Hoover Institution Archives (HI), Stanford, California.

14 Bryce N. Harlow to Dwight D. Eisenhower, June 8, 1962, Box 7, Special Names Series, Dwight D. Eisenhower Post-Presidential Papers, DDEL.

15 Robert Alan Goldberg, *Barry Goldwater* (New Haven: Yale University Press, 1995), 154–155.

16 Richard Reeves, *President Kennedy: Profile of Power* (New York: Simon and Schuster, 1993), 465–466; Lewis L. Gould, "Never a Deep Partisan: Lyndon Johnson and the Democratic Party," in *The Johnson Years,* vol. 3, *LBJ at Home and Abroad,* ed. Robert A. Divine (Lawrence: University Press of Kansas, 1994), 24–25.

17 Richard M. Nixon, "Dixie Democrats Fatal Error," Oct. 30, 1966, Box 23 (6626-g), James J. Kilpatrick Papers, Alderman Library, University of Virginia, Charlottesville.

18 James J. Kilpatrick, notes of interview with Richard Nixon, Jan. 11, 1968, Box 23 (6626-g), Kilpatrick Papers.

19 Graham, *Civil Right Era,* 303.

20 "Remarks by Governor Rockefeller," June 3, 1968, Folder 1717, Box 76, POS, Rockefeller Gubernatorial Papers, RG 15, RFA.

21 "Richard M. Nixon–Positions on Record," May 6, 1968, Box 22, Graham T. Molitor Papers, RAC.

22 "Richard M. Nixon–Summary Analysis," May 6, 1968, Box 22, Molitor Papers.

23 Nixon to J. Strom Thurmond, Jan. 2, 1967, Campaign 1968 Correspondence 501 (Strom Thurmond File), NPPP, RNLB.

24 Lewis Chester, Godfrey Hodgson, and Bruce Page, *An American Melodrama: The Presidential Campaign of 1968* (New York: Viking Press, 1969), 448; Theodore H. White, *The Making of the President, 1968* (New York: Pocket Books, 1970), 279; Harry S. Dent, Jr., *The Prodigal South Returns to Power* (New York: Wiley, 1978), 97–99; Richard M. Nixon, *RN: The Memoirs of Richard Nixon* (New York: Grosset and Dunlap, 1978), 304–305; Strom Thurmond Oral History, Feb. 1, 1974, Southern Oral History Program, University of North Carolina, Chapel Hill, 13–15 (SOHP); Harry S. Dent, Jr., Oral History, Feb. 22, 1974, 25–26, SOHP.

25 Nixon handwritten comment (NHC) on Thurmond to Nixon, July 2, 1968, Campaign 1968 Correspondence 501 (Strom Thurmond File), NPPP, RNLB.

26 Jonathan Rieder, "The Rise of the 'Silent Majority,'" in *The Rise and Fall of the New Deal Order, 1930–1980,* ed. Steve Fraser and Gary Gerstle (Princeton, N.J.: Princeton University Press, 1989), 243–268. An account which plays down Nixon's appeals to the South is John N. Mitchell interview with A. James Reichley, Sept. 18, 1969, 3, Box 2, A. James Reichley Interview Transcripts, Gerald R. Ford Library (GRFL), Ann Arbor, Michigan. For Nixon's statements on desegregation, see Richard M. Nixon handwritten notes, July 8, 1968, Richard M. Nixon Collection, HI; Richard M. Scammon and Ben J. Wattenberg, *The Real Majority* (New York: Coward-McCann, 1970), 200–211.

27 Richard A. Watson, *The Presidential Contest* (New York: Wiley, 1984), 86; White, *Making of the President, 1968,* 545–547.

28 Fred LaRue to Harlow, Feb. 18, 1969, Box 35, Confidential Files (CF), White House Special Files (WHSF), NPM.

29 H. R. Haldeman meeting notes, Aug. 8, 1970, *Papers of the Nixon White House,* pt. 5, *H. R. Haldeman Notes of White House Meetings, 1969–73,* ed. Joan Hoff-Wilson (Lanham, Md.: University Publications of America, 1989), Fiche 30 *(PNWH).*

30 Annotated news summary (ANS), March 1969, *PNWH* pt. 6, ser. B, *Annotated News Summaries,* Fiche 3; Alexander P. Butterfield to Ehrlichman, Mar. 27, 1969, Box 8, Harry S. Dent, Jr., Files, WHSF, NPM.

31 Nixon to Ehrlichman, Jan. 16, 1969, Box 1, President's Personal Files (PPF); Thurmond to Nixon, Jan. 29, 1969; Harlow to H. R. Haldeman, Jan. 31, 1969; Harry Dent to Ehrlichman, and Haldeman to Dent, Feb. 6, 1969, Box 49, H. R. Haldeman Files, WHSF, NPM; *Columbia (S.C.) Record*, July 29, 1969, Box 204, Rogers C. B. Morton Papers, Margaret I. King Library, University of Kentucky, Lexington; Dent to Nixon through Ehrlichman and Haldeman, Feb. 3, 1969, *PNWH*, pt. 6, ser. A, *Documents Annotated by the President*, Fiche 7.

32 Nixon to Haldeman, Sept. 22, 1969, Box 229, Haldeman Files, NPM; NHC on Dent to Nixon, Apr. 30, 1969, *PNWH*, 6A, Fiche 15; Dent to Southern Chairman, July 15, 1969, Box 8, Dent Files, WHSF, NPM; *New York Times*, Dec. 7, 1969, 1, 60.

33 NHC on Dent to Nixon, Dec. 8, 1969, *PNWH*, 6A, Fiche 49; John Brown to Dent, Dec. 11, 1969, Box 2, Dent Files, NPM.

34 Butterfield to Ehrlichman, Mar. 11, 1969, Box 3, Haldeman Files, CDF, NPM; Dent to Nixon, Dec. 11, 1969, *PNWH*, 6A, Fiche 51 (quotation).

35 Nixon to Haldeman and Ehrlichman, Jan. 18, 1971, Box 3, PPF, NPM; Nixon to Haldeman, Jan. 31, 1972, Box 230, Haldeman Files, NPM; Colson to Haldeman, Dec. 22, 1970, Box 1, Colson Files, NPM.

36 John D. Ehrlichman meeting notes, Aug. 4, 1970, *PNWH*, pt. 3, *John D. Ehrlichman Notes of Meetings with the President*, Fiche 17.

37 Haldeman meeting notes, July 11, 1970, *PNWH* 5, Fiche 69.

38 H. R. Haldeman Diary, Apr. 15, 1971, in *The Haldeman Diaries: Inside the Nixon White House*, ed. H. R. Haldeman (Santa Monica, Calif.: SONY Corporation, 1994), CD-ROM.

39 Haldeman Diary, Jan. 17 and 29, 1971; *St. Louis Post-Dispatch*, Mar. 21, 1971, B3; John Ehrlichman, *Witness to Power: The Nixon Years* (New York: Simon and Schuster, 1982), 235–236.

40 NHC on Dent to Nixon, Feb. 3, 1969, *PNWH*, 6A, Fiche 7.

41 *New York Times*, Feb. 29, 1969, 29; *Memphis Press-Scimitar*, Nov. 12, 1969, 4; Haldeman to Dent and Harlow, Feb. 13, 1969, Box 49, Haldeman Files, NPM; Dent to Mitchell, July 7, 1969, Box 8, Dent Files, NPM; Dent to Dwight Chapin and Ehrlichman, Aug. 13, 1969, Box 204, Morton Papers.

42 Dent to Moynihan, July 15, 1969, Box 2, Dent Files, NPM.

43 Nixon to Ehrlichman, Sept. 22, 1969, Box 228, Haldeman Files, NPM.

44 Haldeman to Ehrlichman, Jan. 18, 1971, Box 84, Staff Secretary Files, NPM; Hullin to Staff Secretary, Aug. 25, 1971, Box 57, Ehrlichman Files, NPM.

45 John Campbell to Edward Morgan, July 22, 1971, Box 9, Human Rights (HU), White House Central Files (WHCF), NPM; see also Harry Dent

interview with A. James Reichley, Apr. 3, 1978, Box 1, Reichley Transcripts, GRFL.

46 Phillips, *Emerging Republican Majority,* 461–474.

47 Haldeman meeting notes, Jan. 8, 1970, *PNWH,* 5, Fiche 14.

48 NHC on Kevin Phillips column, Sept. 25, 1970, *PNWH,* 6A, Fiche 97; Brown to Ehrlichman, Oct. 12, 1970, Action Memo P839, Box 42, Staff Secretary Files, NPM.

49 Eisenhower to Meade Alcorn, Aug. 30, 1957, Box 25, Dwight D. Eisenhower Diary Series, Whitman File, Eisenhower Papers.

50 Arthur S. Fleming Oral History, June 2 and 3, 1988, 42, DDEL.

51 Nixon to Charles H. Percy, Mar. 21, 1959, Box 50, William P. Rogers Papers, DDEL.

52 L. Arthur Minnick meeting notes, July 23, 1957, Box 4, Legislative Meeting Series, Staff Secretary Records, DDEL.

53 "To Protect Social Security: Remarks of Richard M. Nixon," Oct. 29, 1966, Box 49, Political Files, Bourke B. Hickenlooper Papers, Herbert Hoover Library (HHL), West Branch, Iowa.

54 NHC on George P. Shultz to Nixon, Mar. 27, 1972, Box 2; ANS, Feb. 17, 1973, President's Office Files (POF), CDF, NPM; column by Richard Nixon for the North American Newspaper Alliance, Apr. 3, 1966, Box 14, Special Names Series, Eisenhower Post-Presidential Papers.

55 Haldeman meeting notes, Jan. 8, 1970, *PNWH,* 5, Fiche 14.

56 NHC on Ehrlichman to Nixon, Oct. 21, 1970, *PNWH,* 6A, Fiche 101.

57 Patrick J. Buchanan to Committee of Six, Feb. 3, 1971, Box 73, Haldeman Files, NPM.

58 Harlow to Arthur F. Burns, Mar. 24, 1969, Box A33, Arthur F. Burns Papers, GRFL.

59 *Republican Battle Line* (August 1969), Box 184, Morton Papers; *Republican Battle Line* (Feb.–Mar. 1969), Box 22 (6626-g), Kilpatrick Papers. See John M. Asbrook to Republican Leaders and Philip M. Crane, "The Nixon Administration . . . The Conservative Mandate," n.d., Box 10, Post-Eisenhower Administration Series, Fred A. Seaton Papers, DDEL.

60 Barry M. Goldwater to Walter Trohan, Feb. 11, 1969, Box 46, Walter Trohan Papers, HHL; President's News Summary, Feb. 13, 1969, *PNWH,* 6B, Fiche 2. Goldwater had written "à la" as "ala." I have corrected this and similar errors throughout where to do so added clarity without altering the writer's meaning.

61 Haldeman Diary, Feb. 21, 1969.

62 Nixon to Buchanan, Apr. 21, 1970, Box 1, PPF, CDF, NPM.

63 Nixon to Haldeman, May 18, 1971, Box 78, Haldeman Files, NPM.

64 Sallyanne Payton interview with author, July 27, 1994, Ann Arbor, Michigan.

65 See Hoff, *Nixon Reconsidered*, 115-144; *New York Times*, Dec. 20, 1967, 22; *Time*, May 3, 1968, 21; Payton interview with author, July 27, 1994; former Equal Employment Opportunity Commission chair William H. Brown III telephone interview with author, Sept. 15, 1994; Leonard Garment interview with A. James Reichley, Oct. 19, 1977, 3, Box 1, Reichley Transcripts.

66 "Excerpts from an Address by Richard M. Nixon in Cincinnati, Ohio," Feb. 12, 1964, PPS 208 (1964).4(1), NPPP, RNLB.

67 "The President's News Conference of September 26, 1969," in *Public Papers of the Presidents: Richard M. Nixon (1969)* (Washington, D.C.: Government Printing Office, 1971), 750 *(PPP)*.

68 Ehrlichman to Robert J. Brown et al., Oct. 1, 1969, Box 51, Ehrlichman Files, NPM.

69 "Text of On-the-Record Interview in 1958 with Richard M. Nixon," Box 47, Joseph and Stewart Alsop Papers, Manuscript Division, Library of Congress (LC), Washington, D.C.

70 Nixon to Ehrlichman and Ken Cole, Dec. 28, 1972, Box 2, POF, CDF, NPM.

71 "Visit with President Nixon, June 5, 1970," Box 5, Richard L. Wilson Papers, HHL.

72 "Richard M. Nixon's Public Record on Civil Rights Measures," n.d., Box 649, General Correspondence, NPPP, National Archives, Pacific Southwest Region, Laguna Niguel, California (NA-LN). *New York Times*, June 16, 1964, 22; Mar. 11, 1965, 19; Mar. 14, 1965, 67; Mar. 21, 1968, 28; Hoff, *Nixon Reconsidered*, 78; John Edward Wilz, *Democracy Challenged: The United States since World War II* (New York: Harper and Row, 1990), 444.

73 Eisenhower to Nixon, Aug. 15, 1953, PPS 307.6, and Martin Luther King, Jr., inscription in *Stride Toward Freedom: The Montgomery Story*, Book 297, Richard Nixon's Den, NPPP, RNLB.

74 Eisenhower to Swede Hazlette, Nov. 18, 1957, Box 18, Name Series, Whitman File, Eisenhower Papers; *New York Times*, Feb. 14, 1956, p. 18; Parmet, *Richard Nixon and His America*, 268; news clipping, Sept. 24, 1957, Box 153, General Correspondence, NPPP, NA-LN.

75 Raymond Price and H. R. Haldeman quoted in Gerald S. Strober and Deborah Hart Strober, eds., *Nixon: An Oral History of His Presidency* (New York: Harper Collins, 1994), 113.

76 "Text of On-the-Record Interview in 1958 with Richard M. Nixon," Box 47, Alsop Papers.

77 All quotations come from Nixon to Clark, July 22, 1960, Box 153, General Correspondence, NPPP, NA-LN.

78 *New York Times,* Oct. 17, 1957, 6.

79 Richard M. Nixon, "Report to the President on Trip to Africa," Apr. 5, 1957, Box 28, Administrative Series, Ann Whitman File, Dwight D. Eisenhower Papers, DDEL.

80 Nixon to Clark, July 22, 1960, Box 153, General Correspondence, NPPP, NA-LN.

81 Nixon to Lewis C. Olive, Jr., July 20, 1956, Box 153, General Correspondence, NPPP, NA-LN. On limited government, see Nixon to George W. Romney, Oct. 31, 1960, Box 15, George W. Romney Papers–Early Series, Michigan Historical Collections (MHC), Bentley Historical Library (BHL), University of Michigan, Ann Arbor.

82 Quotations come from UPI news release, June 17, 1960, and NHC on William P. Rogers to Nixon, June 17, 1960, Box 653, General Correspondence, NPPP, NA-LN.

83 NHC on Ehrlichman to Nixon, July 18, 1970, *PNWH,* 6A, Fiche 85.

84 Haldeman to Nixon, Aug. 4, 1970, Box 138, Haldeman Files, NPM.

85 "What Nixon Said: Civil Rights," 52, Box 1023, John F. Kennedy Pre-Presidential Papers, John F. Kennedy Library (JFKL), Boston, Massachusetts.

86 Robert Dallek, *Flawed Giant: Lyndon Johnson and His Times, 1961–1973* (New York: Oxford University Press, 1998), 324.

87 Department of Health, Education, and Welfare press release, May 17, 1968, Box 52, HU, WHCF, Lyndon B. Johnson Library (LBJL), Austin, Texas.

88 Dallek, *Flawed Giant,* 324; "HEW Guidelines," Box 75, Ramsey Clark Papers, LBJL.

89 Johnson handwritten comment (JHC) on Douglass Cater to Lyndon B. Johnson, Mar. 25, 1966, Box 13, Handwriting File, LBJL.

90 Commissioner of Education to Cater, n.d. [ca. Apr. 15, 1967], Box 51, HU, WHCF, LBJL.

91 Cater memorandum attached to Cater to Secretary John W. Gardner, May 21, 1966, Box 50, HU, WHCF, LBJL.

92 JHC on Cater to Johnson, May 19, 1966, Box 14, Handwriting File, LBJL.

93 Quoted in J. Harvie Wilkinson, *From Brown to Bakke: The Supreme Court and School Desegregation, 1954–1978* (New York: Oxford University Press, 1979), 81.

94 For the Johnson administration's stance, see "Summary of Statement of Policies under Title VI . . . ," Box 50, HU, WHCF, LBJL.

95 *"Green v. New Kent County* (391 US 430: 1968)," in *The Irony of Desegregation Law,* ed. Mark Whitman (Princeton, N.J.: Markus Weiner, 1998), 124.

96 Notes on civil rights meeting, Apr. 14, 1969, Folder: National Strategy Guidelines, Drawer: Civil Rights–HEW, Finch Papers; A. James Reichley, *Conservatives in an Age of Change* (Washington, D.C.: Brookings Institution, 1981), 179–181.

97 Robert H. Finch Oral History, June 19, 1967, 3–4; Mitchell interview with Reichley, Sept. 18, 1969, 3, Reichley Transcripts.

98 Reichley, *Conservatives in an Age of Change,* 180; Robert H. Finch interview with A. James Reichley, Mar. 8, 1978, 5, Reichley Transcripts.

99 Finch interview with A. James Reichley, Mar. 8, 1978, 3, Reichley Transcripts; *Washington Star,* Jan. 30, 1969, 2; *Baltimore Sun,* Feb. 4, 1969, 6.

100 "High Administration Officials . . . ," *National Journal,* Oct. 1, 1971, Box 46, Trohan Papers (first quotation); Mitchell interview with Reichley, Sept. 18, 1969, 3, Reichley Transcripts (second quotation).

101 Memorandum on meeting with Attorney General John N. Mitchell, Feb. 18, 1969, Box D61, Leadership Conference on Civil Rights (LCCR) Papers, LC.

102 Bradley H. Patterson, Jr., to Leonard Garment, "Notes from the First Term," 3, Nov. 28, 1973, Box 1, Leonard Garment Papers, LC.

103 Jerris Leonard to John N. Mitchell, n.d., Box 4, Robert C. Mardian Papers, HI.

104 The Justice Department was willing, for example, to accept phased desegregation plans rather than one that had to go into effect immediately in September 1969. See HEW meeting notes, June 2, 1969, Drawer: Civil Rights–HEW, Finch Papers.

105 Thurmond to Mitchell, May 15, 1970, Box 5, Mardian Papers.

106 Leon E. Panetta to Finch, Apr. 21, 1969, and Panetta to Finch, n.d.; HEW meeting notes, June 2 and 3, 1969, Drawer: Civil Rights–HEW, Finch Papers.

107 G. Paul Jones to Dent, June 3, 1969, Box 1, Mardian Papers.

108 John Couson to Dent, Feb. 6, 1970, Box 1, Mardian Papers.

109 *Charlotte Observer,* Mar. 23, 1969, 9A; *Washington Star,* June 21, 1969, 2; Jerris Leonard interview with A. James Reichley, Oct. 31, 1977, Box 2, Reichley Transcripts.

110 NHC on Ehrlichman to Nixon, Apr. 17, 1969, *PNWH,* pt. 7, *The President's Personal Files,* Fiche 153.

111 ANS, July 10, 1969, *PNWH,* 6B, Fiche 11; Hullin to Staff Secretary, Box 8, HU, WHCF, NPM.

112 Ehrlichman to James Keogh, June 26, 1969, Box 50, Ehrlichman Files, NPM.

113 Haldeman Diary, Feb. 15, 1969.

114 ANS, n.d. [March 1969], *PNWH,* 6B, Fiche 3.

115 Haldeman meeting notes, Feb. 17, 1969, *PNWH,* 5, Fiche 2.

116 Haldeman meeting notes, Mar. 26, 1969, *PNWH,* 5, Fiche 2.

117 Haldeman to Ehrlichman, May 12, 1969, Box 50, Haldeman Files, NPM;
     John D. Ehrlichman, memorandum of meeting, May 15, 1969, Box 50,
     Ehrlichman Files, NPM.

118 Haldeman meeting notes, June 6, 1969, *PNWH,* 5, Fiche 5.

119 Handwritten notes, John N. Mitchell on July 3, 1969, statement, n.d.,
     Drawer: Civil Rights–HEW, Finch Papers.

120 *Los Angeles Times,* July 4, 1969, pt. 1, 18. For a draft of the statement, see
     "School Desegregation Statement," July 3, 1969, Box 8, Dent Files,
     WHSF, NPM.

121 Roscoe and Geoffrey Drummond, "Nixon More 'Mid' than Conserva-
     tive," Folder 253, Box 30, John H. Knowles Papers, RAC.

122 Dent to Nixon, July 8, 1969, Box 2, Dent Files, NPM.

123 *Washington Post,* July 9, 1969, 19.

124 *Washington Star,* July 8, 1969, 3; *Los Angeles Times,* July 9, 1969, pt. 1, 14;
     New York Times, July 11, 1969, 1, 23; *Los Angeles Times,* July 8, 1969, 1;
     Detroit News, July 14, 1969, 16A; *Baltimore Sun,* Aug. 20, 1969, 1; *Wash-
     ington Post,* Aug. 24, 1969, 2; *Washington Post,* Aug. 23, 1969, B1; *New
     York Times,* Sept. 17, 1969, 18; *Detroit News,* Sept. 28, 1969, 13B; *Wash-
     ington News,* Oct. 8, 1969, 20.

125 *Washington News,* Sept. 4, 1969, 14.

126 Russell Rice to Robert Light, May 9, 1969, Box 1, Dent Files, CDF,
     NPM.

127 John F. Sosnowski to Morton, Mar. 21, 1970, Box 219, Morton Papers.

128 John Stennis to Nixon, Aug. 11, 1969, Box 3, Ehrlichman Files, CDF,
     NPM.

129 Dent to Nixon, June 26, 1969, Box 13, HU, WHCF, NPM; Reichley,
     Conservatives in an Age of Change, 92–94; see also Harlow to Staff Secre-
     tary, July 14, 1969, *PNWH,* pt. 2, *The President's Meeting File, 1969-1974,*
     Fiche 69–6–22, and Harlow to Staff Secretary, Aug. 25, 1969, *PNWH,* 2,
     Fiche 69–7–20.

130 Reichley, *Conservatives in an Age of Change,* 9.

131 *Washington Post,* Aug. 21, 1969, 28.

132 *Los Angeles Times,* Nov. 2, 1969, G4.

133 George R. Metcalf, *From Little Rock to Boston: The History of School Deseg-
     regation* (Westport, Conn.: Greenwood, 1983), 41–49; Congressional
     Quarterly, *Nixon: The First Year of His Presidency* (Washington, D.C.:
     Congressional Quarterly, 1970), 49–50.

134 Wicker, *One of Us,* 505.

135 Haldeman Diary, Oct. 30, 1969.

136 Handwritten notes on Finch conversation with Nixon, Apr. 14, 1969, Drawer: Civil Rights–HEW, Finch Papers.

137 *New York Times,* Oct. 31, 1969, 1.

138 Morgan to Ken Cole, Jan. 28, 1970, Box 35, Confidential Files (CF), NPM.

139 Buchanan to Nixon, Feb. 12, 1970, Box 35, Staff Secretary–Courier Files, NPM.

140 Harlow to Staff Secretary, Feb. 13, 1970, Box 13, HU, WHCF, NPM.

141 Haldeman meeting notes, Feb. 19, 1970, *PNWH,* 5, Fiche 16; Haldeman Diary, Feb. 19, 1970.

142 Ehrlichman meeting notes, Aug. 4, 1970, *PNWH,* 3, Fiche 17; Haldeman meeting notes, Aug. 4, 1970, *PNWH,* 5, Fiche 28.

143 Ehrlichman meeting notes, Mar. 19, 1970, *PNWH,* 3, Fiche 13.

144 Haldeman Diary, Feb. 20, 1970. Later, Nixon reminded aides to "play [the] center strategy right down the middle." Haldeman meeting notes, June 3, 1970, *PNWH,* 5, Fiche 24.

145 ANS, Jan. 19, 1970, *PNWH,* 6B, Fiche 22.

146 Haldeman to Nixon, Aug. 4, 1970, Box 138, Haldeman Files, NPM.

147 *Baltimore Sun,* Mar. 25, 1970, 9; *Washington Star,* Mar. 24, 1970, 1.

148 Ehrlichman meeting notes, Mar. 19, 1970, *PNWH,* 3, Fiche 13.

149 Haldeman meeting notes, Aug. 4, 1970, *PNWH,* 5, Fiche 28.

150 Haldeman Diary, Feb. 20, 1970.

151 Blair handwritten comment on Harlow to Stanley Blair, Feb. 23, 1970, Box 35, Series 3, Subseries 5, Spiro T. Agnew Papers, Theodore McKeldin Library, University of Maryland, College Park.

152 Memorandum of conversation between Governor Kirk of Florida and John Ehrlichman, Feb. 12, 1970, Folder 314 [2 of 2], Box 3, Ehrlichman Files, CDF, NPM.

153 See NHC on S. M. Brownell to Nixon, Mar. 12, 1970, *PNWH,* 6A, Fiche 69.

154 Hullin to Brown, Feb. 24, 1970, and Ehrlichman to Cole, Mar. 3, 1970, Box 52, Ehrlichman Files, NPM.

155 Nixon to Haldeman, Ehrlichman, and Henry A. Kissinger, Mar. 2, 1970, Box 229, Haldeman Files, NPM.

156 Dent to Harlow, May 14, 1970, Box 3, Dent Files, NPM; Haldeman meeting notes, Feb. 4, 1970, *PNWH,* 5, Fiche 15.

157 Leon E. Panetta to Finch, n.d.; Leonard Garment to Cole, Jan. 26, 1970; Morgan to Cole, Jan. 28, 1970, memorandum for Kenneth R. Cole, Jr.,

Jan. 23, 1970, Box 35, CF, NPM; George Shultz interview with A. James Reichley, Jan. 4, 1978, Box 2, Reichley Transcripts.

158 George P. Shultz, *Turmoil and Triumph: My Years as Secretary of State* (New York: Scribner's, 1993), 1046.

159 Mardian to Agnew, May 19 and June 5, 1970, Box 3, George W. Romney Post-Gubernatorial Papers, MHC, BHL; Richard C. Van Dusen notes of cabinet committee meeting, Apr. 7, 1970, Staff Correspondence Files, Richard C. Van Dusen Files, General Records of the Department of Housing and Urban Development, RG 207, NA; James Clawson to Mardian, July 24, 1970, Box 11, Mardian Papers.

160 Mardian to Agnew, July 6, 1970, Box 35, Series 3, Subseries 5, Agnew Papers.

161 Gray to Cabinet Committee on School Desegregation, June 19, 1970, Box 35, Series 3, Subseries 5, Agnew Papers.

162 Haldeman meeting notes, Aug. 8, 1970, *PNWH*, 5, Fiche 28.

163 Harlow to Staff Secretary, Aug. 20, 1970, Box 9, HU, WHCF, NPM.

164 Ehrlichman meeting notes, July 28, 1970, *PNWH*, 3, Fiche 17.

165 "Lighter Moments Dept.," July 28, 1970, Box 11, Department of Health, Education, and Welfare Series, Creed C. Black Papers, King Library, University of Kentucky (HEW).

166 Howard A. Glickstein Memorandum to the Files, Aug. 12, 1970, Folder 22, Box 19, Theodore M. Hesburgh Civil Rights Papers, Theodore M. Hesburgh Library, University of Notre Dame, Notre Dame, Indiana.

167 Theodore M. Hesburgh (with Jerry Reedy), *God, Country, Notre Dame* (New York: Ballantine, 1990), 209–210.

168 Gray to Cabinet Committee on Education, June 29, 1970, Box 3, Romney Post-Gubernatorial Papers.

169 V. Bendrick to Gerald R. Ford, July 21, 1970, Folder B163–13, Gerald R. Ford Congressional Papers, GRFL.

170 Jerry Poole to Elliot Richardson, Aug. 14, 1970, Box 3, HEW.

171 Dent to Nixon, Aug. 6, 1970, Box 46, CF, NPM.

172 Haldeman Diary, July 22, 1970.

173 Ibid., July 23, 1970.

174 Ibid., Aug. 10, 1970.

175 Dent to Ehrlichman, Nov. 13, 1969, Box 1, Dent Files, CDF, NPM.

176 Moynihan to Members of the Cabinet Committee on Education, July 23, 1970, Box 3, Romney Post-Gubernatorial Papers.

177 Ehrlichman meeting notes, Aug. 13, 1970, *PNWH*, 3, Fiche 18.

178 Hugh Sloan to Ehrlichman, June 22, 1970; Sloan to Nixon, June 25, 1970; Haldeman to Dent, July 7, 1970; Dent to Nixon, Aug. 6, 1970,

Box 46, CF, NPM; Haldeman meeting notes, July 22, 1970, *PNWH*, 5, Fiche 28.

179 Moynihan to Members of the Cabinet Committee on Education, July 23, 1970, Box 3, Romney Post-Gubernatorial Papers; Haldeman Diary, Aug. 14, 1970; William Safire, *Before the Fall: An Inside View of the Pre-Watergate White House* (New York: DaCapo, 1975), 442–443; Raymond Price, *With Nixon* (New York: Viking, 1977), 209; Dent, *Prodigal South Returns to Power,* 151–152, 188–194.

180 NHC on Morgan to Ehrlichman, Aug. 12, 1970, Box 1, POF, CDF, NPM.

181 NHC on Morgan to Nixon, Aug. 27 (quotation) and 28, 1970; Morgan to Nixon, Sept. 3, 1970, Box 1, POF, CDF, NPM.

182 Harlow to Staff Secretary, Aug. 20, 1970, Box 16, WHCF: Subject Files, Federal Government (FG), CDF, NPM.

183 Kilberg to Cole, Nov. 19, 1970, Box 9, HU, WHCF, NPM.

184 Leonard interview with Reichley, Oct. 31, 1977, Box 2, Reichley Transcripts; U.S. Civil Rights Commission quoted in Joseph M. Samuels, "Busing, Reading, and Self in New Haven," *Integrated Education,* 10 (November–December 1972), 28.

185 Kilberg to Cole, Nov. 19, 1970, Box 9, HU, WHCF, NPM.

186 Paul M. Rilling, "Have Time and Reality Overtaken the Southern Strategy?" *Interplay,* 3 (August 1970), 34–38.

187 Both Mitchell and HEW Secretary Elliot Richardson, Finch's successor, found the work of the cabinet committee and state advisory committees to be enormously successful. Memorandum of telephone conversation between Mitchell and Richardson, Aug. 6, 1970, Box 127, Elliot L. Richardson Papers, LC.

188 Thurmond Oral History, Feb. 1, 1974, 15, SOHP.

189 Larry A. Jobe to Maurice H. Stans, June 2, 1971, Box 67, Commerce Department Files, Maurice H. Stans Papers, Minnesota Historical Society, St. Paul.

190 Thurmond to Stans, Aug. 25, 1970, Box 20, Commerce Files, Stans Papers.

191 *St. Louis Post-Dispatch,* May 26, 1971, 6A; Haldeman Diary, May 25, 1971.

192 Jon M. Huntsman to Dent, June 22, 1971, Action Memo P-1759, Box 48, Staff Secretary Files, NPM.

193 Jobe to Stans, June 2, 1971, Box 67, Commerce Files, Stans Papers; Stans to Thurmond, Sept. 23, 1970, Box 20, Commerce Files, Stans Papers.

194 Nixon to Haldeman, Nov. 12, 1971, Box 230, Haldeman Files, NPM.

195 Murphy and Gulliver, *Southern Strategy,* 228–229.

196 Winton M. Blount to Nixon, Nov. 17, 1970, Box 46, CF, NPM.

197 Robert Marik to Cole and Ed Harper through Jeb S. Magruder, Oct. 21, 1971, Box 46, CF, NPM; Nixon, *Memoirs,* 542.

198 Huntsman to Dent, May 25, 1971, Box 83, Staff Secretary Files, NPM.

199 Haldeman meeting notes, Nov. 25, 1970, *PNWH,* 5, Fiche 37.

200 Haldeman meeting notes, May 7, 1970, *PNWH,* 5, Fiche 23; Stephan Lesher, *George Wallace: American Populist* (Reading, Mass.: Addison-Wesley, 1994), 442; Haldeman Diary, Apr. 28, 1972; William E. Timmons to Nixon, Feb. 22, 1971, Box 46, CF, NPM; Charles W. Colson notes of meetings with the president, June 28 and 30, 1972, Box 16, Colson Files, NPM.

201 Memorandum of telephone conversation, Richardson and Nixon, Jan. 28, 1971, Box 129, Richardson Papers. Haldeman's diary proclaimed that Nixon wanted to abandon FAP in 1970 because of budgetary reasons. Yet he did not discard the program until 1972 out of frustration over lack of congressional support. Haldeman Diary, July 13, 1970, and Parmet, *Richard Nixon and His America,* 560. At any rate, FAP was still alive in 1971.

202 Colson meeting notes, Sept. 17, 1971, Box 15, Colson Files, NPM.

203 NHC on Morgan to Nixon, July 6, 1971, Box 84, Staff Secretary Files, NPM.

204 ANS, Jan. 18, 1972, Action Memo P-1986, Box 50, Staff Secretary Files, NPM.

205 Stephen E. Ambrose, *Nixon,* vol. 2, *The Triumph of a Politician, 1962–1972* (New York: Simon & Schuster, 1989), 524.

206 Memorandum of telephone conversation, Richardson and Nixon, Jan. 28, 1971, Box 129, Richardson Papers.

207 Memorandum of conversation between Nixon, Richardson, and Shultz, Feb. 2, 1971, Folder: Nixon, Richard M.–Memecons, Box 146, Richardson Papers.

208 Haldeman Diary, Nov. 1, 1971. The following year Nixon again waffled between conservative and moderate positions on high court appointments. Haldeman Diary, Sept. 21 and Nov. 27, 1972.

209 Memorandum of telephone conversation, Ehrlichman and Richardson, Sept. 9, 1971, Box 142, Richardson Papers.

210 "Gordon" to Senator Birch E. Bayh, Jan. 28, 1972, Folder: Busing, Box 953, Birch E. Bayh Papers, Lilly Library, Indiana University, Bloomington.

211 Nixon to Ehrlichman, May 17, 1972, Box 3, Ehrlichman Files, CDF, NPM.

212 Edward L. Morgan, Memorandum for the President's File, Mar. 10, 1972, Box 4, POF, CDF, NPM.

213 NHC on Morgan to Nixon, May 24, 1971, Box 1, POF, CDF, NPM.

214 Memorandum of telephone conversation, Richardson and Colson, Dec. 29, 1971, Box 131, Richardson Papers.

215 "DLH" to Colson, Jan. 5, 1972, Box 46, CF, NPM.

216 Memorandum of telephone conversation, Ehrlichman and Richardson, Aug. 13, 1970, Box 127, Richardson Papers.

217 Blum, *Years of Discord,* 417-421.

218 Haldeman Diary, July 20, 1972; Lesher, *George Wallace,* 461-462.

219 Dewey W. Grantham, *The South in Modern America: A Region at Odds* (New York: HarperCollins, 1994), 284-285.

220 See Carter, *Politics of Rage,* 465-468; William C. Berman, *America's Right Turn: From Nixon to Bush* (Baltimore: Johns Hopkins University Press, 1994), 5-20; Mary C. Brennan, *Turning Right in the Sixties: The Conservative Capture of the GOP* (Chapel Hill: University of North Carolina Press, 1995), 120-137; Kenneth O'Reilly, *Nixon's Piano: Presidents and Racial Politics from Washington to Clinton* (New York: Free Press, 1995), 277-329.

221 Michael Kazin, *The Populist Persuasion: An American History* (New York: Basic Books, 1995), 251.

222 Nixon to Hall, Finch, and Bassett, Sept. 7, 1960, Folder 79: Memos from RN, Box 12, Finch Papers.

223 Haldeman Diary, Apr. 22, 1971; Nixon to Haldeman, Sept. 4, 1972, Box 230, Haldeman Files, NPM; Haldeman Diary, Sept. 19, 1972 (quotation).

224 Sallyanne Payton, "Remarks at the Sixth Annual Presidential Conference: Richard M. Nixon," in *Richard M. Nixon: Politician, President, Administrator,* ed. Leon Friedman and William F. Levantrosser (Westport, Conn.: Greenwood, 1991), 40, 183.

225 "Statement of Robert F. Kennedy on Bussing," Sept. 9, 1964, Box 20, Senate Papers, Robert F. Kennedy Papers, John F. Kennedy Library (JFKL), Boston, Massachusetts; Timothy N. Thurber, *The Politics of Equality: Hubert H. Humphrey and the African American Freedom Struggle* (New York: Columbia University Press, 1999), 227-228; "Q&A for ACLU Journal," n.d., Box 2, Speech Series, Nelson A. Rockefeller Vice Presidential Papers, RG 26, RFA.

226 Quoted in *Nixon: An Oral History of His Presidency,* ed. Gerald S. Strober and Deborah Hart Strober (New York: HarperCollins, 1994), 114.

227 Alfred H. Kelly, Winfred Harbison, and Herman Belz, *The American Constitution: Its Origins and Development,* 6th ed. (New York: Norton, 1983), 710.

228 Ronald P. Formisano, *Boston Against Busing: Race, Class, and Ethnicity in the 1960s and 1970s* (Chapel Hill: University of North Carolina Press,

1991); Lawrence J. McAndrews, "Missing the Bus: Gerald Ford and School Desegregation," *Presidential Studies Quarterly*, 27 (Winter 1997), 791–804; *Wall Street Journal*, Mar. 21, 1977, 12.

229 Arthur S. Flemming to Jimmy Carter, n.d., Box 8, Presidential Handwriting File, Jimmy Carter Library (JCL), Atlanta, Georgia.

230 Carter handwritten message to Flemming, Feb. 16, 1977, Box 8, Presidential Handwriting File, JCL.

231 Louis Martin to Carter, Sept. 26, 1978, Box 103, Presidential Handwriting File, JCL.

2. Open Communities versus Forced Integration

1 Robert Weisbrot, *Freedom Bound: A History of America's Civil Rights Movement* (New York: Plume, 1990), 271–272.

2 John Ehrlichman, *Witness to Power: The Nixon Years* (New York: Simon and Schuster, 1982), 223.

3 Alfred H. Kelly, Winfred A. Harbison, and Herman Belz, *The American Constitution: Its Origins and Development*, 6th ed. (New York: Norton, 1983), 605; David Falk and Herbert M. Franklin, *Equal Housing Opportunity: The Unfinished Federal Agenda* (Washington, D.C.: Potomac Institute, 1976), 52; Allen J. Matusow, *The Unraveling of America: A History of Liberalism in the 1960s* (New York: Harper and Row, 1984), 208; Michael Danielson, *The Politics of Exclusion* (New York: Columbia University Press, 1976), 138.

4 David Halberstam, *The Fifties* (New York: Fawcett, 1993), 141; Arnold R. Hirsch, *Making the Second Ghetto: Race and Housing in Chicago, 1940–1960* (New York: Cambridge University Press, 1983), 89–94.

5 Donald R. McCoy and Richard Ruetten, *Quest and Response: Minority Rights and the Truman Administration* (Lawrence: University Press of Kansas, 1973), 217.

6 Robert Frederick Burk, *The Eisenhower Administration and Black Civil Rights* (Knoxville: University of Tennessee Press, 1984), 127.

7 Carl M. Brauer, *John F. Kennedy and the Second Reconstruction* (New York: Columbia University Press, 1977), 205–211; Matusow, *Unraveling of America*, 206–209.

8 "Reaction to Colored Neighbor Nonsense," Box 649, General Correspondence, Richard M. Nixon Pre-Presidential Papers (NPPP), National Archives, Pacific Southwest Region, Laguna Niguel, California (NA-LN).

9 Position paper on housing, n.d., Civil Rights Research File (Housing), NPPP, Richard Nixon Library and Birthplace (RNLB), Yorba Linda, California.

10 "Richard M. Nixon–Summary Analysis–Civil Rights," May 6, 1968, Box 22, Graham T. Molitor Papers, Rockefeller Archive Center (RAC), Sleepy Hollow, New York.

11 Memorandum on Nixon and open housing, July 3, 1968, Box 22, Molitor Papers.

12 "Richard M. Nixon–Summary Analysis–Civil Rights," May 6, 1968, Box 22, Molitor Papers.

13 "Meeting Notes of the President's Leadership Breakfast," Mar. 14, 1968, Box 2, Meeting Notes File, Lyndon B. Johnson Library (LBJL), Austin, Texas.

14 George R. Metcalf, *Fair Housing Comes of Age* (Westport, Conn.: Greenwood, 1988), 80–83; Hugh Davis Graham, *The Civil Rights Era: Origins and Development of National Policy, 1960–1972* (New York: Oxford University Press, 1990), 271; draft letter from Gerald R. Ford, Apr. 4, 1968, and Ford to F. Waldo Lewis, Apr. 23, 1968, Box 44, Robert T. Hartmann Papers, Gerald R. Ford Library (GRFL), Ann Arbor, Michigan.

15 *New York Times,* Mar. 21, 1968, 28.

16 Clarence Mitchell to Richard M. Nixon, Mar. 22, 1968, Box 44, Hartmann Papers.

17 UPI news dispatch, n.d. Box 44, Hartmann Papers; Graham, *Civil Rights Era,* 272.

18 *New York Times,* Mar. 24, 1968, 50.

19 "Remarks Given by George Bush" (plus attached letter), n.d. [1968], PPS 500.16, NPPP, RNLB.

20 Beth J. Lief and Susan Goering, "The Implementation of the Federal Mandate for Fair Housing," in *Divided Neighborhoods: Changing Patterns of Racial Segregation,* ed. Gary A. Tobin (Newbury Park, Calif.: Sage Publications, 1987), 235; Metcalf, *Fair Housing Comes of Age,* 75–85; Irving Bernstein, *Guns or Butter: The Presidency of Lyndon Johnson* (New York: Oxford University Press, 1996), 499.

21 Lewis Chester, Godfrey Hodgson, and Bruce Page, *An American Melodrama: The Presidential Campaign of 1968* (New York: Viking, 1969), 624–625.

22 "Nixon Was the One for Suburbia," *Chicago Defender,* Apr. 7, 1969, Box 177, Rogers C. B. Morton Papers, Margaret I. King Library, University of Kentucky, Lexington.

23 U.S. Department of Justice, *Annual Report of the Attorney General, 1973* (Washington, D.C.: Government Printing Office, 1973), 74. Another source cited twenty-three fair housing suits for 1969; see Congressional Quarterly, *Nixon: The First Year of His Presidency* (Washington, D.C.: Congressional Quarterly, 1970), 52.

24 Daniel P. Moynihan, "Toward a National Urban Policy," July 1969, Box 10, Richard C. Van Dusen Subject Files, Record Group (RG) 207, General Records of the Department of Housing and Urban Development, National Archives (NA), College Park, Maryland.

25 Graham, *Civil Rights Era,* 304–306, 533–534, n.21.

26 "Summary of Nov. 23–24 Meeting of President's Task Force on Urban Renewal," Box 38, Charles L. Clapp Files, Staff Member and Office Files (SMOF), Richard M. Nixon Presidential Materials (NPM), NA.

27 Raymond J. Saulinier to Task Force on Low-Income Housing, Dec. 19, 1969, Box A26, Arthur F. Burns Papers, GRFL.

28 Annotated news summary (ANS), July 23, 1970, *Papers of the Nixon White House,* ed. Joan Hoff-Wilson, pt. 6, ser. B, *Annotated News Summaries* (Lanham, Md.: University Publications of America, 1989), Fiche 30 *(PNWH).*

29 "Guidelines for Task Forces," n.d., Box 38, Clapp Files, NPM.

30 *Los Angeles Times,* July 27, 1995, A20; George W. Romney to John F. Kennedy and Richard M. Nixon, Oct. 14, 1960, Box 15, George W. Romney Papers, Early Series, Michigan Historical Collections (MHC), Bentley Historical Library (BHL), University of Michigan, Ann Arbor.

31 T. George Harris, *Romney's Way: A Man and an Idea* (Englewood Cliffs, N.J.: Prentice Hall, 1967), 195–196, 201–203; Gerald O. Plas, *The Romney Riddle* (Detroit: Berwyn, 1967), 74.

32 Harris, *Romney's Way,* 201.

33 *Washington Post,* July 27, 1995, C5.

34 Edwin O. Guthman and Jeffrey Shulman, *Robert Kennedy: In His Own Words* (New York: Bantam, 1988), 76.

35 Memorandum on Cleveland Governors' Conference, 3, n.d., Box 1, Leonard Garment Papers, Manuscript Division, Library of Congress (LC), Washington, D.C.

36 John D. Ehrlichman telephone interview with author, Feb. 12, 1995, Atlanta, Georgia.

37 Robert Lee Grant with Carl Gardner, *The Star Spangled Hustle* (Philadelphia: Lippincott, 1972), 145.

38 Romney to Kenneth N. Scott, Oct. 8, 1964, Box 363, George W. Romney Gubernatorial Papers, MHC, BHL.

39 Romney to Goldwater, Mar. 25, 1965, Box 363, Romney Gubernatorial Papers.

40 *New York Times,* July 27, 1995, D22; *Los Angeles Times,* July 27, 1995, A20.

41 *New York Times,* Oct. 15, 1970, 43; *Washington Evening Star,* Oct. 9, 1970; "Secretary George W. Romney: Address to HUD Employees," Oct. 14,

1970, 20–31; and "Statement by Secretary George Romney," Oct. 22, 1972, Box 5, Albert Applegate Papers, MHC, BHL.

42 Tom Wicker, *One of Us: Richard Nixon and the American Dream* (New York: Random House, 1991), 265–335; Richard M. Nixon, *RN: The Memoirs of Richard Nixon* (New York: Grosset and Dunlap, 1978), 271–277.

43 Harris, *Romney's Way,* 195. On Romney's stubborn refusal to endorse Goldwater, see Romney to Mr. and Mrs. Hayse Whiteley, Oct. 8, 1964, Box 363, Romney Gubernatorial Papers.

44 Romney to Kennedy and Nixon, Oct. 14, 1960, Box 15, Romney Papers, Early Series.

45 Nixon to Dwight D. Eisenhower, Feb. 20, 1962, Box 14, Special Names Series, Dwight D. Eisenhower Post-Presidential Papers, Dwight D. Eisenhower Library (DDEL), Abilene, Kansas.

46 Nixon to Romney, Nov. 16, 1962, Box 363, Romney Gubernatorial Papers.

47 David Bunn to Henry Wilson, Jan. 12, 1966, Box 11, Handwriting File, LBJL.

48 Memorandum on phone call from Rose Woods to Fred A. Seaton, Apr. 23, 1964, Box 9, Post-Eisenhower Administration Series, Fred A. Seaton Papers, DDEL; memorandum on Cleveland Governors' Conference, n.d., Box 1, Garment Papers, LC.

49 "Nixon Quotes," n.d., Box 23, James J. Kilpatrick Papers (6626-g), Alderman Library, University of Virginia, Charlottesville.

50 Press statement, Apr. 30, 1968, Box 363, Romney Gubernatorial Papers; Nixon, *Memoirs,* 314.

51 Leonard Garment to Nixon, Nov. 26, 1968, Box 54, Leonard Garment Files, SMOF, NPM.

52 Memorandum of telephone conversation with John Whitaker, Sept. 11, 1968, Box 363, Romney Gubernatorial Papers.

53 Ehrlichman, *Witness to Power,* 97.

54 Romney to James Keogh, Sept. 19, 1969, Box 2, George W. Romney Post-Gubernatorial Papers, MHC, BHL.

55 H. R. Haldeman Diary, Mar. 19, 1969, in *The Haldeman Diaries: Inside the Nixon White House,* ed. H. R. Haldeman (Santa Monica, Calif.: Sony Corporation, 1994), CD-ROM.

56 Romney notes on telephone talk with Ehrlichman, Jan. 28, 1971, Box 13, Romney Post-Gubernatorial Papers.

57 Joan Hoff, *Nixon Reconsidered* (New York: Basic Books, 1994), 70; Romney notes on telephone talk with Ehrlichman, Jan. 28, 1970, Box 13, Romney Post-Gubernatorial Papers.

58 Charles Orlebeke to Romney, Feb. 19, 1969, Box 76, and Romney et al, to Nixon, Feb. 14, 1970, Box 76, Van Dusen Subject Files, Record Group (RG) 207; *Detroit News,* Nov. 8, 1970, 13I.

59 H. R. Haldeman meeting notes, Jan. 14, 1970, *PNWH,* pt. 5, *H. R. Haldeman Notes of White House Meetings,* Fiche 14.

60 *Detroit News,* Aug. 4, 1970, 5B.

61 Quoted in Leonard Garment, *Crazy Rhythm: My Journey from Brooklyn, Jazz, and Wall Street to Nixon's White House, Watergate, and Beyond* (New York: Times Books, 1997), 152.

62 Garment to Ehrlichman, Jan. 20, 1972, Box 2, Garment Papers, LC.

63 Ehrlichman interview with author, Feb. 12, 1995.

64 Stephen Hess interview with A. James Reichley, Oct. 21, 1977, Box 1, A. James Reichley Interview Transcripts, GRFL.

65 William Safire, *Before the Fall: An Inside View of the Pre-Watergate White House* (New York: Da Capo, 1975), 248.

66 "George W. Romney Interviewed on *The Evans-Novak Report,*" Feb. 23, 1969, Box 12, Romney Post-Gubernatorial Papers.

67 Memorandum of telephone conversation, Elliot L. Richardson and George W. Romney, Jan. 4, 1972, Box 131, Elliot L. Richardson Papers, LC.

68 *Detroit News,* Apr. 6, 1969, 4B, and Jan. 26, 1969, 22A.

69 Richard C. Van Dusen to Lawrence Thompson, May 3, 1972, Box 9, Richard C. Van Dusen Papers, MHC, BHL; Sallyanne Payton interview with author, July 27, 1994, Ann Arbor, Michigan.

70 Albert Applegate notes of Camp David meeting, May 19 and 20, 1969, Box 3, Applegate Papers, MHC, BHL.

71 Ehrlichman to Nixon, n.d., Box 4, Romney Post-Gubernatorial Papers; "Elements of an 'Open Communities' Policy," n.d., Box 9, Van Dusen Papers, MHC, BHL; Sherman Unger to Romney, Feb. 6, 1970, Box 10, Van Dusen Subject Files, RG 207.

72 Robert A. Sauer to Samuel J. Simmons, Dec. 23, 1969, Box 24, Van Dusen Subject Files, RG 207.

73 Notes of Open Communities Committee, Aug. 15, 1969, Box 10, Van Dusen Subject Files, RG 207.

74 Applegate notes of Camp David meeting, May 19 and 20, 1969, Box 3, Applegate Papers, MHC, BHL.

75 "Balanced Communities" and "Position Paper on Open Communities (II)," n.d., Box 10, Van Dusen Subject Files, RG 207.

76 "Immediate Administrative Actions to Further Open-Community Objectives," n.d., Box 10, Van Dusen Subject Files, RG 207.

77 "A Strategy for Metropolitan Open Communities," n.d., Box 10, Van Dusen Subject Files, RG 207 (both quotations).

78 "Balanced Communities," n.d., Box 10, Van Dusen Subject Files, RG 207.
79 Van Dusen to Romney, Aug. 15, 1969, Box 8, Van Dusen Papers, MHC, BHL.
80 Open Communities Group to Romney, n.d., Box 9, Van Dusen Papers, MHC, BHL; Romney to Rep. Wright Patman, May 27, 1970, Box 10, Van Dusen Subject Files, RG 207.
81 Chapin to Van Dusen, Sept. 19, 1969; Chapin to Romney, Aug. 15, 1969; and Chapin to Open Communities Committee, Sept. 15, 1969, Box 10, Van Dusen Subject Files, RG 207; Jill Quadagno, *The Color of Welfare: How Racism Undermined the War on Poverty* (New York: Oxford University Press, 1994), 108.
82 Chicago Regional Office to Van Dusen, May 4, 1970, Box 35, Staff Correspondence Files, Van Dusen Files, RG 207.
83 "Open Communities: HUD's Legislative Proposal," July 27, 1970, Box 29, Romney Post-Gubernatorial Papers.
84 *Detroit News,* Jan. 11, 1971, 16A; Van Dusen to Ehrlichman and William Timmons, Aug. 14, 1970, Box 9, Van Dusen Papers, MHC, BHL; Danielson, *Politics of Exclusion,* 237.
85 Romney to Ehrlichman, May 12, 1970, Box 14, and Romney note cards for meeting with the president, May 14, 1970, Box 13, Romney Post-Gubernatorial Papers; John D. Ehrlichman meeting notes, May 14, 1970, *PNWH,* pt. 3, *John D. Ehrlichman Notes of Meetings with the President,* Fiche 14.
86 Ehrlichman to Romney and Romney to Ehrlichman, July 16, 1970, Confidential Files (CF), White House Special Files (WHSF), NPM.
87 Romney notes on telephone talk with Ehrlichman, Jan. 28, 1971, Box 13, Romney Post-Gubernatorial Papers.
88 *New York Times,* Dec. 7, 1969, 1.
89 "Housing Resolutions–NAACP 61st Annual Convention," Box 25, Van Dusen Subject Files, RG 207.
90 *Washington Post,* July 27, 1970, Box 29, Romney Post-Gubernatorial Papers.
91 *Detroit News,* July 27, 1970, 4A, and July 29, 1970, 6A.
92 Ibid., July 21, 1970, 1A.
93 Ibid., July 26, 1970, 16A.
94 Ibid., July 27, 1970, 4A.
95 Ibid., July 28, 1970, 1A.
96 Ibid., July 29, 1970, 10B.
97 "Proceedings of Conference between Housing and Urban Development Representatives, City of Warren Officials," July 27, 1970, 11–14, Box 9, Applegate Papers, MHC, BHL.

98 Ibid., 42

99 William C. Whitbeck to Romney, May 19, 1970; Lawrence M. Cox to Romney, May 12, 1970; and Whitbeck to Romney, July 21, 1970, Box 33, Van Dusen Staff Correspondence Files, RG 207.

100 *Detroit News,* Aug. 27, 1970, 3A.

101 *Detroit Free Press,* Aug. 29, 1970, 3A.

102 *Detroit News,* Nov. 4, 1970, 20A.

103 *Detroit Free Press,* Aug. 28, 1970, 6A.

104 Ehrlichman, *Witness to Power,* 232; Ehrlichman meeting notes, Aug. 4, 1970, *PNWH,* 3, Fiche 17.

105 Nixon handwritten comment (NHC) on Ehrlichman to Nixon, Oct. 21, 1970, *PNWH,* pt. 6, ser. A, *Documents Annotated by the President,* Fiche 101.

106 Ehrlichman to Romney, Oct. 22, 1970, Box 2, FG 24, Department of Housing and Urban Development, White House Central Files (WHCF), NPM.

107 Cox to Romney, July 22, 1970, Box 10, Van Dusen Subject Files, RG 207.

108 *St. Louis Post-Dispatch,* June 16, 1971, 2A.

109 Ehrlichman meeting notes, Aug. 9, 1970, *PNWH,* 3, Fiche 18.

110 Ehrlichman meeting notes, Aug. 11, 1970, *PNWH,* 3, Fiche 18.

111 Nixon to Ehrlichman, Jan. 28, 1972, Box 2, John D. Ehrlichman Files, Contested Documents File (CDF), NPM.

112 Haldeman meeting notes, Nov. 7, 1970, *PNWH,* 5, Fiche 35; Haldeman Diary, Nov. 7, 1970.

113 "Romney Presentation," Oct. 1, 1970, Box 22, Van Dusen Staff Correspondence Files, RG 207.

114 Position Paper on "Fair Housing," 5, Nov. 11, 1970, *PNWH,* 3, Fiche 68.

115 Romney to Nixon, Nov. 16, 1970, Box 4, Romney Post-Gubernatorial Papers.

116 Romney to Mitchell, Nov. 24, 1970, Box 1, Romney Post-Gubernatorial Papers.

117 Haldeman meeting notes, Nov. 16, 1970, *PNWH,* 5, Fiche 36.

118 *Detroit News,* Dec. 11, 1970, 1A.

119 Romney to Nixon, Nov. 16, 1970, Box 4, Romney Post-Gubernatorial Papers; Haldeman meeting notes, Dec. 7 and 16, 1970, *PNWH,* 5, Fiche 37–38; John Ehrlichman, Memorandum for the President's File, Dec. 16, 1970, Box 2, Federal Government (FG) 24, HUD, WHCF, NPM; Haldeman Diary, Jan. 2, 1971.

120 Haldeman meeting notes, Jan. 2, 1971, *PNWH,* 5, Fiche 40.

121 On Panetta's dismissal, see Chapter 1. Hickel became a thorn in Nixon's side when he took a very public stance against the Vietnam War. See Hoff, *Nixon Reconsidered,* 57.

122 Commission on Civil Rights press release, Feb. 19, 1970, and General Services Administration news release, Feb. 27, 1970, Folder 10, Box 15, Theodore M. Hesburgh Civil Rights Papers, Theodore M. Hesburgh Library, University of Notre Dame, Notre Dame, Indiana.

123 "Draft Policies for Tenant and Site Selection," Apr. 1, 1970, Box 32, Van Dusen Staff Correspondence Files, RG 207.

124 Simmons to David O. Maxwell, Feb. 8, 1971, Box 8, Romney Post-Gubernatorial Papers.

125 Transcript of White House conversation between Nixon and Ehrlichman, 17-18, Apr. 19, 1971, *PNWH*, pt. 8, *The White House Tapes: The Complete Transcripts*, Fiche 3.

126 Ehrlichman to Nixon, n.d., Box 14, Romney Post-Gubernatorial Papers.

127 Ehrlichman to Garment, Mar. 8, 1971, Box 19, Human Rights (HU), WHCF, NPM.

128 Ehrlichman meeting notes, Apr. 23, 1971, *PNWH*, 3, Fiche 31; Raymond K. Price to Nixon, June 5, 1971, *PNWH*, 6A, Fiche 149; Ehrlichman to Price, May 21, 1971, Box 2, FG 24, HUD, WHCF, NPM.

129 Bradley H. Patterson, Jr., to Garment, "Notes from the First Term," Nov. 28, 1973, Box 1, Garment Papers, LC.

130 Edward Morgan to Ehrlichman, Dec. 28, 1970, Box 19, HU, WHCF, NPM.

131 "HUD Draft of Proposed Presidential Statement," May 5, 1971, Box 13, Romney Post-Gubernatorial Papers; "Statement about Federal Policies . . . ," June 11, 1971, in *Public Papers of the Presidents: Richard M. Nixon (1971)* (Washington, D.C.: U.S. Government Printing Office, 1972), 721-735 *(PPP)*.

132 Maxwell to Romney, Jan. 5, 1971, Box 30, Romney Post-Gubernatorial Papers.

133 George W. Romney, memorandum of telephone conversation with Mitchell, Dec. 17, 1970, and Romney to Mitchell, Jan. 7, 1971, Box 1, Romney Post-Gubernatorial Papers.

134 *St. Louis Post-Dispatch,* Apr. 5, 1971, A1.

135 Ehrlichman to Romney, May 6, 1971, Box 4, Romney Post-Gubernatorial Papers.

136 "Statement about Federal Policies . . . ," June 11, 1971, *PPP, 1971,* 730.

137 Ibid., 730.

138 Ibid., 731.

139 NHC on Price to Nixon, June 5, 1971, *PNWH,* 6A, Fiche 149.

140 *New York Times,* June 16, 1971, 19; Ehrlichman meeting notes, June 15, 1971, *PNWH,* 3, Fiche 34; Metcalf, *Fair Housing Comes of Age,* 123; U.S.

Department of Justice, *Annual Report of the Attorney General, 1971* (Washington, D.C.: Government Printing Office, 1971), 57.

141 U.S. Department of Justice, *Annual Report of the Attorney General, 1974* (Washington, D.C.: Government Printing Office, 1974), 70; *Annual Report of the Attorney General, 1973,* 74.

142 *St. Louis Post-Dispatch,* Sept. 30, 1971; "Project Selection Criteria: Notice of Proposed Rule-Making," Oct. 2, 1971, Box 35, Romney Post-Gubernatorial Papers.

143 Kelly, Harbison, and Belz, *The American Constitution,* 706–707; Garment to H. R. Haldeman, Apr. 28, 1971, Box 77, H. R. Haldeman Files, WHSF, NPM.

144 *Detroit News,* July 5, 1971, 12A; *New York Times,* July 11, 1971, 43.

145 Gloster Current to William R. Morris, May 27, 1971, Box 25, Roy Wilkins Papers, LC.

146 Nixon to Ehrlichman, Jan. 28, 2972, Box 2, Ehrlichman Files, CDF, NPM.

147 Morris to Roy Wilkins, May 27, 1971, Box 25, Wilkins Papers.

148 NHC on "WIN" to John Tower, July 26, 1971, *PNWH,* 6A, Fiche 163.

149 Ehrlichman to Nixon, July 2, 1971, Box 57, John D. Ehrlichman Files, WHSF, NPM.

150 Ehrlichman to Nixon, July 2, 1971, Box 57; Ehrlichman to Shultz, Sept. 30, 1971, Box 58, Ehrlichman Files, NPM (quotation); *New York Times,* Apr. 22, 1976, Box 8, Frederick Lynn May Files, Gerald R. Ford Presidential Papers, GRFL.

151 Memorandum on the Ribicoff Bill, Nov. 30, 1970, Action Memo P1123, Box 44, Staff Secretary Files, WHSF, NPM.

152 Charles W. Colson to Haldeman, Dec. 7, 1970, Action Memo P1123, Box 44, Staff Secretary Files, NPM.

153 Colson to Nixon, Apr. 21, 1971, Action Memo P1491H, Box 46, Staff Secretary Files, NPM. See Congressional Quarterly, *Almanac: 92nd Congress, 1st Session, . . . 1971* (Washington, D.C.: Congressional Quarterly, 1972), 605–606, 7S.

154 Doug Hallett to Colson, Feb. 24, 1972, Box 1, Charles W. Colson Files, CDF, NPM.

155 Ehrlichman to Morgan, Jan. 15, 1972, Box 5, Ehrlichman Files, CDF, NPM.

156 Sherman Unger to Rose Mary Woods, n.d., Box 3, President's Personal File, CDF, NPM.

157 Nixon to Haldeman, Aug. 12, 1972, Box 16, Haldeman Files, CDF, NPM.

158 Danielson, *Politics of Exclusion,* 234–235.

159 The resignation was pushed back until after the election. Memoranda, Romney to Nixon, Aug. 10, 1972, and Romney to Nixon, Nov. 9, 1972, Box 14, Romney Post-Gubernatorial Papers; Danielson, *Politics of Exclusion,* 241–242; James Cannon to Ford, Apr. 28, 1976, Box 8, May Files, GRFL.

160 Dana Mead, memorandum on meeting, Sept. 12, 1973, Box 5, Alexander M. Haig, Jr., Files, WHSF, NPM.

161 *New York Times,* Jan. 9, 1973, 1; Sept. 20, 1973, 1; Oct. 3, 1973, 24; Oct. 4, 1973.

162 Between 1981 and 1985, federal expenditures on public housing fell from $26.1 million to $2.1 million. See Quadagno, *The Color of Welfare,* 114.

163 "Statement about Policies . . . ," June 11, 1971, *PPP, 1971,* 733.

164 Simmons to Romney, Dec. 18, 1970, Box 12, Romney Post-Gubernatorial Papers.

165 *New York Times,* Apr. 21, 1976; News Clipping, "Housing Integration: A Tough '76 Issue," Box 8, May Files, GRFL.

166 *Washington Post,* Apr. 11, 1976, C7.

167 *Washington Evening Star,* Apr. 8, 1976, A1.

168 Ford handwritten comment on "Q&A for American Newspaper Reception," Apr. 13, 1976, Box 24, Presidential Handwriting File, GRFL.

169 "Interview with the President by Helen Anderson et al., Apr. 21, 1976, Box 8, May Files, GRFL.

170 *Baltimore Sun,* Apr. 23, 1976, A1.

171 Ford's Justice Department initiated thirty-one such suits in 1975 and thirty-five the next year. Although Carter favored strengthening fair housing laws, his Justice Department filed an average of nineteen fair housing suits annually. Between 1981 and 1987, during the Reagan administration, Justice averaged fewer than ten fair housing suits per year. U.S. Department of Justice, *Annual Reports of the Attorneys General, 1975–1986* (Washington, D.C.: Government Printing Office, 1975–1986). The annual reports from 1987 to 1991 contain no information on the number of fair housing lawsuits filed. *Wall Street Journal,* Mar. 22, 1979, 2; Dec. 8, 1980, 19; May 6, 1981, 29.

172 Congressional Quarterly, *Almanac: 100th Congress, 2nd Session, . . . 1988* (Washington, D.C.: Congressional Quarterly, 1989), 68–74.

173 U.S. Department of Justice, *Annual Report of the Attorney General, 1992* (Washington, D.C.: Government Printing Office, 1992), 29; U.S. Department of Justice, *Annual Report of the Attorney General, 1993* (Washington, D.C.: Government Printing Office, 1993), 32.

174 Dwight A. Ink to John A. Buggs, Oct. 21, 1974, and Arthur S. Fleming et

al. to the President, December 1974, Box 54, Arthur S. Fleming Papers, DDEL; Danielson, *Politics of Exclusion*, 241–242.

175 Michael J. Vernarelli, "Where Should HUD Locate Assisted Housing? The Evolution of Fair Housing Policy," in *Housing Desegregation and Federal Policy*, ed. John M. Goering (Chapel Hill: University of North Carolina Press, 1986), 224.

176 *Washington Post*, Nov. 5, 1993, A4; *New York Times*, July 8, 1993, A16; *Washington Post*, June 8, 1994, A23.

177 *New York Times*, Mar. 21, 1995, A11.

178 Bureau of the Census, U.S. Department of Commerce, *1970 Census of Housing: General Housing Characteristics, United States* (Washington, D.C.: Government Printing Office, 1971), 1–35; Bureau of the Census, U.S. Department of Commerce, *1990 Census of Housing: General Housing Characteristics, United States* (Washington, D.C.: Government Printing Office, 1992), 6.

179 Gerald David Jaynes and Robin M. Williams, Jr., eds., *A Common Destiny: Blacks and American Society* (Washington, D.C.: National Academy Press, 1989), 141–143.

180 *New York Times*, July 8, 1993, A16.

181 Barriere to Carl Albert, Feb. 1, 1972, Folder 9, Box 238, Albert Collection, Carl Albert Center, University of Oklahoma, Norman.

3. The Art of Compromise

1 Monica Crowley, *Nixon in Winter* (New York: Random House, 1998), 142.

2 Accounts critical of Nixon's record on voting rights include Steven F. Lawson, *In Pursuit of Power: Southern Blacks and Electoral Politics* (New York: Columbia University Press, 1985), 121–157; Herbert S. Parmet, *Richard Nixon and His America* (Boston: Little, Brown, 1990), 595; Tom Wicker, *One of Us: Richard Nixon and the American Dream* (New York: Random House, 1991), 492.

3 John D. Ehrlichman meeting notes, June 19, 1970, Box 1, John D. Ehrlichman Files, Contested Documents File (CDF), Richard M. Nixon Presidential Materials (NPM), National Archives (NA), College Park, Maryland.

4 Accounts favorable to Nixon's voting rights policy include Abigail M. Thernstrom, *Whose Votes Count? Affirmative Action and Minority Voting Rights* (Cambridge, Mass.: Harvard University Press, 1987), 31–42; Stephen E. Ambrose, *Nixon*, vol. 1, *The Triumph of a Politician, 1962–1972* (New York: Simon and Schuster, 1989), 370; Hugh Davis Graham, *The Civil Rights Era: Origins and Development of National Policy, 1960–1972* (New York: Oxford University Press, 1990), 246–265; Joan Hoff, *Nixon Reconsidered* (New York: Basic Books, 1994), 94.

5 Robert Fredrick Burk, *The Eisenhower Administration and Black Civil Rights* (Knoxville: University of Tennessee Press, 1984), 204.

6 Herbert Brownell with John P. Burke, *Advising Ike: The Memoirs of Attorney General Herbert Brownell* (Lawrence: University Press of Kansas, 1993), 218–219; J. W. Anderson, *Eisenhower, Brownell, and the Congress: The Tangled Origins of the Civil Rights Bill of 1956–1957* (Kingsport, Tenn.: Inter-University Case Program and University of Alabama Press, 1964), 134–135, 138.

7 Brownell, *Advising Ike*, 219.

8 Memorandum of telephone conversation, Dwight D. Eisenhower and Lyndon B. Johnson, June 15, 1957, Box 25, Dwight D. Eisenhower Diary Series (EDS), Ann Whitman File, Dwight D. Eisenhower Papers, Dwight D. Eisenhower Library (DDEL), Abilene, Kansas.

9 Ann Whitman Diary, July 10, 1957, Box 9, Ann Whitman Diary Series (AWDS), Whitman File, Eisenhower Papers.

10 "Interview with Vice President Nixon," n.d., Box 50, William P. Rogers Papers, DDEL.

11 "Voter's Guide to Civil Rights and Social Legislation: Recorded Votes of Richard M. Nixon," n.d., Box 29, Roy Wilkins Papers, Manuscript Division, Library of Congress (LC), Washington, D.C.; "Richard M. Nixon's Public Record on Civil Rights Measures," n.d., Box 649, General Correspondence, Richard M. Nixon Pre-Presidential Papers (NPPP), National Archives, Pacific Southwest Region, Laguna Niguel, California (NA-LN); minutes of the cabinet meeting of Dec. 12, 1955, 8, in *Minutes and Documents of the Cabinet Meetings of President Eisenhower (1953–1961)*, ed. Paul Kesaris and Joan Gibson (Washington, D.C.: University Publications of America, 1980), Reel 4, microfilm *(CMPE)*.

12 Burk, *Eisenhower Administration and Black Civil Rights*, 209.

13 Nixon handwritten comments (NHC) on Jackie Robinson to Richard M. Nixon, Jan. 29, 1960, Box 649, General Correspondence, NPPP, NA-LN.

14 Burk, *Eisenhower Administration and Black Civil Rights*, 221–222; "Richard M. Nixon's Public Record on Civil Rights Measures," n.d., Box 649, General Correspondence, NPPP, NA-LN; Robert Dallek, *Lone Star Rising: Lyndon Johnson and His Times, 1908–1960* (New York: Oxford University Press, 1991), 521.

15 Summary of legislative leadership meeting, July 16, 1957, 8, in *President Eisenhower's Meetings with Legislative Leaders, 1953–1961*, ed. William E. Leuchtenburg (Bethesda, Md.: University Publications of America, 1986), Reel 2, microfilm *(EMLL)*.

16 Dallek, *Lone Star Rising*, 525–526; Paul K. Conkin, *Big Daddy from the Pedernales: Lyndon Baines Johnson* (Boston: Twayne, 1986), 140–142.

17 Notes of congressional leadership meeting, Aug. 13, 1957, Box 1, Robert E. Merriam Papers, DDEL.

18 L. Arthur Minnich notes of legislative leadership meeting, Aug. 6, 1957, Box 4, Legislative Meeting Series, Staff Secretary Records, DDEL.

19 Notes of congressional leadership meeting, Aug. 13, 1957, Box 1, Merriam Papers.

20 Minnich meeting notes, Aug. 6, 1957, Box 4, Legislative Meeting Series, Staff Secretary Records, DDEL.

21 Summary of legislative leadership meeting, Aug. 13, 1957, *EMLL*, Reel 2.

22 Nixon to Martin Luther King, Jr., Sept. 17, 1957, PPS 320.107.14, NPPP, Richard Nixon Library and Birthplace (RNLB), Yorba Linda, California.

23 Burk, *Eisenhower Administration and Black Civil Rights,* 226.

24 King to Nixon, Aug. 30, 1957, PPS 320.107.12, NPPP, RNLB.

25 P. L. Prattis to Lyndon B. Johnson, Aug. 8, 1957, Box 50, Rogers Papers.

26 Robinson to Nixon, Aug. 28, 1957, Box 649, General Correspondence, NPPP, NA-LN.

27 Daniel M. Berman, *A Bill Becomes a Law: The Civil Rights Act of 1960* (New York: Macmillan, 1962), 2.

28 Burk, *Eisenhower Administration and Black Civil Rights,* 243–244.

29 Roy Wilkins to Nixon, Sept. 3, 1959, and Nixon to Wilkins, Oct. 5, 1959, Box 820, General Correspondence, NPPP, NA-LN.

30 Theodore M. Hesburgh to Nixon, Dec. 1, 1959, and Nixon to William P. Rogers, Dec. 8, 1959, Box 50, Rogers Papers.

31 "Excerpts of Remarks of Vice President Richard M. Nixon at Milwaukee, Wisconsin," Feb. 8, 1960, in *Papers of the Republican Party,* pt. 2, *Reports and Memoranda of the Research Division of the Headquarters of the Republican National Committee, 1938–1980,* ed. William E. Leuchtenburg and Paul L. Kesaris (Lanham, Md.: University Publications of America, 1987), Reel 2, microfilm.

32 NHC on Robinson to Nixon, Jan. 29, 1960, Box 649, General Correspondence, NPPP, NA-LN.

33 Berman, *A Bill Becomes Law,* 1; *New York Times,* June 21, 1960, Box 820, General Correspondence, NPPP, NA-LN.

34 Congressional Quarterly, *Almanac: 89th Congress, 1st Session, . . . 1965* (Washington, D.C.: Congressional Quarterly, 1966), 536–537; Berman, *A Bill Become Law,* 134–137; Robert J. Cottrol, "Civil Rights Act of 1957" and "Civil Rights Act of 1960," in *Encyclopedia of the American Presidency,* ed. Leonard W. Levy and Louis Fisher (New York: Simon and Schuster, 1994), 1:208–209; Steven F. Lawson, *Black Ballots: Voting Rights in the South, 1944–1969* (New York: Columbia University Press, 1976), 140–249.

35 "Summary Analysis–Richard M. Nixon–Civil Rights," May 6, 1968, Box 22, Graham T. Molitor Papers, Rockefeller Archive Center (RAC), Sleepy Hollow, New York.

36 Robert Weisbrot, *Freedom Bound: A History of America's Civil Rights Movement,* (New York: Plume, 1990), 142.

37 *New York Times,* Mar. 14, 1965, 67.

38 Monica Crowley, *Nixon Off the Record* (New York: Random House, 1996), 18.

39 "Excerpts of Address by Richard M. Nixon in Cincinnati, Ohio," Feb. 12, 1964, PPS 208 (1964).4(1), NPPP, RNLB. Nixon seemed to get these ideas from his friend Raymond Moley. Raymond Moley to Nixon, Feb. 6, 1964, Nixon to Moley, Feb. 12, 1964, and Moley to Nixon, Feb. 14, 1964, Box 293, Raymond Moley Papers, Hoover Institution Archives (HI), Stanford University, Stanford, California.

40 Hugh Davis Graham, "Voting Rights," in *Encyclopedia of the American Presidency,* ed. Leonard W. Levy and Louis Fisher (New York: Simon and Schuster, 1994), 4:1566–67. David L. Norman to Thomas Keeling, Nov. 6, 1968, Box 1, David L. Norman Files, General Records of the Department of Justice, Record Group (RG) 60, NA.

41 "Bill" to Senator Hugh D. Scott, Jr., Apr. 30, 1969, Box 103, Hugh D. Scott, Jr., Papers, Alderman Library, University of Virginia, Charlottesville.

42 Lamar Alexander to Bryce N. Harlow, Feb. 6, 1969, Box 19, Human Rights (HU), White House Central Files (WHCF), NPM; Memorandum for the President's File on meeting with Roy Wilkins on Feb. 7, 1969, Apr. 22, 1969, *Papers of the Nixon White House,* ed. Joan Hoff-Wilson, pt 2, *The President's Meeting File* (Lanham, Md.: University Publications of America, 1989), Fiche 69-2 *(PNWH).*

43 Minutes of meeting of U.S. Commission on Civil Rights, Mar. 3, 1969, Folder 9, Box 21, Theodore M. Hesburgh Civil Rights Papers, Theodore M. Hesburgh Library, University of Notre Dame, Notre Dame, Indiana.

44 Theodore M. Hesburgh to Nixon, Mar. 28, 1969, Folder 19, Box 19, Hesburgh Civil Rights Papers.

45 Alfred H. Kelly, Winfred Harbison, and Herman Belz, *The American Constitution: Its Origins and Development,* 6th ed. (New York: Norton, 1983), 631; Graham, *Civil Rights Era,* 352–353.

46 Congressional Quarterly, *Almanac: 89th Congress, 1st Session, . . . 1965,* 977, 1042; *New York Times,* July 11, 1969, 22, and July 18, 1969, 10.

47 Howard H. Callaway to Gerald R. Ford, Feb. 24, 1969, Box B134, Gerald R. Ford Congressional Papers, Gerald R. Ford Library (GRFL), Ann Arbor, Michigan.

48 Callaway to Mitchell, Feb. 24, 1969, Box B134, Ford Congressional Papers.

49 Clarke Reed to White House Attendees, Mar. 17, 1969, Box 210, Rogers C. B. Morton Papers, Margaret I. King Library, University of Kentucky, Lexington.

50 Graham, *Civil Rights Era,* 358–359; Richard H. Poff note, n.d., Box 370, Richard Harding Poff Papers, Alderman Library, University of Virginia.

51 Press release from Senator Joseph D. Tydings, Apr. 6, 1965, Series VI, Box 11, Joseph D. Tydings Papers, Department of Special Collections, Theodore R. McKeldrin Library, University of Maryland, College Park.

52 Congressional Quarterly, *Almanac: 89th Congress, 1st Session, . . . 1965,* 541; Callaway to Mitchell, Feb. 24, 1969, Box B134, Ford Congressional Papers (quotation).

53 Memorandum on meeting with John N. Mitchell, Feb. 18, 1969, Box D61, Leadership Conference on Civil Rights (LCCR) Papers, LC.

54 Nixon to Mitchell, Feb. 18, 1969, Box 19, HU, WHCF, NPM.

55 Jerris Leonard to Mitchell, Feb. 27, 1969, Box 72, John W. Dean III Files, White House Special Files (WHSF); Leonard to Ehrlichman, June 9, 1969, and Arthur F. Burns to Nixon, June 17, 1969, Box 19, HU, WHCF, NPM.

56 Annotated news summary (ANS), May 24, 1970, *PNWH,* pt. 6, ser. B, *Annotated News Summaries,* Fiche 7.

57 Diary of White House leadership meeting, 91st Congress, June 4, 1969, Box 106, Robert T. Hartmann Papers, GRFL; Mitchell to Ehrlichman, June 18, 1969, Box 19, HU, WHCF, NPM.

58 Summary notes of staff meetings, June 12 and 16, 1969, Box 51, H. R. Haldeman Files, WHSF, NPM.

59 U.S. House of Representatives, Committee on the Judiciary, *Hearings on the Voting Rights Act Extension, 91st Congress, 1st Session, May 14, 15; June 19, 26; July 1, 1969* (Washington, D.C.: Government Printing Office, 1969), 279.

60 Diary of White House leadership meeting, 91st Congress, May 20, 1969, Box 106, Hartmann Papers.

61 Diary of White House leadership meeting, 91st Congress, June 4, 1969, Box 106, Hartmann Papers.

62 Diary of White House leadership meeting, 91st Congress, June 17, 1969, Box 106, Hartmann Papers.

63 Alexander to Bryce N. Harlow and Dale Grubb to Harlow, June 2, 1969, Box 19, HU, WHCF, NPM.

64 Ehrlichman meeting notes, June 17, 1969, Box 19, HU, WHCF, NPM.

65 Diary of White House leadership meeting, 91st Congress, June 17, 1969, Box 106, Hartmann Papers.

66 "Statement of John N. Mitchell," June 26, 1969, in *Hearings on the Voting Rights Act Extension,* 219.

67 Daniel P. Moynihan to Ehrlichman, July 2, 1969, Box 19, HU, WHCF, NPM.

68 "Statement of Mitchell," June 26, 1969, in *Hearings on the Voting Rights Act Extension,* 219.

69 *New York Times,* June 27, 1969, 16.

70 Ibid., June 28, 1969, 30.

71 Ibid., July 2, 1969, 20.

72 Glickstein to Commissioners, June 26, 1969, Folder 19, Box 19, Hesburgh Civil Rights Papers.

73 See the reaction of Representative Edward Hutchinson, Republican of Michigan and a member of the House Judiciary Committee, in typescript notes, Dec. 10, 1969, Box 60, Edward Hutchinson Papers, GRFL.

74 *New York Times,* July 11, 1969, 1.

75 Reed to Southern Chairman, June 30, 1969, Box 210, Morton Papers.

76 "Statement by Mitchell," July 1, 1969, in *Hearings on the Voting Rights Act Extension,* 279; for Harlow's approach to congressional liaison, see A. James Reichley, *Conservatives in an Age of Change* (Washington, D.C.: Brookings Institution, 1980), 85–86; Egil M. Krogh to Edward L. Morgan, Nov. 19, 1969, Box 1, Egil M. Krogh Files, WHSF, NPM; "News Release from Congressman Gerald R. Ford," Dec. 15, 1969, Box 105, Hartmann Papers.

77 Gerald R. Ford to Mr. and Mrs. Sol Bach, Dec. 19, 1969, Box B134, Ford Congressional Papers; undated meeting notes, Box 105, Hartmann Papers.

78 *New York Times,* Dec. 12, 1969, 1.

79 Arnold Aronson to Participating Organizations, Dec. 23, 1969, Box D5, LCCR Papers.

80 Albert B. Britton, Jr., to Scott, July 16, 1969, Box 103, Scott Papers.

81 U.S. Commission on Civil Rights staff memorandum, "Analysis of S. 2507 . . . ," 2, July 8, 1969, Box 103, Scott Papers.

82 Gary J. Greenberg to Jerris Leonard, Mar. 4, 1969, Box 1, Norman Files, RG 60.

83 John W. Dean III to Ehrlichman, May 28, 1969, Box 72, Dean Files, NPM

84 Grubb to Harlow, June 2, 1969, Box 19, HU, WHCF, NPM.

85 Memorandum from William E. Timmons, June 2, 1969, Box 19, HU, WHCF, NPM.

86 Glickstein to Leonard Garment, Jan. 20, 1969, Box 156, Leonard Garment Files, Staff Member and Office Files (SMOF), NPM.

87 Sid Bailey to Scott and Gene Cowen, June 10, 1969, Box 156, Scott Papers.

88 NHC on Bradley H. Patterson, Jr., to Ehrlichman, Dec. 8, 1969, *PNWH*, pt. 6, ser. A, *Documents Annotated by the President,* Fiche 49.

89 Ehrlichman meeting notes, Dec. 9, 1969, *PNWH*, pt. 3, *John D. Ehrlichman Notes of Meetings with the President,* Fiche 7.

90 Garment to Nixon, Dec. 4, 1969, Box 1, Garment Files, NPM.

91 Quoted in John David Skrentny, *The Ironies of Affirmative Action: Politics, Culture, and Justice in America* (Chicago: University of Chicago Press, 1996), 210.

92 *Wall Street Journal,* Jan. 17, 1969, 23.

93 Quoted in Douglas Brinkley, *Dean Acheson: The Cold War Years, 1953–1971* (New Haven: Yale University Press, 1992), 302.

94 Ehrlichman meeting notes, Dec. 3, 1970, *PNWH,* 3, Fiche 22.

95 Fact sheet, "Senator Scott's Record on Civil Rights Legislation," n.d., Box 215, Scott Papers.

96 "Statement by U.S. Senator Hugh Scott on Civil Rights Legislation," Mar. 10, 1960, Box 74, Scott Papers.

97 Clarence Mitchell, "From the Work Bench," *The Afro-American,* Sept. 17, 1963, Box 74, Scott Papers.

98 Gene Cowen to Scott, July 9, 1969, Box 156, Scott Papers.

99 Cowen to Scott, June 25, 1969, Box 156, Scott Papers.

100 Scott handwritten comment on Bart-Jeffrey to Scott, n.d., Box 156, Scott Papers.

101 Scott handwritten note, n.d., Box 32, Scott Papers.

102 Scott to Nixon, Mar. 4, 1970, Box 3, Additional Papers (10,200 unpaginated), Scott Papers.

103 "GOP Leader Helps Scuttle Anti-Busing Bill," *Human Events,* Oct. 21, 1972, Box 163, Scott Papers.

104 Bill to Scott, Jan. 20, 1970, Box 32, Scott Papers.

105 "Unpublished Paper by U.S. Senator Hugh Scott," n.d., Box 64, Scott Papers.

106 Scott to Norman Richardson, Apr. 10, 1974, Box 1, Additional Papers, Scott Papers; H. R. Haldeman Diary, May 18, 1971, in *The Haldeman Diaries: Inside the Nixon White House,* ed. H. R. Haldeman (Santa Monica, Calif.: Sony Corporation, 1994), CD-ROM.

107 David Johnson to Sid Bailey, Dec. 10, 1969, Box 156, Scott Papers.

108 Congressional Quarterly, *Almanac: 91st Congress, 2nd Session, . . . 1970* (Washington, D.C.: Congressional Quarterly, 1971), 193–194.

109 Bart to Senator Scott, Feb. 9, 1970, Box 156, Scott Papers; Michael O'Brien, *Philip Hart: The Conscience of the Senate* (East Lansing: Michigan State University Press, 1995), 101–102.

110 Barry M. Goldwater to Scott, Jan. 20, 1970, Box 156, Scott Papers.

111 Bart to Scott, Feb. 18, 1970, Box 156, Scott Papers.

112 "Outline for Review of Compromise Amendment to the Voting Rights Act of 1969," Feb. 18, 1970, Box 156, Scott Papers.

113 "Statement Explaining the Cooper Amendment," n.d., Box 510, John Sherman Cooper Papers, King Library, University of Kentucky, Lexington.

114 Bart to Scott, Feb. 17, 1970, Box 156, Scott Papers; Congressional Quarterly, *Almanac: 91st Congress, 2nd Session, . . . 1970,* 196.

115 Bart to Scott, Feb. 26, 1970, Box 156, Scott Papers.

116 Congressional Quarterly, *Almanac: 91st Congress, 2nd Session, . . . 1970,* 196.

117 Birch E. Bayh to Charlotte Adler, Jan. 19, 1970, Folder: Voting Age-A, Box 382, Birch E. Bayh Papers, Lilly Library, Indiana University, Bloomington.

118 *Sacramento Union,* Feb. 14, 1967, B6.

119 Congressional Quarterly, *Almanac: 91st Congress, 2nd Session, . . . 1970,* 197; Bart to Senator Scott, Feb. 26, 1970, Box 156, Scott Papers.

120 Bayh to Kathy Akers, Nov. 13, 1969, Folder: Voting Age-A, Box 382, Bayh Papers.

121 *New York Times,* Mar. 14, 1970, 1.

122 NHC on news summary, Mar. 5, 1970, *PNWH,* 6B, Fiche 27.

123 H. R. Haldeman meeting notes, Feb. 21, 1970, *PNWH,* pt. 5, *H. R. Haldeman Notes of White House Meetings,* Fiche 17.

124 Dean J. Kotlowski, "Trial By Error: Nixon, the Senate, and the Haynsworth Nomination," *Presidential Studies Quarterly,* 26 (Winter 1996), 71–91.

125 John Robert Greene, *The Limits of Power: The Nixon and Ford Administrations* (Bloomington: Indiana University Press, 1991), 38–41.

126 Diary of White House leadership meeting, 91st Congress, Mar. 3, 1970, Box 106, Hartmann Papers.

127 Haldeman meeting notes, Mar. 5, 1970, *PNWH,* 5, Fiche 17.

128 Haldeman meeting notes, Apr. 8, 1970, *PNWH,* 5, Fiche 20.

129 Congressional Quarterly, *Almanac: 91st Congress, 2nd Session, . . . 1970,* 21S.

130 Ehrlichman meeting notes, Mar. 17, 1970, *PNWH,* 3, Fiche 13.

131 ANS, n.d. [March 1970], *PNWH,* 6B, Fiche 28.

132 Ehrlichman meeting notes, Apr. 16, 1970, *PNWH,* 3, Fiche 14.

133 "Summary Outline of Statement of Louis H. Pollak," Mar. 10, 1970, Folder: Voting Age-A, Box 382, Bayh Papers.

134 Nixon to Haldeman, n.d., Box 230, Haldeman Files, NPM.

135 Transcript of Nixon broadcast, Oct. 16, 1968, Box 20, HU, WHCF, NPM; Sam Williams to Jack Padrick, Oct. 3, 1968, and typescript note (quotation), n.d., Folder: Youth, Box 17, Annelise Graebner Anderson Papers, HI.

136 William Safire to Haldeman, March 1971, Box 76, Haldeman Files, NPM.

137 Haldeman handwritten notes, n.d., Box 19, HU, WHCF, NPM.

138 Mitchell to James O. Eastland, n.d., Box 28, Dean Files, NPM; Ehrlichman meeting notes, Mar. 18, 1970, *PNWH*, 3, Fiche 13.

139 Tod Hullin to Ehrlichman, Apr. 16, 1970, Box 52, John D. Ehrlichman Files, WHSF, NPM; Timmons to Charles W. Colson, Apr. 29, 1970, Box 59, Charles W. Colson Files, WHSF, NPM.

140 Kotlowski, "Trial by Error," 71-83.

141 Richard Cook to Dwight Chapin through Timmons, Apr. 7, 1970, Box 19, HU, WHCF, NPM.

142 John B. Anderson et al. to Colleague, Apr. 7, 1970, Box 60, Hutchinson Papers.

143 Timmons to Ehrlichman, Apr. 9, 1970, Box 19, HU, WHCF, NPM; *New York Times,* June 18, 1970, 1.

144 Nixon to Ehrlichman, Apr. 13, 1970, Box 1, Dean Files, CDF, NPM.

145 Raymond K. Price to Garment, June 18, 1970, Box 60, Haldeman Files, NPM.

146 Memorandum on voting rights from Garment, June 18, 1970, Box 60, Haldeman Files, NPM.

147 William H. Rehnquist to John W. Dean III, June 18, 1970, Box 1, Dean Files, CDF, NPM.

148 "Veto Message," n.d., Box 28, Dean Files, NPM; Timmons to Nixon, June 18, 1970, Box 20, HU, WHCF, NPM.

149 Ehrlichman to Haldeman, Apr. 15, 1970, Box 52, Ehrlichman Files, NPM.

150 Ehrlichman meeting notes, June 19, 1970, *PNWH*, 3, Fiche 16.

151 Haldeman meeting notes, June 17 and 19, 1970, *PNWH*, 5, Fiche 25.

152 Haldeman meeting notes, June 19, 1970, *PNWH*, 5, Fiche 25.

153 Haldeman meeting notes, June 19, 1970, *PNWH*, 5, Fiche 25.

154 *New York Times,* June 23, 1970, 1.

155 "Voting Rights Signing Statement–Draft–Price," June 17, 1970, Box 60, Haldeman Files, NPM.

156 NHC on "Statement by the President," June 22, 1970, *PNWH*, pt. 7, *The President's Personal File, 1969-1974,* Fiche 244.

157 "Voting Rights Signing Statement–Draft–Price," June 17, 1970, Box 60, Haldeman Files, NPM.

158 *New York Times,* June 23, 1970, 1.

159 J. Strom Thurmond to Nixon, June 23, 1970, Box 2, Garment Files, NPM.

160 ANS, n.d. [September 1970], *PNWH,* 6B, Fiche 32.

161 ANS, Jan. 1, 1971, *PNWH,* 6B, Fiche 39.

162 Dwight L. Chapin to Haldeman, Dec. 21, 1970, and Memorandum for the President's File, Dec. 21, 1970, in *From: the President: Richard Nixon's Secret Files,* ed. Bruce Oudes (New York: Harper and Row, 1989), 192–195.

163 Nixon to Patrick J. Buchanan, Apr. 21, 1970, Box 1, President's Personal File (PPF), CDF, NPM.

164 Ehrlichman meeting notes, July 7, 1970, *PNWH,* 3, Fiche 17.

165 *New York Times,* Aug. 22, 1970, 24.

166 Colson to Kenneth Cole, Dec. 30, 1970, Box 20, HU, WHCF, NPM.

167 Timmons to Ehrlichman, Feb. 22, 1971, Box 20, HU, WHCF, NPM; *St. Louis Post-Dispatch,* July 1, 1971, 1A.

168 Lawson, *In Pursuit of Power,* 299.

169 Joint Center for Policy Studies, "Purpose and Design of the Voting Rights Act," Jan. 14, 1975, Box E36, LCCR Papers.

170 Thernstrom, *Whose Votes Count?* 154–157.

171 Lawson, *In Pursuit of Power,* 168.

172 Aronson to Heads of National Organizations, Apr. 13, 1971, and Ralph David Abernathy to Mitchell, Apr. 22, 1971, Box E37, LCCR Papers; Garment to Thomas Stoel, Mar. 12, 1971, and Garment to Ehrlichman, Apr. 5, 1971, Box 156, Garment Files, NPM.

173 Lawson, *In Pursuit of Power,* 173.

174 Eighty-seven percent of the Justice Department's objections to voting laws between 1965 and 1974 were filed after 1970. See Lawson, *In Pursuit of Power,* 189–190.

175 Joint Center for Policy Studies, "Purpose and Design of the Voting Rights Act," Jan. 14, 1975, Box E36, LCCR Papers.

176 Graham, *Civil Rights Era,* 362.

177 Joint Center for Policy Studies, "Purpose and Design of the Voting Rights Act," Jan. 14, 1975, Box E36, LCCR Papers.

178 Rudolfo de la Garza and Louis DeSipio, "Save the Baby, Change the Bathwater, and Scrub the Tub: Latino Electoral Participation after Twenty Years of Voting Rights Act Coverage," in *Pursuing Power: Latinos and the Political System,* ed. F. Chris Garcia (Notre Dame, Ind.: University of Notre Dame Press, 1997), 73.

179 Memorandum on Voting Rights Act extension, Jan. 13, 1975, Box 24, Presidential Handwriting File, Gerald R. Ford Presidential Papers, GRFL.

180 Newspaper editorial, "Human Rights and Voting Rights," n.d., Box 5, Fernando E. C. De Baca Files, GRFL.

181 Quoted in Thernstrom, *Whose Votes Count?* 50.

182 Press release, Americans for Democratic Action, Apr. 28, 1975, Box E38, LCCR Papers; news clipping, "Mansfield Acts Quickly on Voting Bill," n.d., Box 5, De Baca Files, GRFL.

183 News clipping, "Mansfield Acts Quickly on Voting Bill," n.d., Box 5, De Baca Files, GRFL.

184 David A. Bositis, *The Congressional Black Caucus in the 103rd Congress* (Washington, D.C.: Joint Center for Political and Economic Studies, 1994), 53–68.

185 Lawson, *In Pursuit of Power,* 301.

4. Jobs Are Nixon's Rights Program

1 "Where the Quotas Came From," *Fortune,* May 30, 1994, 174.

2 Elliot Zashin, "The Progress of Black Americans in Civil Rights: The Past Two Decades Assessed," *Daedalus,* 117 (Winter 1981), 239–262; Bruce J. Schulman, *Lyndon B. Johnson and American Liberalism* (Boston: Bedford Books, 1995), 114–123; John Ehrlichman, *Witness to Power: The Nixon Years* (New York: Simon and Schuster, 1982), 223; Joan Hoff, *Nixon Reconsidered* (New York: Basic Books, 1994), 78.

3 James Farmer quoted in *Nixon: An Oral History of His Presidency,* ed. Gerald S. Strober and Deborah Hart Strober (New York: HarperCollins, 1994), 114.

4 Daniel P. Moynihan to Richard M. Nixon, Mar. 19, 1969, 27–28, Oversize Attachment 564, Box 1, Human Rights (HU), White House Central Files (WHCF), Richard M. Nixon Presidential Materials (NPM), National Archives (NA), College Park, Maryland.

5 Nixon to John D. Ehrlichman, Jan. 28, 1972, Box 2, John D. Ehrlichman Files, Contested Documents File (CDF), NPM.

6 Ehrlichman, *Witness to Power,* 231. Nixon also favored job training and welfare reform. Bert Silver to Howard A. Glickstein, Feb. 4, 1970, Box 249, Rogers C. B. Morton Papers, Margaret I. King Library, University of Kentucky, Lexington; memorandum for Howard A. Glickstein, Feb. 2, 1971, Folder 1, Box 20, Theodore M. Hesburgh Civil Rights Papers, Theodore M. Hesburgh Library, University of Notre Dame, Notre Dame, Indiana.

7 David Hawkins, "Jobs Are Nixon's 'Rights' Program," n.d., Morton Papers.

8 *New York Times,* Aug. 28, 1969, 27; statement by the Executive Council of the AFL-CIO, Feb. 10, 1956, Box 441, Official File (OF), WHCF, Dwight D. Eisenhower Papers, Dwight D. Eisenhower Library (DDEL), Abilene, Kansas; *Chicago (Weekly) Defender,* Sept. 20–26, 1969, 8.

9 John D. Ehrlichman meeting notes, Dec. 23, 1969, *Papers of the Nixon White House,* ed. Joan Hoff-Wilson, pt. 3, *John D. Ehrlichman Notes of Meetings with the President, 1969–73* (Lanham, Md.: University Publications of America, 1989), Fiche 8 *(PNWH).*

10 *Equal Employment Opportunity Commission News,* Sept. 28, 1969, Box A10, Arthur F. Burns Papers, Gerald R. Ford Library (GRFL), Ann Arbor, Michigan.

11 Dwight D. Eisenhower to Nixon, Sept. 4, 1953, PPS 307.10, Richard M. Nixon Pre-Presidential Papers (NPPP), Richard Nixon Library and Birthplace (RNLB), Yorba Linda, California.

12 "Report of Meeting with Compliance Officers," 5, May 1, 1957, Box 440, OF, WHCF, Eisenhower Papers.

13 Transcript of press interview by Nixon, Oct. 25, 1955, PPS 307.70; television remarks, Apr. 22, 1956, PPS 307.80; and summary of discussion with representatives of organized labor, Apr. 30, 1957, PPS 307.97.2, NPPP, RNLB.

14 James P. Mitchell to Sherman Adams, Jan. 12, 1955, Box 441, OF, WHCF, Eisenhower Papers.

15 Notes of cabinet meeting, Dec. 18, 1959, 2 and 4, *Minutes and Documents of the Cabinet Meetings of President Eisenhower (1953–1961),* ed. Paul Kesari and Joan Gibson (Washington, D.C.: University Publications of America, 1980), microfilm, Reel 10.

16 H. R. Haldeman meeting notes, Mar. 5, 1970, *PNWH,* pt. 5, *H. R. Haldeman Notes of White House Meetings, 1969–73,* Fiche 17.

17 See Roger Morris, *Richard M. Nixon: The Rise of an American Politician* (New York: Henry Holt, 1990); Garry Wills, *Nixon Agonistes: The Crisis of the Self-Made Man* (New York: New American Library, 1979), 523–546; Theodore H. White, *The Making of the President, 1968* (New York: Pocket Books, 1970), 318–319.

18 "Nixon Answers Questions about Civil Rights," n.d., Civil Rights Position Paper File, NPPP, RNLB.

19 David R. Kochery to the editor of the *New York Times,* Aug. 11, 1960, Committee on Government Contracts File, NPPP, RNLB; *Anderson (S.C.) Independent,* Aug. 19, 1953, Box 28, Administration Series, Ann C. Whitman File, Eisenhower Papers.

20 Ann C. Whitman Diary, Mar. 13, 1956, Box 8, Ann C. Whitman Diary Series (AWDS), Whitman File, Eisenhower Papers.

21 Nixon to Dulles, Sept. 27, 1956, PPS 307.91; Nixon to Ezra Taft Benson, Mar. 2, 1959, PPS 307.134, and Nixon to Clarence Mitchell, Dec. 29, 1955, PPS 307.74, NPPP, RNLB.

22 "Nixon's Record on Job Discrimination," n.d., PPS 307.164.2, NPPP, RNLB.

23 Summary of discussion with representatives of organized labor, Apr. 30, 1957, PPS 307.97.2, NPPP, RNLB.

24 Harry Fleischman to Herbert Hill, Nov. 9, 1960, Box 525, Jay Lovestone Papers, Hoover Institution Archives (HI), Stanford University, Stanford, California; minutes of the meeting of the Government Contract Committee, Sept. 14, 1953, PPS 307.41, and *Chicago Defender,* Oct. 17, 1959, PPS 307, NPPP, RNLB; "Three Negroes Obtain Rodman Jobs Here," Apr. 30, 1960, Box 129, James P. Mitchell Papers, DDEL; *News from NAACP,* Feb. 25, 1960, PPS 307.153, NPPP, RNLB.

25 Jacob Seidenberg, "The President's Committee on Government Contracts, 1953-1960," 227-259 (quotations 231, 235), Box 130, Mitchell Papers.

26 *Philadelphia Tribune,* June 1, 1963, 1, 5, and June 4, 1963, 3; John D. Spellman to John D. Ehrlichman, Sept. 16, 1969, Box 18, HU, WHCF, NPM; *New York Times,* Nov. 8, 1969, 19, and Aug. 28, 1969, 27.

27 *New York Times,* Aug. 30, 1969, 1, 22, and 20.

28 Ibid., Sept. 27, 1969, 18.

29 Hugh Davis Graham, *Civil Rights Era: Origins and Development of National Policy, 1960-1972* (New York: Oxford University Press, 1990), 278-281; Executive Order 11246, Sept. 24, 1965, in *Weekly Compilation of Presidential Documents,* vol. 1, no. 9 Sept. 27, 1965 (Washington, D.C.: Government Printing Office, 1965), 305-309.

30 Graham, *Civil Rights Era,* 188, 278-291; J. Larry Hood, "The Nixon Administration and the Revised Philadelphia Plan for Affirmative Action: A Study in Expanding Presidential Power and Divided Government," *Presidential Studies Quarterly,* 23 (Winter 1993), 146-147.

31 "Philadelphia Plan: Questions and Answers," n.d., Folder 3, Box 18, Laurence H. Silberman Papers, HI.

32 Graham, *Civil Rights Era,* 284-297; Hood, "The Nixon Administration and the Revised Philadelphia Plan," 147.

33 Glickstein to John A. Hannah, Jan. 31, 1969, Folder 19, Box 19, Hesburgh Civil Rights Papers.

34 "The Reluctant Guardians: A Survey of the Enforcement of Federal Civil Rights Laws," 15, Dec. 1969, Box 21, Bradley H. Patterson, Jr., Files, Staff Member and Office Files (SMOF), NPM.

35 Nixon to George P. Shultz, Feb. 18, 1969, Box 24, George P. Shultz Files, 1969-70, General Records of the Department of Labor, Record Group (RG) 174, NA.

36 Moynihan to Shultz, Mar. 3, 1969, Box 17, HU, WHCF, NPM.

37 Richard C. Van Dusen to James D. Hodgson, June 26, 1969, Box 22, Staff Correspondence Files, Richard C. Van Dusen Files, General Records of the Department of Housing and Urban Development, RG 207, NA.

38 George W. Romney to Nixon, n.d., Box 74, Subject Files, Van Dusen Files, RG 207.

39 Shultz to Nixon, July 30, 1969, Box 24, Shultz Files, 1969–70, RG 174.

40 Shultz to Don Slaiman, Feb. 25, 1969, Box 16, Shultz Files, 1969–70, RG 174.

41 George P. Shultz interviewed on *Meet the Press,* Apr. 27, 1969, 8, Box 135, Shultz Files, 1969–70, RG 174.

42 Shultz to Heads of All Agencies, June 17, 1969, Box 3, Commerce Department Files, Maurice H. Stans Papers, Minnesota Historical Society, St. Paul.

43 Shultz to Maurice H. Stans, Oct. 24, 1969, Box 3, Commerce Files, Stans Papers.

44 Graham, *Civil Rights Era,* 238; Arthur A. Fletcher to Heads of All Agencies, June 27, 1969, Folder 5, Box 18, Silberman Papers.

45 *Department of Labor News,* Mar. 31, 1972, Box 142; Sept. 23, 1969, Box 143; and "For Backgrounder on the Philadelphia Plan Vote," n.d., Box 143, Garment Files, NPM.

46 Robert Brown, Memorandum for the President's File, Feb. 7, 1969, *PNWH,* pt. 2, *The President's Meeting File,* Fiche 69-2-2.

47 Harrison A. Williams, Jr., to Clarence Mitchell, Apr. 15, 1969, and "Suggested Questions LCCR Conference with Secy Shultz, DOL," Apr. 25, 1969, Box D63, Leadership Conference on Civil Rights (LCCR) Papers, Manuscript Division, Library of Congress (LC), Washington, D.C.; Glickstein to John A. Hannah, Jan. 31, 1969, Folder 19, Box 19, Hesburgh Civil Rights Papers.

48 Fletcher to Roy Wilkins, June 18, 1969, Box D63, LCCR Papers.

49 NAACP press release, Aug. 7, 1969, Box 27, Roy Wilkins Papers, LC.

50 Notes on meeting with AFL-CIO, n.d., Folder 2, Box 28, Silberman Papers.

51 Elmer B. Staats to Shultz, Aug. 5, 1969, Folder 2, Box 18, Silberman Papers.

52 Everett M. Dirksen to Shultz, Aug. 7, 1969, Everett M. Dirksen Papers, Everett McKinley Dirksen Congressional Leadership Research Center, Pekin, Illinois.

53 Richard M. Nixon, *RN: The Memoirs of Richard Nixon* (New York: Grossett and Dunlap, 1978), 438.

54 United States Senate, Committee on the Judiciary, *Hearings on the Philadelphia Plan, 91st Congress, 1st Session, October 27 and 28, 1969* (Washington, D.C.: Government Printing Office, 1970), 1–45; Congressional Quarterly, *Congressional Quarterly Almanac (1964)* (Washington, D.C.: Congressional Quarterly, 1965), 696; "For Backgrounder on the Philadelphia Plan Vote," n.d., Box 143, Garment Files, NPM.

55 *Department of Labor News,* Sept. 23, 1969, Folder 3, Box 18, Silberman Papers; *Department of Labor News,* Sept. 23, 1969, Box 143, Garment Files, NPM.

56 David Barr to Laurence H. Silberman, Sept. 11, 1969, "Synopsis of Argument"; John N. Mitchell to Shultz, Sept. 22, 1969, Box 18, Silberman Papers.

57 Quotation is from George P. Shultz telephone interview with author, Oct. 17, 1995, Stanford, California; "Notes on the Philadelphia Plan," Feb. 2, 1970, Folder 3, Box 14, Silberman Papers; *Wall Street Journal,* Aug. 11, 1977, 22.

58 George P. Shultz, Memorandum of Meeting of the President, Mar. 13, 1969, Box 16, Shultz Files, 1969–70, RG 174; Leonard Garment to Kenneth Cole, Aug. 22, 1969, Box 1, Garment Files; Bradley H. Patterson, Jr., to Garment, July 11, 1969, Box 28, Patterson Files, NPM.

59 Press conference of George P. Shultz, Aug. 6, 1969, 10, Box 135, Shultz Files, 1969–70, RG 174.

60 William Safire, *Before the Fall: An Inside View of the Pre-Watergate White House* (New York: Da Capo, 1975), 585.

61 Nixon handwritten comment (NHC) on Charles K. McWhorter to Nixon, Dec. 14, 1957, Box 153, General Correspondence, NPPP, National Archives, Pacific Southwest Region, Laguna Niguel, California (NA-LN).

62 United States Senate, Committee on Commerce, *Freedom of Communications Final Report,* pt. 3, *The Joint Appearances of Senator John F. Kennedy and Vice President Richard M. Nixon* (Washington, D.C.: Government Printing Office, 1961), 447.

63 President's Committee on Government Contracts, *Pattern for Progress: Final Report to President Eisenhower from the Committee on Government Contracts* (Washington, D.C.: Government Printing Office, 1961), 14–15.

64 Nixon to Cushman, Dec. 9, 1960, PPS 307.177, NPPP, RNLB.

65 John David Skrentny, *The Ironies of Affirmative Action: Politics, Culture, and Justice* (Chicago: University of Chicago Press, 1996), 193.

66 Nixon to Lt. Lewis C. Olive, July 20, 1956; Nixon to Mrs. John Canning, Feb. 13, 1957; and Nixon to Leonard Clark, July 22, 1960, Box 153, General Correspondence, NPPP, NA-LN; Nixon handwritten notes, "Cam-

paign Leads," Oct. 16, 1970, *PNWH*, pt. 7, *The President's Personal Files,*
Fiche 259; NHC on Franchot J. Swanagan to Nixon, Apr. 23, 1971,
PNWH, pt. 6, ser. A, *Documents Annotated by the President,* Fiche 143.

67 *New York Times,* Dec. 20, 1967, 22.

68 *Detroit Free Press,* Jan. 26, 1969, 3B.

69 "For Backgrounder on the Philadelphia Plan Vote," n.d., Box 143, Garment Files, NPM.

70 Graham, *Civil Rights Era,* 325.

71 "For Backgrounder on the Philadelphia Plan Vote," n.d., Box 143, Garment Files, NPM.

72 Ehrlichman meeting notes, Dec. 23, 1969, *PNWH,* 3, Fiche 8.

73 "Statement by Governor Rockefeller . . . June 17, 1960," Box 6, Nelson A.
Rockefeller Gubernatorial Papers, RG 15, Rockefeller Family Archives
(RFA), Rockefeller Archive Center (RAC), Sleepy Hollow, New York.

74 "Summary Analysis–Ronald W. Reagan–Civil Rights," May 7, 1968, Box
27, Graham T. Molitor Papers, RAC.

75 H. R. Haldeman to Harry S. Dent, Jr., Oct. 31, 1969, Box 2, HU, WHCF,
NPM; annotated news summary (ANS), March 1969, *PNWH* pt. 6, ser.
B, *Annotated News Summaries,* Fiche 3; H. R. Haldeman Meeting Notes,
July 11, 1970, *PNWH,* 5, Fiche 69.

76 Dent to Nixon, Oct. 16, 1969, Box 1, President's Office File (POF), CDF,
NPM.

77 Diary of White House leadership meetings, 91st Congress, July 8, 1969,
Box 106, Robert T. Hartmann Papers, GRFL.

78 John R. Brown III to Ehrlichman and Garment, Jan. 14, 1970, Box 142,
Garment Files, NPM.

79 Ehrlichman meeting notes, Dec. 20, 1969, *PNWH,* 3, Fiche 7.

80 Ehrlichman meeting notes, Dec. 20 and 22, 1969, *PNWH,* 3, Fiche 7.

81 Ehrlichman meeting notes, Dec. 22, 1969, *PNWH,* 3, Fiche 7.

82 Patrick J. Buchanan to Nixon, July 8, 1970, *PNWH,* 2, Fiche 69-7-6;
Ehrlichman meeting notes, Dec. 20 and 22, 1969, *PNWH,* 3, Fiche 7.

83 Diary of White House leadership meetings, 91st Congress, July 8, 1969,
Box 106, Hartmann Papers.

84 *Los Angeles Times,* Dec. 19, 1969, 22; Gerald R. Ford to Colleagues in the
House of Representatives, Dec. 20, 1969, Folder 2, Box 18, Silberman
Papers; Nixon, *Memoirs,* 438.

85 "Statement by the President," Dec. 19, 1969, Box 7, HU, WHCF, NPM;
Patterson to Garment, "Notes from the First Term," Nov. 28, 1973, Box
1, Leonard Garment Papers, LC.

86 *Los Angeles Times,* Dec. 22, 1969, 1; George P. Shultz telephone interview
with author, Oct. 25, 1995, Stanford, California; Harlow to Nixon, Dec.

22, 1969, Box 17, HU, WHCF, NPM; *Wall Street Journal,* Dec. 24, 1969, 2; *Detroit News,* Dec. 23, 1969, 3A.

87 *New York Amsterdam News,* Jan. 3, 1970, 10; William H. Brown III to Nixon, Dec. 24, 1969, Box 17; American Advancement League to Nixon, Dec. 27, 1969, Box 8; Whitney Young to Nixon, July 11, 1969, Box 18; Andrew G. Freeman, Executive Director of Philadelphia Urban League, to Nixon, Aug. 7, 1969, Box 18, all in HU, WHCF, NPM; NHC on Herbert G. Klein to Nixon, Dec. 26, 1969, *PNWH,* 6A, Fiche 55A.

88 ANS, Jan. 17, 1970, *PNWH,* 6B, Fiche 22.

89 Haldeman meeting notes, July 18, 1970, *PNWH,* 5, Fiche 28.

90 NHC on Ehrlichman to Nixon, Oct. 21, 1970, *PNWH,* 6A, Fiche 101.

91 *Department of Labor News,* Feb. 3, 1970, Folder 1, Box 18, Silberman Papers; *Department of Labor News,* Dec. 2, 1971, Box 86, Garment Files, NPM.

92 *Department of Labor News,* Feb. 9, 1970, Folder 1, Box 28, Silberman Papers.

93 *Department of Labor News,* July 9, 1970, Box 270, James D. Hodgson Files, 1970, RG 174.

94 Nelson A. Rockefeller to Peter J. Brennan, Feb. 6, 1973, Box 83, Peter J. Brennan Files, 1973, RG 174; "Status of the Contract Compliance Construction Program," April 1973, Box 4, PQ-Procurement, WHCF, NPM.

95 Joan Hoff Wilson, *Herbert Hoover: Forgotten Progressive* (Boston: Little, Brown, 1975), 79-121.

96 The government imposed its own plans on just five cities. "Status of the Contract Compliance Program," April 1973, Box 4, PQ, WHCF, NPM.

97 *St. Louis Post-Dispatch,* Feb. 11, 1971, 2A; Fletcher to Hodgson, Aug. 26, 1970, Box 270, Hodgson Files, 1970, RG 174.

98 Memorandum of telephone conversation, Elliot L. Richardson and Laurence H. Silberman, Sept. 9, 1970, Box 127, Elliot L. Richardson Papers, LC.

99 Silberman to John Wilks, Aug. 26, 1971, Folder 1, Box 18, Silberman Papers; *Wall Street Journal,* Oct. 28, 1970, 6.

100 William J. Kilberg to E. Carl Uehlein, Jr., Mar. 21, 1972, Box 200, Hodgson Files, 1970-72, RG 174.

101 Van Dusen to Samuel J. Simmons, Jan. 26, 1970, Box 8, Richard C. Van Dusen Papers, Michigan Historical Collections (MHC), Bentley Historical Library (BHL), University of Michigan, Ann Arbor.

102 *Wall Street Journal,* Oct. 10, 1972, 1.

103 Fletcher to Hodgson, May 22, 1970, Box 269, Hodgson Files, 1970, RG 174; *Wall Street Journal,* Oct. 10, 1969, 14, and May 6, 1971, 4; Ronald Reagan to Hodgson, Sept. 16, 1970, Box 270, Hodgson Files, 1970, RG 174.

104 *Department of Labor News,* Mar. 31, 1972, Box 142, Garment Files, NPM.

105 John Barber to John Leslie, Oct. 15, 1970, Box 270 Hodgson Files, 1970, RG 174.

106 *Department of Labor News,* June 18, 1971, Box 142, Garment Files, NPM; Rockefeller to Hodgson, Nov. 10, 1970, Box 269, Hodgson Files, 1970, RG 174; Richard F. Schubert to Hodgson, Jan. 11, 1973, Folder 1, Box 18, Silberman Papers.

107 Press release, United States Commission on Civil Rights, Dec. 15, 1972, Folder 12, Box 15, Hesburgh Civil Rights Papers.

108 Labor Department staff meeting notes, June 30, 1970, Folder 3, Box 13, Silberman Papers.

109 Labor Department staff meeting notes, May 4, 1971, Folder 3, Box 13, Silberman Papers; Noah Robinson to Brennan, May 24, 1973, Box 84, Brennan Files, 1973, RG 174.

110 John V. Lindsay to Frederick O'Neal, Jan. 24, 1973, Box 83, Brennan Files, 1973, RG 174.

111 John A. Buggs to Brennan, July 24, 1974, Folder 29, Box 18, Hesburgh Civil Rights Papers.

112 *St. Louis Post-Dispatch,* June 28, 1971, 1B; *Detroit News,* May 11, 1976, 7A.

113 Garment to Silberman, May 5, 1971, Box 142, Garment Files, NPM.

114 Ehrlichman to John R. Price and Mark Alger, July 2, 1971, Box 58, Garment Files, NPM.

115 Colson to Haldeman, May 6, 1971, Box 2, Colson Files, NPM.

116 John Robert Greene, *The Limits of Power: The Nixon and Ford Administrations* (Bloomington: Indiana University Press, 1992), 134.

117 Ehrlichman to Haldeman, Mar. 2, 1970, Box 58, Haldeman Files, NPM.

118 Nixon to Haldeman, Sept. 21, 1970, Box 138, Haldeman Files, NPM.

119 Colson to Haldeman, Oct. 7, 1970, Box 1, Colson Files, NPM.

120 Colson to George Bell, Aug. 4, 1970, Box 2, Colson Files, CDF, NPM.

121 Colson to Haldeman, July 28, 1971, Box 1, Colson Files, CDF, NPM.

122 Buchanan to Colson and Haldeman, Sept. 13, 1971, Box 3, Colson Files, CDF, NPM.

123 Colson to Haldeman, May 6, 1971, Box 2, and Colson to Ehrlichman, June 9, 1971, Box 15, Colson Files, NPM.

124 Colson to Haldeman, Apr. 30, 1971, and Colson to Haldeman, May 6, 1971, Box 2, Colson Files, NPM.

125 Colson to Cole, June 4, 1971, Box 65, Colson Files, NPM.

126 Colson to Malek, June 4, 1971, Box 10, Colson Files, NPM.

127 Colson to Ehrlichman, June 7, 1971, Box 4, Colson Files, CDF, NPM.

128 Action memo P-1769, Box 48, Staff Secretary Files, NPM; Colson to Ehrlichman, June 28, 1971, Box 7; Colson to Nixon, July 2, 1971, Box 1; Colson to Nixon, July 26, 1971, Box 15, Colson Files, NPM.

129 Colson to Malek, Aug. 26, 1971, Box 19, Colson Files, NPM.

130 Colson to Nixon, n.d., and Colson to Nixon, n.d., Box 20, Colson Files, NPM.

131 Nixon to Colson, Mar. 8, 1971, Box 1, Colson Files, NPM.

132 H. R. Haldeman Diary, July 21, 1971, in *The Haldeman Diaries: Inside the Nixon White House,* ed. H. R. Haldeman (Santa Monica, Calif.: Sony Corporation, 1994), CD-ROM.

133 Haldeman meeting notes, July 31, 1971, *PNWH,* 5, Fiche 55.

134 "Remarks on Accepting the Presidential Nomination . . . ," Aug. 23, 1972, in *Public Papers of the Presidents: Richard Nixon (1972)* (Washington, D.C.: Government Printing Office, 1974), 788 *(PPP); Washington Post,* Sept. 24, 1972, B3.

135 Malek to Nixon, Jan. 22, 1973, Box 6, Frederick V. Malek Papers, HI; *St. Louis Post-Dispatch,* Feb. 24, 1973, 1; Haldeman Diary, Nov. 20, 1972 (quotation).

136 Charles W. Colson meeting notes, Nov. 17, 1972, Box 17, Colson Files, NPM.

137 Buggs to Schubert, Nov. 2, 1973, Folder 26, Box 18, Hesburgh Civil Rights Papers.

138 Buggs to Brennan, Jan. 11, 1974, and Brennan to Buggs, May 8, 1974, Box 54, Brennan Files, 1974–75, RG 174.

139 *New York Times,* Sept. 5, 1972, 14; Nixon to Philip E. Hoffman, Aug. 11, 1972, Box 17, HU, WHCF, NPM.

140 Garment to William Rhatican (plus attachment), Sept. 25, 1972, Box 6, Garment Files, NPM.

141 Nixon to Haldeman, Feb. 28, 1973, Box 16, Haldeman Files, CDF, NPM.

142 Graham, *Civil Rights Era,* 382–390.

143 "The Reluctant Guardians," n.d., 15, Box 21, Patterson Files, NPM; Roger Wilkins to John W. Macy, Jr., Jan. 14, 1969, Box 2, Robert E. Hampton Papers, GRFL.

144 Robert Brown to Harry Fleming, Mar. 3, 1969, Box 17, HU, WHCF, NPM; Brown to Robert E. Hampton et al., Mar. 7, 1969, Box 2, Hampton Papers.

145 Nixon to Heads of Departments, Mar. 28, 1969, Box 17, HU, WHCF, NPM.

146 Hampton to Burns, May 2, 1969, and Hampton to Macy, Aug. 11, 1965, Box 2, Hampton Papers; Glickstein to Theodore M. Hesburgh, Aug. 18,

1970, Folder 24, Box 19, Hesburgh Civil Rights Papers; radio editorial, May 13, 1969, Hampton Papers.

147 Hampton to Cole, Apr. 30, 1969, Box 2, Hampton Papers; Nixon to Heads of Departments, Aug. 8, 1969, Box 17, HU, WHCF, NPM.

148 Robert Brown to Nixon, July 15, 1969, Box 32, Patterson Files, NPM.

149 Cole to Nixon, Aug. 7, 1969, Box 17, HU, WHCF, NPM.

150 *U.S. Civil Service Commission News,* Sept. 4, 1969, Box 2, Hampton Papers.

151 *New York Times,* Feb. 28, 1970, 1.

152 John Brown to Ehrlichman, Mar. 3, 1970, Box 83, Staff Secretary Files, NPM.

153 Hampton to Garment, May 13, 1971, Box 133, Garment Files, NPM.

154 Thad V. Ware to Robert Brown, Dec. 17, 1969, Box 125, Garment Files, NPM; "Black Leadership in the Nixon Administration," n.d., Box 4, Benjamin F. Holman Papers, HI.

155 Hampton to Donald Rumsfeld, Apr. 15, 1975, Box 2, Hampton Papers.

156 Frederick A. Kistler to Hampton, Aug. 26, 1975, Box 2, Hampton Papers.

157 John Campbell to Garment, July 22, 1971 and Hampton to Nixon, Feb. 18, 1971, Box 17, HU, WHCF, NPM.

158 Walter D. Scott to Warren Hendricks, Jan. 31, 1975, Box 7, Fernando E. C. DeBaca Files, GRFL; "Highlights of Nixon Administration Initiatives in Civil Rights and Related Programs," February 1974, Box 4, Garment Papers, LC.

159 *HEW News,* Dec. 12, 1974, Box 20, Joseph L. Rauh, Jr., Papers, LC.

160 J. Stanley Pottinger to Richardson, Dec. 30, 1971, Box 140, Richardson Papers; *Wall Street Journal,* July 27, 1971, 1; Pottinger to Presidents of Institutions of Higher Learning, Aug. 1972, Box 144, Garment Files, NPM; Pottinger to College and University Presidents, Oct. 1, 1972, Box 144, Garment Files, NPM.

161 Memorandum of telephone conversation, Richardson and Pottinger, Oct. 2, 1972, Box 133, Richardson Papers; quoted in attachment to Pottinger to Garment, Aug. 7, 1972, Box 145, Garment Files, NPM.

162 Minutes of meeting of U.S. Commission on Civil Rights, Apr. 9, 1973, Folder 13, Box 21, Hesburgh Civil Rights Papers.

163 "Mr. Pottinger's Red Herrings," n.d., Box 4, Garment Papers, LC.

164 Patterson to Garment, n.d., Box 4, Garment Papers, LC.

165 Patterson to Garment, Sept. 20, 1972, Box 145, Garment Files, NPM.

166 *Washington Post,* Sept. 24, 1973, B3; "New Action in Affirmative Action," *Analysis,* Feb. 1, 1973, Box 20, Rauh Papers.

167 Hyman Bookbinder to Yvonne Price, Sept. 14, 1972, Box E1, LCCR Papers.

168 Nixon to Hoffman, Aug. 11, 1972, and George S. McGovern to Hoffman, Aug. 14, 1972, Box E1, LCCR Papers.

169 Walter J. Leonard to Arthur Herzberg, Dec. 28, 1972, Box 22, Rauh Papers.

170 Haldeman Diary, Jan. 10, 1973.

171 Caspar W. Weinberger to Derek C. Bok, n.d., Box 4, HU, WHCF, NPM; "No More Quotas Says Weinberger," Aug. 1973, Box 26, Anne Armstrong Files, SMOF, NPM; Karen Keesling to Anne Armstrong, July 16, 1974, Box 12, Armstrong Files, NPM.

172 *New York Times,* Apr. 9, 1972, 44; Harold Orlans, "Affirmative Action in Higher Education," *Annals of the American Academy of Political and Social Sciences,* 523 (September 1992), 144.

173 Gerald R. Ford to James G. Cannon, Mar. 10, 1975, Box 24, Presidential Handwriting File, GRFL; Paul H. O'Neill to Ford, Aug. 7, 1975, Box 8, HU, WHCF, GRFL.

174 Gerald David Jaynes and Robin M. Williams, Jr., eds., *A Common Destiny: Blacks and American Society* (Washington, D.C.: National Academy Press, 1989), 375–379.

175 Creed C. Black to Lewis Butler, Feb. 17, 1969, Box 1, Department of Health, Education, and Welfare Series, Creed C. Black Papers, King Library, University of Kentucky; Harry Fleming to Staff Secretary, Apr. 4, 1969, Box 23, Federal Government (FG) 109, Equal Employment Opportunity Commission, WHCF, NPM.

176 *New York Times,* Mar. 28, 1969, 1; NHC on news summary, Mar. 28, 1969, *PNWH,* 6B, Fiche 4.

177 *New York Times,* Mar. 29, 1969, 23.

178 Edward M. Kennedy to Nixon, Mar. 28, 1969, Box 23, FG 109, WHCF, NPM; *Washington Afro-American,* Apr. 1, 1969, Box 177, Morton Papers.

179 William Brown to Robert Brown, Nov. 23, 1970, Box 84, Garment Files, NPM.

180 William Brown to Garment, Nov. 12, 1970, Box 51, Garment Files, NPM.

181 William Brown to Nixon, Nov. 7, 1970, Garment Files, NPM; Brown to Nixon, Dec. 30, 1969, Box 1, FG 109, WHCF, NPM.

182 Shultz to Nixon, June 9, 1971, Box 1, HU, WHCF, NPM.

183 Graham, *Civil Rights Era,* 448.

184 Milton R. Young, Jr., to Hugh Scott, Aug. 19, 1970, Box 114, Hugh D. Scott Papers, Alderman Library, University of Virginia, Charlottesville.

185 Haldeman meeting notes, Dec. 13, 1969, *PNWH,* 5, Fiche 13.

186 Memorandum for Burns, n.d., Box A13, Burns Papers.

187 *Philadelphia Bulletin,* Aug. 12, 1969, 26.

188 Diary of White House Leadership Meeting, 91st Congress, Apr. 4, 1969, Box 106, Hartmann Papers. "Republican Policy Statement on Equal Employment Opportunity Act of 1965," Apr. 26, 1966, PPS 500.10–5.3, NPPP, RNLB.

189 For the debate on this issue, see Jerris Leonard to Ehrlichman, n.d., Box A10, Burns Papers; Richard T. Burress to Cole, Apr. 29, 1969, Box 29, Patterson Files, NPM; William H. Rehnquist to Richard G. Kleindienst, n.d.; "Arthur Burns's Report," n.d.; and Burress to Ehrlichman et al., July 31, 1969, Box 33, Dean Files, NPM.

190 William Brown to Moynihan, Apr. 29, 1969, Box 29, Patterson Files, NPM; "William H. Brown III Interviewed on the 'Today' Show," Aug. 15, 1969, Box A10, Burns Papers.

191 John Anderson et al. to Colleagues, Sept. 17, 1971; form letter, National Organization for Women, Sept. 10, 1971; and "Anti-Civil Rights Forces Prevail in House," Sept. 30, 1971, Box D64, LCCR Papers.

192 John N. Erlenborn and Romano L. Mazzoli to Colleagues, July 16, 1971, Box D64, LCCR Papers; Silberman to Cole, Apr. 6, 1971, Folder 5, Box 27, Silberman Papers; *Wall Street Journal,* Sept. 17, 1971, 2.

193 *Wall Street Journal,* Sept. 15, 1971, 16; William H. Brown III telephone interview with author, Sept. 15, 1994.

194 Stephen Hess to Ehrlichman, May 2, 1969, Box 1, FG 109, WHCF, NPM.

195 Brown interview with author, Sept. 15, 1994.

196 United States Senate, Committee on Education and Labor, *Hearings on Equal Employment Opportunity Enforcement Procedures, 91st Congress, 1st and 2nd Sessions, December 1 and 2, 1969, and April 7–10, 1970* (Washington, D.C.: Government Printing Office, 1970), 32–66.

197 Ziegfried H. Rommel to Nixon, Mar. 17, 1972, Box 29, Patterson Files, NPM. Nixon was prepared to veto a bill providing cease and desist; see Haldeman meeting notes, Jan. 27 and Feb. 19, 1972, *PNWH,* 5, Fiche 70.

198 *New York Times,* Sept. 18, 1973, 1.

199 Ibid., Dec. 11, 1970, 1, and Dec. 12, 1970, 16; *Wall Street Journal,* Dec. 12, 1971, 21, and Jan. 19, 1973, 3.

200 William Brown to Garment, Mar. 14, 1973, Box 51, Garment Files, NPM.

201 *Wall Street Journal,* Sept. 28, 1973, 1, and Aug. 11, 1977, 22.

202 Mitchell to Garment, June 26, 1973, Box 83, Garment Files, NPM.

203 Brown interview with author, Sept. 15, 1994.

204 Jerry Jones to Alexander M. Haig, Jr., n.d., Box 23, Confidential Files (CF), WHSF, NPM.

205 Clarence Mitchell, "Moods and Changes: The Civil Rights Record of the Nixon Administration," *Notre Dame Lawyer,* 49 (October 1973), 70–72.

206 Haldeman meeting notes, Dec. 13, 1969, *PNWH,* 5, Fiche 13.

207 Peter M. Flanigan to Nixon, Apr. 22, 1971, *PNWH,* 6A, Fiche 137.

208 Brown to Garment, Mar. 14, 1973, Box 51, Garment Files, NPM.

209 *Wall Street Journal,* Sept. 28, 1973, 1.

210 *St. Louis Post-Dispatch,* Apr. 20, 1973, 1B.

211 Mitchell, "Moods and Changes," 70–72.

212 *Washington Evening Star,* May 21, 1973, A2.

213 Garment to Ehrlichman, Mar. 19, 1973, Box 51, Garment Files, NPM.

214 Harlow to Haig, July 31, 1973, Box 83, Garment Files; Jones to Haig, n.d., Box 23, CF, NPM.

215 Haig to Harrison Williams, Dec. 7, 1973, Box 12, Alexander M. Haig, Jr., Files, WHSF, NPM; "Meeting with John H. Powell, Jr.," Dec. 7, 1973, Box 23, CF, NPM; Andrew Young to Nixon, Aug. 17, 1973, Box 1, FG 109, WHCF, NPM.

216 Bureau of the Census, U.S. Department of Commerce, *Statistical Abstract of the United States: 1995 (115th Edition)* (Washington, D.C.: Government Printing Office, 1995), 401.

217 *Wall Street Journal,* Apr. 18, 1974, 1.

218 Bureau of the Census, U.S. Department of Commerce, *Statistical Abstract of the United States: 1980,* 101st ed. (Washington, D.C.: Government Printing Office, 1980), 418–419.

219 Haldeman Diary, July 21, 1971.

220 NHC on Flanigan to Nixon, July 26, 1972, Box 2, POF, CDF, NPM.

221 John Sherman Cooper to Samuel Starks, Nov. 17, 1971, Box 117, John Sherman Cooper Papers, King Library, University of Kentucky.

222 Hanes Walton, Jr., *When the Marching Stopped: The Politics of Civil Rights Regulatory Agencies* (Albany: State University of New York Press, 1988), 1–27.

223 Philip Hart and Jacob Javits to Cooper, Sept. 11, 1967, Box 116, Cooper Papers.

224 *St. Louis Post-Dispatch,* Apr. 1, 1973, 1B.

225 John Dumbrell, *The Carter Presidency: A Re-evaluation* (New York: Manchester University Press, 1993), 93.

226 *Wall Street Journal,* Jan. 20, 1981, 1.

227 Ibid., Dec. 18, 1981, 3.

228 David Frost, *"I Gave Them a Sword": Behind the Scenes of the Nixon Interviews* (New York: Morrow, 1978), 177, 263; Nixon, *Memoirs,* 437–438.

229 Nixon, *Memoirs,* 437–438.

230 *Buffalo News,* Dec. 26, 1990, C3.

5. Black Power, Nixon Style

1 "Richard M. Nixon Interviewed . . . ," Oct. 13, 1968, 7, Richard M. Nixon Pre-Presidential Papers (NPPP), Richard Nixon Library and Birthplace (RNLB), Yorba Linda, California.

2 Robert Weisbrot, *Freedom Bound: A History of America's Civil Rights Movement* (New York: Plume, 1990), 222-261; Harvard Sitkoff, *The Struggle for Black Equality, 1954-1992* (New York: Hill and Wang, 1993), 184-209; E. U. Essien-Udom, *Black Nationalism: A Search for an Identity in America* (Chicago: University of Chicago Press, 1962); Floyd B. McKissick, "Black Business Development with Social Commitment to Black Communities," in *Black Nationalism in America*, ed. John H. Bracey, Jr., August Meier, and Elliot Rudwick (Indianapolis: Bobbs-Merrill, 1970), 492-506; William L. Van Deburg, *New Day in Babylon: The Black Power Movement and American Culture, 1965-1975* (Chicago: University of Chicago Press, 1992), 118-119.

3 Malcolm X with Alex Haley, *The Autobiography of Malcolm X* (New York: Ballantine, 1965), 281.

4 "Bridges to Human Dignity Address," Apr. 25, 1968, PPS 208 (1968), 28, NPPP, RNLB.

5 "Statement about Federal Policies Relative to Equal Housing Opportunity," in *Public Papers of the Presidents: Richard M. Nixon, (1971)* (Washington, D.C.: Government Printing Office, 1971), 733 *(PPP)*.

6 Nixon handwritten comment (NHC) on Ray Price to Richard M. Nixon, June 5, 1971, *Papers of the Nixon White House*, ed. Joan Hoff-Wilson, pt. 6, ser. A, *Documents Annotated by the President* (Lanham, Md.: University Publications of America, 1989), Fiche 3 *(PNWH)*.

7 "AG" to "DC," Apr. 8, 1968, PPS 500.10-6.10, NPPP, RNLB.

8 Wire dispatch, n.d., PPS 500.10-7.10, NPPP, RNLB.

9 Anderson to "DC," Mar. 4, 1968, PPS 500.10-6.6, NPPP, RNLB; *New York Times*, Mar. 7, 1968, 1.

10 Patrick J. Buchanan to Nixon, Aug. 15, 1967, PPS 500.10-5.19, NPPP, RNLB.

11 Alan Greenspan to Nixon, Sept. 26, 1967, PPS 500.10-6.10, NPPP, RNLB.

12 Price to Nixon, July 27, 1967, PPS 500.10-5.13, NPPP, RNLB.

13 Draft of position paper, July 17, 1967, PPS 500.10-5.11, NPPP, RNLB.

14 Buchanan to Robert H. Finch, n.d., Folder: Nixon, Richard, Drawer: Mazo to O'Donnell, Private Papers of Robert H. Finch, Pasadena, California.

15 Kenneth Khachigian to Staff, n.d., Box 15, Annelise Graebner Anderson Papers, Hoover Institution Archives (HI), Stanford University, Stanford, California.

16 "Statement by Richard M. Nixon," Feb. 15, 1968, Box 14, Special Names Series, Dwight D. Eisenhower Post-Presidential Papers, Dwight D. Eisenhower Library (DDEL), Abilene, Kansas.

17 "Bridges to Human Dignity," Apr. 25, 1968, PPS 208 (1968).28, NPPP, RNLB.

18 "Bridges to Human Dignity," Apr. 25, 1968, PPS 208 (1968).28, NPPP, RNLB.

19 Maurice H. Stans, "Nixon's Economic Policy toward Minorities," in *Richard M. Nixon: Politician, President, Administrator,* ed. Leon Friedman and William F. Levantrosser (Westport, Conn.: Greenwood Press, 1991), 239–241.

20 Samuel I. Doctors and Anne Sigismund Huff, *Minority Enterprise and the President's Council* (Cambridge, Mass.: Ballinger Publishing Company, 1973), 1–2, 7.

21 Robert McKersie, "Vitalize Black Enterprise," in *Black Business Enterprise: Historical and Contemporary Perspectives,* ed. Ronald W. Bailey (New York: Basic Books, 1971), 103.

22 Hugh Davis Graham, *The Civil Rights Era: Origins and Development of National Policy, 1960–1972* (New York: Oxford University Press, 1990), 316.

23 "Minority Entrepreneurship," n.d. [mid-1968], Box 21, James Gaither Files, Lyndon B. Johnson Library (LBJL), Austin, Texas.

24 Memorandum for Stanley Ruttenberg, n.d. [mid-1968], Box 21, Gaither Files, LBJL.

25 Howard J. Samuels to Maurice H. Stans, Box 3, and Moynihan to Staff Secretary, Feb. 6, 1969, Box 4, Commerce Department Files, Maurice H. Stans Papers, Minnesota Historical Society, St. Paul.

26 Abraham S. Venable to Stans, June 12, 1970, Box 32, Commerce Files, Stans Papers; John David Skrentny, *The Ironies of Affirmative Action: Politics, Culture, and Justice in America* (Chicago: University of Chicago Press, 1996), 67–110, 192–193.

27 James J. Reynolds to Hubert H. Humphrey, Feb. 12, 1968, Box 21, Gaither Files, LBJL.

28 Samuels to Lyndon B. Johnson, June 21, 1968, Box 21, Gaither Files, LBJL.

29 William Welsh to James Gaither, Mar. 26, 1968, and "Mr. Boussalian" to "Mr. Carey," Aug. 9, 1968 (quotation), Box 21, Gaither Files, LBJL.

30 Matthew Nimetz to Joseph A. Califano, Aug. 12, 1968, Box 21, Gaither Files, LBJL.

31 *GOP Fact Sheet,* Feb. 24, 1956, Box 21, Bryce N. Harlow Records, DDEL; "'A New Alignment for American Unity': An Address," May 16, 1968, Box 158, Joseph and Stewart Alsop Papers, Manuscript Division, Library of Congress (LC), Washington, D.C.

32 Joan Hoff, *Nixon Reconsidered* (New York: Basic Books, 1994), 95;
    Richard Nixon, *RN: The Memoirs of Richard Nixon* (New York: Grossett
    and Dunlap, 1978), 6.

33 Minutes of meeting of the Council for Urban Affairs, Mar. 17, 1969, Box
    3, President's Office Files (POF), Contested Documents File (CDF),
    Richard M. Nixon Presidential Materials (NPM), National Archives
    (NA), College Park, Maryland.

34 Quoted in A. James Reichley, *Conservatives in an Age of Change: The
    Nixon and Ford Administrations* (Washington, D.C.: Brookings Institution,
    1981), 56.

35 Annotated news summary (ANS), n.d., Box 2, POF, CDF, NPM.

36 ANS, n.d., Box 2, POF, CDF, NPM.

37 Sallyanne Payton, "Remarks at Hofstra," in Friedman and Levantrosser,
    Richard M. Nixon, 180.

38 *Wall Street Journal,* May 21, 1968, 16.

39 Nixon to Dwight D. Eisenhower, Aug. 18, 1967, Box 14, Special Names
    Series, Eisenhower Post-Presidential Papers, DDEL.

40 *Time,* May 3, 1968, 21; *Wall Street Journal,* May 21, 1968, 16.

41 *New York Times,* Oct. 11, 1968, 32.

42 *Wall Street Journal,* May 21, 1968, 16.

43 *New York Times,* Aug. 7, 1968, 30, and Nov. 1, 1968, 50. There was only
    one brief mention of "Bridges to Human Dignity" in the Leadership
    Conference's files. See Perkins Magurie to Yvonne Price, June 6, 1969,
    Box E27, Leadership Conference on Civil Rights (LCCR) Papers, LC.

44 *Pittsburgh Courier,* Feb. 22, 1969, 6.

45 "Excerpts of Remarks by Governor Nelson A. Rockefeller," May 23,
    1968, Folder 514, Box 26, Press Office (PO), Subseries I, Public Rela-
    tions Files, Nelson A. Rockefeller Gubernatorial Papers, Record Group
    (RG) 15, Rockefeller Family Archives (RFA), Rockefeller Archive Cen-
    ter (RAC), Sleepy Hollow, New York; Jeff Geilich to Richard P.
    Nathan, July 16, 1968, Box 26, Graham T. Molitor Papers, RAC (quota-
    tion).

46 "Nixon: Rebuilding the Ghetto," July 3, 1968, 19, Box 22, Molitor Papers.

47 "Excerpts of Remarks by Governor Nelson A. Rockefeller," May 23,
    1968, Folder 514, Box 26, and "Statement on Small Business," July 12,
    1960, Folder 106, Box 6, PO, Subseries I, Public Relations Files, Rocke-
    feller Gubernatorial Papers, RG 15, RFA.

48 *New York Times,* Oct. 4, 1968, 46, and Oct. 14, 1968, 46. For Humphrey's
    response, see Timothy Thurber, *The Politics of Equality: Hubert Humphrey
    and the African-American Freedom Struggle* (New York: Columbia Univer-
    sity Press, 1999), 206.

49 Price to Nixon, July 27, 1967, PPS 500.10–5.13, NPPP, RNLB.

50 Annelise Anderson to Herbert G. Klein, July 16, 1968, Box 17, Anderson Papers.

51 *New York Times,* Nov. 7, 1968, 21.

52 Ibid., Jan. 14, 1969, 1, and Nov. 7, 1968, 35.

53 Maurice H. Stans, *One of the President's Men: Twenty Years with Eisenhower and Nixon* (Washington, D.C.: Brassey's, 1995), 169.

54 ANS, Mar. 10, 1969, *PNWH,* pt. 6, ser. B, *Annotated News Summaries,* Fiche 3.

55 Buchanan to Nixon, Feb. 18, 1969, Box 3, POF, CDF, NPM.

56 Robert J. Brown to Stans, Feb. 3, 1969, Box 4, George W. Romney Post-Gubernatorial Papers, Michigan Historical Collections (MHC), Bentley Historical Library (BHL), University of Michigan, Ann Arbor; "Statement about a National Program for Minority Business Enterprise," Mar. 5, 1969, *PPP, 1969* (Washington, D.C.: Government Printing Office, 1971), 197–198; Stans, *One of the President's Men,* 169.

57 Alexander P. Butterfield, memorandum for the President's File, Mar. 25, 1969, *PNWH,* pt. 2, *The President's Meeting File,* Fiche 69–3–23; minutes of the meeting of the Council for Urban Affairs, Feb. 12, 1969, *PNWH,* 2, Fiche 69–2–9; minutes of the meeting of the Council on Urban Affairs, Feb. 17, 1969, *PNWH,* 2, Fiche 69–2–16; Peter M. Flanigan to Nixon, Sept. 15, 1969, Box 7, Federal Government (FG) 21, Department of Commerce, WHCF, NPM.

58 NHC for minority business enterprise meeting, Oct. 13, 1969, *PNWH,* pt. 7, *The President's Personal Files, 1969–74,* Fiche 183.

59 John D. Ehrlichman meeting notes, Apr. 11 and Nov. 11, 1972, *PNWH,* pt. 3, *John D. Ehrlichman Notes of Meetings with the President, 1969–1973,* Fiche 44 and 56.

60 Harry S. Dent, Jr., to Bryce N. Harlow and John D. Ehrlichman, Dec. 22, 1969, Box 4, Harry S. Dent, Jr., Files, White House Special Files (WHSF), NPM.

61 Harry S. Dent, *The Prodigal South Returns to Power* (New York: Wiley, 1978), 159.

62 ANS, n.d., *PNWH,* 6B, Fiche 12; NHC on Ehrlichman to Nixon, July 29, 1969, *PNWH,* pt. 6, ser. A, *Documents Annotated by the President,* Fiche 29.

63 H. R. Haldeman Diary, Feb. 28, 1970, in *The Haldeman Diaries: Inside the Nixon White House,* ed. H. R. Haldeman (Santa Monica, Calif.: Sony Corporation, 1994), CD-ROM.

64 Ehrlichman meeting notes, Apr. 26, 1971, *PNWH,* 3, Fiche 31.

65 Stans, *One of the President's Men,* xv.

66 Stans to Ehrlichman, Sept. 2, 1971, Box 4A, Commerce and Personal Papers, Stans Papers.
67 *Wall Street Journal,* Mar. 6, 1969, 8.
68 Stans to Robert P. Mayo, Feb. 19, 1969, Box 3; Flanigan to Stans, Oct. 29, 1969, Box 14; Stans to Henry Ford II, Sept. 18, 1969, Box 14; Stans to R. A. Kroc, July 9, 1969, Box 3, Commerce Files, Stans Papers.
69 Handwritten note, Stans to Venable, Nov. 24, 1969, and *Department of Commerce News,* Nov. 6, 1969, Box 68, Commerce Files, Stans Papers.
70 Venable to Interagency Committee Members, Feb. 2, 1970, Box 23, Commerce Files, Stans Papers.
71 *Department of Commerce News,* Nov. 6, 1969, Box 68, Commerce Files, Stans Papers.
72 Flanigan to Stans, Oct. 2, 1969, Box 14; Venable to Stans, Box 32, Commerce Files, Stans Papers.
73 Robert Sansone to Stans, July 10, 1970, Box 33; Arthur Singer to Stans, July 29, 1971, Box 41, Commerce Files, Stans Papers.
74 Statement of Maurice H. Stans before the Senate Select Committee on Small Business, Oct. 15, 1969, 1 and 3, Box 14, Commerce Files, Stans Papers.
75 Frederick Lynn May to William Casselman II, July 30, 1974, Box 2, Frederick Lynn May Files, Gerald R. Ford Presidential Papers, Gerald R. Ford Library (GRFL), Ann Arbor, Michigan.
76 Memorandum of meeting, Mar. 19, 1970, Box 68; Roeser to Stans, June 26, 1969, Box 14, Commerce Files, Stans Papers.
77 Moynihan to staff secretary, Feb. 6, 1969, 2, Box 4, Commerce Files, Stans Papers.
78 Stans to George W. Romney, May 21, 1970, Box 7, Albert Applegate Papers, MHC, BHL; Roeser to Stans, Apr. 23, 1969; Robert M. Smalley to Stans, Aug. 29, 1969, *Department of Commerce News,* Sept. 11, 1969, Box 14, Commerce Files, Stans Papers; staff meeting notes, Feb. 18, Mar. 10, July 7, July 22, and Aug. 19, 1969, Box 2A, Commerce and Personal Papers, Stans Papers; minutes of meeting of the National Advisory Council for Minority Business Enterprise, Oct. 13, 1969, 1, Box 6, Commerce Files, Stans Papers.
79 *Wall Street Journal,* July 10, 1969, 1; *National Journal,* June 30, 1970, 132.
80 Stans, *One of the President's Men,* 173.
81 Ibid., 173; *National Journal,* June 30, 1970, 132.
82 "Minority Business Enterprise," n.d., Box 2, May Files, GRFL; Charles H. Alexander to Jan T. Dykman, Feb. 18, 1969, Box 68, Commerce Files, Stans Papers.

83 *Black Enterprise*, 3 (January 1971), 14–18; United States Small Business Administration, *SBA Profile: Who We Are and What We Do* (Washington, D.C.: Government Printing Office, 1994), 20; Graham, *Civil Rights Era*, 314; Venable to Stans, Box 33, Commerce Files, Stans Papers; Hilary Sandoval, Jr., to Robert Brown, Nov. 23, 1970, Box 2, Procurement (PQ), WHCF, NPM; *Wall Street Journal*, July 10, 1969, 1.

84 Stans, *One of the President's Men*, 147.

85 Jack Crawford to Robert C. Mardian, Feb. 13, 1970, Box 1, Robert C. Mardian Papers, HI.

86 Venable to Stans, Sept. 25, 1970, Box 32, Commerce Files, Stans Papers.

87 Staff meeting notes, Sept. 22, 1971, Box 2A, Commerce and Personal Papers, Stans Papers.

88 May to Casselman, July 30, 1974, Box 2, May Files, GRFL.

89 *New York Times*, Apr. 27, 1969, 62; United States Senate, Committee on Banking and Currency, Subcommittee on Small Business, *Hearings on Federal Minority Enterprise Program, December 9–12, 1969* (Washington, D.C.: Government Printing Office, 1970), 154.

90 "A Legislative and Enforcement Program for the 91st Congress and the Administration, 1969–70," 1, Box E13, LCCR Papers.

91 *New York Times*, Dec. 30, 1969, 49.

92 *Wall Street Journal*, July 10, 1969, 1; Whitney M. Young, Jr., to Stans, Nov. 5, 1969, Box 14, Commerce Files, Stans Papers.

93 Venable to Young, Dec. 4, 1969, Box 14; Stans to Vernon E. Jordan, Jr., Dec. 13, 1971, Box 54, Commerce Files, Stans Papers.

94 Jackie Robinson to Stans, Nov. 25, 1969, Box 14; Robinson to Nixon, Feb. 9, 1970, Box 21, Commerce Files, Stans Papers.

95 "In Harlem Hope Mingles with Skepticism," *New York Times*, Dec. 14, 1969, Box 21, Commerce Files, Stans Papers.

96 Milton O. McGinty to William A. Raspberry, July 25, 1970, Box 62, Commerce Files, Stans Papers.

97 Venable to Stans, Nov. 19, 1970, Box 31, Commerce Files, Stans Papers.

98 U.S. Senate, Subcommittee on Small Business, *Hearings on Federal Minority Enterprise Program*, 2.

99 Moynihan to Staff Secretary, Oct. 17, 1969, Box 7, FG 21, WHCF, NPM.

100 Memorandum to Heads of Departments and Agencies, Oct. 18, 1969, Box 2, PQ, WHCF, NPM.

101 John D. Ehrlichman to Nixon, Nov. 21, 1969, Box 2, PQ, WHCF, NPM.

102 Moynihan to Staff Secretary, Oct. 17, 1969, Box 7, FG 21, WHCF, NPM.

103 Robert L. Kunzig Oral History, Sept. 8, 1972, 1–5, DDEL; Ted Trimmer to Bradley H. Patterson, Jr., Nov. 17, 1969, Box 2, PQ, WHCF, NPM.

104 Nixon to Heads of Departments and Agencies, Dec. 5, 1969, Box 7, FG 21, WHCF, NPM.

105 George J. Pantos to Stans, n.d., [November 1969], Box 3, Commerce Files, Stans Papers.

106 Thomas S. Kleppe to Stans, July 2, 1971, Box 54, Commerce Files, Stans Papers.

107 Nate Bayer to Kenneth Cole through John Evans, June 19, 1972, Box 3, PQ, WHCF, NPM; Kleppe to Stans, July 2, 1971, Box 54, Commerce Files, Stans Papers.

108 Melvin Laird to Sandoval, Sept. 2, 1970, Box 2, PQ, WHCF, NPM.

109 Sandoval to Ehrlichman, Dec. 10, 1970, Box 2, PQ, WHCF, NPM.

110 Ehrlichman to Sam Wyly, Oct. 1, 1970, Box 2, PQ, WHCF, NPM.

111 Shultz to Ehrlichman, Jan. 13, 1971, Box 2, PQ, WHCF, NPM.

112 Theodore H. Elliott to Henry A. Kissinger, Nov. 21, 1970, Box 2, PQ, WHCF, NPM.

113 Richard C. Van Dusen to Undersecretaries, Mar. 19, 1970, Box 8; draft memorandum to undersecretaries, n.d., Box 9, Richard C. Van Dusen Papers, MHC, BHL.

114 Dick Dunnell to Van Dusen, Feb. 13, 1970, Box 27, Subject Files, Richard C. Van Dusen Files, General Records of the Department of Housing and Urban Development, RG 207, NA.

115 "Los Angeles Minority Building Contractors Plan," n.d., Box 27, Van Dusen Subject Files, RG 207.

116 Samuel J. Simmons to Van Dusen, Dec. 1, 1970, Box 27, Van Dusen Subject Files, RG 207.

117 Draft memorandum to Heads of Departments and Agencies, Box 26, Van Dusen Subject Files, RG 207.

118 NHC on Garment to Nixon, July 20, 1971, Box 3, HU, WHCF, NPM.

119 Venable to Glen M. Anderson, Jan. 21, 1971, Box 54; J. Strom Thurmond to Stans, Aug. 25, 1970, Box 20, Commerce Files, Stans Papers.

120 Jay I. Leanse to Stans, Jan. 13, 1971, Box 54, Commerce Files, Stans Papers.

121 Senate Republican memo on minority business enterprise, Apr. 16, 1970, Box 130, John Sherman Cooper Papers, Margaret I. King Library, University of Kentucky, Lexington.

122 Ronald Reagan to Stans, May 7, 1971, Box 54, Commerce Files, Stans Papers.

123 "Statement of John G. Tower," July 14, 1971, Box 55, Commerce Files, Stans Papers.

124 Stans handwritten comment on Venable to Stans, Mar. 24, 1970, Box 32, Commerce Files, Stans Papers.

125 "Address by Richard C. Van Dusen," Apr. 13, 1972, Box 9, Van Dusen Papers, MHC, BHL; Ciro P. Farina to Members of the Interagency Task Force, Dec. 28, 1971, Box 137, Leonard Garment Files, Staff Member and Office Files (SMOF), NPM; Cole to Garment, Aug. 17, 1970, Box 1, Garment Papers, LC; Robert Brown to Peter G. Peterson, June 30, 1972, Confidential Files (CF), WHSF, NPM.

126 "Highlights of Nixon Administration Initiatives in Civil Rights and Related Programs," February 1974, Box 4, Garment Papers, LC.

127 Arthur S. Fleming et al. to the President, n.d., Box 57, Arthur S. Fleming Papers, DDEL.

128 Roeser to Stans, June 18, 1969, Box 68, Commerce Files, Stans Papers.

129 Stans to Flanigan, Oct. 17, 1969, Box 4; Murray Wiedenbaum to Capital Development Task Force, Box 23, Commerce Files, Stans Papers.

130 Charls E. Walker to Stans, May 26, 1971, Box 45, Garment Files, NPM.

131 Walker and Stans to Nixon, Box 45, Garment Files, NPM.

132 *New York Times,* Jan. 8, 1970, 15; Arthur F. Burns to Garment, Mar. 10, 1970, Box 32, Commerce Files, Stans Papers; Harry F. Byrd, Jr., to Gene Cowan, Oct. 19, 1971, Box 46, Garment Files, NPM.

133 *Department of Commerce News,* Oct. 2, 1970, Box 46, Garment Files, NPM.

134 Stans to Leanse, Oct. 19, 1970, Commerce Files, Stans Papers; F. E. Agnew to Garment, Sept. 14, 1971; Louis K. Eilers to Garment, Sept. 10, 1971; and Robert W. Reneker to Garment, Sept. 8, 1971, Box 45, Garment Files, NPM.

135 Venable to Stans, Apr. 11, 1971, Box 67, Commerce Files, Stans Papers; Garment to Cole, June 11, 1971, and Garment to Patterson, June 21, 1971, Box 46, Garment Files, NPM.

136 Walker to Garment, Nov. 10, 1971, Box 46, Garment Files, NPM.

137 William E. Simon to Frank Carlucci, Apr. 26, 1973, Fiche 4, Box 15, William E. Simon Papers, GRFL; "Minority Business Enterprise: A Timely Opportunity," n.d., 5, Box 2, May Files, GRFL; "Highlights of the Nixon Administration Initiatives in Civil Rights and Related Programs," February 1974, Box 4, Garment Papers, LC.

138 *New York Times,* Feb. 21, 1971, Box 67, Commerce Files, Stans Papers.

139 Minutes of the National Advisory Council on Minority Business Enterprise, Nov. 16, 1970, Box 23, Commerce Files, Stans Papers.

140 Patterson to Garment, "Notes from the First Term," Nov. 28, 1973, 5, Box 1, Garment Papers, LC.

141 Stans to Nixon, Dec. 17, 1970, Box 7, FG 21, WHCF, NPM.

142 Ehrlichman to Cole, Nov. 24, 1970, Box 54, John D. Ehrlichman Files, WHSF, NPM.

143 Stans to Garment, Jan. 22, 1971, Box 41, Commerce Files, Stans Papers.

144 "Special Message to Congress . . . ," Oct. 13, 1971, *PPP, 1971,* 1041–46.

145 Stans to Nixon, July 21, 1971, *PNWH,* 6A, Fiche 173; Lawrence Imhoff to Stans, June 9, 1969, Box 54, Commerce Files, Stans Papers.

146 NHC on Shultz to Nixon, Sept. 17, 1971, *PNWH,* 6A, Fiche 173.

147 Shultz to Nixon, Sept. 17, 1971, *PNWH,* 6A, Fiche 173; Larry Jobe to Stans, June 2, 1971, Box 67, Commerce Files, Stans Papers.

148 Congressional Quarterly, *Nixon: The Fourth Year of His Presidency* (Washington, D.C.: Government Printing Office, 1973), 46A, 47A; James T. Lynn to Laurence H. Silberman, June 29, 1972; Silberman to Lynn, July 11 and 18, 1972; and Lynn to Silberman, Sept. 5, 1972, Folder 11, Box 17, Laurence H. Silberman Papers, HI; *Questions and Answers about MBDA's Business Assistance to Minority Entrepreneurs* (Washington, D.C.: Government Printing Office, 1993), 1–3.

149 Quoted in Robert Brown to Nate Sayer, Oct. 16, 1972, Box 50, CF, NPM. See also Frederic V. Malek to Robert Brown et al., Mar. 3, 1972, and Cole to Malek, Feb. 29, 1972, Box 7, FG 21, WHCF, NPM; *New York Times,* Nov. 18, 1972, 70.

150 Herbert S. Parment, *Richard Nixon and His America* (Boston: Little, Brown, 1990), 601.

151 Hullin to Ehrlichman, Jan. 26, 1973, Box 5, Ehrlichman Files, CDF, NPM.

152 Donald Carruth memorandum, n.d. Box 1, Alexander M. Haig, Jr., Files, CDF, NPM.

153 Kleppe to Henry M. Paulson, Sept. 27, 1973, Box 1, Haig Files, CDF, NPM.

154 Carruth memorandum, n.d., and Kleppe to Henry M. Paulson, Sept. 27, 1973, Box 1, Haig Files, CDF, NPM.

155 Jonathan J. Bean, *Beyond the Broker State: Federal Policies toward Small Businesses, 1936–1961* (Chapel Hill: University of North Carolina Press, 1996), 147.

156 Parment, *Richard Nixon and His America,* 601.

157 Stans to Nixon, June 27, 1969, Box 1, President's Personal File (PPF), CDF, NPM.

158 Fleming et al. to the President, n.d., Box 57, Fleming Papers; May to Cole, Sept. 17, 1974, Box 2, May Files, GRFL.

159 May to John Calhoun, Nov. 7, 1974, Box 32; Ford to Secretary of State et al., Dec. 11, 1974, Box 2, May Files, GRFL.

160 "Minority Business Programs Seek to Resist Recession, Infighting," n.d., Box 2, May Files, GRFL.

161 John C. Whitaker, "Nixon's Domestic Policy: Both Liberal and Bold in Retrospect," *Presidential Studies Quarterly,* 26 (Winter 1996), 143.

162 Maurice H. Stans, "Nixon and His Bridges to Human Dignity," *Presidential Studies Quarterly*, 26 (Winter 1996), 181–183.

163 Whitaker, "Nixon's Domestic Policy," 143.

164 George R. LaNoue, "Social Science and Minority 'Set-Asides,'" *Public Interest*, 62 (Winter 1993), 49.

165 George R. LaNoue, "Split Visions: Minority Business Set Asides," *Annals of the American Academy of Political and Social Sciences*, 523 (September 1992), 106.

166 LaNoue, "Social Science and Minority 'Set-Asides,'" 50; W. Avon Drake and Robert D. Holsworth, *Affirmative Action and the Stalled Quest for Black Progress* (Urbana: University of Illinois Press, 1996), 70–114.

167 LaNoue, "Social Science and Minority 'Set-Asides,'" 50.

168 *Time*, June 15, 1987, 20; *Wall Street Journal*, Apr. 21, 1995, B2.

169 "On Their Own: For Minority-Owned Firms, the Federal Government's 8(a) Program Can Be Too Much of a Good Thing," *Wall Street Journal*, May 21, 1995, R23.

170 "$4 Billion Worth of Temptation," *Time*, June 15, 1987, 20.

171 Hugh Davis Graham, "Richard Nixon and Civil Rights: Explaining an Enigma," *Presidential Studies Quarterly*, 26 (Winter 1996), 102–103; *New York Times*, Mar. 10, 1996, "Week in Review," 2.

172 Hoff, *Nixon Reconsidered*, 97; Whitaker, "Nixon's Domestic Policy," 143.

173 Drake and Holsworth, *Affirmative Action and the Stalled Quest for Black Progress*, 100.

174 Michael D. Woodard, *Black Entrepreneurs in America: Stories of Struggle and Success* (New Brunswick, N.J.: Rutgers University Press, 1997), 33.

175 John W. Handy, *An Analysis of Black Business Enterprises* (New York: Garland Publishing, 1989), 62–64.

176 See Woodard, *Black Entrepreneurs in America*, 241.

177 Stans to Nixon, Apr. 15, 1970, Box 32, Commerce Files, Stans Papers.

178 "Remarks by Richard C. Van Dusen," Apr. 13, 1972, Box 9, Van Dusen Papers, MHC, BHL; Stans to Nixon, Mar. 28, 1972, Box 7, FG 21, WHCF, NPM; Stans, *One of the President's Men*, 175–176.

179 "Minority Business Programs Seek to Resist Recession, Infighting," n.d., Box 2, May Files, GRFL.

180 *Jet*, Feb. 24, 1971, 20–25, and Sept. 27, 1971, 46–50; *Ebony* (August 1973), 32–179.

181 "Roy Wilkins–N.A.A.C.P.–Outlook for Minority Business," Box 27, Roy Wilkins Papers, LC.

182 "Jesse L. Jackson," in *Political Profiles: The Nixon/Ford Years*, ed. Eleanora W. Schoenebaum (New York: Facts on File, 1979), 325–326.

183 Donald Bogle, "The Jeffersons," in *Blacks in American Films and Television: An Encyclopedia* (New York: Garland, 1988), 282–284.

184 Stans, "Nixon and His Bridges to Human Dignity," 180.

185 *Black Enterprise* (September 1971), 36–39; *New York Times,* June 27, 1971, 33.

186 Ehrlichman meeting notes, Mar. 14, 1972, *PNWH,* 3, Fiche 44.

187 Leon E. Panetta to Robert H. Finch, Oct. 17, 1969, Box 3, Mardian Papers.

188 *New York Times,* Feb. 17, 1973, 1; *Wall Street Journal,* June 24, 1974, 13.

189 James Cavanaugh, Memorandum for the President's File, Nov. 29, 1973, *PNWH,* 2, Fiche 73–11–25.

190 Dana Mead to Nixon through Cole and Harlow, Mar. 18, 1974, Folder: ExHU 2–1 Education–Schooling–States and Territories–Alabama to Iowa 1/1/73–8/9/74, HU, WHCF, NPM.

191 Vernon E. Jordan, Jr., to Dana S. Creel, Oct. 15, 1970, Box 231, Series 4–Grants, Rockefeller Brothers Fund Archives, RAC.

192 Nixon to H. R. Haldeman, Sept. 22, 1969, Box 229, H. R. Haldeman Files, WHSF, NPM.

193 Robert J. Brown, Memorandum for the President's File, May 20, 1970, *PNWH,* 2, Fiche 70–5–17.

194 H. R. Haldeman meeting notes, May 20, 1970, *PNWH,* pt. 5, *H. R. Haldeman Notes of White House Meetings, 1969–1973,* Fiche 23.

195 Ehrlichman meeting notes, June 3 and 12, 1970, *PNWH,* 3, Fiche 16; Haldeman meeting notes, *PNWH,* 5, Fiche 24; Patterson to Garment, Nov. 28, 1973, 5, "Notes from the First Term," Box 2, Garment Papers, LC.

196 Robert Brown to Garment, Jan. 5, 1970, and Garment to Robert Brown, Jan. 8, 1970, Box 2, Garment Papers, LC; Robert Brown to Nixon, Jan. 9, 1970, Box 2, Garment Files, NPM; Vivian Henderson to Robert Brown, Jan. 22, 1970, Box 11, Chester Finn Papers, HI.

197 Garment to Nixon, May 19, 1970, Box 49, Garment Files, NPM.

198 John D. Ehrlichman, *Witness to Power: The Nixon Years* (New York: Simon and Schuster, 1982), 236.

199 James Cavanaugh, Memorandum for the President's File, Nov. 29, 1973, *PNWH,* 2, Fiche 73–11–25.

200 John F. Kennedy to John D. Rockefeller, May 21, 1963, Box 105, Series 4–Grants, Rockefeller Brothers Fund Archives.

201 Kennedy handwritten comment on Kennedy to Laurance S. Rockefeller, Aug. 6, 1963, Box 105, Series 4–Grants, Rockefeller Brothers Fund Archives.

202 "News about the $50 Million "Crash" Program for United Negro Colleges," Jan. 27, 1964, Box 105, Series 4–Grants, Rockefeller Brothers Fund Archives.

203 Hugh Davis Graham, *The Uncertain Triumph: Federal Education Policy in the Kennedy and Johnson Years* (Chapel Hill: University of North Carolina Press, 1984), 217.

204 NHC on James E. Cheek to Nixon, July 22, 1970, *PNWH*, 6A, Fiche 86.

205 Haldeman to Ehrlichman, June 29, 1970, Box 4, Haldeman Files, CDF, NPM. See also Haldeman meeting notes, June 26, 1970, Box 1, Haldeman Files, CDF, NPM.

206 "Press Conference of Robert H. Finch and Robert J. Brown," July 23, 1970, Box 11, Finn Papers.

207 "Federal Agencies and Black Colleges," n.d., Box 49, Garment Files, NPM.

208 Finn to Moynihan, June 8, 1970, Box 11, Finn Papers; Richard P. Nathan to Robert Brown, Feb. 16, 1971, Box 49, Garment Files, NPM.

209 Edwin Harper to Ehrlichman, May 12, 1971, and Hullin to Nathan, May 28, 1971, Box 3, HU, WHCF, NPM.

210 James Cavanaugh, Memorandum for the President's File, Nov. 29, 1973, *PNWH*, 2, 73-11-25.

211 Elliot L. Richardson to Nixon, May 4, 1972, Box 14, Bradley H. Patterson, Jr., Files, SMOF, NPM.

212 Kenneth Cole, Memorandum for the President's File, Dec. 2, 1971, *PNWH*, 2, Fiche 71-11-28.

213 Frank A. Rose to Garment, Jan. 9, 1973, Box 6, Garment Files, NPM.

214 Patterson to Garment, Jan. 30, 1973, Box 14, Patterson Files, NPM.

215 David N. Parker to Cavanaugh and Stanley S. Scott, Nov. 27, 1973, Box 4, HU, WHCF, NPM.

216 John Matlock, "The Effect of Desegregation Policies on Historically Black Public Colleges and Universities," in *Black Colleges and Universities: Challenges for the Future,* ed. Antoine Garibaldi (New York: Praeger, 1984), 209.

217 "Highlights of the Nixon Administration Initiatives in Civil Rights and Related Social Programs," February 1974, Box 4, Garment Papers, LC.

218 Sherman J. Jones and George B. Weathersby, "Financing Black Colleges," in *Black Colleges in America: Challenge, Development, Survival* (New York: Teacher's College Press of Columbia University, 1978), 130.

219 Mary Carter-Williams, "Student Enrollment Trends in Black Colleges: Past, Current, and Future Perspectives," in Garibaldi, *Black Colleges and Universities,* 223; Jordan to J. Quigg Newton, President of the Common-

wealth Fund, May 3, 1971, Folder 1419, Box 83, Series 1–Administrative and Historical, Commonwealth Fund Archives, RAC.

220 Frank Bowles and Frank A. DeCosta, *Between Two Worlds: A Profile of Negro Education* (New York: McGraw-Hill, 1970), 250.

221 United Negro College Fund Annual Report 1970, Folder 1419, Box 83, Series 1–Administrative and Historical, Commonwealth Fund Archives.

222 "United Negro College Fund Annual Report, 1975," 10, Box 231, Series 4–Grants, Rockefeller Brothers Fund Archives; Louis Martin to Jimmy Carter, Sept. 26, 1978, Box 103, Presidential Handwriting File, Jimmy Carter Library, Atlanta, Georgia.

223 Antoine Garibaldi, "Black Colleges: An Overview," in *Black Colleges and Universities*, 3.

224 Graham, *The Uncertain Triumph*, 217.

225 Nixon to Anthony Maxwell, Oct. 31, 1972, Box 7, FG 21, WHCF, NPM.

226 Hoff, *Nixon Reconsidered*, 115–137; Haldeman Diary, July 13, 1970.

6. A Cold War

1 Adam Fairclough, *To Redeem the Soul of America: The Southern Christian Leadership Conference and Martin Luther King, Jr.* (Athens: University of Georgia Press, 1987), 40.

2 Richard M. Nixon notes on meeting with Martin Luther King, Jr., June 13, 1957, PPS 320.107.69.1–8, Richard M. Nixon Pre-Presidential Papers (NPPP), Richard Nixon Library and Birthplace (RNLB), Yorba Linda, California.

3 Taylor Branch, *Parting the Waters: America in the King Years, 1954–63* (New York: Simon & Schuster, 1989), 219; Richard M. Nixon to Martin Luther King, Jr., Sept. 22, 1958, PPS 320.107.17, NPPP, RNLB.

4 King to Nixon, Aug. 30, 1957, PPS 320.107.12, NPPP, RNLB.

5 Nixon to King, Sept. 17, 1957, PPS 320.107.14, NPPP, RNLB.

6 King inscription in *Stride toward Freedom: The Montgomery Story* (New York: Harper & Brothers, 1958), Richard Nixon's Den, Book 297, RNLB.

7 Branch, *Parting the Waters*, 219.

8 Handbill, n.d., Folder 12: Richard M. Nixon, Box 2, Private Papers of Robert H. Finch, Pasadena, California.

9 Charles K. McWorter to Robert H. Finch, Feb. 2, 1958, Box 2, Finch Papers.

10 Nixon to Leonard Hall et al., Sept. 7, 1960, Folder 79: Memos from RN, Box 12, Finch Papers.

11 Nixon to King, Sept. 22, 1958, PPS 320.107.17 NPPP, RNLB.

12 Nixon to JDH, Jan. 12, 1960, Box 820, General Correspondence, NPPP, National Archives, Pacific Southwest Region, Laguna Niguel, California (NA-LN).

13 Charles K. McWorter to Donald Hughes, Aug. 23, 1960, Box 820, General Correspondence, NPPP, NA-LN.

14 David J. Garrow, *Bearing the Cross: Martin Luther King, Jr. and the Southern Christian Leadership Conference* (New York: Random House, 1986), 144–148.

15 Clarence Mitchell to Nixon, PPS 320.107.62; Allison L. and Elizabeth B. Bayless to Nixon, PPS 320.107.34; and Claudia E. Whitmore to Nixon, PPS 320.107.47, NPPP, RNLB.

16 "R" to "Pat," n.d., PPS 320.107.26.2, NPPP, RNLB.

17 E. Frederic Morrow Oral History, Apr. 15, 1968, Butler Library, Columbia University, New York.

18 Quoted in Louis Martin Oral History, Apr. 7, 1966, 50, John F. Kennedy Library (JFKL), Boston, Massachusetts.

19 Quoted in Edwin O. Guthman and Jeffrey Shulman, eds., *Robert Kennedy, In His Own Words: The Unpublished Recollections of the Kennedy Years* (New York: Bantam, 1988), 69.

20 Robert H. Finch Oral History, June 19, 1967, 51–52, Butler Library, Columbia University.

21 Richard M. Nixon, *Six Crises* (New York: Warner Books, 1979), 429.

22 Morrow Oral History, Apr. 15, 1968, 141.

23 Sargent Shriver interview with Anthony Shriver, fall 1988, 24, "Kennedy's Call to King," JFKL.

24 Franklin Williams interview with Anthony Shriver, fall 1988, 100, "Kennedy's Call to King," JFKL.

25 Finch Oral History, June 19, 1967, 51.

26 Nixon, *Six Crises,* 477–478.

27 Nixon handwritten comment (NHC) on "GG" to Robert H. Finch, Nov. 15, 1960, PPS 320.107.30.1, NPPP, RNLB.

28 Martin Luther King, Jr., Oral History, Mar. 9, 1964, 12, JFKL.

29 Cornel West, foreword to Jackie Robinson (with Alfred Duckett), *I Never Had It Made: An Autobiography* (Hopewell, N.J.: Ecco Press, 1995), ix–x.

30 Jules Tygiel, *Baseball's Great Experiment: Jackie Robinson and His Legacy* (New York: Oxford University Press, 1983), 196.

31 Maury Allen, *Jackie Robinson: A Life Remembered* (New York: Franklin Watts, 1987), 121–122.

32 Transcript of Richard M. Nixon interviewed by Brian Lamb on *Booknotes,* Mar. 1, 1992 (Lincolnshire, Ill.: C-SPAN, 1992), 21; Richard

Nixon, *Seize the Moment: America's Challenge in a One-Superpower World* (New York: Simon and Schuster, 1992), 105.

33 "Incident Recalled by Harrison McCall and Dictated by Him," Jan. 3, 1959, Box 649, General Correspondence, NPPP, NA-LN.

34 Allen, *Jackie Robinson,* 115.

35 Sallyanne Payton interview with the author, July 27, 1994, Ann Arbor, Michigan.

36 John D. Ehrlichman meeting notes, Dec. 12, 1972, *Papers of the Nixon White House,* ed. Joan Hoff-Wilson, pt. 3, *John D. Ehrlichman Notes of Meeting with the President, 1969–1973* (Lanham, Md.: University Publications of America, 1989), Fiche 58 *(PNWH).*

37 Quoted in notes on conversation between Jackie Robinson and Rose Mary Woods, Nov. 1, 1957; and for Robinson's praise of Nixon's support for the 1957 act, see Jackie Robinson to Nixon, Aug. 18, 1957, both in Box 649, General Correspondence, NPPP, NA-LN.

38 "Jack Roosevelt Robinson Interviewed on *Viewpoint,*" Dec. 14, 1957, Box 649, General Correspondence, NPPP, NA-LN.

39 *New York Post,* Dec. 30, 1959, Box 649, General Correspondence, NPPP, NA-LN.

40 Nixon to Robinson, Jan. 16, 1960, Box 649, General Correspondence, NPPP, NA-LN.

41 Rose Mary Woods to Nixon, Mar. 30, 1960, Box 649, General Correspondence, NPPP, NA-LN.

42 Woods to Nixon, May 10, 1960, Box 649, General Correspondence, NPPP, NA-LN.

43 *New York Times,* July 2, 1960, Box 649, General Correspondence, NPPP, NA-LN.

44 *New York Post,* July 29, 1960, and Associated Press dispatch, Sept. 3, 1960, Box 649, General Correspondence, NPPP, NA-LN.

45 Robinson, *I Never Had It Made,* 140.

46 Paul W. Keyes to Nixon, Sept. 5, 1962; Keyes to H. R. Haldeman, Sept. 6, 1962; and Victor Lasky to Finch, Haldeman, and Herbert Klein, Sept. 13, 1962, Folder: Jackie Robinson, Drawer: Omott-Schechter, Finch Papers.

47 Arnold Rampersad, *Jackie Robinson: A Biography* (New York: Knopf, 1997), 369.

48 Robinson, *I Never Had It Made,* 175, 209; Robinson to Nelson A. Rockefeller, Oct. 7, 1964, and Robinson to Ann Whitman, Jan. 1, 1968, Folder 2078, Box 207, Nelson A. Rockefeller Papers, Personal Projects, Record Group (RG) 4, Rockefeller Family Archives (RFA), Rockefeller Archive Center (RAC), Sleepy Hollow, New York.

49 Robinson, *I Never Had It Made,* 235; "An Exchange of Letters: Jackie Robinson and Malcolm X," in *The Jackie Robinson Reader,* ed. Jules Tygiel (New York: Dutton, 1997), 246.

50 Robinson to Warren M. Dorn, Mar. 27, 1969, Folder: Jackie Robinson, Drawer: Omott-Schechter, Finch Papers.

51 Robinson, *I Never Had It Made,* 238–240.

52 Bryce N. Harlow, Memorandum for the Record, Dec. 28, 1960, Box 2, Miscellaneous Series, Ann C. Whitman File, Dwight D. Eisenhower Papers, Dwight D. Eisenhower Library (DDEL), Abilene, Kansas.

53 *Washington Post,* May 1, 1969, K8; Leonard Garment, *Crazy Rhythm: My Journey from Brooklyn, Jazz, and Wall Street to Nixon's White House, Watergate, and Beyond* (New York: Times Books, 1997), 171–172; *Washington Post,* Apr. 30, 1969, D1.

54 Garment, *Crazy Rhythm,* 172; *Washington Post,* May 1, 1969, K8.

55 *Washington Post,* May 1, 1969, K8 (both quotations).

56 "Honoring Duke Ellington Wins Nixon Black Friends," *The Afro-American Voter* (March–April 1969), 10.

57 H. R. Haldeman Diary, Feb. 14, 1969, in *The Haldeman Diaries: Inside the Nixon White House,* ed. H. R. Haldeman (Santa Monica, Calif.: Sony Corporation, 1994), CD-ROM.

58 Theodore M. Hesburgh (with Jerry Reedy), *God, Country, Notre Dame: The Autobiography of Theodore M. Hesburgh* (New York: Ballantine, 1990), 208; Theodore M. Hesburgh to Nixon, Mar. 6, 1969, Box 1, Federal Government (FG) 90, Commission on Civil Rights, White House Central Files (WHCF), Richard M. Nixon Presidential Materials Staff (NPM), National Archives (NA), College Park, Maryland (quotation).

59 Roy Wilkins to Participating Organizations, Oct. 2, 1968, Box E15, Leadership Conference on Civil Rights (LCCR) Papers, Manuscript Division, Library of Congress (LC), Washington, D.C.; Roy Wilkins (with Tom Mathews), *Standing Fast: The Autobiography of Roy Wilkins* (New York: Viking Press, 1982), 333.

60 Roy Wilkins handwritten draft, "Speech–Leadership Conference on Civil Rights–Wash., D.C.–28 Jan. 1969," Box 76, Roy Wilkins Papers, LC.

61 All quotations from Robert J. Brown, Memorandum for the President's File, Feb. 7, 1969, *PNWH,* pt. 2, *The President's Meeting File,* Fiche 69-2-2.

62 Raymond K. Price, Jr., Notes for the President's File, May 13, 1969, *PNWH,* 2, Fiche 69-5-11.

63 Ralph David Abernathy, *And the Walls Came Tumbling Down: An Autobiography* (New York: Harper & Row, 1989), 554.

64 Ibid.
65 Price, Notes for the President's File, May 13, 1969, *PNWH,* 2, Fiche 69-5-11.
66 Patrick J. Buchanan to Nixon, April 29, 1969, Box 3, President's Office Files (POF), Contested Documents File (CDF), NPM.
67 Diary of White House Leadership Meetings, 91st Congress, May 13, 1969, Box 106, Robert T. Hartmann Papers, Gerald R. Ford Library (GRFL), Ann Arbor, Michigan.
68 Haldeman Diary, May 13, 1969.
69 Daniel P. Moynihan to Ralph David Abernathy, May 1, 1969, Box 92, John C. Whitaker Files, WHSF, NPM; Richard M. Nixon, *RN: The Memoirs of Richard Nixon* (New York: Grosset & Dunlap, 1978), 436 (quotation).
70 Annotated news summary (ANS), May 20, 1969, *PNWH,* pt. 6, ser. B, *Annotated News Summaries,* Fiche 7.
71 Haldeman Diary, May 13, 1969.
72 John Ehrlichman, *Witness to Power: The Nixon Years* (New York: Simon & Schuster, 1982), 228.
73 Nixon, *Memoirs,* 436.
74 Payton interview with the author, July 27, 1994.
75 "Carl Rowan Commentary," July 15, 1969, Box 57, Leonard Garment Files, Staff Member and Office Files (SMOF), NPM.
76 *Detroit News,* July 14, 1969, 16A, and Dec. 22, 1969, 6B.
77 Aronson to Participating Organizations, Nov. 13, 1969, and Jan. 30, 1970, Box D5, LCCR Papers.
78 *New York Times,* Jan. 13, 1970, 26.
79 Nixon to Haldeman, Dec. 11, 1970, Box 229, H. R. Haldeman Files, White House Special Files (WHSF), NPM.
80 Buchanan to Haldeman, Dec. 21, 1972, Box 106, Haldeman Files, NPM.
81 Marvin Caplan to John Morsell et al., Sept. 23, 1970, Box E18, LCCR Papers.
82 "A Legislative and Enforcement Program for the 91st Congress and the Administration," January 1969, Box E13, LCCR Papers.
83 Haldeman Diary, Feb. 27, 1970.
84 Nick Thimmesch, "Black Progress Increases with Less Fanfare," July 24, 1971, Box 50, Garment Files, NPM.
85 Richard L. Wilson, "Visit with President Nixon, June 5, 1970," Box 5, Richard L. Wilson Papers, Herbert Hoover Library (HHL), West Branch, Iowa.
86 ANS, Dec. 29, 1969, *PNWH,* 6B, Fiche 21; Ehrlichman meeting notes, Dec. 15, 1969, *PNWH,* 3, Fiche 7 (quotation).

87 ANS, n.d. Box 2, POF, CDF, NPM.

88 ANS, Jan. 9, 1970, *PNWH*, 6B, Fiche 22.

89 John R. Brown III to H. R. Haldeman and Leonard Garment, Dec. 31, 1969, Box 1, Garment Files, NPM.

90 Haldeman handwritten comment on Harry S. Dent to Haldeman, Dec. 8, 1969, Box 55, Haldeman Files, NPM. See also Charles Evers and Andrew Szanton, *Have No Fear: The Charles Evers Story* (New York: John Wiley, 1997), 273–298.

91 Haldeman handwritten comment on Brown to Haldeman and Garment, Dec. 31, 1969, Box 1, Garment Files, NPM.

92 Howard A. Glickstein to Hesburgh, Dec. 24, 1969, Folder 2, Box 18, Theodore M. Hesburgh Civil Rights Papers, Theodore M. Hesburgh Library, University of Notre Dame, Notre Dame, Indiana.

93 Aronson to Participating Organizations, Sept. 19, 1969, Folder 20, Box 19, Hesburgh Civil Rights Papers; Hesburgh, *God, Country, Notre Dame*, 208.

94 NHC on Moynihan to Nixon, Jan. 16, 1970, *PNWH*, pt. 6, ser. A, *Documents Annotated by the President*, Fiche 60.

95 James Farmer, *Lay Bare the Heart: An Autobiography* (New York: Plume, 1985), 325.

96 *New York Times*, Mar. 3, 1970, 40.

97 Ibid., Mar. 8, 1970, E-1; Nixon handwritten notes for press conference, Mar. 21, 1970, *PNWH*, pt. 7, *The President's Personal Files: The President's Speech File, 1969–74*, Fiche 221 (quotation).

98 Robert Dallek, *Flawed Giant: Lyndon Johnson and His Times, 1961–1973* (New York: Oxford University Press, 1998), 224.

99 Ibid., 326.

100 NHC on John D. Ehrlichman to Nixon, Mar. 9, 1970, *PNWH*, 6A, Fiche 68.

101 H. R. Haldeman meeting notes, May 12, 1970, *PNWH*, pt. 5, *H. R. Haldeman Notes of White House Meetings, 1969–1973*, Fiche 23.

102 Caplan to Morsell et al., Sept. 23, 1970, Box E18; "Statement of Roy Wilkins," May 25, 1972, Box E3, LCCR Papers.

103 Leonard Garment, memorandum for the President's File, May 13, 1970, *PNWH*, 2, Fiche 70-5-10; *New York Times*, June 18, 1971, 19.

104 Bruce Rabb, Memorandum for the File, June 5, 1970, Box 57, Garment Files, NPM.

105 *New York Times*, June 30, 1970, 1.

106 Garment to Stephen G. Spottswood, June 30, 1970, Box 8, Leonard Garment Papers, LC.

107 Spottswood to Garment, July 1, 1970, Box 8, Garment Papers, LC.
108 Garment to Nixon via Haldeman, June 30, 1970, Box 8, Garment Papers, LC; Daniel P. Moynihan, Report to the President, July 24, 1970, Box 2, John D. Ehrlichman Files, CDF, NPM.
109 NHC on Moynihan to Nixon, June 30, 1970, *PNWH,* 6A, Fiche 82.
110 "NAACP Sees Another Term for Nixon," July 27, 1971, Box 15, Charles W. Colson Files, WHSF, NPM.
111 Haldeman Diary, July 18, 1970.
112 Haldeman meeting notes, July 13, 1970, *PNWH,* 5, Fiche 27.
113 Haldeman meeting notes, July 14, 1970, *PNWH,* 5, Fiche 27.
114 ANS, Oct. 10 or 11, 1970, *PNWH,* 6B, Fiche 34.
115 Glickstein to Commissioners, Aug. 6, 1970, Folder 24, Box 19, Hesburgh Civil Rights Papers.
116 Hesburgh memorandum, n.d., Folder 4, Box 20, Hesburgh Civil Rights Papers.
117 Ehrlichman meeting notes, Nov. 4, 1970, *PNWH,* 3, Fiche 20.
118 Hesburgh, *God, Country, Notre Dame,* 212.
119 ANS, Feb. 9, 1970, *PNWH,* 6B, Fiche 25.
120 Brown to Nixon, Apr. 16, 1969, Box 86, Garment Files, NPM.
121 Moynihan to Nixon, Jan. 16, 1970, *PNWH,* 6A, Fiche 60.
122 All quotations come from Donald Rumsfeld to Nixon, July 20, 1970, Box 2, Human Rights (HU), WHCF, NPM.
123 NHC on Moynihan to Nixon, Jan. 16, 1970, *PNWH,* 6A, Fiche 60.
124 Rogers C. B. Morton to Charles S. Gubser, Oct. 28, 1970, and Morton to George W. Althouse, Nov. 24, 1970, Box 219, Rogers C. B. Morton Papers, Department of Special Collections, Margaret I. King Library, University of Kentucky, Lexington.
125 *The Black Silent Majority Committee Newsletter* (January 1971), 3, Box 219, Morton Papers.
126 Ibid., 6.
127 Haldeman meeting notes, Feb. 9, 1970, *PNWH,* 5, Fiche 15.
128 Dwight Chapin to Hugh Sloan, Jr., July 8, 1970, Box 2, HU, WHCF, NPM.
129 Haldeman Diary, Apr. 2, 1970.
130 Ibid., Feb. 7, 1970.
131 Rabb, Memorandum for the President's File, June 5, 1970, Box 57, Garment Files, NPM.
132 Haldeman Diary, Mar. 5, 1970.
133 Haldeman meeting notes, Apr. 30, 1970, *PNWH,* 5, Fiche 15.
134 Sloan to Nixon, July 9, 1970, Box 2, HU, WHCF, NPM.
135 Haldeman meeting notes, Aug. 5, 1970, *PNWH,* 5, Fiche 29.

136 Haldeman Diary, Mar. 5, 1970.

137 Robert J. Brown, Memorandum for the President's File, July 15, 1970, *PNWH*, 2, Fiche 70–7–12.

138 Nixon to Haldeman, Mar. 16, 1970, Box 228, Haldeman Files, NPM.

139 Haldeman meeting notes, Apr. 1, 1970, Box 1, Haldeman Files, CDF, NPM.

140 President's news summary, Feb. 19, 1970, *PNWH*, 6B, Fiche 26.

141 Joan Hoff, *Nixon Reconsidered* (New York: Basic Books, 1994), 287; Huey P. Newton, *War against the Panthers: A Study of Repression in America* (New York: Harlem River Press, 1996), 43–90.

142 Tom Charles Huston to Haldeman, Dec. 11, 1969, Box 4, Haldeman Files, CDF, NPM.

143 NHC on memo, Moynihan to Nixon, Jan. 16, 1970, *PNWH*, 6A, Fiche 60.

144 President's news summary, Aug. 3, 1969, *PNWH*, 6B, Fiche 13.

145 ANS, Aug. 3, 1969, *PNWH*, 6B, Fiche 13; Robert J. Brown, Memorandum for the President's File, Oct. 6, 1972, *PNWH*, 2, Fiche 72–10–1.

146 *St. Louis Post-Dispatch*, Feb. 12, 1971, 9B.

147 Haldeman to Charles W. Colson, Box 67, Haldeman Files, NPM.

148 Ed Harper to Ehrlichman, Dec. 29, 1971, Box 10, Egil M. Krogh Files, WHSF, NPM.

149 "Remarks at the Dedication of the Dwight D. Eisenhower National Republican Center," Jan. 15, 1971, in *Public Papers of the Presidents: Richard Nixon (1971)* (Washington, D.C.: Government Printing Office, 1972), 37 *(PPP)*.

150 Haldeman to Chapin, Dec. 1, 1970, Box 3, HU, WHCF, NPM.

151 Haldeman meeting notes, Dec. 17, 1970, *PNWH*, 5, Fiche 38.

152 Ehrlichman meeting notes, Dec. 15, 1970, *PNWH*, 3, Fiche 23.

153 Nixon to Finch, Jan. 20, 1970, Box 230, Haldeman Files, NPM.

154 *National Enquirer*, Dec. 31, 1972, *PNWH*, 6B, Fiche 194; Leonard Garment, Memorandum for the President's File, Nov. 16, 1970, *PNWH*, 2, Fiche 70-11-16; "Remarks on Presenting the Heart-of-the-Year Award . . . ," in *PPP, 1972* (Washington, D.C.: Government Printing Office, 1974), 143–144.

155 *National Enquirer*, Dec. 31, 1972, *PNWH*, 6B, Fiche 194.

156 President's news summary, July 28, 1969, *PNWH*, 6B, Fiche 12; *New York Times*, July 25, 1970, 10.

157 *Philadelphia Inquirer*, Feb. 3, 1971, Box 133, Garment Files, NPM.

158 *New York Times*, Mar. 26, 1971, 1.

159 "Garment Points," n.d., Box 48, Garment Files, NPM.

160 Nixon to Honorable Charles C. Diggs, Jr., May 18, 1971, and George P. Shultz to Nixon, May 18, 1971, Box 37, Hartmann Papers.

161   *St. Louis Post Dispatch,* May 19, 1971, 2A.

162   *Wall Street Journal,* Nov. 11, 1968, 1; Moynihan to Nixon, Feb. 1, 1969, *PNWH,* 6A, Fiche 7.

163   NHC on Moynihan to Nixon, Feb. 1, 1969, *PNWH,* 6A, Fiche 7.

164   NHC on letter to the President, Apr. 29, 1969, *PNWH,* 6A, Fiche 15.

165   Moynihan to Ehrlichman, Aug. 7, 1969, Box 1, Garment Files, NPM; Haldeman meeting notes, July 27, 1970, *PNWH,* 5, Fiche 28.

166   Nancy J. Wiess, *Whitney M. Young, Jr., and the Struggle for Civil Rights* (Princeton: Princeton University Press, 1989), 175–190; Whitney M. Young, Jr., "The Negro and Self Help," Nov. 14, 1960, Box 529, Sub-series 3, Series 1, General Education Board Archives, RAC; Robert W. Scrivner to RBF Files, June 26, 1968, Box 75, Series 4–Grants, Rockefeller Brothers Fund Archives, RAC.

167   Scrivner to RBF Files, Aug. 7, 1968, Box 75, Series 4–Grants, Rockefeller Brothers Fund Archives.

168   Whitney M. Young, Jr., to Scrivner, Dec. 18, 1968, Box 75, Series 4–Grants, Rockefeller Brothers Fund Archives.

169   Young to NUL Staff, Dec. 15, 1970, Box 476, National Urban League Papers, pt. 3, LC; *New York Times,* July 21, 1970, 34.

170   Bradley H. Patterson, Jr., to Garment, "Notes from the First Term," Nov. 28, 1973, Box 1, Garment Papers, LC.

171   William Safire to Alexander Butterfield, Dec. 22, 1970, *PNWH,* 2, Fiche 70-12-20.

172   Patterson to Garment, "Notes from the First Term," Nov. 28, 1973, Box 1, Garment Papers, LC.

173   Transcript, "Press Conference of Whitney Young," Dec. 22, 1970, Box 3, HU, WHCF, NPM.

174   Safire to Butterfield, Dec. 22, 1970, *PNWH,* 2, Fiche 70-12-20.

175   Patterson to Garment, "Notes from the First Term," Nov. 28, 1973, Box 1, Garment Papers, LC.

176   Young to Nixon, Dec. 24, 1970, Box 3, HU, WHCF, NPM.

177   Patterson to Garment, "Notes from the First Term," Nov. 28, 1973, Box 1, Garment Papers, LC.

178   NHC on memo, Ehrlichman to Nixon, Jan. 11, 1971, *PNWH,* 6A, Fiche 115.

179   Nixon to Ehrlichman, Feb. 8, 1971, Box 2, Ehrlichman Files, CDF, NPM.

180   Ehrlichman to Finch, Jan. 9, 1971, Box 5, Ehrlichman Files, CDF, NPM.

181   "Eulogy by the President," n.d. *PNWH,* pt. 7, *The President's Personal Files, 1969–74,* Fiche 295; "Eulogy Delivered at Burial Services for Whitney M.

Young, Jr., in Lexington, Kentucky," Mar. 17, 1971, *PPP, 1971,* 437 (quotation).

182 Haldeman meeting notes, Mar. 23, 1971, *PNWH,* 5, Fiche 45.

183 *Chicago Defender,* Mar. 22, 1971, Box 35, Staff Secretary–Courier Files, SMOF, NPM.

184 Garment to Colleagues, May 11, 1971, Box 70, Bradley H. Patterson, Jr., Files, SMOF, NPM.

185 Ehrlichman, *Witness to Power,* 240.

186 Ibid.; Vernon E. Jordan, Jr., to Garment, Oct. 14, 1971, Box 70, Patterson Files, NPM.

187 Ehrlichman meeting notes, July 20, 1971, *PNWH,* 3, Fiche 35.

188 Memorandum of telephone conversation, Elliot L. Richardson and John D. Ehrlichman, July 13, 1972, Box 132, Elliot L. Richardson Papers, LC.

189 *Louisville Courier-Journal,* Nov. 28, 1996, 1.

190 Sallyanne Payton to Cole via Krogh, Feb. 9, 1972, Box 10, Krogh Files, NPM.

191 Jeffrey Donfeld, Memorandum for the President's File, July 1, 1971, *PNWH,* 2, Fiche 71-6-27; Robert J. Browm, Memorandum for the President's File, Oct. 10, 1972, *PNWH,* 2, Fiche 72-10-8; Robert J. Brown, Memorandum for the President's File, Oct. 17, 1972, *PNWH,* 2, Fiche 72-10-15; Stanley S. Scott, Memorandum for the President's File, Aug. 10, 1972, *PNWH,* 2, Fiche 72-8-6.

192 "Black Americans," n.d., Box 47, Confidential Files (CF), WHSF, NPM.

193 *Jet,* Aug. 24, 1972, 21.

194 Richard A. Watson, *The Presidential Contest* (New York: John Wiley, 1984), 86.

195 Haldeman Diary, Feb. 14, 1973.

196 *New York Times,* Jan. 21, 1969, 22.

197 "Garment Points," n.d., Box 48, Garment Files, NPM.

198 Augustus Alven Adair, "Black Legislative Influence in Federal Policy Decisions: The Congressional Black Caucus, 1971–1975" (Ph.D. diss., Johns Hopkins University, 1976), 126–127, 136; Richard Champagne and Leroy N. Rieselbach, "The Evolving Congressional Black Caucus: The Reagan-Bush Years," in *Blacks and the American Political System,* ed. Huey L. Perry and Wayne Parent (Gainesville: University of Florida Press, 1995), 144; Carol M. Swain, *Black Faces, Black Interests: The Representation of African Americans in Congress* (Cambridge, Mass.: Harvard University Press, 1993), 40.

199 *Washington Post,* Aug. 16, 1974, Box A12, President Ford Committee Records, GRFL.

200 Burton I. Kaufman, *The Presidency of James Earl Carter, Jr.* (Lawrence: University Press of Kansas, 1993), 110–111. See also *Wall Street Journal*, July 26, 1977, 30.

201 Thomas Byrne Edsall with Mary D. Edsall, *Chain Reaction: The Impact of Race, Rights, and Taxes on American Politics* (New York: Norton, 1991), 172–255.

202 Stanley S. Scott to Editor, Jan. 15, 1975, Robert T. Hartmann Files, GRFL; Ford handwritten comment on "Meeting with Key Black Civil Rights Leaders," Oct. 25, 1974, Box 24, Presidential Handwriting File, GRFL.

203 Watson, *The Presidential Contest*, 86.

204 Norman C. Amaker, *Civil Rights and the Reagan Administration* (Washington, D.C.: Urban Institute Press, 1988), 28.

205 Dan T. Carter, *From George Wallace to Newt Gingrich: Race in the Conservative Counterrevolution, 1963–1994* (Baton Rouge: Louisiana State University, 1996), 65, 76–78, 99.

206 Kenneth A. Jordan and Modibo M. Kadalie, "Black Politics During the Era of Presidents Reagan and Bush," in *Black Politics and Black Political Behavior: A Linkage Analysis,* ed. Hanes Walton, Jr. (Westport, Conn.: Praeger, 1994), pp. xxxv–xxxix.

7. Challenges and Opportunities

1 Quoted in Joan Hoff, *Nixon Reconsidered* (New York: Basic Books, 1994), 28.

2 Quoted in Rebecca L. Robbins, "Self-Determination and Subordination: The Past, Present, and Future of American Indian Governance," in *The State of Native America: Genocide, Colonization, and Resistance,* ed. M. Annette Jaimes (Boston: South End Press, 1992), 104.

3 Francis Paul Prucha, *The Great Father,* vol. 2, *The United States Government and the American Indians* (Lincoln: University of Nebraska Press, 1984), 609–610, 667–671, 686 (quotation), 919, 945.

4 Graham D. Taylor, *The New Deal and American Indian Tribalism: The Administration of the Indian Reorganization Act, 1934–1945* (Lincoln: University of Nebraska Press, 1980), 17–29; Prucha, *Great Father,* 2:944.

5 See Prucha, *Great Father,* 2:962–963; Taylor, *New Deal and American Indian Tribalism,* 17–29; Alison Bernstein, *American Indians and World War II: Toward a New Era in Indian Affairs* (Norman: University of Oklahoma Press, 1991), 105–110; "The IRA Record and John Collier," in *Indian Self-Rule: First-Hand Accounts of Indian-White Relations from Roosevelt to Reagan,* ed. Kenneth R. Philp (Logan: Utah State University Press, 1995), 107–108.

6 Prucha, *Great Father,* 2:919.

7 Ibid., 1029.

8 Vine Deloria, Jr., "The Evolution of Federal Policy Making," in *American Indian Policy in the Twentieth Century,* ed. Vine Deloria, Jr. (Norman: University of Oklahoma Press, 1985), 250; Prucha, *Great Father,* 2:1045 (quotation).

9 Address by Orme Lewis, assistant secretary of the Department of the Interior, Aug. 13, 1953, Box 11, Bryce N. Harlow Records, Dwight D. Eisenhower Library (DDEL), Abilene, Kansas.

10 Donald L. Fixico, *Termination and Relocation: Federal Indian Policy, 1945–1960* (Albuquerque: University of New Mexico Press, 1986), 158–163; Prucha, *Great Father,* 2:1085 (quotation).

11 "The Forgotten American," Mar. 6, 1968, 2, Box 18, Fred Bohen Files, Lyndon B. Johnson Library (LBJL), Austin, Texas.

12 Stewart L. Udall to Joseph Califano, Mar. 2, 1968, Box 122, White House Central Files (WHCF), Speech File (SP), LBJL; "Ending Moons of Neglect," *New York Times,* Mar. 9, 1968, Box 18, Bohen Files, LBJL.

13 Handwritten note, n.d. [Mar. 1968], Folder 4, Box 140, Stewart L. Udall Papers, Department of Special Collections, Main Library, University of Arizona, Tucson.

14 Califano to Lyndon B. Johnson, Mar. 5, 1968, Box 122, SP, WHCF, LBJL.

15 Emma Rosalie Gross, "American Indian Policy Development, 1968–1980" (Ph.D. diss., University of Michigan, 1986), 119–147; William Vanden Heuvel and Milton Gwirtzman, *On His Own: Robert F. Kennedy, 1964–1968* (Garden City, N.Y.: Doubleday, 1970), 107–109; "The American Indian–An American Tragedy," *Washington Report from Senator Robert F. Kennedy,* Feb. 1968, Box 4, Speeches and Press Releases, Robert F. Kennedy Senate Papers, John F. Kennedy Library (JFKL), Boston, Massachusetts.

16 Hazel Whitman Hertzberg, "The Indian Rights Movement, 1887–1973," in *Handbook of North American Indians,* ed. William E. Sturtevant, vol. 4, *History of Indian-White Relations,* ed. Wilcomb E. Washburn (Washington, D.C.: Smithsonian Institution, 1988), 318–323; James T. Patterson, *Grand Expectations: The United States, 1945–1974* (New York: Oxford University Press, 1996), 638.

17 Vine Deloria, Jr., *Behind the Trail of Broken Treaties: An Indian Declaration of Independence* (New York: Delacorte Press, 1974), 23.

18 *Pomona Progress-Bulletin,* Feb. 2, 1949, PPS Scrapbook 1 (1949), Richard M. Nixon Pre-Presidential Papers (NPPP), Richard Nixon Library and Birthplace (RNLB), Yorba Linda, California.

19 Richard M. Nixon to Mrs. Philip Lord, Mar. 25, 1959, Box 367, General Correspondence, NPPP, National Archives, Pacific Southwest Region, Laguna Niguel, California (NA-LN).

20 Quoted in Angie Debo, *A History of the Indians of the United States* (Norman: University of Oklahoma Press, 1970), 341.

21 *Baltimore Sun,* Mar. 31, 1968, PPS 500.111.3, NPPP, RNLB.

22 Nixon to National Congress of American Indians, Sept. 27, 1968, Box 1, Indian Affairs (IN), White House Central Files (WHCF), Richard M. Nixon Presidential Materials (NPM), National Archives (NA), College Park, Maryland.

23 Arthur F. Burns to Nixon, Mar. 7, 1969, Box 10A, Arthur F. Burns Papers, Gerald R. Ford Library (GRFL), Ann Arbor, Michigan.

24 Nixon to NCAI, Sept. 27, 1968, Box 1, IN, WHCF, NPM.

25 Patrick J. Buchanan, Memorandum for the President, Mar. 24, 1970, *Papers of the Nixon White House,* ed. Joan Hoff-Wilson, pt. 2, *The President's Meeting File* (Lanham, Md.: University Publications of America, 1989), Fiche 70–3–22 *(PNWH).*

26 Quoted in Tom Wicker, *One of Us: Richard Nixon and the American Dream* (New York: Random House, 1991), 518.

27 Nixon to Andrew T. D'Amico, Feb. 16, 1970, Box 1, IN, WHCF, NPM.

28 Daniel McCool, "Indian Voting," in Deloria, *American Indian Policy in the Twentieth Century,* 116–130.

29 H. R. Haldeman to James Keogh, Jan. 13, 1969, Box 10A, Burns Papers.

30 See Nixon to Haldeman, May 13, 1970, in *From: The President: Richard Nixon's Secret Files,* ed. Bruce Oudes (New York: Harper and Row, 1989), 130–131, quoted in *New York Times,* Oct. 8, 1969, 29.

31 Annotated news summary (ANS), Sept. 21, 1969, *PNWH,* pt. 6, ser. B, *Annotated News Summaries,* Fiche 15.

32 Nixon to John D. Ehrlichman, Nov. 30, 1970, Box 12, H. R. Haldeman Files, Contested Documents File (CDF), NPM.

33 Nixon handwritten comment (NHC) on Daniel P. Moynihan to Nixon, Jan. 16, 1970, *PNWH,* pt. 6, ser. A, *Documents Annotated by the President,* Fiche 60.

34 Haldeman to Keogh, June 29, 1970, Box 60, H. R. Haldeman Files, White House Special Files (WHSF), NPM.

35 John D. Ehrlichman, *Witness to Power: The Nixon Years* (New York: Simon and Schuster, 1982), 103.

36 Minutes of Fifteenth Council for Urban Affairs Meeting, July 11, 1969, Box 3, President's Office Files (POF), CDF, NPM.

37 John D. Ehrlichman telephone interview with the author, Feb. 6, 1995, Atlanta, Georgia.

38 "Nixon and the Indian," *Commonweal,* Sept. 4, 1970, 433.

39 Keogh to Haldeman, Feb. 14, 1969, Box 10A, Burns Papers.

40 Patrick Agan, *Hoffman vs. Hoffman: The Man and the Actor* (London: Robert Hale, 1986), 49–51; *Wall Street Journal,* Apr. 6, 1973, 8. See Iron Eyes Cody (with Collin Perry), *Iron Eyes: My Life as a Hollywood Indian* (New York: Everest House, 1986).

41 Leonard Garment to Ehrlichman, Dec. 24, 1969, Box 101, Leonard Garment Files, Staff Member and Office Files (SMOF), NPM.

42 Burns to Nixon, Mar. 7, 1969, and Stephen Bull to Ehrlichman, Mar. 20, 1969, Box 10A, Burns Papers.

43 Bull to Ehrlichman, Mar. 20, 1969, Box 10A, Burns Papers; Ehrlichman to Nixon, Nov. 3, 1969, Box 51, John D. Ehrlichman Files, WHSF, NPM.

44 Walter J. Hickel to John C. Whitaker, Apr. 21, 1969, Box 375, Rogers C. B. Morton Papers, Margaret I. King Library, University of Kentucky, Lexington.

45 Whitaker to Garment, Oct. 6, 1969, Box 1, IN, WHCF, NPM.

46 *New York Times,* Oct. 9, 1969, 24; Garment to Jerry Pettis, Dec. 12, 1969, Box 1, IN, WHCF, NPM; Garment to Hickel, June 25 and Sept. 8 and 29, 1970, Box 378, Morton Papers.

47 Jack D. Forbes, *Native Americans and Nixon: Presidential Politics and Minority Self-Determination, 1969–1972* (Los Angeles: American Indians Studies Center, University of California at Los Angeles, 1981), 35–36.

48 NHC on Ehrlichman to Nixon, Nov. 3, 1969, Box 1, IN, WHCF, NPM.

49 Garment to Ehrlichman, Feb. 20, 1970, Box 35, Bradley H. Patterson, Jr., Files, SMOF, NPM.

50 Ehrlichman telephone interview with the author, Feb. 6, 1995; Bradley H. Patterson, Jr., exit interview with Terry W. Good, Sept. 10, 1974, 42, NPM.

51 Agnew to Mrs. Roman S. Gibbs, Dec. 28, 1972, Box 35, Series 3, Subseries 5, Spiro T. Agnew Papers, Theodore R. McKeldin Library, University of Maryland, College Park.

52 Reverend Robert T. Newbold, Jr., to Agnew, Nov. 15, 1966, Box 2, Series 2, Subseries 2, Agnew Papers.

53 *Baltimore Sun,* Nov. 2, 1968, Folder: Civil Rights [1967–68], Box 1, Series 2, Subseries 2, Agnew Papers; *Washington Evening Star,* Mar. 8, 1967, D3.

54 *Baltimore Afro-American,* Sept. 30, 1967, Box 1, Series 2, Subseries 2, Agnew Papers.

55 *Washington Post,* Apr. 16, 1968, Folder: Racial Agnew [1968], Box 3; *Baltimore Sun,* June 21, 1968, Box 1, Series 2, Subseries 2, Agnew Papers.

56 C. D. Ward to Agnew, Feb. 18, 1971, Dec. 19 and Nov. 15, 1972, Box 37, Series 3, Subseries 5, Agnew Papers.

57 Ward to Agnew, July 13, 1970, and press release, July 20, 1970; quoted in William Youpee to Agnew, Apr. 27, 1973, Box 37, Series 3, Subseries 5, Agnew Papers.

58 Agnew to Mrs. Roman S. Gibbs, Dec. 28, 1972, Box 35, Series 3, Subseries 5, Agnew Papers.

59 Agnew to Gwinn Owens, Oct. 17, 1972, Box 36, Series 3, Subseries 5, Agnew Papers.

60 *New York Times,* Nov. 30, 1969, 80; Hoff, *Nixon Reconsidered,* 35; Alcatraz Chronology, Aug. 3, 1970, Box 33, Garment Files, NPM.

61 *New York Times,* Nov. 30, 1969, 80.

62 *San Francisco Chronicle,* June 12, 1971, Box 34, Garment Files, NPM; Troy Rollen Johnson, "The Indian Occupation of Alcatraz Island, Indian Self-Determination and the Rise of Indian Activism" (Ph.D. diss., University of California at Los Angeles, 1993), 179.

63 Garment to Ehrlichman and Shultz, July 28, 1970, Box 10, Egil M. Krogh Files, WHSF, NPM.

64 Bradley H. Patterson, Jr., to Garment, "Notes from the First Term," Nov. 28, 1973, Box 1, Leonard Garment Papers, Manuscript Division, Library of Congress (LC), Washington, D.C.

65 "Alcatraz Chronology," Aug. 3, 1973, Box 33, Garment Files; Robert Robertson to Indians of All Tribes, Mar. 31, 1970, Box 1, IN, WHCF, NPM; Johnson, "The Indian Occupation of Alcatraz Island," 176–177.

66 Commandant, U.S. Coast Guard, to Executive Director, National Council on Indian Opportunity, July 17, 1970, and Krogh to Ehrlichman, Aug. 13, 1970, Box 10; Krogh to Ehrlichman, Mar. 5 and June 10, 1971, Box 4, Krogh Files, NPM.

67 Krogh to Ehrlichman, Mar. 5, 1971, Box 4, Krogh Files, NPM.

68 Geoffrey C. Shepard to Krogh, Nov. 27, 1970, Box 10, Krogh Files, NPM.

69 Garment to Ehrlichman, Dec. 14, 1970, Box 1, Garment Papers, LC.

70 Ehrlichman handwritten comments on Garment to Ehrlichman, Jan. 21, 1971, Box 34, Garment Files, NPM; Patterson exit interview, Sept. 10, 1974, 33, NPM; Garment to Ehrlichman, Dec. 14, 1970, Box 1, Garment Papers, LC (quotation).

71 Ehrlichman to Garment, July 9, 1970, Box 1, IN, WHCF, NPM.

72 Patterson to Garment, "Notes from the First Term," Nov. 28, 1973, Box 1, Garment Papers, LC.

73 "Alcatraz Chronology," Aug. 3, 1973, Box 33, Garment Files, NPM; Patterson to Garment, "Notes from the First Term," Nov. 28, 1973, Box 1, Garment Papers, LC.

74 Patterson exit interview, Sept. 10, 1974, 32, NPM; Leonard Garment, *Crazy Rhythm: My Journey from Brooklyn, Jazz, and Wall Street to Nixon's*

White House, Watergate, and Beyond (New York: Times Books, 1997), 224–225; *San Francisco Chronicle,* June 11, 1971, Box 34, Garment Files, NPM.

75 "Points Concerning Alcatraz," Jan. 26, 1970, Box 1, IN, WHCF, NPM.

76 Patterson to Garment, "Notes from the First Term," Nov. 28, 1973, Box 1, Garment Papers, LC; William Timmons and Gene Cowen to Alexander, Nov. 26, 1969, Box 1, Federal Government (FG) 173, National Council on Indian Opportunity, WHCF, NPM; Agnew to Hickel, Jan. 30, 1970, Box 376, Morton Papers; *New York Times,* July 24, 1970, 28; Barbara Greene to Garment, Mar. 27, 1970, Box 100, Garment Files, NPM.

77 Draft memorandum, n.d., Box 105, Garment Files, NPM.

78 Agnew to Nixon, n.d., Box 108, Patterson Files; Patterson to Garment, Apr. 2, 1970, and Garment to Agnew, n.d., Box 105, Garment Files, NPM.

79 Patterson to Garment, Apr. 2, 1970, Box 105, Garment Files, Nixon Presidential Materials; Tod Hullin to Ehrlichman, Apr. 23, 1970, Box 52, Ehrlichman Files, NPM.

80 Donald Rumsfeld to Cole, May 19, 1970, Box 67; George P. Shultz to Cole, May 19, 1970, Box 68, Patterson Files, NPM; "Origin of the Message," n.d., Box 106, Garment Files, NPM.

81 Ehrlichman made the request through Kenneth Cole, his deputy. Patterson exit interview, Sept. 10, 1974, 23–24, NPM; Patterson to Garment, "Notes from the First Term," Nov. 28, 1973, Box 1, Garment Papers, LC.

82 "Special Message to the Congress on Indian Affairs," July 8, 1970, in *Public Papers of the Presidents: Richard Nixon (1970)* (Washington, D.C.: Government Printing Office, 1971), 567, 566 *(PPP)*.

83 Hickel to Nixon, July 20, 21, and 29, 1970, Box 379, Morton Papers; "Special Message to the Congress on Indian Affairs," July 8, 1970, in *PPP, 1970,* 571–572.

84 Garment to Harrison Loesch, Barbara Greene, and Woody Sneed, June 24, 1970, Box 146, Garment Files, NPM.

85 Charles A. Fagan III to Maurice H. Stans, July 10, 1970, Box 22, Commerce Department Files, Maurice H. Stans Papers, Minnesota Historical Society, St. Paul.

86 *New York Times,* July 12, 1970, E3.

87 Ibid., July 9, 1970, 18.

88 Ibid., July 15, 1970, 38.

89 *Detroit News,* July 23, 1970, 7B.

90 American Indian Press Association (AIPA) news release, Aug. 9, 1974, Box 9, Patterson Files, NPM.

91 Patterson to Garment, Oct. 26, 1976, Box 4, Bradley H. Patterson, Jr., Files, GRFL.

92 "Special Message to the Congress on Indian Affairs," July 8, 1970, in *PPP: 1970*, 573; Jack Caulfield to John W. Dean III, Feb. 16, 1971, Box 39, John W. Dean III Files, WHSF, NPM.

93 Lewis H. Butler to Garment, May 25, 1970, Box 105, Garment Files, NPM.

94 Ward to Agnew, Nov. 15, 1972, Box 37, Series 3, Subseries 5, Agnew Papers.

95 Patterson exit interview, Sept. 10, 1974, 24, NPM.

96 John J. Bodine, "Taos Pueblo," in Sturtevant, *Handbook of North American Indians*, vol. 9, *Southwest*, ed. Alonzo Ortiz (Washington, D.C.: Smithsonian Institution, 1979), 263; Garment, *Crazy Rhythm*, 226; Agnew to Hickel, Feb. 13, 1970, Box 377, Morton Papers.

97 Garment, *Crazy Rhythm*, 226.

98 "Selected Editorial Opinion on Blue Lake," in Garment to Nixon, Apr. 17, 1970, Box 1, IN, WHCF, NPM; Agnew to Hickel, Feb. 13, 1970, Box 377, Morton Papers; *New York Times*, July 10, 1970, 1.

99 Agnew to Hickel, Feb. 13, 1970, Box 377, Morton Papers.

100 Garment to Nixon, Apr. 17, 1970, Box 1, IN, WHCF, NPM.

101 Quoted in Barbara Greene to Hullin, Apr. 21, 1970, Box 100, Garment Files, NPM.

102 Hullin to Ehrlichman, Apr. 17, 1970, Box 52, Ehrlichman Files; Barbara Greene to Hullin, Apr. 21, 1970, Box 100, Garment Files, NPM; Memorandum for the President, July 8, 1970, Box 1, IN, WHCF, NPM.

103 Clinton P. Anderson to Hickel, Mar. 12, 1970, Box 1, IN, WHCF, NPM.

104 BeLieu to Ehrlichman, Apr. 17, 1970, Box 3, Harry S. Dent, Jr., Files, WHSF, NPM.

105 Kenneth BeLieu to Ehrlichman, Apr. 22, 1970, Box 100, Garment Files, NPM.

106 Ward to Agnew, Nov. 30, 1970, Box 38, Series 3, Subseries 5, Agnew Papers.

107 Agnew to Hickel, Feb. 13, 1970, Box 377, Morton Papers; Garment to Nixon, Apr. 17, 1970, Box 1, IN, WHCF, NPM; Hullin to Ehrlichman re: Domestic Affairs Meeting, Apr. 17, 1970, Box 52, Ehrlichman Files, NPM; Wicker, *One of Us*, 519.

108 Patterson to Garment, "Notes from the First Term," Nov. 28, 1973, Box 1, Garment Papers, LC; quoted in memo, Bobbie Greene to Ken [Cole], Nov. 5, 1970, Box 1, IN, WHCF, NPM.

109 Bobbie Greene to BeLieu, Nov. 10, 1970, Box 1, IN, WHCF, NPM; Patterson to Garment, "Notes from the First Term," Nov. 28, 1973, Box 1, Garment Papers, LC.

110 *New York Times,* Dec. 3, 1969, 1; Patterson to Garment, "Notes from the First Term," Nov. 28, 1973, Box 1, Garment Papers, LC.

111 Timmons to Ehrlichman, Dec. 3, 1970, Box 1, IN, WHCF, NPM.

112 Garment to BeLieu, Dec. 9, 1970, Box 1, IN, WHCF, NPM.

113 Kilberg to Dwight Chapin, Dec. 8, 1970, Box 1, IN, WHCF, NPM.

114 John D. Ehrlichman meeting notes, Nov. 23, 1971, *PNWH,* pt. 3, *Notes of Meetings with the President, 1969–73,* Fiche 40, Frame B11.

115 "Signing Ceremony for H.R. 471 Blue Lake Bill," Dec. 15, 1970, and Bull to Haldeman via Chapin, Dec. 14, 1970, Box 1, IN, WHCF, NPM.

116 Quoted in William R. Hunt, *Alaska: A Bicentennial History* (New York: Norton, 1976), 154.

117 Ibid., 156–157; Ernest S. Burch, "The Land Claims Era in Alaska," in Sturtevant, *Handbook of North American Indians,* vol. 5, *Arctic,* ed. David Damas (Washington, D.C.: Smithsonian Institution, 1984), 657; Congressional Quarterly, *Almanac: 92nd Congress, 1st Session, . . . 1971* (Washington, D.C.: Congressional Quarterly, 1972), 828.

118 Norman A. Chance, "Alaska Eskimo Modernization," in Sturtevant, *Handbook of North American Indians,* 5:655 (quotation); Congressional Quarterly, *Almanac: 92nd Congress, 1st Session, . . . 1971,* 828.

119 Nixon to Representative Howard Pollock, Sept. 17, 1968, Box 1A, Burns Papers.

120 "Statement of the Secretary of the Interior," Apr. 29, 1969, Box 1A, Burns Papers; "Index to Extracts of Hearing Record on Alaska Native Land Claims," Box 9, Patterson Files, NPM.

121 Tom Cole to Burns, Apr. 28, 1969, Box 1A, Burns Papers; Bud Krogh, Memorandum for the Alaska File, July 25, 1969, Box 1, Krogh Files, NPM.

122 Patterson exit interview, Sept. 10, 1974, 24–25, NPM; Kilberg to Patterson and C. D. Ward, Jan. 11, 1971, Box 9, Patterson Files, NPM.

123 Bobbie Greene to Whitaker, Apr. 1, 1970, Box 8, Patterson Files, NPM.

124 Congressional Quarterly, *Almanac: 92nd Congress, 1st Session, . . . 1971,* 828; William Byler to "Friend," Oct. 20, 1970, Box E1, Leadership Conference on Civil Rights (LCCR) Papers, LC; *Tundra Times,* May 13, 1970, Box 9, Patterson Files, NPM.

125 *Tundra Times,* May 20, 1970, 2; *Anchorage Daily Times,* Oct. 21, 1970, 1; "Statement of Charles Edwardsen, Jr.," Oct. 20, 1970, Box 9, Patterson Files, NPM; *Anchorage Daily News,* Oct. 21, 1970, 1; Alaska Federation of Natives to Agnew, Feb. 28, 1971, Box 7, Patterson Files, NPM; Donald R. Wright to Nixon, Feb. 20, 1971, Box 100, Garment Files, NPM.

126 Patterson to Garment, "Notes from the First Term," Nov. 28, 1973, Box 1, Garment Papers, LC.

127 Ehrlichman meeting notes re: Stevens, n.d., Box 32; Kilberg to Patterson, Jan. 22, 1971, Box 100; "Various Positions on the Alaska Native Land Claims Legislation," n.d., Box 32, Garment Files, NPM; Garment to Ehrlichman, Mar. 5, 1971, Box 7, Patterson Files, NPM; Frank A. Bracken to Rogers C. B. Morton, Mar. 3 and 5, 1971, Box 314, Morton Papers; Patterson exit interview, Sept. 10, 1974, 25–27, NPM.

128 Memorandum for the Record on Alaska Native Claims, meeting with John Ehrlichman, Mar. 12, 1971, Box 314, Morton Papers.

129 Patterson to Garment, "Notes from the First Term," Nov. 28, 1973, Box 1, Garment Papers, LC.

130 Harry Dent to Russell Train, Ehrlichman, and Whitaker, Mar. 13, 1970, Box 260, Morton Papers.

131 Bobbie Kilberg, Memorandum for the President's File, Apr. 6, 1971, *PNWH,* 2, Fiche 71-4-4.

132 Patterson to Garment, "Notes from the First Term," Nov. 28, 1973, Box 1, Garment Papers, LC; Patterson exit interview, Sept. 10, 1974, 27.

133 Patterson exit interview, Sept. 10, 1974, 27, NPM.

134 Max Friedersdorf to Timmons, Sept. 23, 1971, Box 32, Garment Files, NPM; Congressional Quarterly, *Almanac: 92nd Congress, 1st Session, . . . 1971,* 830.

135 Garment to Nixon, Nov. 1, 1970, Box 31, Garment Files, NPM; *New York Times,* Nov. 2, 1971, 26, and Dec. 20, 1971, 9.

136 Congressional Quarterly, *Almanac: 92nd Congress, 1st Session . . . 1971,* 828–829; John C. Whitaker, "Nixon's Domestic Policy: Both Liberal and Bold in Retrospect," *Presidential Studies Quarterly,* 26 (Winter 1996), 145; *The Economist,* May 25, 1996, 31; Linda Kruger and Graciela Etchart, "Forest-Based Economic Development in Native American Lands: Two Case Studies," in *American Indian Policy: Self-Governance and Economic Development,* ed. Lyman H. Legters and Fremont J. Lyden (Westport, Conn.: Greenwood Press, 1994), 202–204; Chance, "Alaska Eskimo Modernization," in Sturtevant, *Handbook of North American Indians,* 5:646–656.

137 Hunt, *Alaska,* 156–157; Burch, "The Land Claims Era in Alaska," in Sturtevant, *Handbook of North American Indians,* 5:660.

138 Kruger and Etchart, "Forest-Based Economic Development in Native American Lands," 202.

139 *The Economist,* May 25, 1996, 31.

140 Caulfield to Dean, Feb. 16, 1971, Box 39, Dean Files; Frank C. Carlucci to Cole, Mar. 8, 1972, Box 50, Patterson Files, NPM.

141 Memorandum for Ed Harper, June 24, 1971, Box 98, Garment Files, NPM.

142 Whitaker to Ehrlichman, Mar. 22, 1973, Box 325, Morton Papers.

143 Brad to Tod, Sept. 20, 1971, Box 2, IN, WHCF, NPM.

144 Patterson to Garment, Mar. 5, 1973, Box 76, Patterson Files, NPM; Cole to Kilberg, Mar. 9, 1971, Box 2, IN, WHCF, NPM.

145 Ward to Agnew, Mar. 16, 1972, Box 37, Series 3, Subseries 5, Agnew Papers.

146 AIPA news release, Sept. 10, 1973, Box 18, Patterson Files, NPM.

147 Garment to Butler and Loesch, May 26, 1970, Box 27, Patterson Files, NPM; "Special Message to the Congress on Indian Affairs," July 8, 1970, in *PPP, 1970,* 569–571; Patterson to Garment, Mar. 5, 1973, Box 76, Patterson Files, NPM.

148 Prucha, *Great Father,* 2:1140; "Statement on Signing the Education Amendments of 1972," June 23, 1972, in *PPP, 1972* (Washington, D.C.: Government Printing Office, 1974), 701–703.

149 Patterson to Garment, Mar. 5, 1973, Box 76, Patterson Files, NPM; AIPA news release, Jan. 30, 1971, Box 35, Patterson Files, NPM.

150 Memorandum for Ed Harper, June 24, 1971, Box 98, Garment Files, NPM.

151 *Wall Street Journal,* Sept. 22, 1972, 1; Kilberg to Ehrlichman, June 1, 1971, and Ehrlichman to Agnew, Oct. 21, 1971, Box 2, IN, WHCF, NPM; Bradley H. Patterson, Jr., "The Federal Executive Branch and the First Americans: A Trustee's Report," *Civil Rights Digest* (Fall 1973), Box 8, Norman E. Ross, Jr., Files, GRFL; Morton to Agnew, n.d., Box 3, IN, WHCF, NPM.

152 AIPA news release, Aug. 9, 1974, Box 9, Patterson Files, NPM.

153 Patterson to Garment, Mar. 5, 1973, Box 76, Patterson Files, NPM.

154 AIPA news release, Aug. 9, 1974, Box 9, Patterson Files, NPM; Agnew to Maurice H. Stans, n.d., Box 5; Fagan to Stans, July 10, 1970, Box 22, Commerce Files, Stans Papers.

155 U.S. Bureau of the Census, *Statistical Abstract of the United States: 1974,* 95th ed. (Washington, D.C.: U.S. Government Printing Office, 1974), 30.

156 AIPA news release, Aug. 9, 1974, Box 9, Patterson Files, NPM.

157 AIPA news release, July 1971, Box 72, Patterson Files, NPM; William Youpee to Louis R. Bruce, Sept. 22, 1971, Box 316, Morton Papers.

158 Morton to All Assistant Secretaries, Sept. 17, 1971, Box 316, Morton Papers; Kilberg to Patterson, Sept. 23, 1971, Box 2, IN, WHCF, NPM; Garment to Ehrlichman, Oct. 1, 1971, and Garment to John N. Mitchell, Oct. 1, 1971, Box 72, Patterson Files, NPM; Mitchell to Ehrlichman, Feb. 28, 1972, Box 2, IN, WHCF, NPM.

159 "Department of Justice Press Conference of Honorable J. Stanley Pottinger," Aug. 13, 1973, Box 20, Patterson Files, NPM; Earle D. Goss to Patterson, Aug. 27, 1970, Box 115; T. K. Cowden to Garment, May 1,

1970; Loesch to Garment, Aug. 3, 1970; Hickel to Clifford M. Hardin, June 30, 1970; and Cowden to Hickel, July 14, 1970, Box 115, Garment Files, NPM.

160 Ralph E. Erickson to Garment, Jan. 18, 1972, Box 115, Garment Files, NPM.

161 Agnew to Nixon, Jan. 21, 1972, Box 115, Garment Files, NPM.

162 Timmons to Cole, Mar. 10, 1972, and Garment to Nixon, May 3, 1972, Box 115, Garment Files, NPM; "Statement on Signing Executive Order . . . ," May 20, 1972, in *PPP, 1972,* 609–610.

163 Memorandum for Ed Harper, June 24, 1971, Box 8, Garment Files, NPM.

164 Minutes of Fifteenth Council for Urban Affairs Meeting, July 11, 1969, Box 3, POF, CDF, NPM.

165 "Excepts from Remarks by Commissioner of Indian Affairs Louis R. Bruce," May 21, 1970, Box 317, Morton Papers.

166 "Policy Statement on Redelegation on Authority," n.d., Box 317, Morton Papers; Garment to Ehrlichman, Nov. 27, 1970, Box 316, Morton Papers.

167 *New York Times,* Aug. 15, 1971, 12; issue paper, "Personnel," n.d., Box 316, Morton Papers; *St. Louis Post-Dispatch,* Aug. 18, 1971, 4B.

168 Both quotations come from Whitaker to Ehrlichman, Mar. 22, 1971, Box 325, Morton Papers.

169 AIPA news release, n.d., Box 40, Patterson Files, NPM; handwritten memorandum, n.d., Box 316, Morton Papers.

170 Kilberg to Cole, Jan. 8, 1971, and Kilberg to Shepard, Mar. 3, 1971, Box 79, Krogh Files, NPM.

171 "Special Message to Congress on Executive Branch Reorganization," Mar. 25, 1971, in *PPP, 1971* (Washington, D.C.: Government Printing Office, 1972), 481.

172 Ehrlichman meeting notes, Nov. 23, 1971, *PNWH,* 3, Fiche 40, Frame B11.

173 Resolution of the Executive Committee of NCAI, n.d., Box 100, Garment Files, NPM; *Arizona Republic,* Sept. 11, 1971, 1; *Albuquerque Tribune,* Sept. 10, 1971, Box 316, Morton Papers.

174 "Morton to Block Officials Opposing Indian Self-Rule," *New York Times,* Oct. 5, 1971, 18; ibid., Jan. 9, 1972, 1, and Dec. 1, 1972, 27.

175 AIPA news release, Aug. 9, 1974, Box 9, Patterson Files, NPM.

176 FBI Report, "The American Indian Movement: A Record of Violence," Jan. 30, 1974, Box 8, Ross Files, GRFL; Garment, *Crazy Rhythm,* 228: "A Characterization of the American Indian Movement," n.d., Box 9, Patterson Files, NPM.

177 *New York Times,* Oct. 31, 1972, 31; "Chronology of Events," n.d., Box 152, Garment Files, NPM; Garment, *Crazy Rhythm,* 230–231; Patterson exit interview, Sept. 10, 1974, 33, NPM.

178 Patterson exit interview, Sept. 10, 1974, 35, NPM.

179 Egil M. Krogh handwritten notes, n.d., Box 13, Krogh Files, NPM.

180 Patterson exit interview, Sept. 10, 1974, 34, NPM.

181 "Chronology of Events," n.d., Box 152, Garment Files, NPM.

182 Patterson exit interview, Sept. 10, 1974, 34, NPM.

183 "Trail of Broken Treaties . . . ," n.d.; Garment to Morton; "Decision to Finance Travel Expenses for Return of Indians to their Homes," n.d., Box 67, Patterson Files, NPM.

184 Ehrlichman telephone interview with the author, Feb. 6, 1995.

185 H. R. Haldeman Diary, Nov. 15, 1972, in *The Haldeman Diaries: Inside the Nixon White House,* ed. H. R. Haldeman (Santa Monica, Calif.: Sony Corporation, 1994), CD-ROM.

186 Ehrlichman meeting notes, Dec. 6, 1972, *PNWH,* 3, Fiche 57.

187 Carlucci to Hullin, Dec. 26, 1972, Box 6, FG 19, Department of Interior, WHCF, NPM.

188 *New York Times,* Nov. 12, 1972, E5.

189 All quotations come from "Messages Received from Tribal Leaders Re 'Trail of Broken Treaties' Activities," n.d., Box 30, Human Rights (HU), WHCF, NPM.

190 Hoff, *Nixon Reconsidered,* 37.

191 Garment, *Crazy Rhythm,* 238; Hoff, *Nixon Reconsidered,* 37; *St. Louis Post-Dispatch,* Mar. 1, 1973, 1, 4A; *New York Times,* Mar. 5, 1973, 1, 26.

192 Joseph T. Sneed to Henry E. Petersen, Apr. 16, 1973, Box 32, HU, WHCF, NPM.

193 Patterson to Garment, Apr. 27, 1973, Box 76, Patterson Files, NPM.

194 Patterson to Garment, n.d. and Mar. 1, 1973, Box 76, Patterson Files, NPM.

195 *New York Times,* Feb. 11, 1971, 56; *St. Louis Post-Dispatch,* Mar. 1, 1973, 1, 4A.

196 Prucha, *Great Father,* 2:728–729, 1119; "Wounded Knee, 1973," *Los Angeles Times,* Mar. 2, 1973, pt. 2, 6; Garment, *Crazy Rhythm,* 236 (quotation).

197 Patterson exit interview, Sept. 10, 1974, 38, NPM.

198 Ehrlichman meeting notes, Mar. 27, 1973, *PNWH,* 3, Fiche 62.

199 Shepard to Cole, n.d., Box 32, HU, WHCF, NPM.

200 Weinberger to Garment, Mar. 14, 1973, Box 76, Patterson Files, NPM.

201 Patterson to Garment, Apr. 12, 1973, Box 76, Patterson Files, NPM; Hoff, *Nixon Reconsidered,* 41.

202 Volney F. Warner to Generals Alexander M. Haig, Jr., and Creighton Abrams, Mar. 12, 1973, Box 76, Patterson Files, NPM.

203 Garment to Cole, n.d., Box 76, Patterson Files, NPM.

204 NHC on Cole to the President, Apr. 20, 1973, *PNWH,* 6A, Fiche 282.

205 Hank Adams to Vine Deloria, Jr., May 16, 1973, and Garment to Dean Sneed, Apr. 7, 1973, Box 76, Patterson Files, NPM.

206 Quotation and subsequent information come from Adams to Deloria, May 16, 1973, Box 76, Patterson Files, NPM.

207 *New York Times,* May 7, 1973, 1, 77; Garment to the Headsman and Chiefs of the Teton Sioux, May 15, 1973, Box 68, Patterson Files, NPM.

208 Patterson exit interview, Sept. 10, 1974, 39, NPM.

209 Garment handwritten comment on Dennis J. Banks to Patterson, Dec. 17, 1973, Box 9, Patterson Files, NPM.

210 *St. Paul Dispatch,* Apr. 3, 1974, Box 75, Patterson Files, NPM.

211 Patterson to Garment, June 18, 1974, Box 9, Patterson Files, NPM.

212 Shepard to Fred Malek, Apr. 12, 1973, Box 35, Garment Files, NPM.

213 Joseph T. Sneed to Benjamin F. Holman, n.d., Box 4, Benjamin Holman Papers, Hoover Institution Archives (HI), Stanford University, Stanford, California.

214 FBI report, "The American Indian Movement: A Record of Violence," Jan. 30, 1974, Box 8, Ross Files, GRFL.

215 Holman to Sneed, May 1, 1973, Box 4, Holman Papers; FBI Report, "The American Indian Movement: A Record of Violence," Jan. 30, 1974, Box 8, Ross Files, GRFL; FBI Director to the President et al., Feb. 27, 1974, Box 9, Patterson Files, NPM.

216 Whitaker to Ehrlichman, Mar. 22, 1973, Box 35, Patterson Files, NPM.

217 ANS, Mar. 19, 1973, *PNWH,* 6B, Fiche 231.

218 Patterson to Cole, Mar. 13, 1973, Box 76, Patterson Files, NPM.

219 *New York Times,* Mar. 17, 1973, 14.

220 Gary Orfield quoted in "Indian Policy, 1945–1960," in Philp, *Indian Self-Rule,* 138; Congressional Quarterly, *Almanac: 93rd Congress, 1st Session, . . . 1973* (Washington, D.C.: Congressional Quarterly, 1974), 587; Prucha, *Great Father,* 2:1135–38; press release, "Statement by the President," Dec. 22, 1973, Box 50, Patterson Files, NPM.

221 Congressional Quarterly, *Almanac: 93rd Congress, 2nd Session, . . . 1974* (Washington, D.C.: Congressional Quarterly, 1975), 587; Prucha, *Great Father,* 2:1144–46; Fred Russell to Nixon, n.d., Box 379, Morton Papers.

222 Garment, *Crazy Rhythm,* 243; Gerald R. Ford to the Secretary of the Treasury et al., Aug. 26, 1976, Box 178, FG 229, United States Civil Service Commission, Gerald R. Ford Presidential Papers, GRFL.

223 AIPA news release, Aug. 9, 1974, Box 9, Patterson Files, NPM; Arrell M. Gibson, "Indian Land Transfers," in Sturtevant, *Handbook of North American Indians*, 4:228.

224 AIPA news release, Aug. 9, 1974, Box 9, Patterson Files, NPM.

225 Roger L. Nichols, "Indians in the Post-Termination Era," *Storia Nordamericana*, 5, no. 1 (1988), 71.

226 Whitaker, "Nixon's Domestic Policy," 145.

227 LaDonna Harris to Sarah Weddington, Oct. 6, 1978, Box 3, IN, WHCF, Jimmy Carter Library, Atlanta, Georgia.

228 Fixico, *Termination and Relocation*, 203 (quotation); Kelly, "United States Indian Policies, 1900–1980," in Sturtevant, *Handbook of North American Indians*, 4:79; Patterson to Ronald Nessen, Oct. 18, 1976, Box 4, Patterson Files, GRFL.

229 Prucha, *Great Father*, 2:1123–24.

230 Nichols, "Indians in the Post-Termination Era," 83–86.

231 Kelly, "United States Indian Policies, 1900–1980," 79; Prucha, *Great Father*, 2:1123–24.

232 Kelly, "United States Indian Policies, 1900–1980," 79.

233 Ibid., 80.

234 Peter N. Carroll, *It Seemed Like Nothing Happened: America in the 1970s*, 2nd ed. (New Brunswick, N.J.: Rutgers University Press, 1990), 254.

235 Gibson, "Indian Land Transfers," 229; C. Patrick Morris, "Termination by Accountants: The Reagan Indian Policy," in *Native Americans and Public Policy*, ed. Fremont J. Lyden and Lyman H. Legters (Pittsburgh: University of Pittsburgh Press, 1992), 65–69, 70–76.

236 Kelly, "United States Indian Policies, 1900–1980," 79–80.

237 Nichols, "Indians in the Post-Termination Era," 83–84.

238 Morris, "Termination by Accountants," in Lyden and Legters, *Native Americans and Public Policy*, 77; Prucha, *Great Father*, 2:1123.

239 U.S. Bureau of the Census, *1970 Census of Population, Subject Reports: American Indians* (Washington, D.C.: U.S. Government Printing Office, 1973), 120; U.S. Bureau of the Census, *Statistical Abstract of the United States: 1989*, 109th ed. (Washington, D.C.: U.S. Government Printing Office, 1989), 39.

240 U.S. Bureau of the Census, *Statistical Abstract of the United States: 1996*, 116th ed. (Lanham, Md.: Bernan Press, 1996), 50, 476.

8. Stops and Starts

1 John Andrews, Memorandum for the President's File, Aug. 6, 1971, *Papers of the Nixon White House*, ed. Joan Hoff-Wilson, pt. 2, *The President's*

Meeting File (Lanham, Md.: University Publications of America, 1989), Fiche 71–8–1 *(PNWH)*.

2 Jo Freeman, *The Politics of Women's Liberation: A Case Study of an Emerging Social Movement and Its Relation to the Policy Process* (New York: David McKay, 1975), 205.

3 Annotated news summary (ANS), May 24, 1969, *PNWH,* pt. 6, ser. B, *Annotated News Summaries,* Fiche 7.

4 Susan M. Hartmann, *From Margin to Mainstream: American Women in Politics Since 1960* (New York: Alfred A. Knopf, 1989), 77.

5 Richard L. Wilson, "Visit with President Nixon, June 5, 1970," Box 5, Richard L. Wilson Papers, Herbert Hoover Library (HHL), West Branch, Iowa.

6 H. R. Haldeman meeting notes, Feb. 20, 1970, *PNWH,* pt. 5, *H. R. Haldeman Notes of White House Meetings,* Fiche 16.

7 John D. Ehrlichman meeting notes, Feb. 14, 1972, Box 1, John D. Ehrlichman Files, Contested Documents File (CDF), Richard M. Nixon Presidential Materials (NPM), National Archives (NA), College Park, Maryland.

8 Monica Crowley, *Nixon Off the Record* (New York: Random House, 1996), 205.

9 Nixon handwritten comment (NHC) on "Political Media Analysis," Sept. 25, 1972, Box 3, President's Office File (POF), CDF, NPM.

10 Both quotations come from Julie Nixon Eisenhower, *Pat Nixon: The Untold Story* (New York: Simon and Schuster, 1986), 68, 321.

11 Monica Crowley, *Nixon in Winter* (New York: Random House, 1988), 369.

12 Theodore H. White typescript notes of airplane conversation with Nixon, Nov. 21, 1967, Box 32, Theodore H. White Papers, John F. Kennedy Library (JFKL), Boston, Massachusetts.

13 Richard M. Nixon to John D. Ehrlichman, Nov. 30, 1970, Box 2, Federal Government (FG) 22, Department of Labor, White House Central Files (WHCF), NPM.

14 "Nixon Press Conference, Cincinnati, Ohio," Feb. 12, 1964, 3, Box 10, Series 22, New York Office, Nelson A. Rockefeller Gubernatorial Papers, Record Group (RG) 15, Rockefeller Family Archives (RFA), Rockefeller Archive Center (RAC), Sleepy Hollow, New York.

15 Hartmann, *From Margin to Mainstream,* 73.

16 Daniel P. Moynihan to Nixon, Aug. 20, 1969, Box 21, Human Rights (HU), WHCF, NPM.

17 "Humor, 5/24/71," Folder: B-10, RHF Humor, Speeches by Subject File, Drawer B, Private Papers of Robert H. Finch, Pasadena, California.

18 Garment handwritten comment on Hugh W. Sloan, Jr., to Robert J. Brown et al., Apr. 16, 1970, Box 2, Leonard Garment Files, Staff Member and Office Files (SMOF), NPM.

19 Kathryn F. Clarenbach and Betty Friedan, President, to Nixon, Mar. 14, 1969, Box 30, Robert H. Finch Files, SMOF, NPM.

20 "Excerpt from Tape of Press Briefing," May 15, 1969, Box 39, Charles L. Clapp Files, SMOF, NPM.

21 Dwight Chapin to H. R. Haldeman, Jan. 21, 1972, Box 21, HU, WHCF, NPM.

22 Chapin to David Parker, June 26, 1972, Box 21, HU, WHCF, NPM.

23 Haig handwritten comment on Bruce A. Kerli to Alexander M. Haig, Jr., Feb. 19, 1974, Box 12, Anne Armstrong Files, SMOF, NPM.

24 Helen Delich Bentley to Nixon, n.d., Box 28, Finch Files, NPM.

25 *Wall Street Journal,* Aug. 19, 1969, 1.

26 Ibid., Jan. 19, 1973, 4.

27 Ibid., Mar. 6, 1973, 1.

28 Ibid., Mar. 12, 1974, 1.

29 Quoted in Joan Hoff, *Nixon Reconsidered* (New York: Basic Books, 1994), 101.

30 "Stenographic Transcript of Informal Press Conference," July 17, 1960, 7, Folder 107, Box 6, Press Office Series, Rockefeller Gubernatorial Papers, RG 15, RFA.

31 Democratic National Committee Press Release, May 2, 1964, Box 1, Press Conferences, Transcripts of Interviews, and Dedication Ceremonies of Stewart Udall, Records of the Office of the Secretary of the Interior, RG 48, NA.

32 James N. Giglio, *The Presidency of John F. Kennedy* (Lawrence: University Press of Kansas, 1991), 267–270; Susan M. Hartmann, "Women's Issues and the Johnson Administration," in *The Johnson Years,* vol. 3, *LBJ at Home and Abroad,* ed. Robert A. Divine (Lawrence: University Press of Kansas, 1994), 56.

33 Memorandum for President Lyndon B. Johnson Regarding Staff Meeting, January 20, 1967, Folder: HU-3, Equality of Women, Box 57, Confidential Files (CF), Lyndon B. Johnson Library (LBJL), Austin, Texas.

34 "Statement by Richard M. Nixon," Oct. 16, 1968, Box 7, Armstrong Files, NPM.

35 Bentley to Nixon, n.d., Box 28, Finch Files, NPM.

36 Carol Reavis to Robert H. Finch, Nov. 17, 1970, Box 29, Finch Files, NPM.

37 Friedan to Nixon, May 11, 1968, Civil Rights Research File, Richard M. Nixon Pre-Presidential Papers (NPPP), Richard Nixon Library and Birthplace (RNLB), Yorba Linda, California.

38 Clarenbach and Friedan to Nixon, Mar. 14, 1969, Box 30, Finch Files, NPM.

39 Hugh Davis Graham, *The Civil Rights Era: Origins and Development of National Policy, 1960–1972* (New York: Oxford University Press, 1990), 397; Peterson to Rogers C. B. Morton, May 28, 1969, Box 205, Rogers C. B. Morton Papers, Department of Special Collections, Margaret I. King Library, University of Kentucky, Lexington.

40 Minutes of Republican National Committee, June 27, 1969, 25, 47 (quotation), *Papers of the Republican Party,* pt. 1, *Meetings of the Republican National Committee, 1911–1980,* ser. B, *1960–1980,* Reel 7.

41 Peterson to Morton, May 28, 1969, Box 205, Morton Papers.

42 "Excerpt from Tape of Press Briefing," May 15, 1969; Vera Glaser to Arthur F. Burns, May 23, 1969; "Some Suggestions for Equalizing Opportunities," June 4, 1969, Box 39, Clapp Files, NPM.

43 Florence P. Dwyer to Nixon, July 8, 1969, Box 39, Clapp Files, NPM.

44 Bobby D. Spears to James M. Miller, Nov. 13, 1969, Folder 2, Box 29, Laurence H. Silberman Papers, Hoover Institution Archives (HI), Stanford University, Stanford, California; Joan Hoff, *Law, Gender, and Injustice: A Legal History of U.S. Women* (New York: New York University Press, 1991), 234–235; Clarenbach and Friedan to Nixon, Mar. 14, 1969, Box 30, Finch Files, NPM (quotation).

45 "A Partial Listing of Existing Discriminations against Women in the United States," June 4, 1969, Box 39, Clapp Files, NPM.

46 Clarenbach and Friedan to Nixon, Mar. 14, 1969, Box 30, Finch Files, NPM.

47 Cynthia Harrison, *On Account of Sex: The Politics of Women's Issues, 1945–1968* (Berkeley: University of California Press, 1988), 119–137; Tom Cole to Burns, Apr. 10, 1969, Box 170, Garment Files, NPM.

48 Memoranda for the File, Aug. 20 and Sept. 5, 1969, Box 39, Clapp Files, NPM; press release, Task Force on Women's Rights and Responsibilities, Oct. 1, 1969, Box 39, Clapp Files, NPM; Graham, *Civil Rights Era,* 400.

49 Burns to Virginia R. Allan, Sept. 12, 1969, Box A26, Arthur F. Burns Papers, Gerald R. Ford Library (GRFL), Ann Arbor, Michigan.

50 All quotations come from "Presidential Task Force on Women's Rights and Responsibilities, Summary of First Meeting, September 25–26, 1969," Box 39, Clapp Files, NPM.

51 Allan to Nixon, Dec. 15, 1969, Box A26, Burns Papers.

52 Larry Higby to Leonard Garment, Feb. 19, 1970, Box 209, H. R. Haldeman Files, White House Special Files (WHSF), NPM.

53 Haldeman handwritten comment on Peter Flanigan to Haldeman, Feb. 16, 1970, Box 209, Haldeman Files, NPM.

54 Alice L. Beeman to Charles L. Clapp, Mar. 18, 1970, Box 39, Clapp Files, NPM.

55 Dwyer to Nixon, Mar. 24, 1970, Box 39, Clapp Files, NPM.

56 Clapp to Garment, Apr. 10, 1970, and Garment to Ehrlichman, Apr. 15, 1970, Box 39, Clapp Files, NPM.

57 Unsigned typescript note, n.d., Box 39, Clapp Files, NPM.

58 Peterson to Morton, June 12, 1970, Box 259, Morton Papers.

59 Charles W. Colson to Garment, Apr. 22, 1970, Box 30, Finch Files, NPM.

60 Morton to Dent, June 5, 1970, Box 260, Morton Papers.

61 Joan Hoff-Wilson, introduction to *Rights of Passage: The Past and Future of ERA,* ed. Joan Hoff-Wilson (Bloomington: Indiana University Press, 1986), xi.

62 Mary Frances Berry, *Why ERA Failed: Politics, Women's Rights, and the Amending Process of the Constitution* (Bloomington: Indiana University Press, 1986), 57; Christine A. Lunardini, *From Equal Suffrage to Equal Rights: Alice Paul and the National Woman's Party, 1910–1928* (New York: New York University Press, 1986), 169; Edith Mayo and Jerry K. Frye, "The ERA: Postmortem of a Failure in Political Communication," in Hoff-Wilson, *Rights of Passage,* 80.

63 Harrison, *On Account of Sex,* 21, 117; Hartmann, "Women's Issues and the Johnson Administration," 57; "Press Comments on President's Message," January 1957, Box 245, General Correspondence, NPPP, National Archives, Pacific Southwest Region, Laguna Niguel, California (NA-LN).

64 Quoted in Stephen E. Ambrose, *Eisenhower,* vol. 2, *The President* (New York: Simon and Schuster, 1984), 412.

65 Josephine V. Terrill to Nixon, Nov. 10, 1946, PPS 1.423; Nixon to Terrill, Nov. 14, 1946, PPS 1.425, NPPP, RNLB.

66 Quoted in Hoff, *Nixon Reconsidered,* 105.

67 Alice Paul Oral History, 388, Regional Oral History Office, Bancroft Library, University of California, Berkeley; "What the Republican Party Has Done for Women," n.d., Box 245, General Correspondence, NPPP, NA-LN.

68 Paul Oral History, 388.

69 Robert L. King to Nina R. Price, Oct. 31, 1955, Box 552, General Correspondence, NPPP, NA-LN; Paul Oral History, 388.

70 Nixon to Amelia Haines Walker, Sept. 23, 1959, Box 552, General Correspondence, NPPP, NA-LN.

71 Nixon to "WWS," Oct. 6, 1959, Box 552, General Correspondence, NPPP, NA-LN.

72 Nixon to Walker, Oct. 13, 1959, Box 552, General Correspondence, NPPP, NA-LN.

73 NHC on Nixon to Walker, Oct. 13, 1959, Box 552, General Correspondence, NPPP, NA-LN.

74 Walker to Nixon, Oct. 19, 1959, Box 552, General Correspondence, NPPP, NA-LN.

75 "Governor Rockefeller Gives His Support to Equal Rights for Women Amendment," Aug. 19, 1959, Box 552, General Correspondence, NPPP, NA-LN; Charles K. McWorter, Memorandum for the File, Aug. 22, 1959, Box 245, General Correspondence, NPPP, NA-LN.

76 John Reagan McCrary to Nixon, Feb. 3, 1960, Folder 57: Campaign Suggestions, Box 10, Finch Papers.

77 McWorter to Finch, Apr. 2, 1960, Box 552, General Correspondence, NPPP, NA-LN.

78 Nixon to Finch, July 13, 1960, Folder 79: Memos from RN, Box 12, Finch Papers.

79 Nixon to Finch, July 18, 1960, Folder 79: Memos from RN, Box 12, Finch Papers.

80 Nixon to Emma Guffey Miller and Perle Mesta, Sept. 2, 1960, Box 552, General Correspondence, NPPP, NA-LN.

81 "Statement by Former Vice President Richard M. Nixon," n.d. [1968], Civil Rights Research File, NPPP, RNLB.

82 Rose Mary Woods to "WWS," Jan. 15, 1960, Box 552, General Correspondence, NPPP, NA-LN.

83 *Washington Evening Star,* Mar. 30, 1960, A15.

84 Annelise Anderson to Alan Greenspan, July 18, 1968, Box 17, Annelise Graebner Anderson Papers, HI.

85 Patrick J. Buchanan to Ehrlichman and Haldeman, Feb. 15, 1973, Box 109, Haldeman Files, NPM.

86 *Newsweek,* Aug. 24, 1970, 16.

87 *Time,* Aug. 31, 1970, 17.

88 *New Yorker,* Sept. 5, 1970, 27.

89 *New York Times,* Aug. 27, 1970, 30.

90 *New Yorker,* Aug. 22, 1970, 30.

91 Hoff, *Nixon Reconsidered,* 106; Elizabeth Duncan Koontz to the Vice President et al., July 23, 1970, Box 270, Records of the Secretary of Labor, James D. Hodgson, 1970, RG 174, Department of Labor, NA; *New York Times,* Aug. 11, 1970, 1, 23; Dent to Ehrlichman and William E. Timmons, May 7, 1970, Box 21, HU, WHCF, NPM.

92 Aileen C. Hernandez to Nixon, Sept. 25, 1970, Box 22, HU, WHCF, NPM; Garment to Nixon, n.d., 6, Box 39, Clapp Files, NPM.

93 Timmons to Staff Secretary, Moynihan to Staff Secretary, and Donald Rumsfeld to Kenneth Cole, May 27, 1970, Box 35, Confidential Files

(CF), WHSF, NPM; Patterson to Garment, May 27, 1970, Box 30, Finch Files, NPM.

94 Colson to Cole, Jan. 2, 1970, in *From: The President: Richard Nixon's Secret Files*, ed. Bruce Oudes (New York: Harper and Row, 1989), 85.

95 Harlow handwritten comments on memorandum from John Campbell, n.d., Box 3, WHCF, Subject Files, CDF, NPM.

96 Garment to Cole, May 27, 1970, Box 30, Finch Files, NPM.

97 Garment to Ehrlichman and Garment to Nixon, n.d., Box 39, Clapp Files, NPM.

98 *New York Times*, Aug. 18, 1970, 18; Oct. 9, 1970, 11; Oct. 14, 1970, 1; Oct. 18, 1970, E6.

99 Anne Armstrong to Lyn Nofziger, Mar. 8, 1971, Box 7, Armstrong Files, NPM.

100 Frederic V. Malek to Ehrlichman, July 14, 1971, Box 82, Haldeman Files, NPM.

101 Jacqueline G. Gutwillig to Finch, July 20, 1971, Box 28, Finch Files, NPM.

102 Malek to Ehrlichman, July 14, 1971, Box 82, Haldeman Files, NPM.

103 Bentley et al. to Nixon, July 20, 1971, Box 28, Finch Files, NPM.

104 Nancy Woloch, *Women and the American Experience*, 2nd ed. (New York: McGraw-Hill, 1994), 552; John C. Whitaker, "Nixon's Domestic Policy: Both Bold and Liberal in Retrospect," *Presidential Studies Quarterly*, 26 (Winter 1996), 145-146.

105 All quotations come from Barbara Franklin, Memorandum for the Files, Aug. 4, 1971, Box 28, Finch Files, NPM.

106 Malek to Ehrlichman, July 14, 1971, Box 82, Haldeman Files, NPM.

107 Garment to Ehrlichman, July 23, 1971, Box 4, Garment Files, NPM.

108 Garment to Ehrlichman, July 21, 1971, Box 4, Garment Files, NPM.

109 Garment to Ehrlichman, July 23, 1971, Box 4, Garment Files, NPM.

110 Hullin to Garment, Sept. 20, 1971, and Garment to Nixon, n.d., Box 1, Leonard Garment Papers, Manuscript Division, Library of Congress (LC), Washington, D.C. See also memorandum of telephone conversation, Elliot L. Richardson and Leonard Garment, Sept. 20, 1971, Box 130, Elliot L. Richardson Papers, LC.

111 Garment to Nixon, Oct. 1, 1971, Box 36, Staff Secretary Files–Courier Files, SMOF, NPM.

112 NHC on Garment to Nixon, Oct. 6, 1971, *PNWH*, pt. 6, ser. A, *Documents Annotated by the President*, Fiche 178.

113 Constance Stuart Oral History, Aug. 15, 1988, NPM; John Ehrlichman, *Witness to Power: The Nixon Years* (New York: Simon and Schuster, 1982), 137-139.

114 H. R. Haldeman Diary, Oct. 21, 1971, in *The Haldeman Diaries: Inside the Nixon White House* (Santa Monica, Calif.: Sony Corporation, 1994), CD-ROM. See also Eisenhower, *Pat Nixon*, 321–322.

115 Hoff, *Nixon Reconsidered*, 109.

116 Garment to Ehrlichman, July 21, 1971, Box 4, Garment Files, NPM.

117 Franklin, Memorandum for the Files, Aug. 4, 1971, Box 28, Finch Files, NPM. See also Eisenhower, *Pat Nixon*, 322.

118 Julie Nixon Eisenhower to Nixon, n.d., *PNWH*, pt. 7, *The President's Personal Files*, Fiche 58.

119 Quoted in Rose Mary Woods to Ehrlichman, Feb. 2, 1972, Box 35, CF, NPM.

120 Quoted in Woods to Ehrlichman, Jan. 20, 1972, Box 3, WHCF, Subject Files, CDF, NPM.

121 NHC on memo, Ehrlichman to Woods, Jan. 27, 1972, Box 3, WHCF, Subject Files, CDF, NPM.

122 John Dean to Nixon through Ehrlichman, Mar. 14, 1972, Box 21, HU, WHCF, NPM; Nixon to Hugh Scott, Mar. 18, 1972, Box 86, Garment Files, NPM; Freeman, *Politics of Women's Liberation*, 220.

123 Armstrong to Haldeman and Ehrlichman, Feb. 16, 1973, Box 109, Haldeman Files, NPM; Kehrli to Haldeman, Mar. 13, 1973, and NHC on Kenneth Cole to Nixon, Mar. 8, 1973, *PNWH*, 6A, Fiche 276; Joan Hoff-Wilson, introduction to *Rights of Passage*, 39.

124 Buchanan to Ehrlichman and Haldeman, Feb. 15, 1973, Box 109, Haldeman Files, NPM.

125 Hoff, *Law, Gender, and Injustice*, 321–327; Elizabeth Pleck, "Failed Strategies, Renewed Hope," in Hoff-Wilson, *Rights of Passage*, 112; Hartmann, *From Margin to Mainstream*, 137; Berry, *Why ERA Failed*, 70–85.

126 Berry, *Why ERA Failed*, 3; Hoff, *Law, Gender, and Injustice*, 322–326.

127 Hartmann, *From Margin to Mainstream*, 137.

128 Pleck, "Failed Strategies, Renewed Hope," 109.

129 National Woman's Party Press Release, Aug. 17, 1968, Box 30, Finch Files, NPM.

130 Graham, *Civil Rights Era*, 218–232; Hartmann, "Women's Issues and the Johnson Administration," 60.

131 Patricia Zelman, *Women, Work, and National Policy: The Kennedy-Johnson Years* (Ann Arbor: UMI Research Press, 1982), 116.

132 "Summary of Proposed Part 60-20, OFCC Rules," n.d.; James D. Hodgson to Arnold R. Weber et al., May 2, 1970, Folder 3, Box 29, Silberman Papers.

133 Laurence H. Silberman to John L. Wilks, n.d.; Hodgson to Weber et al., May 2, 1970; Wilks to Hodgson and Fletcher, Apr. 7, 1970, Folder 3,

Box 29, Silberman Papers; Garment to Cole, June 3, 1970, Box 39, Clapp Files, NPM.

134 "Title 41–Public Contracts and Property Management, Chapter 60," n.d., Folder 3, Box 29, Silberman Papers.

135 Edward Aguirre to Weber, May 15, 1970, Folder 3, Box 29, Silberman Papers.

136 Mary H. Hilton to Silberman, May 28, 1970, Folder 3, Box 29, Silberman Papers.

137 Hodgson to Representative Edward I. Koch, Aug. 21, 1970, Box 270, James D. Hodgson Files, 1970, RG 174, National Archives, College Park, Maryland.

138 Dwyer to Hodgson, July 27, 1970, Box 270, Hodgson Files, 1970, RG 174.

139 Patsy T. Mink to Hodgson, July 1, 1970, Box 270, Hodgson Files, 1970, RG 174.

140 Edith Green to Hodgson, Sept. 16, 1970, Box 269, Hodgson Files, 1970, RG 174.

141 Ann F. Scott to Hodgson, July 27, 1970, Box 270, Hodgson Files, 1970, RG 174.

142 Bernice Sandler to Hodgson, July 8, 1970, Box 270, Hodgson Files, 1970, RG 174.

143 Quoted in Wilks to Hodgson et al., July 29, 1970, Box 270, Hodgson Files, 1970, RG 174; Margaret Chase Smith to Hodgson, July 29, 1970, Box 270, Hodgson Files, 1970, RG 174; *NOW Press Release,* May 13, 1971, Box 241, Hodgson Files, 1971, RG 174.

144 Hodgson to William L. Safire, Aug. 25, 1970, Box 269, Hodgson Files, 1970, RG 174.

145 "James D. Hodgson," in *Political Profiles: The Nixon-Ford Years,* ed. Eleanora W. Schoenebaum (New York: Facts on File, 1979), 299–302; Department of Justice Press Release, July 20, 1970, Box 39, Clapp Files, NPM; *Wall Street Journal,* July 21, 1970, 8; *U.S. Department of Labor News,* July 31, 1970, Folder 3, Box 29, Silberman Papers.

146 Koontz to Hodgson, July 29, 1970, Folder 3, Box 29, Silberman Papers; Wilks to Beeman, Aug. 21, 1970, Box 270, Hodgson Files, 1970, RG 174; Wilma Scott Heide and Ann Scott to Hodgson, Aug. 10, 1970, Folder 3, Box 29, Silberman Papers.

147 Hodgson to Silberman, Aug. 1, 1970, Folder 3, Box 29, Silberman Papers.

148 Wilks to Silberman and Fletcher, Dec. 1, 1970, Folder 3, Box 29, Silberman Papers.

149 *U.S. Department of Labor News,* Jan. 19, 1971, Folder 3, Box 29, Silberman Papers; Wilks to Hodgson and Silberman, Apr. 15, 1971, Box 241, Hodgson Files, 1971, RG 174.

150 NOW Press Release, May 13, 1971, Box 241, Hodgson Files, 1971, RG 174; quoted in Catherine East to George Grassmuck, Mar. 17, 1971, Box 29, Finch Files, NPM.

151 Silberman to Wilks, Mar. 22, 1971, Folder 2, Box 29, Silberman Papers.

152 Wilks to Hodgson, n.d., Folder 5, Box 29, Silberman Papers.

153 Nash to Gerald L. Paley, June 23, 1971, and Nash handwritten comment on Paley to Peter G. Nash, June 22, 1971, Folder 5, Box 29, Silberman Papers.

154 Hodgson handwritten comment on Wilks to Hodgson, Aug. 5, 1971, Folder 5, Box 29, Silberman Papers.

155 *Washington Daily News,* Apr. 28, 1972, Box 57, Armstrong Files, NPM.

156 *U.S. Department of Labor News,* Dec. 2, 1971, Box 86, Garment Files, NPM.

157 Graham, *Civil Rights Era,* 410.

158 Ibid., 412 (quotation).

159 Frederick L. Webber to Silberman, Dec. 23, 1971, Folder 5, Box 29, Silberman Papers.

160 ANS, n.d., *PNWH,* 6B, Fiche 12.

161 *Wall Street Journal,* Apr. 10, 1969, 17, and Aug. 11, 1969, 26; *New York Times,* May 16, 1970, 1, and Aug. 26, 1970, 4; Dent to Herbert Klein, June 23, 1969, Box 2, Harry S. Dent, Jr., Files, WHSF, NPM.

162 Malise C. Bloch to Grassmuck, Oct. 26, 1970, Box 28, Finch Files, NPM.

163 ANS, July 24, 1970, *PNWH,* 6B, Fiche 33.

164 Haldeman to Finch, Sept. 8, 1970, Action Memo P615, Box 42, Staff Secretary Files, NPM.

165 John D. Ehrlichman meeting notes, Dec. 31, 1970, *PNWH,* pt. 3, *John D. Ehrlichman Notes of Meetings with the President,* Fiche 24.

166 Grassmuck to Finch, Feb. 25, 1971, Box 29, Finch Files, NPM.

167 Malek handwritten comment on Weber to John Campbell, Mar. 9, 1971, Box 29, Finch Files, NPM.

168 Finch handwritten comment on Malek to Finch and Donald Rumsfeld, Mar. 10, 1971, Box 29, Finch Files, NPM.

169 NHC on Finch to Nixon, Apr. 15, 1971, *PNWH,* 6A, Fiche 135.

170 Franklin, Memorandum for the File, Aug. 16, 1971, Box 26, Armstrong Files, NPM.

171 Malek to Morton, June 23, 1971, Box 379, Morton Papers; Malek to George W. Romney, July 1, 1971, Box 26, Armstrong Files, NPM.

172 *Maine Sunday Telegram,* Aug. 27, 1972, Box 21, HU, WHCF, NPM.

173 "Fact Sheet: Women in the Federal Government," n.d. [1973], Box 31, Armstrong Files, NPM; *Maine Sunday Telegram,* Aug. 27, 1972, and "Key Facts on Women," n.d., Box 21, HU, WHCF, NPM.

174 As Hugh Davis Graham has argued in *Civil Rights Era*, 412.
175 *St. Louis Post-Dispatch*, Aug. 28, 1972, 2A; Jean Hawkins to Morton, Aug. 15, 1973, Box 338, Morton Papers.
176 Rose Mary Woods, memorandum, n.d., Box 4, President's Personal File (PPF), WHSF, NPM.
177 Mrs. Tobin Armstrong to Jean L. McCarrey, Apr. 5, 1974, and Harriet to Judy, Apr. 17, 1974, Box 22, HU, WHCF, NPM.
178 Higby handwritten comment on Dick Moore to David Parker, Jan. 31, 1973, Box 109, Haldeman Files, NPM.
179 *Wall Street Journal*, Nov. 29, 1974, 21.
180 "Nixon Stalwarts Speak Out," n.d., Box 11, Armstrong Files, NPM.
181 Vera Hirschberg to Armstrong, Feb. 27, 1974, Box 12, Armstrong Files, NPM.
182 NHC on Rita E. Hauser to Nixon, Feb. 5, 1969, *PNWH*, 6A, Fiche 7.
183 Hauser to Safire, Mar. 2, 1970, Box 21, HU, WHCF, NPM; Hauser to Nixon, Apr. 12, 1971, Box 82, Haldeman Files, NPM.
184 Colson to Parker, May 4, 1971, Box 10, Charles W. Colson Files, WHSF, NPM; Presidential Courier to San Clemente, July 10, 1971, Box 36, Staff Secretary–Courier Files, NPM.
185 Ehrlichman meeting notes, Aug. 11, 1970, *PNWH*, 3, Fiche 18.
186 NHC on Hauser to Nixon, Oct. 1, 1973, Box 13, Alexander M. Haig, Jr., Files, WHSF, NPM.
187 Hauser to Ehrlichman and Garment, Sept. 14, 1970, Box 3; Hauser to Garment, Mar. 7, 1972, Box 86, Garment Files, NPM.
188 Judith Sealander, *As Minority Becomes Majority: Federal Reaction to the Phenomenon of Women in the Work Force, 1920–1963* (Westport, Conn.: Greenwood Press, 1983), 146–147.
189 Cole to Robert J. Brown, May 7, 1969, FG 23, Department of Health, Education, and Welfare, WHCF, NPM.
190 Burns to Nixon, Apr. 25, 1969, Box 1, FG 23, WHCF, NPM.
191 Finch to Garment, May 1, 1970, Box 30, Finch Files, NPM; John Irving to Arthur Fletcher, Aug. 18, 1970; Silberman to Hodgson, Aug. 18, 1970; Silberman to Fletcher et al., Nov. 20, 1970; "Secretary's Staff Meeting–December 1, 1970"; and Silberman to Fletcher, Jan. 29, 1971, all in Folder 6, Box 13, Silberman Papers; Mary Frances Berry, *The Politics of Parenthood: Child Care, Women's Rights, and the Myth of the Good Mother* (New York: Viking, 1993), 132.
192 ANS, *PNWH*, 6B, Fiche 4.
193 Ehrlichman meeting notes, n.d. [1969], *PNWH*, 3, Fiche 1, Frames B3–B4.
194 Ehrlichman meeting notes, n.d. [1969], *PNWH*, 3, Fiche 1, Frame A6.

195 Ehrlichman meeting notes, Nov. 12, 1969, *PNWH,* 3, Fiche 5.

196 Ehrlichman meeting notes, n.d. [1969], *PNWH,* 3, Fiche 1, Frames B3–B4.

197 NHC on William V. Shannon, "A Radical, Direct, Simple, Utopian Alternative to Day-Care Centers," June 6, 1972, *PNWH,* 6A, Fiche 218.

198 *New York Times,* June 9, 1971, 22; memorandum of telephone conversations, Richardson and Clark MacGregor, May 21, 1971, and Richardson and George Shultz, May 21, 1971, Box 129, Richardson Papers.

199 Ehrlichman meeting notes, July 24, 1971, *PNWH,* 3, Fiche 36.

200 Ehrlichman to Ziegler, Nov. 6, 1971, Box 58, Ehrlichman Files, NPM.

201 ANS, Nov. 11, 1971, *PNWH,* pt. 4, *The John Ehrlichman Alphabetical Subject Files, 1969–1973,* Fiche 33.

202 Buchanan to Ehrlichman and Haldeman, Nov. 19, 1971, Box 86; Colson to Haldeman, Dec. 8, 1971, Box 87, Haldeman Files, NPM.

203 "Veto of the Economic Opportunity Amendments of 1971," Dec. 10, 1971, in *Public Papers of the Presidents: Richard Nixon (1971)* (Washington, D.C.: U.S. Government Printing Office, 1972), 1176 *(PPP).*

204 Memorandum of telephone conversation, Richardson and Charles Colson, Dec. 29, 1971, Box 131, Richardson Papers.

205 Memorandum of telephone conversation, Richardson and John D. Ehrlichman, Dec. 8, 1971, Box 129, Richardson Papers.

206 Constance Stuart to Ehrlichman, Feb. 1, 1972, Box 3, FG 15, Domestic Council, WHCF, NPM; *St. Louis Post-Dispatch,* Aug. 21, 1972, 1A.

207 Hoff, *Law, Gender, and Injustice,* 245; "What Is the Nixon Administration's Position on Child Day Dare?" n.d., Box 33, Armstrong Files, NPM; Berry, *Politics of Parenthood,* 142.

208 Berry, *Politics of Parenthood,* 146 (quotation), 142–146, 193.

209 Ellen Willis, foreword to Alice Echols, *Daring to Be Bad: Radical Feminism in America, 1967–1975* (Minneapolis: University of Minnesota Press, 1989), vii.

210 David J. Garrow, *Liberty and Sexuality: The Right to Privacy and the Making of Roe v. Wade* (New York: Macmillan, 1994), 335–388; Woloch, *Women and the American Experience,* 526.

211 Echols, *Daring to Be Bad,* 174–175.

212 NHC on Burns to Nixon, Mar. 19, 1969, *PNWH,* 6A, Fiche 10; *Wall Street Journal,* Sept. 15, 1969; Nixon to the Vice President et al., July 25, 1969; and White House Press Release, Mar. 16, 1970, Box 2, Chester E. Finn Papers, HI.

213 Moynihan to Moore, Sept. 10, 1970, Box 2, Finn Papers.

214 NHC on Moynihan to Nixon, Dec. 17, 1969, *PNWH,* 6A, Fiche 53.

215 "Richard M. Nixon in Question and Answer Session," Apr. 24, 1968, PPS 208.1968.17A, NPPP, RNLB.

216 *Wall Street Journal,* Sept. 15, 1969, and press release of the United States Catholic Conference, July 18, 1969, Box 2, Finn Papers.

217 Colson to Haldeman, Nov. 13, 1970, Box 46, Colson Files; Buchanan to Ehrlichman, Haldeman, and Colson, Sept. 23, 1971, Box 3, Patrick J. Buchanan Files, WHSF, NPM; Ehrlichman to Laird, Mar. 4, 1971, Box 55, Ehrlichman Files, NPM.

218 Ehrlichman meeting notes, Mar. 23, 1971, *PNWH,* 3, Fiche 28; Nixon to Laird, Mar. 24, 1971, Box 75, and "Statement," Apr. 2, 1971, Box 76 (quotations), Haldeman Files, NPM.

219 Brigadier General James D. Hughes to Haldeman, Apr. 26, 1971, Box 77, Haldeman Files, NPM.

220 Haldeman meeting notes, Apr. 10, 1972, *PNWH,* 5, Fiche 74.

221 *New York Times,* Mar. 17, 1972, 1; Gordon Strachan to Haldeman, May 3, 1972, Box 120, Haldeman Files; *Washington Post,* May 22, 1972, Folder: Women–Abortion, Box 50, Armstrong Files; *New York Times,* May 11, 1972, Box 120, Haldeman Files, NPM.

222 Hauser to Ehrlichman, Aug. 28, 1972, Box 28, Colson Files, NPM.

223 Haldeman meeting notes, Oct. 10, 1972, *PNWH,* 5, Fiche 86.

224 Tod Hullin to Franklin, Aug. 19, 1972, Box 61, Ehrlichman Files, NPM.

225 Ehrlichman meeting notes, Feb. 15, 1973, *PNWH,* 3, Fiche 60.

226 "Transcript of Richard Nixon Interviewed by Brian Lamb on C-SPAN's *Booknotes,*" Feb. 23, 1992 (Washington, D.C.: C-SPAN, 1992), 10; Jessamyn West, "Abortion," in *Encyclopedia of the Republican Party,* ed. George Thomas Kurian and Jeffrey D. Schultz (Armonk, N.Y.: M. E. Sharpe, 1997), 1:68; Karen O'Connor, "Abortion," in *Encyclopedia of the American Presidency,* ed. Leonard W. Levy and Louis Fisher (New York: Simon and Schuster, 1994), 1:3–5.

227 Quoted in Monica Crowley, *Nixon Off the Record* (New York: Random House, 1996), 109.

228 Robert Alan Goldberg, *Barry Goldwater* (New Haven: Yale University Press, 1995), 331–333.

229 Hartmann, *From Margin to Mainstream,* 109.

230 Attachment to Ruth Beasley to Birch E. Bayh, Aug. 27, 1970, Box 382, Birch E. Bayh Papers, Lilly Library, Indiana University, Bloomington.

231 Bayh handwritten comment on Beasley to Bayh, Aug. 27, 1970, Box 382, Bayh Papers.

232 "Title Nine's Effect . . . ," Mar. 14, 1975, Box 14, Patricia Lindh and Jeanne Holm Files, GRFL; "Statement by the President," Aug. 19, 1972, Box 28, Armstrong Files, NPM.

233 Hartmann, *From Margin to Mainstream,* 109; Gwendolyn H. Gregory to Armstrong, Sept. 28, 1973, Box 28, Armstrong Files, NPM.

234 Hullin to Dana Mead and Jim Cavanaugh, Feb. 20, 1974, Box 30, Bradley H. Patterson, Jr., Files, SMOF, NPM.

235 Hartmann, *From Margin to Mainstream,* 109; "Muscle in Bias Laws" and "Women's Groups Sue HEW, Labor," n.d., Box 14, Lindh and Holm Files, GRFL.

236 NHC on Geoff Shepard to Nixon through Cole, May 17, 1974, *PNWH,* 6A, Fiche 241.

237 Bradley H. Patterson, Jr., to Garment, June 4, 1974, Box 30, Patterson Files, NPM; Timmons to Garment, Apr. 17, 1974, Box 28, Armstrong Files, NPM.

238 Jean Spencer to Armstrong, June 4, 1974, Box 12, Armstrong Files, NPM; *Wall Street Journal,* June 19, 1974, 3; John Buggs to Peter E. Holmes, n.d., Box 55, Arthur S. Fleming Papers, Dwight D. Eisenhower Library (DDEL), Abilene, Kansas.

239 "Title IX–Civil Rights," June 1975, and *Washington Post,* June 8, 1975, Box 14, Lindh and Holm Files, GRFL.

240 Ford handwritten comment on Weinberger to Ford, Feb. 28, 1975, Box 14, Lindh and Holm Files, GRFL.

241 *Washington Post,* June 8, 1975, Box 14, Lindh and Holm Files, GRFL.

242 *New York Times,* June 16, 1997, 1A, and *USA Today,* Mar. 3, 1997, 9C.

243 *Washington Post,* July 7, 1997, A1 and A10.

244 *USA Today,* Oct. 29, 1997, 5C.

245 *Washington Post,* June 25, 1997, C10; quotations from E. J. Dionne, "Nothing Wacky about Title IX," *Washington Post,* May 13, 1997, A17; *Christian Science Monitor,* Dec. 19, 1995, 13, and Mar. 28, 1997, 1; *New York Times,* Feb. 22, 1998, sec. 8, 1.

246 *Los Angeles Times,* June 18, 1997, A5; quoted in *Washington Post,* June 25, 1997, C10.

247 Howard A. Glickstein to Garment, May 1, 1970, Box 30, Finch Files; Cole to Garment, Nov. 1, 1971, Box 21, HU, WHCF, NPM.

248 Frank Carlucci to Cole, Jan. 8, 1972, Box 21, HU, WHCF, NPM.

249 Congressional Quarterly, *Almanac: 92nd Congress, Second Session, . . . 1972* (Washington, D.C.: Congressional Quarterly, 1972), 732–733.

250 "United States Senator Bill Brock," Apr. 19, 1973, Box 28, Armstrong Files, NPM; Hartmann, *Margin to Mainstream,* 111; Hirschberg to Armstrong, July 11, 1973, and Hirschberg, Memorandum for the Record, Aug. 2, 1973, Box 8, Armstrong Files, NPM.

251 Garment to Armstrong, Nov. 9, 1973, and Weinberger to Armstrong, Nov. 12, 1973, Box 28; Wilfred H. Rommel to Armstrong, Jan. 18, 1974,

and Hirschberg to Armstrong, Feb. 4, 1974, Box 12, Armstrong Files, NPM; Congressional Quarterly, *Almanac: 93rd Congress, 2nd Session, . . . 1974* (Washington, D.C.: Congressional Quarterly, 1974), 165, 170, 134H; "United States Senator Bill Brock," May 14, 1974, Box 28, Armstrong Files, NPM.

252 Hartmann, *From Margin to Mainstream*, 112, 110 (quotation).

253 Graham, *Civil Rights Era*, 476.

254 Woloch, *Women and the American Experience*, 562; *New York Times*, Mar. 26, 1995, 15.

255 *Los Angeles Times*, Nov. 11, 1995, D2.

256 Doris-Jean Burton, "Child-Care," in *Supplement to Dictionary of American History: AARP–Lyme Disease*, ed. Robert H. Ferrell and Joan Hoff (New York: Charles Scribner's Sons, 1996), 1:114–115.

257 "Conversation with the President," Jan. 2, 1972, in *PPP, 1972* (Washington, D.C.: U.S. Government Printing Office, 1974), 17.

258 Hoff, *Law, Gender, and Injustice*, 321.

259 F. Lynn May to Cole through Shepard, June 18, 1974, Box 42, Frederick Lynn May Files, GRFL.

260 NHC on news summaries, Mar. 22, 1969, *PNWH*, 6B, Fiche 3, and Nov. 25, 1971, *PNWH*, 6B, Fiche 66.

261 ANS, Apr. 8, 1969, *PNWH*, 6B, Fiche 5; Aug. 24, 1970, *PNWH*, 6B, Fiche 31; October 1971, *PNWH*, 6B, Fiche 34, Frame 29.

262 ANS, Mar. 22, 1969, *PNWH*, 6B, Fiche 3; Apr. 8, 1971, *PNWH*, 6B, Fiche 5.

Epilogue

1 Leonard Garment, *Crazy Rhythm: My Journey from Brooklyn, Jazz, and Wall Street to Nixon's White House, Watergate, and Beyond* (New York: Times Books, 1997), 220.

2 James Keogh, *This Is Nixon* (New York: G. P. Putnam's Sons, 1956), 85.

3 Richard L. Wilson, "Visit with President Nixon, June 5, 1970," Box 5, Richard L. Wilson Papers, Herbert Hoover Library (HHL), West Branch, Iowa.

4 Roger Wilkins, "Racism Has Its Privileges," in *Double Exposure: Poverty and Race in America*, ed. Chester Hartman (Armonk, N.Y.: M. E. Sharpe, 1997), 174.

5 Gerald David Jaynes and Robin M. Williams, Jr., eds., *A Common Destiny: Blacks and American Society* (Washington, D.C.: National Academy Press, 1989), 312; Wilkins, "Racism Has Its Privileges," 174–175; Hugh Davis Graham, *The Civil Rights Era: Origins and Development of National Policy, 1960–1972* (New York: Oxford University Press, 1990), 453.

6 *USA Today,* Apr. 17, 1997, 8A.

7 *New York Times Book Review,* Apr. 14, 1996, 16.

8 Salim Muwakkil, "Affirmative Action, R.I.P.," in Hartman, *Double Exposure,* 185.

9 Maxine Waters, "Scapegoating," ibid., 178.

10 *The Economist,* "Affirmative Action: Why Bosses Like It," ibid., 180.

11 David L. Kirp, John P. Dwyer, and Larry A. Rosenthal, *Our Town: Race, Housing, and the Soul of Suburbia* (New Brunswick, N.J.: Rutgers University Press, 1995), 4.

12 Richard M. Nixon to John D. Ehrlichman, Jan. 28, 1972, Box 2, John D. Ehrlichman Files, Contested Documents File (CDF), Richard M. Nixon Presidential Materials (NPM), National Archives (NA), College Park, Maryland.

13 Quoted in Kirp, Dwyer, and Rosenthal, *Our Town,* 5.

14 Charles M. Haar, *Suburbs under Siege: Race, Space, and Audacious Judges* (Princeton: Princeton University Press, 1996), 6; Kirp, Dwyer, and Rosenthal, *Our Town,* 8, 181.

15 Haar, *Suburbs under Siege,* xi.

16 Kirp, Dwyer, and Rosenthal, *Our Town,* 174.

17 Ibid., 188.

18 Haar, *Suburbs under Siege,* 186–209; Kirp, Dwyer, and Rosenthal, *Our Town,* 176–195.

19 Memorandum for President's File, Sept. 11, 1970, *Papers of the Nixon White House,* ed. Joan Hoff-Wilson, pt. 2, *The President's Meeting File* (Lanham, Md.: University Publications of America, 1989), Fiche 70-9-6 *(PNWH);* S. Steven Karalekas to President's File, Sept. 25, 1972, *PNWH,* 2, Fiche 72-9-24.

20 John N. Mitchell to Heads of Divisions, July 21, 1970, Box 3, Human Rights (HU), White House Central Files (WHCF), NPM.

21 Nixon to Desi Arnaz, Jan. 27, 1969, and Nixon to Barry M. Goldwater, Jan. 27, 1969, Box 1, HU, WHCF; Ken Cole to Nixon, Aug. 29, 1972, Box 38, Staff Secretary–Courier Files, White House Special Files (WHSF), NPM; "Nixon Administration Accomplishment Report," July 5, 1974, 12, Folder: Hispanic Americans, Anne Armstrong Files, Staff Member and Office Files (SMOF), NPM; John D. Ehrlichman meeting notes, July 2, 1970, Box 1, Ehrlichman Files, CDF, NPM; Julie Leininger Pycior, *LBJ and Mexican Americans: The Paradox of Power* (Austin: University of Texas Press, 1997), 183–187.

22 Quoted in "Nixon Administration Accomplishment Report," July 5, 1974, 21, Folder: Hispanic Americans, Armstrong Files, NPM.

23 Nixon to Ehrlichman, June 28, 1971, Box 2, Ehrlichman Files, CDF, NPM.

24 Elliot L. Richardson to Nixon, Nov. 29, 1972, Box 147, Elliot L. Richardson Papers, Manuscript Division, Library of Congress (LC), Washington, D.C.

25 "Special Message to the Congress on Older Americans," Mar. 23, 1972, and "Memorandum about Age Discrimination in Federal Employment," Sept. 13, 1972, in *Public Papers of the Presidents: Richard Nixon (1972)* (Washington, D.C.: Government Printing Office, 1974), 461–485, 868–869 *(PPP);* Hugh Davis Graham, "The Politics of Clientele Capture," in *Redefining Equality,* ed. Neal Devins and Davison M. Douglas (New York: Oxford University Press, 1998), 112.

26 Congressional Quarterly, *Almanac: 92nd Congress, 2nd Session, . . . 1972* (Washington, D.C.: Congressional Quarterly, 1972), 953–958; "Statement on Signing the Rehabilitation Act of 1973," in *PPP, 1973* (Washington, D.C.: Government Printing Office, 1975), 823–824; Edward D. Berkowitz, "A Historical Preface to the Americans with Disabilities Act," *Journal of Policy History,* 6, no. 1 (1994), 103–107; J. Stanley Pottinger to Richardson, Aug. 22, 1973, Box 199, Richardson Papers; Herbert S. Parmet, *George Bush: The Life of a Lone Star Yankee* (New York: Scribner, 1997), 424–425.

27 Cabinet Committee on Opportunities for the Spanish-Speaking People, Box 7, Fernando E. C. De Baca Files, Gerald R. Ford Library (GRFL), Ann Arbor, Michigan.

28 *Civil Service News,* May 14, 1970, Box 2, Robert E. Hampton Papers, GRFL; George R. LaNoue and John C. Sullivan, "Presumptions for Preferences: The Small Business Administration's Decisions on Groups Entitled to Affirmative Action," *Journal of Policy History,* 6, no. 4 (1994), 439–467.

29 Colson to Ehrlichman, Dec. 20, 1971, 22, Box 4, HU, WHCF, NPM.

30 *Washington Post,* July 28, 1995, A10; *Los Angeles Times,* Nov. 24, 1996, M5; *New York Times,* Jan. 16, 1997, D4, and Nov. 18, 1996, B10.

31 *Los Angeles Times,* Aug. 1, 1995, B9; *New York Times,* Jan. 16, 1997, D4, and Nov. 18, 1996, B10; *Wall Street Journal,* Jan. 15, 1997, B6.

32 Burton I. Kaufman, *The Presidency of James Earl Carter, Jr.* (Lawrence: University Press of Kansas, 1993), 110.

33 Quoted in Keogh, *This Is Nixon,* 89.

34 *New York Times,* July 17, 1992, A14.

35 Ibid., Jan. 21, 1997, A14.

36 Quoted in William C. Berman, *America's Right Turn: From Nixon to Clinton,* 2nd ed. (Baltimore: Johns Hopkins University Press, 1998), 165.

37 "President's Radio Address," Oct. 16, 1993, in *PPP, 1993,* vol. 2 (Washington, D.C.: Government Printing Office, 1994), 1647; "Remarks at the

Funeral Service for President Richard Nixon," Apr. 17, 1994," in *PPP,
1994,* vol. 1 (Washington, D.C. Government Printing Office, 1995), 782.

38 *Los Angeles Times,* Apr. 13, 1997, M5; *Washington Post,* Aug. 24, 1996,
A23; *USA Today,* Nov. 17, 1997, 8A.

39 John David Skrentny, *The Ironies of Affirmative Action: Politics, Culture,
and Justice in America* (Chicago: University of Chicago Press, 1996), 189.

40 Spiro T. Agnew to Nixon, Mar. 16, 1972, Box 93, H. R. Haldeman Files,
WHSF, NPM.

41 *Christian Science Monitor,* Sept. 30, 1997, 3; *New York Times,* Oct. 12,
1997, 17.

42 *Christian Science Monitor,* Sept. 30, 1997, 3.

43 *Los Angeles Times,* Apr. 13, 1997, M5.

44 John Ehrlichman, *Witness to Power: The Nixon Years* (New York: Simon
and Schuster, 1982), 223.

45 Nixon to Ehrlichman, May 17, 1972, Box 3, Ehrlichman Files, CDF,
NPM.

46 Following the GOP's victory in the congressional elections of 1994, Jesse
Jackson quipped, "We survived George Wallace. We'll survive Newt
Gingrich." *New York Times,* Nov. 13, 1994, 32.

47 *New York Times,* Nov. 20, 1994, sec. 4, 6; "The Southern Captivity of the
GOP," *Atlantic Monthly* (June 1998), 55–72.

48 Quoted in Monica Crowley, *Nixon Off the Record* (New York: Random
House, 1996), 108, 198.

49 Roger Wilkins, "Remarks at Hofstra," in *Richard M. Nixon: Politician,
President, Administrator,* ed. Leon Friedman and William F. Levantrosser
(Wesport, Conn.: Greenwood Press, 1991), 186.

50 Joan Hoff, *Nixon Reconsidered* (New York: Basic Books, 1994), 91.

51 Stanley I. Kutler, *The Wars of Watergate: The Last Crisis of Richard Nixon*
(New York: Norton, 1990), xiv.

52 Stanley I. Kutler, *Abuse of Power: The New Nixon Tapes* (New York: Free
Press, 1997).

53 Stewart Alsop, off-the-record interview with Nixon, 1955, Box 47,
Joseph and Stewart Alsop Papers, LC.

54 Stephen E. Ambrose, *Nixon,* vol. 2, *The Triumph of a Politician, 1962–1972*
(New York: Simon and Schuster, 1989), 407.

55 Nixon to Haldeman, Aug. 14, 1972, Box 4, President's Personal File
(PPF), NPM.

56 Ehrlichman meeting notes, Feb. 2, 1970, Box 1, Ehrlichman Files, CDF,
NPM.

57 Nixon to Ehrlichman, Nov. 30, 1970, Box 12, Haldeman Files, CDF,
NPM.

58 Nixon to Ehrlichman, Nov. 30, 1970, Box 12, Haldeman Files, CDF, NPM.

59 Tom Wicker, *One of Us: Richard Nixon and the American Dream* (New York: Random House, 1991), 487.

60 "Remarks at the Dedication of the Lyndon Baines Johnson Library in Austin, Texas, May 22, 1971," in *PPP, 1971* (Washington, D.C.: Government Printing Office, 1972), 656.

Select Bibliography

Manuscript Collections

Abilene, Kansas

Dwight D. Eisenhower Library
Dwight D. Eisenhower Papers
–Post-Presidential Papers
–Ann Whitman File
Arthur S. Flemming Papers
Bryce N. Harlow Records
Robert Humphreys Papers
Robert E. Merriam Papers
James P. Mitchell Papers
Gerald D. Morgan Papers
E. Frederic Morrow Records
William P. Rogers Papers
Fred A. Seaton Papers
Staff Secretary Records
White House Central Files
–Confidential File
–Official File

Ann Arbor, Michigan

BENTLEY HISTORICAL LIBRARY, UNIVERSITY OF MICHIGAN
  Albert Applegate Papers
  George W. Romney Papers
  Richard C. Van Dusen Papers
GERALD R. FORD LIBRARY
  Arthur F. Burns Papers
  Thomas G. Cody Papers
  James E. Connor Files
  Fernando E. C. De Baca Files
  Gerald R. Ford Papers
  –Congressional Papers
  –Vice Presidential Papers
  Robert A. Goldwin Papers
  Robert E. Hampton Papers
  Robert T. Hartmann Files
  Robert T. Hartmann Papers
  Edward Hutchinson Papers
  Myron Kuropas Files
  Patricia Lindh and Jeanne Holm Files
  Frederick Lynn May Files
  Bradley H. Patterson, Jr., Files
  President Ford Committee Records
  Presidential Handwriting File
  A. James Reichley Interview Transcripts
  Norman E. Ross, Jr., Files
  William E. Simon Papers (microfiche)
  White House Central Files
  –Federal Government (FG)
  –Human Rights (HU)

Atlanta, Georgia

JIMMY CARTER LIBRARY
  Presidential Handwriting File
  White House Central Files
  –Indian Affairs (IN)

Austin, Texas

LYNDON B. JOHNSON LIBRARY
  Fred Bohen Files
  Ramsey Clark Papers

Confidential Files
James Gaither Files
Handwriting File
Meeting Notes File
White House Central Files
–Human Rights (HU)
–Speeches (SP)

Bloomington, Indiana

LILLY LIBRARY, INDIANA UNIVERSITY
Birch E. Bayh Papers

Boston, Massachusetts

JOHN F. KENNEDY LIBRARY
John F. Kennedy Pre-Presidential Papers
Robert F. Kennedy Papers
Theodore H. White Papers

Charlottesville, Virginia

ALDERMAN LIBRARY, UNIVERSITY OF VIRGINIA
James J. Kilpatrick Papers
Richard Harding Poff Papers
Hugh D. Scott, Jr., Papers

College Park, Maryland

THEODORE R. MCKELDIN LIBRARY, UNIVERSITY OF MARYLAND
Spiro T. Agnew Papers
Joseph D. Tydings Papers
NATIONAL ARCHIVES
General Records of the Department of Housing and Urban Development, Record Group 207
–Albert Applegate Files
–Richard C. Van Dusen Files
General Records of the Department of the Interior, Record Group 48
–Stewart L. Udall Files
General Records of the Department of Justice, Record Group 60
–David L. Norman Files
General Records of the Department of Labor, Record Group 174
–Peter J. Brennan Files
–James D. Hodgson Files
–George P. Shultz Files

RICHARD M. NIXON PRESIDENTIAL MATERIALS STAFF, NATIONAL ARCHIVES
Anne Armstrong Files
Patrick J. Buchanan Files
Charles L. Clapp Files
Charles W. Colson Files
Confidential Files
Contested Documents File
John W. Dean III Files
Harry S. Dent, Jr., Files
John D. Ehrlichman Files
Robert H. Finch Files
Leonard Garment Files
Alexander M. Haig, Jr., Files
H. R. Haldeman Files and Diary
Egil M. Krogh Files
Frederic V. Malek Files
Bradley H. Patterson, Jr., Files
President's Office Files
President's Personal File
Staff Secretary Files
John C. Whitaker Files
White House Central Files
–Federal Government (FG)
–Human Rights (HU)
–Indian Affairs (IN)
–Procurement (PQ)
White House Tapes

Laguna Niguel, California

NATIONAL ARCHIVES–PACIFIC SOUTHWEST REGION
Richard M. Nixon Pre-Presidential Papers

Lexington, Kentucky

MARGARET I. KING LIBRARY, UNIVERSITY OF KENTUCKY
Creed C. Black Papers
John Sherman Cooper Papers
Rogers C. B. Morton Papers

Norman, Oklahoma

CARL ALBERT CENTER, UNIVERSITY OF OKLAHOMA
Carl Albert Collection

Notre Dame, Indiana

THEODORE M. HESBURGH LIBRARY, UNIVERSITY OF NOTRE DAME
  Theodore M. Hesburgh, C.S.C., Papers

Pasadena, California

PRIVATE PAPERS OF ROBERT H. FINCH (COURTESY STORAGE AT OCCIDENTAL
COLLEGE LIBRARY AND RICHARD NIXON LIBRARY AND BIRTHPLACE)

Pekin, Illinois

EVERETT McKINLEY DIRKSEN CONGRESSIONAL LEADERSHIP RESEARCH
CENTER
  Everett McKinley Dirksen Papers

St. Paul, Minnesota

MINNESOTA HISTORICAL SOCIETY
  Maurice H. Stans Papers

Sleepy Hollow, New York

ROCKEFELLER ARCHIVE CENTER
  Commonwealth Fund Archives
  General Education Board Archives
  John H. Knowles Papers
  Graham T. Molitor Papers
  Rockefeller Brothers Fund Archives
  Rockefeller Family Archives
  –Record Group 2, Office of Messrs. Rockefeller Files
  –Record Group 4, Nelson A. Rockefeller Personal Papers
  –Record Group 9, Winthrop Rockefeller Papers (microfilm)
  –Record Group 15, Nelson A. Rockefeller Gubernatorial Papers
  –Record Group 26, Nelson A. Rockefeller Vice Presidential Papers

Stanford, California

HOOVER INSTITUTION ARCHIVES, STANFORD UNIVERSITY
  Annelise Graebner Anderson Papers
  Chester E. Finn, Jr., Papers
  Benjamin F. Holman Papers
  Jay Lovestone Papers
  Frederic V. Malek Papers
  Robert C. Mardian Papers
  Sidney P. Marland, Jr., Papers

Raymond Moley Papers
Richard M. Nixon Collection
Laurence H. Silberman Papers
John G. Veneman Papers

Tucson, Arizona

UNIVERSITY OF ARIZONA LIBRARY
Stewart L. Udall Papers

Washington, D.C.

LIBRARY OF CONGRESS
Joseph and Stewart Alsop Papers
Association of Former Members of Congress Papers
Leonard Garment Papers
Leadership Conference on Civil Rights Papers
National Urban League Papers
Joseph L. Rauh, Jr., Papers
Elliot L. Richardson Papers
Roy Wilkins Papers

West Branch, Iowa

HERBERT HOOVER LIBRARY
Bourke B. Hickenlooper Papers
Herbert Hoover Papers
Walter N. Thayer Papers
Walter Trohan Papers
Richard L. Wilson Papers

Yorba Linda, California

RICHARD NIXON LIBRARY AND BIRTHPLACE
Richard M. Nixon Pre-Presidential Papers

Interviews and Oral Histories

Author's Interviews

William H. Brown III, Sept. 15, 1994, Philadelphia, Pennsylvania (telephone)
John D. Ehrlichman, Feb. 6, 1995, Atlanta, Georgia (telephone)
Theodore M. Hesburgh, C.S.C., Oct. 24, 1995, Notre Dame, Indiana
Sallyanne Payton, July 27, 1994, Ann Arbor, Michigan
George P. Shultz, Oct. 17, 1995, Stanford, California (telephone)

Suffragists Oral History Project, Regional Oral History Office, Bancroft Library,
University of California, Berkeley, California

Alice Paul, May 10–12, 1973

Oral History Program, California State University, Fullerton, California

Robert H. Finch, June 17, 1981

Oral History Research Office, Butler Library, Columbia University, New York

Robert H. Finch, Aug. 14, 1967
Stephen Hess, June 14, 1972
Kenneth B. Keating, Feb. 2, 1968
Robert L. Kunzig, Sept. 8, 1972
E. Frederic Morrow, Apr. 15. 1968

Dwight D. Eisenhower Library, Abilene, Kansas

Herbert Brownell, Feb. 24, 1977
Robert E. Cushman, Mar. 4, 1977
Arthur S. Flemming, June 2 and 3, 1988
Robert E. Hampton, Feb. 6, 1975
Bryce N. Harlow, May 30, 1974
E. Frederic Morrow, Feb. 23, 1977

A. James Reichley Interview Transcripts, Gerald R. Ford Library,
Ann Arbor, Michigan

Harry S. Dent, Jr., Apr. 3, 1978
Robert H. Finch, Mar. 8, 1978
Leonard Garment, Oct. 19, 1977
Bryce N. Harlow, Nov. 3, 1977
Stephen Hess, Oct. 21, 1977
Barbara Greene Kilberg, Dec. 1, 1977
Richard Kleindienst, Aug. 30, 1977
Jerris Leonard, Oct. 31, 1977
John N. Mitchell, Sept. 18, 1969
Sonny Montgomery, Nov. 9, 1977
Daniel P. Moynihan, July 13, 1978
Richard M. Nixon, Sept. 28, 1967
Leon Panetta, Sept. 19, 1977
Bradley H. Patterson, Jr., Nov. 11, 1977
Richardson Preyer, Oct. 21, 1977
Raymond K. Price, Mar. 2, 1978

George P. Shultz, Jan. 4, 1978
Louis Stokes, Sept. 15, 1977
David Treen, Oct. 5, 1977
John G. Veneman, Sept. 12, 1977

Lyndon B. Johnson Library, Austin, Texas

Clifford L. Alexander, Nov. 1, 1971, and June 4, 1973
James Farmer, July 20, 1971
J. Strom Thurmond, May 7, 1979
Roy Wilkins, Apr. 1, 1969

John F. Kennedy Library, Boston, Massachusetts

"Kennedy's Call to King: Six Perspectives," Fall 1988
  Louis Martin
  Sam Proctor
  Sargent Shriver
  Franklin Williams
Martin Luther King, Jr., Mar. 9, 1964
Louis Martin, Apr. 7, 1966

Oral History Collection of Former Members of Congress, Manuscript Division, Library of Congress, Washington, D.C.

Charles E. Goodell, June 6, 1979
Martha W. Griffiths, Oct. 28 and 30, 1979
Hugh D. Scott, Jr., Sept. 13, 1976

Richard M. Nixon Presidential Materials Staff, National Archives, College Park, Maryland

Charles W. Colson, Jan. 12, 1973, and June 15 and Sept. 21, 1988
Bradley H. Patterson, Jr., Sept. 10, 1974
Elliot L. Richardson, May 31, 1988
Constance Stuart, Aug. 15, 1988

Southern Oral History Project, Wilson Library, University of North Carolina, Chapel Hill, North Carolina

Harry S. Dent, Jr., Feb. 22, 1974
J. Strom Thurmond, Feb. 1, 1974
George C. Wallace, July 15, 1974

Index

A. Philip Randolph Institute, 102

Abernathy, Ralph David, 132, 159, 166, 167–170, 197

Abortion rights, 223, 248, 250–252, 257

Acheson, Dean, 84

Affirmative action: as policy, 8, 21, 97–98, 130, 155–156, 263; post-Nixon reactions to, 96, 149, 261–262, 265–266; women's rights and, 110, 116, 121, 123, 240–248, 257; white-collar workers and, 115–122; colleges and universities and, 116–117, 123, 266; enforcement of, through litigation, 119–120. *See also* Hiring goals; "Hometown plans"; Philadelphia Plan

Africa, 11, 159, 270

African Americans: as voting bloc, 7, 17, 20, 48, 73, 128, 134, 165–166; higher education and, 8, 121, 125, 127, 151–155, 260; racial strife and, 47, 76, 101, 106, 127–128, 174, 219, 263; office holding and, 51, 94, 114, 164, 182, 186;

Jewish Americans and, 117; middle-class expansion among, 131, 151, 176, 261; minority enterprise, reactions of, 132, 139–140; in mass media, 151; polarization and, 158, 185–187; invitations to White House events and, 175, 178–179; as "silent black majority," 176–178; politics of, contrasted with Native Americans, 188–189, 192, 219; government recognition of rights of, 263

Afro-American Voter, The (magazine), 166–167

Age discrimination, 264

Agnew, Spiro T.: school desegregation and, 6–7, 20, 34; as Nixonian, 13; Native American policy and, 194, 196–198, 200, 201, 202, 207, 208, 209, 210, 213, 214, 220; as governor, 197; sexism of, 226; on civil rights policies, 268

Alaska Federation of Natives (AFN), 204, 205, 206

Alaska Native Claims Settlement Act (1971), 203–206, 207

Alaska natives, 189, 196, 202, 204

Alaska Statehood Act (1958), 204

Alcatraz Island, seizure of, 195, 198–199, 201, 202, 213, 218

Aleuts, 149, 204

Alexander, Clifford L., 118

Alexander v. Homes County, 31–32, 34, 36–37

Allan, Virginia R., 230–231

Allen, James B., 236

Allott, Gordon, 203, 207, 210

Ambrose, Stephen E., 270, 276n23

American Conservative Union, 23

American Federation of Labor-Congress of Industrial Organizations (AFL-CIO), 99–100

American Hellenic Educational Progressive Association, 263

American Indian Movement (AIM), 192, 201, 212–215, 217, 218

American Indian Press Association, 218–219

American Jewish Committee, 117

Americans for Democratic Action, 120

Americans with Disabilities Act, 265

American Telephone and Telegraph Company (AT&T), 120–121

Anderson, Annelise G., 234

Anderson, Clinton P., 202–203

Anderson, John B., 90

Andrews, John, 222, 223

Antiballistic missile (ABM) program, 30, 203

Antiwar protests, 72, 89, 92

Appointments: to federal courts, 17, 164, 182; of Southerners, 19; to Supreme Court, 19–20, 39, 85, 86, 88–89, 91, 107, 170, 237–238; of African Americans, 51, 114, 164, 182, 186; of women, 164, 223, 224, 227–228, 237–238, 240, 244–247, 257; of Spanish-surnamed persons, 264

Apprenticeships, 99

Arizona, 95, 218

Armed forces, desegregation of, 4

Armstrong, Anne, 236, 239, 246, 255

Arnaz, Desi, 264

Arts funding, 10

Asian Americans, 9, 114, 149, 262

Athletics (Title IX), 252–255, 260

Bailey, Pearl, 180, 183

Baltimore Afro-American (newspaper), 197

Banks, Dennis J., 212–214, 216–217, 218

Banks, minority-owned, 127, 141, 144–145

Bayh, Birch E., 86–88, 236, 245, 252, 255, 260

Beeman, Alice L., 231

"Benign neglect" policies, 5, 173–174, 176, 178, 204

Bentley, Helen Delich, 227, 236, 244

Between Two Worlds (Carnegie Commission), 155

Bewley, Tom, 10

Bickel, Alexander M., 33

Bilingual education, 264, 265

Black capitalism, 126, 127–133, 136, 139, 140. *See also* Minority business enterprise

Black colleges, 8, 125, 127, 151–155, 260

Black Economic Union (BEU), 147

Black Enterprise (magazine), 151

Black Panther Party (BPP), 179

Black Power, 125–126, 132, 156, 223

Black separatism, 5, 14, 144

Black Silent Majority Committee, 177

Blair, Stanley, 33

Bloch, Malise C., 245

"Blockbusting," 45, 48

Blue-collar workers, 98, 99–115, 107, 112, 143

Blue Lake, N. M., 202–203, 207

Bond, Julian, 184

Bookbinder, Hyman, 117

Bracken, Frank A., 205, 206

Bradley, Bill, 263

Brando, Marlon, 195, 216
Brennan, Peter J., 113, 114, 226
"Bridges to Human Dignity" (radio broadcasts), 129, 135, 143
Brimmer, Andrew F., 139, 145, 155
Brock, William, 255
Brooke, Edward W., 176, 180
Brown, Dee, 215
Brown, James (singer), 184
Brown, Jim (football player), 147, 184
Brown, Robert J.: staff responsibilities of, 115, 178; fair employment and, 115; minority business enterprise and, 141, 142, 143, 144; political underhandedness and, 147, 148; black colleges and, 152–153; on civil rights policies, 176; women's rights and, 248
Brown, William H., III, 98, 118–121, 122, 179, 247
Brownell, Herbert A., 72–73
Brown II (1955), 27
Brown v. Board of Education (1954), 4, 18, 24, 27, 32, 37, 159
Bruce, Louis R., 196, 201, 211–212
Buchanan, Patrick J.: on Nixon's political style, 12, 23, 171; school desegregation and, 31–33; on Colson, 112; on civil disorders, 127–128; on the black vote, 128; staff responsibilities of, 133; election strategies and, 184; women's rights and, 234, 239, 249, 251
Buckley, James L., 66, 131–132
Buggs, John, 114
Bull, Stephen, 196
Bunche, Ralph J., 172
Bureau of Indian Affairs (BIA): criticism of, 188, 192; reform of, 192, 195, 196, 201, 211–212, 220; funding of, 208–209; seizure of, 210, 213–214, 218. *See also* Wounded Knee siege
Bureau of the Budget, 56, 130, 136. *See also* Office of Management and Budget (OMB)
Burns, Arthur F., 10; staff responsibilities of, 49, 195, 229; voting rights and, 79, 80, 81;

bank deposit program and, 145; Native American policy and, 195–196, 204; sexism of, 226; women's rights and, 228, 229–230, 248
Burrell, Berkeley G., 148
Bury My Heart at Wounded Knee (Brown), 215
Bush, George H. W.: civil rights record of, 24; school desegregation and, 35; "southern strategy" and, 41, 42, 185–186; fair housing and, 47–48; affirmative action and, 124, 187; minority business enterprise and, 148, 149; Willie Horton ad and, 186; abortion rights and, 252; disabled persons and, 265
Busing, 8, 12, 16, 18, 32, 33, 55, 155, 260, 262; constitutional amendments on, 39, 40, 171, 237; moratorium on, 39, 86; reactions to, 42–43; "southern strategy" and, 184, 268
Butler, Lewis H., 201
Buzhardt, J. Fred, 19
Byrd, Harry F., 16, 145

Cabinet Committee on Opportunities for Spanish-Speaking People (CCOSSP), 264, 265
California, 56, 95, 143–144, 150, 174, 263
Callaway, Howard H. "Bo," 78, 79
Cambodian incursion, 72, 89, 93
Campaign finance, 148
Carlucci, Frank C., 213, 255
Carnegie Commission on Higher Education, 155
Carswell, G. Harrold, 20, 88–89, 90, 91
Carter, Jimmy: school desegregation and, 43; fair housing and, 68; affirmative action and, 123–124; minority business enterprise and, 148–149; black colleges and, 155; Congressional Black Caucus and, 185; appointments by, 186; Native American policy and, 219, 220; women's rights and, 250, 252; civil rights record of, 266–267
Cater, Douglass, 26–27

Catholics, 7, 22, 60, 251
Celler, Emanuel, 77, 89
Chamberlain, Wilt, 133
Chapin, Dwight, 226
Cheek, James E., 153
Chicago Defender (newspaper), 183
Child care programs, 223, 248–250, 256–257
Child Development Act, 249
China, 208
Cisneros, Henry G., 69–70
Citizen's Advisory Council on the Status of Women, 229, 235
Civil disorders, 47, 72, 76, 89, 92, 192, 210–211, 213–219, 234–235, 266. *See also* Racial strife
Civil Rights Act (1957), 73–74, 160, 164
Civil Rights Act (1960), 75, 85
Civil Rights Act (1964), 24, 85, 99, 102, 104–105, 108, 115, 119, 229, 238, 242
Civil Rights Commission: school desegregation and, 35, 175; fair housing and, 62; voting rights and, 74–75, 78, 82–83; affirmative action and, 102, 104; minority business enterprise and, 144; Hesburgh appointment to, 167, 173; women's rights and, 223; expansion of, 248, 255
Civil Service Commission, 98, 115–116, 122
Clay, William L., 181
"Clean Elections" bill, 148
Cleaver, Eldridge, 179
Clinton, Hillary Rodham, 224
Clinton, William Jefferson: minority business enterprise and, 148, 149; speeches of, 186, 267; women's rights and, 254–255; limited government and, 263; affirmative action and, 266; civil rights record of, 267–268
Cole, Kenneth, 113, 147, 207, 216, 239
Colleges and universities, 116–117, 123, 248, 252–255, 266. *See also* Black colleges

Collier, John, 190
Colmer, William, 78
Colson, Charles W.: staff responsibilities of, 13, 20, 23, 112; school desegregation and, 66; voting age and, 89–90; racial views of, 112; affirmative action and, 112–113; welfare reform and, 112, 113; Fletcher and, 113; women's rights and, 231, 235, 247, 249, 251; bilingual education and, 265
Commission on Population Growth, 49, 251
Commission on the Status of Women, 247
Committee on Equal Employment Opportunity, 101
Congress: fair housing and, 47, 56, 66; school desegregation and, 66; voting rights and, 73–74, 77–78, 80, 82–84, 86–88, 90; redistricting and, 94, 96; affirmative action and, 104–105, 108, 118–119, 123; antipoverty measures and, 129–130; minority business enterprise and, 136–137, 140, 142, 143, 146–147; Black Caucus, 146, 180–181, 185; Native American policy and, 190–191, 200–201, 202–210, 217–218, 220; women's rights and, 232, 235–236, 238, 247, 249, 255, 257; age discrimination and, 264; disabled persons and, 264–265; "southern strategy" and, 268–269
Constitutional amendments: on busing, 39, 171, 237; on voting age, 89, 94; on women's rights (ERA), 223, 230, 232–240, 252, 255, 257, 260
Construction trades, 99, 142–144. *See also* Philadelphia Plan
Cook, Marlow W., 87
Cooke, Terrence, Cardinal, 251
Cooper, John Sherman, 123
Corporations, 117, 120, 122, 131, 136, 148, 266
Cox, Lawrence M., 59
Credit, financial, 248, 255
Crow, John, 211, 212

Daley, Richard J., 26, 65
Dallek, Robert, 5
Dawes Act (1887), 190, 204
Day care programs, 223, 248–250, 256–257
Dean, John W. III, 238
Deer, Ada, 217
Deloria, Vine, Jr., 192, 195
Dent, Harry S., Jr.: staff responsibilities of, 13, 23; appointment of, 19; "national strategy" and, 20; welfare reform and, 21; school desegregation and, 21, 30, 33–34, 36; voting rights and, 80; affirmative action and, 107; black capitalism and, 134–135; women's rights and, 244–245
Department of Commerce, 127, 134
Department of Defense, 142, 216
Department of Health, Education, and Welfare (HEW), 26–28, 117, 145, 153, 245, 264
Department of Housing and Urban Development, 56, 64–65, 66, 69, 103, 246. See also Fair housing
Department of Justice: school desegregation and, 16, 23–24, 27, 28, 30, 37; re-election strategy and, 39; fair housing and, 44, 48, 55, 60, 63–64, 67, 69; voting rights and, 75, 83, 94–95; affirmative action and, 119–120; Native American policy and, 209, 210; Wounded Knee siege and, 216; women's rights and, 242, 246; credit, financial and, 255; organized crime terminology in, 263
Department of Labor, 101–102, 103, 110, 145, 243–244, 246, 248
Department of the Interior, 209, 246. See also Bureau of Indian Affairs (BIA)
Dionne, E. J., 254
Dirksen, Everett M., 47, 80–81, 104–105, 118, 119, 169
"Dirty tricks," 38–39, 53, 208
Disabled persons, 264–265
Dole, Robert J., 265–266, 269
Douglas, Paul, 73

Drummond, Geoffrey, 30
Drummond, Roscoe, 30
Dunlop, John T., 117
Dwyer, Florence P., 228–231, 236, 241

East, Catherine, 229, 230
East Europeans, 114, 263
Ebony (magazine), 151
Economic Development Administration (EDA), 145–146, 209
Economic Opportunity Amendments (1971), 249–250
Economist, The (magazine), 206
Ehrlichman, John D.: staff responsibilities of, 12, 23, 49, 112, 174, 195, 196; as Nixonian, 13–14; welfare reform and, 21, 196; domestic policy agenda and, 22, 40; school desegregation and, 33; Romney and, 50, 60–61, 67; fair housing and, 57, 59, 62–63, 65–67; voting rights and, 89, 91, 94; affirmative action and, 109, 112, 115; minority business enterprise and, 140, 141, 142, 146, 147; black colleges and, 152–154; civil rights leaders and, 169, 178; National Urban League and, 183; Native American policy and, 196–197, 200, 201, 202, 205–206, 212, 213; Watergate and, 218; women's rights and, 225, 231, 235, 238, 245, 248, 250; "southern strategy" and, 268
Eisenhower, Dwight D.: record of, 4, 22, 46; voting rights and, 72–74; fair employment and, 99; Small Business Administration and, 130; Native American policies and, 191; women's rights and, 233
Eisenhower, Julie Nixon, 238
Elderly citizens' rights, 264
Ellender, Allen J., 142
Ellington, Duke, 166–167, 183
Employment opportunity. See Fair employment
Employment quotas. See Hiring goals
Enterprise zones, 44–45, 69
Equal Credit Opportunity Act (1974), 255

Equal Employment Opportunity Act (1972), 117, 120

Equal Employment Opportunity Commission (EEOC), 5, 117–120, 209, 240, 247

Equal Pay Act (1963), 238, 247, 257

Equal Rights Amendment (ERA), 223, 230, 232–240, 252, 255, 257, 260

Ervin, Sam J., 78, 82, 86–87, 105, 235–236

Eskimos, 149, 204. *See also* Alaska natives

Ethnic neighborhoods, 60, 68–69

Evers, Charles, 11, 171, 172–173

Executive Orders: on armed forces desegregation, 4; on fair housing, 16, 46; on affirmative action, 101, 115–116, 240; on minority business enterprise, 134, 136, 146, 149; on Native American policy, 210, 220; on women's rights, 240, 242

Fair employment, 4–5, 6, 8, 98–100, 116, 159, 256. *See also* Affirmative action; Hiring goals

Fair housing, 44–70, 262; policy statements on, 14, 46, 62–65, 135; executive orders and, 16, 46; enforcement of, through litigation, 44, 48, 55, 60, 63–64, 65, 69, 263; withholding of federal funds and, 45, 49, 54, 56, 58, 61; open communities and, 54–59; ethnic neighborhoods and, 60, 68–69; working group on, 62–63; regulation of, 62, 64–65, 69; reactions to, 64–65

Fair Housing Act (1968), 5, 44–45, 47–48, 55

Family and Parental Leave Act, 257

Family Assistance Plan (FAP), 21, 23, 39, 67, 112, 113, 156, 248–249

Family planning services, 251

Farmer, James, 11, 97, 173, 174, 177

Faubus, Orval, 24, 164

Federal Acknowledgment Project, 220

Federal Bureau of Investigation (FBI), 179, 217

Federal Communications Commission, 244

Federal courts: appointments to, 17, 164, 182; school desegregation and, 27, 29; voting rights and, 75, 83, 94–95; affirmative action and, 96, 119–120; black colleges and, 151–152; Native Americans and, 220; women's rights and, 229, 236, 242. *See also* Supreme Court

Federal procurement, 125, 127, 130, 141–144

Finch, Robert H., 27–30, 63, 152, 153, 162, 168, 225, 227, 245, 248

Fisher, Frank, 66

Flanigan, Peter M., 231

Flemming, Arthur S., 43, 176, 264

Fletcher, Arthur A., 98, 103–104, 105, 106, 111, 113, 174, 177, 248

Ford, Gerald R.: school desegregation and, 43; fair housing and, 47, 68; Romney's resignation and, 53; voting rights and, 77, 79, 82, 88, 95–96; affirmative action and, 108, 117; minority business enterprise and, 148; black colleges and, 155; Congressional Black Caucus and, 185; "open door policy" of, 186; Native American policy and, 209, 220; women's rights and, 237–238, 250, 253–254, 255

Ford Foundation, 152

Ford Motor Company, 136

Franklin, John Hope, 261, 268

Freedom of choice plans, 18, 27, 37–38

Friedan, Betty, 227, 235

Funding, withholding of: school desegregation and, 26, 28–29, 37, 56; fair housing and, 45, 49, 54, 56, 58, 61; colleges and universities and, 116, 152–154; athletics and, 253

Garment, Leonard: policy agendas and, 1, 12, 174–175, 259; arts funding and, 10; school desegregation and, 13, 14, 33, 35; fair housing and, 14, 62; voting rights and, 14, 84, 90–91, 94; on Romney, 52; liberalism of, 53; affirmative action and, 105, 112, 114, 118, 121; minority business enterprise and, 141–146; black colleges and, 152–153; civil rights leaders and, 166, 177, 182; Congressional Black Caucus and, 181; National Urban League and, 183; Native American policy and, 195, 197, 198–199, 200–201, 202, 205–206, 207, 209, 210, 211–213, 216–217; executive branch reorganization and, 211; staff responsibilities of, 218; women's rights and, 225, 231, 235, 236–237, 238, 253, 255, 257

Gaston County v. United States, 78, 79–80, 94

Gay rights, 257

General Allotment Act of (1887), 190, 204

General Services Administration (GSA), 62, 137

Georgia, 28, 79

Gifford Pinchot National Forest, 210

Gingrich, Newt, 41–42, 269

Glaser, Vera, 228–229, 230, 231

Glass Ceiling Commission, 256

Glickstein, Howard A., 35, 78, 173, 175, 255

Goldwater, Barry M., 17, 20, 23, 41, 50–51, 87, 203, 252, 264

Government contracts, 99–102, 103–104, 110, 159; set-asides in, 125, 141–142, 149, 265; Section 8(a) programs and, 138, 141–142, 147–148

Graham, Hugh Davis, 2, 106, 371n174

Gramm, Phil, 269

Gray, L. Patrick, 34

Great Society programs, 7, 22, 23, 127, 138, 191

Green, Edith, 241, 242, 252

Greenspan, Alan, 128, 133

Green v. New Kent County, 27

Gregory, Gwendolyn, 252–253

Gregory, Jack, 194

Griffin, Robert P., 203

Griffiths, Martha W., 235

Griggs v. Duke Power Co., 115

Gurney, Edward J., 34

Hagerty, James C., 100

Haig, Alexander M., Jr., 121, 226

Haldeman, H. R.: on Nixon, 6, 23; domestic policy agenda and, 11; staff responsibilities of, 13, 23, 112, 133; on Romney, 52; on Garment, 53; affirmative action and, 109, 114; black colleges and, 152; civil rights leaders and, 169, 172–173; White House events and, 175, 178–179; "silent black majority" and, 177; election strategies and, 184; racial views of, 184; Native American policies and, 193, 203; sexism of, 226; women's rights and, 231, 239, 251

Hamilton, Charles V., 176

Hamilton, Clarence, 214

Hampton, Robert E., 115–116, 121

Hansen, Derek, 147

Hansen, Tom, 254

Hardin, Clifford M., 210

Harlow, Bryce N., 17, 33–34, 53, 82, 88–89, 91, 141, 235

Harris, Fred R., 202, 203

Harris, LaDonna, 219

Harris, Patricia Roberts, 69

Hart, Philip A., 7, 53, 86–87, 123, 260

Hartke, Vance, 78

Hatfield, Mark O., 203

Hauser, Rita E., 247, 251

Havasupai land claims, 218

Hawkins, David, 98

Hayden, Carl, 232

Haynsworth, Clement F., Jr., 20, 86, 88, 90, 107

Heckler, Margaret M., 228, 236

Heclo, Hugh, 2

Hesburgh, Theodore M., 13, 75–76, 78, 158, 167, 173, 175–176

Hess, Stephen, 53, 119

Hickel, Walter J., 62, 196, 198, 204, 210, 211

Higher Education Act (1965), 153–154, 155
Higher Education Amendments (1972), 208, 252–255, 260
Hill, Herbert, 104
Hills, Carla A., 67
Hills v. Gautreaux, 65
Hiring goals, 8, 101–102, 114; Philadelphia Plan and, 85, 103–105, 110; differentiation from quotas, 105, 114, 122–124, 143, 244; Civil Service Commission and, 115–116; colleges and universities and, 116–117, 123; corporations and, 120, 266; women's rights and, 240–247
Hispanic-Americans, 7, 95–96, 114, 130, 149, 262, 263–264, 265
Hodgson, James D., 110, 241, 242–243, 248
Hoff, Joan, 2
Holmes v. Alexander, 260
Holt, Leila, 234
"Hometown plans," 98, 110–111, 114, 121, 122
Hook, Sidney, 117
Hoover, Herbert, 12, 110
Hoover Commission on Government Organization, 190–191
House of Representatives: Appropriations Committee, 142; Banking and Currency Committee, 56; Judiciary Committee, 81, 82, 236; Select Committee on Small Business, 137
Housing and Community Development Act (1974), 69
Housing and Urban Development Act (1968), 55
Housing desegregation. *See* Fair housing
Hruska, Roman L., 80
Hullin, Tod, 147, 253
Humphrey, Hubert H., 19, 42, 48, 66, 130, 132–133, 264
Huston, Tom Charles, 179

Illinois, 26, 29, 56, 65, 95, 101, 111
"Independent Conservative Party," 42

Indiana University, 252, 253
Indian Claims Limitation Act (1982), 220
Indian Financing Act (1974), 218
"Indian New Deal," 190
Indian Reorganization Act (1934), 190
Indian Self-Determination Act (1975), 218
Individual initiative solutions. *See* Black capitalism
Inflation. *See* Wage and price controls
Irish-Americans, 60, 263
Italians, 7, 20, 60, 263

Jackson, Henry M. "Scoop," 68, 203, 206, 260
Jackson, Jesse, 95, 123, 151, 266, 268
Jackson, Samuel C., 54–55, 66
Jackson State University, student killings at, 91, 152
James v. Valtierra, 64
Javits, Jacob R., 78, 119, 123
Jenkins, John L., 138
Jet (magazine), 151
Jewish Americans, 10, 117, 123, 175, 270
Job Corps, 138
Johnson, Lyndon B.: rights record of, 4–5, 6; racial views of, 11; "southern strategy" of, 17; school desegregation and, 26–27, 30, 172; fair housing and, 46, 47; on Nixon, 51; voting rights and, 73–74, 76, 94–95; affirmative action and, 97, 101–102, 115, 130, 172, 240; minority business enterprise and, 129–130, 137; black colleges and, 153; "benign neglect" and, 174; Black Panthers and, 179; speeches by, 186, 191; Native American policies and, 191; sexism of, 227; women's rights and, 232; age discrimination and, 264
Jordan, Vernon E., 155, 183
Josephy, Alvin M., 194–195, 196, 201
Judicial appointments. *See* Federal courts; Supreme Court
Jury trials, 73–74, 160

Kaufman, Burton I., 266
Kelly, Lawrence C., 220

Kemp, Jack F., 45, 69

Kennedy, David M., 144

Kennedy, Edward M., 7, 66, 78, 87–88, 193–194, 203, 208, 209, 260

Kennedy, Ethel, 199

Kennedy, John F.: rights record of, 4–5, 6, 162; "southern strategy" of, 17, 164–165; school desegregation and, 30; fair housing and, 46; on Romney, 50; jury trial amendment and, 73, 161; affirmative action and, 97, 101; black colleges and, 152–153; speeches by, 186; Native American policies and, 191; sexism of, 227; women's rights and, 229, 232

Kennedy, Robert F., 42, 161–162, 191, 193

Kennedy Park Homes Ass'n v. City of Lackawanna, N.Y., 63

Kent State University, student killings at, 72, 91, 93, 152, 199

Kerner Commission, 262

Kilberg, Barbara Greene, 197, 200–201, 202–203, 204–205, 211

Kilberg, William J., 110

King, Martin Luther, Jr., 11, 17, 24, 74, 159–162, 172, 182–183

King, Martin Luther, Sr., 162

Kirk, Claude, 33

Kissinger, Henry A., 10, 226

Kleppe, Thomas, 147–148

Knauer, Virginia H., 244

Knowland, William, 73–74

Koontz, Elizabeth Duncan, 242, 243

Krogh, Egil M., 199, 204

Kunzig, Robert L., 141–142

Kutler, Stanley I., 270

Labor unions, 16, 100–101, 103, 104, 106, 107, 109, 113–114, 121

Laird, Melvin R., 142, 217

Land claims, Native American, 189, 196, 201, 202–206, 207, 209, 210, 218, 219–220

Law and order, 93, 127, 128–129, 132, 167

Lawson, Steven, 96

Leadership Conference on Civil Rights, 104, 132, 139, 170–171, 174, 175

Leonard, Jerris, 28, 35, 48, 79–80

Lerner, Max, 201

Lewis, Orme, 191

"Liberal feminism," 229, 230, 241, 247

"Liberals for Muskie," 39

Lindsay, John V., 111

Literacy tests, 71, 75–84, 87, 92–93, 96

Lodge, Henry Cabot, 165

Loesch, Harrison, 201, 210, 212

Louisiana, 36, 152

Lowery, Fred, 164

Low-income housing, 45, 49, 54–55, 60, 62, 67, 69, 263

Lynn, James T., 67

MacDonald, Peter, 188, 210, 212

Macy, John, 227

Maine, 220

Malcolm X, 125–126

Malek, Frederic V., 113, 147, 236–237, 245–247

Manatos, Mike, 47

Mansfield, Mike, 73, 87, 96, 118

Mardian, Robert C., 34

Marijuana, legalization of, 251

Martin, Louis, 161

Massachusetts, 43, 56

Matter of Simple Justice, A (Women's Rights Task Force), 230–231

May, Catherine D., 228

May, F. Lynn, 257

McClaughry, John, 143

McClellan, John L., 38

McCoy, Donald R., 4

McCrary, John Reagan, 233

McCulloch, William, 77, 79–80, 82

McDonalds Corporation, 136

McGinty, Milton O., 140

McGovern, George S., 40, 42, 66, 117, 123, 202, 203, 208, 246

McKissick, Floyd, 125–126, 132, 179

McNair, Robert E., 30

McPherson, Harry, 240

Means, Russell, 188, 212–217, 218

Meany, George, 99–100, 104, 107–108, 112, 113

Meese, Edwin, III, 149

Menominee Restoration Act, 217–218

Mexican-American Legal Defense and Education Fund, 95

Mexican-Americans, 9, 20, 60, 78, 95–96, 114, 130, 194

Michigan, 37, 40, 42, 56–59, 66, 111

Miller, Emma Guffey, 232, 234

Milliken v. Bradley, 42

Minimum income programs, 14, 248

Mink, Patsy T., 241, 242

Minorities: office holding and, 94; affirmative action and, 114, 123; federal jobs and, 116; respect for institutions of, 126, 151, 152, 189, 220; middle class expansion by, 261; "forgotten," 263

Minority Business Development Agency, 148

Minority business enterprise, 8, 133–140, 141–146, 149–151, 155–156; reactions to, 38, 132–133, 139–140; cabinet committee on, 134, 136; floundering of, 136–139; policy statements on, 141, 143; Native Americans and, 206, 208. *See also* Black capitalism; National Advisory Council on Minority Business Enterprise

Minority businesses, 129, 260; banks, 127, 141, 144–145; construction firms, 142; white ownership of, 147, 149; definition of, 148

Minority Enterprise Small Business Investment Corporations (MESBICs), 136, 138–139, 146–147, 149–150

Mississippi, school desegregation in, 30–31, 37

Missouri, 63–64, 102

Mitchell, Clarence, 47, 78, 82–84, 85, 92, 95, 109, 120–121, 166, 170, 171, 175

Mitchell, James P., 99–100, 101

Mitchell, John N.: on domestic policy, 1; school desegregation and, 27–30, 63,

290n187; fair housing and, 44, 63–64; Romney's firing/resignation and, 61; voting rights and, 71, 79–84, 88–89, 94–95; affirmative action and, 105; antitrust and, 131; Native American policy and, 210; women's rights and, 235; organized crime terminology and, 263

Mitsubishi Motors, 266

Model Cities program, 53

"Modern Republicanism," 3, 22, 259, 267

Moley, Raymond A., 17

Molitor, Graham T., 18, 132

Morgan, Edward L., 36, 40

Morris, William R., 65

Morrow, E. Frederic, 161–162

Morsell, John A., 170

Morton, Rogers C. B., 205, 207, 210, 211–212, 228, 231, 245–246

Moynihan, Daniel P.: "benign neglect" and, 5, 173–174, 176, 178; racial views of, 11; staff responsibilities of, 12; welfare reform and, 14, 21, 48, 196; fair housing and, 48, 55; voting rights and, 81; affirmative action and, 97–98, 105; minority business enterprise and, 140, 141; civil rights leaders and, 169, 175; "silent black majority" and, 176–177; political strategy advice of, 194; women's rights and, 225; population growth and, 250–251

Muskie, Edmund S., 38–39, 66, 179, 244

Muwakkil, Salim, 261

Nash, Peter G., 243

Nathan, Richard P., 154

National Advisory Commission on Civil Disorders, 127

National Advisory Council on Minority Business Enterprise, 49, 134, 137, 139, 145, 229

National Association for the Advancement of Colored People (NAACP), 20, 57, 65, 73–74, 101, 104, 111, 175

National Collegiate Athletic Association (NCAA), 253

National Congress of American Indians (NCAI), 192, 196, 212, 216
National Council on Indian Opportunity (NCIO), 196, 200, 201
National Insurance Association, 178
National Organization for Women (NOW), 227–228, 229, 235, 239, 240, 242, 243
National Tribal Chairmen's Association (NTCA), 216–217
National Urban League, 139, 158, 181–183
National Woman's Party, 232, 233–234
National Women's Political Caucus, 224
Native American policy, 7, 14, 152, 188–221, 260; self-determination and, 8, 126, 156, 188, 191–192, 193, 195–197, 200, 206, 217–218, 219–220, 260; land claims and, 189, 196, 201, 202–206, 209, 210, 218, 219–220; termination of tribes, 190–193, 195, 200, 204, 207, 217–218; education and, 191, 208; revenue sharing and, 197, 208; presidential statement on, 200–201, 202, 209; water rights and, 209–210; reaction to, 220; separatism and, 189, 220
Native Americans: business ownership and, 130; set-asides for, 149; politics of, contrasted with African Americans, 188–189, 192, 219; assimilation of, 190, 193, 221; urban, 192, 196, 201, 209, 210, 214; as voting bloc, 193–194; in mass media, 195; militancy of, 195, 198–199, 201, 202, 210–211, 212–216, 218; surveillance of, 217; federal courts and, 220; government recognition of rights, 263, 265
Neighborhood integration, 8, 14, 60, 68–69, 262. See also Fair housing
New Federalism, 18, 110, 200
New Jersey, 56, 262–263
Newman, Wallace, 10, 193
"New Thrust" program, 181
New York, 56, 66, 95, 111

New York Times, 82, 133, 173, 191, 197, 201
Nichols, Roger L., 219
Nixon, Pat, 224, 235, 237–238, 250, 251
Nixon, Richard M.: "southern strategy" of, 1, 14, 16–20, 31, 32, 38, 40, 41–43, 76–77, 88, 157, 161, 183–184, 185–186, 268; racial views of, 2, 9–11, 25, 127, 163–164, 169, 177, 193, 194, 261, 270; speeches of, 5, 167, 172, 180, 186, 193, 255; as vice president, 6, 8, 10, 22, 24, 25, 71–76, 99–101, 106, 158–159, 192, 233; personality of, 6, 131, 170–171, 180, 270; administrative style of, 7, 12–13, 21, 23, 52, 63, 133, 137, 140, 189, 271; philosophy of, 8, 15, 20, 24, 25–26, 72, 99, 106, 122, 126, 130–131, 134; class bias of, 9, 10, 24, 100, 122, 223, 248; populism of, 9, 122, 131, 177; conservatism of, 11–12, 22–23, 39, 41–42; in 1960 election, 16–17, 42, 75, 106, 161–162, 234; in 1968 election, 16, 18–19, 44, 48, 52, 76–77, 106, 125–127, 128–129, 133, 190, 225, 251; celebrity endorsements of, 17, 163–165, 167, 180, 183, 184; national strategy of, 20, 80, 165, 269; in 1972 election, 38–39, 40, 42, 109, 113–114, 117, 183–184; firings by, 53, 60–62, 67, 118, 151, 158; as congressman, 73, 192, 232, 233; radio broadcasts of, 129; sexism of, 223–225, 248, 257; family of, 224–225, 238; on same-sex marriages, 247
Nixonians: grassroots pressure and, 3, 242; class bias of, 8, 13–14, 156, 177; fair housing and, 49; fair employment and, 111; affirmative action and, 155–156; sexism of, 156, 225–226, 229; civil rights leaders and, 158, 169, 175; Native American policy and, 189, 208–209; women's rights and, 223
Nordwall, Adam, 198

O'Brien, Larry, 66
Office of Economic Opportunity, 138, 209

Office of Federal Contract Compliance (OFCC), 101–102, 104, 241, 242
Office of Indian Civil Rights, 210
Office of Management and Budget (OMB), 153–154, 217. *See also* Bureau of the Budget
Office of Minority Business Enterprise (OMBE), 38, 125, 127, 133–140, 145–146, 147, 148, 208
Ogilvie, Richard, 26
Ohio, 102
Olympic Committee, U. S., 254
Open communities, 45, 54–59, 68. *See also* Fair housing
"Open door policy," 176, 179–184, 245
"Operation Breakthrough," 52
Organic Act (1884, Alaska), 204

Panetta, Leon E., 28, 34, 62, 151, 155
Patman, Wright, 56
Patterson, Bradley H., Jr., 28, 63, 182; Philadelphia Plan and, 105; affirmative action and, 108, 117; minority business enterprise and, 146; Native American policy and, 197, 198–199, 200, 201, 203, 205–208, 211–212, 213, 215, 216, 217–218, 220; executive branch reorganization and, 211; women's rights and, 253
Patterson, John, 165
Paul, Alice, 232, 233
Payton, Sallyanne, 3, 131, 163–164, 184
Pennsylvania, 101, 102
Percy, Charles H., 47, 140
Peterson, Elly M., 53, 228, 231
Philadelphia Plan, 85, 99–115, 122, 240, 265
Phillips, Kevin, 22
Pine Ridge Indian Reservation, 214–216
Pipelines, Alaskan, 205
Pittsburgh Courier, 132
Pleck, Elizabeth, 240
Poff, Richard H., 79, 80, 81, 236, 238
Polish-Americans, 7, 20, 114, 263
Poll taxes, 4, 73, 75
Population growth issues, 250–251

Pornography, 257
Pottinger, J. Stanley, 98, 116–117, 123
Poverty, 127–128, 129–130, 220–221
Powell, John H., Jr., 121
Powell, Lewis F., 237
Prattis, Percy L., 74
Pre-clearance of voting laws, 71, 79, 82–85, 87, 92–96
Presidential election rules, 81, 94
President's Committee on Government Contracts, 99–101, 106
Presley, Elvis, 93
Price, John R., 112
Price, Raymond K., 13, 62–63, 90–92, 128, 133, 169
Private schools, 25
Project OWN, 130
Public facilities, desegregation of, 4–5, 16–17
Public housing, 67, 69. *See also* Fair housing
Public relations (PR), 7, 20, 154, 158, 171, 217, 245
Puerto Ricans, 130, 194

Quotas. *See* Hiring goals

Racial polarization, 158, 185–187
Racial strife, 7, 47, 76, 101, 106, 127–128, 174, 219, 263
Racism, white, 57, 128
Randolph Institute, 102
Rape, 257
Rauh, Joseph L., Jr., 95–96, 120
Reagan, Ronald: rights record of, 24; "southern strategy" of, 41–42, 185–186; school desegregation and, 43; public housing and, 67; union discrimination and, 107; affirmative action and, 111, 124, 187; minority business enterprise and, 143–144, 148, 149; Native American policy and, 220–221; abortion rights and, 252
Reavis, Carol, 227
Redistricting, Congressional, 94, 96
"Red Power," 192, 198, 223

Referees, voting, 74–75
Registrars, voting, 74, 76
Rehnquist, William H., 91, 236, 237–238
Reid, Charlotte T., 228, 236
Residency requirements, voting, 81, 84, 87, 92
Revenue Act (1971), 250
Revenue sharing, 12, 52–53, 180, 197, 208
Reverse discrimination, 115–116, 137
Revised Order 4, 240–242, 243–244, 246–247, 248
Reynolds, Gerald, 268
Reynolds, James J., 130
Rhode Island, land claims in, 220
Ribicoff, Abraham A., 66
Richardson, Elliot L., 39, 40, 63, 153, 245, 249, 250, 290n187
Richmond, City of v. Cronson, 149
Riegle, Donald, 90
Robertson, Robert, 198–199, 200
Robinson, Jackie, 17, 74–75, 139–140, 159, 163–165, 183
Rockefeller, Laurance S., 153
Rockefeller, Nelson A., 16, 18, 42, 47, 107, 132, 226, 233, 251
Rockefeller Brothers Fund, 152–153
Roeser, Thomas F., 137, 138
Roe v. Wade, 252
Rogers, William P., 74–75, 161, 224, 270
Romney, George W.: as administration dissenter, 13, 49–54; fair housing and, 45, 50, 54–67, 70; Goldwater and, 50–51; leadership style of, 50–51, 53, 57; firing/resignation of, 53, 60–62, 67; affirmative action and, 103; women's rights and, 246
Roosevelt, Eleanor, 224, 232
Roosevelt, Franklin D., 8, 11, 114, 190, 219
Roosevelt, Theodore, 8, 202, 210
Rose, Frank A., 154
Rowan, Carl, 170
Ruetten, Richard T., 4
Rumsfeld, Donald, 200
Russell, Richard B., 32

Safire, William, 10, 54
Same-sex marriages, 247
Samuels, Howard J., 130
Sandler, Bernice, 242–243
Sandoval, Hilary, 138, 142
San Francisco Chronicle, 199
"Scattered-site" housing, 65, 69, 155, 260
Schlafly, Phyllis, 239
School desegregation, 6, 21, 23–43, 159, 170, 171, 270; enforcement of, through litigation, 4, 16, 18, 23–24, 27–31, 33, 37, 42, 260; policy statements on, 14, 29–30, 32, 33, 36, 46, 55, 135, 174, 178; de jure/de facto segregation and, 16, 32–33, 42, 174; freedom of choice plans and, 18, 27, 37–38; withholding of federal funds and, 26, 28–29, 37, 56; cabinet committee on, 34, 40, 290n187; reactions to, 35, 42; Civil Rights Commission and, 35, 175; Ribicoff Amendment and, 66; voting rights and, 72. *See also* Black colleges; Busing
Schools, tribal, 191, 208
Schultz, George P.: on domestic policy, 12; school desegregation and, 34, 63; affirmative action and, 103–105, 110, 112, 118, 242; minority business enterprise and, 142, 146; National Urban League and, 183; Native American policy and, 200; women's rights and, 241
Scott, Ann F., 242–243
Scott, Hugh D., 7, 78, 80, 81, 85–89, 108, 118, 238, 260
Section 8(a) contracts, 138, 141–142, 147–148
Seidenberg, Jacob, 101
Senate: Appropriations Committee, 119, 142; Interior Committee, 202–203, 207; Judiciary Committee, 73, 87; Republican Policy Committee, 143; Subcommittee on Constitutional Rights, 86–87
Separatism, 5, 14, 126, 144, 156, 189, 220
Set-asides in federal contracts, 125, 141–142, 149, 265
Sexism, 225–227, 229, 241, 246, 248
Shannon, William V., 249

Shannon v. Romney, 62

Shepard, Geoffrey C., 199, 215, 253

Silberman, Laurence H., 105, 110–111, 241, 242–243, 248

"Silent black majority," 176–178

"Silent majority," 22, 259

Simmons, Samuel J., 54, 62, 66, 67, 143–144, 150

Small, Melvin, 2

Small Business Act (1953), 138

Small Business Administration (SBA), 129–130, 133, 137–139, 141–142, 145–149, 264

Smith, Margaret Chase, 225, 242

Sneed, Joseph T., 217

Social Security programs, 22

Sons of Italy Supreme Council, 263

South Carolina, 29, 36

Southwest Development Act (1967), 264

Speeches: inaugural, 5, 167, 172, 186, 267; civil rights, 157, 186, 191, 193; State of the Union, 172, 180, 255; Native American policy, 196

Spottswood, Stephen G., 65, 174–175, 178

Staats, Elmer B., 102, 104, 108

Stans, Maurice H., 133, 135–139, 141, 143–146, 148, 150–151, 155, 209

States' rights, 17–18, 75, 82, 87–88, 89, 111, 250

Stennis, John, 30

Stern, Mark, 6

Stevens, Ted, 205, 206

Stokes, Louis, 117

Strickland, Rennard, 194

Student loan programs, 208, 252

Sundquist, James Q., 2

Supreme Court: school desegregation and, 4, 18, 24, 27, 31, 33, 42, 260; appointments to, 19–20, 39, 85, 86, 88–89, 91, 107, 170, 237–238; fair housing and, 63–64, 65; voting rights and, 78, 79–80, 94; redistricting and, 94; affirmative action and, 115; on law and order, 128; set-asides and, 149; abortion rights and, 252. *See also* Federal courts

Surveillance of dissidents, 179, 217

Swann v. Mecklenberg County, 39

Taos Pueblo, 189, 202–203, 207

Task Force on Low-Income Housing, 49

Task Force on Women's Rights and Responsibilities, 49, 223, 229–231, 235, 241, 244

Tax incentives, 25, 44, 129

Texaco Oil Company, 266

Texas, 47–48, 56, 78–79, 95, 110, 142

Textile mills, discrimination in, 103–104

Thurmond, Strom, 18–19, 28, 30, 35–36, 38, 92, 143

Time (magazine), 131

Timmons, William E., 56, 75–83, 90–91, 203, 207, 253

Title IX (athletics), 252–255, 260

Tower, John, 35–36, 83, 144

"Trail of Broken Treaties," 213, 214, 215

Truman, Harry S., 4, 11, 46, 232

Tucker, Sterling, 181

Tunney, John, 209

Tydings, Joseph D., 79

Udall, Morris K., 68

Udall, Stewart L., 204, 226–227

Underhandedness, political, 38–39, 53, 147–148

Unger, Sherman, 55, 66

United Auto Workers, 113

United Negro College Fund, 153, 154, 155, 178

Upicksoun, Joseph, 214

Urban League. *See* National Urban League

Van Dusen, Richard C., 54, 56, 59, 66, 103, 111, 142–144, 150

Venable, Abraham S., 129, 137–138, 139, 140, 144

Victor, Wilma, 211, 212

Vietnam War, impact of, 7, 72, 89, 91, 93, 109, 113, 208

Virginia, 27, 79, 149, 160
Vocational programs, 24, 264
Voluntary action programs, 52
Voting rights, 4, 5, 71–96, 159, 160, 170; literacy tests and, 71, 75–84, 87, 92–93, 96; pre-clearance rules and, 71, 79, 82–85, 87, 92–96; referees and, 74–76; enforcement of, through litigation, 75, 83, 94–95; nationalization of, 78–80, 82, 87, 95; residency rules and, 81, 84, 87, 92; age requirements and, 85, 87–91, 93–94, 260; reactions to, 92
Voting Rights Act (1965), 5, 71, 76, 77–85, 87, 92
Voting Rights Act (1970), 7, 14, 72, 85–93, 237, 260

Wage and price controls, 109, 113, 146
Walker, Charls, 144–145
Walker Amelia Haines, 233
Wallace, George C., 6, 9, 19, 38–40, 48
Wall Street Journal, 131
Want ads, gender differentiated, 240–241
Ward, C. D., 197, 200, 201, 207–208
Warner, Volney F., 216
Watergate, impact of, 117, 154, 218, 253, 270
Water rights, 209–210
Waters, Maxine, 262
Watkins, Arthur V., 191
Weber, Arnold R., 183, 245
Weinberger, Caspar W., 117, 216, 250, 255
Welfare reform, 6, 14, 21, 23, 48, 196. *See also* Family Assistance Plan (FAP)
Whitaker, John C., 196, 207, 212, 217, 219
White-collar workers, 115–122, 261
White ethnics, 7, 20, 60, 114, 263, 265
Whitman, Ann, 72
Wicker, Tom, 2, 12, 271
Wiggins, Charles P., 236, 238
Wilentz, Robert, 263
Wilkins, Roger, 261, 269
Wilkins, Roy: school desegregation and, 30, 170; on fair housing policies,
64–65; relationship with Nixon, 75, 161, 166, 167–168, 174; voting rights and, 78, 84, 92, 170; on affirmative action, 104; on minority business enterprise, 151; on civil rights policy, 166, 168, 171
Wilks, John L., 241, 242, 243
Williams, Franklin, 162
Williams, Harrison A., Jr., 104, 119
Willis, Ellen, 250
Wilson, Pete, 266
Wilson, Richard (tribal leader), 214–215, 216
Wilson, Richard L. (journalist), 24, 171, 224, 261
"Womanpower," 223–224
Women: business ownership and, 148–149, 156; appointments to federal office and, 164, 223, 224, 227–228, 237–238, 240, 244–247, 257; as voting bloc, 233–234, 245; civil disorder and, 234–235
Women's Bureau, 235
Women's Business Ownership Act (1988), 149
Women's Educational Equity Act (1974), 255–256
Women's Equity Action League (WEAL), 242, 252
Women's rights, 222–258, 263, 265; movements for, 14, 229, 232; task force on, 49, 223, 229–231, 235, 241, 244; affirmative action and, 110, 116, 121, 123, 240–248, 257; child day care and, 223, 248–250, 256; empowerment and, 223–225, 257; staff attitudes toward, 225–227; enforcement of, through litigation, 229, 236, 242; credit, financial and, 248, 255; Title IX (athletics) and, 252–255, 260. See also Abortion rights; Equal Rights Amendment (ERA)
Woods, Rose Mary, 46, 234, 248, 246
Wounded Knee siege, 210–211, 214–216, 218
Wright, Donald R., 204, 206

Yakima, 189, 210
Young, Milton T., Jr.,
  118–119
Young, Whitney M., Jr., 130,
  181–183

Young Americans for Freedom, 23
Youpee, William, 209

Ziegler, Ronald, 226
Zoning laws, 45, 54, 56–57, 63–64, 262